W9-AVE-190

improving the teaching
of reading

EMERALD V. DECHANT
Fort Hays State University

improving the teaching of reading

THIRD EDITION

Prentice-Hall, Inc., Englewood Cliffs, New Jersey 07632

Library of Congress Cataloging in Publication Data

DECHANT, EMERALD V.
   Improving the teaching of reading.

   Bibliography: p.
   Includes index.
   1. Reading (Elementary) I. Title.
LB1573.D345 1964, 1970, 1982   372.4′1   81–15355
ISBN 0-13-453423-9   AACR2

Editorial production/supervision by Virginia Cavanagh Neri
Interior design by Cathie Mick Mahar
Cover design by Suzanne Behnke
Manufacturing buyer: Edmund W. Leone

Printed in the United States of America

10 9 8 7 6 5 4 3 2 1

ISBN 0-13-453423-9

PRENTICE-HALL INTERNATIONAL, INC., *London*
PRENTICE-HALL OF AUSTRALIA PTY. Limited, *Sydney*
PRENTICE-HALL OF CANADA, LTD., *Toronto*
PRENTICE-HALL OF INDIA PRIVATE LIMITED, *New Delhi*
PRENTICE-HALL OF JAPAN, INC., *Tokyo*
PRENTICE-HALL OF SOUTHEAST ASIA PTE. LTD., *Singapore*
WHITEHALL BOOKS LIMITED, *Wellington, New Zealand*

This book is lovingly dedicated to my parents,
Mr. and Mrs. Cornel J. Dechant.

contents

preface

This third edition of *Improving the Teaching of Reading* attempts to retain from the earlier editions those aspects that reflected sound educational practice and research, but goes well beyond the earlier editions in certain key areas. Thus, it presents:

1. A broadened description and definition of reading. Since the second edition, it is more common and more fashionable to use terms like psycholinguistics, encoding, recoding and decoding, surface and deep structure, sign system, cue systems, feature analysis, and semantic and syntactic cues in describing reading.

2. A refocus on the eye-movements in reading. It is once again fashionable to study eye-movements. Eye-movements are exceedingly valuable evidence of what the pupil is doing visually while reading and for interpreting the effects of visual deviations upon reading.

3. A continuing emphasis on reading as a perceptual process. Recognition of a word is not reading and the word does not of itself contain meaning; rather, reading more commonly involves the taking of meaning *to* the symbol.

4. A broadened understanding of reading as a language and communication process. The interrelationships between reading, thinking, and language and the effects that listening, speaking, and knowledge of grammar have on reading are carefully delineated.

5. A careful analysis of the variables that affect the learner's ability to read. We are gradually coming to a better understanding of the variables that explain achievement or failure in reading.

6. An emphasis on the enabling skills or the readiness factors that make it possible for the pupil to be a reader and without which the pupil is likely to have great difficulty in learning to read.

7. A discussion of the different methods of word identification, of their variant purposes, and of their role in developing a code system for identifying words. The book identifies the aspects or elements that should permeate all teaching of word identification skills.

8. A discussion of the variant ways of introducing reading to the reader (language experience, basal reader, individualized reading), of organizing a classroom lesson (directed reading activity), and of the various word-identification strategies (within-word cues, meaning cues, and use of the dictionary). The book deals with both the *what* and the *how*—the skills the pupil must learn and the method of developing the reading skills.

9. A discussion of the phoneme/grapheme correspondences without which the coding system, referred to earlier, cannot be developed.

10. A description of the eight categories of morphemic or structural-analysis skills and the significance of this knowledge in both word identification and comprehension.

11. A discussion and analysis of the word meaning or vocabulary skills and their development; of the various comprehension skills, including comprehension of units of increasing size and comprehension on different levels such as inferential and critical comprehension; of reading for learning or study-type reading; of developing rate of comprehension; and of reading in the content areas, with specific suggestions for developing specific skills.

12. A discussion of oral reading and its development, including suggestions for dealing with oral reading errors or miscues.

13. An outline of remedial procedures for helping the pupil who is drifting or has drifted into trouble in reading.

14. A discussion of how to plan a good reading program, how to organize for slow learners, and corrective and remedial readers, and how to plan an effective reading lesson, including a discussion of skill or task training, process or ability training, and process-task training.

There are few questions in education that have clear-cut answers. This book does not pretend to have all the answers. Perhaps the most that can be done is to somehow merge theoretical knowledge and practical know-how. It is not enough that teachers have a knowledge of the reading process; they must know how to use this knowledge. I hope this book both increases the teacher's knowledge base, and also helps him or her to become better at applying what is known. The teacher is the crucial determinant of a good reading program. There is no substitute for good teaching.

EMERALD V. DECHANT

improving the teaching of reading

PART

1

reading—an overview

Part I consists of three chapters. Chapter 1 examines variant definitions of reading. Chapter 2 deals with the sensory and perceptual nature of the reading process. Chapter 3 considers the linguistic and communicative aspects of reading.

It is practically impossible to discuss in detail within a few hundred pages all the phases of a complete reading program, and this book does not propose to do so. Rather, it attempts to provide answers to a few basic questions: What is reading? (Chapters 1 to 3); Who is the learner or who must be taught? (Chapters 4 and 5); How can the pupil become ready for the tasks required for successful reading? (Chapters 6 and 7); How does the pupil learn to read? (Chapter 8); What is to be learned or what must be taught? (Chapters 9 to 15); What can the teacher do when the pupil fails to learn to read? (Chapter 16); and How should the reading program be organized? (Chapter 17).

This book is concerned with reading method and with the actual teaching of reading. Thus, the book is written first and foremost for the practitioner or the teacher-in-service. The first concern has been to meet the needs of the classroom teacher. Nevertheless, the book should be of particular value to the remedial teacher, the reading specialist, and the reading supervisor; it should also meet the needs of those students preparing to become teachers. Administrators and state department personnel should find it helpful in obtaining a better understanding of the reading process.

Every attempt has been made throughout the book to relate psychological theory and research to practice. In actual teaching, the results of such attempts can sometimes be rather frustrating, but this should not keep the teacher from theorizing and engaging in research or from applying theory to practice.

The transition for us as individuals from what we know to what we do is always a great leap. Perhaps an even greater transition exists between what researchers as a group have learned and what the individual teacher practices in the classroom. The challenge facing teachers today, as always, is the improvement of classroom practice in the light of present knowledge. This is particularly true in the field of reading, where research has been above the ordinary. We hope that this book will help to familiarize the teacher with what is presently known about reading and reading instruction.

1

THE NATURE OF THE READING PROCESS: A DEFINITION OF READING

Definitions of reading are divided into two major types: (1) those that equate reading with interpretation of experience generally; and (2) those that equate reading with interpretation of graphic symbols. The first is a broader category and encompasses the second; most reading definitions are related to one or both. Let us consider more closely some of the definitions which make up these categories.

READING AS INTERPRETATION OF EXPERIENCE

With the first type of reading definition, in which reading is equated with the interpretation of experience generally, we might speak of reading pictures, reading faces, or reading the weather. We read a squeaking door, a clap of thunder, a barking dog. The golfer reads the putting greens, the detective reads clues, the geologist reads rocks, the astronomer reads stars, the doctor reads the symptoms of illness, and the reading teacher reads the symptoms of reading disability.

The definition of reading that has come out of the Claremont College Reading Conference fits this first category. In the Conference's Eleventh Yearbook, Spencer (1946) wrote, "In the broadest sense, reading is the process of interpreting sense stimuli. . . . Reading is performed whenever one experiences sensory stimulation." Benjamin Franklin in *Poor Richard's Almanac* had such a definition in mind when he wrote: "Read much, but not too many books."

Perhaps the reading-readiness program—in which experience with the concrete object is emphasized, visual and auditory discrimination are stressed, and children are required to interpret pictures and conversation—is closest to the meaning of reading implied in the first type of definition.

Reading as interpretation of experience has implications for both the reading teacher and the pupil learning to read. One implication is that teachers of reading must become experts in reading children. The teacher of reading must understand children and must be able to identify the personal differences in children which may lead to achievement differences between pupils.

A second implication is that the teacher needs to become expert in reading the symptoms of reading success and reading disability. One lesson learned the hard way in combating major diseases is that many people die from treatable diseases because someone either ignored the symptoms or did not read them correctly. In a similar fashion, children may become reading disability cases because someone ignored or misread the symptoms of reading disability.

A third implication is that the teacher must develop expertness in reading the causes of reading disability. Smith and Carrigan (1959) note that clinicians are like a small group of bystanders standing next to a river full of drowning people who are being swept seaward. The clinicians can pull out a few, but the rest are lost. Few clinicians are willing to go upstream to find out how the people got into the river in the first place. Yet reading teachers clearly need to know how the disabled reader gets into the river of reading disability. To do this they need to be able to read the causes of reading disability. It is not enough to know the symptoms; symptom must be related to cause. Only in this way are prevention and remediation of reading disability possible.

Still another implication of reading as interpretation of experience is that pupils must be readers of experience before they can become readers of graphic symbols. The pupil cannot read symbols without having experience—without having those experiences that give the symbol meaning.

READING AS INTERPRETATION
OF GRAPHIC SYMBOLS

Turn now to the second type of definition of reading, that which equates reading with the interpretation of graphic symbols. Most definitions of reading given in professional textbooks are of this second type. DeBoer and Dallmann (1960: p. 19) consider that reading "involves the comprehension and interpretation of ideas symbolized by the written or printed page." In a later book (Dallmann, Rouch, Char, and DeBoer 1978: p. 33) the authors note that their emphasis is on "reading as a process involving meaningful reaction to printed symbols." Bond and Tinker (1967: p. 22) point out that "reading involves the recognition of printed or written symbols which serve as stimuli for the recall of meanings built up through the reader's past experience." Harris and Sipay (1975: p. 5) define reading as "the meaningful interpretation of written or printed verbal symbols." Gibson (1966) says that reading "is receiving communication; it is making discriminative responses to graphic symbols; it is decoding graphic symbols to speech; and it is getting meaning from the printed page." The present writer (Dechant 1970: p. 19) has defined reading as "the process of giving the significance intended by the writer to the graphic symbols by relating them to one's own fund of experience."

All these definitions of reading have certain elements in common; in particular, they all note that reading is an interpretation of graphic symbols. Reading is thus perceived as a twofold process:(1) identification of the symbols; and (2) association of appropriate meanings with them. Reading requires identification *and* comprehension.

Another aspect of reading that is frequently emphasized in definitions of reading is that it is a language and communication process—the process of putting the reader in contact and communication with ideas. Reading always involves an interaction between the writer and reader. It is the culminating act of the communication process, initiated by the thoughts of the writer and expressed through the symbols on the page. Without a reader, communication via the printed page is impossible; writing has no purpose without a reader. Thus, a team of experts, under the sponsorship of the U. S. Office of Education, defined reading as an interaction by which meaning encoded in visual stimuli by an author becomes meaning in the mind of the reader.

Other descriptions of reading emphasize that reading requires higher-order thinking. Reading requires the communication of a message or of meanings and the apprehension of meanings; and meaning occurs on several levels, from literal comprehension to interpretative reading, from concrete interpretation to abstract interpretation, and from simple reaction to evaluation of what has been decoded. Reading is so difficult to analyze because it involves the most intricate workings of the human mind. It is a genuine cognitive process. Reading is thinking through print.

Thorndike (1917) maintained years ago that the reading of a paragraph involves the same sort of organization and analysis as does thinking. It includes learning, reflection, judgment, analysis, synthesis, problem-solving behavior, selection, organization, comparison of data, determination of relationships, and critical evaluation of what is being read. Einstein noted that reading is the most difficult task that man has ever devised for himself. Hildreth (1958) has pointed out that reading requires inference, weighing the relative importance of ideas and meanings, and seeing the relationships among them.

Examine now more closely two important aspects of the reading process: (1) the language or sign system of reading which the reader must identify and recognize and in which the messages are formulated or encoded; and (2) the decoding or comprehension process in which the reader must engage.

THE SIGN SYSTEM

The purpose of all communication is the sharing of meanings; the purpose of all reading is comprehension of meanings. But it is the sign system, the symbols or words, that must carry the burden of meaning between the communicators or between the writer and the reader. The symbol is the writer's or speaker's tool for awakening meaning in the reader or listener. James (1890: p. 356) noted that language is "a system of signs, different from the things signified, but able to suggest them."

The focus for many years in the teaching of reading has been on the development of quick and easy recognition of the sign system—the alphabetic writing or the graphic language system. The teacher was interested in helping the beginning reader to perceive the significant contrastive features of the letters in words and to identify letters and words with facility and accuracy. Research focused on feature analysis (analysis of the written symbols) or on the analysis of the surface structure of the language. Reading teachers spent most of their time and energy on the perceptual aspects of letter and word identification and on methods of word identification.

The last fifteen years have seen the emergence of numerous methods of teaching reading (*ITA, Words In Color, Diacritical Marking System,* and so forth) whose major concern is with the alphabetic nature or the featural aspects of printed materials.

Even more significant has been the writing of linguists such as Bloomfield (1942), Bloomfield and Barnhart (1961), and Fries (1963). Bloomfield and Fries define reading as the act of turning the stimulus (the graphic shape) on a surface back into speech. Bloomfield differentiated between the *act of reading* (recognition of letter-sound or grapheme-phoneme correspondences) and the *goal of reading* (comprehension).

The central thesis of the Bloomfield method is that there is an inseparable relationship between the words as printed and the sounds for which the letters are conventional signs, and that converting letters to meaning requires from the beginning a concentration upon letter and sound to bring about as rapidly as possible an automatic association between them. Bloomfield's system is a linguistic system of teaching reading which separates the problem of the study of word form from the study of word meaning. Bloomfield felt that initial teaching of reading for meaning is incorrect, and that meaning will come quite naturally as the alphabetic code or principle is discovered.

Reading is thus basically described by Fries and Bloomfield as recoding printed symbols into sound and then extracting meaning from sound. The early linguists focused primarily on the problems of beginning reading and more specifically on the problems of word recognition.

In Bloomfield's approach to reading, readers who have not previously dealt with the words, γνῶθι σαυτόν, must make two adjustments: (1) They must visually identify the symbols (which makes reading a sensory process, requiring proper use of the eyes and to some extent proper eye movements; and a word-identification process, requiring the discrimination of one visual stimulus from another and the application of the appropriate method of word identification); and (2) they must associate sound with the symbols (which makes reading a recoding process).

Reading thus involves visual identification of the symbol and pronunciation of the symbol. The reader must identify the symbols, but must also be able to translate them into sounds: γνῶθι σαυτόν, becomes *gnothi-sauton*.

Unfortunately, excessive concern with the sign system or the identification of letters and words may actually handicap the pupil. Poor readers have to focus most of their processing capacity on the visual aspects. Also, beginning readers often become so engrossed with the mechanical aspects of reading, with word identification and pronunciation, that they fail to understand the need for comprehension.

Nevertheless, pupils must learn to identify letters and words, they must become familiar with the letter sequences, and they must acquire a sight vocabulary. Later chapters will concentrate on these facets of the reading process, but one must remember that they form only one aspect of reading. There are other aspects that are perhaps more important, and we turn now to examine one of them.

THE IMPORTANCE OF DECODING OR COMPREHENSION

If reading were simply a word-identification or word-naming process, children would be good readers when they could name the printed symbols. However, reading is much more than simple recognition of the graphic symbols. Reading is more than the mere ability to pronounce the words on the printed page, to match the written word with the spoken code, to go from the graphic code to the spoken code. It is more than a matching of phoneme and grapheme: this is recoding, but it is not decoding. Decoding occurs only when meaning is associated with the written symbol and only when the meaning that the writer wanted to share with the reader has been received by the reader.

Few today would accept Flesch's description of reading, as cited by Harris and Sipay (1975: p. 5): "I once surprised a native of Prague by reading aloud from a Czech newspaper. 'Oh, you know Czech?' he asked. 'No I don't understand a word of it,' I answered. 'I can only read it.' " Nor would there be any great enthusiasm for Reed's (1965: p. 847) view: "Anyone who has learned to read can read many sentences whose meanings are almost completely unknown to him." Reading without meaning is pure verbalism.

Decoding is effected through the use of semantic and syntactic cues. Consider first the semantic cues.

Role of Semantic or Experientially Derived Meanings

The reading of graphic symbols consists of two processes: the visual process involved in bringing the stimuli to the brain, and the mental processes involved in interpreting the graphic symbols after they get to the brain. When the light rays from the printed page strike the retinal cells of the eyes, signals are sent along the optic nerve to the visual centers of the brain. This is not yet reading. The signals must be interpreted; the reader must give significance to the graphic symbols by bringing meaning to them. The critical element in reading often is not what is on the page, but rather what the graphic symbols signify to the reader. As was noted earlier, (Dechant 1970: p. 19), reading thus might be described in a general way as "the process of giving the significance intended by the writer to the graphic symbols by relating them to one's own fund of experiences."

Reading is a perceptual process, an interpretative process, a conceptual and thinking process. Conceptual thought is required to react with meaning. Readers interpret what they read, associate it with their past experience, and project beyond it in terms of ideas, relations, and categorizations.

Reading can be viewed as a process of forming tentative judgments and interpretations, and of verifying, correcting, and confirming guesses. To comprehend a passage, readers must be in a continuously alert, anticipatory frame of mind, suspending judgment and correcting or confirming guesses as they go along. A pupil, upon meeting the word *run* in a sentence, calls upon the meaning (for example,"to move swiftly") that she has learned to associate with that word and projects that meaning on the text. The pupil makes an educated guess that the meaning of the word is "to move swiftly" and as she continues to read, she verifies and confirms that meaning. Sometimes the pupil finds that her projection is not accurate (for example, if the word is used as a part of a phrase like "a cattle run," "a run on the bank," or "the ordinary run of people"); or the pupil may find that she cannot read the sentence because her experience has not been adequate enough to make use of the semantic context.

Reading as decoding or as an interpretative process focuses on the semantic information or cues. Semantic cues are meaning-bearing cues based on experience; they are bundles of experience which have been given vocabulary tags by an author (Hoskisson and Krohm 1974). When the reader associates meaning with a symbol, a meaning acquired through experience, the reader is utilizing a semantic cue and is making use of the semantic context.

The fact is that readers cannot be proficient readers of graphic symbols without previously having been proficient readers of experience. Reading always involves a reading of past experience. Meaning is supplied by the readers as they process the symbols by relating them to experience. The word *boat* may have no meaning for a pupil who has never experienced, handled, seen, or sailed a boat.

In reading, an adequate response demands much more than mere identification and recognition of the configuration. There simply is not a one-to-one correspondence between the stimulus (the graphic input) and the response: what the reader must add is the sum total of the retained and organized effects of past experience. According to Hurvich and Jameson (1974), the individual perceives his world in terms of "what he is" as much as "what it is."

Writers have frequently noted the experiential content of perception. James (1890: p. 103) pointed out long ago that "whilst part of what we perceive comes through our senses from the object [word] before us, another part always comes. . . out of our head." Horn (1937), suggested that the writer does not really convey ideas to the readers but merely stimulates them to construct ideas out of their own experience.

And, the one who takes the most experience and information to the printed page gains the most. Chall (1947) gave an information test about tuberculosis to about one hundred sixth and eighth graders. She then had them read a selection on tuberculosis and gave them a test on the selection. Those children who already knew the most about tuberculosis also made the best comprehension scores on the reading selection. Chall noted that we read in order to gain experience and yet it is also true that we get more out of reading if we have more experience. Thus, "Reading typically is the bringing of meaning *to* rather than the gaining of meaning *from* the printed page" (Smith and Dechant 1961: p. 22). The reader is stimulated by the writer's words, but in turn invests those words with his or her own meaning.

Meaning is thus output (what the reader brings by way of past experience to the printed page) as well as input (the new meanings that the reader gets from the printed page).

It is not enough to put one's own stamp of meaning on the words. Langman (1960) notes that to read is to comprehend the meaning of visually presented word sequences, that the reader must follow the thought of the writer. Thus the reader may and even must gain meaning from the printed page. This occurs when the writer's symbols stimulate readers to combine or reconstruct their own experiences in a novel way or to construct new meanings through the manipulation of relevant concepts already in their possession (Tinker and McCullough 1975). Comprehension occurs only when the reader's reconstruction agrees with the writer's intended message.

Role of Language or Syntactic Structures in Meaning

Decoding is also effected through syntax or the syntactic content. Recent discussions of the nature of the reading process have thus broadened the description of reading by focusing on language structures.

Lefevre (1962, 1964), a linguist, started the emphasis on language structures. He stressed syntactical cues, both intraword (such as inflections) and interword (such as sentence structure), and maintained that the "grasp of meaning is integrally linked to grasp of structure" (1964: p. 68). Only by reading structures can full meaning be attained. Or to put it another way, unless readers correctly translate the printed text into the intonation pattern of the writer, they may not be getting the meaning intended. If readers read the text the way the writer would like it to have been said, true communication of meaning may be possible.

Lefevre thus adapted linquistic ideas to meaningful reading. He suggested an analytical method of teaching reading, emphasizing language patterns. He emphasized in particular that meaning comes only through the grasping of the language structure exemplified in a sentence.

Walcutt, Lamport, and McCracken (1974: pp. 41-42), noting that syntax concerns itself with meaning-bearing patterns, point out that the word *dogs* is easily understood on a surface level as two morphemes, (*dog* and *s*), expressing a recognized relationship among certain animals. There are, however, very noticeable differences among the statements "Dogs make good pets," "It's a dog's life," and "He's gone to the dogs," all of which employ the same two morphemes. The illustrations clearly show that meaning comes through syntax by intonation patterns, word-form changes, and the use of structure and function words.

Lefevre's ideas were more clearly outlined by psycholinguists such as Chomsky (1957, 1970), Goodman (1966, 1970), and Ruddell (1974). All reject the notion that reading is simply sequential word recognition. Reading is not the adding up, as it were, of the meanings of individual words; it is not simply a sequential perception and identification of letters and words. These theorists emphasize that all languages, and hence all sentences, have a surface structure and a deep structure. Sounds or written words are the surface representation of a message; meaning, both syntactic and semantic interpretation, is the deep level. The deep structure gives the meaning of the sentence; it is the sentence structure, the way the words are used in the sentence, that at least partially determines the meaning of the individual words.

The transformational-generative grammar model, advocated by Chomsky, suggests that grammar or the rules of syntax are a set of rules by which sense is made out of language. Grammar is the link between sound or graphic symbols, and meaning. Syntax mediates between the visual surface structure and the deep structure or meaning.

Syntax permits the grouping or ordering of words to suggest specific nuances of meaning. For example, the same words might be grouped in different ways to suggest various meanings: "The weak girl is playing a game of tennis"; or "The girl is playing a weak game of tennis." Readers must first recognize the distinction in arrangement before they can perceive the distinction in meaning. To read the word *runs*, for example, the reader must know whether it is a noun or a verb. The formal distinction between *runs* as a verb and *runs* as a noun ("He runs home"; "The runs on the bank were many") is syntactic in nature. Or again, an adjective can be given a noun meaning by syntax: "The *best* is not good enough for him."

Goodman (1967) notes that reading is a selective process, involving partial use of available minimal language cues (graphic, semantic, and syntactic). Readers, as they process this partial information, confirm, reject, or refine their tentative decisions in the course of reading. Goodman notes that readers utilize all three kinds of information (graphic, semantic, and syntactic) simultaneously. Certainly, without the graphic input there would be no reading, but the reader uses syntactic and semantic information as well.

Smith (1971) points out that fluent readers maximize the use of cues contained in the semantic and syntactic language and minimize their dependence on feature analysis or surface structure. They operate at a deep structure level and predict as they read, sampling the surface structure as they test out their predictions. When the predictions are not confirmed, they then engage in more visual analysis.

Wardhaugh (1969) suggests that when a person reads, the processing itself is not just a matter of processing visual signals in order to convert these signals into some kind of covert speech, or of recoding printed symbols into sounds and then extracting meaning from sound. This conversion is merely the beginning of the process, because semantic and syntactic processing are necessary in addition to the processing of the visual signals. Wardhaugh notes that one cannot read a foreign language by simply being able to vocalize the print; this is more in the nature of barking at print.

The import of all this is that readers will do a better job of decoding if they understand language structures or the patterned regularities among the elements of a sentence. The presumption is that increasing knowledge of syntax (rules for ordering words in sentences), in addition to increasing knowledge of semantics (word meanings), will result in improved ability to process sentences (Frasure and Entwisle 1973). It is not enough to focus on the semantic or referential meaning (what the symbol *steeple* represents, or in other words, its referend); the good reader also uses structure to decode meaning. The language structure, the syntax, the word order, the inflectional endings, and the intonation patterns all redundantly define the meaning of a symbol. Because language structures communicate meanings, the better one's knowledge of language structure, the less need one has for visual information.*

Words acquire meaning as a consequence of occurring in sentences. And for this reason, it is almost impossible to read a sentence correctly without mastery of the grammar of a language. Syntax determines how the semantic associations of a given symbol or word are to be interpreted; it determines which of the many

---

* This is perhaps the best reason for using the Language Experience Method, especially with children whose oral language structures deviate substantially from the written language structures used in commercial materials.

meanings that might be associated with a word is the appropriate one in the sentence or in the syntactic and structural context in which the word is placed. The pupil who has become a word reader has fallen into the error of not reading the phrase or sentence unit that gives meaning to the word.

Poor readers, in contrast to good readers, maximize the graphic input and minimize the semantic and the syntactic input. They are so involved in working out the pronunciation of the word that they have little time left to attend to meaning. Steiner, Wiener, and Cromer (1971) found that poor readers fail to extract contextual cues essential for identification, and that they fail to utilize such cues in identification even when they are presented with them: "They seem to be identifying words as if the words were unrelated items uneffected by syntactical or contextual relationships."

The good reader, on the other hand, processes only a part of the available surface information, attending selectively to the more important words (Willows 1974). Good readers concentrate most of their processing ability on the extraction of meanings, using both semantic and syntactic contexts in reading, and seem to employ an analysis-by-synthesis strategy of reading for meaning. They sample the text to validate linguistic expectancies of the information content of the text rather than analyzing the passage in a word-by-word manner (Hochberg 1970). They maximize their reliance on semantic and syntactic information so they can minimize the amount of print-to-speech processing (recoding or graphophonemic analysis) they have to do (Pearson 1978). Sometimes, unfortunately, they are so entranced with meaning that they make careless errors in recoding words accurately.

THE CUE SYSTEMS IN READING

The discussion thus far has in a general way identified three basic systems operating in reading that can cue meaning: the sign system or the graphic cues; the semantic cues; and the syntax or the syntactic cues. These translate themselves generally into two phases: identification of the symbols; and association of meaning with the symbols. Reading is clearly a synthesis of recognizing and comprehending, in which the absence of either makes true reading impossible (Harris and Sipay 1975).

Good readers can deal with the graphic cues in reading, but they also can handle the decoding phase. This later process requires the association of meanings with symbols. It is a twofold process: Readers must associate semantic meaning (generally acquired through experience) with the symbols; but they must also associate syntactic meaning with them. In other words, there are two contexts in reading (the semantic and the syntactic) and readers must use both of them if they expect to be good readers. The good reader thus utilizes three kinds of information simultaneously: the graphic input; the semantic input; and the syntactic input. Figure 1-1 illustrates these relationships.

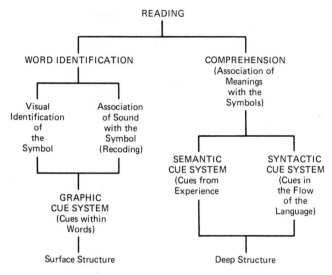

Figure 1-1 The Graphic, Semantic, and Syntactic Relationships

Reading as a sensory process focuses on the graphic input or information, on the letters used in printing, and on their sequencing in words; reading as a perceptual process focuses on the semantic information or cues; reading as a language process is concerned with the syntactic information, or structure, as provided, for example, by word order, inflectional endings, and intonation patterns. Reading is message reconstruction (like the reading of a map) and for the most part comprehension of meaning depends on using all the information or cues available.

A SYNTHESIS

The description of reading that has been developed to this point is twofold: (1) Reading is a complex language system; (2) it is a complex cognitive skill aimed at obtaining information. The reader is constantly processing information.

The following statements summarize basic knowledge about the reading process. They attempt to relate what is known about reading as a language and cognitive process.

1. *Encoding.* The writer translates or encodes a thought, idea, or message into written symbols.
2. *Decoding.* The reader decodes or reconstructs the message encoded graphically by the writer.
3. *Reading is a language and communication process.* Statements 1 and 2 describe the interaction between the writer and the reader. They define the communicative

nature of reading. Communication (and hence comprehension) occurs when the reconstruction agrees with the writer's intended message.

4. *Reading is a sensory process and a word-identification process.* The reader must identify the graphic symbols or develop a perceptual image of the graphic stimulus by fixating on the graphic cues and making discriminative visual responses to them. The graphic cue is the sign in reading. Letters and words are the sign system in which messages are encoded. Communication requires such a sign system. The word-identification process is completed when the reader has formed a perceptual image of the graphic symbol and has associated sound with it.

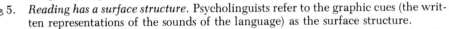

5. *Reading has a surface structure.* Psycholinguists refer to the graphic cues (the written representations of the sounds of the language) as the surface structure.

6. *Reading requires a knowledge of the critical differences between words.* The reader's problem is to discover the critical differences between two letters or words. Readers must learn to look for the distinctive features of the graphic symbols or of the visual configuration that differentiates one word from another. This is not so much a matter of knowing how to look as of knowing what to look for.

7. *Reading frequently requires recoding, not simply decoding.* Recoding is the process of going from the written code to the spoken code.

    a.   A common model for reading has been based on the reconstruction of a spoken message from a printed text, with readers thus making the same meaning responses to the printed text that they would make to the spoken message.

    b .   Visual symbols (graphemes) represent sound (phonemes), not concepts or meanings. The printed word is a phonetic code for the auditory-vocal language.

8. *Reading has a deep structure.* It is this deep structure which gives meaning to the graphic symbols. Reading has as its central purpose the effective communication of meaning. Meaning is mediated through (a) semantic cues; and (b) syntactic cues.

    a.   *Semantic Cues:* Meaning is supplied by readers as they process the symbolic system by relating it to their experiences and conceptual structures.

        (1)   Meaning is not a property of language. The words themselves have no intrinsic meaning.

        (2)   Semantic decoding leads to tentative meaning choices that are tested against the syntactic information.

    b.   *Syntactic Cues:* Meaning is also dependent upon the reader's ability to process sentence patterns that signal information or redundantly confirm the use of a word.

    c.   The reader must be able to deal efficiently with both the surface and the deep structure. The better the reader's knowledge of language, the less need exists for visual information from the printed page.

9. *Syntax is the link between written symbols and meaning.* The two levels of language (surface and deep structure) are related through grammar or syntax. Grammar is the link between graphic symbols and meaning. The rules of syntax determine how the particular visual-semantic associations should be interpreted.

10. *Reading is a process of testing hypotheses.* Readers make a meaning choice or guess consistent with the graphic cues. If they can make a readable choice, they test it for semantic and grammatical acceptability. If the choice is semantically and grammatically acceptable, they assimilate a new meaning or integrate it with prior meanings. Readers check the validity of their guesses by asking whether they produced language structures as they know them, and whether they make sense.

11. *Reading requires acquisition of the writer's meaning.* It is not enough to put one's

own stamp of meaning on the words. The reader must follow the thought of the writer.

SUMMARY

Chapter 1 has reviewed various definitions of reading, classified definitions into those that define reading as interpretation of experience and those that define reading as interpretation of graphic symbols, and discussed the importance of the sign system, decoding, and semantic and language structures.

Reading always involves a sign system—the words or symbols on the printed page; decoding—the association of meaning with the symbols; a semantic context—the word meanings; and language structures—the syntax that mediates between the surface structure and meaning.

The chapter has presented the view that readers can be good readers only if their past experience has furnished them with a cognitive base relevant to the information contained in a particular written communication (Hollander 1975). It was also noted that the reader's level of experience with language itself, with syntactic and idiomatic usage, will play a significant role in determining the level of reading comprehension.

Finally, the basic theme of the chapter has been that reading is clearly a process which is complete only when comprehension is attained. Reading requires a sign system in which messages are formulated, but the critical element is that the reader reconstruct the message encoded in the written language. Full comprehension occurs when the reconstruction agrees with the writer's intended message.

Meaning is supplied by readers as they process the symbolic system by relating it to experience and conceptual structures. Good readers often can go directly to meaning by using syntactic and semantic redundancy. They use the words around a given word (semantic context) and the way the word functions in the sentence (syntactic context) to identify the word. The beginning reader must put letters together to form words. The two levels of language (words and meaning) are related in a complex way through the rules of grammar. Grammar is the link between words and meaning. The rules of syntax determine how the particular visual-semantic association should be interpreted.

QUESTIONS FOR DISCUSSION

1. Discuss the types of reading definitions and give two illustrations of each type.
2. If reading is interpretation of experience, what are the implications for the reading teacher?
3. Explain what is meant when we say that reading is a language and a communication process?
4. What is meant by recoding, decoding, encoding?

5. Why is reading often described as a thinking process?

6. Distinguish between the surface and the deep structure of language.

7. Explain the following: Decoding is effected through syntax; syntax mediates between the visual surface structure and meaning.

8. Compare and contrast the cue systems in reading.

9. Why in the definition of reading is it necessary to include the words "giving the significance intended by the writer to the graphic symbols"?

10. Reading in this chapter is described as "the bringing of meaning to the printed page." What are the implications of this for the beginning reader; for the slow learner or reader; for rate improvement training; and for reading in the content area?

2

THE SENSORY AND PERCEPTUAL NATURE OF READING

Chapter 1 described the nature of the reading process. Two points emerged from this analysis: (1) Reading cannot occur without identification of the symbol; and (2) reading requires the association of meaning with the symbol, hence comprehension. Reading is thus a sensory and a perceptual process. Chapter 2 elaborates on the perceptual and sensory nature of reading more fully, beginning with the sensory nature of the reading process.

READING: A SENSORY PROCESS

Reading begins as a sensory process and ends up being a word-identification process. The eyes bring the stimuli to the reader—the eyes process the printed symbols—and it is only through vision that the reader is able to deal with the significant contrastive shapes and features of the graphic symbols which form the sign system or the surface structure in reading. It is vision that allows the reader to identify the word and to then recognize the word on subsequent occasions.

Reading also includes the vocal and subvocal muscular responses made at the sight of the word and the eye movements made during reading. Efficiency in reading often depends on the oculomotor habits of the reader.

The real significance of vision in reading is that our imaging or perceptual processes, indeed our ability to read with meaning, are clearly dependent upon the stimulus information received through the eyes (Smith 1971). Children must have attained certain levels of visual efficiency and maturation before they are ready to begin reading. Visual efficiency is described in detail in Chapter 5. Here the emphasis is on the visual behavior, or eye movements, of the person engaged in reading.

The Eye Movements In Reading

Emile Javal in 1878 was the first to report on the nature of eye movement during reading. He described the eyes as moving "par saccades"—by jerks or little jumps with intervening fixation pauses (Griffin, Walton, and Ives 1974). Tinker (1933) found that photographs of eye movements record the approximate center of the field of vision. This fixation field is called the point of fixation. However, when fixating on this point, one also sees and recognizes a part of the peripheral visual field.

In reading there is no continuous sweep of the eyes across the page. The eyes proceed in quick, short movements with pauses interspersed. Eye movements are characterized by fixations, interfixation movements, regressions or refixations, and return sweeps. The time elements in reading are fixation time and movement time.

A fixation is the stop the eye makes so that is can react to the graphic stimuli. It is the pause for reading. Because the input of visual information resulting in perception is not continuous, the material is divided into chunks that are reassembled by the brain into a spatiotemporally continuous visual world (Gaardner 1970). During the fixation pause the reader recognizes letters, words, or possibly phrases. The intake process is suspended and the inner process of reading occurs.

Taylor, Frackenpohl, and Pettee (1960) report that the average first grader makes about 224 fixations per 100 words; the average college student, about 90 (see Table 2-1). The fixation time varies according to the difficulty of the material from about 0.22 seconds for easy reading materials to 0.32 seconds for objective test items. Smith (1978) notes that the prolongation of a fixation in reading indicates that the viewer can make little sense of what is being looked at.

The size of the unit recognized during a single fixation (its length in terms of words) depends upon the physical characteristics of the material and upon the reader's facility in word recognition, familiarity with the material being read, and ability to assimilate ideas. Fixation frequency, on the other hand, is determined by the purposes of the reader, the reader's familiarity with the content, the difficulty of the material, and the format in which the materials are presented.

To understand the role that the fixation pause plays in reading, it is

Table 2-1* Averages for Measurable Components of the Fundamental Reading Skill

Grade†	1	2	3	4	5	6	7	8	9	10	11	12	Col.
Fixations (incl. regressions) per 100 words	224	174	155	139	129	120	114	109	105	101	96	94	90
Regressions per 100 words	52	40	35	31	28	25	23	21	20	19	18	17	15
Average span of recognition (in words)	.45	.57	.65	.72	.78	.83	.88	.92	.95	.99	1.04	1.06	1.11
Average duration of fixation (in seconds)	.33	.30	.28	.27	.27	.27	.27	.27	.27	.26	.26	.25	.24
Rate with comprehension (in words per minute)	80	115	138	158	173	185	195	204	214	224	237	250	280

* Stanford E. Taylor, Helen Frackenpohl, and James L. Pettee, *Grade Level Norms for the Components of the Fundamental Reading Skill* (Huntington, New York: Educational Developmental Laboratories, Inc., 1960), Bulletin No. 3, p. 12. Reprinted by permission.

† First grade averages are those of pupils capable of reading silently material of 1.8 difficulty with at least 70 percent comprehension. Above grade one, averages are those of students at midyear reading silently material of midyear difficulty with at least 70 percent comprehension.

necessary to be familiar with two terms, namely, the perception span and the recognition span.

The perception (or visual) span is the amount (usually conceived in terms of numbers, letters, or words) that is *seen* in a single fixation. This can be measured by a tachistoscopic exposure. Poor readers frequently have a wider visual span than good readers because they do not organize what they see.

The recognition span is the amount that is *seen and organized* in a single fixation, ordinarily the number of words that are recognized and understood during a single fixation. The size of the recognition span is obtained by dividing the number of words read, by the number of fixations made while reading: $\frac{\text{Number of words read}}{\text{Number of fixations}}$. This span varies with the difficulty of the material or with the knowledge of the reader. The less readers know about what they are reading, the less they will be able to apprehend in a single fixation.

A wide span of recognition contributes to a wide eye-voice span in oral reading and to a wide eye-memory span in silent reading. A narrow span of recognition contributes to a narrow eye-voice span and forces the pupil to pronounce each word as it is recognized in order to obtain meaning from the text. Such pupils cannot keep their eyes several words ahead of their voice and thus carry the context mentally.

Thought-unit reading is sometimes wrongly identified with the concept of phrase seeing or with the suggestion that it is possible or even common to read three or four words per fixation. Thought units are not visual units. The reader groups words, using a knowledge of syntax to do so. Meaning depends upon the syntactic (not visual) structure that the reader projects on a series of words. Even though pupils read in thought units, they rarely comprehend more than one word per fixation. Thought units generally consist of a series of fixations.

A regression is a reverse movement. It is a return to a previously fixated syllable, word, or phrase, for a repeat fixation; or a return to material that was missed because the eye movement overreached the perceptual span. It is a fixation in a right-to-left direction on the eye-movement photograph. It is a saccade that goes in the opposite direction from the line of type—from right to left along a line (Smith 1971, 1978).

Regressions are likely to occur when the flow of thought is interrupted, out of habit or a lack of confidence which leads the pupil to feel the need for constant re-reading; when eye deficiencies prevent accurate perception; when directional attack in seeing is inadequate; or simply because certain material has been missed. The flow of thought may be broken in a number of ways: through failure to recognize the basic meaning of a word; failure to recognize the meaning suggested by the context; failure to relate the meaning of one word to that of other words; or failure to relate the meaning of a word to the conditions under which it is being used.

Although regressions may result in immature reading, a certain amount of regression may be desirable. A regression may well be a means by which pupils correct themselves. Regressions for verification, for phrase analysis, and for re-examination of a previous sentence seem especially useful. Regression thus may at times be just as productive an eye movement as a saccade in a forward direction (Smith 1971, 1978).

The number of regressions made per 100 words varies from reader to reader. The average first grader makes about 52; the average ninth grader about 20; and the average college student about 15. (For averages for the other grades see Table 2-1.) The regressions of the poor reader are usually not for verification or for phrase analysis. They tend to occur within the same word and thus are caused primarily by inaccuracies in seeing. The really good reader makes about 9 or 10 regressions per 100 words.

After a line is read, the eyes make a return sweep to the beginning of the next line. The return sweep takes from 0.04 to 0.05 seconds. Inaccuracies here may require refixation. For example, the proper line may be missed entirely, or the eyes may fix on a point before or after the first word of the new line.

Figure 2-1 illustrates the various components of the movements of the eye as recorded by the eye-movement camera.

Developmental Aspects of Eye Movement

When researchers in reading first succeeded in recording eye movements, many concluded that to improve reading it was merely necessary to improve eye movements. Poor readers obviously made many more regressions and required more fixations per line than did good readers. It seemed logical that if the number of regressions and fixations could be reduced, reading would be improved. Some theorists consequently held that eye movements were major determinants of reading facility; others, however, held that eye movements were only symptoms of good or poor reading; and still others indicated that they might be either causes or symptoms or both. Oculomotor behavior has since come to be regarded primarily as a symptom of underlying perceptual and assimilative processes, or of central cerebral processes, especially comprehension. The generally held opinion is that efficient reading results in efficient eye movements rather than vice versa.

Eye-movement skills develop rapidly during the first four grades with perhaps a slight improvement between grades six and ten. Apart from the age of the reader, however, the research indicates that eye movements vary with the material, as the difficulty of the material increases, and as the individual takes greater pain to read well. The difficulty of the material rather than the nature of the subject matter is the crucial determinant.

Immature readers generally do not vary their eye movements with the difficulty of the reading matter or with a change of purpose. The good readers, on the other hand, employ more efficient eye movements, which result in better word recognition, word analysis, and comprehension. Poor readers make extra fixations and regressions because they do not understand; they need training to improve word recognition and comprehension rather than training in eye move-

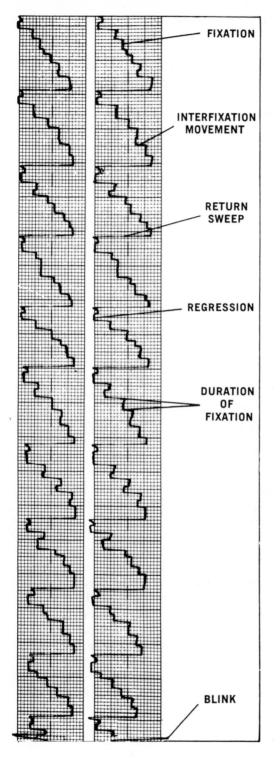

FIXATION

INTERFIXATION
MOVEMENT

RETURN
SWEEP

REGRESSION

DURATION
OF
FIXATION

BLINK

Figure 2-1 Components of Eye Movement. EDL/McGraw Hill, Educational Developmental Laboratories, Inc. A Division of McGraw-Hill, Huntington, N. Y. 11743.

ment (Schubert and Torgerson 1972). When children make many regressions, that itself indicates that that they are having difficulty. The regressions are best understood as symptomatic of the difficulty, rather than being its cause (Smith 1971, 1978).

Under certain conditions, both good and poor readers show irregularities in their eye movement. And, although eye-movement surveys indicate that a great number of children have not developed the habit of perceiving materials in a left-to-right progression, while making a minimum number of fixations and regressions (Taylor 1959), one should remember that most of these surveys involve situations that are somewhat atypical. The pupil's eye movements might be different in normal reading.

However, Griffin, Walton, and Ives (1974) found that poor readers had less efficient eye movements even when allowance was made for differences in decoding words and comprehension. The poor readers had more regressions and omitted more materials. They were less efficient regardless of the type of material used. Some sequenced saccadic eye movements too rapidly, thus skipping material; others sequenced too slowly, resulting in over fixation.

The Eye-Voice and Eye-Memory Spans

The eye memory span is the distance the eyes have traveled ahead of the point at which interpretation occurs. The eye-voice span is the distance the eyes have moved ahead of the point at which pronunciation occurs; it is the number of words or letter spaces by which the visual processing is ahead of the oral reading (Golinkoff 1975-1976). Mature readers have a wide eye-memory span and a wide eye-voice span. They do not commit themselves to an interpretation until they have read a sufficient amount of material. Such readers delay their interpretation of the visual intake until they have perceived enough material to grasp a thought unit, and they keep in mind a sufficient amount of context so as to make the best interpretation.

Generally in silent reading, the mature reader has a memory span of from 15 to 20 letters. In oral reading it is slightly less. The eye-voice span of good comprehenders tends to be about 13.8 letter spaces and that of poor comprehenders tends to be about 8.7 letter spaces. The average eye-voice span is approximately 3 words for second graders and 4.5 words for fourth graders (Levin and Turner 1966). It tends to increase with age and is influenced by the meaningfulness of the material. Rate improvement depends, to a great extent, on the shortening of the fixation pauses and on the lengthening of the eye-memory and eye-voice spans.

Eye-Movement Screening

Eye-movement screening probably provides the best objective evidence of precisely what the individual is doing visually while reading; furthermore, it confirms the effects of the visual deviations upon reading as no other diagnostic tool can do (Spache 1976). A study of the pupil's eye movements during reading may provide cues to the pupil's more basic word-recognition and comprehensive difficulties.

The best screening device is the EDL/Biometrics Reading Eye II.* It records eye movements instantly on heat-sensitive paper. A small mirror can satisfy most needs for observing eye movements, however. By placing a mirror on a table between the child and the examiner, the number of fixations per line can be counted. Another approach consists of punching a hole in the center of a page of reading material. As one person reads, another looks through the hole and observes the eye movement.

Through an analysis of the recorded pattern of the individual's eye movements, it is possible to obtain information about the number of fixations per 100 words; the number of regressions per 100 words; the average span of recognition

$$\left(\frac{100 \text{ words read}}{\text{Number of fixations}} \right);$$

the average duration of fixation

$$\left(\frac{\text{Number of seconds of reading time}}{\text{Number of fixations}} \right);$$

the rate of comprehension; the pupil's directional attack

$$\left(\frac{\text{Number of regressions per 100 words}}{\text{Number of fixations per 100 words}} \right);$$

and the pupil's relative efficiency in reading

$$\left(\frac{\text{Number of words read per minute}}{\text{Number of fixations per 100 words } + \text{ Number of regressions per 100 words}} \right).$$

The reading efficiency score can be converted to a grade-level reading score. As the pupil advances in reading maturity, there should be fewer fixations per 100 words, a wider recognition span, a shorter duration of fixation, more rapid reading, better directional attack, and more fluent reading.**

READING: A PERCEPTUAL
AND THINKING PROCESS

Consider now a second point, namely, that reading is a perceptual process. This concept was introduced in Chapter 1 under the heading, "The Importance of

---

* Available from Educational Developmental Laboratories (McGraw-Hill), 1221 Avenue of the Americas, New York, New York, 10020.

** For a profile of eye movement, see *Diagnosis and Remediation of Reading Disabilities* (Dechant 1981a: p. 58).

Decoding or Comprehension." Reading is certainly more than vision or eye movements. Reading is much more than simply recognizing the graphic symbols.

Reading is more than a sensory process; it is more than the simple recognition of the graphic symbol or words. It is more than a skill to be learned through practice; it is even more than the arousal of meaning or the gaining of meaning from printed symbols. It is also a perceptual, conceptual, and thinking process. Conceptual thought is required to react with meaning to the word, the sentence, or a paragraph, and reading occurs only when meaning is brought to graphic stimuli. Reading is a progressive apprehension of the meanings and ideas represented by a sequence of words; it includes seeing the word, recognizing the word, being aware of the word's meaning, and relating the word to its context. The reader is stimulated by the author's printed words but must in turn invest those words with meaning.

Chapter 1 noted that the reader must use graphic, semantic, and syntactic cues to be a good reader. This section focuses on the importance of the semantic cues. It points out that printed pages do not of themselves transmit meaning. The essence of meaning comes from the reader's fund of experience. Thus, both ocular *and* interpretative factors are essential for reading.

Although reading begins with sensation and with the subsequent recognition of the symbol, the critical element in the reading act is not so much what is seen on the page as what is signified by the symbol; the significant element is the reader's interpretative response to the written symbol.

Such an interpretative response to the symbol requires perception. An examination of the perceptual process should make possible a better understanding of the reading process.

The Nature of Perception

Perception is a consciousness of the experiences evoked by a symbol—a process whereby sensory stimulation is translated into organized experience, or percept. Perception concerns itself with the way one processes information that comes through the senses. Perception is initiated by a stimulation of the sense organs which in reading are the eyes. Atkinson (1971: p. 106) notes that perception involves "the interaction of the sensory systems with those parts of the brain that are concerned with storage and retrieval of past experiences." Perception is a sensation clothed with the perceiver's wealth of past experience.

In perception, the perceiver always goes beyond what the senses provide. Perception goes beyond the sensory data and involves information that is not present to the senses. In looking at a chair, one's senses are not really in contact with the chair at all. What strikes the rods and the cones of the retina is a series of light rays that are reflected from the chair. In looking at a circle one organizes the incoming impulses into a circle even though the pattern (the Gestalt) on the retina is not circular. Although the light rays *cause* the perception, the perceiver perceives not the light rays, but the chair or table. The perceiver's *behavior* is determined by the object and not by the light rays.

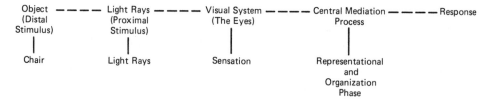

Figure 2-2   The Perceptual Process

As a result, the cognitive theorist draws a distinction between the light rays (the proximal stimuli) and the object (the distal stimulus). Generally, psychologists refer to the proximal stimulus simply as the stimulus. Figure 2-2 illustrates the various steps in perception.

The world as it *appears* is very different from the actual physical world (for example, electromagnetic waves are clearly not perceptible); indeed, the world that is perceived is a construction, the end result of events that occur in the nervous system. The physicist describes a situation as electromagnetic vibrations of varying wavelength, but the perceiver experiences color, or hues of red, green, or blue. Only when a wavelength of 470 nanometers strikes the eye, does the perceiver perceive blue; yet hues and tones have no existence other than as contents in the consciousness of human beings, as mental events. Thus, one's perceptions roughly correspond to the physical phenomenon, but they are clearly not the same thing. Perception is not a phenomenon which is understandable by an analysis of the microscopic events that underlie it.

In instances of figure-ground reversal (see Figure 2-3), perception depends as much on the characteristics of the perceiver as on the characteristics of

Figure 2-3   Figure Reversal. Clifford Morgan and Richard King, *Introduction to Psychology*, © 1975, p. 341. Reprinted by permission of McGraw-Hill, New York.

the stimuli. Whether one sees two faces or a vase depends upon one's mental set, and yet the proximal stimuli (the light rays) are the same. Obviously the same proximal stimuli can become signs for various distal objects.

The phenomenon of apparent movement, generally called the phi-phenomenon, clearly demonstrates that in perception the perceiver goes beyond what the senses provide. Motion pictures are an excellent example of apparent movement. The projected images from the individual frames of the film have no movement—the movement is only apparent. The light in the neon advertising sign is also perceived as moving from one place to another, but actually as the light in one place is turned off, another light goes on.

Certainly what is apprehended by the viewer involves data not presently available to the senses. There is an implication here that in some way the incoming sensory data are retained, processed, and reorganized by the viewer. Some intermediary step takes place between the sensory input and the response. This intermediary step or process is called perception. Perception thus lies between the sensory processes on the one side and the cognitive processes on the other. Perceptual problem solving results in a percept, and cognitive problem solving results in a concept.

Perception obviously involves more than the transmission of nerve impulses by the sensory system. The information is interpreted by the brain, which constructs an image from a composite of information extracted from the retinal pattern and from information from past visual inputs retrieved from memory. The inner image, mental experience, or percept which results is not an exact photographic copy of the optical pattern thrown on the retina by an object. Thus, the comparison of the eye to a camera is not an entirely accurate analogy. The fact is that one does not see the retinal image; one sees with the aid of the retinal image (Neisser 1971), and with this information one constructs the internal representations of objects called "conscious experience." As indicated earlier, the study of eye movement shows that because of the narrowness of foveal vision (the point of clearest vision) and because the eye movements or saccades occur every twentieth of a second, the inner visual world must be constructed on the basis of information taken in during many distinct fixations.

In summary, perceptual research clearly indicates

1. That perception always goes beyond what the senses provide.
2. That both the external stimulus and a central cerebral process determine what is finally perceived.
3. That what is perceived is dependent upon the perceiver's past experience. People perceive the world in terms of "what they are" as much as "what it is."

Perception and Reading

The view of perception just presented seems to be in agreement with what is known of the nature of the reading process. The perception of a graphic symbol must of necessity involve the simple perception of forms (the printed word) as a means of learning to read. But the more complex perception of the word must come to include the organization and modification of various sensory data in order that a particular series of printed letters (the word) may evoke meaning.

Words on the printed page have no meanings of their own since meaning is not inherent in the word. Reading, then, like perception, must go beyond the sensory data. Meaning comes at least partly from within the reader. Reading occurs only when the reader understands what the symbol represents. Reading requires interpretation. Korzybski notes that reading is the reconstruction of the events behind the symbols. And Semelmeyer (1957) points out that reading should bear the same relationship to experiences or events that a map bears to the territory which it is supposed to represent.

Readers do not see the object, person, or experience of which the author writes. Their eyes are in contact with a word, in fact with the light rays that are reflected by the word. It is impossible for readers to see meaning, and yet they take meaning to the word. Readers must be perceiving something beyond what they see. They must be—and are—using information that is not present to the senses. Their reactions to the printed word must be determined by the experiences that they have had with those objects or events for which the symbol stands. The reader cannot stop with a simple recognition of the symbol. Unfortunately, readers, especially poor readers, sometimes become so engrossed with the mechanical aspects of reading, with word identification and with pronunciation, that they fail to understand the need for comprehension.

Good readers are gatherers, processors, and consumers of information (Smith 1971) rather than simple reactors to stimuli (Boneau 1974). They are active and selective information-gatherers who both gain and create knowledge. Their brains are constantly processing information, and incoming information is continually being tested, reformulated, and acted upon in the light of prior experience. Readers extract meaning from what they read on the basis of the visual information (the surface structure of the language) they receive from the environment through their receptor systems, but also on the basis of the deep structure of language and the knowledge and experiences contained within their brain and which are available to memory (Smith 1971). Language and what is read cannot be comprehended unless the receiver (the reader or listener) makes this critical, active contribution.

Although earlier psychologists used somewhat different terminology, they noted similar characteristics of perception and hence of reading. Lange (1902: p. 8) wrote, "The mind apprehends outer impressions in accordance with its wealth of knowledge gained through former activity." He noted as well that "we see and hear not only with the eye and ear, but quite as much with the help of our present knowledge, with the apperceiving content of the mind" (1902: p. 21).

The Major Determinants of Meaning

To this point, reading has been described as a perceptual process. Indeed, without perception there is no true reading, for it is through perception that the graphic symbol achieves meaning.

It seems appropriate here to discuss further some of the factors which influence perceptions and consequently meanings. What are some determinants of the meaning which the individual will bring to the graphic symbol? Are there ways in which a group of pupils can be helped to have similar understandings of the materials they read? And how can "discommunication" between reader and writer be reduced?

The major determinants of meaning seem to include one's experience, culture, and native endowment; one's ability to reconstruct experience; one's previous experience in concept formation; one's affective state; and the context in which the word occurs. The more alike these elements are in both communicator and perceiver, the better the communication tends to be.

Perhaps concern should first be given to the very personal nature of perception and of the meanings taken to the printed word.

PERSONAL NATURE OF PERCEPTION AND MEANING

Perception and meaning are very personal. If a group of persons were to look at the same object of art, there likely would be as many different interpretations (perceptions) of that art object as there were viewers. Lange, noting that of the same landscape the poet's image differs greatly from that of the botanist, and the painter's from that of the geologist, remarked:

> Were we in perception chiefly passive, could the things of the outer world impress themselves immediately upon our minds and thus stamp their nature upon it, they would necessarily always leave behind the same ideas, so that a variety of apprehension would be impossible and inexplicable. (1902: pp. 3-4)

Porter (1958) points out that each human being represents literally billions of varied experiences which have been assimilated and ordered in specific ways, and each attempt at communication, at understanding or being understood, bears the mark of this prodigious personal context. He suggests that no word can ever mean precisely the same thing to any two individuals.

PHYSIOLOGICAL, BIOLOGICAL-NEUROLOGICAL FACTORS

The cognitive representation (for example, of the meaning of the word *democracy*) is personal because it is based on the individual's past experiences, but it is also based on the individual's organizational response characteristics, which are in turn the result of biological inheritance. The perceptual content is both experiential and biological. Studies show that "higher" animals perceive relationships which "lower" animals cannot. The spider monkey, for example, cannot grasp the principle of similarity, but the chimpanzee does so very readily.

Lashley (1949) notes that all animals learn but not all can learn the same thing. What is learned differentiates their organizational ability and this essentially seems to be biologically determined. It is not too presumptuous to presume that the same mechanisms operate in children.

Thus, although meaning must develop from experience, the process is rooted in biology, and frequently it is not the experience that guarantees the solution of the problem, but rather the organizational pattern or biological inheritance into which the experience is fitted. If the pupil lacks the ability to organize the stimuli or to develop habit linkages, or if no trace, or record, is left by the neural activities, there is little hope that perception will reach a level adequate for thinking, reasoning, or reading, or even for simple recall or rote memorization.

PAST EXPERIENCES

One's specific life experiences are, as has already been noted, a major determinant of the nature of the interpretation that one will give to an event or to a word. The individual is a storehouse of past experiences which in turn are the bases for interpretation of the new experiences or stimuli.

A chick that previously tried pecking at a bitter-tasting caterpillar will reject it in a second situation simply at the sight of it. The chick now responds to the caterpillar on the basis of its past learning. The chick is said to "know" that the object is bitter-tasting.

The backwoods boy who has known a *road* to be the painfully rocky mule path along a gullied hillside might give an unusual interpretation of the sentence, "All roads lead to Rome." And the child who has lived all her life in the city or near a superhighway is likely to take to the lines of the poem, "Let me live in my house by the side of the road and be a friend to man" numerous memories of the roar of speeding vehicles and the odors of gas fumes and speed-heated tires—hardly the peaceful atmosphere the poet intended to project.

Although each child's interpretation of the two quotations will become more accurate as his or her experiences, real or vicarious, become more extensive, there will always remain some elements of their original perceptions.

CULTURE

The culture in which we have lived is surely another major determinant of what a word will mean to us. Smith (1956: p. 23) noted that "our interpretation of what we read, in fact our very readiness to learn to read, is largely a function of those human groups and institutions with which we have been associated."

Language and culture are closely related. The language—the words and idioms—frequently becomes encrusted with historic and cultural meaning. Anshen (1957) notes that language is indispensable not only for the construction of the world of thought but also for the construction of the world of perception, both of which constitute the ultimate nexus of an intelligible communion between people.

PHYSICAL AND EMOTIONAL FACTORS

One's physical state also influences one's perceptions and meanings. The child who is ill and the healthy youngster will have quite different reactions to such phrases as "hot dogs and mustard" or "turkey stuffed with dressing."

Perception may also be dependent on the emotive quality of one's past experiences. The word *cave*, for example, will be interpreted differently by the youngster who has enjoyed security while digging or exploring caves and by the youngster whose experience with a cave was one of terror and panic. The emotional state of the reader may distort, color, or completely change meaning to such an extent that communication becomes impossible.

Perceptual Veridicality

The consideration of factors which influence perception and hence reading has indicated that no two persons will have exactly the same perceptions of the same object or, as applied to reading, of the same word. However, individuals do seem to strive to achieve the closest possible agreement between the realities of their environment and their own perceptions of them. In other words, the individual is striving for perceptual veridicality. Perception, unfortunately, rarely is totally veridical. Due to the various and varying factors which influence it, perception is at best an inadequate and approximate representation of concrete reality.

In reading, veridicality is especially difficult to attain. Words are abstractions that have acquired their meaning from specific experiences. And if experience has been inadequate or the symbolic processes of perceiving have caused inaccuracies or have left deeply entrenched inaccurate interpretation, a high degree of veridicality may be almost impossible. The pupil's meaning for the word will be inadequate.

Words permit the writer to share experiences with readers. Readers do not directly see or experience the object, person, place, sensation, or event of which the author writes. They see or experience them through the symbols that stand for them and evoke their perception of them. There is thus no direct or invariable connection between the symbol and the referend, the datum, object, event, or sensation. Verbal symbols are at best inadequate substitutes for direct experience.

Brunswik (1957) refers to the degree of distal-proximal similarity as "ecological validity." Herrick (1956) suggests that the validity of a perception is in its predictive value as a guide for action. The meaning of "tractor" that might be aroused by the word *caterpillar* may be adequate in one response situation; in another situation such a response to the word would not be validated in action. The word might then more appropriately suggest the concept "larva."

Perceivers call upon their previous experience and generally assume that the perception which was most successful in the past is most likely to be correct now. They interpret sensory data on the basis of their past experience. When they find their perception to be in error, they must change their interpretation even though the retinal image has not changed. When one has a great deal of relevant and consistent experience to relate to stimulus patterns, the probability of the success of one's prediction or perception as a guide to action is high. When experience is limited or inconsistent, the reverse holds true.

The situation in reading is quite similar. Pupils commonly make substitutions when they read. Studies have shown that when good readers err, they tend to substitute words that harmonize with the context. Poor readers on the other hand, substitute words that do not fit contextually. Perhaps this is because of the greater experience underlying the good reader's perception. As Norberg noted (1953, 1956), the observer perceives whatever represents, for him, the most likely prognosis for action based upon his experience. Thus, the good reader's prognosis is superior to that of the poor reader primarily because the good reader's experience is superior.

Generally, the greater the number of experiences and the richer their quality, the greater are the chances for veridicality both in perception and in reading. But even the most veridical perception may be an inadequate representation, as indeed the "best" interpretation in reading may be equally inadequate. Complete comprehension is extremely difficult to attain. Perception normally remains a representation.

Problems of Communication

There are many possibilities for faulty communication between writer and reader, and there is little likelihood that any two readers ever will give exactly the same interpretation to any given paragraph. Perfect communication is rare. Not only are readers' experiences usually different (and hence also their meanings, ideas, and concepts), but frequently they are not familiar with all the ways of expressing meaning. They are also, of course, not completely familiar with the writer's specific modes of expression. Finally, words can only create a symbolic representation in the mind—never exact reality.

Generally, the writer and the reader communicate only if they are capable of assigning some common meaning to a symbol. This means that they must have had some commonality of experience. And usually they must be able to make a generic response to their experience. Thus, Bruner (1957b: p. 125) notes, "If perceptual experience is ever had raw, that is, free of categorical identity, it is doomed to be a gem serene, locked in the silence of private experience."

Fortunately, because experiences tend to be more similar than different, perceptions of reality or the interpretations given to sentences (or the comprehension of them) are similar enough to allow for communication between one person and another, between writer and reader.

SUMMARY

Chapter 2 has described reading as a visual skill while noting that success in reading depends more on the underlying perceptual and assimilative processes than on visual efficiency and the peculiar oculomotor habits of the individual reader. Faulty eye movements are not so much a cause of poor reading as a symptom of poor reading; nevertheless, the opening portion of the chapter looked intensely at eye movements in reading because reading is a visual process and eye-movement screening provides the best objective evidence of precisely what the individual is doing visually while reading. It was further noted that reading efficiency depends upon making a minimum number of fixations and regressions while preceiving reading material in a left-to-right fashion.

This chapter has also expanded on the nature of perception and its significance for reading. Because reading is a perceptual process, in which the graphic symbols are retained, processed, and reorgainized by the reader, we can make the following observations:

1. Recognition of a word is not reading. The printed word itself possesses no meaning. The pupil must react with meaning, and this frequently requires the organization of previous experiences.
2. Perception of a word or the meaning taken to a word or series of words is usually representational, not representing wholly or completely the meaning intended. Children use previous experience to interpret the words of others. At times their perceptions are in error.
3. The meaning comes from the learner rather than from the word.
4. The central process that controls the readers' particular reactions to printed materials is termed cognition and depends on adequate neural functioning
5. The sum total of the readers' biology and experiences and their perception of them—in other words, the total field of psychological, physical, physiological, and social forces as they impinge upon the readers' perceptions at the moment of action—determine their reactions to words. Simply put, all readers read something of themselves into the written or printed word.
6. Communication is the process of understanding another's perceptions and meanings.

QUESTIONS FOR DISCUSSION

1. Is it desirable to develop the eye movements of the reader? In your answer discuss the relationship between eye movements and the central processes of comprehension.
2. Reading is said to be a thinking process. Find four reading passages that illustrate the thinking processes of analysis-synthesis, problem solving, inference, and organization.
3. What is the relationship between degrees of comprehension and experiential background?
4. Discriminate between thought-unit reading and the suggestion that the child should learn to read two or three words per fixation. Does a fixation constitute a thought unit? What are the implications of recent findings in this area with regard to the development of the child's memory and retention span?
5. Compare a child's development of a percept of "chair" with his perception of the word *cat*.
6. Discuss the following statements:
    a. Reading should bear the same relationship to experiences or events that a map bears to the territory which it is supposed to represent.

    b.   Reading is the development or creative construction of meaning in response to external stimuli, usually written words.

    c.   Comprehension, or the apprehension of meaning, is a direct function of (1) the number of words one knows and (2) the number of meanings that one associates with each word.

    d.   The specific meaning elicited by a word is a function of the context in which it occurs.

3

READING: A LANGUAGE AND COMMUNICATION EXPERIENCE

Chapter 1 noted that in addition to being a sensory and perceptual process, reading is also a language and communication process; that it is a process of putting the reader in contact and communication with ideas; and that writing has no purpose without a reader. Communication from writer to reader occurs only if the reader can take meaning to the printed page; and without the reader, communication via the printed page is impossible.

This chapter deals with a broad range of topics, beginning with reading as communication. Other topics include the meaning of language, oral language proficiency, listening proficiency, knowledge of grammar, and speech defects. All of these aspects of language, though complex areas of study in their own right, are relevant to the understanding of reading.

READING AS COMMUNICATION

Early in this book it was suggested that the teaching of reading functions best when it is one phase of the total communicative process. There are good reasons why the teacher of reading needs to understand communication and language:

1. The child's proficiency in communication and language skills, both speaking and listening, is one of the best indicators of the child's readiness for beginning reading.
2. The teacher cannot understand the reading process without understanding communication and oral language development.
3. The more alike the patterns of language structure in the reading material are to the patterns of language structure used in speaking, the better the pupil's comprehension tends to be.
4. Language is a system of responses by which individuals communicate with each other (interindividual communication); it is a system of responses that facilitates thinking and cognition (intraindividual communication); and it is a measure of cognitive development.
5. Disabled readers frequently are retarded in language, often beginning to speak later than is usual.

Communication is the heart of the language arts. Without communication listening or reading cannot occur. Reading takes place only when the child shares the ideas that the communicator intends to convey.

Communication always involves two elements: (1) the ideas or experiences that are to be communicated; and (2) the signs or symbols that are used to convey these ideas or experiences. The signs or symbols may be natural or conventional. The distress cries of children, their tears, cries, and yawning, are natural signs. Words and numbers are conventional symbols. They are conventional because they have no meaning of their own.

Communication is not only a human characteristic. The bee that engages in a dance to inform a fellow worker of the distance and direction of a new supply of food is communicating. The cluck of the hen that sends her chicks scurrying is also communication. Even a traffic light or a temperature control system communicates.

Communication is thus a sensorimotor process involving the use of signs. It includes the motor reactions of the signmaker—the speaker or writer—and the reception of the sign by the listener or reader. In human communication, these signs are symbols or words, and they receive their meaning from and through experience. Reading is the culminating act of the communicative process, initiated by the thoughts of the writer and expressed through the signs or symbols on the printed page.

Terms from communication theory that have special significance in understanding reading are *communication channel, limited channel capacity, noise,* and *redundancy* (Smith 1978). Consider these terms more closely:

1. *Communication channel.* The writer (transmitter) and the reader (receiver) are two ends of a communication channel through which information flows. As a message passes through the communication channel, it takes on a variety of forms. At each part of the communication process it is possible that the message will be changed in some way.
2. *Limited channel capacity.* As in any communication system, there is a limited channel capacity in the communication system of the reader. For example, there is

a limit to the speed at which the eye can travel over a passage of text while making information-gathering fixations. The amount of information that can be acquired in a single fixation is also limited.

3. *Noise.* A message or communication may be confused or made less clear by extraneous signals called noise. Because all communication channels have limited capacities, noise may overload the system and prevent the transmission of informative signals. In reading, noise may be a type face that is difficult to read, poor illumination, or distraction of the reader's attention. Smith (1971, 1978) notes that because of noise, reading is intrinsically more difficult for the beginning reader than for the experienced reader.

4. *Redundancy.* Redundancy exists whenever information is duplicated by more than one source. Presenting a word both visually and orally is a form of redundancy that helps the learner. In reading, it is immediately apparent that the larger the context, the greater the redundancy. And the more redundancy there is, the less visual information the skilled reader requires to identify words.

Conversely, the less redundancy there is, the more visual information is needed. Lack of experience with life itself, with materials and their content, and with words and their identification, are major inhibitors to redundancy. When readers must get a great amount of visual information, when they must identify every single letter or even every word, they will be slow readers and will usually have difficulty reading for meaning.

THE MEANING OF LANGUAGE

Reading is not only communication; it is communication through language, albeit written language. Proficient readers are those who can make appropriate associations between written and spoken symbols, who understand language structures, and who have an adequate language base that allows them to bring meaning to the printed page. The teacher of reading needs to have some basic understandings about language. The discussion that follows will elaborate upon the meaning of language, the philosophy and sociology of language, and the role of language in thinking.

The Definition of Language

Soffietti (1955) notes that language refers to "the systemized set of vocal habits by means of which the members of a human society interact in terms of their culture." Sapir (1921) suggests that language is a purely human method of communication through a system of voluntarily produced symbols. Ruddell (1974: p. 20) defines language "as a system represented by sound symbols with conventional meanings shared by members of a linguistic group."

Definitions of language generally emphasize the following characteristics (see, especially, Jolly 1972: pp. 322-341; Ruddell 1974: p. 64: Wilson 1972: p. 37):

1. Language is a human attribute.
2. Language is in part acquired behavior, but it is also largely instinctive. The child is equipped biologically both to use and to learn language. In all cultures the onset of

language is age correlated, and the process of first-language learning occurs in a rapid, smooth, and predictable sequence. Any child can learn any of the world's languages, because he or she spontaneously emits the sounds of all language. The acquisition strategy is the same for all babies everywhere in the world. Children are born ready to speak a language, namely, the baby talk of childhood, that they gradually modify to approximate the language of their parents. They start with a language of their own, not from nothing.

3. Language is verbal symbolic behavior. Language is primarily oral in nature. Indeed, some cultures have not developed a written language.

4. Language is systematic and patterned behavior, having a definite form or structure. The speaker cannot indiscriminately alter the sequence of words. He does not say, "The man fat in sit can there."

5. Language is generally reflexive behavior. After the child has acquired language, language tends to become almost completely reflexive behavior.

6. Language has individual and social significance, being a primary tool of communication.

7. Language is a system actualized as sounds or phonemes.

8. Language has an intonation pattern which gives it its melody and rhythm and which includes pitch, stress, and juncture.

9. The connection between the symbol and its meaning is conventional, arbitrary, learned, and traditional.

10. Lexical items and grammatical patterns convey meaning to those who know the code. English has a characteristic group of grammatical patterns, having a definite form or structure.

11. Writing is a recodification of speech. The alphabet and the punctuation represent speech sounds and intonation patterns.

12. English is based on an alphabetical principle.

13. English is spoken in dialects of which standard English is only one.

14. Language is an open system, allowing the speaker to say new utterances that may never have been said before. The child is clearly able to generate sentences.

15. Words can be used at a distance in time and space from their referents.

This last point calls for a comment. If, for example, some balmy afternoon you look out of the window and see water dripping from the trees, you infer that it is raining. The water itself is a sign of the rain. The word *water*, on the other hand, does not have a direct connection with rain. One may use it and rain need not fall.

Furthermore, except for the fact that humans have conventionally agreed among themselves that the word "rain" should be used when the vapor in the atmosphere condenses and falls in watery form, the word "flour" might be used. However, if one wants to communicate with others, it is necessary to abide by common conventions. Communicators must assign similiar meanings to the same symbol. As noted earlier, a word that has a private definition does not communicate, but instead represents a perceptual experience in the raw and is "doomed to be a gem serene, locked in the silence of private experience" (Bruner, 1957b).

Consider now the parameters of a sociology and philosophy of reading.

The Philosophy and Sociology
of Language*

The philosopher of language deals with the question, "Are words just words, or do they mirror reality and the world, bear meaning, and act as a medium of communication?"

Western thought has always considered that language is about something. Unless words express reality, one is just bantering words about or engaging in empty verbalism.

Nor is this a uniquely Western concept. The Chinese philosopher Hsun Tzu noted that "names have been fixed to denote realities," that they have a content "determined by an identity of reaction in man . . . to the same things, to the same stimuli" (Anshen 1957: p. 13).

The identity of reaction by various humans undergirds all human certainties. The word thus laden with the experience of the ages becomes an entity upon which all social relations rest.

Through language, we symbolize and order our concepts of the universe. Words are symbols of reality and permit their uses to manipulate knowledge concerning reality. Language allows us to speak of things not in sight, to project into the future, to hold on to reality, to fix it in experience, and to make it available when needed.

The word makes concepts usable. No better illustration of this can be had than the water-pump experience of Helen Keller:

> We walked down the path to the well-house, attracted by the fragrance of the honeysuckle with which it was covered. Someone was drawing water and my teacher placed my hand under the spout. As the cool stream gushed over one hand she spelled into the other the word *water*, first slowly, then rapidly. I stood still, my whole attention fixed upon the motions of her fingers. Suddenly I felt a misty consciousness as of something forgotten—a thrill of returning thought; and somehow the mystery of language was revealed to me. I knew then that "w-a-t-e-r-" meant the wonderful cool something that was flowing over my hand. That living word awakened my soul, gave it light, hope, joy, set it free! . . . I left the well-house eager to learn. Everything had a name, and each name gave birth to a new thought. (1920: pp. 23–24)

In this incident, Helen Keller became aware of the representational function of symbols. The endless job of associating each symbol with a specific object was now over. She had learned that a word can be used to signify and to order the events, ideas, and meanings of the world about her.

What has been said about language applies with equal force to writing and reading. Reading is a language process. People interact with one another through speech and writing, through listening and reading. Listening is the other half of talking, and reading is the other half of writing. A culture becomes a

---

*See Dechant (1965b).

civilization only when it possesses a written language and when there are readers of the history of that culture. Reading is an indispensable means of communication and participation in a civilized society.

When writing and reading became a means of communication and of recording and encoding facts, a sociology of reading was born. Concern then was focused on who reads what and why. An immediate interest developed in questions such as the motives for reading; the amount and kind of material read by members of different social classes; the levels of difficulty of reading materials; and the social effects of reading.

As a result of various inquiries into these questions, the social role of reading became unmistakably clear. Reading is both a social and a socialization process. It is a self-defining process. Reading is quite frequently done in a social group and always involves some degree of social interaction between the writer and the reader. Furthermore, in this society, people who cannot read tend not to perceive themselves as "enfranchised"members of the group or society.

Experience indicates that reading does in fact affect the social understandings, interests, attitudes, beliefs, judgments, morals, and behavior of the reader. Words mold our thinking, direct our action, and permit us to share genius.

The Role of Language in Thinking

As skills in language develop, language serves an increasingly significant role in thinking. Adults are prone to tell youngsters to keep still, but the child continues to drip speech. The child's thinking and mental imagery are so closely associated with the vocal expression that the child finds it difficult to separate them (Van Riper and Butler 1955: p. 4).

The little boy talks to himself as he tries to understand the mechanisms of the toy plane in front of him. The little girl carries on a full conversation with her stuffed elephant. What the adult only thinks, the child both thinks and speaks.

The close relationship between language and thought and between implicit speech and reading has been generally acknowledged. Langer (1948: p. 103) writes: "In language we have the free, accomplished use of symbolism, the record of articulate conceptual thinking; without language there seems to be nothing like explicit thought whatever." Laurita (1973) notes that speech is not merely a by-product of thinking but is also a means of thought.

There is little doubt that a certain amount of vocal behavior and lip and tongue movement accompany many thought processes and most reading. Experiments show that students preparing for an examination actually become hoarse after four hours of intensive study. Hebb (1958: pp. 59-60) suggests that some verbal behavior may play a vital role in problem solving, but he adds that sentence construction shows that thought and speech are not entirely the same process. Our thought processes run well ahead of our articulations.

Consider now the relationship between language and reading. Inadequate language development is admittedly a common cause of poor reading. It is strange but true, nonetheless, that reading theory and teaching have concerned themselves largely with psychological, sociological, physical, and neurological matters but have not concerned themselves rigorously enough with language. As indicated earlier, reading must be regarded as a language-related process; it must be studied in relation to language; and progress in reading occurs most readily when it is taught as one phase of the total communicative process. Kirk and Elkins (1975) report that the academic difficulties of 29 percent of learning-disabled children are attributable to language disorders. There is a strong indication that for some children, reading failures are often secondary to primary language disturbances (verbal expression and comprehension) and that with these children it is necessary to emphasize the primary linguistic skills prior to reading.

Pearson (1978) notes that the failure of diagnosticians to look at reading failure in the context of language has been one of the most serious educational shortcomings. He adds that it has led to situations where it is common to treat a child whose basic problem is a language difference as if he had a reading deficiency. Clearly, if the pupil cannot formulate sentences or turn ideas into words, the deficiency is in general language ability.

The major aspects of language that are most significant for reading readiness and achievement are (1) listening comprehension; (2) clarity of pronunciation; (3) vocabulary knowledge; and (4) mastery of sentence structure or knowledge of sentence sense. Consider first listening comprehension.

LISTENING AND READING PROFICIENCY

There is ample evidence that language training should include experience and training in listening. Listening is the first language art that the child develops, and together with speaking, it has an important effect on the development of competency in reading. Reading success depends upon the pupil's aural-oral experience with words.

Listening requires a cultivation of auditory abilities. It involves the same basic perceptual and mental processes as reading and, indeed, in certain cases may be a more suitable method of learning than is reading. *The language is the same in all the language arts: only the media for communication are different.*

Listening, if it is to be learned at all, must be taught early in life. Carhart (1947) points out that the capacity for mastering new sound discriminations diminishes with age. Children learn to speak fluently the language they hear, regardless of race or nationality. However, when adults learn a new language, they have what native speakers think of as a foreign accent. This is so because

adults have fixed their habits of listening. They do not notice the subtle differences in the phonetic elements of the two languages; instead, they hear the
new language as though it were identical with their native tongue.

Listening goes beyond the mere recognition of sounds. Good auditory
acuity does not necessarily result in good listening. Adequate hearing is only the
first step in listening. Ross (1966) found that good listeners rated higher than poor
listeners on intelligence, reading, socioeconomic status, and achievement, but not
on a hearing test. Two listeners, even with the same hearing acuity, often receive
widely different messages from the same sound.

Listening Skills

There are varying degrees of ability in listening, and these abilities
develop sequentially. The good listener can

1. Recognize differences in phonemes.
2. Recognize morphemes.
3. Interpret sentences modified by intonation.
4. Recognize the role that pitch plays in speech.
5. Identify the speaker's purpose.
6. Develop empathy with the speaker.
7. Use context clues to understand.
8. Anticipate what is being said.
9. Listen for the main ideas.
10. Listen for and remember details.
11. Follow oral directions.
12. Mentally summarize what has been said.
13. Listen between the lines.
14. Identify transitional elements.

Children need training in these skills, and studies indicate that these skills
can be developed.

There are many reasons for improving the listening skills of children.
Skill in listening is closely related to proficiency in many academic areas. Reading
is not learning. It is only one of the media for learning, and for some children it is
an inferior medium. In fact, some studies indicate that up to about the fifth grade
(mental age of ten) children generally learn more and remember better through
listening than through reading. For children in the lower grades, for children
who are poor readers, and perhaps for boys generally, listening is an important
means for achievement.

Generally, the lower the reading ability and the lower the scholastic aptitude, the greater is the advantage of listening over reading. However, since
reading allows the pupil to go back and reread, reading becomes more effective as
the difficulty of the material increases.

Listening ability also is basic to the learning of reading. Coefficients of correlation between scores on listening and reading tests vary from .25 to .80. Does this mean that improvement in listening will lead to improvement in reading? Hollingsworth (1964) reviewed the literature on this point and concluded that listening does indeed have a positive effect on reading achievement. This is not surprising. Listening and reading have basic similarities. Both involve the reception and interpretation of linguistic messages and of ideas from others. Reading demands sight and comprehension; listening calls for hearing and comprehension.

Other relationships between listening and reading are as follows:

1. Listening (and speaking) provides the vocabulary and the sentence structure that serve as a foundation for reading. In a very real sense children read with their ears, mentally pronouncing the words to themselves.
2. Listening and reading utilize similar verbal factors, but they also encompass factors unique to each skill.
3. Without the ability to hear and interpret sounds, the child cannot learn phonics. Training in listening (and speaking) develops auditory discrimination which in turn serves as a basis for phonetic analysis in reading.
4. Ability to listen to and provide an ending for a story is a good indicator of readiness for reading.
5. Words most easily read are those that have been heard and spoken.
6. Listening ability (for example, if scores on a listening comprehension test are higher than reading comprehension scores) is an indicator of the pupil's potential ceiling in reading ability.

Children learn language by ear. The vocabulary and skills in language structure that children bring to school were learned first through listening. In fact, if it were not for these learnings, children would not, or at least only rarely, learn to read. The teacher of reading should take advantage of these previous learnings, helping children to associate the visual symbols with the sounds previously learned. If children have not learned to listen, they must be taught.

Development of the Listening Skill

The listening skill must be consciously fostered in the school. Alert teachers play a major role here. They provide an adequate physical environment, and they see to it that children have visual as well as auditory contact with one another. Teachers are also able to discover children with hearing defects and to adjust learning tasks to fit these children's needs.*

* For a listing of test instruments useful in assessing the listening skill, see Dechant (1981a: p. 16); and for commercial materials designed specifically for teaching the listening skill, see Dechant (1981b: pp. 26-30).

Teachers promote the listening habit mostly by being good listeners themselves and by providing the proper psychological climate for listening. They have high regard for what the child says, help children to formulate a purpose for listening, encourage children to listen for new words and ideas, and provide the opportunities for listening. They introduce new words, read good literature, and point out sound differences and similarities in words.

Listening can be taught through conversation, dramatization, telling stories, singing songs, reading poems, and reading or speaking of rhymes. Children should be encouraged to engage in "show and tell" exercises, in debates, quiz shows, and discussions. They ought to discuss topics informally, ask questions, make plans, give reports, follow directions, criticize, and evaluate what others have said. Each of these activities creates multiple opportunities for listening by other pupils. The tape recorder, record player, radio, television, telephone, piano, and band instruments are particularly useful in developing the listening skill.

The last ten years have witnessed the development of listening centers in classrooms all over the country. Such centers include autoinstructional devices consisting of a tape recorder or record player, a number of earphones, and response sheets which are filled in by the pupil.

EXERCISES FOR DEVELOPIING LISTENING SKILL

Exercises designed to develop the listening skill include the following:

1. The teacher has the pupils listen to a series of scrambled words (*elephants I saw the*) and has the pupils put the words into a meaningful sequence. This exercise (A-Seq-8, from *Teach*, Walker Educational Book Corporation) teaches the pupil to order words according to semantic and syntactic cues. The pupils are told to begin with *I* in the exercise above: *I* _____ _____ _____.
    Another exercise (A-Seq-9, from *Teach*) teaches the pupils to remember and retell a story sequence.

2. The teacher gives directions for making a simple toy and has the pupils carry out the directions. This activity teaches the ability to follow a thought sequence, a skill needed for successful reading comprehension.

3. The teacher asks the pupils to listen for the main idea of a paragraph, story, or poem.

4. The teacher reads a poem or short story and asks the pupils to submit a title for the poem or story.

5. The teacher starts a whispered message around the room from child to child and the last child repeats it aloud. In this activity, the emphasis is on accuracy in relaying the message from one to another.

6. Pupils prepare short talks on a favorite topic. Other pupils in the class should be ready to state the organization of the talk. This exercise teaches the skill of listening to (and reading for) the organization.

7. The teacher reads a short paragraph containing a sentence (or two) that is not in harmony with the context. The pupils are required to identify the out-of-context sentence.

8. Pupils listen to two different broadcasts or recordings with the same news content, one giving a factual report, and the other giving an analysis. Pupils should analyze the two reports, studying the vocabulary used and looking for indications of distortion. This exercise teaches critical listening, and the techniques learned should be useful in critical reading.

9. The teacher uses the tape recorder to record the children's speech and then gives them an opportunity to hear themselves. The teacher should guide the pupils in what to listen for. Later, before beginning reading, the pupils should identify their purposes for reading.

10. The pupils learn to listen for language signals such as *first, there are several ways, furthermore, several suggestions are,* or *on the other hand.* In reading, the pupils need to look for similar language signals.

ORAL LANGUAGE PROFICIENCY AND READING

Communication may involve expression through speaking and writing, or reception and comprehension through listening and reading. The concern in this section is with the effects of the expressive speaking skills on the receptive reading skills. Speaking provides the vocabulary and the sentence patterns for reading. Words and sentences most easily read are those that have been spoken (and heard).

The pupil's proficiency in reading, and certainly in word identification and recognition, is dependent upon the ability to articulate, enunciate, and pronounce the sounds met in the language. Oral language proficiency basically requires the following abilities: to speak without abnormal hesitation; to articulate and enunciate clearly; to pronounce words correctly; to associate words with experiences; to talk in simple sentences; and to tell a simple story. Above everything else, in learning to read the child must perceive the relationships between the spoken and the written language. The pupil must learn that what can be said also can be written and read.

Conversely, lack of vocabulary knowledge, a lack of sentence sense, and the inability to articulate and understand spoken language are among the chief causes of reading disability. To these should be added certain kinds of speech defects. Speech defects generally related to reading disability are those in which speech is characterized by indistinctness, by blurring of the consonant sounds, by a thick quality, or by the rapid, jerky, stumbling patterns seen in cluttering.

The teacher of reading is especially concerned with clarity of pronunciation. It is essential that children learn to articulate all the vowels and the consonants without distortion, omission, substitution, addition, or transposition; that children learn to enunciate all syllables clearly; that they learn to pronounce accurately; that they give the total visual form its proper sound; and that they accent the appropriate syllable or syllables. *Children generally must learn the alphabet of sound* (the phonemes) *before they can be taught the alphabet of letters* (the graphemes).

Reading teachers must know the sound system and the basic principles of language structure. They should be as interested in the development of good speech as is the speech correctionist. Reading teachers are teachers of language and communication skills. They know that development in reading closely parallels development in speech. They realize that if the child has not acquired the needed language facility *before* entering school, the child must be given the opportunity to do so *in* school.

Teachers of reading must familiarize themselves with phonemics, or the discrimination and production of the phonemes of language. They must have an elementary knowledge of the physiology of speech. They must know how to analyze words for their specific sounds.

The Physiology of Speech

Speech consists of the sound waves that are emitted by the human vocal mechanism. These sound waves strike the ear of another and elicit meaning from the recipient. The result of some of these sounds are the vowels and consonants.

THE VOWELS

Children learn quite early to articulate the short and long vowels. The production of the vowels begins with a muscular contraction of the lungs which forces a steady, unobstructed airstream through the trachea, larynx, and pharynx to the outside. *Webster's Dictionary* describes a vowel as a speech sound "in the articulation of which the oral part of the breath channel is not blocked and is not narrowed enough to cause audible friction."* Sometimes the air passes through the oral cavities to the outside; sometimes it passes through the nasal cavities.

The larynx contains the vocal cords. In normal respiration the cords are widely separated at the back end of the larynx. This produces unvoiced sounds. When the cords are almost closed, the forcing of air through the narrow opening sets the cords into vibration and produces a voiced sound. Vowels are voiced sounds.

The size and shape of the mouth and the position of the lips and tongue determine what vowel will be produced. For example, the sounds /ĭ/ (bit) and /ĕ/ (bet) are produced by spreading or flattening the lips; the sounds /o͝o/ (book), /ȯ/ (ball), and /o͞o/ (boot) are produced by rounding the lips.

THE CONSONANTS

Consonants are produced by obstructing the airstream much as a stricture in hose obstructs the passage of water. Appendix I details how the consonant sounds are produced. Table 3-1 summarizes the twenty-five consonant sounds of the language.

* *Webster's Third New International Dictionary*, Philip B. Gove, ed. (Springfield, Mass.: G. & C. Merriam Company, 1967).

Table 3-1   The Consonant Sounds of the Language

PLOSIVES		FRICATIVES		NASALS	SEMIVOWELS	
Voiced	*Unvoiced*	*Voiced*	*Unvoiced*	*Voiced*	*Voiced*	*Unvoiced*
/b/	/p/	/th/	/th/	/m/	/r/	/h/
/d/	/t/	/v/	/f/	/n/	/l/	/hw/
/g/	/k/	/z/	/s/	/ng/	/y/	
		/zh/	/sh/		/w/	
		/j/	/ch/			

Emerald Dechant, *Diagnosis and Remediation of Reading Disabilities,* © 1981, p. 151.
Reprinted by permission of Prentice-Hall, Inc., Englewood Cliffs, N.J.

Developmental Stages of Articulatory Development *

Experience has shown that the child must have reached a certain level of oral language maturity before beginning reading. The reading teacher is thus interested in the "speech age" of the child—the age when the child can produce the various phonemes. Consonant sounds generally develop in a definite order. By the age of seven the average child articulates correctly the consonants and consonant blends 90 percent of the time.

Poole (1934) studied 140 preschool children over a period of three years and found that the rate of development in articulation is similar among boys and girls between the ages of two and one-half and five and one-half. After this girls develop more rapidly and attain the same degree of proficiency by six and one-half that boys attain only at seven and one-half. Poole also found that there is a regular progression in articulation development. Table 3-2 summarizes these findings and indicates at what age certain sounds had been mastered by the 140 children in her group.

The *s* and *z* sounds are listed twice because after the age of five, when

Table 3-2   Ages When Children Normally Have Mastered the Consonant Sounds

AGES	CONSONANTS
3.5	b,p,m,w,h
4.5	d,t,n,g,k,ng,y
5.5	f,v,z,s
6.5	sh,zh,l,th,
8.0	z,s,r,wh,ch,j

Emerald Dechant, *Diagnosis and Remediation of Reading Disabilities,* © 1981, p. 152. Reprinted by permission of Prentice-Hall, Inc, Englewood Cliffs, N.J.

* For assessment of articulatory ability, see Dechant (1981a: pp. 151-153); for materials for teaching articulation skills, see Dechant (1981b: pp.31-34).

dentition causes a spacing between the teeth, they become distorted in a lisp. This lisp disappears when normal dentition is reestablished.

Although serious deviation from normal speech development is not too frequent among first graders, quite commonly children have difficulty with *ch*, *zh*, *sh*, *l*, *th*, *z*, *s*, *r*, and *wh*. The average child does not attain complete mastery of *s*, *l*, *r*, and *th* or their blends until the age of eight years.

What are the implications of all this for reading? If pupils cannot sound the individual phoneme, if they have not developed the clarity of pronunciation mentioned earlier, they probably will not be good oral readers, they will have difficulty with phonics and with learning the proper phoneme-grapheme correspondences, and they may also have difficulty in transmitting meaning.

Lyle (1970), for example, found that retarded early speech development and substantial incidence of articulatory defects between the ages of two and one-half and four are closely related to subsequent reading disability. And yet, developing listening comprehension is more relevant to reading achievement than is becoming a competent speaker of standard English (Harris and Sipay 1975).

KNOWLEDGE OF
GRAMMAR AND READING

The introduction to this chapter alluded to the significance of grammar for reading. If one accepts Chomsky's formulation, then grammar is the link between sounds or graphic symbols and meaning; it mediates between the surface and the deep structure. Grammar has only one basic function: to make utterances clearer.

Grammar consists of morphology and syntax. Morphology is a study of word structure, and syntax is a study of how words are grouped into utterances. Morphology allows for the introduction of minute changes into the word to bring out a special meaning; the various uses of *s* (*cats*, *cat's*, *hits*) are examples of this. Syntax is the grouping of words to suggest variant (and specific) nuances of meaning; for example, "The boy sat in a chair with a broken arm" or "The boy with a broken arm sat in a chair." Readers must first recognize the distinction in arrangement before they can perceive the distinction in meaning.

In addition to phonemes, morphemes, and words, there are certain other characteristics about the utterance that add to and develop meaning. The suprasegmentals of stress, pitch, and juncture convey phonemic differences and change meanings. The loudness of the voice may change, or certain words may be stressed more than others. The pitch may be either low, normal, high, or extra high. High pitch is often associated with heavier stress. In speaking, utterances are combined by what are termed *plus junctures* and are ended by *terminal junctures*. The plus junctures separate words. The terminal junctures are usually accompanied by falls or rises in pitch; they differentiate one phrase unit from another or one type of sentence from another. Phrasing depends on the placement of the junctures.

Junctures or pauses in speech are indicated in writing by punctuation. Punctuation in writing is not so much an aid to writing as it is to reading. The writer knows what the sentences mean and does not need grammatical aids to get at the meaning.

As indicated earlier, genuine reading proficiency is the ability to read language structure. The best reader is one mentally aware of the stresses, elongations of words, changes of pitch and intonation, and rhythms of the sentences. Improper phrasing, wrong emphasis on words, and improper pitch and intonation impair the ability to read a sentence with full meaning.

Words do not give meaning to sentences; rather, words receive their meaning from the sentence or the verbal and syntactic context of which they are a part. The pupil who has become a word reader has fallen into the error of not reading the phrase unit that gives meaning to the word. The word must be looked upon merely as one element in a series of elements that constitute a sentence. The sentence circumscribes the word, giving it the distinct meaning intended by the writer. The word *run* means many things, depending upon its usage in the sentence.

If the pupil reads something the way the writer would like it to have been said, true communication of meaning is possible. Conversely, it is almost a certainty that if pupils do not develop sentence sense, they are well on the way to becoming disabled readers. Lefevre (1964) stressed that misapprehending the relationships between spoken and printed language patterns is the most decisive element in reading failures.

Children find it particularly difficult to read passive sentence patterns, appositives with commas ("John, my grandson, was . . ."), infinitives used as subjects ("To work is good"), conjunctive adverbs (*therefore, hence, so, nevertheless, since*), paired conjunctions (*neither-nor*), clauses used as subjects ("What you do is your problem"), and absolute constructions ("There being nothing left to do, let's get . . .").

What is the school's role in teaching language structure and usage? By the age of four most children have learned the fundamental structural features of their language and know the mechanics of grammar in a practical way. They can form sentences, handle subjects and predicates, and punctuate their spoken sentences by pauses and inflections. Without the benefit of formal instruction, they apply the rules of grammar in their speech. By the time they get to school they have an adequate and usable grammar system, and they use syntax cues to work out the meanings of new words.

It is doubtful that sentence analysis, parsing, and diagramming have any place in the elementary school. The early grades generally lay the foundation for grammar, but principles, generalizations, and definitions are left for the junior high and high school years.*

---

* For a discussion of what grammar skills to teach and not to teach in the elementary school, see *Improving the Teaching of Reading* (Dechant 1970: pp. 147-149).

SPEECH DEFECTS AND
READING DISABILITY

Up to this point, the discussion has centered upon the influence of listening ability, oral language proficiency, and a knowledge of grammar upon reading achievement. Consider now the speech defects and their effect on reading.

Children with reading problems frequently have speech problems. And these affect their perfomance in oral reading and in the learning of phonics and reading. Children with speech defects are often at a disadvantage in learning to read because they cannot associate a sound with its appropriate letter or word.

Speech is considered to be defective when it is not easily audible; is not easily intelligible; is vocally unpleasant; deviates in respect to specific sound reproduction; is labored in production; lacks conventional rhythm, stress, tonal quality, or pitch; or is inappropriate in terms of the age, sex, or physical development of the speaker. Speech tends to be defective if more attention is paid to how one speaks than to what one says.

There is adequate evidence that poor readers exhibit numerous articulatory defects. Sonenberg and Glass (1965), in a study of forty children between the ages of seven and sixteen who were remedial readers, found that only two of these children were free from articulatory errors, and 47 percent had difficulty with auditory discrimination. They point out that most of those who had difficulties in auditory discrimination often made the following sound substitutions: *k-g, b-d, p-d, t-k, w-wh, f-t, d-t, t-l, t-unvoiced th, f-unvoiced th, p-m, p-g,* and *f-v,* substitutions which also frequently show up as reading reversals. It may be that the problems of articulation, auditory discrimination, and reversals are basically one and the same problem.

Articulatory Defects

Articulatory defects (dyslalia) are speech deficiencies characterized by the imperfect production of phonetic elements and are accompanied by distortions, additions, substitutions, or omissions of certain speech sounds. Lisping, cleft palate speech, delayed speech, and speech characterized by dialect are classified as articulatory defects.

The average child of eight years of age is able to articulate 90 to 95 percent of the sounds needed in speech. Some children, however, engage in baby talk, indistinct speech, tongue twisting, or lisping, and these children may be confused by their own defects, because the words sound one way when they say them and another way when they hear them spoken by someone else. This frequently leads to faulty word recognition and comprehension in reading. Common articulatory errors are:

1. Addition of speech sounds—"athelete" for athlete, "chimaney" for chimney.
2. Distortion of speech sounds—"Shister" for sister. This occurs in lateral lisps when the air escapes over the sides of the tongue.

3. Omission of speech sounds—"baw" for ball, "kool" for school, "tink" for think, "wat" for what, "sining" for singing.
4. Substitution of speech sounds—"fumb" for thumb, "wawipop" or "jajipop" for lollypop, "tap" for cap, "dive" for give, "wed" or "jed" for red, "doe" for go, "twy" for try, "choe" for shoe, "toap" for soap, "thoap" for soap, "shoap" for soap, "wery" for very, "ketch" for catch, "fink" for think, "jike" for like, "kin" for can, "bat" for bad, "bak" for bag, "tite" for kite.
5. Transposition of speech sound—"aks" for ask.
6. Slurring of speech sounds—not giving enough duration to the sound.
7. Delayed speech—inappropriate for the child's age level.
8. Foreign or regional dialect or accent—"thoid" for third.

The most common articulation defect is a functional defect, and it decreases with age. This articulatory defect is usually overcome without therapy as the child matures. Some children have poorly developed auditory discrimination skills at the age of six, but these may mature by the age of eight. They hear sound differences at seven or eight years of age that the average child hears at six years.

Errors of articulation may result also from faulty sound discrimination, missing or misarranged teeth, a high or narrow hard palate, a sluggish or too large tongue, cleft palate, cleft lip, retarded speech development, or cerebral palsy. Occasionally, articulatory defects may result from frustration with early attempts at speech. Parental pampering, parental encouragement of baby talk, or inadequate speech standards in the home may lead children to develop carelessness in speech.

Children also frequently do not use the speech equipment that they possess. Many errors in articulation stem from lazy and indolent jaws, lips, tongue, or soft palate. The child drops end consonants, especially *t*, *d*, and *ng*; frequently changes *t* to *d* as *dudy* for *duty;* and uses contractions such as *woncha, lemme,* and *gimme.* To overcome this, children should be encouraged to overemphasize lip movements and should engage in choral reading and speaking. Tongue twisters such as "Peter Piper picked a peck of pickled peppers" are especially helpful.

Delayed speech, or slowness in learning to talk, is closely related to reading disability and is associated with multiple factors. Lesions in the dominant hemisphere, shifts in handedness, confused hand preference, impaired hearing, mental subnormality, paralysis, or lack of speech stimulation in the home are commonly associated with it. Parents may delay children's speech development by inadvertently punishing their early speech production. Intense shock, fright, or shame associated with the production of speech may keep children form making further attempts. Sometimes children are allowed to form a relationship with their parents and siblings that does away with the need for speech. Twins are said to be at a disadvantage in speech production because they get along with each other and understand each other so well that they frequently are not motivated to learn to speak.

Lisping is an example of distorted speech. It is of two kinds: *frontal* and *lateral*. In frontal lisping, the *th* is substituted for *s*; frontal lisping occurs when the child, while attempting to make the *s* sound, allows the tongue to protrude between the teeth. Lateral lisping occurs when the child makes the *s*, *sh*, and *ch* sounds inaccurately, by allowing the air to pass over the sides of the tongue. Lisping also may be due to faulty occlusion between the upper and lower teeth, loss of the front teeth, hearing defects, or malformation of the teeth or jaws. To stop lisping, children must be able to close their teeth tightly, with tongue remaining inside the mouth, and air being blown through the teeth.

SUMMARY

A summary of the interrelationships between language skills and reading is now in order. The following statements restate some key interrelationships identified in this chapter and include additional observations:

1. For some children, reading failure is often secondary to primary language disturbances (verbal expression and comprehension), and with these children it is necessary to emphasize the primary linguistic skills prior to reading.

2. The major aspects of language that are most significant for reading readiness and achievement are vocabulary knowledge, mastery of sentence structure, clarity of pronunciation, listening comprehension, and the absence of major speech defects. Their opposites are associated with reading failure.

3. Children generally must learn the alphabet of sound (the phonemes) before they can be taught the alphabet of letters (the graphemes).

4. The maturational rate for articulation skills differs from child to child. Some children may not be ready to master sound discriminations until the age of eight or nine. By the age of two and one-half the child uses most of the vowel sounds. By the age of seven the average child articulates correctly the consonants and consonant blends 90 percent of the time. Children at seven have most difficulty with *ch*, *zh*, *sh*, *l*, *th*, *z*, *s*, *r*, and *wh*; most do not attain complete mastery of *s*, *l*, *r*, and *th* until the age of eight.

5. If children cannot sound the individual phoneme and if they have not developed clarity of pronunciation, they will have difficulty with phonics and with learning the proper phoneme-grapheme correspondences, and they will not be good oral readers.

6. Development in articulation is probably more significant for reading success than is auditory discrimination. If articulation development is adequate, poor auditory discrimination may have less significance for reading.

7. Development of listening comprehension is more relevant to reading achievement than is becoming a competent speaker of standard English.

8. An inability to communicate may erect emotional barriers to progress in reading. The speech defect alone generally does not cause reading disability. It is the emotional reactions to speech difficulties that can cause reading difficulties.

9. Poor readers frequently have difficulty with auditory discrimination and exhibit numerous articulatory defects. They frequently substitute sounds (*k-g*, *b-d*) and have special difficulty with *r*, *s*, *l*, *k*, *sh*, *th*, *ch*, and *f*. The most common substitutions are those of an unvoiced sound for a voiced sound. The articulation errors of

disabled readers are characterized by additions, distortions, omissions, slurring, delayed speech, and dialect. Many speech problems are caused by dialect or by the bilingual background of the learner.

10. Neurological lesions in the language centers may impair both speech and reading.

11. The inadequacy of auditory association and discrimination (when the sounds of a word are not associated with the muscular movements required to produce them) may predispose an individual to both speech and reading difficulties. Oral reading and the learning of phonics are almost always more difficult for the person with a speech defect.

12. The evidence of a relationship between speech defects (especially those characterized by indistinctness, blurring of the consonants, thick quality, or cluttering) and reading deficiencies is certainly sufficient to warrant early attention to any speech difficulties.

13. Factors suggestive of future reading difficulty are slowness in learning to talk (retarded speech development) and substantial incidence of articulatory defects between the ages of two and one-half and four.

14. To prevent reading disability, language training should accompany reading instruction every step of the way. Every reading lesson should be an extension of language and a means of developing the child's linguistic skill. There is little point in teaching children to read until they can use sentence language in conversation. And it is unwise for the reading text to run any considerable distance ahead of the child's own oral language expression; otherwise, the pupil is virtually trying to learn a foreign language, and valuable instructional time is lost.

15. Children's comprehension of speech and their oral use of language should be checked frequently. Appraisal of the linguistic competency of all, especially slow learners and language-handicapped youth, should be a part of the diagnostic and remedial program. Children whose phonological system or dialect differs from that of the language used by teachers have enormous difficulty with auditory discrimination tasks and are likely to experience reading difficulties.

Development in reading closely parallels development in speech and listening. Reading involves the same language, the same message, and the same code as are involved in hearing spoken words.

The following conclusions are especially pertinent in understanding reading:

1. *Reading is communication.* Communication involves the transmission of meaning, and this occurs in the reading process. Without the communication of meaning there is no reading.

2. Reading meets all the criteria of language, albeit a written language. *Reading is a linguistic process.*

3. Reading is language, and language involves thought. *Reading is* thus *a thinking process.*

QUESTIONS FOR DISCUSSION

1. Why must the teacher understand the communication process?
2. What is the meaning of (a) communication; (b) language; (c) symbol?
3. What are the two basic elements of all communication?

4. Why is communication rarely perfect?
5. Can you define (a) communication channel; (b) limited channel capacity; (c) noise; and (d) redundancy?
6. Identify five characteristics of language.
7. What is the significance of the study of the philosophy of language?
8. Illustrate how the experience of Helen Keller demonstrates that words make concepts usable.
9. Identify five criteria of an effective listener.
10. What language skills are significant for reading readiness?
11. What are the implications for the teaching of reading in the studies that suggest that thought is accompanied by a certain amount of vocal behavior?

PART II

the nature
of the learner

The emphasis in Part I was on the nature of the reading process. In Part II the emphasis is upon the learner. Reading is a response made by a learner. Reading must be learned by a learner. It is thus interrelated with the learner's total growth and development.

Chapters 4 and 5 attempt to identify the child who learns to read well and the child who frequently ends in failure. These chapters are designed to help the teacher to become a better reader of the causes of reading disability, to study the correlates of reading achievement and proficiency, and to study the child to see if there are any inhibitory factors preventing the response for successful reading. They are designed to help the teacher to understand children in general, children on the level on which the teacher is teaching, and the individual child in the classroom.

Teachers are interested in why certain children have more difficulty than do others. Certain principles of behavior, growth, and development can be stated:

1. The development of each child is *caused*. In general, there is a reason why the child either achieves or fails to achieve in reading.
2. The causes of development are multiple and complex. Achievement in reading and disability in reading must be viewed as complex processes, explainable only by a group of related causes or factors
3. Development is a continuous process. What happens at one stage of development influences subsequent stages. Each stage of a child's development is an outgrowth of an earlier stage, not simply an addition to it.
4. Development and growth are generally orderly and gradual. All children go through the same genetic and developmental sequences. Children usually learn to walk only after learning to stand; they learn to speak only after a certain amount of experience in listening. However, some children may skip one of the itermediate steps, or because of structural defects, the order may be altered.
5. Growth sequences generally are sufficiently predictable to permit the teacher to develop norms for the average child. These norms, however, must not become standards by which individual pupils are rated. It is no more ridiculous to expect children of one class to wear shoes of the same size than to expect them to achieve equally.
6. Children usually develop as a unified whole. Children's physical, social, emotional, and intellectual growth are generally unified. The growth curve for any given child in each of these areas is usually high, average, or low. Thus, the relative rates of growth tend to remain constant from childhood to adulthood. However, not all aspects of growth proceed along an even front.
7. There are wide variations in growth and development. Not all children reach a plateau or make a spurt at the same time. Because of the vast differences in children in heredity and environment, and nature and nurture, each child is different in some degree from any other child. The rate of growth and the ceiling of potential levels of achievement vary considerably, even though the developmental sequence is fairly constant. Sex differences in growth and development are particularly noticeable.

The premises of Part II are the following:

1. Reading is a developmental task. It is a response made by a learner and must be *learned* by a learner.

2. The pupil's readiness for this developmental task, which is termed reading, and the reading-achievement level that the pupil will attain depend upon the pupil's overall growth and development. Reading cannot be completely understood until all the developmental aspects of living and learning in general are understood.

3. Growth and development are variable and so is achievement in reading. Each child's growth in reading is unique. The uniqueness of the individual is a fundamental principle of human life. (Tyler 1969)

4. It is imperative that the teacher understand the causes for the variability in achievement.

5. The absence of those factors (such as adequate experience) which are associated with good achievement in reading may cause reading deficiency and even reading disability.

6. There is for each child a teachable moment for learning to read and for learning every subsequent reading skill. This teachable moment depends on factors with which the next few chapters are concerned.

Chapters 4 and 5, presenting the developmental position, seek to identify factors that explain the symptoms and the causes of reading disability. They seek in addition to identify typical developmental sequences and behavior that is appropriate at a given point in time. Adequate learning is presumed to flow from healthy development, and inadequate learning indicates a malfunction in some antecedent development or a disruption of the sequential developmental pattern. Because there is a sequential pattern, it is assumed there is a time when the organism is most ready to learn a certain behavior. This point in time is the teachable moment, or the time when the pupil is most easily taught.

The above enunciated principles have important implications for the understanding and teaching of reading. If it were possible to divorce reading from other fundamental aspects of growth, it might be possible to produce similar achievements in all children. But this is not possible. Experience shows that the range in achievement levels by the second grade is commonly about four grades. By the sixth grade this range may have increased to as much as seven grades. The reading levels of seventh graders vary from the second to the eleventh grade. As a consequence, all teachers face the responsibility of utilizing, extending, and adapting assignments to the reading abilities of students who differ as much as six or eight or even more grades in reading competence.

4
THE LEARNER

Chapter 4 summarizes significant data about maturation, experience, intelligence, attention, interest, and personal-social development that have a bearing on the pupil's readiness *for* and achievement *in* reading. However, before evaluating the specific effects of each of these, consider in a general way the correlates of readiness for and achievement in reading.

THE CORRELATES
OF READING READINESS
AND ACHIEVEMENT

The teacher needs to ask: When is the pupil ready to read? When is the pupil ready to advance to the next stage of instruction? What is needed for adequate achievement in reading?

The human system is subject to development of two sorts: biological and environmental. Since both aspects of development affect readiness for and achievement in reading, success in reading will depend on adequate experiential background, as well as on adequate intelligence, and adequate physical, visual, auditory, and neurological development. As noted in Chapter 3, pupils must have had an adequate language background and must be able to enunciate, articulate, and pronounce accurately. They should be able to express themselves clearly to others and to speak in simple sentences. Pupils also need to have adequate social-emotional development and must be interested in becoming readers. They need to be able to detect perceptual likenesses and differences, to remember word forms, and to associate symbols with pictures and objects. And pupils must have the benefits of an adequate instructional program.

These factors are inextricably interrelated. Obviously, no one single factor determines a child's success. Conversely, it is rarely a single factor that explains reading disability. It is the pattern, the complex of correlates, with which the teacher must be concerned. The child must have a certain degree of readiness in each significant area, because each in its own way may contribute to reading disability or prevent future growth. It is illogical to expect to produce a successful reader by promoting growth and development in a few specifics while ignoring others. The teacher must examine the composite of interacting factors and on the basis of them must identify each pupil's overall readiness for reading. If there is one factor that interferes with learning to read, it needs to be identified.

Now examine more closely each of the factors that are related to achievement or lack of achievement in reading, beginning with maturation.

MATURATION AND READING

Baller and Charles (1961) note that maturation is an unfolding of potentials that individuals possess by virtue of their biological inheritance from a particular heritage. Children develop their biological inheritance through maturation, and they acquire their social inheritance through learning. Maturation and learning are indispensable, interweaving factors.

Maturation is a primary determinant of a pupil's readiness for learning in general and for reading in particular. Readiness can and does result from an internal unfolding of the pupil's biological potential; this might be described as maturational or constitutional readiness. Readiness thus may mean that the organism is mature enough to make the responses required for learning. Readiness then is defined as the developmental stage at which constitutional factors have prepared the pupil for instruction; it is an intrinsic state of the organism.

Readiness can also refer to the extrinsic acculturation of the organism. This is referred to as building readiness and is dependent upon appropriate learning experiences, practice, and integration of information. Building readiness is then synonymous with filling gaps in experience.

Bruner (1962) adds a slightly different dimension when he observes that readiness for learning depends more on the teacher's ability to translate ideas into the language and concepts at the age level being taught than on pupil maturation. Pestalozzi in 1802 said it very beautifully when he wrote: "To instruct man is nothing more than to help nature develop in its own way, and the art of instruction depends primarily on harmonizing our messages, and the demands we make upon the child, with his powers at the moment."

A variant of Bruner's position is one that suggests that readiness depends at least in part on a fit between the child's abilities (which are a product of the child's genetic endowment, maturation, experience, and learning) and the way the child is taught (Harris and Sipay 1975). Reading readiness may also be described as the teachable moment for beginning reading instruction and for teaching each of the reading skills.

The pupil's readiness for and achievement in reading are certainly affected by maturational delays—by inadequacies and delays in the development of physical-physiological functions. The teacher cannot do much about these except to time instruction to them. The teacher is more effective in dealing with developmental delays in which the experiential factors play a dominant role.

Maturational changes are usually orderly and sequential. The nervous system develops regularly according to its own intrinsic pattern. There thus seems to be very little benefit in rushing the maturation process. For example, one doesn't teach the child to swing a bat before he or she is capable of lifting a bat. Practice needs to wait for maturation.

Teaching and other environmental stimulations such as readiness programs are not useless, however. Children need appropriate environmental stimulation if maturational development is to progress at an appropriate rate. But the teacher should not overemphasize the importance of either maturation or experience learning. Too much concern with maturation may lead to useless postponing of what could be learned; too much emphasis on learning or experience may lead to futile attempts at teaching the child before the child is ready.

Teachers of reading must be careful not to push children beyond their maturational level. The timing of instruction is especially important in preventing reading disability. Instruction should march slightly ahead of maturation. However, it might be better to err by going too slowly than by going too fast. Rousseau put it aptly when he wrote of his Emile, "I would much rather he would never know how to read than to buy this knowledge at the price of all that can make it useful. Of what use would reading be to him after he had been disgusted with it forever" (1899: p. 83).

It would be a serious indictment of teachers if children became reading disability cases because of the teacher's failure to recognize the child's maturational readiness. It is true that reading disabilities are sometimes the result of predisposing conditions within the child having gone unrecognized, but for the most part such disabilities are brought about by other factors in the child's environment.

Consider now a few summarizing observations:

1. There are varying degrees of biological-maturational readiness for undertaking learning. Pupils generally become ready for specific learning tasks at different ages.

2. Pupils develop reading skills most readily if skills are built upon the natural foundation of maturational, and indeed experiential, development. Pupils put most effort into tasks that are neither too difficult not too simple, that are within their range of challenge, that are possible for them but not necessarily easy.

3. Children should not be forced into readiness for beginning reading or for any subsequent reading skill before maturational development is adequate. Such premature training may lead to no improvement, to only temporary improvement, or to actual harm and reading disability. The pupil may learn to fear, dislike, or avoid the task. Premature training may destroy the natural enthusiasm for a given activity, and it is doubtful that drill and exercises will ever be a substitute for maturation. Timing of instruction is very important in the prevention of reading disability.

4. Generally, the more mature the learner is, the less training is needed to develop a given proficiency.

5. The teacher can promote readiness for a given learning task by filling the gaps in the pupil's experience. The child whose difficulty is basically maturational, who is a slow developer, may best be helped by being given the opportunity to catch up.

6. Maturational delays are evident in some disabled readers. They are manifested by (1) difficulties with the orientation of figures in space (spatial disorientation), in telling right from left, with reversals of letters and words, and with confusion of handedness (especialy at ages five to seven and one-half); (2) difficulties in the ordering and sequencing of sounds in time (temporal disorientation); (3) difficulties in relating two or more perceptual modalities, or in establishing an association between the meaning and sounds of letters and the visual pattern of letters (intermodal difficulties); (4) immature or defective visual discrimination and recall of asymmetric figures, and poor visual-motor patterning (inability to copy a triangle); (5) inability to distinguish a visual pattern or figure embedded in a background; (6) delayed or inadequate spoken language; (7) inadequate visual development; (8) inadequate auditory-discrimination skills (auditory discrimination may reach its peak on an average only about the age of nine); and (9) an inability (on the upper grade levels) to organize what is being read.

    In cases of a maturational lag or a delay in the development of specific neurological functions, the neural tissues may have failed to develop at a rate comparable to that of the child's age-mates, and performance is affected adversely. Such a reading difficulty tends to run in families and is commonly more prevalent on the father's side of the family.

EXPERIENTIAL BACKGROUND AND READING

Experience is clearly another of the prime bases for all educational development. Innate ability alone cannot explain the pupil's academic achievement. The reason for this is fairly clear. Concepts develop from experience and their richness and scope are in direct proportion to the richness and scope of the child's experiences.

The differences in reading achievement that are seen daily in the classroom are at least partially explained by differences in experience. Those with favored experience tend to do well in reading; those with inadequate experience tend to have difficulty in reading.

Experience is a broad term that can include socioeconomic background, culture, the instruction received, and the timing (whether reading was introduced early or late). Each of these factors plays a significant role in the pupil's reading development. Consider first the socioeconomic factors.

Socioeconomic Factors

In American society, unfortunately, not every child has an equal opportunity for experience. Those from middle and upper socioeconomic homes have a decided advantage over those from lower socioeconomic homes. And these experiential differences are likely to result in differential achievement in reading in favor of the child from the middle- and upper-class home.

Most studies show that pupils from upper socioeconomic homes come to school more ready than those from lower socioeconomic homes to learn the tasks needed for success. The middle-class home contains "a hidden curriculum" (Henry 1963) which permits the pupil to deal appropriately with school experiences. Benson (1969) notes that in middle-class communities the number of children retarded in reading is between 10 and 20 percent, whereas in low socioeconomic areas it can be as high as 80 percent. Barton (1962) found in a survey of 1200 teachers that the most important single determinant of success in reading in school was socioeconomic status. The evidence also shows that black children do not on an average read as well as white children, not because of an absence of symbolic activity, but because the black student, especially from lower socioeconomic groups, has a different cultural base whose language is different from that of the white middle class. It may well be that students from lower socioeconomic homes are at a distinct disadvantage in learning to read because they have spoken and heard language patterns that interfere with the comprehension of standard materials, both oral and written.

Frasure and Entwisle (1973), studying kindergarten, first-, and third-grade children, found evidence for significant semantic development between the ages of five and eight for all children. However, performance based on syntax improved more with age, with the middle-class children making use of syntactic information earlier than lower socioeconomic children. Since lack of sentence sense, or the inability to use syntactic cues, is often associated with reading deficiency, this study has significance for understanding the problems of children from lower socioeconomic homes.

In summary, the studies indicate that the crucial elements associated with low socioeconomic status which appear to cause reading difficulties are

1. A dearth of reading materials in the home. (Thorndike 1973)
2. Parents' not reading regularly to their children before they enter school and during the primary years. (Chomsky 1972)

3. A cultural base in which the language is different from that of the school. Children from lower socieconomic homes often lack sentence sense or exhibit an inability to use syntactic cues.
4. An inadequacy in auditory-discrimination skills.
5. Reading materials in the school which present experiences generally alien to those of children in lower socioeconomic groups.

The opposites of each of the above (for example, the ready availability of reading materials in the home) are associated with reading achievement.

Most studies have shown that children from homes that provide a rich background of experience are generally ready to attack the printed page. When children have had experience with books and magazines, when they have had opportunities to make trips, to go to summer camp, to hear standard English being spoken, to be read to, *and* attend a nursery school, they tend to develop an interest in reading and generally are proficient at it. Their potential for understanding concepts and meaning is greater than that of children who lack this background. They are ready to bring meaning *to* the printed page. The symbols on the page are empty unless the reader endows them with meaning. For this the pupil needs the appropriate experience.

Cultural Factors

Culture refers to the traditions, beliefs, customs, values, and mores of a group of people. It is the most pervasive of the environmental determinants. It is a form of learning that begins at birth and that permeates all behavior, including patterns of thought, communication, and use of symbols. It determines how one perceives oneself and others.

The cultural differences that appear to have special significance for reading are those that affect thought and language. Culture shapes thoughts and language. If a culture lacks certain experiences, people in that culture will not develop the concepts or language expressions that might accompany those experiences. Cultural differences, especially those which often express themselves in dialect, account for many academic difficulties.

Whorf (1939-1940) found that where a culture and a language have developed together, there are significant interrelationships between the general aspects of grammar and the characteristics of the culture as a whole. The words a child uses, how they are uttered, and how they are strung together, clearly reflect the child's social boundaries (Entwisle 1977). Social selection determines which phones become phonemes, what the vocabulary of the language shall be, and what the sentence structure shall look like. The Eskimo language, for example, has thirty words for different kinds of snow; the Aztecs use the same word for *cold*, *ice*, and *snow*. The Paiute, a desert people, have a language that permits detailed description of topical features, a necessity in a country where complex directions are needed for location of water holes. The subcultures in this country (black, Chicano, rural, mountain, Indian) determine children's speech and vocabulary. Examples from these subcultures are words such as *gas head, chitlings, pik, Bo Didley, Dixie Hummingbirds,* or *Uhuru.*

Because reading is a language process, culture has a very direct impact on reading. Reading materials, the amount and types of material read, the motives for reading, the skill with which one reads, and the meanings that are ascribed to printed materials are to a great degree culturally and socially determined. And although the causes of the differences among children in reading educability are frequently debatable, social and cultural factors may often play an important role.

Instructional Inadequacies

Instructional provisions constitute further variables of reading achievement or failure. The child's readiness for reading and the level of achievement attained in reading depend on the instructional program received. Of course, reading disability may be the result of innate factors within the child, but it is perhaps more often the result of factors within the environment, factors for which good instruction may compensate or which poor instruction may aggravate. Children may not be ready for some instructional programs until the age of seven, whereas they may be ready for others at the age of five. Poor teaching may be a cause of reading disability or lack of achievement in reading. Poor teaching is no less a handicap than is poor vision.

Instruction may be inadequate because it is not adapted to the individual and the individual's needs, because it is unsystematic, or because the management of the skill-development process is poor. It may also suffer because the teacher uses a single method exclusively or accepts a low level of mastery of word recognition in the primary grades.

Reading achievement may be inadequate because classroom stimulation has been inadequate. Pupils may not have had enough practice in reading, or their teachers may have been consistently inexperienced. Children have less difficulty in reading when their teachers have more experience.

Finally, whenever the teacher makes inappropriate choices in regard to pacing, reinforcement, cognitive style, and modality, it is likely that the chances of reading disability are increased (Otto and Chester 1976).

Reading disability is also related to numerous other factors that may be grouped under the general heading of institutional variables: whether classes will be grouped heterogeneously or homogeneously; the type of control exercised in the classroom; the library facilities; the expectations that the administration and staff have of the pupils; grading practices; and the size of the instructional unit. Other things being equal, the child must have reached a more advanced developmental stage to be as successful in a class of thirty-six pupils as in a class of twelve or thirteen pupils. Very telling among the institutional deficiencies is a lack of appropriate materials. Every child has a right to read; a child's right to read readable materials is just as basic. Some children do not learn to read because there is a dearth of instructional materials.

A solution to many of the problems created by institutional inadequacies is teaching excellence. Educational ills are not solved by spending more money, by bringing in consultants or retaining outmoded in-service programs, by gadgets, mechanical devices, or the latest approaches. Outstanding instructional programs in reading can be achieved only through outstanding instruction.

Timing of Introduction to Reading

The question must naturally be asked: When is the child ready for reading? The answers are complex. On the one hand, one frequent cause of reading disability is a too early introduction to reading. As is noted later, the eyes at the age of six are often not physiologically ready to cope with the reading of graphic symbols; auditory discrimination may not be adequate until age nine; and surely many six-year-old children are not emotionally and socially ready to cope with the intra- and interpersonal pressures of the classroom.

On the other hand, Durkin (1966a, 1966b), in various and continuous studies of early and nonearly readers, found significantly higher achievement among the early readers. She reports that even after six years of instruction in reading, the early readers, as a group, achieved better than their classmates of the same mental age who did not begin to read until the first grade.

Studies (Sutton 1964; Plessas and Oakes 1964; Brzeinski 1964; Brzeinski et al. 1967; Durkin 1966a, 1966b; and Hall, Moretz, and Statom 1973) show that the children who learn to read early manifest an interest in learning to print either simultaneously or prior to developing an interest in reading. These "pencil and paper kids" eagerly respond to their word-filled world. They move from scribbling and drawing to copying forms and letters of the alphabet, to naming the letters, to questions about spelling, to ability to read. They want to see their names in print. They are curious, conscientious, persistent, and self-reliant. They become intensely interested in projects (such as making a calendar) for long periods of time. Their attention spans are long for their age, and their memories and concentration are good. They have parents or siblings who read to them, their mothers have frequently played a key role in encouraging early achievement; they tend to be girls and to come from upper socioeconomic homes.

There is little doubt that three-, four-, five-year-olds can be taught to read. The important question is: Is this desirable: do children who seem ready for an early start in reading suffer adverse effects when taught?

The research data generally indicate that if the reading materials are interesting and suited to their level, and if the teaching method and teacher expectancies are adapted to their intellectual maturity, children may learn to read at mental ages considerably below six and one-half. An important consideration, however, is that the younger the pupils, the lower, it appears, should be the teacher-pupil ratio.

It would seem that if teachers of reading are expert in reading children, they will not push children beyond their maturational level. The timing of instruction is especially important in preventing reading disability. Reading disability is too often caused by starting children in a reading program before they are ready for it. Such children cannot handle the day-by-day learning tasks and find themselves further and further behind as the time goes by. They become frustrated and develop antipathy toward reading. They actually learn *not to read.* This is quite different from and far more serious than not learning to read.

Another caution seems indicated. It may be dangerous to emphasize one phase of education or one developmental task at the expense of another. Although it is possible to teach very young children to read and to type, Bugelski (1964: p. 59) notes that "typing is not a substitute for geography, nor is reading a substitute for tying one's shoes." It may be far better to help children develop an adequate language background.

The question, When is the child ready to read?, has no decisive answer, then. No single criterion applies to all children. The question is meaningless without knowing the circumstances of learning. The teacher must determine *for each child* what program is suitable and avoid programs that would result in either too much hurry or too much delay.

A few summary observations about the educational implications of experiential background can now be made:

1. Experience is one factor that accounts for differences among children, and lack of experience may be a cause of reading disability.
2. Differences in learning ability among children are related to their biological potentials but also to their environmental opportunities. Some children become reading-disability cases because their environment does not call forth their potential.
3. Children from middle-class homes have an advantage because their homes contain "a hidden curriculum" which permits them to deal appropriately with first school experiences.
4. Although high socioeconomic status is not a completely accurate indicator of reading achievement, the broadness of experience and the added language facility that are associated with it can result in superior achievement in reading by equipping the pupil with the tools for meaningful reaction to the printed page.
5. Reading disability is positively associated with lack of experience and with lower socioeconomic status. Readers who are identified as "disadvantaged readers," in particular, exhibit the symptoms that result from deprived experience and most clearly show their deficiency through inadequacies in language formulation.

    Children from lower socioeconomic homes suffer from the lack of reading materials in the home, tend to have poorer auditory-discrimination skills, are slower to use syntactic cues in reading, and often do not develop sentence sense.
6. Cultural differences are also related to reading achievement or lack of it. They translate themselves into dialect and account for many academic difficulties, including difficulties in articulation. Culture determines the amount and types of material read, the motives for reading, the skill with which one reads, and the meanings that are ascribed to printed materials.
7. Where lack of experience is a prime cause of reading disability, instructional modifications should include
    a. Emphasis on oral language-skill development.
    b. Use of the language-experience approach.
    c. Use of experience charts and pupil-prepared materials.

d. Provision of stimulating nursery-school and kindergarten experiences, especially for children from lower socioeconomic homes.

e. Provision of readiness programs for children who are bilingual, come from lower socioeconomic homes, or are slow learners.

8. Poor teaching may be a major cause of reading disability; conversely, teacher excellence may be the best solution to educational ills.

9. Too early introduction to reading can cause children to learn to dislike reading and can thwart development in reading. The decision as to what is too early depends on an understanding of the children and their preschool experiences; on within classroom adjustments; and on harmonizing instruction with maturation and with the principle of individual differences. Moore and Moore (1975) suggest that the evidence of research in child development and early-childhood education supports later, not earlier, school-entrance age.

It is extremely difficult to identify the respective roles of heredity and environment, of maturation and experience, of the biological bases and the environmental determinants of behavior.

Maturation (genetically determined growth) and experience and learning (environmentally induced growth) are not opposing forces; they interact to shape behavior. Both nature and nurture are important for most human traits. In most instances, the interaction of genetics (maturation) and experience is so close that no one knows for sure where genetic capacity stops and learning begins.

There are, nonetheless, sensitive points in the maturation process when certain kinds of learning occur most easily and when experience imprints its mark most deeply. These are the teachable moments.

And finally, understanding may have come full circle: heredity and learning, maturation and experience, are seen most clearly as products of each other (London 1975). One inherits the ability to learn from experience. As Harris (1962: p. 3) puts it, "Without maturation the child cannot learn; without experience he has nothing to learn."

INTELLECTUAL DEVELOPMENT AND READING

Intelligence is an extremely important determinant of reading readiness and general reading achievement. It is a function of both biology and environment. Biology sets the limits to children's mental development, but how close children come to attaining their potential depends upon the environment and the use that they make of that environment. It depends upon opportunity, challenge, desire, nutrition, rest, self-discipline, aggressiveness, the need to achieve, and the learner's self-concept. Harris and Sipay (1975: p. 242) note that most psychologists believe that "the intellectual functioning of an individual involves the intimate interplay between an inborn potential for development, which varies from one person to another, with environmental conditions which strongly influence the degree to which this potential is realized."

Intelligence can be defined as "cognitive potential" or as the ability to profit from experience. Wechsler (1944) defined it as the aggregate or global capacity of the individual to act purposefully, to think rationally, and to deal effectively with his environment.

Inadequacy or failure of development of the brain, because of gene deficiency, can become a major cause of inadequate intellectual functioning and probably of reading disability. Experience has also shown that the brain, and hence the intellectual functioning of the child, may be damaged by infection, birth trauma, toxic agents, or endocrine disorders. It may be damaged by pressure upon the fetus, faulty position of the fetus, severe temperature changes, or overexposure to X-rays; it is also vulnerable to premature separation of the placenta, umbilical-cord complications, drug overdosage of the mother, use of psychotropic medications, delayed breathing of the infant, or forceps delivery. Barbiturates may produce asphyxiation in the fetus; the mother also can pass on diseases that interfere with normal fetal brain development, some common ones being smallpox, German measles, scarlet fever, syphilis, and tuberculosis.

Painkilling (meperidine or Demerol, promazine or Sparine, promethazine or Phenergan, scopolamine or Hyoscine, and secobarbital or Seconal) and inhalant anesthetic drugs given to women during childbirth can cause brain damage to the baby, affecting thinking ability and motor skills, and apparently lowering the I.Q.

The teacher is essentially an environmentalist. Even though teachers cannot add to children's basic capacity, they can do much to encourage children to develop their potential. Children commonly have a much greater mental capacity than they use. The teacher's task is to challenge children's existent capacity rather than to try to produce increments to their native endowment.

Examine now more closely two terms that have received considerable emphasis in the measurement of scholastic aptitude, namely, the mental age (M.A.) and the intelligence quotient (I.Q.).

Mental Age

The pupil's scholastic aptitude is usually expressed as a mental age or an intelligence quotient. Mental age refers to the *level* of mental growth that has been achieved. It is the pupil's score on an intelligence test expressed in age units, or put another way, it is the average age of the individuals who attained that score in the standardization process. An average six-year-old child will have a mental age of six; an average child of ten, a mental age of ten; an average youth of fifteen, a mental age of fifteen.

Intelligence Quotient

The intelligence quotient, or I.Q., refers to the *rate* of mental growth. Recall the simple formula, distance equals rate multiplied by time ($D = R \times T$). An analogous formula may be used in thinking about mental age and

I.Q.: MA = IQ × CA. In the formula, *MA* refers to the distance that the pupil has traveled mentally; *IQ* refers to the rate at which the pupil has been going; and *CA* refers to the length of time that the pupil has been at it.

If an I.Q. of 120 means that the person has advanced at the rate of 1.2 years mentally for each year of chronological life (up to the age of fifteen or sixteen), and if an I.Q. of 80 means that the pupil has advanced 0.8 of a year mentally for each year of chronological life, the formula, MA = IQ × CA (where IQ represents the conventional I.Q. divided by 100), is easy to understand and to use. A ten-year-old boy with an I.Q. of 120 has a mental age of twelve (MA = IQ × CA = 1.2 × 10). Another ten-year-old with an I.Q. of 80 has a mental age of eight (MA = IQ × CA = 0.8 × 10). The first boy has attained the mental level of the average twelve-year-old; the second, the mental level of the average eight-year-old.

I.Q. may also be defined in terms of a relative position within a defined group of persons. An I.Q. tells how much above or below the average an individual is when compared with persons of the same age. It measures the person's ability relative to persons of the same age group.

Studies have shown that the I.Q. is normally distributed. The distribution of scores is plotted on what is called a normal curve (see Figure 4-1). The curve is merely a graph showing some type of score on the baseline; the height of the curve at any given point indicates the number of cases that fall at that point. The curve shows the distribution of I.Q.s and the percentage of persons that have a given I.Q.

The I.Q. is certainly not an adequate criterion of reading readiness or achievement. However, it is significant in that it puts a ceiling upon individual achievement. Individuals with an I.Q. below 25 have little chance of learning to

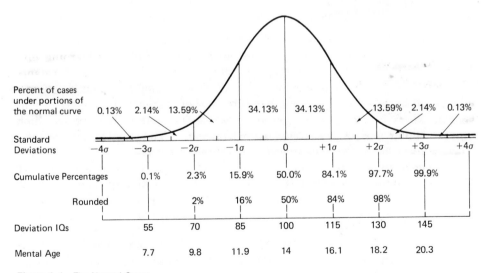

Figure 4-1 The Normal Curve

read; those with an I.Q. below 50 will experience extreme difficulty with abstract materials; and those with an I.Q. between 50 and 70 will rarely be able to read above a fourth-grade level.

The I.Q. is also an important long-range predictor of the child's performance. The child with an I.Q. of 150 who is only six years old may not be as efficient a reader as the child with an I.Q. of 100 who is ten years old. With time, however, the chances are that the six-year-old will reach a higher level of reading proficiency.

Mental age is generally a much better indicator of reading readiness and achievement than is I.Q., especially at the early age levels. The ability to read requires many skills that come only with age, which the mental age takes into account.

Correlations between intelligence and reading ability vary from about .35 in the first grade to about .65 in the sixth grade. These findings suggest that mental age is actually a more basic determinant of reading success when children have reached the stage at which they *read to learn* than it is when they are *learning to read*.

Although there is ordinarily a fairly high correlation between mental-age scores and reading-test scores, so long as the correlation is imperfect, other factors are operating. Clearly, it is impossible to predict reading readiness on the basis of intellectual development or mental-age scores alone.

High intelligence-test scores do not guarantee success in reading. Research indicates that the great majority of poor readers have I.Q.s between 80 and 110 and that frequently the readers who are the most severly retarded in relation to their mental age have I.Q.s of 110 to 130 or more.

Cognitive Development and Reading Disability

Reflect now on the relationship between cognitive development (or the lack of it) and reading disability. Disabled readers exhibit low learning efficiency; their verbal I.Q. score tends to be significantly below their performance I.Q. score; they have poor memories for sequences; they think on a concrete rather than on an abstract level; they have difficulty remembering what they read; they have a small recognition and speaking vocabulary for their age; their overall reading score is substantially below grade level; and they cannot deal with quantitative relationships and concepts or think critically.

Their low learning efficiency is indicated at age five by their inability to name colors, shapes (circle, square, triangle), sizes (big, little), or their own body parts (arm, leg, nose). They cannot give their name, age, address, or telephone number. They do not understand the meaning of *today, tomorrow,* or *yesterday.* They cannot count to twenty or recite the alphabet and cannot label experiences, ideas, or objects. They cannot make the associations required for learning, being unable to associate appropriate experiences and meanings with symbols. This inability is often referred to as an associative-learning disablity.

Low learning efficiency is sometimes caused by lack of opportunity and experience or even by poor sensory mechanisms which prohibit the pupil from acquiring experience.

The discussion now allows for a few summarizing educational applications:

1. Intelligence is a product of inherited structure developed by environmental stimulation and opportunity; it is an alloy of endowment and experience. Intelligence is subject to environmental variation. Scholastic-aptitude tests do not discriminate between ignorance (simply not knowing because of lack of opportunity) and stupidity (low intelligence).

2. Scholastic-aptitude-test scores do reflect differences among children; low scores are associated with poorer achievement and high scores are associated with better-than-average achievement.

3. The teacher needs to stimulate children. Children do not develop best on their own; they need challenging encounters with their environment. It may be necessary to expand the intelligence level of some children in much the same way that the life expectancy of all Americans has been extended. Long life-spans typify some families, but the life-spans of all can be improved.

4. The measured I.Q. of some children, especially the experientially deprived, diminishes with increasing age, apparently as a cumulative result of environmental deprivation.

5. Scholastic-aptitude-test scores serve their primary purpose by helping teachers to gear the instructional program to the ability level of the pupils.

6. Teachers need to be very careful when interpreting low scholastic-aptitude-test scores as to what is the true cause of reading disability. For example, a child who does not have adequate sensory mechanisms to acquire experience or to acquire it adaquately tends to do poorly on the tests; the cause of reading disability in this case may well be inadequate sensory development.

7. In investigating whether intelligence is the cause of the pupil's reading deficiency, the teacher should check (a) whether the pupil shows any of the symptoms associated with inadequate gene development; (b) whether there is any indication of intrauterine problems or birth trauma (whether the child was premature or there was a complication of pregnancy); and (c) whether the child's experience has been deficient.

8. The learner most likely to perform significantly below grade level in reading as a result of intellectual deficiency is the slow learner (I.Q. below 90).

9. Disabled readers have cognitive deficiencies, generally associated with low learning efficiency and with associative-learning disability, and often explainable by educational and cultural deprivation.

10. Specifically, intellectual inadequacies may show themselves in the following ways:
    a. The pupil has difficulty in organizing what he or she is reading or studying, especially at the upper-grade levels.
    b. The pupil's cognitive style is characterized by shorter attention span, distractibility, impulsivity, difficulty in associating graphemes and phonemes, and difficulty with part-whole and figure-ground relationships; it is usually two or three years below what is characteristic for the age.
    c. The pupil cannot integrate the meaningfulness of printed material.
    d. The pupil cannot generalize from word to concept. Symbolic abilities are im-

paired, with the result that the pupil cannot come up with the proper symbolic designations (*height* for "tallness," *summer* for "hot weather").

e. The pupil is unable to infer the main idea from a paragraph or to grasp cause-effect relationships.

f. The pupil has difficulty engaging in abstract thinking.

ATTENTION FACTORS AND READING*

Inability to pay attention, together with an accompanying distractibility and impulsiveness, may well be the major problem of disabled readers. Selective attention to graphic stimuli includes the ability to attend to the appropriate stimuli as well as the capacity to inhibit stimuli that are irrelevant to the task at hand. Proficient readers move from whole to detail and from detail to whole. They peripherally attend to the whole when focusing on the part and to the parts when focusing on the whole. Like a camera, they may take in breadth while subsuming detail, or they may focus sharply upon detail while subsuming the whole.

Attention capacity develops with age; some children develop greater proficiency and at an earlier age than do others. Thus, whenever success depends on the ability to use and sustain selective attention (and it certainly does so in reading), some children must be expected to perform inadequately.

Very young children appear to be captured by one aspect of a stimulus, attending to it to the relative exclusion of all other aspects; in other words, their attention is overexclusive. Poor readers seem to share this characteristic with young children.

Specifically, the pupil who is a disabled reader exhibits these characteristics:

1. *Short attention span.* The pupil cannot remember words, forgets instructions, cannot recall events in a story, and so forth. The causes for short attention spans include immaturity, low intelligence, inadquate motivation, low basal-metabolic rate, a hyperthyroid condition, or low socioeconomic level. Minority children often have short attention spans.

2. *Inability to easily shift attention.* The pupil perseverates excessively.

3. *Inability to withold attention from stimuli.* The pupil is very distractible, excitable, and hyperactive, shows rapid shifts of attention, cannot screen out distractions, and cannot sit still in class.

4. *Marked impulsivity.*

5. *Attention given equally to all stimuli.* The pupil's attention is not selective.

---

* For an extended discussion of the role of attention in learning and reading, see Ross's *Psychological Aspects of Learning Disabilities and Reading Disorders* (1976). Ross considers learning disability to be the result of "delayed development in the capacity to employ and sustain selective attention" (p.61).

Attention getting is enhanced when the teacher emphasizes the distinctive features of the stimulus; uses novelty, change, and surprise; and reduces the pauses that intervene between the alerting message and the material to be presented.

INTEREST AND READING

Reading for and achievement in reading are also dependent upon the pupil's motivational readiness, and poor reading or reading failure may be caused by lack of interest. To achieve in reading, the child must want to learn.

Children generally come to school wanting to learn to read. However, when children are disabled readers, they almost certainly do not want to read. Teachers must know how to get the disabled reader interested in reading and they must also be concerned with the type and the readability of reading materials that will encourage extensive reading and that will raise the pupil's general level of reading interests and tastes.

This section gives consideration to motivation, without which the pupil will not read, and to an interest in reading and its development. Consider first motivation.

The Framework of Motivation*

Motivation is the *why* of human behavior. It initiates, sustains, and directs behavior toward a goal. It arouses learners, moves them, wakes them up as it were, and tenses them just enough for action.

Casual observation suggests that behavior and learning are motivated. Woodworth (1921) pointed to the importance of recognizing motivation as a psychological principle when he wrote, "We have to find room . . . for action persistently steered in a certain direction by some cause acting from within the individual. We must find room for internal states that last for a time and direct action" (p. 71). This cause within the individual that directs action is termed motivation.

To understand and predict the behavior or action of an organism, it is necessary to understand the organism's motives; to influence its behavior, it is helpful to provide incentives and rewards.

There are still many mysteries about motivation. Teachers are befuddled time and time again because the pupil does not want to learn what they are trying to teach.

Thorndike (1917) recognized that practice is not the sole determinant of learning; it does not in itself cause learning. Thorndike recognized that improvement in performance requires certain motivations. He found that learners im-

* See Dechant's "Motivation Revisited" (1977).

prove in performance only if they are interested in their work and interested in improving themselves, if the material to be learned has special significance for them, if they are attentive to the situation, and if they have a problem-solving attitude. Each of these conditions has major significance for reading.

Much of an infant's behavior is controlled by physiological motives or visceral needs; an infant cries when hungry or thirsty. Teachers, however, dealing with older children, are likely to be more concerned with the psychological than with the physiological aspects of motivation. They are interested in the conscious direction of children's activity.

Goldstein (1934) suggested that normal behavior corresponds to a continual change of tension, and that tension of a certain level impels the organism to actualize itself through activity. For Goldstein, there is only one basic drive, namely, self-actualization. The organism performs those acts which are most important for the whole organism. Human beings are thus perceived as striving toward self-maintenance and toward the actualization of their potential.

In the classroom, psychological motives are paramount. Self-esteem, self-realization, curiosity, and security; a need to be adequate and successful; and a desire to belong are the motives that most commonly energize children's behavior. Children learn more readily and retention is more permanent when they want to learn, when they actively participate in the learning task, when they perceive the meaningfulness of the task, or when they are moving toward a goal.

There are also habit motives. Habits are formed through the repetition of some act that satisfies a motivating condition. However, once well formed, habits no longer need to draw on other motives for energy. They acquire their own ability to energize. Pupils may learn to read because they are motivated by basic personal needs. But gradually, as the pupils become skilled in reading, reading acquires a motivating, self-propelling force of its own. It becomes an interest in its own right.

The variables of learning are numerous, but motivation is primary. Reduce motivation to zero and all other factors pale into insignificance. Without it, intelligence and many other positive factors are neutralized; with it, the pupil can make amazing compensations for such negative factors as physical deficiency, limited experience, and even low intelligence. Often the root of the reading difficulties of a given pupil is the mental attitude of the pupil. The pupil may not like school and may like reading even less. And without motivation, the pupil will simply not develop into a mature reader.

The solution to the reluctant reader's problem begins then with a change of attitude. Pupils will not be adequate readers until they want to read.

The Role of Interest

Interests are positive attitudes of attraction toward objects or events. They are learned responses which predispose the organism to certain lines of activity and which facilitate attention. Interest is the set of attending, the tendency to give selective attention to something.

Interests arise through the interaction of basic needs and the means used to satisfy them. The child who is interested in reading is usually the child for whom reading satisfies the basic needs of personal adequacy or self-esteem, esteem of others, curiosity, or success.

Teachers are concerned with two somewhat distinct relationships of interest to reading—*interest in reading* (whether pupils will read and how much they will read) and *reading interests* (areas in which they will read). The first aim in reading should be to produce children who want to read and who do read. Examine then how children develop and maintain an interest in reading.

Developing a Permanent Interest in Reading

The interest of the child must somehow be captured if the child is to learn to read, but reading must also become an habitual activity. Wheat (1955) points out that as a child learns to read, reading enters the child's mental makeup as a permanent mode of behavior. The learner learns to use reading as a means of enjoyment, studying, and thinking, and will arrange work and play time in order to provide time for reading. Reading is soon a dominating interest that comes from within. Indeed, it is at this point that reading acquires a motivational force of its own.

It is now generally recognized that to promote the reading habit and to produce a generation of booklovers, there is no other factor so powerful as interest. Interest determines not only the areas within which children will make their reading choices, but more important, it determines how much children will read or even whether they will become "readers" at all.

Acquiring an ability to read is pointless unless that ability is used. The school's first aim should be to produce children and adults who want to read and who do read (Southgate 1973). As Strickland (1957) has said, a reader "is not a person who can read; he is a person who does read." The reading habit may be the most important academic aim of the school. Psycholinguists emphasize that pupils grow in reading ability primarily by reading. Smith (1978: p. v) notes, "Children learn to read by reading."

One of the teacher's prime concerns, then, is that pupils do read. The kindergarten teacher, especially, is more interested in fostering interest in reading than in developing specific reading skills, but even the primary teacher should not be so busy teaching reading skills that he or she neglects to develop readers. Although children usually come to school with an attitude favorable to reading, this attitude is not necessarily self-perpetuating. Seventh graders probably read more than they ever did before; by the time they are through high school their reading may have decreased tremendously. Few high school graduates habitually read books. An impressive proportion of young people recall that they virtually stopped reading, or at least stopped enjoying reading, in high school.

The development of interest in reading has been described as a "lure and ladder" procedure. The child must be lured to reading by parents and teachers. If reading is important to these surrogate figures, reading will ordinarily also be important to the child.

Determinants of Reading Interest

Among the correlates of reading interest are ability, socioeconomic and cultural factors, intelligence, and sex differences. Children who exhibit skill in a given area of activity are likely to read in that area, for example, the student who is skilled in crafts may be an avid reader of books dealing with scouting or camping but may find most historical novels or biographies boring.

SOCIOECONOMIC AND CULTURAL FACTORS

The exact nature of the role of socioeconomic status in determining whether a child will become a "reader" and what the pupil's choice of reading matter might be is not clear. There is some indication that the proportion of time spent in book reading is not highly related to socioeconomic status, but that the specific type of reading done may be highly related.

INTELLIGENCE AS A FACTOR

Intelligence also plays a major part in determining what students will read. Generally, the areas of interest of more intelligent students are on a slightly higher level than are those of less intelligent students, and the more educated tend to read more than the less educated. Students with high I.Q.s read books that are more difficult and more adult. They read nonfiction and have a greater interest in historical novels, science, mystery, literary classics, biographies, autobiographies, and mysteries.

SEX DIFFERENCES

Generally, it is found that girls are more interested in reading than are boys. Norvell made extensive studies of the reading interests of children in grades three through six (1958) and seven through twelve (1950). He found that during the high school years the most powerful determinant of reading interest is the sex of the reader.

On the basis of his study of children in grades four to twelve, Thorndike (1941) felt that the sex of the reader is "conspicuously more important" than is age or intelligence in determining what children will read.

A 1974 study (Beta Upsilon Chapter) reports that the interests of seven-to twelve-year-old children were based on factors such as content, plot, humor, and characterizations. Conclusions drawn from this study were:

1. Children at all age levels most often mentioned content. Girls mentioned plot and character more than boys at age twelve; girls showed greater interest in people and make-believe; boys showed more interest in science, sports, and transportation.

2. Excitement was the most often mentioned stylistic trait, followed by humor and information.
3. Animals were the favored content, with a slacking off of interest in them at age eleven and twelve.
4. Interest in mystery grew with age.
5. Reading interests start to vary with the sex of the reader at about age eleven.

Techniques and Materials for Developing Interest in Reading

Stott (1973) notes that the overriding causes of reading failure are lack of attention, withdrawal from the learning task, and *nonuse* of cognitive and perceptual powers. The largest variable in cognitive functioning is not the quality or level of cognitive thought, but rather whether it occurs or not.

Motivational and cognitive variables are substantially interdependent, with the prime mover being motivation. Because a pupil's cognitive development depends to a great degree on the *use* of his or her mental faculties, the unmotivated child ends up with poor conceptual equipment. Thus cognitive inefficiency may be merely a lack of cognition.

Disabled readers, more than other readers, tend to have poor concentration and to have difficulty in maintaining sustained motivation and effort. In fact, many have an aversion to reading.

Low motivation is not always caused by "within-self" factors. It may be caused by materials that are too difficult or uninteresting, by lack of purpose, or by a home environment which does not encourage achievement.

Pupils whose problem is essentially motivational may be helped by awareness of their progress. The material should also be interesting and on the pupils' instructional level. The teacher needs always to set a purpose for pupil reading. Good remedial teachers compensate for pupils' short attention spans, constantly involve pupils in activities, and motivate them by their own love of reading, by reading stories and poems aloud to them, and by helping them to discover in books the way to a world of information and adventure.

More than anything else, the teacher must get the pupil to read. The teacher may promote interest in reading in the following ways:*

1. Develop charts to be placed on the reading table containing pupil-made jokes, riddles, statements, and stories. Other charts may contain famous sayings, a poem, or a list of words.
2. Provide a wide selection of easy reading materials—materials which pupils *may* read, not *must* read.
3. Guide pupils to books which they can read independently. While interest in a book is a powerful motivational factor, interest alone is not enough to make a difficult book easy to read.

* See, also, Roeder and Lee's "Twenty-five Teacher-Tested Ways to Encourage Voluntary Reading" (1973).

4.   Help each child to find materials of appropriate content and difficulty. Do not emphasize literary content only. Generally, the content should provide adventure, action, humor, romance, or surprise. The stories should be about children, about heroes and heroines, about people with whom the reader can identify.

5.   Use book exhibits, book fairs, book advertisements, periodicals, and bulletins to stimulate interest in reading.

6.   Give children an opportunity to share their reading experiences through book reports, panels, or round-table discussions. Encourage pupils to discuss the author, plot, theme, setting, and style.

7.   Develop a book club or hobby club. Choose a "Book of the Week." Devote an assembly to a particular author or invite a favorite author to school.

8.   Introduce children to the reading topic by illustrating the content with TV, films, recordings, and other audiovisual aids. Give an introduction to the book to create interest. Whet children's curiosity.

9.   Provide class time for library reading.

10. Stay in the background. A pupil's recommendation of a book carries more weight than the recommendations of ten teachers.

11. Suggest the sports page, magazines, or even the comics to children who do not read.

12. Have pupils keep a record of the books they have read.

13. Help pupils to look upon themselves as readers. Self-concept is closely related to reading success. Pupils who do not see themselves as readers, are not likely to develop the reading habit.

Finally, the good teacher introduces the disabled reader to the literature of low-difficulty-level, high-interest materials. These materials are especially useful with slow learners, with disadvantaged or experientially deprived children, and with disabled readers—in other words, with pupils reading substantially below their ability level or significantly below grade level. They permit the teacher to match the pupil's interests and reading ability.*

PERSONAL AND SOCIAL DEVELOPMENT OF THE LEARNER

Consider now the personal and social development of the learner and its relation to reading achievement or failure. Educators have long debated what the goals of the school program are or should be. On one thing all are agreed. The student is the focal point of this program. In essence, educators believe that good education generally (and reading instruction particularly) should enhance the personal and social adjustment of the student.

* For a listing of such readers, see Dechant (1981b: pp. 247–255).

Personal Maladjustment:
A Cause of Reading Failure

Studies show that the incidence of maladjustment among poor readers is greater than among good readers. At times, personal maladjustment precipitates and may even cause problems with reading. To the extent that emotional disturbances block adequate learning, they interfere with reading development and may cause disability. Painful emotional events during early efforts at reading may turn the young learner against reading. The young learner may also transfer feelings of resistance from the parent to the teacher, or from eating to reading. A youngster may seek gang approval by not learning to read or may exert so much energy in repressing aggressive impulses that little is left for intellectual effort. Difficulties in adjusting to a new environment, poor parent-child relationships, sibling rivalry, lack of encouragement from home, and negative attitudes of parents to learning in general may all lead to failure. Children may be afraid that they are "no good" and thus are sure that they cannot learn to read. Reading makes such children feel "bad inside." Other children may be afraid of making mistakes. They don't want to be wrong, because at home they have learned that it is "bad" to be wrong. Still others use reading failure as a way of punishing the adult. They demonstrate their independence by refusing to read. Their attitude is: "I'll show you." Among the factors that have a special bearing on reading disability in certain children is a low frustration tolerance. Such children are easily discouraged, cry easily, fight readily, give up too quickly, are quarrelsome or argumentative, tear up their work, destroy games, and the like.

The teacher must be slow in attributing the reading difficulties of even one pupil to emotional or social problems. More commonly the reverse is true. Nevertheless, it is not uncommon to find that secondary emotional and behavioral disorders often mask the true nature of a reading handicap and often become the stated reason for referral. This fact alone may explain why the ratio of boys to girls referred to reading centers is approximately four to one.

Reading Failure:
A Cause of Personal Maladjustment

Research indicates that most children come to school with rather well-adjusted personalities and that personal maladjustment is more frequently an effect rather than a cause of reading failure.

The child who cannot read is deprived of a means of widening personal interests, of satisfying the need for new experiences, of filling leisure time, and of promoting emotional and social adjustment. Reading failure gives a sense of inadequacy, threatens the child's self-esteem and social acceptance, and tends to breed more failure.

There is no substitute for success in reading. Conversely, a reading disability is a disability in almost every area of learning. Reaing failure poses an important problem to any child. Persistent reading failure, whatever its cause, is certain to block the child from performing a basic developmental task. Thus, reading failure may become a significant cause of emotional distress and behavior disorder.

Maladjustment and Reading Failure: Interacting Factors

It is not always easy to establish whether personality maladjustment is the cause, the effect, or a concomitant circumstance. The relationship between reading disability and emotional and social maladjustment is frequently circular in nature. Early reading failure leads to maladjustment, and personal maladjustment in turn prevents further growth in reading. It is also quite conceivable that in certain cases reading failure and personal maladjustment have their own distinct causes. Even when the child is both emotionally maladjusted and a disabled reader, it is quite possible that one complex of factors caused the emotional maladjustment, whereas a different set of factors caused the reading disability.

Generally, if the reading failure is caused by emotional factors, the child will have difficulties in other academic areas also. If the emotional problem was caused by failure in reading, the emotional difficulty is reduced when the child learns to read.

In summary;

1. Emotions are reactions to environmental stimuli that also motivate behavior.
2. Some types of emotion facilitate learning, and some hinder or prevent learning.
3. The relationship between maladjustment and learning to read might be any of the following:
   a. Maladjustment causes reading failure.
   b. Reading failure causes maladjustment.
   c. Maladjustment and reading failure have a common cause.
   d. Maladjustment and reading failure have each their own distinct cause.
   e. The relationship is circular: maladjustment causes reading failure, and the reading failure in turn increases the maladjustment; or reading failure causes maladjustment, which in turn increases the reading failure.

Types of Treatment

Because of the intimate relationship between emotional adjustment and reading, therapy and remedial reading are frequently combined in dealing with reading disability cases.

In a detailed study of 500 disabled readers, Klasen (1972) found that 65 percent of the children showed anxiety, 92 percent showed some element of psychopathology, 63 percent were handled successfully by reading therapy alone, and 28 percent needed psychotherapy.

Various forms of therapy (art therapy, language therapy, drug therapy, play therapy, psychodrama, group-interview therapy, sociodrama, and individual-interview therapy) have been found to help the pupil to overcome emotional difficulties and to achieve in reading. For severely emotionally disturbed children who are also reading disability cases, therapy combined with the remedial reading program appears to be most successful. The greater the intensity of the emotional problem, the greater tends to be the need for both therapy and individual instruction.

Lawrence (1976) reports on three experiments that involved counseling of disabled readers. In each of the three experiments the students who received counseling showed significantly greater improvement in reading achievement than the students who received reading instruction only.

Therapy may remove pressures and tensions and clear the way for attentive concentration on the reading material. In some cases it may remove a fear of reading and allow the child to develop attitudes favorable to reading. Thus, the pupil may be led from a negative to a positive identification with reading.

Eisenberg (1966) notes that no single pattern of psychopathology is characteristic of the disabled reader. Poor readers may be adjusted or maladjusted; they may run the gamut of personal deviation. There is no one-to-one relationship between type of adjustment difficulty and type of reading retardation.

Among the more common patterns are anxiety states which preclude attention to academic tasks, passive-aggressive syndromes, and low self-esteem. Eisenberg adds that reading difficulty is in itself a potent source of emotional distress. Ineptness in reading penalizes the retarded reader in all subjects and leads to the pupil's misidentification as a dullard. However begun, adjustment difficulties and reading disability are often mutually reinforcing, and therapy may be necessary before response to remedial reading techniques can be expected.

Obviously, many of the special, intensive treatments that have been tried with seriously disabled readers cannot be used in the typical classroom. Some of them are far too time-consuming, and others require clinical training beyond that possessed by most teachers. They have been mentioned here as illustrations of what can be done and has been done in the way of remediation.

Although therapy designed to alleviate underlying emotional disturbances will not be a cure-all for reading problems, the evidence certainly suggests that when pupils are not accessible to reading instruction because of emotional disturbance, they should be treated by someone who is expert in psychotherapy. It may be necessary to intervene in pupils' lives through counseling and psychotherapy to help them to achieve at an optimum level.

The import of this section is that it is almost impossible to have serious difficulties in reading without experiencing some adjustment difficulties or without a strong emotional overlay. A major portion of reading disability often involves the student's self-image and self-concept.*

* For a discussion of the relationship between the self-concept and reading disability, see Dechant's *Diagnosis and Remediation of Reading Disabilities* (1981a: pp. 52-54).

SUMMARY

Why study the correlates or the factors that have been analyzed in this chapter? What do maturation, experience, intellectual development, attention, motivation, and the personal-social development of the learner have to do with reading achievement? *An understanding of these factors* (and indeed of those that will be examined later) *reduces costly trial and error in instruction and very often prevents reading disability and failure.* The timing of instruction and too early introduction to reading are issues which need to be considered because not all children mature at the same rate or have the same experiential readiness; not all children have the same rate of intellectual development that assures them an equal level of intellectual readiness before the age of six; and not all are equally attentive or motivated, or have adequate personal and social development.

Readiness for reading clearly depends upon the ripening of the potentials that individuals possess by virtue of their biological inheritance. If learning is to occur, the learner must be in a state of readiness. This is the developmental state at which constitutional factors have prepared the child for instruction. It is the teachable moment. Without maturation the child cannot learn. Timing of instruction is extremely important in prevention of reading difficulties.

Adequate maturation alone will not assure success in reading. It must be accompanied by adequate experience. Those with favored experience (above average socioeconomic background, appropriate cultural base, and good instruction) tend to do well in reading, and those with inadequate experience tend to do poorly. Inadequacies in experience, differences in culture, and inadequate instruction account for many reading difficulties. Conversely, optimum experience provides the child with a hidden curriculum, as it were.

Intelligence is a third factor that is closely related to reading. It is a mix of maturation and experience. The slow learner is perhaps most affected by intellectual deficiency, but many disabled readers show the effects of inadequate intellectual functioning, of cognitive deficiencies, and of difficulties in attention.

Perhaps the most important correlates of reading achievement are attention, motivation, and interest. They make learning to read possible. To be a good reader the pupil must be attentive to the reading task, must want to read, and must be at least generally interested in what is being read.

Lastly, the relationship between personal-social factors and reading is an important one. Adjustment difficulties at times interfere with learning to read; more frequently, reading difficulties lead to adjustment problems.

QUESTIONS FOR DISCUSSION

1. What are the premises of this chapter? State five basic principles of growth and development, and point out how they apply in the teaching of reading.
2. What is the developmental position?
3. Summarize the correlates of reading readiness and achievement.

4. Define maturation and the implications it has for timing of instruction.

5. Give three descriptions of readiness and discuss their application to reading.

6. What are the factors that determine experiential readiness for reading? Discuss the import of each of these for reading readiness.

7. What are the crucial elements associated with low socioeconomic status that appear to cause reading disability?

8. Outline instructional inadequacies and their implications for reading.

9. Define mental age and intelligence quotient, and discuss their respective importance for reading.

10. Disabled readers have various attention difficulties. What are they?

11. Discuss the importance for reading of motivation, interest, and psychological and habit motives.

12. In two parallel columns, list conditions under which reading failure leads to personal maladjustment and personal maladjustment leads to reading failure.

13. Is it possible to raise all children's reading proficiency to the same level?

14. What is the advantage for reading of a broad experiential background?

15. Discuss the reasons for identifying, at least in a general way, the pupil's intellectual capacity, and discuss the implications of this for the pupil's reading achievement.

16. If it is recommended that a child have a mental age of six for beginning reading, and if intelligence-test scores indicate that a given child's I.Q. is approximately 120, at what age would that child be mentally ready for beginning the teaching of reading?

17. Discuss the reasons for and against delaying reading instruction.

5

ADDITIONAL CORRELATES OF READING READINESS AND ACHIEVEMENT

Reading is a complex process. It is a composite of many skills, habits, and attitudes. It is an act, a performance, or a response that the reader makes to the printed page. Unfortunately, certain factors may prohibit making the response. Chapter 5 reviews such factors. Its concern is with the physical-physiological factors that affect reading performance: general physical conditions, sex-related correlates, visual and auditory deficiencies, and neurological inadequacies. Consider first those physical conditions which are of a general nature.

GENERAL PHYSICAL CONDITIONS

The child is both physical and physiological. Functions such as vision, hearing, and thought are possible only through the operation of organs of the body (the eye, ear, or brain). If the organ is defective, the function is likely to be impaired. This may lead to serious reading difficulties, especially in the case of vision, hearing, and thought. In general, good health is conducive to good reading, and poor health is often associated with reading deficiency.

Numerous studies have dealt with the effect upon reading disability of glandular dysfunction, particularly underfunctioning of the pituitary glands, vitamin deficiencies, endocrine disturbances, nerve disorders, nutritional and circulatory problems, and systematic changes in metabolism (Park and Schneider 1975). Other studies have stressed the effects of conditions such as adenoids, infected tonsils, poor teeth, rickets, asthma, allergies, tuberculosis, rhumatic fever, and prolonged illnesses. Tumefaction of the pituitary gland, for example, may lead to a reduction in eye span and consequently to an increase in the number of fixations. Hyperthyroid conditions may prevent normal fixation on what is being read and thus lead to daydreaming, poor attention, slow word recognition, and general fatigue. Diabetes mellitus is associated with visual defects, excessive regressions, and loss of place in reading.

The eating habits of children are related to their overall functioning and may also may be a direct cause of poor learning. Poor nutrition and food additives are receiving increasing attention as causative agents of disability. Preliminary evidence at least hints at a direct link between food additives and a blood-sugar level that does not remain constant and hyperkinesis (Feingold 1975).

Livingston (1975) intimates that the brains of perhaps one million infants in utero and young children in early life have been so adversely affected by malnutrition that subsequent school learning is seriously hampered. Read (1972) suggests that hunger and malnutrition may have a direct bearing on children's self-concept, on their motivation to achieve, and on their attitude toward the environment generally. A perinatal condition that appears to be related to reading disability is birth weight (Balow 1974).

Complications of pregnancy and birth and prematurity, often brought about by physical conditions, are sometimes additional causes of reading disability. It is possible that such complications may trigger an inherited disposition to a developmental lag.

Sometimes a lowering of the child's basic vitality is closely related to the functions required for successful reading. For example, the basal metabolic rate (BMR) affects the convergence of the eyes. If the rate is low, children may not be able to aim the eyes properly in binocular vision, and thus may frequently regress, omit words, lose their place, and become fatigued. And fatigue makes it difficult to become interested in a reading task: attention suffers and comprehension is usually lowered; as nervous tension builds up, children become uninterested, disgusted, and may even turn from reading completely.

The teacher must be cautious in interpreting the relationship that these factors seemingly have to reading deficiency. Generally, physical inadequacies contribute to rather than cause reading problems. Illness keeps children from school and causes them to miss important phases of instruction. Any physical inadequacy makes it difficult to become enthusiastic about learning and may result in lowered vitality, in depletion of energy, in slower physical development, and even inadquate mental functioning. Physical inadequacies cause children to center attention on them and away from learning.

Schiffman (1967) cautions that there is no known relationship between errors of biochemical functioning and any *specific* reading syndrome.

THE SEX OF THE LEARNER
AND READING ACHIEVEMENT

Teachers have always been concerned with differences in achievement between boys and girls. One of the more obvious differences is in achievement in reading. Girls as a group achieve better than boys in reading. They learn to read earlier, and fewer of them are significantly retarded in reading. They also seem generally to perform better than boys in English usage, spelling, and handwriting. In general, the ratio of reading disability among children is about three or four boys to one girl. Girls maintain their superiority in reading, English usage, and spelling through the upper elementary, junior high, and high school years. *Reading in America*, a reading report of the National Assessment of Educational Progress (1976) indicated that females continue to perform better in reading than males, with the differences being greatest at age seventeen.

Girls and boys also exhibit differences in other areas. For example, the incidence of stuttering, night and color blindness (about 5 percent of boys are color-blind), left-handedness, ambidexterity, high-frequency hearing loss, and brain damage is substantially greater among boys. Boys also tend to lisp and lall more and are less proficient than girls in visual acuity, in auditory and visual discrimination, and in listening skills.

The brain-control center is on the same side as the dominant hand five times more frequently among boys than among girls (Sexton 1969). The fontanelle closes later in boys, and their bones and muscles develop strength later than do those of girls. Female superiority is shown also in wrist movement, fine-finger movement, manual dexterity, clerical aptitude, verbal fluency, and rote memory. Boys show superiority in spatial relationships, problem solving, and mechanical aptitude.

Numerous attempts have been made to explain the apparently genuine differences between boys and girls in reading and language achievement. In general, the explanations have emphasized either heredity or environment. Consider the hereditary factors first.

It has been suggested that girls have an inherited language advantage. They do in fact reach maturity about a year and a half earlier than boys. Throughout childhood there are detectable differences in physiological maturity, in favor of girls, indicated by the age of the eruption of teeth and X-ray studies of bone development (Harris and Sipay 1975).

Generally, by the twentieth month of life, girls also show some superiority in the production of speech sounds. In the prelinguistic or babbling stage no appreciable differences are noticeable, but differences appear in the second year of life. However, Durrell (1940) found that even when children are equated on oral language achievement, there are still twice as many reading-disability cases among boys as among girls.

Some studies have indicated that intelligence is more variable among boys than among girls, that more boys than girls have extremely low as well as extremely high intelligence quotients. This would lead one to expect that the reading ability of boys might also be more variable and that a larger number of boys would be poor readers (Vernon 1957).

Environmental factors have probably been given more consideration than biological factors. Bentzen (1963) advances the hypothesis that boys' problems stem from the stresses put on their immature organisms by a society that fails to make appropriate provisions for the biological age differential between boys and girls.

Firester and Firester (1974) stress that strong social forces (the excessively feminine atmosphere within the school) make it difficult for boys to cope. The prevalence of women teachers in the elementary school may be a determining factor. Gentile (1975) found that at least in one grade, male tutorship was associated with greater gains in the reading achievement of Mexican-American boys.

Girls are generally promoted on lower standards of achievement than boys, are less frequently retained in a class, and use reading activities for recreation more often. In addition, before coming to school girls engage in numerous activities that may better prepare them for reading. In their weaving, sewing, and doll playing they have more opportunity to develop near vision and motor coordination. Reading materials are generally more in accordance with the interests of girls.

A major factor that has not received the emphasis that it deserves is the attention or the lack of attention children give to reading. Boys put into booths that resemble an airplane cockpit appear to learn more during the reading hour than do girls: apparently their attention improves with this arrangement. Research generally indicates that girls are more attentive during the reading hour than are boys.

Certainly, not all reading-disability cases are referred to the reading clinic for reading disability alone. It is quite possible that many boys, manifesting their reading problems through aggressive tendencies, are referred for their aggressive behavior. Boys are generally more openly aggressive and exhibit more behavior problems. The reading problems of well-behaved tractable girls may go undetected, or may be taken care of in the classroom. A study by Naiden (1976) of 14,700 students, or the entire fourth, sixth, and eighth grade school population in the Seattle Public Schools, found that the ratio of boys to girls with significant deficit in reading was three to two, not the three or four to one reported in most studies of reading-clinic populations. Naiden added that her data indicated that there are large numbers of female students with serious reading deficits who are not finding their way to the reading diagnostician.

That there are sex differences in readiness and reading achievement in favor of the girls in this country can hardly be questioned. There are also vast differences among boys themselves: most six-year-old boys are less mature than the average six-year-old girl, but a significant number may be more mature. What educational implications do these differences have? One recommendation, based on these differences, has been that boys begin first grade later than girls. A second recommendation is that separate reading norms be devised for girls and boys.

Educational provisions must ultimately be concerned with the individual student. It is not enough to know what is best for the group. It is not enough to know what type of reading program would benefit most boys or girls. Teachers must prescribe for the individual boy and girl, and as soon as they attempt this it becomes apparent that differences other than sex play a significant role in reading achievement. The solution probably lies in a delay of formal reading instruction until the child is ready for it and in an early provision of experiences that will prepare the child for reading.

VISUAL EFFICIENCY AND ACHIEVEMENT IN READING

The next two sections are concerned with the pupil's perceptual development and ability to process information, especially as it relates to vision and hearing. The constructions of the "imaging" or perceptual processes are clearly dependent upon the stimulus information received through the eyes (Smith 1971). Perception is initiated by stimulation of the sense organs; in reading these are the eyes.

Visual defects are obvious handicaps to reading efficiency. They cause discomfort and fatigue, they act as irritants, and they lower the efficiency of the individual. However, deficiencies in sequential processing, both visual and auditory, are often more closely related to poor reading achievement than are visual and auditory deficiencies as such.

Visual Readiness

Children must have attained certain levels of visual maturation before they are ready to begin reading. They should have become able to focus the eyes at distances of 20 inches or less, as well as to focus at 20 feet or more. They should have acquired some skill in depth perception, binocular coordination, ability to center, and ability to change fixation at will. And they must be able to see clearly, singly, and for sustained periods.

A major concern is the age at which a child achieves sufficient proficiency in these visual skills to begin reading. The question may be phrased: When are the child's seeing processes sufficiently mature for learning to read?

There is some justification to question the current educational procedures concerning the age for beginning formal instruction in reading. The eyes of some children are often not mature enough to cope with the printed page before the age of eight. Unfortunately, too many teachers fail ro recognize the relationship in first-grade children between visual immaturity and failure in reading.

Children are born farsighted. This prevents adequate focus of the image of near objects in the retina. As the eyeball lengthens, farsightedness gradually decreases and the child becomes capable of adapting to the demands of near vision. At age six, however, the pupil is often still too farsighted to clearly see such small stimuli as the printed word. As will be seen later, teaching Johnny to read at an early age may be a major factor in causing myopia or nearsightedness. Whether formal instruction in reading at age six causes reading disability is not as firmly established.

Examine now the various visual defects and the effects that they may have on reading.

Types of Defective Vision

Teachers of reading need to become familiar with the various types of visual defects if for no other reason than that they need to make different classroom adjustments for these defects. Three types of defects are discussed here: lack of visual acuity, refractive errors, and binocular difficulties.

LACK OF VISUAL ACUITY

Visual acuity or keenness of vision does not seem to have the significance for reading achievement that some other visual factors have. First, reading is a near-point task. One could fail the visual acuity test at 20 feet but possess good visual acuity at 16 inches. Secondly, to read the average book, one needs only 20/60 visual acuity. Nevertheless, acuity is important. Each child should probably have at least 20/30 acuity at far point. Any significant differences, especially if the left eye is poor, should be checked further.

The emmetropic or normal eye sees with 100 percent of acuity only a very small portion of the visual field, perhaps no more than four or five letters. When a book is held 16 inches from the eyes, the reader sees about 2.25 inches of printed material. The book, incidentally, should be held at a slight angle; looking up from one's work and glancing into the distance has a restful effect on the eyes.

REFRACTIVE ERRORS

Refractive errors are due to damage, disease, or weakness in the lens or other portion of one or both eyes, causing a defect in the conformation of some portion of one or both eyes. Generally, refractive errors can be corrected by glasses. Glasses, however, do not increase the sensitivity of the eyes. They help the eye to focus and lessen eye strain, but they frequently fail to provide normal vision.

Myopia or nearsightedness is perhaps the most common among the refractive errors. The myopic eyeball is too long, with the result that the light rays (and hence the image) come into focus in front of the retina, instead of on the retina. This forces the reader to hold the book closer than the normal 16 inches or so. Distant vision is generally blurred. Concave lenses are usually prescribed for myopic conditions.

Hyperopia or hypermetropia is generally known as farsightedness. Where the myopic eye is too long, the hyperopic eye is too short. In this case the image falls behind the retina, and near vision is blurred. To remedy this condition, convex lenses are prescribed.

Another type of refractive error, **astigmatism,** is the inability to bring the light rays to a single focal point. Vision is blurred and distorted. The underlying cause is an uneven curvature of the front or cornea of the eye: the cornea is spoon-shaped rather than spherical. Unless the distorted image is corrected by the use of cylindrical lens, the child fatigues easily and usually dislikes close work or prolonged distant vision. Astigmatism is a major cause of ocular asthenopia or eyestrain. Headaches are common, similar letters and words are confused, and the pupil experiences difficulty in sustained reading.

BINOCULAR DIFFICULTIES

As a rule, apparently, it is the left eye which does the majority of the leading, suggesting that the eyes are not synchronistically moving together during saccadic movement. Presumably, when the deviations become too large, binocular difficulties occur.

Binocular difficulties, or lack of fusion, have the effect of giving the child a double image (diplopia). The two eyes do not move in unison and they either do not aim correctly or they give conflict reports. When the ocular maladjustments are minor the child may compensate for them. If the maladjustments are major the child may see two of everything, or the two images may be so badly blurred that he sees neither image clearly. Usually the individual suppresses one stimulus. When the image can be suppressed only partially or only temporarily, a blurred image results and the reader is likely to lose her place, to omit words, or to regress. Continued suppression of the vision of one eye can lead to functional blindness of that eye. When the child uses only one eye, repressing the use of the other even though both eyes are structurally intact, the condition is described as amblyopia or the "lazy-eye" condition. Sometimes a patch is used over the good eye to correct the amblyopic condition.

To read with efficiency and ease, the reader can either become monocular (people blind in one eye must do this) or develop an efficient binocular system. Anything between these two extremes is likely to cause fusion problems and to lead to difficulties in reading. To see clearly, the lenses of the two eyes must be in focus. The images must fuse correctly, giving one mental picture.

An inability to fuse correctly is manifested by mixing of letters and words, inability to follow lines across a page, loss of place, and slowness in reading. Fusion difficulty is often caused by a paralysis of an eye muscle. Strabismus is an instance of severe imbalance, and heterophoria is a form of mild imbalance.

Strabismus (from the Greek word meaning to squint) is a muscular imbalance stemming from an incoordination of the muscles that move the eyeball. The eyes are actually aiming in different directions. Each of the eyes has six muscles that must function together if the eye is to aim correctly. This is made somewhat more difficult because the eyes are set in a movable base, the head. Sometimes one eye aims too far outward (exophoria, or wall eyes), too far inward (esophoria, or crossed eyes), or in a different vertical plane from the other eye, where one eye focuses higher than the other (hyperphoria). A severe case of strabismus may result in double vision; a less severe case, in a general blurring of the image. Hyperphoria may lead to jumping of lines or misplacement of a word to a line above or below.

Heterophoria is a milder form of imbalance which results in fatigue. As the reader tires, the eyes tend to deviate even farther. Attempts to counteract this increase fatigue. The pupil becomes inattentive and irritable, loses the place, omits, and regresses.

Some research indicates that myopic children with phoric, or visually deviant, conditions read about as well as do children without phoria, but that children with phorias at far point have poorer reading skills.

Two other conditions related to fusion problems are **aniseikonia** and **astereopsis**. Aniseikonia occurs whenever there is a difference in size or shape between the two ocular images. As a result, fusion is difficult and the reader may become tense, experience fatigue, and develop headaches.

Astereopsis, which is a weakness in the ability to perceive depth and which gives a tridimensional effect, occurs because the two eyes receive slightly different images; often it is the best indication of binocular difficulties.

Figure 5-1 summarizes the more common visual defects that are present among school children.

Symptoms of Eye Disturbances

Teachers of reading cannot be satisfied with a general knowledge of eye defects. They need to know the individual pupil's eye condition well enough to answer a number of specific questions. Does the pupil need special reading materials? When should the pupil wear glasses? Does the pupil require special lighting? Can the pupil read for prolonged periods of time?

To answer these questions the teacher frequently must seek help from a vision specialist. Perhaps the teacher's chief responsibility here is to be familiar with the symptoms of eye defects. A knowledge of these will help the teacher to detect visual problems before they have become visual defects.

The symptoms of visual difficulty are many. They may be categorized

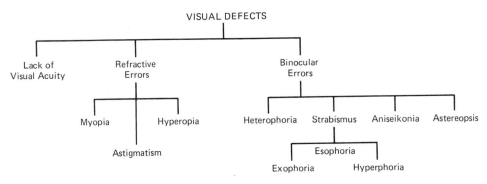

VISUAL DEFECTS

Lack of Visual Acuity — Refractive Errors — Binocular Errors

Myopia — Hyperopia — Astigmatism

Heterophoria — Strabismus — Aniseikonia — Astereopsis

Esophoria — Exophoria — Hyperphoria

Figure 5-1 The More Common Visual Defects. Emerald Dechant, *Diagnosis and Remediation of Reading Disabilities,* © 1981, p. 174. Reprinted by permission of Prentice-Hall, Inc., Englewood Cliffs, N. J.

under four headings: general complaints; specific and visible conditions of the eye; symptomatic behaviors of the child; and avoidance symptoms in the child.

General complaints include such problems as headaches, dizziness, inability to see well, blurred vision, double vision, fatigue, inability to see the blackboard, letters and lines running together, and nausea.

Eye conditions that need attention are red-rimmed, encrusted, or swollen eyelids; watering of the eyes; recurring sties or lid inflammation; eyes or pupils unequal in size; drooping of one or both eyelids; eyes crossing inward, turning outward constantly, or wandering occasionally; and eyes "shaking" or oscillating.

Behaviors that are indicative of visual problems are difficulty in reading or in work requiring close vision; skipping of words or lines; rereading; losing the place; slow reading; frowning; excessive blinking; squinting; holding the book to close or too far away; rubbing the eyes frequently; shutting one eye; tilting the head forward; stumbling over small objects; sensitivity to light; inability to detect color; assuming poor sitting position; poor alignment in writing; confusion of letters such as *o* and *a, e* and *c,* and *n* and *m;* reversals in reading; writing "up- or down-hill" even if the paper is lined; finger pointing while reading; tenseness and nervousness.

Avoidance symptoms include avoidance of close work, shunning of reading tasks, and avoidance of sustained reading.

It must be recognized that many of these signs and symptoms are common during colds and other illnesses, but any persistence of these complaints indicates the need for an eye examination.

Eye Defects and Reading Difficulties

Eye defects of one sort or another increase throughout the grades and may play an important role in reading inadequacy. Generally, the incidence of myopia does not distinguish the good reader from the poor reader. In fact, myopia may be associated with better than normal progress. There appears to be a greater incidence of hyperopia among poor readers (Hartlage 1976). Severe hyperopia affects the ability of the eyes to converge. There is some indication that perhaps 10 to 15 percent of first graders are so farsighted that they are unable to use their eyes in deciphering print without developing headaches, fatigue, or nervousness. Hyperopia also appears to have an adverse effect on reading if it is linked to phorias, when it is present in one eye while the other is normal or myopic, if it is a present above fifth-grade level, or when it is accompanied by a squint (Spache 1976). Astigmatism may be a handicap to successful reading when the learner has a severe case or when it is present in only one eye.

Failure of the eyes to function together, as in strabismus, often has a serious impact on reading development. Taylor (1962) reports that a survey of some 2000 children with academic difficulties showed that 95 percent of these had difficulties with fusion. When the deviations are vertical, as when one eye focuses higher (hyperphoria), readers frequently lose their place and fixate at a point either below or above the line they should be reading. Such readers frequently complain of not understanding what they are reading. When the deviations are lateral in nature, the convergence may be insufficient as in exophoria, or excessive as in cross eyes, or esophoria. Exophoria seems to occur more frequently among poor readers than does any other heterophoric condition; it leads to ommissions, regressions, and loss of place, and results in greater divergent movements at the beginning of lines. As noted earlier, phorias combined with far-sightedness are particularly related to reading problems. Difficulties with aniseikonia also seem to be more common among poor readers than among good readers.

Deficiencies in binocular control lead to inadequate word perception and the consumption of an excessive amount of energy in maintaining single vision. The pupil fatigues easily, is easily distracted, tends to have poor comprehension, constantly moves the head, and has difficulties in concentrating.

Other eye movements associated with varying degees of reading inefficiency are convergence and divergence, accommodation (adusting the shape of the lens to the distance), compensation (compensating for head movements while reading), pursuit (using smooth movement to read signs while driving or to read moving print on a screen) and physiological nystagmus (employing involuntary, oscillating eye movements, or an involuntary, rapid, back-and-forth movement of the eyeball) (Griffin, Walton, and Ives 1974).

In adjusting to distance, the lenses and the posture of the eyes must be carefully coordinated. The eyes separate or diverge for distance and converge for near-point focusing. While this is going on, the lenses bulge or flatten to keep the image clear. The accommodation-convergence reflex is often not mature before the age of six (Spache 1976). Ocularmotor pursuit (ocular mobility) is the ability to track a moving target without moving the head. This ability is needed to shift the eyes along a line in a book, to shift from one line to the next, and to make quick and accurate shifts of vision between the desk and the chalkboard (Pope 1976).

It is difficult to evaluate the specific effect of various visual disturbances on a given child. The eyes can make amazing accommodations so that words may be seen clearly. With the proper motivation pupils may learn, despite visual handicaps. They can ignore a distortion from one eye if they see clearly with the other.

The fact is that some children with defective vision become good readers and that others without any visual difficulty do not learn to read. However, this does not indicate that good vision is unimportant to reading. Eye defects are a handicap to both good and poor readers.

Eames (1959) lists the following ways of helping children with visual difficulties:

1. Control the glare in the classroom by eliminating highly polished, glass-topped, or highly reflective surfaces.
2. While teaching, do not stand directly in front of the light source.
3. Shield light sources so that the light does not shine directly into children's eyes.
4. Arrange students in the classroom so that the light comes over the left shoulder of right-handed children and over the right shoulder of left-handed children.
5. Write on the blackboard in large letters at or slightly above the level of the children's eyes.
6. Use large-size materials: heavily printed charts and maps, large sheets of paper, and sight-saving texts.
7. Seat children either near or away from the light, depending on the nature of their visual difficulty.
8. Provide students with ample rest periods.
9. Use only black and white materials with color-blind students.
10. Do not try to change the "eyedness" of the child.

Visual Screening Tests

Screening tests may be used by the classroom teacher to detect visual problems. They are useful in locating difficulties that require referral to a specialist.

In the past, the *Snellen Chart Test*, designed by Snellen in Utrecht in 1862, was the acceptable screening test. It consists of rows of letters, or *E*s, in varied positions. The pupil being examined stands 20 feet from the chart and names progressively smaller letters. The test identifies nearsightedness and measures visual acuity at a distance of 20 feet, but it fails to detect astigmatism and farsightedness. Since nearsightedness is frequently associated with good reading rather than with poor reading, the test is not too helpful in reading diagnosis. The Snellen Test letters should be used with children who can read and the Snellen E letters with those who cannot read.

The *American Medical Association* (A.M.A.) *Rating Reading Card* may be used to supplement the Snellen Test. It is similar to the Snellen but is read at a distance of 14 inches. The child who fails on this test and succeeds on the Snellen chart is probably farsighted; when the results are reversed, the child is probably nearsighted.

A perhaps even more helpful visual screening test is the *Keystone School Vision Screening Test.* (Mast Development Company) which uses telebinocular and stereoscopic slides to check whether the student has normal sharpness and clarity of vision and whether the eyes work together efficiently as a team. It provides binocular screening, testing vision with both eyes open, and tests total visual efficiency both at far point and at normal reading distance.

AUDITORY EFFICIENCY AND ACHIEVEMENT IN READING

Some children are handicapped in reading because they are not able to discriminate between the various phonetic elements of words; they do not hear and do not speak the sounds correctly, and thus they confuse words. This confusion leads to an inability to associate the sound with the appropriate printed symbol or to deal with phonics. Hearing may consequently bear as close a relationship to reading proficiency as does vision.

Auditory adequacy includes hearing, listening, and comprehension. It encompasses auditory *acuity*, auditory *discrimination*, auditory *blending* or auditory *synthesis* of sounds, auditory *comprehension*, and auditory *memory*.

Auditory acuity, or hearing, is the process by which sound waves are received, modified, and relayed along the nervous system by the ear. It is the recognition of discrete units of sound. Auditory discrimination is the ability to discriminate between the sounds or phonemes of a language. Auditory blending is the ability to reproduce a word by synthesizing its component parts. It is especially significant in synthetic phonics. Finally, hearing is not complete until the hearer can comprehend (listening comprehension) and remember (auditory memory) what has been heard. Disabled readers almost always do poorly on auditory memory tests. Auditory memory seems to have a special significance for reading at the first-grade level and in phonics-oriented programs.

The emphasis in this section is on auditory acuity, or the pupil's ability to recognize discrete units of sound. Smith (1977) notes that "auditory acuity is not essential for reading, although it may be a prerequisite for reading instruction," and for this reason it is of concern to the reading teacher.

Normal conversation has an intensity of about 50 decibels. The decibel is a unit in the measure of sound intensity variation or loudness above a sound that is barely audible. Thus, someone who has a 50-decibel hearing loss in the speech range of sound would be aware of conversation only as a barely audible sound. Normal acuity is variously defined. Some believe that a hearing loss of as little as 6 decibels puts one in the hard-of-hearing group; others put the cutoff point at 15 or more decibels. Because of the difference in definition, writers have reported percentages of hearing deficiencies ranging from 2 to 20 percent. Generally, it is estimated to be about 2.5 percent (Hull et al. 1976).

Types of Auditory Deficiency

There are basically two kinds of auditory deficiency or loss: conductive loss and nerve loss. A conductive loss is a loss in loudness and stems from an impairment in the conductive process in the middle ear which reduces the intensity of sound reaching the inner ear. (The outer ear consists of the auditory canal; the middle ear consists of the eardrum, the malleus or hammer, the incus or anvil, and the stapes or stirrup; and the inner ear consists of the round window, the oval window, the semicircular canals, and the cochlea. See Figure 5-2.)

In a conductive loss, there may be wax in the ear blocking the external canal, the eardrum may be punctured, or there may be a malfunction of the three small ossicles or bones in the middle ear. This kind of loss reduces hearing ability, affecting the loudness with which one hears speech, but if the loudness of the sound is increased, the individual hears and understands. Persons with a conduc-

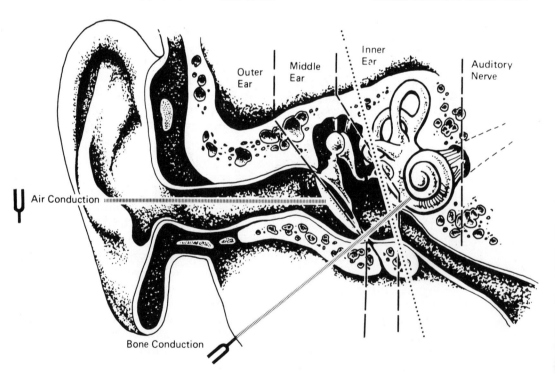

Figure 5-2   The Human Ear. F. N. Martin, *Introduction to Audiology,* second edition © 1981, p. 4. Reprinted by permission of Prentice-Hall, Inc., Englewood Cliffs, N. J.

tive loss can hear their own voice through bone conduction. Because the voices of others sound much softer than their own, they may try to compensate by speaking softly so as to conform to the voices of others around them.

When the sound passes through the entire peripheral mechanism of the external, middle, and inner ear, the sound is heard through air conduction. When the sound is introduced by mechanically vibrating the skull and only the inner ear is stimulated, the sound is heard through bone conduction. Thus, bone-conduction hearing tends to be normal as long as the inner ear is intact. A wax (cerumen) buildup in the external auditory canal or a fluid buildup in the middle ear (serous otitis) will affect air-conduction hearing, but may not affect bone-conduction hearing. Such a hearing loss is termed a conductive hearing loss.

A nerve (sensorineural) or perceptive loss stems from an impairment or lesion of the end organ, the cochlear hair cells, or the auditory nerve of the ear, and affects clarity and intelligibility of speech. It is a hearing loss resulting in a combined defect in the external, middle, and inner ear, affecting both air and bone conduction. A person with such a loss hears but may not understand the speech of others.

Since high-frequency loss is often associated with sensorineural deafness, high-tone nerve loss prevents the individual from hearing and distinguishing certain speech sounds, especially such sounds as /f/, /v/, /s/, /z/, /sh/, /zh/, /th/, /t/, /d/, and /k/. Articulation generally is affected. The pupil may speak too loudly or may develop monotony in the voice, may show signs of frequently misunderstanding the teacher, and may be inappropriately thought of as mentally retarded. Low-tone losses generally affect hearing of the consonants /m/, /g/, /b/, and /h/ and the vowels. An early emphasis on consonant sounds, blends, and digraphs in phonics teaching, especially if the emphasis is on synthetic phonics, presents some difficulty for children with high-tone losses.

Symptoms of Hearing Defects

Behaviors symptomatic of hearing problems are

1. Pupils are inattentive or indifferent when the teacher is talking or during class discussion.
2. Pupils turn their heads toward the speaker, cup their hands behind their ears, or tend to favor one ear; when listening to the radio or TV, they frequently request that the volume be turned up.
3. Pupils complain of ringing or buzzing in the ears; they have discharging ears or frequently complain of earaches.
4. Pupils listen with a tense or blank facial expression; they have a tendency to watch the speaker's face.
5. Pupils confuse words with similar sounds. They ask that statements, instructions, and directions be repeated and often answer questions with an unrelated answer.
6. Pupils hear the speech of others but may not understand what they hear. They do not follow the trend of thought during oral discussions.

7. Pupils have special difficulty with the sounds /f/, /v/, /s/, /z/, /sh/, /zh/, /th/, /t/, /d/, /p/, /g/, /k/, and /b/.
8. Pupils' speech is poorer than one would expect for children of their age. Speech is in a monotone or the pitch is unnatural.
9. Pupils fail to respond to phonic instruction.
10. Pupils' pronunciation is faulty and enunciation is indistinct.
11. Pupils breathe through the mouth or hold the mouth open while listening.

Tests of Hearing

The hearing of every child consistently exhibiting the symptoms of hearing difficulty just enumerated should be tested. A loud, ticking watch may be used as a simple test. Normally a child can hear the ticking up to a distance of about 48 inches. Anything below 20 inches probably indicates hearing deficiency. For a more accurate test an audiometer may be used. Audiometers produce sounds of different frequency and intensity levels for the purpose of measuring auditory sensitivity. They permit the audiologist to obtain an audiogram of an individual's hearing in terms of frequency and intensity by producing tones that can be varied in intensity and in cycles per second, allowing for the measurement of acuity of low, medium, and high tones.

Some audiometers are similar to a portable phonograph, with several connected telephone receivers that permit individual testing or the simultaneous testing of as many as ten children. For group testing with such an instrument children must be able to write numbers, although in individual testing a teacher could record a child's answers.*

Educational Implications

In general, a hearing level of −10 to 25 decibels (db) is considered to be within the normal range for most children. When the pupil's hearing ranges between 11 to 15 decibels, the pupil should be seated close to the teacher. When the hearing level falls between 15 and 25 decibels, the pupil may have difficulty sustaining attention and may benefit from a hearing aid. When the hearing level falls between 25 and 40 decibels, the pupil has difficulty hearing faint speech or distant sounds, may benefit from lip-reading instruction, may need speech training, and at the upper (35 db) level should have a hearing aid. Children with a 40 decibel loss across the speech range will have particular difficulty with /ch/, /f/, /k/, /s/, /sh/, /th/, and /z/. Between the hearing level of 41 to 55 decibels, the hearing loss is substantial and the pupil can understand speech only up to about 3 to 5 feet away. The pupil needs a hearing aid, auditory training, lip reading, speech correction, and preferential seating. When the hearing level is between 56

---

* For a discussion of audiometric testing and for an analysis of audiograms (graphs indicating how loud in decibel levels the sound must be for a person to hear at different pitch or frequency levels) useful in reading diagnosis see Dechant's *Diagnosis and Remediation of Reading Disabilities* (1981a: pp. 54–63).

and 70 decibels, the pupil has difficulty hearing even with a hearing aid. Conversation must be loud to be understood, and the pupil may need to be placed in a special class for the hearing impaired. Such a pupil usually cannot learn to speak without aid. When the hearing level is 71 or more, the pupil cannot learn speech through hearing; ordinarily, the school is unable to meet the needs of such pupils.

Persons whose hearing level is 71 db or more are considered to be deaf; anyone whose level is 35 to 69 db is considered to be hard-of-hearing.

Loss of hearing, even a mild hearing loss, is associated with retardation in school and with speech problems, and it can aggravate a reading deficiency. Without the ability to discriminate speech sounds children cannot isolate the separate sounds in words, and they thus find phonics training incomprehensible. Auditory factors may be especially important when there is a severe hearing loss, when the specific hearing loss involves high-tone deafness (lowered acuity for sounds of high pitch) or when instruction puts a premium on auditory factors. The exclusive use of the phonic method with children who have suffered a hearing loss may prevent achievement in reading. If hearing losses are dissimilar in the two ears, children may have difficulty in localizing sounds or in telling where sound comes from. The teacher needs to make sure of having such children's attention before speaking to them.

The child will be at a disadvantage if the teacher fails to distinguish between mistakes in reading and differences in pronunciation (Labov 1965). The pupil, who reads "I write wif a pin," has read correctly, but may not have spoken the way the teacher would speak. Admonishing this child for poor reading may only hurt the pupil. In fact, the child may not be able to hear the difference between *with* and *wif* or *pen* and *pin*, even under the most favorable of instructional procedures. Hearing loss, in such instances, precipitated the misarticulation, and the pupil may be best served by a speech therapist.

Inadequate auditory perception is twice as common as is hearing loss in children with learning disablities. Furthermore, studies show that the percentage of children with auditory-perception problems is higher than average among children in low socioeconomic groups and is even higher among disadvantaged children who belong to racial minorities or come from bilingual homes (Arnold and Wist 1970; Deutsch et al. 1967).

NEURAL ADEQUACY AND ACHIEVEMENT IN READING

Understanding of reading requires understanding the functioning of the brain. The brain controls the rest of the body by sending commands, as it were, through a network of eighty-six major nerves that expand into thousands of smaller nerves. The nerves spread from the brain through the brain stem down the spinal cord. The nerves may be likened to miles of telephone wire; the brain, to a central switchboard. The impulses travel through the neural network, transmitting sensory data and messages.

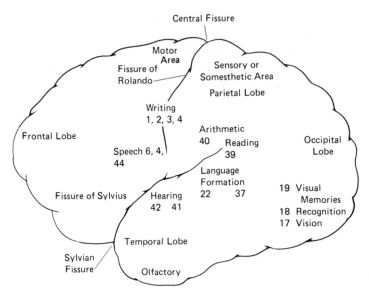

Central Fissure

Motor Area

Fissure of Rolando

Sensory or Somesthetic Area

Parietal Lobe

Writing 1, 2, 3, 4

Arithmetic 40   Reading 39

Frontal Lobe

Speech 6, 4, 44

Occipital Lobe

Language Formation 22   37

19 Visual Memories

Fissure of Sylvius   Hearing 42 41

18 Recognition

17 Vision

Temporal Lobe

Sylvian Fissure

Olfactory

Figure 5-3 The Brain. Adapted from Emerald Dechant, *Diagnosis and Remediation of Reading Disabilities,* © 1981, p. 185. Reprinted by permission of Prentice-Hall, Inc., Englewood Cliffs, N. J.

However, brain activity is much more complex than a telephone switchboard connection operating strictly as an electrical system. The brain is an intricate and enormous information-processing and decoding system in which neurons are the biological wires that carry information in the form of tiny electrochemical impulses (London 1975).

Recent experiments with electrical stimulations of the brain have given much information concerning the projection areas of the brain. Figure 5-3 shows the auditory, visual, motor, somesthetic, and olfactory areas. Two fissures, the central or Fissure of Rolando and the Sylvian fissure, separate the brain into lobes: the frontal lobe, the parietal lobe, the temporal lobe, and the occipital lobe. The sense organs are connected with their special projection areas in the cortex, and the essential sensory processes occur there. An injury to the visual projection area, for example, may cause blindness.

The functions of the brain, however, are not restricted to the projection areas. More than three-fourths of the brain consists of association areas.

The brain must have memory in order to relate the information of the moment with that of the past and to recognize its significance. This means millions of functional correlations, countless hookups of sensory centers with one another and with motor centers, and repeated exchanges of data for analysis, comparison, and synthesis. These elaborative functions of the cortex are performed by the association areas.

The nerve impulse travels from the retina along the optic nerve to visual area 17 in the occipital lobe. This area is concerned with seeing but not with recognition. In areas 18 and 19 recognition and visual memory occur. There, the words are recognized as words. In area 39 (the angular gyrus) the meaning of the word is comprehended. This part of the brain deals with the interpretation of symbols (letters, words, syllables). A lesion here will interfere with the ability to read. In area 39, the association of sounds and visual symbols occurs. Thus, since reading is commonly an association of a visual symbol with an auditory symbol, this part is of major importance in reading.

LATERAL-CEREBRAL DOMINANCE

A condition thought to be dependent on the development of the brain is cerebral or lateral dominance. Lateral dominance implies that one cerebral hemisphere is more important in behavior or functionally more efficient than the other; it refers to the consistent use of and preference for the muscles of one side of the body. The dominant hemisphere is on the side opposite the preferred hand. Since most persons are right-handed, the dominant hemisphere for most is the left hemisphere.

Research data indicate that the left hemisphere is also the dominant hemisphere for speech in most people. Newborn children show greater left-sided electrical response to speech (Molfese 1973). Broca was the first to ascribe speech dominance to the cerebral hemisphere contralateral to the preferred hand (McNeil and Hamre 1974). Rossi and Rosadini (1967) found, however, that even for most left-handed people the dominant hemisphere for speech was the left hemisphere, with 98.6 percent of the right-handed and 71.4 percent of left-handed showing speech dominance in the left hemisphere.

Speech musculature, until at least four or five years of age, is served by both hemispheres simultaneously. It is a bilateral function, permitting recovery of articulation following unilateral injury or excision. The young child can tolerate damage to the language hemisphere because the function can be transferred to the other hemisphere. In older children such damage will lead to aphasic disorders. The left hemisphere, however, seems to be primarily responsible for language processes, including the differential verbal labeling of letter and word shapes.

There are exceptions to the general rule of lateral dominance. Some persons are ambidextrous with neither hemisphere being dominant (thus exhibiting lack of dominance); some exhibit crossed laterality, being left-eyed and right-handed or vice versa; and in others dominance changes from activity to activity. Do these conditions hinder reading proficiency?

Related concerns are: directional confusion (inability to identify left from right), ear dominance, and crossed dominance (preferred hand and preferred eye are on opposite sides).

Orton (1928) suggested that in learning to read the pupil develops memory traces, or engrams, for words, both in the dominant (left for the average individual) and the nondominant (right) hemisphere, but that those in the nondominant hemisphere normally are mirror images of the former and thus are suppressed. Orton added that if cerebral dominance is well developed by the time reading begins, reading proficiency is not affected. If, however, no special dominance is developed, or if the engrams or memory traces in the right hemisphere become active, reading difficulties occur, and the child will read once with a left and then with a right orientation.

In cases of lack of dominance (as in the ambidextrous person), the engrams of each hemisphere are equally dominant, and readers may become confused and indecisive in their reading. They will sometimes read in a left-to-right direction and at other times reverse the direction. Letters and words are reversed because such readers sometimes use the mirror images developed in the nondominant hemisphere.

Although Orton did not concern himself with the left-handed, similar difficulties may arise for them. Left-handed people have a natural tendency to move their arms and hands towards the left, away from the body, in writing, and it is presumed that it is also most natural for them to move their eyes from right to left in attacking words. If they follow this natural tendency in reading, they will see little difference between the printed words and their mirror images. This results in reversals of words and word forms. There is indeed substantial evidence that left-handedness, a symptom of right-cerebral dominance, is frequently associated with poorer reading.

Studies of reading-disability cases, especially those showing up in reading clinics, have provided further evidence for a relationship between poor reading and lack of or undeveloped dominance. Harris (1956) reports a high proportion of reading-disability cases develop preference for one hand later than the age of nine. In a later study (1957) he suggests that if tests are sufficiently discriminative, genuine relationships between reading disability and laterality are found. Harris and Sipay (1975) note that they have become convinced that there is more than a chance relationship between lateral dominance and reading disability.

Silver and Hagin (1966), in an intensive study of eighteen subjects over a period of years, concluded that the persistence of anomalies of laterality, even when maturation in perceptual areas has occurred, suggests that for some children "reading disability may be a basic biologic defect resulting from the failures to establish clear-cut cerebral dominance." They used the arm-extension test in which the subjects extend their arms straight out with fingers spread, to determine cerebral dominance. Children over six years old generally hold one arm slightly higher than the other in this test; if the right arm is held higher, it indicates that the left hemisphere is dominant. Silver and Hagin reported with regard to these studies that children who showed an abnormality on the arm-extension test (their left hand was held higher but they wrote right-handed) also had a 90 percent likelihood of having a reading problem.

Many reading disabilities also exhibit directional confusion. Alexander and Money (1967) and Money, Alexander, and Walker (1965) believe that defective direction sense (confusion in applying the terms *left* and *right* first to oneself and later to others) and defective space-form perception, themselves the result of a maturational lag or a developmental defect, may explain some cases of reading retardation. They found that right-left spatial orientation normally becomes established between the ages of eleven and fourteen, but dyslexic boys of age eleven through fourteen made significantly more errors on the test than did the standardization group.

Cohen and Glass (1968) found significant relationships between knowledge of left and right (and hand dominance) and reading ability, but not so in the fourth grade. Testing 429 second graders, Ginsburg and Hartwick (1971) found that left-right confusion was significantly associated with reading errors.

Ear dominance is a recent area in which research tends to support the concept of cerebral dominance. Newborn children are better able to discriminate the right sides of two dichotic verbal messages, indicating left-cerebral dominance. (Entus 1975) In dichotic listening experiments, two different stimuli (the words *bake* and *mash*) are presented simultaneously, one in each ear. Normal children tend to respond as though they hear the right-ear stimulus first, indicating a left cerebral dominance for verbal processing. Children with learning disabilities or reading disabilities often exhibit a mixed or left-ear dominance. They frequently perform significantly worse in overall right-ear superiority.

Not all researchers come to the same conclusion as did Orton. Many consider that dominance is not an either-or proposition; rather it is a matter of degree. To some degree everyone is two-handed; the embryo is completely symmetrical, and the development of a dominant hand is a gradual process with the dominance of one hand over the other increasing with age. Furthermore, a different hand may be preferred for a different function.

At one time it was thought that the preferred use of one eye over the other was an indication of the dominance of one cerebral hemisphere. More recent knowledge of eyedness (Stephens, Cunningham, and Stigler 1967; Cohen and Glass 1968) has furnished little evidence for this belief. The nerves from each eye are connected to both hemispheres of the brain. In each eye the right half of the visual field in the retina is related to the right cerebral hemisphere, and the left half is related to the left hemisphere.

Gardner (1973) notes that although a causal relationship between incomplete lateralization and reading disability has yet to be confirmed, a correlation between a developmental lag in the attainment of dominance and reading problems is well documented. He reports that Bernard Sklar, working at UCLA's Brain Research Institute, used a computer to analyze the electroencephalogram (EEG) data of a group of normal and a group of dyslexic readers. Computer analysis showed that the EEGs of the two groups differed in three ways: the disabled readers showed less synchronization between the two hemispheres of their brains, more synchronization within each hemisphere, and generally more theta waves. Sklar believes the first two findings support the theory that reading disability is related to incomplete cerebral dominance.

Summarization of the data leads to the following observations:

1. Both cerebral hemispheres have equal potential for language until four or five years of age.
2. The left hemisphere is the language hemisphere and is also the dominant hemisphere for most individuals.
3. Some individuals, however, are left-handed and hence right dominant; some are ambidextrous and hence lack dominance; some are right-handed, left-eyed, or vice versa, thus showing crossed dominance; and some experience directional confusion.
4. Orton felt that mixed or incomplete dominance and directional confusion hinder development in reading.
5. Data favorable to Orton's position:
   a. Some studies show a relationship between left-handedness and reading disability.
   b. Reading disability cases, especially in clinics, develop hand preference later than the age of nine.
   c. Ambidextrous individuals show evidence of hemispheric conflict.
   d. Defective direction sense seems related to reading disability.
   e. Children with learning or reading disabilities often exhibit a mixed or left-ear dominance.
6. Views contrary to Orton:
   a. Dominance is not an either-or proposition but depends on the function in question.
   b. There is little evidence that eyedness or crossed dominance is related to reading disability.
7. Recent evidence seems to indicate that though a causal relationship is not absolutely certain, the relationship between dominance and reading problems is more than simple chance.
8. The brain's two hemispheres are programmed to process information differently, with the left hemisphere being the locus of speech and the right hemisphere processing information such as the orientation of objects in space and the recognition of visual form. It is probable that if something interferes with the development of hemispheric asymmetry, problems in academic tasks could be expected to follow. Disabled readers in fact show less than the normal amount of difference in electrical activity between the hemispheres. The relationship of dual-cerebral asymmetry to sidedness preferences and left-right spatial awareness is not known. It may be that body laterality, lateral awareness, and brain asymmetry are completely independent, but the prospect of a functional interdependency among them is strong.

READING: A LEARNED PROCESS

Consider now the final statement about reading to be made in this chapter, namely, that reading is also a *learned* process. The same laws of learning that govern all learned processes govern the pupil's learning to read.

Learning theories are generally divided into stimulus-response or behavioral theories, and field or cognitive theories. The behavioral model holds that all learning is habit formation, a connection between a stimulus and a response. The connection is referred to as an S-R bond. The S-R theorist focuses on the response or the observable action: the learner learns an action or a response. For the S-R theorist, conditioning is the clearest and most simple instance of a response to a stimulus. Learning is defined as the acquisition of new behavior patterns (or the changing of behavior) by the strengthening or weakening of old patterns as a result of practice or training.

The best contemporary exponent of behaviorism is B. F. Skinner. In Skinnerian terminology, all behavior can be understood, predicted, and controlled in terms of habits established or shaped by a process of successive approximation: by the reinforcement of a response in the presence of a particular stimulus.

Reinforcement determines whether conditioning in fact takes place. A particular S-R bond will be established only if the responding organism is reinforced in a particular way in the presence of a particular stimulus.

The process of setting up the type of behavior that one wants to reinforce is known as shaping. Shaping of behavior does not wait until the learner's response is exactly correct; at first it may be necessary to reinforce gross approximations to the final response. Behavior is thus molded into shape by a process of successive approximation. It is through shaping that the very fine discriminations required in reading are produced. Through a process of chaining, elaborate sequences of behavior—like those required in reading—are built up. The behaviorist view explains *why* learning takes place; it takes place because of reinforcement.

The cognitive model perceives the learner as a consumer of information. The cognitive theorist does not believe that language skills can be explained as habits established by the conditioning of S-R bonds. Rather, the cognitive theorist points out that readers extract meaning from what they read on the basis of the visual information (the surface structure of the language) but also on the basis of the deep structure of language and of the knowledge and experiences contained within their brain. Cognition is the central brain process that determines the reader's particular reaction to graphic symbols.

Cognitive theorists are interested more in what children know and understand than in what they do. They believe strongly that learning is guided by intervening mental processes which are labeled cognition, thought, or perception. To the cognitive psychologist, what is interesting is the unobservable manner in which information is acquired and organized by the brain (Smith 1971).

Theorists like Smith (1971: pp. 68-80) reject the behaviorist view for the following reasons:

1. There is no simple correspondence between writing and meaning.
2. Skill in language production and comprehension cannot have developed through

the establishment of S-R bonds because practically all the sentences one speaks or reads are novel ones.

3. Perception is a constructive process, adding something to the stimulus aspects. The reader makes decisions on the basis of two kinds of evidence: current information received from the environment by the reader's receptor systems, and stored information available in the memory. Writing cannot be comprehended unless the reader makes this critical, active contribution.

4. Since sentence meaning cannot be determined on a sequential word-by-word basis, information from several printed words has to be held in short-term memory. The load on short-term memory is reduced by "chunking" information into larger units—by storing words rather than letters, or meanings rather than words.

The following few statements summarize in a general way the major learning principles that are applicable in the teaching of reading:

1. All learning involves a stimulus (S), a response (R), and a connection between the stimulus and the response. The pupil is stimulated by words, sentences, and paragraphs (S) and responds with meaning (R).

2, Learning proceeds best when the learners understand what they are doing.
   a. Teachers need to be aware that sometimes the pupil comes up with the correct response by accident or by guessing, without understanding why the answer is correct.
   b. The teacher needs to determine whether to reward the correct response, the correct process, or only the correct response when it is accompanied by the correct process. Pupils are not best served when the teacher simply feeds phonogram-phoneme relationships to them and cares only if the right response comes back. Pupils are not best served when the teacher rewards guesses or accidental solutions.

3. Pupils learn by doing. Learning occurs under conditions of practice, and overlearning is of crucial importance to beginning readers and to poor readers. Children generally become better in word recognition the more frequently they see the word. However, practice or repetition, per se, does not cause learning. Children's practice must be both motivated and rewarded, and it should be slightly varied from session to session.

4. Students learn best when they are psychologically and physiologically ready to respond to the stimulus. They will not respond unless they are motivated, and they cannot learn unless they respond. Their performance will improve only if they are interested in their work, if they are interested in improving themselves, if the material to be learned has special significance for them, and if they are attentive to the situation. Students must recognize their reading problems as ones they want to solve. Reduce motivations to zero, and there is no performance and hence no learning.

5. Students cannot learn without doing, but they will not *do* without being rewarded. The teacher must divide the learning situation into numerous small steps and must reward the learning of each discrete step.

6. Each activity (the reading of this sentence, for example) consists of a complex of individual movements. Improvement and learning are not necessarily attained by *much reading* but rather by increasing the number of *correct movements in reading* (such as moving from left to right, proper identification of the word, association of the proper meaning with the word, and development of proper eye

movements) and by reducing the number of incorrect movements (such as excessive regressions and improper word attack) in the complex of movements comprising the total act. Improvement occurs because learners gradually replace the erroneous movements they are still making with correct ones. Thus, additional practice gives more opportunity to master the myriad of movements comprising a complex total performance.

This view of the learning of a skill certainly emphasizes the need for the teaching of specific habits. Telling a disabled reader to "read" is not specific enough. The teacher needs to teach specific habits in specific situations. This requires careful job analysis, leading to an identification of all specific movements. The curriculum, methods, and materials must be so specific that they will serve as proper stimuli to call forth appropriate responses. It is not enough to identify large all-embracing abilities, such as gaining a sight vocabulary. It is necessary to break the broad area into basic subskills, such as the ability to discriminate between sounds, to see elements within a word, and to blend the elements into the total word.

7. When a stimulus is followed by a response, there is a tendency for the same response to occur when the stimulus recurs (law of contiguity). The child who responds to *was* with *saw*, tends to respond again with *saw* on the next presentation of the stimulus, *was*. In the classroom, much teaching follows this contiguity principle. The teacher shows the child a card containing the word *cat* and says "/kat/," and the assumption is that the child will, upon subsequent occasions, say the word *cat* when the same printed stimulus is presented alone.

It is important that the teacher not permit the learner to leave a learning situation without performing the response correctly. The child should not get by with approximations of the correct answer. The child should not be permitted simply to get a general idea. Partially correct answers, such as reading *their* for *them*, are in fact totally wrong.

8. If the student tends to repeat the response that was made most recently in the presence of the stimulus (law of relative recency), the teacher should exercise great care, expecially with the beginning and the disabled reader, not to permit extraneous materials to come between the stimulus and the response. The teacher must see to it that when the response is made, it is made to the proper stimulus and not to any of many other possible stimuli that may have intervened. Too frequently in teaching, by the time the proper response occurs, the original stimulus situation has disappeared. The teacher must take great care that the necessary stimuli are so distinct for the student that they cannot help but see the connection between a given stimulus and the right response.

9. Teachers will make fewer mistakes in teaching if they analyze all the variables in behavior. There are multiple causes of behavior.

SUMMARY

Chapter 5 has continued the analysis of the correlates of reading disability begun in Chapter 4, focusing on general physical conditions, the sex of the learner, visual deficiency, auditory deficiency, and neural inadequacy. Again, perhaps the major reason for making this analysis is that it reduces costly trial and error and very often prevents reading disability and failure.

Poor readers and poor students frequently exhibit low levels of motivation and high levels of fatigue. They have low motivation to achieve, show little enthusiasm for learning, have a low energy level, daydream a lot, their attention is poor, and they are often fatigued. This chapter has sought to account for these behaviors and their effect on achievement in reading.

Another correlate of reading disability is the sex of the learner. It is a fact that boys are more likely to have reading disabilities than are girls. Girls read earlier than boys and continue this superiority through life. The chapter has examined both biological and environmental explanations for these differences.

A third correlate of reading achievement is visual skill. Eye defects, unless they are of a gross nature, are rarely an absolute bar to the child's becoming a good reader, but they do result in uncomfortable and inefficient reading. Success in reading depends more on the underlying perceptual and assimilative processes than on visual efficiency. And yet reading disability can be clearly aggravated by inadequate sensory development or by visual deficiencies.

Another major correlate of reading ability is auditory adequacy. A key reading skill is the ability to deal with phoneme-grapheme correspondences, and to do this the pupil must have mastered certain auditory-discrimination skills. Auditory acuity, auditory discrimination, auditory blending, auditory comprehension, and auditory memory all play a role in reading performance. They are especially important in oral reading and phonics. Auditory defects are most likely to hinder reading success when there is a severe hearing loss, when hearing loss involves deafness for high tones, and when instruction puts a premium on auditory factors.

Finally, the chapter has considered neural adequacy and its effect on reading performance. It is quite probable that biologically determined or hereditary defects and brain injuries are basic causes of reading disability in at least some cases. Neurological lesions or cerebral imbalance may impair both reading and speech and may influence handedness. Mixed laterality frequently seems to be related to retarded speech and retarded linguistic development.

This chapter, and Chapter 4 as well, should have cautioned the teacher in the interpretation of reading failures. Not all children can learn to read with ease. Some children want to learn but have little success. They are motivated; they are not lazy or indifferent; but because they are handicapped intellectually, experientially, physically, or physiologically, learning to read is difficult.

Certainly, of one thing we are sure: one should not diagnose a pupil as remedial without checking out the factors that have been discussed in this and the preceding chapter.

It is extremely difficult to establish clear-cut cause-and-effect correlates, but a cluster of factors may at times constitute a syndrome that leads to a better diagnosis and a clearer determination of remediation. A cluster of organic factors, for illustration, may include soft signs of neurological dysfunction, motor awkwardness, poor performance in motor tests, and low spatial-test scores. Another cluster, indicating deficiency in auditory processing, might include slow language development, inadequate articulation, poor performance in auditory discrimination, poor test scores in sound blending, poor auditory memory, and inability to learn phonics (Lerner 1976).

The import of Chapters 4 and 5 is this: Teachers should not devote most of their time and effort to finding out how the average individual performs. It is true that poor readers often come from homes of lower socioeconomic standing, tend to dislike school, have more auditory and visual defects, and cannot analyze or synthesize well. But many good readers have similar problems and characteristics, and yet they do not become poor readers. What is the explanation? The whole complex of causes, correlates, and reasons why children fail in reading presents a new pattern of organization for each individual. All children have their own organization and their own rate and level of growth and development.

Reading achievement is variable because children are different. They have different biological and environmental backgrounds, and if teachers are to know how and when to teach what, they must know and understand those factors that make children different.

In general, the psychology of individual differences indicates:

1. Children achieve at different rates.
2. The differences in achievement increase as children advance through school, going from as much as four grades at the first-grade level to as much as nine or ten grades at the sixth-grade level.
3. Native endowment or biology plays a large role in children's development. Biological characteristics are prime factors in making children individuals.
4. Intraindividual differences may be as great or greater than the differences between individuals.
5. The achievements of individuals are often marked by spurts and plateaus.
6. Environmental factors may serve as equalizers among individuals. They may tend to make unequals more equal and more similar.
7. The rate of teaching (pacing) must be suited to the child's pace of learning.

QUESTIONS FOR DISCUSSION

1. List and discuss types of commonly found physiological defects which are related to reading failure.
2. Discuss the question of when the child's eyes are ready for reading. What is meant by visual adequacy?
3. What are the general types and symptoms of defective vision? What are the common refractive errors and binocular difficulties.
4. What relationships have been observed between eye defects and reading proficiency?
5. What are the relationships between hearing and reading?
6. Can you give an explanation for the apparent differences in achievement in reading among boys and girls?
7. Discuss the relationship between neural functioning and achievement in reading.
8. Elaborate on the statement: Not all children can learn to read with ease.

PART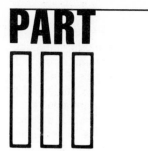III

developing readiness for reading

Part III outlines a program for developing reading readiness and for introducing the pupil to reading. It is not enough for teachers to know what promotes or hinders reading readiness; they must know how to develop this readiness. Part III consists of two chapters: Chapter 6, "Developing Reading Readiness" and Chapter 7, "Introducing the Pupil to Reading." These chapters are designed to develop the enabling or readiness skills without which the pupil cannot learn to read. Chapter 6 deals principally with the development of concepts, of auditory and visual-perception skills, of preferred modes of learning, and of intersensory modality strength. Chapter 7 continues the emphasis on reading readiness, but also introduces the formal teaching of basic reading skills; it deals with letter recognition, left-to-right progression, acquisition of a sight vocabulary, utilization of phonics and context, readiness materials, and evaluation of reading-readiness tests.

6

DEVELOPING READING READINESS

Reading readiness has been defined as the developmental stage at which constitutional and environmental factors have prepared the child for reading instruction. Reading readiness also may be described as the teachable moment for reading: the point in time when the pupil is ready to learn how to read. Chapters 4 and 5 discussed the constitutional and environmental factors that may interfere with the child's readiness for and achievement in reading. Perhaps it would be valuable for the reader to refer back to the section on maturation in Chapter 4 for a description of readiness as well as for a statement of the significant principles of readiness.

The reading teacher must not only know what factors promote or prohibit adequate reading performance but must also identify each pupil's specific readiness in each of them. The reading program must be individualized for each pupil.

The concern in this chapter and in Chapter 7 is with the development of readiness, the development of the enabling skills that make it possible for pupils to learn to read. The particular concern is with those readiness elements that can be and usually are developed through classroom instruction and that can be taught well in advance of formal reading instruction (Rosner 1974). There are, of course, many other enabling skills, such as motivation and interest, that are just as significant: these also need careful cultivation.

It is not easy to list in sequence the major skills and attitudes that must be developed in the kindergarten and early first grade. However, research and experience indicate that for success in reading the child should either possess or develop in school certain minimum levels of proficiency in a number of areas. At the same time, the teacher of reading should not forget that some children may come to school fully prepared for reading. A readiness program may only be frustrating for these children; and they are ready for reading.

The first requisite for beginning reading is an interest in reading. Children generally come to school wanting to learn to read. When they have discovered that what can be said also can be written, they show an even greater interest. The most frequently repeated phrase during the readiness period is "What does it say?"

After the child's interest and attention have been obtained, major teaching tasks remain. Classroom instruction must provide for the following:

1. Development of speaking and listening skills (see Chapter 3)
2. Development of concepts
3. Development of auditory-perception skills
4. Development of visual-perception skills
5. Knowledge of the alphabet (development of letter recognition)
6. Training in left-to-right progression and in reading on a line
7. Acquisition of a sight vocabulary
8. Acquisition of simple word-identification skills
9. Ability to associate meanings with printed symbols (simple comprehension skills)

Figure 6-1 illustrates the various facets of the readiness program.

A good readiness program is directed toward the development of proficiency in these areas. The pupil must develop proficiency in each area in the day-to-day activities in the classroom. This chapter focuses on the development of concepts and the development of auditory- and visual-perception skills, the development of children's preferred modes of learning, and the development of intersensory modality strength. (The development of the other skills is discussed in Chapter 7.) Begin with the development of concepts.

THE DEVELOPMENT OF CONCEPTS

Chapter 2 noted that children can learn to conceptualize, with experience being a prime determinant of whether or not a child will develop a given concept.

Children go through stages as they learn to interpret words. Concrete and specific concepts probably develop first. Gradually, children engage in more complex, abstract thinking.

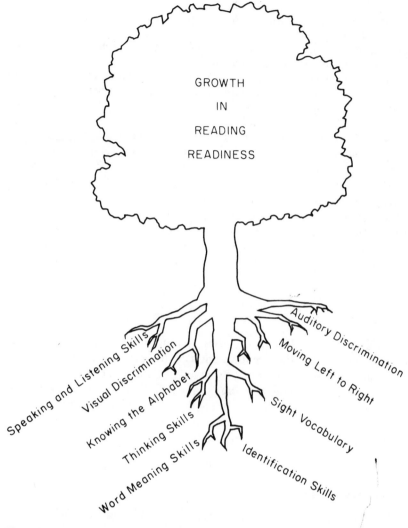

GROWTH

IN

READING

READINESS

Speaking and Listening Skills

Visual Discrimination

Knowing the Alphabet

Auditory Discrimination

Moving Left to Right

Thinking Skills

Sight Vocabulary

Word Meaning Skills

Identification Skills

Figure 6-1 The Readiness Tree.

However, not all children are capable of thinking on an abstract level. Goldstein and Scheerer (1941) found that aphasics are incapable of abstracting; they cannot use a word in its generic sense. Young children and frequently poor readers as well tend to be like aphasics in the level of their interpretations. In one study, aphasics, when asked to give the names of the animals they saw at the zoo, replied, "A polar bear, a brown bear, a black bear, a lion, and a monkey." Each name given in this reply represents a specific animal indicating an inability to generalize "bears" (Goldstein 1936).

The evidence suggests certain general conclusions:

1. Differences in abstracting ability or in the ability to think in categories differentiate the superior or more mature reader from the poor less mature reader, as a rule (Lundsteen 1974).
2. The greater the number of concepts that the reader has fixed through words, the better tends to be his or her understanding of what is read.
3. The more specific the reader's reaction to printed words, the less effective tends to be the communication between writer and reader; the more generic the reaction, the more effective tends to be the communication.

Examine now the steps or levels in the development of concepts. The development of meanings or concepts follows a characteristic pattern. First, children must learn to discriminate one object from another. Gradually, with repeated experience with similar objects, children acquire new layers of meaning and their perceptions become increasingly wider, richer, more diversified, and more complex. They learn to identify the essential and the nonessential characteristics of the various realities in their environment. They proceed from simple experience to concept via abstraction and finally arrive at categorization. They are able to categorize when they can group objects or experiences into classes.

The Percept

The initial perceptual level, or the first step in the development of meaning, is the differentiation of realities within one's environment or one's experience with concrete reality. It is characterized by reaction on a concrete level. At this level each object is distinct, having no commonalities with any other objects. The end result is a percept. It is an impression of an object obtained solely through the senses. A chair, for example, is differentiated from a table without actual identification of the object as a chair. Differentiation at this level is partly based on shape.

Perceptual Schematism

A higher level of reaction is termed "perceptual schematism" by Scheerer (1959). The term refers essentially to the internal representation in perception. On this level the incoming sensory data are grouped into their most natural gestalt or organization. The object with a back and four legs is perceived as a chair. The configuration takes on meaning. This meaning allows the perceiver to react with the experience of sameness upon subsequent contact with another representative object. The object now looks familiar. The perceiver recognizes it as an object he or she has seen before. Chairs can vary within a certain range (their inessential characteristics may change within a prescribed limit) and the perceiver will still react with "Ah, another chair." If the variants are too great in the light of the perceiver's experience, recognition will not occur.

This stage is often confused with abstraction. Children may perceive the similarities, but they are not thinking abstractly because they do not perceive the essential and invariant characteristics.

Contextual Perception

The percept may have a third meaning. An object can take on meaning by being characteristically associated with other objects or experiential events. Thus, a hammer is recognized as something that can be used in a certain way. Whether the pupil *recognizes* the hammer or not (whether it is familiar and can be identified as to its use or meaning) depends on previous experience.

Perception of Differences

One of the best ways of leading children to the development of concepts is to give them an opportunity to experience both examples and nonexamples of the concept under consideration. An example of a concept contains all the basic features; a nonexample contains only some or none of the essential features. If one were to teach the concept *cat*, one would necessarily show children cats of various kinds, sizes, and colors. One might also show them dogs, chickens, or other animals. The children would learn to identify the individual objects and would also learn to discriminate one from the other.

At this level of conceptual development the emphasis is on simple and clear-cut examples. The cats are all the domestic kind. Only later would the children be introduced to the various shadings and meanings that might be associated with the concept *cat*.

The child's meaning for an object may omit certain characteristics or it may include too many. Young children tend to overgeneralize. To them, all men are daddy and all women are mother. Errors of overgeneralization are errors in discrimination of similar objects, persons, or events. Only through experience will children learn that one man is their daddy, another is their uncle, and another is their grandfather.

Abstract Concept

The next stage in conceptual development is the concept itself, which is actually the end result of abstraction. Abstraction isolates the essential properties, and the end result might be termed an abstract concept. Scheerer provides a definition of an abstract concept:

> Concepts are psychologically operative when the invariant relationship between the properties of an object, an action, or an idea is grasped, and when the communality of characteristics that is invariant can be abstracted from a variety of changing aspects. (1954: p. 126)

A concept thus requires both abstraction (this isolates the property—abstract concept) and generalization (this applies it to several objects). A word is the verbal expression of a concept.

The development of a concept requires a distillation of the essential and invariant similarities from a series of related objects or events. To form an adequate concept of *chair* the activation of some (and probably several) of the receptor processes will have taken place in response not only to one chair but to several kinds of chairs.

Categorization

Finally, children must learn to categorize. They must group their experiences into classes. Abstraction isolates the basic characteristic (such as *chairness, beauty*); categorization applies it to more objects. Scheerer notes:

> The name for an individual object in daily life does not refer to the specific uniqueness of the object; the name signifies the object as a representative of a category—an exemplification of all the possible variations allowed for by its invariant characteristics. (1954: p. 126)

Bruner (1957a) suggests that to categorize is to render discriminably different things equivalent; it is to group objects, events, and people into classes; and it is to respond to them in terms of their class membership rather than their uniqueness.

At this stage of the development of meaning, the child may be able to use the word *cat* to refer to an even broader class of objects, one that includes lions, tigers, leopards, jaguars, cougars, lynxes, wildcats, and cheetahs, all of which belong to the cat family.

Figure 6-2 summarizes the process of the development of meaning. It illustrates how the perceiver moves from sensation to perception and more specifically from concrete percept to concept and categorization.

Piaget's Model of Cognitive Development

Perhaps at this point brief allusion ought to be made to Piaget's model of cognitive development, which as been outlined by Dechant and Smith (1977: pp. 39-42). Our interest here is principally in what Piaget terms the preoperational period, the concrete operational period, and he formal operational period.

The preoperational period, from approximately age two to age seven, covers the important period when rapid growth of language occurs. During the preconceptual period (age two to four), children rapidly learn to represent objects and the world by symbolic means. For example, 50 percent of children at age two can identify common objects, such as a cup. However, children tend to orient their activities on the basis of appearances. They are easily misled by what they see. For them, language is not something apart from objects and experiences. The name of the thing inheres in the thing itself: a chair is called a chair, a rocker is something else entirely.

In the latter part of stage two (age four to seven), the intuitive period, children move from near-total dependence on sensation and perception to the in-

Figure 6-2 The Development of Meaning

CONCRETE ——→ ABSTRACT

	Step I		Step II		Step III	Step IV
	Percept (Level I)	Perceptual Schematism (Level II)	Contextual Perception (Level III)	Perception of Differences (Level IV)	Concept (Level V)	Categorization (Level VI)
	Simple discriminations of concrete reality. A chair is differentiated from a table without actual identification of the object as a table. Shape is a key factor in the discrimination.	The configuration takes on identity; the object with the back and four legs is termed a chair and upon subsequent experience with a similar object the perceiver will say, "Ah, another chair." Similarity or sameness is a key element.	At this level there is an extension of meaning. Thus, a chair can be used to wash the ceiling or to send a man to his death. Objects will take on new meanings dependent upon the context in which they are used. Pupils learn that words can have multiple meanings or referents.	This is the beginning of concept formation. The perceiver can see similarities among chairs generally, but discriminates chair from rocker, from high chair, etc. This is more than the simple discrimination of difference that occurs in Level I.	The concept is the product of abstraction. It requires (1) perception of communality or sameness (2) perception of invariant characteristics (3) abstraction of invariant characteristics from a variety of changing aspects The learner perceives "chairness" or "catness."	The perceiver can think of the object (cat) as representative of a class or category—as an exemplification of all possible variations permitted by its invariant characteristics (lions, tigers, leopards, cougars, etc.). He can identify the "cat" family.

itial stages of logical thought. They can now group objects into classes by noting similarities and differences, but they still pay attention to one aspect of an object to the neglect of other aspects. They can also form the concept *fruit*, relating *orange* and *apple*.

Piaget believes that the average four-year-old child can manage reading skills, and the fact is that most children experience their initial, formal reading instruction between the ages of four to seven.

Beginning about age seven, children enter the concrete operational period and develop the capability of carrying out logical operations. They can classify according to one or more criteria. They are less dependent upon their own perceptions and motor actions and show a capacity for reasoning. They can now make transformations. They notice that, in pouring liquid from a short glass into a tall glass, nothing is added and nothing has been taken away. They can also transform and manipulate sentences. Such operations suggest that in this period thought and language are freed from dependence upon sensation and perception, but mental activity is still tied to concrete or physical situations or experiences.

At about age eleven to fifteen children attain the fourth and mature stage of mental development, Piaget's formal operations period. They are able to deal with abstract relationships instead of just with things. Whereas concrete-operational children reason only from directly observed data, their older counterparts are freed from dependence on directly experienced events and begin to deal with conditional, suppositional, and hypothetical statements and propositions.

Although the sequence of these stages of cognitive development and the overall order within the stages are the same for all individuals, not all children pass through the stages of intellectual growth in exactly the same way or at exactly the same rate. As children acquire more experience, their concepts broaden, become clearer, and are hierarchically organized. Concepts are also less egocentric and less concrete and take on conventionalized significance.

ACTIVITIES FOR TEACHING MEANING

Chapter 12 outlines how the development of concepts may be encouraged through a series of activities. There the emphasis is on the teaching of meaning beyond the primary level. Let us confine ourselves here to those activities that help the teacher to develop the conceptual readiness required by pupils on the kindergarten/first-grade level.

The following activities are especially appropriate:

1. Give children an opportunity to deal with concrete objects.
2. Label objects in the classroom.
3. Use pictures and art activities to expand children's concepts. Teach children to interpret pictures.

4. Encourage conversation and storytelling.
5. Use description, riddle, and rhyme games.
6. Use audiovisual aids.
7. Use dramatization, including marionette and puppet shows.
8. Teach children to make and use picture dictionaries.
9. Use oral and written directions.
10. Teach categorization skills with words and objects.

A discussion of each of these activities follows.

Experience with the Concrete Object

A natural activity in the kindergarten is to have children bring toys and objects to school and then tell the other children about them. This "bring-and-tell" activity, besides being language training, is interesting to children and extends their fund of meanings.

Demonstrations, models, exhibits, and dioramas also serve to expand children's knowledge of meanings and vocabulary. Experiences may be broadened by models of houses and vehicles, and by plant and geological specimens. Children may help construct a play house, a play town, a toy store, an airplane, or a fire engine. Science activities, such as collecting shells and rocks or caring for an aquarium, develop and clarify children's concepts of the real world that is symbolized by words. Children may discuss the seasons and the weather. They may care for plants and study about vegetables and flowers.

They learn the meaning of *pint, quart,* and *gallon* by handling and seeing such containers. A measuring cup may be used to develop meaning for *half, fourth,* or *third.* The height of the door, the weight of a bag of potatoes, or a foot rule are simple referents useful in teaching measurement concepts.

Concepts develop most easily through sense impressions. Visits for example, to farms, food markets, factories, trains, museums, circuses, newspaper plants, creameries, planetariums, zoos, fire departments, bakeries, airplanes, post offices, school buildings, libraries, and stores provide experience backgrounds for many words. Preparatory activities should familiarize children with the objects they will be seeing. They need to know what to look for. After the trip they need exercises in association with the experience and the symbol. They may draw pictures of what they saw or they may develop an experience chart about their trip.

In developing meanings, teachers also should make use of children's sense of touch, taste, smell, and hearing. Kindergarten children like to handle objects. Nails, bolts, washers, screws, ball bearings, pliers, files, screwdrivers, and hammers fascinate them. Teachers may blindfold children and ask them to identify by touch—fur, bark, screen, soft flannel-like leaves, satin, sandpaper, and thistles.

Young learners like to make sounds and to discriminate sounds made in the world about them. Meanings are broadened through exercising the sense of smell, a very delightful activity. Children may never have matched a specific smell to paint, varnish, ink, oil, soap, fingernail polish, shoe polish, gasoline, or catnip.

An interesting game is "My Nose Tells Me." A blindfolded pupil is asked to identify foods or objects by smell. Apples, onions, vinegar, leather, bananas, oranges, or pepper may be used. On more advanced levels children should "hear" and "see" the meanings of words like *stealthily, drowsy, steaming,* or *smoking.*

Labeling

Labeling of objects in the classroom begins in the kindergarten. For example, labels can be put on the desks, chairs, doors, windows, and pictures. Children's names can be put on their kindergarten rugs. Children can label the pictures in scrapbooks. In the upper grades, labeling is a useful way for teaching technical vocabularies. Pupils can provide labels for collections of insects, leaves, rocks, shells, woods, and snakes; they can label both the materials and the apparatuses used in class.

Signs and directions are additional means for teaching children to associate meanings with printed symbols. Signs, such as "Put milk bottles here," "Stop," "Go," and "Grocery Store," are effective teaching devices.

Learning to Read Pictures

Children are frequently introduced to the meaning of a word through the use of pictures. Children's books commonly have pictures accompanying the text. The pictures are clues to the story, and the text often merely represents the conversation of one of the persons identified in the picture. Children should be encouraged to observe what is happening in a picture, to figure out what has happened before and what will happen next, and to decide what the characters in the picture might be saying.

Pictures may also be used to teach the multiple meanings of words, to develop meanings for prepositions, to understand the meanings of opposites, and to develop an understanding of sequential thought. The exercise in Figure 6-3 is illustrative.

The meaning of the words *up* and *down*, for example, can be illustrated by simple drawings of someone ascending and descending stairs. The child draws a red circle around the girl going up the stairs and a blue circle around the boy coming down the stairs. Art exercises also are effective for illustrating processes and for demonstrating the steps required in making something.

Conversation and Storytelling

In actively constructing sentences, stories, and experience charts, children enlarge their vocabulary and increase their number of usable concepts while at the same time correcting misconceptions and inadequacies in meaning. Suppose, for example, that the word *potato* appears in a sentence. The teacher may ask, "What kind of potatoes have you seen?" or "Where are potatoes

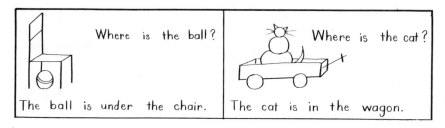

Figure 6-3 Meanings of Prepositions. Adapted from Mary E. Platts, *Spice* (Stevensville, Mich.: Educational Service, Inc., 1973), p. 118. Reproduced by permission.

generally grown?" Children need a lot of experience with words, and encouraging them to speak is one way of helping them to get this experience.

Numerous language activities can be planned for children. We already have mentioned the bring-and-tell activity. Children may also tell a story about a picture, describe their own art work, or tell of their experiences the previous evening or on the way to school. They may be asked to select a title for a picture, to play word games, or to tell the sequence of events in a story that was read to them.

Description, Riddle, and Rhyme Games

In description games one side of a card contains a description and the other contains the correct word. The children hear the description and then are asked to identify what has been described—in other words, to give the word on the card. In another version of this exercise, students are given three words from which they select the one that identifies what has been described.

Riddles are of two kinds: *Who am I?* and *What am I?* The following riddles are illustrative:

My coat is red
My tail is bushy
I'm shrewd and cunning
I'm the sly_____.

Rhymes are useful in developing meaningful listening. For example:

Johnny jumped over the wall
Only to have a terrible . . .
(fall)

Audiovisual Aids

We have already spoken of pictures and their usefulness in teaching meaning. Slides, filmstrips, television, radio, and disk and tape recordings bring into the classroom numerous experiences that might never be had first-hand. Certain words—for example, *satellite, rocket, pyramid, buffalo, raccoon, por-*

123

cupine, bellows, caboose, andirons, bronco, cactus, coyote, catacomb, penquin chariot, cathedral, and *knight*—become real only when illustrated visually. In the upper elementary grades, charts, maps, diagrams, and graphs are especially useful for teaching relationships.

Film readers appear to have special values. Not only can children see and hear while using the film, but they can then read the same words and content in a correlated reader.

Dramatization: Marionette and Puppet Shows

Acting out the activity frequently is the best way to teach the meaning of words like *hop* and *skip*. Some form of dramatization is also often effective in teaching prepositions such as *into, upon, below, above, behind, through, around,* or *before;* in teaching such action words as *snaillike, trippingly, hesitantly, haltingly, nervously, clumsily, quickly, safely, quietly;* and in teaching feeling words such as *sadness, confusion, elation, anger, disgust,* and *fear.* Sometimes a short dramatization is useful in teaching the meaning of abstract terms such as *love, courage, cooperation,* and *appreciation.*

Making and Using Picture Dictionaries

Children like to construct their own dictionaries. Each new word they meet is included in the dictionary and is accompanied by a picture. The dictionary might start out as 26 pages, each headed by a captial and lowercase letter of the alphabet. When the child has mastered writing, a description may accompany each word. Action words can be accompanied by action pictures. Words like *here, there, wherefore, therefore,* and *why* should be explained by using them in sentences.

There are of course, many published picture dictionaries. These are especially helpful in developing meanings for a word and in developing alphabetizing skills. Some of the common picture dictionaries are:

1. *Picture Book Dictionary* (Children's Press)
2. *Illustrated Golden Dictionary* (Golden Press)
3. *My First Golden Dictionary* (Golden Press)
4. *Grosset Starter Picture Dictionary,* (Grosset & Dunlap)
5. *Young Reader's Color-Picture Dictionary for Reading, Writing, and Spelling* (Grosset & Dunlap)
6. *The Picture Dictionary for Children* (Grosset & Dunlap)
7. *Words I Like to Read and Write,* grades 1-2; *Words to Read, Write, and Spell,* grades 2-4 (Harper & Row)
8. *Pixie Dictionary* (Holt, Rinehart, and Winston)
9. *My Self-Help Dictionary* (The Macmillan Company)
10. *Picture Dictionary for Primary Grades* (Noble and Noble)
11. *My Little Dictionary* (Scott, Foresman)
12. *The Charlie Brown Dictionary* (Prentice-Hall)

13. *Little Golden Picture Dictionary* (Western Publishing)
14. *Golden Picture Dictionary* (Western Publishing)
15. *My Dictionary*, 1970 (William Morrow)
16. *My First Picture Dictionary* (William Morrow)

Oral and Written Directions

As has already been mentioned, teachers can help to develop word meanings by posting directions on the bulletin board or blackboard. They also may ask children to carry out certain actions. "Get your colors, Jose," or "Pass the napkins, Pam" are examples of spoken directions.

Two games, the "Do This" game and the "Yes and No" game, are suitable activities. Each game requires a set of cards. "Do This" gives directions and "Yes and No" asks questions. The child selects a card, reads it aloud, and either carries out the desired directions or answers the question. The "Do This" cards contain statements like the following: "Stand up and then sit down"; "Stand up and point to the left"; "Point to the sky"; "Clap your hands"; or "Give the number that follows five." The "Yes and No" cards contain questions like the following: "Can a dog fly?"; "Can birds sing?"; "Are cats bigger than lambs?"; or "Are there boys in our class?" If the responses to the directions or questions show that the child does not possess the concept involved, the card is put on the bottom of the pack. If the response is adequate, the child keeps the card. The child with the most cards wins the game.

Fitting Objects and Words into Categories

In reading, children are constantly required to think in categories. Initially the exercises used to teach this skill should be pictorial in nature.

A more advanced activity requires children to place words into appropriate categories. In one column is a list of words; opposite the list are certain categories under which the words may be appropriately grouped.

WORDS		CATEGORIES	
Turkey	Pumpkin pie	Christmas	Thanksgiving
Mistletoe	Tree		
Bell	Cranberry sauce		
Santa Claus			

Other headings for the category columns, for example, may be things to eat, things to make, things to wear, things that float, things that are mineral, things that are vegetable, things that move, things that are found in the country, things that are found in the city, things that grow, things that run, things that crawl, or things that have wheels. For a single exercise, generally three classifications, such as things to eat, things to wear, and things that run, are adequate.

Children might be asked to sort articles into the following three categories: things found in a grocery store, things found in a hardware store, and things found in a clothing store. Or they could group words according to color: words that might be appropriately used here are *apple, avocado, beet, bread, butter, carrot, cherry, chocolate, corn, egg, grass, milk, orange, pea, peach, pear, potato, snow, squirrel, strawberry, tomato,* and *watermelon.*

Additional Thought-Initiating Activities

Numerous activities not classifiable under the broad categories suggested above promote the development of concepts necessary for beginning reading. One of these concepts is the meaning of symbols. The child must learn that the word stands for an idea or concept and thus for the real thing. Without this knowledge the child will always be merely a word caller.

In introducing children to reading, it is important for the teacher to use the knowledge of thousands of spoken words which children already possess. Children have meanings for these words but cannot decipher their printed form. They need to associate the sound of the word with its form. The skill consists of using the beginning consonant sound of the word together with the context to identify the specific word.   An exercise which teaches this skill calls for the teacher to read aloud a series of sentences, omitting the final word. The pupil may be told that the words should begin with a specific letter or sound. Sample sentences are

1.   I went swimming in a _____ (brook)
2.   In the birdhouse I saw a _____ (bird)
3.   I use a bat to hit a _____ (ball)
4.   I can ride a _____ (bike)

In these exercises the pupil uses the first consonant of the word in order to arrive at the correct word. Later, in actual reading, this skill will be useful in identifying words: the pupil will think of a spoken word that fits both the context and the initial letter.

Exercises such as those suggested above should enable students

1.   To use picture clues to meaning.
2.   To develop simple concepts, such as top-bottom, left-right.
3.   To develop sentence sense or the ability to recognize proper grammatical language and complete sentence structure.
4.   To understand the meaning of simple prepositions such as *on, under, over, next to, behind, in front of,* and the like.
5.   To follow directions.
6.   To understand and use the pronouns *I, me, we, you, he, she, her, him.*
7.   To classify familiar objects.
8.   To recognize the central idea, note details, and draw simple conclusions.
9.   To associate meanings with spoken words.

Materials designed to develop meaning skills are listed in Chapter 12, p. 292.

Now consider the second enabling or readiness skill identified in this chapter, namely, skill in auditory perception, especially auditory discrimination.

DEVELOPING AUDITORY- PERCEPTION SKILLS

Auditory-perception skills include auditory discrimination, auditory blending, auditory comprehension, auditory figure-ground discrimination, and auditory memory. The readiness program deals with each of these. Begin with auditory discrimination.

Auditory Discrimination

Among the auditory-perception skills, auditory discrimination, especially of phonemes and spoken words, has been given primary attention by teachers of reading, and rightfully so. Auditory discrimination is the ability to discriminate between the sounds, or phonemes, of the language. It is the ability to tell whether two spoken words are alike or slightly different.

It is evident that this skill is essential to readiness for reading and to successful achievement in reading. If children cannot *hear* sounds correctly, especially if this condition appears early in life or is congenital, they normally cannot learn to *speak* them correctly. Children cannot pronounce distinctions that they cannot hear. Furthermore, if they confuse or distort sounds in speech, it is frequently impossible for them to associate the correct sound with the appropriate visual symbol. Thus, inadequate auditory discrimination leads to improper speech and ultimately to an incorrect association of sound and printed symbol. Whether students will profit from phonics instruction is to a large measure dependent upon their auditory-discrimination skills, or the ability to differentiate between sounds in words. One fact appears to be clear: students who learn to read easily are usually those who notice and discriminate sounds in spoken words.

Beginning readers have no concept of the phoneme and do not perceive that speech can be analyzed into phonemes in a definite sequence. However, children need to know what a phoneme is if they are to understand how the alphabet works as a code for speech. Children must learn that words consist of sounds, that sounds follow sequentially, that the same sound may occur in more than one word, and that one word generally has sounds that are different from the sounds of other words. And they need to realize that words that sound alike frequently look alike. The facts concerning auditory discrimination are these:

1. Approximately 20 percent of the normal speaking population has poor auditory-discrimination ability.

2. There is a positive relationship between auditory discrimination and reading (Strag and Richmond 1973; DeHirsh and Jansky 1970; Rosner 1973). Hammill and Larsen (1974), however, did not find that auditory perceptual deficits explained reading deficiency. Groff (1975) likewise questioned the relationship between auditory discrimination and reading achievement and called for more intensive investigation of the pros and cons of the issue.

3. On the primary-grade level, auditory discrimination may be more closely related to reading efficiency than is mental age (Harrington and Durrell 1955; Nila 1953).

4. Auditory discrimination may be more significantly related to early reading achievement than is visual discrimination (Linder and Fillmer 1970).

5. Poor auditory discrimination is related positively to inaccuracies in articulation and pronunciation.

6. Development in articulation is probably more significant for reading success than is auditory discrimination. If articulation development is adequate, poor auditory discrimination may have less significance for reading.

7. The ability to match a picture with a spoken word that has the same sound at the beginning as the name of the picture is a significant predictor of reading.

8. Poor discrimination of vowels and of the consonants /m/, /g/, /b/, and /h/ may reflect a low-tone hearing loss; poor discrimination of /f/, /v/, /s/, /z/, /sh/, /zh/, /th/, /t/, /d/, and /k/ may reflect a high-tone loss.

9. Children have varying degrees of ability in auditory discrimination. Auditory-discrimination ability rarely shows any significant development after eight or nine, but rarely is fully developed before the age of eight (Turaids, Wepman, and Morency 1972; Morency 1968).

10. Auditory-discrimination ability is most needed in programs with a strong phonic emphasis.

Some writers suggest that children whose auditory discrimination is slow in developing should receive the benefits of direct intervention to improve their less developed modality; others suggest that the pupils might be separately grouped for reading. Certainly it would appear that children with a developmental delay in articulation because of slowness in auditory-discrimination development might benefit from an emphasis on visual learning until, in maturing, they can correct their own articulation errors.

In developing auditory discrimination always start with sounds the pupil has already learned to discriminate. Start teaching the recoding skills with words that pupils know by sight.

Causes commonly adduced to explain poor auditory-discrimination skills are inadequate maturation; inattentiveness; a receptive aphasia caused by a neurological lesion; a hearing loss of 15 decibels or more (especially high-frequency hearing losses); or dialect (children from minority groups, as indeed those of low socioeconomic status, tend to have inadequate auditory-discrimination skills).

Sample exercises useful in developing the auditory-discrimination skills include:

1. List the names of children beginning with the /b/ sound. Have pupils give other words *beginning* with the /b/ sound.

2. Have pupils come to the blackboard and draw a line around any pictures whose names begin like the name of the key picture.

bug

3. Provide pupils with three pictures and ask them to encircle the two pictures whose names begin with the same sound.

4. Show a card with the picture of a bell and a bat and say, "This is a bell and this is a bat. Do they *begin* with the same sound?" (See *Teach*, A-D-2, Walker Educational Book Corporation.)

5. Have pupils deal with directives such as, "Listen to two words—*name* and *nine*. Do they begin with the same sound?" and "Listen to the two words I say—*small* and *big*. Do they end with the same sound?"

6. After teaching a given sound, for example, /b/, present the pupils with a mimeographed page of pictures. Ask them to put a line through the objects whose names do not begin with the sound /b/.

7. Show a card with a picture of a fish and a brush and say, "This is a fish and this is a brush. Do these words *end* with the same sound?" (See *Teach*, A-D-3.)

8. Have pupils associate consonant sounds with the appropriate visual symbol. The pupils identify each picture, say its name, and then locate the letter that symbolizes the beginning sound of the picture.

b
h

b
h

b
h

b
h

* The figures on this page are from Emerald Dechant, *Diagnosis and Remediation of Reading Disabilities*, © 1981, pp. 251, 282. Reprinted by permission of Prentice-Hall, Inc. Englewood Cliffs, N. J.

9.   Have pupils indicate whether two nonsense syllables (*gat-gat, fin-fid*) sound the same or different.

Auditory Memory

Some pupils cannot remember words spoken to them. They have a very short auditory memory and retention span. They have a poor memory for auditory sequences and are unable to tell how many sounds there are in spoken words. They cannot sequence auditorially.

Auditory memory span was studied before the turn of the century by Jacobs (1887). A short, sequential memory span may result in inaccuracies of articulation or in reversals of phonemes or syllables in spoken words; it may show itself as reversals of words in sentences or as slowness in developing syntactic phrasing ability; it may lead to substitutions, distortions, omitted words, and the like when reading aloud; and it may result in spelling errors and reversals when writing. Writing and spelling depend upon the ability to hold in mind the sequential order of the word. Reading requires the association of an auditory sequence of speech sounds with a visual sequence of letter symbols.

The ability to recall sequences is developmental in nature, with children gradually becoming able to recall longer series of digits. There is generally little change in scores on tests of auditory sequential memory between the seventh and eighth year; most significant changes occur between ages six and seven.

The following exercises develop attention, and recognition, and recall of precise sequences:

1.   Have children dial on a telephone three, four, and five digits. Children generally manage three digits (3-8-6) by age three and one-half, four digits by age four and one-half, and five digits by seven and one-half. This exercise is especially helpful in developing sustained attention.

2.   Have the children listen to long and short sound patterns on the buzzer board, toy flute, or telegraph keys. The teacher taps out a pair of patterns (____./____.) (.   ./____ ____). Children must indicate when the two patterns sound alike or different. This task teaches recognition and recall of precise sequences of sounds or the patterns within words. Both phonic analysis and structural analysis of words requires the ability to deal with the patterns of sounds within words. (See *Teach*, A-Seq. 4, Walker Educational Book Corporation.)

3.   Pronounce two similar words (*floor, door*); then repeat one of them, and have the children remember if the first or second word was repeated.

4.   Say two words (*chair, cap*) whiie the children's eyes are closed; then, with eyes open, have children select from four pictures the one in which the sequence (*chair, cap*) is pictured.

5.   Have children repeat a series of words (from two to six) from memory.

6.   Have children repeat spoken digits of increasing length from memory.

Auditory Blending

Some pupils have difficulty with auditory synthesis, sequential decoding, or blending; they cannot blend phonemes to form a complete word; they cannot sequence auditorally or synthesize sounds into meaningful speech. Such pupils tend to have difficulty with phonics.

Auditory blending is particularly important in grades one and two, when pupils are learning to read, when reading is taught by a synthetic phonic method, and when pupils must analyze words into syllables to arrive at the pronunciation of a word. It appears to have less bearing on reading achievement after the fundamentals of reading have been mastered.

The inability to blend makes it difficult to read unfamiliar words. Even though many children learn blending incidentally, Ramsey (1972) reports that 40 percent of the errors made by second graders on a test of unfamiliar words resulted from difficulties in blending.

Blending generally takes four forms:

1. Sounding and blending of each letter: c/a/t, /kŭh/ /ă/ /tŭh/.
2. Sounding of the beginning consonant and the following vowel and blending these with the final consonant: ca-t, /kă/-/t/.
3. Sounding of the initial consonant and joining it to the vowel and ending consonant (the phonogram): c-at, /k/-/ăt/.
4. Sounding of the beginning consonant and following vowel (kă), sounding of the vowel and the final consonant /ăt/, and then blending them (kă/ăt) to form the word cat /kăt/.

Each of the blending approaches has its problems. Letter-by-letter sounding and blending (b/a/t) often results in a distortion of the individual sounds. When pupils are asked to blend a beginning consonant with a phonogram (b/at), they tend to develop the habit of looking first at the end of the word. This may cause difficulties for pupils who reverse. Joining the vowel to the beginning consonant (ba/t) makes it difficult to know whether to give the vowel its long or short sound.

It seems preferable to blend the beginning consonant with the phonogram. There are two ways of teaching the phonogram: either by blending a and t, or by teaching it as a unit (at). The latter in many instances is easier than teaching the blending of a and t.

The teacher develops the blending skill in the following manner:

1. Have the pupil form the mouth in preparation for saying the initial consonant but then have him or her say the following vowel instead: b-ȳ. This technique is especially effective when the initial consonant is unvoiced and when the syllable ends in a vowel.
2. Have the pupil join the beginning consonant to the ending phonogram. In this technique the single syllable is divided into two parts: the beginning consonant and the ending phonogram: k-ăt.

3. Use an auditory method, with the teacher pronouncing the word in parts (*sh/eet*) and the pupil being required to combine the parts to form the whole word. Pupils do not see the printed word in this approach.

4. Use an auditory-visual method, with the teacher showing the pupils a card with the word *feet* on it and say: "This word is *feet*. Now I am going to make the word . . ."—with this, the teacher folds down a flap on which is written *sh* so as to make the word *sheet*. If the pupils can pronounce the word, it is assumed they can blend *sh* in the initial position. Haddock (1978) found that the auditory-visual method was more effective than the auditory method.

5. Using alphabet letters of cardboard or felt, identify the word *fat* for the pupil. Separate the letters, gradually separating the sounds at the same time. Then slide the letters together, blending with your voice at the same time. For example, first say, "/rap/." Then separate the *r* from the rest of the word and say, "/r/ . . . /ap/." Slide the *a* away and say "/r/ . . . /a/ . . . /p/." Blend the word together again, moving the letters together as you connect the sounds with your voice. Make certain that the pupils see the visual stimulus at the same time that they hear the word. Then have the pupils go through the same process.

Auditory Comprehension

Some pupils have a poor listening-comprehension ability for their age. They cannot comprehend or understand what is spoken and frequently misunderstand the teacher; they cannot recall oral directions when asked to repeat them. The difficulty is often caused by a high-frequency hearing loss. The reader is referred to Chapter 3, pp. 41, where listening or auditory comprehension is discussed in detail.

Auditory Figure-Ground Discrimination

Some pupils cannot focus attention on a relevant sound (such as the teacher's voice) while ignoring irrelevant sounds (hall noises, pencil sharpeners). Auditory figure-ground discrimination is known as focus-field discrimination. Pupils are aided in making auditory figure-ground discriminations by amplification of the sound (Johnson 1969). Amplifying the sound may serve the same function that color does in print.*

DEVELOPING VISUAL-PERCEPTION SKILLS

Learning to read also requires visual discrimination of letters and words. Visual or form discrimination depends on gross and fine motor skills; visual-motor integration or eye-hand coordination; discrimination of figure and ground; visual closure; perception of part-whole relationships, and of constancy; and visual

---

* For further assessment of auditory-perception skills, see Dechant 1981a: pp. 66-68, and for commercial materials designed as aids in teaching auditory-perception skills, see Dechant 1981b: pp. 15-25.

memory. Pupils who lack proficiency in these are said to have a visual-perceptual deficit.

Consider these areas in more detail.

Ever since there has been concern with identifying the factors that are indicative of both reading readiness and achievement, visual discrimination of letters and words has been accorded a primary position.

Form discrimination involves the ability to distinguish among stimuli on the basis of essential details of shape.* Visual perception of form is critical to the ability to discriminate letters and numerals in reading. It is involved in distinguishing between △ and □, and later in discriminating between *A* and *H* or recognizing the difference between *h*, *n*, and *m*.

Visual discrimination, the ability to visually analyze and synthesize printed words, includes (1) the ability to identify letter symbols visually; (2) the ability to develop a gestalt for a word or to experience the "flash" or global identification of a word as a whole; and (3) the ability to recall visually familiar letters and words.

Prospective readers must be able to sort out and distinguish differences between visual stimuli. They must be able to note similarities and differences in the forms of objects, pictures, geometric figures, and words. Generally, kindergarten and first-grade children have learned to discriminate between gross figures and objects. They see the difference between a cat and a dog and between circles, squares, and triangles. They have also learned something about words. Long before they come to school they have identified signs such as "Stop," "Wichita," and "Kansas." They have noted that some words are long and others short, that some have ascending letters and others have descending letters, and that some words look alike and that others look different.

Unfortunately, not all children can identify words visually. For some, visual discrimination of shape, pattern, and form is so weak that it interferes with their ability to recognize letters and words (Spache 1976). They cannot distinguish differences between visual stimuli on the basis of essential details of shape. Although most children come to school with adequate visual acuity, some are immature in visual perception. They cannot identify words, and this is shown in wild guessing at words, and in frequent errors of omission, in additions, substitutions, repetitions, mispronunciations, hesitations, and the like. Such children make frequent requests for help with the same word and have special difficulty with similar-appearing words. They have difficulty with matching exercises, being unable to match forms, numerals, or letters. These inadequacies, however, although they often appear to be caused by a perceptual handicap, may also be due to inattention.

Eye-hand coordination, or visual-motor integration, involves coordinating what the eye *sees* with what the hand *does*. Eye-hand coordination is in-

---

* Descriptions given here are from the *Teaching Resources Catalog* (Boston: Teaching Resources Corp. 1979), pp. 58-59.

volved in activities such as using scissors, stringing beads, catching and throwing a ball, tying shoelaces, buttoning a shirt, or writing.

Defective visual-motor function is one of the major causes of reading disability. Young children with this deficit cannot reproduce a design although the model is before them, and cannot copy shapes, abstract designs, sequences, or draw geometric figures.

After the initial scribbling stage, young children tend to produce all closed shapes in a roughly circular form. This is followed by a differentiation of curved and straight lines, with drawing of oblique lines coming at about five years of age. Correct copying of complex oblique lines such as those in a diamond occurs at about the age of seven. The developmental ages for various forms are these: circle, three years; square, four to four and one-half years; triangle, five years; triangle in a circle or circle in a square, six years; diamond in a circle, seven years. Less than 50 percent of the five-year-olds can copy a triangle, whereas 95 percent of the six-year-olds can do so. Copying of diamonds is a difficult task for the five- to six-year-old child; the vertical diamond (◊) is easier than the horizontal (◇) diamond. Children of preschool age tend to rotate horizontal configurations to the vertical. When the same tendency occurs in six-year-olds, it probably indicates perceptual immaturity. The visual-motor function reaches maturity between the ages of six and eight.

Errors in form reproduction at times are caused by poor motor control. In general, if pupils recognize errors of reproduction, the difficulty is probably motoric; if they do not, the difficulty is probably perceptual.

Figure-ground discrimination involves the ability to locate and focus on one stimulus or detail at a time while ignoring other irrelevant stimuli, and to shift attention appropriately. This skill is needed to discriminate letters from the word, to focus on one word or symbol on a page, and to maintain one's place on a page in reading. Pupils who are deficient in this skill see the word on the page as an undifferentiated design. Seiderman (1976) found that a significant number of poor readers in his study had deficits in discerning the relationships between a figure and its background.

Visual closure is the ability to identify an object from an incomplete presentation; it is the ability to fill in the missing parts in a picture so as to identify a stimulus even though the total stimulus is not provided: for example recognizing b__s__b__ll as baseball. Visual closure is a significant factor in fluent, rapid, and mature reading.

Perception of parts-to-whole relationships involves the ability to integrate parts into a meaningful whole and to separate a whole into its component parts, a skill which is needed in spelling and reading. Spoken words are made up of individual speech sounds; written words, which represent spoken words, are made up of individual letters; and sentences are made up of individual words. Pupils who are deficient in this area (and many poor readers are) cannot attend simultaneously to the parts (letters) and the whole (word). They have difficulty in discriminating words because they cannot take in the entire word while also seeing its parts. They have special difficulty with words that look alike, and they cannot visually blend parts into a whole; they are unable to synthesize a word out of its component letter parts. Good readers on the other hand, are able to attend simultaneously to the parts and to the whole.

Constancy refers to the concept that a particular figure remains the same, regardless of changes in other properties such as shape, orientation, size, or color. Understanding this concept enables a child to recognize that △ ▷ ◺ ▲ are all triangles; that *A*, *a*, *a*, a, are all the same letter.

Visual memory is the ability to remember the sequence of letters in words. Many words use exactly the same letters but in a different sequence (*ate*, *eat*, *tea*). Visual memory is particulary important in spelling and writing, but also in reading.

Disabled readers tend to have difficulty remembering letters and words. They cannot recall how words looked (or sounded), have a faulty memory for letter sequences, or show an inappropriate spatial order of the graphemes, with resultant odd and peculiar spellings. Early on, Hinshelwood (1917) suggested that disabled readers have a memory deficit caused by a lesion in the angular gyrus of the left hemisphere. Kass (1966) found that poor readers in the early grades have a poorer sequential visual memory than good readers of the same grade level.

Causes of Visual-Discrimination Difficulties

Causes of visual-discrimination difficulties are quite varied. Consider two. Visual defects can obviously interfere with visual discrimination of form. Among the factors commonly mentioned are

1. Severe astigmatism, especially when it occurs in only one eye. It causes a blurring of the image.
2. Binocular difficulties, caused by a paralysis of an eye muscle or by a lack of proper muscle balance. This causes a mixing of letters and words. Strabismus may cause a general blurring of vision or in severe cases a doubling of vision.
3. Hyperopia, especially when it is linked with phorias or when it is present in only one eye. The pupil's eyes at age six also may be too farsighted to see such a small object or image as a letter or number.

Children from lower socioeconomic homes also generally score poorly on perceptual tests. Wheelock and Silvaroli (1967) found a significant difference in visual-discrimination ability among kindergarten children from high and low socioeconomic groups. The children from the lower extreme of the socioeconomic continuum lacked visual-discrimination ability and seemed to profit most from training in making instant responses of recognition to the capital letters.

Activities for Developing Visual-Discrimination Skills

Remediation of visual-discrimination deficits has been chancy at best. There is serious doubt (Hammil and Larsen 1974) whether information-processing deficits such as difficulties in visual perception can be successfully remediated. We do not know whether to attempt to strengthen the processing weakness (the visual-perceptual deficit), or to compensate for the weakness and teach to pupils' strengths. And yet, these learners cannot be left to themselves (Samuels 1973).

Pupils need to be taught that letters are conglomerates of features and that words are conglomerates of letters. A letter is a complex pattern of lines, edges, angles, and orientations. Montgomery (1977) notes that twenty-three letters of the alphabet can be formed using small circles (○), short sticks (ı), long sticks (ı), and looped sticks (ᒧ). The teacher must help pupils to identify these features of letters and words. Pupils must learn what to look for. Most of them already know how to look.

The ultimate goal of all visual-discrimination activities is to help pupils improve their letter and word-recognition skills. Pupils will not be readers until they see differences in shapes; perception of likes and similarities is simply not enough. Reading requires the ability to distinguish each word from every other word. Pupils must thus be relatively more skilled in noting the differences among words than in noting the similarities.

Presenting h to pupils 50 times and telling them that it is h because it has an ascender does not help them to discriminate the letter (Smith 1978). Pupils learn what they need to learn only when h is contrasted with another letter (n, for example) and when they learn that h and n are not functionally equivalent.

Numerous studies (for example, Whisler 1974) indicate that practice in visual discrimination and in visual memory does in fact increase word-discrimination skills and reading performance. However, visual-discrimination activities do not have equal relevance.

The matching of nonword forms and pictures appears to have questionable value in improving letter or word perception. The learning in the former often does not transfer to performance on the latter (Muehl and King 1967). Training in perceptual material appears to have an effect only if there is ecological validity: the training sample must be drawn from the same population as that to which one wishes to generalize (Montgomery 1977).

Matching is a diagnostic tool. If pupils cannot match forms or letters, they are not ready to draw images or write symbols. Pupils must learn matching in order to respond consistently to b as b and to *was* as *was*. Fortunately, most first-grade children appear to be able to match one capital letter with its twin and one lowercase letter with its duplicate.

The normal sequence in developing a visual memory for form is (1) tracing the original figure; (2) matching identical forms; (3) drawing the form with dots; (4) copying the form with the original form available for comparison; and (5) reproducing the form from memory.

The various modes of learning forms can be grouped under two terms: simultaneous discrimination and successive discrimination. In simultaneous discrimination a student matches a printed symbol to its duplicate while both are visible. In successive discrimination, which is a better developer of visual memory, a student is required to locate an example of the symbol after the stimulus card has been removed (Hall 1976b).

Barrett (1965) found that being able to discriminate, recognize, and name letters and numbers was the best single predictor of first-grade reading achievement, but pattern copying and word matching were also strongly related. Visual discrimination of letters and words had a slightly higher value than visual discrimination of geometric designs and pictures. Auditory discrimination, language facility, and story sense also contributed to the prediction of first-grade reading.

In a later study, Barrett (1967) found that recognition of letters had the highest correlation with beginning reading achievement; discrimination of the beginning sounds of words had the next highest correlation; and ending sounds, shape completion, ability to copy a sentence, and discrimination of vowel sounds in words were also positively related.

Association of a name with a configuration is neither necessary nor primary in the discrimination process. Discrimination must be made before names can be applied.

In visual-discrimination exercises, the emphasis is not on reading; the teacher does not specifically teach the pupils to associate a printed word with a spoken word or with an object or experience. The pupils must note differences in words. They should be able to verbalize the differences in words: the difference in inital letters, final letters, or in the general form of the words. The pupils must be taught what to look for so they can identify words as distinct units of language.*

Although visual-perception exercises, especially visual-discrimination exercises that do not involve actual discrimination and perception of letters and words, may not have a direct bearing on performance in reading, the correlation between visual-perception skills (form discrimination, figure-ground discrimination, closure, and the like) and reading is of a sufficient magnitude that perception of forms other than letters should at least be evaluated. The following exercises are useful in developing various visual-perception skills, including visual discrimination of letters and words:

1. Check pupils' discrimination of gross form; of pictures, objects, and geometric figures; and of colors. Check their ability to fit together the pieces of a puzzle.

2. Have pupils select from four pictures (for example, three pictures of a dog and one of a cat) the one that is different from others. Geometric designs and letters may also be used.

3. Present each pupil with a copy of his or her name. Have pupils note the differences and similarities between their names and the names of some classmates.

4. Have pupils trace dotted outlines of a design.

5. Have pupils identify the missing parts of a picture.

* For assessment of adequacy in visual perception, see Dechant 1981a: p. 64–66; for commercial materials designed to develop visual perception skills, see Dechant 1981b: p. 35–45.

6. Have pupils circle a shape in a row of different shapes that looks exactly like the one at the start of the row:

7. Have pupils match basic forms— ⬯, ◇, ▭, ○, △, ☐ —with larger similar forms pasted on or drawn on a file folder (see *Teach*, (V-MR-1). This exercise teaches accurate matching and discrimination of basic forms. It is a recognition task.

8. Show the pupils one of the forms in item 6, cover it, and then ask them to select from the six forms the one that they were shown (see *Teach*, V-MR-2). This exercise teaches accurate visual recall.

9. Have pupils copy designs similar to those in term 7.

10. Have pupils select from three forms the one that completes a figure:

This exercise, from *Teach*, V-MR-3, teaches accurate perception of form through closure of an incomplete figure.

11. Have pupils draw a circle around the first letter (or letter group) and then have them draw a circle around all those letters that match the first letter or letter group:

m	*n m n n m m w v u m*
f	*fhxt blftkt dvkgx vxkd tftk*
bl	*macg wrubl pudl theer gizuk*
dup	*duup stip sor stun shoorx*
pg	*pacg tripg storil mamis herrp fragg*
X	*W L X M Y X*

This exercise (see *Teach*, V-FG-G) teaches accurate perception of form against a distracting background. It teaches figure-ground discrimination.

12. Show the pupils a picture or geometric design, remove the sitmulus, and have them draw from memory what they saw. If the first drawings are imprecise, show the image a second time and let the pupils try again.

13. Show the pupils a picture and ask them to enumerate the various items or bits of detail in the picture.

14. Have the pupils select from three sets of figures the one set that they were shown for ten seconds:

* The art on this page is from Emerald Dechant, *Diagnosis and Remediation of Reading Disabilities*, © 1981, p. 260, 261. Reprinted by permission of Prentice-Hall, Inc., Englewood Cliffs, N. J.

15. Show a word to the pupils for two seconds and then ask them to select the word from a list of words. This exercise teaches memory for letter sequence.

16. Have pupils mark the letter or letters that look like the first combination in each row:

ab. . . . . . . ba   la   ab
fl . . . . lf   fl   fi
gh. . . . . . . hg   ph   gh

Visual-discrimination activities on the readiness level should help pupils to

1. See similarities and differences in pictures, forms, letters, numbers, and the like.

2. Identify letters.

3. Attend to letter order (*on-no*).

4. Attend to letter orientation (*d-b*).

5. Attend to word detail (*boy-buy*)

6. Develop adequate visual memory and note visual sequences.

7. Trace, match, and copy a simple form.

8. Trace, match, and copy letters and words.

9. Print their own names.

DEVELOPING THE PUPIL'S PREFERRED MODE OF LEARNING

To this point the discussion has centered upon the development of concepts, of auditory-perception skills, and of visual-perception skills. Consider briefly the development of a preferred mode of learning and of intermodality strength. These concepts are not often dealt with in books such as this, but they clearly warrant the teacher's attention.

Although the research is ambivalent on the concept of preferred modes, there does seem to be some validity for matching the instructional approach to the child's sensory strength. The idea began with Charcot, who in 1886 suggested that each person had a preferred modality.

The question is really twofold: (1) Do children's modality preferences have any significance for learning? (2) Does reading instruction geared to a child's preferred modality actually facilitate faster and better learning?

Research indicates that developing recognition for a word is not a unimodal experience—not simply a visual memory, an auditory memory, a kinesthetic gestalt, or a tactile sensation. Spache (1976), however, suggests that certain techniques (such as the *Mills Learning Methods Test*)* can help to ascer-

* For a description of the *Mills Learning Methods Test*, see Dechant 1981a: p. 70.

tain the kind of word-recognition lesson that appears to work best for a given pupil. Making use of this knowledge can help the pupil to experience success and thus can be recommended as good practice in teaching.

Assessment of the child's preferred mode of learning is done in two ways: (1) by administering tests (for example, the Mills test) specifically designed to do this; or (2) by measuring competency in such subskills as auditory discrimination, blending or memory, visual perception and discrimination, and word analysis.

The assumption is that if children do well on tests of auditory discrimination, for example, but poorly on tests of visual discrimination, it indicates that they have strength in one modality, but a weakness in another. Thus, if children demonstrate phonic mastery, it is assumed that they have the auditory abilities required to be proficient in that area and that for them the auditory modality is an efficient avenue to learning.

It is further assumed that children with reading difficulties who do well on auditory-discrimination, blending, and memory tests may be expected to respond to reading instruction that is strongly phonetic in approach.

Remediation should emphasize teaching to children's strength rather than to their weaknesses. Students must be given the opportunity to do what they are good at, while at the same time they are helped to become more proficient in areas in which they are weak. It would also seem reasonable to utilize instructional materials that are congruent with each learner's particular strengths in perception, imagery, and recall.

DEVELOPING INTERSENSORY MODALITY STRENGTH

Reading requires the pupil to integrate one modality with another, as in moving from visual letter shapes to auditory letter sounds. The pupil looks at the word *cat* and says "/kăt/." Sometimes a pupil cannot do this.

There appear to be two basic types of functional anomalies: (1) malfunctioning within a part (for example, visual processes); and (2) malfunctioning of the interactions among parts (for example, visual-motor processes) (Beery 1967). The latter difficulty is integrative. Learning disabilities appear to be closely associated with integrational difficulties. According to Beery, disabled readers have more difficulties in visual-tactual and visual-kinesthetic coordination than do those who are not disabled in reading.

It is no accident that many of the remedial methods (Gillingham and Stillman 1966; Fernald 1943, 1966) emphasize multisensory integration. The success of these methods may flow from their stress on coordination of functions rather than on the development of isolated functions. Presumably, if pupils can look at a word, pronounce it, and associate with it the meaning that they previously associated with the spoken word, intersensory processing is intact.

SUMMARY

Chapter 6 has examined the teaching and development of some of the enabling or readiness skills— especially conceptual, visual, and auditory skill development. Conceptual development assures that pupils either have or will develop the meanings without which the symbols on the printed page are empty and without purpose. Auditory and visual discrimination are necessary if pupils are to (1) identify the spoken word, (2) identify the written word, and (3) make the proper association between the spoken and written word. Without proficiency in these two areas, pupils will not be able to master the phonic skills. They will not be able to learn the phoneme-grapheme correspondences.

QUESTIONS FOR DISCUSSION

1. Define reading readiness.
2. Discuss how a field trip to a fire station might help children to develop conceptual thinking and thereby improve their readiness for reading.
3. What is the purpose of picture storybooks and picture dictionaries in the readiness program?
4. Examine one of the reading-readiness manuals, especially one of those offered by a basal-reading series, and list the skills in which the series gives practice.
5. What are the stages of development in conceptualization?
6. What factors in reading readiness are most amenable to training?
7. Discuss five activities that are useful in teaching conceptualization.
8. What do we know about the development of auditory-discrimination skills?
9. Discuss five activities that teach auditory discrimination.
10. What is the value of teaching matching of objects, pictures, and letters to beginning readers?
11. Is there any identifiable sequence in teaching visual-discrimination skills, especially of the letters of the alphabet, and is it desirable to follow such a sequence?
12. Discuss the following statement: Reading readiness is the teachable moment for each of the reading skills.

7

INTRODUCING
THE PUPIL
TO READING

Chapter 7 continues the exploration of readiness factors begun in Chapter 6. It focuses more directly on the development of skills actually used in reading, such as letter recognition and left-to-right progression, and introduces the first reading skills, namely, the acquisition of a sight vocabulary and the use of phonics and context to identify words. In addition, this chapter suggests readiness materials and evaluates assessment of readiness. Begin with the teaching of letter recognition.

DEVELOPING LETTER
RECOGNITION

Before teaching individual letter discrimination the teacher should

1. Check on pupils' discrimination of gross form: pictures, objects, geometric figures..
2. Check on pupils' ability to visualize spatial relationships and to think and reason spatially. Reversals are often an instance of confusion in spatial and visual location.

3. Check on pupils' ability to trace a design and on their ability in eye-hand coordination and visual-motor skills.

Identifying the Letters

Turn your attention now to the task of developing a visual knowledge of the alphabet. Letter discrimination is an absolutely necessary skill if the pupil is to master phonics or the associations between the written and the spoken symbols.

To be readers, children must learn to discriminate every letter from every other letter and every word from every other word; they must learn to distinguish between the capital and lowercase forms; and they must recognize the letter when it is written in either manuscript or cursive form. It is only after pupils have identified the symbol that they can associate meaning with it, either semantic or syntactic meaning or both.

The question is simply: How does the child discriminate and name each of the twenty-six letters? Individual letters cannot be sounded out like words: they do not spell their names.

Unfortunately, no one knows what the truly distinctive features of letters are. Not enough is known about the human visual system to say what it "looks for, "but it is assumed that the closed feature of the o and the ascender feature of the b, the short, long, and looped sticks, the height and slant of the letters, and the tail on some letters are all distinctive features.

Rather than relying on repetition to build recognition of a letter, it is better to point out to the learner the specific feature or features that distinguish one letter from another letter. The teacher can and should use color, ABC books, letter cards, picture dictionaries, film strips, and the like to reinforce the image and to fix the association between the letter shape and its name. Color is especially useful with pupils who have difficulties in figure-ground discrimination and is a definite aid to visual perception among kindergarten children.

The following observations summarize thinking in this area:

1. Children have a tendency to confuse b and d; p and b; p and d; p and g; u and n; m and w; o and e; o and c; e and c; and g and b. These letters might be profitably introduced at different times to minimize interference.
2. Some children cannot develop visual discrimination. They may have to rely on auditory or kinesthetic discriminations, for which special approaches must be used.
3. Children from lower socioeconomic homes may initially profit most from training which requires them to make instant-recognition responses to capital letters rather than to lowercase letters (Wheelock and Silvaroli 1967).

The following techniques will prove helpful in both developmental and remedial teaching in that they provide an environment where the pupil can discover significant differences among letters:

1. Put the names of some children on the chalkboard and let pupils see the differences and similarities between their own names and the names of others.

2. Point out that the individual squiggles that compose each name are called *letters,* and that letters are conglomerates of features, consisting of lines, angles, circles, or semicircles.

3. Teach pupils to develop a discrimination for the letter by using verbal description: ''The letter *t* looks like a cross.''

4. Point out that each letter has a *name.* Select a few lowercase consonant letters (such as *b, h, m, n, p, t*) and one of the vowels (*a, e, i, o, u*) and write these letters on the chalkboard one by one, giving each its name.

5. Point out and discuss the specific features that distinguish one letter from another. The pupils must learn what to look for.

6. Provide pupils with a mimeographed page of groups of letters and have them encircle the letter in each group that is different:

ssk	*mim*	*ppb*
hyh	*nmn*	*ssa*
bbd	*rrz*	*nnv*

7. Teach each letter as one that circles to the right (*b, p, h, m, n, r*) or to the left (*c, a, d, q, e, f*). This exercise is particularly helpful with pupils who have a reversal tendency. Pupils need to discover what the critical dimensions of difference are, to distinguish between curving left, curving right, and obliqueness, for example.

8. Identify each letter with a key word: *b* with *bee; c* with *cat; s* with *sun.*

9. Develop flash cards for each letter.

10. Present the letter to be taught in color.

These exercises are essentially designed to help children to develop a memory for the visual configuration of a letter. Kinesthetic techniques useful in teaching letter discrimination or in reinforcing discrimination are

1. Have pupils trace over a letter (using a finger or pencil) superimposed over a picture: for example, *b* superimposed over a picture of a ball.

2. Use dot-to-dot sheets that use numbers and whose end product is a letter.

3. Have pupils trace dotted letters, saying the name of the letter while they trace it.

4. Have pupils write the letter in clay or sand.

5. Have pupils copy the letter with the image of the letter available to them.

6. Have pupils write the letter from memory.

7. Have pupils *walk through* a large letter on the floor.

Pupils need to respond appropriately to both lowercase and capital letters. They need to be taught that the same name is given to all forms—manuscript or printed, capital or lowercase—of a letter. An exercise like the one shown in the accompanying illustration, which requires the pupil to draw a line between the capital letter and the appropriate lower-case letter, teaches this skill. The pupil, as perceiver, must determine whether *A* and *a* are equivalent—a discriminative task which will not be easy for every pupil.

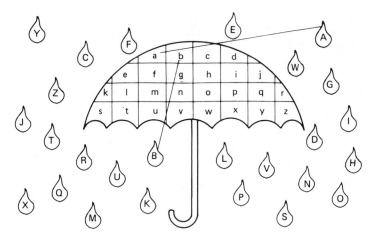

Emerald Dechant, *Diagnosis and Remediation of Reading Disabilities*, © 1981, p. 264.
Reprinted by permission of Prentice-Hall, Inc., Englewood Cliffs, N. J.

Naming the Letters

Earlier, the importance of learning the names of the letters of the alphabet was indicated. Although the research on this point is somewhat ambivalent, the following statements are an attempt to summarize the data and emphasize the key points:

1. Knowledge of letter names is positively related to reading readiness; it is one of the best predictors of the child's readiness for reading (Nicholson 1958; Barrett 1965, 1967). Ohnmacht (1969) did not find this to be true in his study, however.
2. Lack of ability to name the letters of the alphabet is predictive of reading failure (Olson 1958; DeHirsch, Jansky, and Langford 1966).
3. The value of letter naming is that it is a way of labeling symbols, making it easier to discriminate and to remember them (Robeck 1972; Samuels 1973).
4. Ability to name letters may indicate higher intelligence, favored socioeconomic status, and progress in cognitive ability (Samuels 1972). Certainly, the child who is able to name letters can discriminate between variant letter shapes, can make proper associations, and has had the motivation to learn (Walcutt, Lamport, and McCracken 1974).
5. Phoneme-grapheme knowledge may be more significant than is grapheme-name knowledge (Jenkins, Bausell, and Jenkins 1972).
6. Children who know the alphabet tend to be good readers, but teaching letter names will not turn a poor reader into a good one (Smith 1977).

Although the studies do not indicate that pupils should be able to name all the letters or know them in alphabetical order, even this latter knowledge is not without value. Eventually, pupils will find it necessary to file their words, to locate them, and to use the picture dictionary.

The names of both capital and small letters should be taught first, but from the start pupils should realize that each letter also represents a sound. Some children will have learned to identify letters and to name them by the time they enter kindergarten. Others will have to be taught in school.

Exercises designed to develop letter-naming ability include the following:

1. Present the alphabet in random order and require pupils to give the letter names.

    I A B S C D F E P T M L R
    Z J U H G W X Q K V Y N O

    r o h l m y t v k p z i a
    l u s n b c q w d t x g e

2. Have pupils circle the two letters that have the same name:

    W L n w m u

3. Have pupils circle the letters in each row that have the same name as the fist letter:

    L . . . j f l k L

Writing the Letters

The pupil must also learn to write the letters of the alphabet, in both manuscript and cursive form. The ability to write the letters dictated is an important indicator of first-grade reading achievement.*

At present, manuscript (or script, printscript, or printing) is the first mode of writing taught the child. It was introduced into this country in 1921 by Marjorie Wise. It consists of sanserif letters, that is, letters without ornamentation.

The chief reason for using manuscript writing is that the child is readier for it. Manuscript writing is easier to acquire, simpler, more legible, and seems to have more transfer value than cursive writing. In manuscript writing the letters are not joined, and the form of the letters is like that met in reading. This permits children to compare what they write with what they read. Children experience less difficulty with the straight vertical lines, circles, and part circles used in manuscript writing than with the more complex forms used in cursive writing.

TRAINING IN LEFT-TO-RIGHT PROGRESSION

Reading is a left-to-right activity, and this is a new concept for young children. They have not been taught to observe directions in their everyday perceptions. A dog looks like a dog whether the eye movement is from left to right or from right to left. However, in reading a word this is not so. The letters, *s-a-w*, read from

---

* For a listing of commercial materials designed to aid in the development of letter knowledge, see Dechant 1981b: pp. 46–53.

left to right represent *saw*, but read from right to left represent *was*. Thus, one of the first requirements in learning to read is the learning of new habits of perception. Children must perceive from left to right. They must learn to identify their right and left hands, to experience objects on the right and objects on the left, so that gradually the concepts of "leftness" and "rightness" will acquire meaning. They must learn to read through words by proceeding form left to right. The order of the letters in a word symbolizes the time order in which the sounds are made.

The term commonly used to indicate that the pupil is making the wrong directional attack on words is reversing. Reversing may be defined as the tendency to reverse letters, parts of words, or even whole words. This tendency may be observed occasionally in very young children who have difficulty in putting on their clothes the right way or in children who fail to remember right and left distinctions.

Reversals of letters showing right-left symmetry (*p* and *q*, and *b* and *d*) are called static reversals. When the sequence of letters is reversed and a new word is formed (*was* for *saw*), the reversal is termed a kinetic reversal. Other types of reversals involve various transpositions of letters (*animal-aminal*). There are numerous kinds of transpositions (such as initial letter to an internal position, terminal letter to an initial position, internal letter to a different internal position). The parts of phrases and compound words may also be transposed as when *in the house* becomes *house in the*, or *barnyard* becomes *yardbarn*. Finally, letters within words may be inverted while reading: *way* becomes *may*; *help* becomes *yelp*; or *n* is confused with *u*.

It is interesting to note that only in the cases of static reversals (*b-d*) is the second letter a mirror image of the first. The word *no* is not a mirror image of *on*. Thus, in the other types of reversals the difficulty is not one of letter orientation, but rather one of letter sequence.

There are variant points of view as to the origin of reversals. Orton (1928) suggested that reversals are indicative of defective neurological organization or inadequate development of cerebral dominance and are prime factors in reading disability. More specifically, reversals are said to be indicative of perceptual disorders that reflect impaired neurological processes or developmental deficits or delays. Orton inferred that in the case of confused dominance, the child would attack the written word with a left orientation on one occasion and with a right orientation at another time.

Another view (Krise 1949, 1952) suggests that reversals result from a lack of familiarity with the relationship between symbols and their background. Reversals are thus perceived as resulting from an inability to perceive space relations or from difficulties in perceiving figure-ground relations.

Actually, Fildes (1923) made this suggestion as long ago as 1923. She concluded that the tendency of younger children toward mirror writing was only part of their general tendency to reproduce forms of any kind without apparent heed to the position that they occupy in space.

Moyer and Newcomer (1977) advance the view that, except for static reversals (*b-d*), reversals result from the pupil's unfamiliarity with the concept of directionality as it relates to letter and word discrimination. The problem is thus perceived as one of letter sequence.

Stott (1973) suggests that reversals or errors of temporal integration are caused when the pupil advances from the decoding of individual graphemes to the standard combinations. Any slight uncertainty about the phonemic value of a letter may permit a following letter, about which there is no uncertainty, to be decoded ahead of it, thus producing a reversal. This happens especially when a consonant follows a vowel (*at*), since consonants tend to be better known.

It also happens with impulsive children who are psychologically unable to inhibit a hypothesis for action long enough to enable its consequences to be mentally rehearsed. Impulsive children, according to Werner (1948), respond to the first dominant stimulus and thus are unable to use the most salient features that distinguish words from one another. They cannot delay or inhibit their first response. Such pupils impulsively select the first solution that comes to mind. They need to learn to scan the word, looking for salient features. These are often larger chunks than a single letter; more commonly they are phonograms.

Perceptual skills develop with age. During the early school years, reversals have been considered to be normal phenomena. The data in fact indicate that among kindergarten children the incidence of reversals is as high as 90 percent. It drops sharply between the ages of six and seven and one-half and is about 50 percent by the end of that period.

At the kindergarten level, then, it is common for children to experience reversals, but it is also common to explain them developmentally or as a result of lack of maturation. Indeed, it is quite likely that some children reverse because we try to teach letter and word discrimination before they are maturationally ready.

Most children eventually obtain the developmental level needed for success, and reversals disappear from their behavior at that point. However, this is not always the case. When reversals continue beyond the second or third grade, they become a serious problem. After those years, children who reverse generally do not make normal progress in reading.*

In summary, causes commonly adduced to explain reversals are

1. Defective neurological organization; or inadequate, mixed, or left dominance.
2. Inadequate maturation.
3. Lack of familiarity with the relationship that exists between symbols and their background; inability to perceive figure-ground relationships.
4. Tendency to reproduce forms without apparent heed to the position that they occupy in space; inadequacy in spatial relationships.

---

*For assessment of dominance, directionality, spatial perception, and reversal tendency, see Dechant 1981a: pp. 72-74; for a listing of materials to develop proper directional attack see Dechant 1981b: pp. 54-58.

5. Unfamiliarity with the concept of directionality as it relates to letter and word discrimination: The pupil may not have learned that directionality is a distinguishing feature in letter perception, or may have developed the habit of perceiving from right to left.

6. Uncertainty about the phonemic value of a letter permitting the following, better known, letter to be decoded ahead of it.

7. Impulsivity: The pupil responds to the first dominant stimulus.

8. Visual defects: difficulties with fusion and eye coordination.

9. Exclusive use of the whole word or configuration method: If a word is taught as a gestalt or total configuration, the pupil has no need to differentiate between right and left.

10. Overemphasis of the final sounds (word families) of words in instruction.

11. Too rapid reading.

12. Inspecting parts of a word in a wrong order because of regressive eye movements.

13. Difficulty of the materials: Reversals increase as the difficulty level of the material increases.

The elimination of reversals in reading is not easy. No one method has proved completely effective. The following exercises suggest activities that are suitable both for prereaders and for children at more advanced grade levels:

1. Teach children the meaning of left and right by showing them the difference between their right and their left hand or by playing the game "Simon Says." Here the child receives an oral direction, sometimes with and sometimes without the words, "Simon Says." When the direction is not preceded by these words and the child carries out the direction, the child is out of the game. The teacher's directions should emphasize distinctions between right and left, as in "Put your right foot forward" or "Raise your left hand."

2. Teach letters such as *b* and *p* with letters which circle to the right (*B, P, J, p, b, h, m, n, r*), and *d* and *q* with letters which circle to the left (*c, a d, q, e, f*).

3. Teach children that the orientation or direction of letters is the basis for the same-different judgment; children's attention must be directed toward the directional differences. (Moyer and Newcomer 1977)

   Moyer and Newcomer's intervention scheme is the following:

   a. Teach the discrimination task early, beginning with simultaneously-matching-to-sample task. This requires the pupil to select from *b, d, p, q*, the letter that matches in orientation a sample letter *b*. The sample is available for comparison.

   b. After the above task has been mastered, the pupil is required to remember the orientation of the letter without having the sample available for comparison.

   c. After memory for the direction of the letter has been developed, teach the letter names.

   The authors note that if older pupils read *dig* for *big*, first have them name the letters of the words. If these are correct, the error probably was caused by haste or inattention. If they name the letters incorrectly, have them do the simultaneous-matching task. If they can do this, see if they can remember the orientation of the letters without the benefit of a sample. If they can do this, the problem is one of inability to name the letters. Moyer and Newcomer add that if pupils cannot do the simultaneous-matching task even after training, it may be presumed that the possibility of a perceptual or neurological problem exists.

4. Have pupils draw an arrow pointing to the right under the first letter of a word.

5. Point out to pupils that the left side of a word is the beginning of that word and that the right side is the end of that word.

6. Use mechanical devices such as the *Controlled Reader* (Educational Developmental Laboratories) to demonstrate the reading sequence. This particular machine permits thought units to appear in a left-to-right sequence.

7. In referring to a line of print, to a caption under a picture, or to written directions on the bulletin board, sweep the hand from left to right while indicating that in reading this is the required direction.

8. Demonstrate to children how meaning is distorted when the word is read from right to left. "Jim was in the barn" is quite different from "Jim saw in the barn." Some success may be obtained by teaching the pupil what a reversal is, how it is made, and what the results look like.

9. Color the first letter in the word that is often reversed.

10. In demonstrating left-to-right progression in monosyllabic words, put each letter in a block and number the blocks in a left-to-right direction. Another version requires the children to simply number the letters from left to right.

11. Permit children to write only one word on a line. The first letter is placed at the extreme left edge of the paper.

12. Require pupils to cover the word with a card which they then move slowly to the right, thus exposing one letter at a time in a left-to-right progression. The same process may be followed in reading an entire line of print.

13. Have pupils engage in choral reading.

14. Provide alphabetizing and dictionary exercises.

15. Encourage children to type the words with which they are having difficulty.

16. Have pupils trace the word. As they trace the word, they should speak out each part of the word. Pupils should continue tracing until they can reproduce the form from memory.

17. Have pupils put their hands on images of their own hands and ask them to raise two symmetrical fingers (1-1, 3-3, 5-5) or two asymmetrical fingers (left 4-right 2, left 3-right 1, left 4-right 5). (See illustration on page 151.) See *Teach,* BI-3; Silver and Hagin 1976.

18. Have children engage in all types of left-right discrimination activities by giving them directions such as "Stamp your left foot"; "Tap your right knee"; or "Move to the left of John." Have children sort right and left gloves, shoes, and the like, as well.

19. Have children follow layout maps requiring turns to go from one place to another.

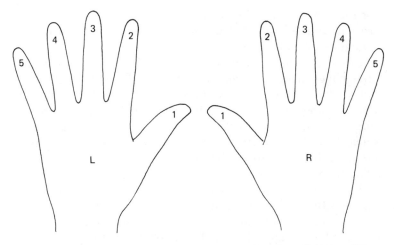

L   R

Emerald Dechant, *Diagnosis and Remediation of Reading Disabilities,* © 1981, p. 269.
Reprinted by permission of Prentice-Hall, Inc., Englewood Cliffs, N.J.

ACQUISTION OF A SIGHT VOCABULARY

Turn your attention now to the acquisition of a sight vocabulary. It is not enough that pupils can identify the letters, or that they can hear separate sounds in words, or indeed that they move from left to right in word identification. Pupils must be able to identify words and associate sounds and meanings with them if they are to be readers.

The goal of all word-identification strategies is the acquisition of a sight vocabulary. This is absolutely necessary if pupils want to become readers. Poor readers are such because they have an unusually small sight vocabulary for their age or grade level. The acquisition of a sight vocabulary provides a foundation on which to learn word attack and other reading skills.

The term *sight vocabulary* refers to (1) all those words that pupils come to know instantly or can recognize on sight (their recognition vocabulary); (2) the basic core or high-utility words, without which pupils cannot make use of context (the Dolch list is a compilation of such words—see Figure 8-2 in Chapter 8); and (3) the group of words that present an unusual amount of difficulty because of their similarity (*went, want*), that are nonphonetic or nonalphabetic and so represent inconsistent and irregular spelling patterns (*come, was*), or that are frequently reversed (*saw, was*). Naturally, there is a certain degree of overlap in these three groupings.

In teaching sight words, once pupils have mastered the basic phonic skills and the diacritical markings, the teacher should present the word, not as a word to be learned totally by memory, but as one that has some regularities. For example, the word *his* is sounded as /hĭz/. Color may be used to let the pupil know where the irregularity is. In this case (*his-hiz*), the *s* and the *z* would be colored. Pupils need to be taught what to look for.

Difficulty with sight words generally shows itself in two ways in particular: (1) Children have an unusual amount of difficulty with high-utility words, the core words without which it is impossible to use the context in reading, and (2) children ask again and again for help with the same word.

Some children have special difficulty with words which have a graphic similarity (such as *who-how; but-put; tired-tried; ever-even*). Such children need to be taught to note the salient features of letters and words.

The following list includes most of the basic words that children in the primary grades need to learn. It includes three types of words: the Dolch words, the words from Johnson's first and second grade list (Johnson and Pearson 1978: pp. 15 and 16), and some of the more common words that are alphabetically irregular. Words designated by (1) appear in the Dolch list; those designated by (2) appear in Johnson's list; and the remainder are additional alphabetically irregular words that the pupil needs to learn.

a (1, 2)	aunt	bury
able (2)	away (1, 2)	busy
about (1, 2)	back (2)	but (1, 2)
above (2)	be (1, 2)	buy (1)
across (2)	bear	by (1, 2)
after (1, 2)	beautiful	calf
again (1, 2)	because (1, 2)	call (1)
against	been (1, 2)	called (2)
ago	before (1, 2)	came (1, 2)
air (2)	behind (2)	can (1, 2)
all (1, 2)	believe (2)	car (2)
almost (2)	best (1, 2)	carry (1)
alone (2)	better (2)	change (2)
along	between (2)	child
already (2)	big (1, 2)	children (2)
always (1, 2)	black (1, 2)	church (2)
am (1, 2)	blood	city (2)
America (2)	blue (1)	clean (1)
American (2)	board (2)	climb
an (1, 2)	book (2)	close (2)
and (1, 2)	both (1, 2)	cold (1)
another (2)	boy (2)	come (1, 2)
answer	bread	coming
any (1, 2)	break	company (2)
anything (2)	bring (1)	cough
are (1, 2)	brother (2)	could (1)
around (1, 2)	brought (2)	country
as (1, 2)	brown (1)	cousin
ask (1, 2)	build	cover
at (1, 2)	built	cruel
ate (1)	bull	cut (1, 2)

day (2)
days (2)
dead
deaf
death
did (1, 2)
didn't (2)
different (2)
do (1, 2)
does (1, 2)
dog
done (1, 2)
don't (1, 2)
door (2)
double
dove
down (1, 2)
dozen
draw (1)
drink (1)
each (2)
early (2)
earth
eat (1)
eight (1)
end (2)
enough (2)
even (2)
ever (2)
every (1, 2)
eye
eyes (2)
face (2)
fall (1)
far (1, 2)
fast (1)
father
feel (2)
feet (2)
field
find (1, 2)
first (1, 2)
five (1, 2)
flood
floor
fly (1)
for (1, 2)
found (1, 2)
four (1, 2)
friend
from (1, 2)
front (2)
full (1, 2)

funny (1)
gave (1, 2)
get (1, 2)
girl (2)
give (1, 2)
glove
go (1, 2)
God (2)
goes (1)
going (1, 2)
gone (2)
good (1, 2)
got (1, 2)
great (2)
green (1)
group (2)
grow (1)
guard
guess
guide
had (1, 2)
half
hand (2)
hard (2)
has (1, 2)
have (1, 2)
having (2)
he (1, 2)
head (2)
heard (2)
heart
heaven
height
help (1, 2)
her (1, 2)
here (1, 2)
high (2)
him (1, 2)
his (1, 2)
hold (1)
home (2)
hot (1)
hour
house (2)
how (1, 2)
hurt (1)
I (1, 2)
idea (2)
if (1, 2)
I'm (2)
in (1, 2)
into (1, 2)
is (1, 2)

it (1, 2)
its (1, 2)
it's (2)
jump (1)
just (1, 2)
keep (1, 2)
key
kind (1, 2)
knew (2)
know (1, 2)
last (2)
laugh (1)
learn
leave (2)
left (2)
let (1, 2)
light (1, 2)
like (1, 2)
lion
little (1, 2)
live (1)
lived
log
long (1, 2)
look (1, 2)
lose
love (2)
made (1, 2)
make (1, 2)
making (2)
man (2)
many (1, 2)
may (1, 2)
me (1, 2)
mean (2)
men (2)
miss (2)
money (2)
month
more (2)
morning (2)
most (2)
mother (2)
move
Mr. (2)
Mrs. (2)
much (1, 2)
music (2)
must (1, 2)
my (1, 2)
myself (1)
name (2)
need (2)

never (1, 2)
new (1, 2)
next (2)
night (2)
no (1, 2)
none
not (1, 2)
now (1, 2)
of (1, 2)
off (1, 2)
office (2)
often
old (1, 2)
on (1, 2)
once (1)
one (1, 2)
only (1, 2)
open (1, 2)
or (1, 2)
other (2)
ought
our (1, 2)
out (1, 2)
outside (2)
over (1, 2)
own (1, 2)
part (2)
party (2)
past (2)
people (2)
pick (1)
place (2)
plan (2)
play (1, 2)
please (1)
point (2)
present (2)
pretty (1)
prove
pull (1)
push
put (1, 2)
ran (1)
read (1)
ready
real (2)
really (2)
red (1, 2)
ride (1)
right (1, 2)
road (2)
roll
room (2)

rough
round (1)
run (1, 2)
said (1, 2)
same (2)
saw (1, 2)
say (1, 2)
says (2)
school (2)
see (1, 2)
seen (2)
set (2)
seven (1)
sew
shall (1)
she (1, 2)
shoe
short (2)
should (2)
show (1, 2)
sign
sing (1)
sister
sit (1)
six (1, 2)
sleep (1)
small (1, 2)
so (1, 2)
some (1, 2)
someone
something (2)
sometime
sometimes (2)
son
soon (1, 2)
sound (2)
start (1)
started (2)
steak
still (2)
stop (1)
street (2)
sugar
sure (2)
swap
table (2)
take (1, 2)
talk
taste
tell (1, 2)
ten (1)
than (2)
thank (1)

that (1, 2)
the (1, 2)
their (1, 2)
them (1, 2)
then (1, 2)
there (1, 2)
these (1, 2)
they (1, 2)
thing (2)
things (2)
think (1, 2)
this (1, 2)
those (1, 2)
thought (2)
three (1, 2)
through (2)
time (2)
to (1, 2)
today (1, 2)
together (1, 2)
told (2)
too (1, 2)
took (2)
top (2)
touch
tough
toward
town (2)
trouble
truth
try (1)
turn (2)
two (1, 2)
under (1, 2)
until (2)
up (1, 2)
upon (1)
us (1, 2)
use (1, 2)
used (2)
very (1, 2)
walk (1)
want (1, 2)
wanted (2)
war
warm (1)
was (1, 2)
wash (1)
watch
water (2)
way (2)
we (1, 2)
wear

weather	whose (2)	work (1, 2)
weight	why (1, 2)	world (2)
well (1, 2)	wife (2)	would (1, 2)
went (1, 2)	wild	write (1)
were (1, 2)	will (1, 2)	year (2)
west (2)	wind	years (2)
what (1, 2)	wish (1)	yellow (1)
when (1, 2)	with (1, 2)	yes (1)
where (1, 2)	wolf	yet (2)
which (1, 2)	woman	you (1, 2)
white (1)	women (2)	young
who (1, 2)	won	your (1, 2)
whole (2)	won't	
whom	word	

Ten words (*a, and, be, I, in, of, the, to, we, you*) make up 25 percent of all words in ordinary writing. The following words make up nearly 50 percent of all words in ordinary writing:

a	can	he	not	the	with
all	do	I	of	this	would
and	for	if	on	time	you
are	from	in	one	to	your
as	get	is	our	very	yours
at	go	it	put	was	
be	good	letter	she	we	
been	had	me	so	when	
but	have	my	that	will	

The teaching of sight words takes many forms.* Useful approaches include the following:

1. Emphasize configuration cues and picture cues. Direct the pupils' attention to the word's physiognomy, its shape, length, and contour, as it is fashioned by the letters, especially the ascenders, descenders, and double letters.
2. Direct the pupils' attention to the word's morphemic cues: inflectional endings, prefixes, suffixes, and the like. Help pupils to identify the word through an examination of the elements within the unidentified word itself. Unfortunately, poor readers are often deficient in aural-oral vocabulary and lack the sentence sense to make best use of morphemic analysis.
3. Use the directed or guided reading activity method (DRA), described in Chapter 8, pp. 172.
4. Use word or flash cards.
5. Use picture-word cards which associate the printed form with a picture of the word. Picture cues may offer children their first means to make use of the context. They are particularly helpful to disabled readers when the words are similar.
6. Have children develop and use picture dictionaries.

*For a listing of commercial materials designed to teach the basic sight words, see Dechant 1981b: pp. 59-69.

7. Use mechanical devices such as the *Language Master*, the *Mast Electronic Card Reader*, and the like. For a description of these see p. 190.

8. Supplement the DRA method with spelling, tracing, writing, and so forth, using the VAKT method (see Chapter 8, pp. 198).

9. Use both color and the linguistic principle of minimal difference to teach pupils where the significant difference between words is. Pupils need to be taught the salient features of words.

   Smith (1978) notes that attempting to teach one word at a time, writing the word on a variety of surfaces and occasions, and repeatedly reminding the pupils: "This is *cat*," will not teach the pupils to identify the word. The pupils must learn how to discriminate the word from any other word. They must be able to see what the word is *not*.

10. A simple but effective exercise presents the word to be taught in dotted outline form within the context of a meaningful phrase. The pupils read the phrase, trace the word and say it, and again read the phrase.

chair ꞇꞇꞇꞇ table   ꞇꞇꞇꞇ is the time?

Emerald Dechant, *Diagnosis and Remediation of Reading Disabilities*, © 1981, p. 274.
Reprinted by permission of Prentice-Hall, Inc., Englewood Cliffs, N.J.

   The sight words to be taught in this manner are the core words found in the Dolch and similar word lists. The most difficult words are words like *but, if, the,* and *their* because they lack strong semantic associations.

11. Have children *see* the word (on the blackboard, flash card); *discuss* the word in class; have children *use* the word; have children *define* the word; and let children *write* the word. Use games, worksheets, and extensive reading to reinforce recognition of the word.

UTILIZING PHONICS AND CONTEXT JOINTLY

Although phonics instruction and the use of contextual cues are discussed more fully in Chapters 9 and 10, even at the kindergarten and first-grade level the pupil needs to acquire at least a rudimentary understanding of each of these.

   Teaching children to use the beginning sound of a word to identify a word in a sentence read aloud to them was discussed in Chapter 6. There are some kindergarten children who can be taught how to use the beginning sound of a word, together with the other words in a sentence (the context), to identify the word. In general, as soon as children have mastered initial consonants, they can combine this skill with the use of context to arrive at the word. The cue supplied by the first letter helps the reader to identify the specific word that meets the meaning and syntactic requirements of the sentence in which the word is placed.

Children must be taught to use sentence meaning plus partial pronunciation to unlock words. In the sentence, "Jimmy fell _____ the stairs," the deleted word is readily filled in by using context cues. The child who knows that the missing word begins with the letter *d* is even more certain that the missing word is *down*. Unfortunately, poor readers often cannot use the beginning consonant and the context to identify the word; they are unable to associate a spoken word with a printed word in context.

Swenson (1975) notes that pupils need to integrate their expectation "about the probability with which a particular word with its unique shape will occur" and their recognition of some grapheme-phoneme correspondences with the meaning of the text. And Smith (1977) remarks, "It is the sense of the text (or the meaning) that enables readers to use spelling-to-sound correspondences effectively."

Pupils become increasingly responsive to context between the ages of seven and nine. They learn to read words in context correctly even though they make mistakes on the same words in isolation. Pupils move more and more to coping with reading as an aspect of language. They want their responses to make sense, both on the level of single words and on the level of language structure (Schlieper 1977).

The basic cause adduced to explain some pupils' inability to use phonic skills together with context in word identification is that such pupils do not listen critically to themselves; they have not developed a feedback system that allows them to effect a perfect match between the sound they make in subvocal speech and the printed symbol, and to check whether the word sounded makes sense in the sentence.

The following exercises* teach the phonic-context skill:

1. Have the pupil circle the word that makes the best sentence: "Will you (*king, sing*)."

2. Have the pupil draw a line under the picture (of fire, match, or stove) that fits with a spoken statement such as: "Mary burned her fingers playing with something that she should not have played with. She played with something that begins in the same way her name begins."

READINESS MATERIALS

Each of the basal-reading series (see page 169) has a reading-readiness program. In general, these programs are designed to teach children to use letter-sound associations with context to decode printed words. They provide exercises which enable pupils to use the spoken context, to distinguish letter forms from one

_____

* For materials designed to teach the phonic-context skill, see Dechant 1981b: pp. 141-144.

another, to listen for beginning sounds, to associate letter sounds and forms, and to make use of the first letter of a printed word.

In addition to the readiness materials that accompany the various basal-reading series, there have been developed books, games, audiovisual aids, readers, and other supplementary materials to help children through the preparatory stage of reading. These materials are designed to develop children's discrimination skills and such reading-readiness abilities as the ability to follow a story sequence, to associate meaning with pictures and words, to see relationships, to sense likenesses and differences, and to identify a printed symbol.

ASSESSING
READING READINESS

Observing children and recording these observations on readiness inventories are a good means for identifying the child who is ready for reading. Teachers have for years made use of informal techniques to gauge a child's readiness and have been rather successful in their efforts. This chapter, however, is particulary concerned with those aspects of reading readiness that may be more easily and more accurately determined through standardized tests, particularly the reading-readiness tests and the predictive scales.

Readiness Tests

Readiness tests are so named because the are specifically designed to measure readiness for reading. In some respects they are similar to scholastic-aptitude tests and measure similar abilities. They appraise various types of mental functioning that are related to success in reading, such as ability to perceive likenesses and differences in letter and word forms, ability to follow directions, auditory-description ability, and auditory memory.

Visual- and auditory-discrimination abilities, and such mental functions as discrimination of form, letter naming and recognition, direction following, copying of and memory for design, eye-hand and motor coordination, auditory blending, listening comprehension, rhyming ability, auditory memory, and recognition of grapheme-phoneme correspondences, are also measured in the reading-readiness tests.

Readiness tests have not been used as profitably as they might be. For a *group* of beginning readers, readiness tests would appear to be adequate predictors of readiness for reading (the intercorrelations between reading-readiness test scores and reading scores at the end of first grade generally range between .50 and .70), and they do identify areas of strength as well as deficits. If teachers capitalized on the strengths as identified in readiness tests and if they intervened early to remediate deficits, surely the reading disabilities of many students could be prevented.

The readiness tests may not predict with sufficient accuracy the reading achievement of *individual* pupils. A good score on a reading-readiness test does not necessarily mean that the pupil is ready for reading. However, some of the children who do well on readiness tests but later fail to learn to read may well have been the recipients of inadequate instruction rather than of poor measurement.

The following readiness tests seem especially useful:

1. *American School Reading Readiness Test* (Bobbs-Merrill). This group test measures picture vocabulary, discrimination of forms, letter-form recognition, letter-combination recognition, word matching, following directions, and memory for designs. Testing time is 30 minutes.

2. *Boehm Test of Basic Concepts*, 1971 (Psychological Corporation). Grades K-2; testing time is 30-45 minutes. This group picture test is designed to appraise the young child's mastery of 50 basic concepts commonly found in preschool and primary-grade instructional materials. A Spanish version of the test is available. Each form of the test consists of 50 sets of multiple-choice pictures presented in 2 booklets. Statements are read aloud to children by the examiner. Concepts measured relate to space, quantity, and time.

3. *CTBS Readiness Test*, 1977 (CTB/McGraw-Hill). This test measures letter names, letter forms, listening for information, letter sounds, visual discrimination, and sound matching. Testing time is 2 hours, 39 minutes. The test provides a reading estimate, which projects the pupils' expected reading performance in first grade.

4. *Gates-MacGinitie Readiness Skills Test*, 1969 (Teachers College Press). Grades K.8-1.2. This test, for use at the end of kindergarten or the beginning of grade one, consists of 7 subtests: listening comprehension, auditory discrimination, visual discrimination, following directions, letter recognition, visual-motor coordination, and auditory blending. An 8th subtest, word recognition, is included for simple identification of those children who already have some reading skill. It is recommended that administration of the test be divided into 4 separate parts over a 2-day period. It takes about 30 minutes to administer each part of the test.

5. *Harrison-Stroud Reading Readiness: Profiles*, 1956 (Houghton Mifflin). For grades K-1. This test measures the ability to use symbols and context, to make visual and auditory discriminations, to use context and auditory clues, and to give the names of letters.

6. *Macmillan Reading Readiness Test*, Revised edition (Macmillan). This test measures for visual discrimination, auditory discrimination, vocabulary and concepts, letter names, and visual-motor skills.

7. *Metropolitan Readiness Test*, 1976 (Psychological Corporation). Level I (kindergarten) of the test measures auditory memory, rhyming, letter recognition, visual matching, school language and listening, quantitative language, and copying. Level II (end of kindergarten, beginning of grade 1) measures beginning consonants, sound-letter correspondence, visual matching, finding patterns, school language and listening, quantitative concepts, quantitative operations, and copying. Testing time is 80 to 90 minutes for each level.

8. *Murphy-Durrell Prereading Phonics Inventory*, 1976 (Borg-Warner Educational Systems). (See p. 408 for a discussion of this test.)

9. *Walker Readiness Test for Disadvantaged Preschool Children*, Ages 4-6.5 (Bureau of Research, U.S. Office of Education). This is an individually administered nonverbal test available in English, Spanish, or French. It measures likenesses, differences, numerical analogies, and missing parts. Testing time is 10 minutes.

Recently, various attempts (Jansky and DeHirsch 1972; McLeod 1969; Hoffman 1971; Banks 1970) have been made to facilitate early identification of those children who are likely to fail in learning to read. It would obviously be desirable if we could locate at an early age those children who are likely to have trouble, so as to head off future problems.

Silver and Hagin (1976) developed a screening battery for detecting kindergarten children vulnerable to learning and reading failure, entitled *Search*. It consists of ten tests including three of visual perception (discrimination, recall, and visual-motor control); two of auditory perception (discrimination and rote sequencing); two of intermodal perception (articulation and intermodal dictation); and three of directionality (directionality, finger schema, and praxis). The instrument is designed to be administered at the end of kindergarten, but may be given to children ranging from five and one-quarter to six and two-thirds years of age. Testing time is about 20 minutes.

Vulnerability to learning and reading failure, according to Silver and Hagin, is presumed to flow from inadequate neurophysiological maturation in the skills needed for learning to read. The syndrome is characterized by difficulty with the orientation of figures in space (spatial disorientation) and in the ordering of sounds in time (temporal disorientation). It is symptomatologically reflected in (1) immature and defective visual discrimination and recall; (2) inability to distinguish a visual pattern or figure embedded in a background; (3) immature visual-motor function, characterized by directional confusion; (4) difficulty with the temporal sequencing of auditory stimuli; and (5) difficulty in directionality.

The child with a Search score of 5 or below is vulnerable to reading failure. When the score is 4 or 5, children tend to have developmental problems; deficit perceptual training seems appropriate for these children. When the score is from 0 to 3, the child may have a neurological problem. In addition to the basic syndrome of spatial and temporal disorientation, the child may show problems in impulse control, hyper- and hypoactive motility, difficulty in sustaining attention, poor ocular convergence, immaturity in abstract thinking, muscle tone and synergy inadequacies, and abnormalities in reflexes. In such a case the perceptual defects tend to be more pervasive, more tenacious, and more resistant to treatment. Perceptual-deficit instruction is necessary because the child has not acquired the skills needed for reading proficiency through the normal interaction of maturation and formal and informal experiences prior to first grade.

There certainly is some validity in Hillerich's (1978) criticism of some efforts at predicting reading failure. Hillerich's (1974) prekindergarten PDQ (Prediction with Diagnostic Qualities) scale measures those elements that are necessary for *success*. The difference in approach is not merely a semantic one. It is important that we not become too satisfied with our ability to predict failure. Our emphasis rather should be to identify what the pupil needs to become a successful reader.

SUMMARY

Chapter 7 has focused on letter recognition, training in left-to-right progression, acquisition of a sight vocabulary, utilization of phonics and context, readiness materials, and assessment of reading readiness. Although the various readiness skills have been discussed separately in this and the previous chapter, they must be developed simultaneously. The child should advance in each on a somewhat even front. Each day the teacher needs to help children grow in conceptual thinking, auditory discrimination, visual discrimination, knowledge of the alphabet, and the ability to deal with reading as a left-to-right activity. The teacher begins with each child at the level that child has attained in each of these skills. And each of the readiness tasks is further developed in the first and second grade.

Children also need to learn that words stand for the real thing—that they have meaning. They need to learn to use the context and the beginning sound of a word in order to identify the word that makes sense in the sentence.

QUESTIONS FOR DISCUSSION

1. What is the distinctive skill necessary for developing recognition of the letters of the alphabet?
2. Which letters are most likely to cause children identification difficulties?
3. What is the value of being able to name the letters of the alphabet before beginning school?
4. What are the major types of reversals, what are the major causes of reversals, and how are reversal difficulties overcome?
5. What are the three meanings of the term *sight vocabulary*?
6. What is the significance of learning the core words of the language?
7. How can the pupil be taught to use phonics together with context to identify words?
8. What are the purposes of the various readiness tests and the predictive reading scales?

learning to read

Part IV of this book is composed of eight chapters. It is the heart of the book, in that it is devoted primarily to the problems of teaching the child to read. Chapter 8 is perhaps the most significant chapter. It attempts to delineate the process of word identification and presents principles and guidelines for reading method.

Chapters 9 and 10 put special emphasis on the development of phonics skills; Chapter 11 discusses the structural or morphemic analysis skills; Chapter 12 deals with word-meaning skills; Chapter 13 discusses higher-level comprehension skills or reasoning with words; Chapter 14 deals with the development of functional reading skills; and Chapter 15 is concerned with the development of oral reading skills. The section begins with an examination of the methods of word identification.

8

METHODS
OF WORD
IDENTIFICATION

Reading is essentially a twofold process (see Figure 8–1). Reading cannot occur unless the pupil can identify and recognize the printed symbol, and generally the pupil must also be able to give the visual configuration a name. Even so, it is only one aspect of the reading process. Meaning, too, is an absolute prerequisite in

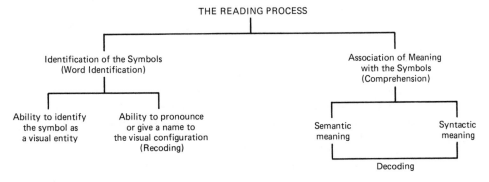

Figure 8-1 The Reading Process

reading. Perhaps too much emphasis in reading instruction has been placed on word identification and not enough on comprehension. The simple fact is that almost every formal reading method today emphasizes the identification process. For effective reading pupils need to be able to identify words immediately at sight and to be able to recode them. But they also must be able to decode or associate meaning with the graphic symbols.

The emphasis in this chapter is on word identification, but before getting into the specifics of word identification, it may be useful to see how the pupil is formally introduced to reading.

INTRODUCING THE PUPIL TO READING

The pupil is commonly introduced to formal reading experiences through the experience chart and the language-experience approach, the basal reader, or individualized reading. Consider first the experience chart and the language-experience approach. It is "each child's avenue to reading something that is interesting and personal" (Zintz 1980: p. 94).

The Experience Chart and the Language-Experience Approach

Children have a natural inclination to want to talk about their experiences, either as individuals or as a part of a group. They may want to describe a mountain trip, the bottling of a soft drink, the planting of a garden, or the harvesting of wheat. Teachers should use this language activity to introduce reading. They may print the anecdotal description on the blackboard or on chart paper, or in other words develop an experience chart.

The experience chart capitalizes on the pupil's natural language. It is a simple, meaningful, and highly motivating introduction to reading. The vocabulary normally is simple; the sentences are short; and three or four sentences complete the story.

The steps in making an experience chart are usually the following:

1. Provide for commonality of experience.
2. Have children discuss their experiences.
3. Record on chart paper or on the blackboard the key ideas or story.
4. Have children read the chart as a whole, one sentence at a time.
5. Isolate parts of the chart for specific emphasis, selecting words and phoneme-grapheme correspondences that should be taught.
6. Have children read the chart as a whole again.
7. Make a file of experience charts and label them "Our Big Book."
8. Have the children read the stories occasionally.

The child comes to school with a well-developed speaking language. This language reflects his or her home background and may deviate somewhat from the language that will be taught in school. Experience charts allow for a gradual transition to the formalized language in books. Moving from the known (child's spoken language) to the unknown (the written language) is good educational procedure, and experience charts make this possible.

Developing experience charts also teaches children the natural relationships between the language arts. The pupils have already learned that what they can think they can say. Now they learn that what can be said can be written and what can be written can be read. The pupils learn that sounds can be put into written form and that the beginning sounds, middle sounds, and ending sounds can be graphically symbolized.

The experience approach began in the 1920s when Flora J. Cooke at the Chicago Institute and later at the Francis Parker School began putting children's oral expressions on the blackboard. It grew and developed as part of the Progressive Education Movement. The latter de-emphasized the importance of systematic and sequential presentation of material in favor of purpose, interest, and meaning. In 1934 Nila Smith termed this approach the "experience method," and recently it has been termed the language-experience approach.

The language experience approach is presented in *Language Experiences in Reading* (LEIR) program, grades 1–4, by Roach Van Allen, Richard L. Venezky, and Harry T. Hahn (Encyclopedia Britannica, 1974). *Teaching Reading as a Language Experience*, by Mary Anne Hall (Charles E. Merril, 1976) provides a description of a total language-experience program. *Language Experience Activities* by Roach Van Allen and Claryce Allen (Houghton Mifflin, 1976) presents 250 language activities useful in a language-experience program.

Hall (1976a) notes that the cornerstones of the language-experience approach are language and experience. The pupils' language determines the language patterns of the reading materials and their experiences determine its content. Perhaps the greatest advantage of the language-experience approach is that the written language is real, natural, and relevant to the pupils. The approach is particularly useful as a way of teaching beginning reading skills or as a lead-in to the basal reading series. It can also stand alone, but generally conventional instructional materials are needed in the latter half of first grade.

The language-experience approach is not a method. It is rather a philosophy about the type of materials to use in beginning reading. Perhaps the major objection (Rystrom 1974) to it is that the materials derived from stories which children dictate are based on children's present performance rather than on their language potential. Materials based upon what the child knows do not extend performance levels. Part of learning to read is learning to identify and interpret words not normally used in one's speech. It is for this reason that children need to read materials other than those which they have constructed.

In the language-experience approach children are asked to talk, write, and read about their own experiences in their own language. It thus prevents a mismatch between the student's oral language and the written language of the instructional material. The language-experience approach also deals with the problems of the reluctant reader and the disadvantaged reader. It has a built-in motivational element because children like to read what they have written. The language-experience approach assures that the reading materials, the words, the meanings, and the language patterns will already be within the children's linguistic experience, and within their control. And when children's own stories are used for reading instruction, there is a perfect match between the thoughts of the writer and the reader. The materials then contain words and meanings the child is interested in and wants to know.

Some psycholinguists believe that the stories should be recorded in the language patterns of the child, whether grammatically correct or not. Others suggest that the vocabulary and the sentences be simplified and be made grammatically correct. Materials should always be written with standard spelling.

The Basal Reading Program

Although most teachers use experience charts or the language-experience approach, few have thought of this as comprising the total reading fare. The need for sequential development in reading skills is difficult to satisfy by these means alone. Most children profit greatly from a steady progression through graded materials.

Such graded materials have come to be known as basal reading materials. They are designed to provide continuity in reading development and to provide training in all the basic reading skills. They aim at systematic instruction. They lead the pupil by logical and sequential steps to the mastery of the basic reading skills. In most schools the basal reader is still the most important material used in the reading program.

The basal reading program consists of a rather complete complement of teaching materials, including comprehensive teacher guides. However, the major components of basal programs are the readers which today are graded in difficulty from preprimers to sixth- or eigth-grade readers, or by levels.

Each of the basal readers is usually accompanied by a workbook that leads the child step by step through a carefully developed program of instruction. The workbook introduces the vocabulary and provides the experiential background needed for successful reading. It is especially useful in meeting individual needs, in stimulating interest in reading, in providing opportunities for practice, in varying instructional procedures, and in making optimum use of pupil and teacher time. The workbook offers the repetition, self-competition, and day-to-day records that make it possible for the pupil to grow and for the teacher to diagnose and to remediate the pupil's inadequacies. A teacher's manual is also provided to guide the teacher in day-to-day and even minute-to-minute teaching.

It is important to note that workbooks and manuals may work also *against* good reading instruction. Teachers may become too reliant upon one or both. It is true as well that basal readers in their attempt to provide systematic instruction, controlled vocabularies, gradual and sequential introduction of skills, and mastery of the basic reading skills through repetition and ready-made seatwork have perhaps failed to some degree in providing purposeful reading. Be that as it may, they have been shown to be helpful in developing reading proficiency in most children and certainly have helped thousands of teachers, especially inexperienced teachers, to offer a fully developed reading program.

A list of the major basal reading series includes the following:

Pathfinder, 1978 (Allyn & Bacon). Grades K-8; graded by levels, 1-20.

American Book Reading Program, 1977 (American Book). Grades K-6; graded by levels, A-N.

Sunrise Basic Reading Series, 1976 (Behavioral Research Laboratories). This is a K-6 basic reading series, based on a linguistic approach to reading. Level I consists of 2 student texts (*The Color Poppits* and *The Lost Letters*). These teach colors, left-right, top-bottom relationships and circling, underlining, drawing dots, and matching. *The Lost Letters* introduces the 26 letters; pupil learns to trace and copy the letters. Level II consists of *What the Letters Say* and *The Earwinkles Words* and teaches phoneme-grapheme correspondences.

Keys to Reading, 1980 (Economy) Grades 1-8; graded by levels, 1-16.

Keytext, 1978 (Economy). Grades 1-6; 14 non-graded levels for pupils reading below grade level.

Reading 360, 1973 and *Reading 720*, 1976 (Ginn). Grades K-8.

Reading 720, Rainbow Edition, 1979 (Ginn). Fifteen-level program for grades K-8.

Bookmark Reading Program, 1979 (Harcourt Brace Jovanovich). Grades K-8; graded by levels, 1-14.

Design for Reading, 1973 (Harper & Row). Grades K-8; graded by levels, 1-21.

Reading Basics Plus, 1977 (Harper & Row). Grades K-8; graded by levels, A-H.

Reading Perspectives, 1975 (D.C. Heath and Company). Grades Primer to grade 6.

Holt Basic Reading System, 1977 (Holt, Rinehart and Winston). Grades K-8; graded by levels, 1-17.

The Houghton Mifflin Readers, 1974 (Houghton Mifflin). Grades K-8; graded by levels, 1-14.

Houghton Mifflin Reading Series, 1976, 1978 (Houghton Mifflin). Multi-level program for grades K-8; levels A-O.

Reading for Meaning Series, 1977 (Houghton Mifflin). Grades K-6.

Laidlaw Reading Program, 1980 (Laidlaw). Grades Readiness-6; graded by levels, 1-13.

Lippincott's Basic Reading Series, 1975 (J.B. Lippincott Company). Grades 1-8; graded by levels, A-M.

Macmillan Reading Program, 1974 (Macmillan). Grades K-6; levels 1-14.

The New Macmillan Reading Program, 1976 (Macmillan). Provides 36 clearly-defined instructional levels from K-6.

Macmillan Series R, 1980 (Macmillan). Grades K-8.

New Practic Readers, 1978 (McGraw-Hill). Grades 1-6; levels A-G.

Reading for Concepts, 1977 (McGraw-Hill). Grades 2–6; levels A-H.

Merrill Linguistic Reading Program, 1975 (Charles E. Merrill). Consists of 11 readers and skill books, grades K-6; graded by levels, A-K.

Headway Program, 1979 (Open Court). Grades K-6, levels A-J.

The Young America Basic Reading Program, 1978 (Rand McNally). Level I, Readiness to Level 15, grade 8.

Reading House Series, 1976 (Random House). Grades K-6.

SRA Reading Program, 1976 (SRA). Grades K-6; includes *Basic Reading Series*, K-2, and *Comprehensive Reading Series*, 3–6.

Reading Unlimited, 1977 (Scott, Foresman and Company). Grades K-6, levels 1–21.

New Open Highways Programs, 1975. (Scott, Foresman). Grades K-8.

Basics in Reading, 1978 (Scott, Foresman). Grades K-8.

The Individualized Reading Program

Two philosophies or procedures of using reading materials have been emphasized through the years. One of these, certainly the most prevalent in the past and the present, emphasized the sequential nature of materials. It is the basal reader approach which was just described. The second approach assigns greater responsibility to the learner in determining the continuity of learning. This latter approach has often been termed individualized reading. It makes the learner and the learner's stage of development the major referents and relates instructional materials to them.

Interest in individualized reading began in the early 1960s. In their thorough discussion of this approach, Veatch and Acinapuro (1978) describe individualized reading as a self-selecting personalized approach. They emphasize use of the child's own language, particularly words that the child finds interesting and meaningful (it thus incorporates the language-experience approach), self-selection of reading materials, the individual teacher-pupil conference, and specific task or needs grouping.

The philosophical base of this approach is Olsen's (1952) concepts of seeking, self-selection, and pacing. Individualized reading thus suggests that children seek what they are physiologically and psychologically ready for, and that they show their readiness through the spontaneous selection of the materials that they want to read.

Self-selection is considered to be a necessary aspect of individualized reading. Teachers have always encouraged children to explore reading materials apart from those they have used in the classroom. In individualized reading, the pupil is encouraged to take a more active part in the selection of the materials.

The advantages claimed for individualized reading are many. Perhaps the most significant is the attitudinal change in the learner. Pupils seem to be more interested in reading. They read more at home. They show more interest in improvement and develop more favorable attitudes toward school in general. They often show improvement in work habits, self-motivation, and self-confidence. They seem to engage in more independent thinking and show better self-management.

In individualized reading, the purposes for reading are primarily individual and only secondarily group-related. The group serves as a sounding board for the individual to test the accuracy of the ideas acquired and to permit each child the luxury of sharing the knowledge and insight that has been acquired.

The teacher thus works with the individual, detecting the pupil's needs and providing for these needs as the pupil's work reveals them. The teacher keeps an accurate record of pupils' accomplishments and inadequacies and helps them to pace activities in accordance with interests, aptitudes, and previous achievements.

Individualized reading does not seem suitable for pupils who cannot work independently or who cannot select or pace themselves wisely, and it is not economical when instruction can be provided more simply and in less time in a group situation than in a one-to-one teacher-pupil conference.

The disadvantages of individualized reading include the danger of insufficient skill development; the heavy clerical burden that is put on the teacher; the difficulty of providing for an adequate number of individual conferences; the problem of judging the difficulty of books and of guiding children in the selection of books; the teacher's need to be familiar with a great number of books; and classroom control (Zintz 1980).

If the individualized reading approach is used, the teacher should keep a card on each book which includes questions to test the pupil's comprehension, the numbers of those pages that have material suitable for oral reading, and a list of the vocabulary. The program needs to make provision for the progressive development of skills. Children should generally make their selections from a list or shelf of books preselected by the teacher. Each such shelf of books might contain one basic reader that the child must read prior to going on to other books.

The effectiveness of the program depends on the number and quality of the reading materials. The need for many basal and supplementary readers, magazines, and tradebooks on all levels of instruction in such a program is obvious. Equally important is the teacher's familiarity with the content and the reading difficulty of the books.

In summary, the reading program needs to lead pupils beyond their level of conceptualization and language acquistion or competency. Once pupils have learned to read their own name, they should be introduced to reading through the language-experience approach. This approach may be continued until the pupil runs out of steam, as it were, or until the pupil would benefit from exposure to new experiences and new language symbols and patterns.

It is at this point that the basal-reading series has much to offer. It is not being suggested that the language-experience approach be totally discontinued. Rather, it should run parallel to the basal program with the teacher going back to it whenever it is appropriate. The transition from language experience to basal reading may occur very quickly for some children; for others, it may not occur until well into first grade.

The next section discusses the directed reading activity, in which the sixth, or final, step is designed to provide enrichment and follow-up activities in the daily reading lesson. It is here that individualized reading seems to fit best. Every reading lesson should allow for some free and wide reading. Each child should daily experience the pleasure of reading. Individualized reading, allowing for self-selection of a book from works that are written on the pupil's own independent level (where the pupil knows 99 percent of the words and where his or her comprehension level is 90 percent or more), provides this in an optimal way.

THE DIRECTED READING ACTIVITY

Whether the pupil is introduced to reading through the language-experience approach, through the basal reader, through individualized reading, or a combination of all three, there is a continuous need to structure the introduction and the teaching of basic skills, both word identification and comprehension skills. The directed reading activity (DRA) provides an easily adaptable format for doing this.

The steps of a directed or guided reading activity or lesson are the following:

1. *Building readiness for reading a selection by building concept and vocabulary background, by creating interest and motivation, and by creating a purpose for reading.* This step includes having pupils study the pictures that illustrate the story, relating the concepts in the story to the previous experiences of the class, teaching new vocabulary words, and establishing a purpose for silent reading by asking pupils to answer specific questions while they are reading.

   The pupils must be helped to develop the concepts necessary to participate successfully in the thinking and problem-solving process that reading is. If there is a concept gap between the learner and the content of the story, the teacher must try to fill it.* The pupils must also be taught strategies for identifying and decoding words that may be new to them. In the sections that follow, five methods for doing this are described.

   Setting a purpose for reading or setting overall goals for comprehension usually takes the form of a global question that requires the learner to read the entire selection and synthesize what has been read (Pieronek 1979). The global question may be written on the chalkboard. The global question develops a "searching attitude on the part of the reader" (Singer 1978). It may take the form of "As you read the story I want you to think of the following question . . . ".

2. *Guided silent reading.* In planning the directed reading (and thinking) activity, the teacher needs to divide the story into appropriate segments. On the primary

---

* For an outstanding description of the DRA see Pieronek 1979.

level a segment may not be more than three or four lines. Pupils are aided when the teacher sets a single purpose for each of the segments.

3. *Checking comprehension: Literal, organizational, inferential, evaluative, creative, and integrative comprehension is sampled and tested.* The questions on the beginning reading levels should call for a literal interpretation of what has been read. If four questions are asked about the content, three questions should be literal questions and one question might be an inferential one. On the basis of the pupil's response to these questions, the teacher can ascertain whether the materials are on the pupil's instructional or teachable level. If the comprehension score falls below the 70 to 75 percent level, it probably indicates that the material is too difficult for the pupil.

   If pupils can write out their answers, the teacher may have them do that periodically to check on each child's level of comprehension. Subgroups of four or five might also be formed in which pupils collectively work out the answer.

4. *Oral rereading of the material.* This reading allows the teacher to evaluate the pupil's oral reading comprehension, to evaluate the pupil's ability in phrasing, and ability in giving the proper intonation; it also permits the teacher to diagnose pupil problems. When the pupil reads orally, the teacher observes errors of omission, hesitation, substitution, pronunciation, reversals, and the like. If the pupil makes more than five errors per one hundred words, it suggests that the materials are not on the pupil's instructional level and that they are too difficult for the learner.

   The oral reading must be purposeful. The reader should have something to convey and there should be a listening audience. It is good practice to integrate oral reading with Step 3; thus, the teacher may ask students to read aloud those specific sentences that answer the questions posed, to read a particular part of the story to prove an answer, and so forth.

5. *Extending word recognition and comprehension skills.* This may take the form of reviewing phonic skills, working with the dictionary, tracing over dotted outlines of words, making a booklet of rhymes, writing a story, building words with alphabet cards, doing a practice exercise on a duplicated exercise sheet, learning to add *s* at the end of the word, dividing two-syllable words into their parts, doing exercises requiring the use of context in conjunction with the beginning consonant to identify a new word, using programmed worksheets, and so forth. This step involves the development of those word recognition and comprehension skills in which the pupil is deficient, as indicated in Steps 3 and 4. Students should be grouped into needs and skills subgroups in which specific content is emphasized.

6. *Enrichment and follow-up activities.* This phase involves supplementary reading, dramatization, creative activities, art work, writing, shared oral reading, or searching encyclopedias and other books for additional information. The purpose of this step is to foster a love for reading. Students should be allowed to read materials written on their independent level—that is, materials on which they would experience very few word recognition or comprehension difficulties.

The DRA is not a method of teaching reading. It is a model for organizing and structuring a reading lesson and for teaching reading in the content areas. The six steps outlined here describe a basal reading lesson in a general way. However, the DRA can serve as a model for almost any reading lesson and any reading method can be fit into it. It just so happens that frequently, when a basal reading series is used, the teacher organizes the reading lesson around the DRA.

WORD IDENTIFICATION
AND WORD RECOGNITION

We are now ready to take a more intensive look at the word-identification process. This will concern us for the remainder of this chapter, but will also be the primary concern in Chapters 9, 10, and 11.

Three questions need to be considered: (1) How do children learn to identify the printed word? (2) How do they discriminate it from every other word? and (3) How do they recognize it upon seeing it again in a different context?

Perhaps this discussion should begin with a discrimination between word identification and word recognition. *Word identification* refers to the ability to develop a visual memory for a word not previously encountered or learned. It is the initial acquaintance with a word.

A broader definition extends the meaning of word identification to include the recall of the spoken symbol that the visual symbol represents. It is thus defined as the first unlocking of the pronunciation of a word. It seems preferable to use the word *recoding* rather than *decoding* for this process. For effective reading the pupil needs to be able to identify the word immediately at sight and be able to recode or pronounce it. Pupils who excel in word identification can readily identify the printed word, but they can also identify the spoken word that the printed word represents. At times pupils may be able to go directly to the meaning of the word without having to go through the auditory image, but in general pupils pronounce the word and associate with it the meaning that they previously associated with the spoken word.

Word recognition is the perception and recollection of a previously identified word. It is a subsequent acquaintance. In this case the pupils recognize the word form as one that they previously identified and now know. Identification and recognition are not the same process and the means of identifying a word may be completely different from the means of recognition.

ACQUISITION OF SIGHT
VOCABULARY

As indicated in Chapter 7, the acquisition of a sight or recognition vocabulary is the primary goal of word-identification instruction. It is hoped that readers will eventually commit the word so well to memory that they can respond to it spontaneously without having "to figure it out." Each word thus becomes a sight word that is instantly recognized. Efficient reading depends on having a vast store of words that are recognized at sight. This is precisely what disabled readers do not have. Furthermore, because of their inadequate sight vocabulary and inability to handle the core words of the language (for example, the 220 words in the Dolch list as presented in Figure 8-2), disabled readers cannot obtain the necessary context cues needed to work out the meaning of the sentence.

1. by	at	a	it	sit	me	to	the
2. in	I	be	big	not	of	we	so
3. did	good	do	go	red	too	seven	walk
4. all	are	any	an	six	start	show	stop
5. had	have	him	drink	put	round	right	pull
6. its	is	into	if	no	on	or	old
7. ask	may	as	am	yellow	you	your	yes
8. many	cut	keep	know	please	pick	play	pretty
9. does	goes	going	and	take	ten	they	today
10. has	he	his	far	my	much	must	together
11. but	jump	just	buy	own	under	off	over
12. black	kind	blue	find	out	new	now	our
13. fast	first	ate	eat	open	one	only	once
14. help	hot	both	hold	try	myself	never	two
15. brown	grow	bring	green	us	up	upon	use
16. four	every	found	eight	with	white	was	wash
17. from	make	for	made	shall	she	sleep	small
18. around	funny	always	because	who	write	would	why
19. long	let	little	look	some	very	sing	soon
20. away	again	after	about	wish	well	work	will
21. cold	can	could	clean	ran	read	run	ride
22. full	fall	five	fly	then	tell	their	them
23. before	best	better	been	see	saw	say	said
24. live	like	laugh	light	that	there	these	three
25. her	here	how	hurt	when	which	where	what
26. down	done	draw	don't	thank	those	this	think
27. give	get	gave	got	want	went	were	warm
28. came	carry	call	come				

Figure 8-2 The Dolch Basic Sight Word List. From E. W. Dolch, *Dolch Basic Sight Word Test.* © 1942 by Garrard Publishing Company, Champaign, Ill.

Perhaps the first question the teacher needs to deal with is: Should teaching emphasize high-interest words, those words that are used most frequently or that the pupil will encounter again and again (the core words), or should it emphasize words that contain consistent and easily decodable letter-sound relationships?

Authorities disagree as to what the initial recognition vocabulary should include and also on how to teach it (Smith and Johnson 1976). The language-experience and the individualized reading approaches suggest that the initial words to be learned should be high-interest words or words that children like to learn. The basal readers are based on the thesis that the words initially taught should be those which are used most frequently in language and that children will encounter again and again (for example, *the, in, it, there, them*). Linguists, especially Bloomfield and Fries, and the modified alphabet approaches such as the Initial Teaching Alphabet (ITA), suggest that the initial vocabulary should consist of words that contain consistent and easily recognizable letter-sound relationships. The good teacher probably uses a combination of all three.

The reading teacher certainly needs to be familiar with the core words that were identified in Chapter 7. Among these are the Dolch words. The 220 words in the *Dolch Basic Sight Word List* (see Figure 8–2) represent approximately 60 percent of all running words in primary grade materials.* They are important words without which the pupil cannot use context in reading.

If pupils know up to 75 of the Dolch words, they may be reading on a preprimer level; up to 120, on the primer level; up to 170, on the first-reader level; up to 210, on the second-reader level; and up to 220, on the third-reader level (McBroom, Sparrow, and Eckstein 1944). Pupils are given credit for knowing the word if they can pronounce it or if they correct the word immediately after mispronouncing it.

Johns (1971-1972) developed the following list of basic sight words for older, disabled readers.

1. more	15. world	29. used	43. united	57. yet
2. than	16. still	30. states	44. left	58. government
3. other	17. between	31. himself	45. number	59. system
4. such	18. life	32. few	46. course	60. set
5. even	19. being	33. during	47. war	61. told
6. most	20. same	34. without	48. until	62. nothing
7. also	21. another	35. place	49. something	63. end
8. through	22. white	36. American	50. fact	64. called
9. years	23. last	37. however	51. though	65. didn't
10. should	24. might	38. Mrs.	52. less	66. eyes
11. each	25. great	39. thought	53. public	67. asked
12. people	26. year	40. part	54. almost	68. later
13. Mr.	27. since	41. general	55. enough	69. knew
14. state	28. against	42. high	56. took	

Teaching strategies to be used in developing a sight vocabulary were discussed in Chapter 7. Consider now the word-identification strategies in more detail.

WORD-IDENTIFICATION STRATEGIES

First graders have already learned much about reading. The pupils have looked at, heard, and used words. When pupils begin first grade, they are required to take a more systematic approach to identifying words, especially those core words

---

* See also E.W. Dolch, "A Basic Sight Vocabulary," *The Elementary School Journal*, 36, (1936), 456-460. The Dolch Basic Sight Cards are available from Garrard Publishing Company.

that were identified in the previous section. The pupils must learn to look at the word, speak the pronunciation, and understand the meaning. They must learn that a printed word has a shape or configuration, that it has a pronunciation, and that it has a meaning. Reading commonly is a *see, say,* and *comprehend* process.

The previous section described *what* pupils must learn; this section describes the *how*: namely, those strategies which pupils must learn to apply if they are to be efficient identifiers of words. The significant word-identification strategies are the configuration cues, the morphemic cues, the phonic cues, the spelling, the syllabication cues, the semantic and syntactic context cues, and the use of the dictionary. These strategies are used in every method of teaching reading and can be categorized as cue systems within words, meaning cues, and cue systems that may be found in dictionaries:

I. CUE SYSTEMS WITHIN WORDS
    A. Configuration Cues: word's physiognomy, its shape, length, and contour.
    B. Morphemic Cues (Strutural Analysis Cues):
        1. Inflectual endings and changes
        2. Compound words
        3. Contractions
        4. Hyphenated words
        5. Affixes: prefixes and suffixes
        6. Syllabication cues and accent
    C. Phonic Cues: Sound-letter relationships or phoneme-grapheme interrelationships, including recurrent spelling patterns and phonograms. The spelling of a word or the letter sequence is a significant cue to the pronunciation of the word.
II. MEANING CUES
    A. Picture Cues: They increase the ease with which beginners can be initiated into contextual reading.
    B. Semantic Context: The meaning of the sentence in which the word occurs narrows the number of words that are possible in that situation.
    C. Syntactic Context: Cue systems in the flow of language which include
        1. Patterns of word order: These identify the sentence patterns (noun-verb, noun-verb-noun, noun-verb-noun-noun, and noun-linking verb-noun) and identify the sentence as a declaratory sentence, an interrogatory sentence, an exclamatory sentence, or as an active or passive pattern.
        2. Intonation patterns: These suprasegmental phonemes represent the rhythm or the melody of the language and include pitch, stress, or accent, and junctures or pauses in speaking or reading. Juncture in writing is conveyed by punctuation marks and spacing between words.
        3. Structure or function words (articles, auxiliary verbs, prepositions, conjunctions).
        4. Redundancy cues: In the sentence, "The boys eat their lunches," there are at least four cues that the subject is plural).
III. DICTIONARY CUES: The dictionary tells how the word is pronounced and what its meaning is.

First consider the cue systems within words: the configuration cues, the morphemic cues, and the phonic cues. Configuration cues generally refer to the word's physiognomy or general appearance as it is fashioned by its shape or contour, its length, and its letters, especially by the ascenders, descenders, and double letters: thus, book = ⬚ . Obviously a word can be identified by its shape. Children early note that words have specific shapes or configurations, that some are short and others are long, and that some have ascending letters and some have descending letters.

Morphemic cues also have a demonstrated usefulness in word identification. Morphemic or structural analysis refers to the identification of a word through an examination of the meaningful elements or the morphemes within the unidentified word, such as the root itself, the prefixes and suffixes, the inflectional endings and changes, and the separate units making up a compound word. By analyzing the structure of a long, unknown word and identifying its meaningful parts, the pupil is more likely to understand the meaning of the word and indirectly to work out its pronunciation.

Morphemic analysis is best used in combination with context and phonic analysis. The unknown word is divided into its parts, the parts are sounded, and they are then blended into the whole word. Finally, the resultant word is tested to see if it makes sense in the sentence. Obviously, this technique works best if the word is within the pupil's aural-oral vocabulary. Unfortunately, the poor reader is often deficient in aural-oral vocabulary and lacks the sentence sense to make best use of morphemic analysis.

The third set of within-word cues are the phonic cues. If readers are to progress in reading, they must notice separate sounds in spoken words, must see differences in printed letters and words, and must see the relationship between the spoken word and the written word. Readers must be able to turn sound symbols into letter symbols and letter symbols into sound symbols. This is what phonics is all about.

Phonics helps pupils to identify a word by helping them to work out the pronunciation of the unknown word. It gives pupils a cue to the name of a configuration by showing them where the significant difference in words lies. It may be the only method that allows pupils to tap the thousands of words that are already in the their aural-oral vocabulary. Smith (1978) notes that phonics serves as a sentinel; it alone may be inadequate to help readers decipher an unknown word, but it will protect them from making implausible renditions of the symbol.

The content of phonics instruction is the phoneme-grapheme relationships. There are more than 250 such relationships, involving combinations of twenty-six letters and forty-four sounds or phonemes.

Meaning cues include picture cues and the semantic and syntactic context. They are cues that readers use when they anticipate what word best completes a sentence in terms of meaning. First consider picture cues. Reading in its earliest stages often involves picture reading, association of sound with the total word, and use of context to get at the meaning intended.

The preprimer introduces children to picture reading. At that level picture cues are very strong cues to meaning and hence to identification. The picture gives clues to the meaning of the words and is the child's first attempt to use the text (although in this case it is only picture context) to infer what the word is. The teacher points out that the picture is trying to tell the reader the same thing that the words convey.

As the children look at the picture of Tip and Tom (Figure 8–3), for example, the teacher may point out the specific details in the picture. Pointing to the title of the story, the teacher may show the children that this is a story about Tip and Tom and that the title tells them this. Then, making certain that the children are looking at the words, the teacher says, "This says, 'Tip and Tom.'"

Figure 8-3   Tip and Tom

The evidence on the use of pictures is conflicting. When too many pictures accompany preprimer and primer materials, reading often becomes an exercise in picture reading, rather than in identification and understanding of the elements that characterize the word. The pictures may even be distracting to a few beginners. Robeck and Wilson (1974) found that learners remember the most from their reading when deeper involvement is required and when picture cues are kept at a minimum. In some linguistic reading programs illustrations are omitted so that pupils must concentrate on the linguistic word patterns.

Denberg (1976-1977), however, found that increasing the amount of available information through the medium of pictures had a strong facilitative effect on word identification, and that the additional pictorial information actually encouraged beginners to use the incomplete information they were able to extract from the printed page rather than to bypass it. Pictures thus may increase the ease with which beginners can be initiated into contextual reading and may enhance the fluency of their reading.

Picture cues may be especially helpful to the disabled reader when the words being presented are similar or when the concept in the text is too difficult for the pupil to develop through the use of words alone.

The major meaning cue, however, is the context: both the semantic context and the syntactic context, and including both typographic and stylistic cues. Context analysis aids word recognition when the pupil can use the context (both semantic and syntactic) to infer what the unknown word is, either by using the meaning that will complete the thought or by using the sentence structure. Readers have a meaning for a word in their semantic memory, but the particular meaning that readers bring to the word is influenced by the sentence or syntactic context in which the word is placed.

Pupils must ask themselves from the beginning: Does the word (that I have identified) make sense in the sentence? The skill taught here is one of inferring meaning. Leary (1951) points out the value of teaching a word in context.

> Train a child to anticipate probable meaning, to infer an unknown word from its total context, to skip a word and read on to derive its probable meaning, to check the context clue with the form of the word, to search the context for a description or explanation that will identify the word, and he will have acquired the most important single aid to word recognition. For, regardless of what word he perceives, if it doesn't "make sense" in its setting, his perception has been in error.

Readers thus use contextual analysis when they identify unfamiliar words by examining their semantic or syntactic environment. Smith and Barrett (1974, 1979) note that context analysis is the process of figuring out a word by the way in which it is used in a sentence. Context cues are especially useful when the arrangement of words in a sentence is such that only one word is likely to fit into a particular slot in that sentence (Arnold and Miller 1976). Heilman (1972) notes that the one ability that sets good readers apart from poor readers is the degree to which they can use context to get at unknown words.

If context cues do in fact aid word identification, it is reasonable to expect that good comprehenders in reading are also good word identifiers. Golinkoff (1975-1976), in a summary of the relevant research, found this to be so. Good comprehenders are capable of rapid and accurate word recognition. They have automatized the basic recoding skills (ability to work out the pronunciation of the word). The recoding rate differentiates good from poor comprehenders.

Poor comprehenders tend to treat each symbol as a separate entity, unmodified by the symbols around it. It may well be that poor comprehenders have such a low degree of success in reading precisely because they have to focus too much on the word's phonological features.

In Chapter 7, it was noted that the effectiveness of context analysis is increased when it is combined with phonic analysis.

In the beginning reading exercises, the teacher should be careful:

1. That context clues are not overemphasized.
2. That the reading exercise does not contain too many strange words.
3. That the pupils do not become frustrated in their attempts to unlock the word.

Finally, readers can resort to the dictionary for word identification, especially at the upper-grade level.

Few readers become very proficient in reading unless they learn most of the above ways of identifying words. Good readers have so automatized their use of cues that they appear to be unaware of which cue they are using at the moment. Persons who have mastered the process of reading may lose sight of the many factors which must mesh if success in reading is to be achieved. Nevertheless, beginning reading instruction proceeds best when pupils show consistent and measurable growth in mastering and applying letter-sound relationships, in acquiring a sight vocabulary, and in the ability to profit from context clues. (Heilman 1976).

METHODS OF TEACHING WORD IDENTIFICATION

Turn now to the more formal methods of word identification. The history of the teaching of reading is replete with various methods used to help the child to identify and recognize the printed symbol. These approaches have been labeled the synthetic, the analytic, and the analytic-synthetic methods.

Synthetic Methods

Methods that begin with word elements, with letters (alphabet spelling method), with sounds (synthetic phonic method), or with syllables (syllable method) are called synthetic methods. They are so called because the letters, sounds, and syllables must be combined or synthesized to form words.

The Alphabet Method

Probably the earliest formal attempt to teach the reading of our language was a synthetic method—the alphabet approach. Each new word was spelled out. The pupil looked at the word *cat*, spelled it *see-ay-tee*, and pronounced the whole word. Even the Greeks and the Romans appear to have used this method. The *New England Primer* in 1690 and the *Webster American Spelling Book* in 1793 were based on the alphabet method. The child first learned to recognize (memorize) the letters and gradually proceeded toward the word and the sentence.

Although the letter may be the crucial unit in writing and spelling, its validity as a unit for reading is not easily established. Certainly the chief weakness in the alphabetic method is that the sounds of the names of letters do not always indicate the sounds to be used in pronouncing the words.

Recent studies, as indicated in Chapter 7, show that the ability to name the letters is positively related to reading success. Pupils who have learned to associate a name with a letter have already learned a basic reading skill. They have learned how to discriminate one visual configuration from another (an *a* is different from a *b*) and have associated a sound and consequently a name and a meaning with that symbol.

THE SYNTHETIC PHONIC METHOD

The second synthetic method to be used by teachers was the phonic method. It was originated by Ickelsamer in 1534 and was introduced to America in 1782 by Noah Webster. The alphabet method starts with the name of the letter; the phonic method, on the other hand, starts with the phonetic sound of the letter. The pupil learns the sounds represented by the letters and gradually proceeds to the sounding of the consonant-vowel and vowel-consonant combinations and ultimately to words.

Unfortunately, sounds as well as letters lack meaning, and most of the various letters in the English language may be used to suggest many different sounds. It is easy to see a portion of the problem involved when one considers the sounds represented by *ou* in the following words: *sour, pour, would, tour, sought, couple.*

THE SYLLABLE METHOD

The third synthetic method is the syllable method. Here syllables are combined to form words. Since morphemic or structural analysis is based on syllable analysis, a syllable approach is an essential aspect of today's reading program. Groff (1971) has adduced much interesting evidence suggesting that the phonogram is the natural unit for the beginner and that it is the most useful unit in learning how to decode words.

Glass and Burton (1973) found that most pupils in their study (second and fifth graders) used a letter-clustering approach associated with sounds or a sound-cluster approach in decoding words. Swenson (1975) found that in matching consonant-vowel-consonant (cvc) trigrams, first-grade average readers attended more to the vc letters than to single letters, and poor readers employed the first letter only.

Sullivan, Okada, and Niedermeyer (1971) note that when they contrasted the single-letter approach in teaching of word attack with letter combinations (vc or vcc) taught as single grapheme-phoneme units, of the forty-eight first graders, those of high ability learned best through the letter-combination approach, and those of low ability learned best through the single-letter approach.

Analytic Methods

Historically, the analytic methods of teaching word identification are three: the word method, the phrase method, and the sentence method. They are called analytic methods because they begin with the word, phrase, or sentence, and these larger units are then broken down or analyzed into their basic elements.

THE WORD METHOD

The word method is the most common analytic method in use today. It was introduced in Europe in 1648 by Comenius in his book, *The Orbis Pictus*, and was proposed in the United States in 1828 by Samuel Worcester. Various sense avenues may be used in teaching the word method. One method of teaching reading which begins with the total word, but whose emphasis is on sound or phonics, is termed analytical or whole-word phonics. The linguistic methods of Bloomfield and Fries also fit here. Another word method emphasizes the kinesthetic sense avenues and is termed the kinesthetic method. This method is most frequently associated with the name of Fernald (1943). It has been used very successfully with remedial readers and with brain-injured children.

THE SENTENCE METHOD

The sentence method of teaching reading was emphasized especially in the early 1900s by Huey (1912). Huey suggested that the sentence, not the word or letter, was the true unit in language, and he argued that therefore it was also the true unit in reading.

Lefevre (1961) suggests an analytical method of teaching reading, emphasizing language patterns. He believes that meaning comes only through the grasping of the language structures exemplified in a sentence. Meaning thus depends on intonation, word and sentence order, grammatical inflections, and certain key function words. Only by reading structures, Lefevre suggests, can full meaning be attained. Or to put it in another way, unless readers correctly translate the printed text into the intonation pattern of the writer, they may not be getting the meaning intended.

It may well be that the sentence (or indeed the story) is the basic unit of reading (that meaning depends on intonation, word and sentence order, and so forth), but the word or letter may still be the basic unit of identification and recognition. Meaningful reading seems to occur only when the reader comprehends the total sentence unit. However, few would suggest that the pupil should learn to *identify* sentences as units. The word seems to be the largest linguistic unit that readily lends itself to identification. Thus, although the sentence method and the linguistic method of Lefevre may be the way one should read, they may have less significance for identification.

Psycholinguists also emphasize that the good reader is one who can read the deep structures of language, who can make optimal use of both semantic and syntactic cues. Good readers operate at the deep structure level, predict as they read, sample the surface structure as they test out predictions, and use semantic and syntactic cues to identify words. But even the good reader may have to resort to other strategies of word identification. Certainly the beginning reader and the poor reader are more likely to focus on discriminating one symbol from another. Disabled readers are generally weak in using syntactic context to identify words. They fail to extract contextual cues essential for identification. Not every reader can play the psycholinguistic guessing game with equal proficiency.

Figure 8–4 summarizes the methods of teaching word identification. It identifies the specific synthetic and analytic methods and makes note of the combination or eclectic method as well.

Figure 8–5 categorizes the word methods. Later in the chapter discussion

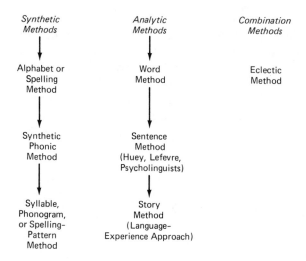

Synthetic Methods	Analytic Methods	Combination Methods

Alphabet or Spelling Method — Word Method — Eclectic Method

Synthetic Phonic Method — Sentence Method (Huey, Lefevre, Psycholinguists)

Syllable, Phonogram, or Spelling–Pattern Method — Story Method (Language–Experience Approach)

Figure 8-4 Methods of Teaching Word Identification

will center on three whole-word methods. It will be seen that it is common to begin with a whole-word method; that should this method not succeed, one may have to switch to a synthetic phonic method; and that it may prove best to use an eclectic or combination method that incorporates elements of each of the other methods.

The sentence and story methods, in that they best illustrate how one reads rather than how one identifies words, have greatest meaning when one considers modes of introducing reading to pupils, that is, through the language-experience, basal, or individualized-reading approaches. Before looking in detail at each of the five main methods of word identification, examine the question of whether it is more appropriate to begin with an analytic method or a synthetic method or some combination of the two.

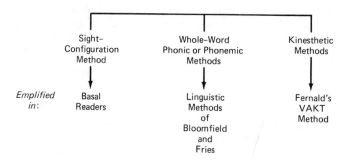

Emplified in:

Sight–Configuration Method — Basal Readers

Whole-Word Phonic or Phonemic Methods — Linguistic Methods of Bloomfield and Fries

Kinesthetic Methods — Fernald's VAKT Method

Figure 8-5 Word Methods

DEVELOPING A CODING SYSTEM

The issues (Smith 1971, 1978) that present themselves are:

1. Should reading teaching begin with an analytic approach or the whole word or with a synthetic approach or a part of the word? Is reading normally a process of serially processing words letter by letter or are the letters processed simultaneously in parallel as when the reader recognizes syllables as chunks or words as wholes (Smith 1971: p. 127)? The question is not whether letters or the configuration can be used to identify words, but whether the reader normally or necessarily uses one or both of them.
2. When pupils identify the word, what do they see? Do pupils see the total configuration or do they react to the parts of the word? Furthermore, what do pupils see when they see a whole?
3. What are the distinctive features of words? What features of a stimulus configuration are so distinctive that they constitute a significant difference?

The previous section noted that there are basically two theories of word identification: whole-word identification and letter-by-letter or syllable-by-syllable identification. The arguments for beginning with the whole word are these:

1. Reading is the process of securing meaning, and it would seem that from the beginning the child should be dealing with meaningful language units. Thus, the child from the beginning should be introduced to the smallest linguistic unit that can stand alone in a sentence and that has meaning. This is the word. Pupils should learn that they are responding to a symbol with which it is possible to associate meaning. Words have meanings; the sounds of the individual letters in a word do not.
2. The child has had numerous experiences with words, listening to them and speaking them. The child has had an aural-oral experience with them.
3. There are many words that cannot be learned letter by letter or sound by sound. These words often defy phonic analysis.
4. The word is as easily identifiable as is the letter.

The letter-by-letter or syllable-by-syllable approach also has some strong points in its favor:

1. The reader appears to be sensitive to individual letters in the identification of a word. The reader quickly notes that the word *percieve* is misspelled in this sentence.
2. When decoding is difficult, as it often is for the beginning reader and the disabled reader, the reader resorts to serial letter-by-letter processing. Even mature readers must at times analyze words into their parts. Terry, Samuels, and LaBerge (1976) indicate that the beginning reader characteristically processes each letter of a word before recognizing the word.
3. Children pay particular attention to the parts of words when they are required to discriminate between similar-appearing words. Four- and five-year-old children and poor readers generally tend to identify words by certain key letters, letter ar-

rangements, or other outstanding characteristics, and for this reason confuse them with other words having the same letters or characteristics.

4. Eye-movement studies indicate that children rarely see a total word per fixation. In the first grade not more than one-half of a word is usually seen. This means that the child must look at the parts of words, retain them in memory, and combine them mentally to form the total word.

5. Marchbanks and Levin (1965), in a study involving fifty kindergarten children and fifty first-grade children, found that specific letters were much more important in determining recognition than was the overall shape of the word. The initial letter was the most salient cue, next came the final letter, and finally the middle letter. The least used cue was the word shape. These findings were generally supported in studies by Timko (1970) and Williams, Blumberg, and Williams (1970).

Over the history of reading, particularly since 1920, whole-word methods have been broadly accepted. The pupil obviously must learn the word as a configuration people , but a configuration that is identified only by length and shape has two basic deficiencies: It helps little in the identification of other words, forcing the pupil to learn each word as a totally independent squiggle, and it does not help the pupil to discriminate between similar-appearing configurations such as *people* and *purple*. The question is: How does the reader differentiate between *people* and *purple*? How do the configurations of each of these words become differentiated? The discussion that follows addresses itself to these questions. The points to be made are

1. Beginning readers really "see" the word's configuration clearly only when they can "see" the elements or features that individualize the word, hence when they have a perception of the word's structure. The most basic structural elements or featural aspects that distinguish one word from another are the letters or graphemes, but these appear in a definite order in words. It is thus the sequence of the letters that individualizes each word's visual configuration, giving it idiosyncratic identity. It is the sequence of letters that individualizes and gives featural identity to the configurations of *eat*, *ate*, and *tea*, each of which is composed of the same letters.

2. If word identification includes the unlocking or the "seeing" of the pronunciation of a printed word, then readers must do more than simply identify the sequence of letters. They must learn that the sequence of letters represents or stands for a sequence of sounds. The reader who can identify and turn a sequence of letters into a sequence of sounds knows the grapheme-phoneme interrelationships or correspondences. The pupil who can convert the letter sequence *people* into the sound sequence /pēpl/ has learned to individualize and to discriminate the configuration people .

3. The basic structural unit, or pattern, or gestalt in words, thus is not the configuration per se; it is the word's configuration as it is individualized by the sequence of letters and the phoneme-grapheme interrelationships. When pupils learn a gestalt for a word that is based on the perception of these interrelationships, they learn a *code* that is applicable to other words. Figure 8–6 summarizes the observation just made.

4. The code teaches the pupil how words are structured and how the arrangement of the letters in a word controls the way the letters function.

5. In unlocking the pronunciation of the symbol *phlogiston*, it is almost certain that most readers will pronounce the word as /flŏg/ĭs/tŭn/ or /flō/gĭs/tŭn/. It is the se-

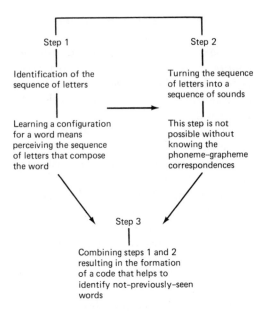

Step 1
Identification of the
sequence of letters

Step 2
Turning the sequence
of letters into a
sequence of sounds

Learning a configuration
for a word means
perceiving the sequence
of letters that compose
the word

This step is not
possible without
knowing the
phoneme–grapheme
correspondences

Step 3

Combining steps 1 and 2
resulting in the formation
of a code that helps to
identify not-previously–seen
words

Figure 8-6   Steps in Developing a Coding System

quence of letters and the knowledge of the grapheme-phoneme interrelationships, in other words the code the pupil has learned, that permits this. It is especially significant that the *ph* is converted to /*f*/, but also that the word can be divided in two different ways, resulting in the assignment of different values to the vowels.

Good word identifiers are differentiated from poor identifiers in that the good identifiers learn a system or a code for identifying words that permits them to reconstruct the sequence of letters in words (Bruner 1957a). Poor identifiers often learn simply by rote. Good identifiers learn that words in the English language follow certain structural laws and that it is the intraword redundancies that identify the word's structure. Three-year-olds are using a coding system or the "transitional probabilities" that characterize the English language when they use regular endings to create words such as *selled*, *runned*, or *mans* for the irregular *sold*, *ran*, or *men*, and so do the first graders who read *come* as /kōm/.* Because these children are dealing with an irregularity, they make an error. Thus, the letter sequence is not an exact indication of the pronunciation of a word, but the system is a valuable cue in perhaps 85 percent of the cases.

The best way of developing the code appears to be through an understanding of the phoneme-grapheme interrelations or phonics. Such learning maximizes the transfer of learning. The pupil is in a sense taught to be a better

* Bruner (1957a) refers to this coding system as the "transitional probabilities"; Gibson and Levin (1975) speak of "conditional redundancies of English orthography."

guesser by knowing the phonogram-phoneme interrelationships. The basic contribution of phonics instruction may be that it requires pupils to visually study the word. Phonics instruction forces pupils to look at the parts of a word and thus may lead to a somewhat different perception than if the word were perceived strictly by concentrating on the configuration alone. Through phonics pupils may learn to more adequately scrutinize the configuration and thus may develop the habit of being unsatisfied with a general, overall view of a word.

The discussion has now come full circle. It has been observed that generally pupils should begin with the whole word, that they need to identify the word's configuration in a way that is based on an understanding of the parts, and that they need to develop a code that can be used in the understanding of other words. It thus affirms that for effective word identification, the pupil needs both an analytic and a synthetic approach. From the beginning, the pupil needs to see the word both as a unit and as made of parts that individualize that unit. Montgomery (1977) notes that the essence of pattern recognition lies in paying attention to detail, not in isolation, but in relation to the whole structure.

The development of the code or the study of the phoneme-grapheme correspondences will be the focus of Chapters 9 and 10.

The remainder of this chapter will examine in detail each of the major methods of developing or teaching word identification, beginning with the sight-configuration method.

THE SIGHT-CONFIGURATION METHOD

Numerous methods of teaching word-identification skills have emerged as distinctive approaches to the word-identification tasks. This section will consider (1) the configuration method; (2) the linguistic method; (3) the kinesthetic method; (4) the phonic method; (5) the eclectic method; and (6) some additional approaches to word identification. Each of these methods of word identification fits into the directed reading lesson described earlier; however, a complete reading lesson involves more than simply word identification. Begin now with the configuration method.

As already indicated, in perhaps 95 percent of all classrooms the teacher introduces the child to reading through a basal reading series and in many of these situations the child is taught to identify words by a whole-word sight-configuration method. Unquestionably, many beginning readers identify words through their general shape and configuration. They see the word as a unified shape rather than as a collection of related letters.

The configuration method generally emphasizes (1) the word's length (words like grandmother, elephant, Christmas, Halloween are readily identifiable by their length) or (2) the word's shape, configuration, or physiognomy (ascending and descending letters identify a word and give it shape). It combines the visual and auditory modalities, but the emphasis is clearly on visual discrimination of the total word. Using this method alone, the pupil will not learn the code which was described earlier.

The steps of the sight-configuration method are

1. Present the word clearly written in manuscript on a 4-by-6-inch card (or on the chalkboard). Pupils tend to learn to identify a word more efficiently when the word is presented in isolation, rather than in sentence context, or with a picture, or both (Singer, Samuels, and Spiroff 1973–1974).

2. Pronounce the word, making sure that the pupils look at the word as it is pronounced.

3. Have the pupils pronounce the word, again making sure that they look at the word when it is pronounced.

4. Present the word in a written-sentence context (on the back of the 4-by-6-inch card or on the chalkboard). Then

    a. Read the sentence to the pupils.

    b. Have the pupils read the sentence aloud.

    c. Have the pupils identify and underline the word that is being taught.

5. Present the word orally in another teacher-made sentence.

6. Have the pupils make a sentence using the word. Write this sentence on another card or on the chalkboard. Older pupils should write the sentence themselves.

7. Have the pupils read the sentence aloud; let pupils first identify the word and then underline it, frame it, or trace it in color.

8. Present the word in isolation again and have the pupils sound it.

9. After teaching various words using the above techniques, present the words at random to test retention of the word.

Of course, using the above method with a group of children may require some modifications. It is important that the word be introduced in a sentence and that the pupils look at the word while saying it. Sight configuration puts major emphasis on visual scrutiny. Pupils need to learn to inspect the word with great care, seeing both the whole and its parts. Other means of reinforcing the visual image of the word are

1. Using flash or picture word cards which associate the printed form with a picture of the word.

2. Developing and using picture dictionaries.

3. Using tachistoscopes.

4. Using card games.

5. Using the word in a spelling lesson.

6. Using the word in meaningful written and spoken contexts.

Flash cards, even though they often encourage dependence upon the wrong type of visual cues (for instance, a broken corner on the card on which the word appears), can be used to build sentences, to test knowledge of words that have been taught, and to develop speed of recognition. Preferably, the word cards should have a word and a picture on one side and only the word on the opposite side. The cards must be opaque.*

Some cards containing visual material come with strips of magnetic recording tape mounted on them. One of the two recording tracks on the tape is prerecorded and serves as an intructor, while the second track is used for recording student response. The child tries to identify the word on the card and then places it into a machine or card reader and listens as a recorded voice pronounces the word. Both printed, prerecorded cards and blank cards can be purchased for these machines or card readers.

Card readers individualize instruction and motivate and challenge the pupil. They are self-directed and self-paced. They include dual-track recording and playback capabilities. Pupils record their response, and then immediately compare it with the information on the instructor track.

Card readers available include:

1. *Califone Card Reader*, Model 4400B, (Califone). Preprepared card reader programs to be used with the Califone card reader include *Directional Phonics* (grade 1-adult); *Transitional Phonics* (grade 3-adult); *Confused Words* (grade 1-adult); *Confused Word Phrases* (grade 1-adult); *Context Vocabulary* (grade 4-adult); *Common Phrases* (remedial readers); *Instant Words I* (grades 1-3); *Instant Words II* (grade 4 and older low achievers); *Instant Word Phrases I* (grades 1-3); *Instant Word Phrases II* (grade 4 and older low achievers).

2. *Language Master* (Bell & Howell). The *Console Language Master Instructional Device*, either Model 717BW or 715B, allows teachers to prepare their own programs. Preprepared programs include *Here Comes Howie* (Readiness level); *TRG Sound System* (K-8); *Phonics Program* (grades 1-6); *Linguistic Word Pattern Program* (grades 1-3); *Vocabulary Mastery* (grades 5-12); *TRG Sight Vocabulary Program* (grades 1-6); *Word Picture* (grades 2-6); *STAR* (Comprehension, grades 5-9).

3. *Voxcom* (Tapecon). The Voxcom is a cassette tape recorder that can receive a separate card reader attachment. An auditory-instruction track can also be added. A prerecorded *Phonics and Word Instruction program* is available.

4. *Skill Master Audio Card Player* (Educators Publishing).

5. *Mast Electronic Card Reader* (Mast).

Teachers of reading should take advantage of a word's general configuration which can be an important clue to the identification of the word. The con-

---

* Commercial, illustrated word cards are the *Dolch Picture Word Cards*, (Garrard Publishing Company). These cards teach 95 common nouns.

figuration method may be the only usable method for a few children who cannot analyze the word into its parts, or have such poor auditory-discrimination skills that they cannot deal with phonics.

However, the configuration method is not without its drawbacks. Asking children to recognize words by length and shape alone ignores the fact that printed letters and words are symbols of sound. As pupils broaden their reading experience, the configuration method becomes less useful with similar-appearing words. Young children and poor readers, being prone to attend to certain key letters, letter arrangements, or "outstanding" characteristics, are generally helped little when they meet other words with similar characteristics. The word *purple* may be identified by the one ascending and the two descending letters. The configuration looks like this: ⌐⌐⌐ Unfortunately, the word *people* has the same visual configuration and the ascending and descending letters fall in the same place. Obviously, it is impossible to discriminate between the two words on the basis of configuration alone. Learning to recognize the word *monkey* by its "tail" (*y*) may help for a while, but soon the child will be required to deal with *penny, funny, sunny.*

Disabled readers are often thus disabled because as they are introduced to words at an ever increasing rate they find it harder and harder to make the fine discriminations required to identify the words. The problems of visual discrimination do in fact increase proportionately as the rate of the introduction of new words increases. The memory load that is created by having to learn hundreds of new and ever less discriminable words becomes quickly excessive and may partially contribute to the negative reading attitudes that one sees so frequently among third and fourth graders. As the differences between configurations become ever finer, with letters curving left and right (*b-d*) and upward and downward (*n-u*), the disabled reader, especially, becomes confused, loses confidence, and turns against reading. Disabled readers, perhaps more so than any other readers, must be freed from having to memorize thousands of words as independent squiggles. They must learn to analyze words that are not in their recognition vocabulary.

The major problems with the configuration method are that it does not develop a reliable identification for the configuration. The words *people* and *purple*, as already noted, have the same configuration, shape, or physiognomy, but it requires more than this to discriminate one from the other. Thus, even after identifying a word's shape or length, one is hard put to use this knowledge in identifying other words. The word's shape, as such, has relatively little transfer value. It is not a code that can be used elsewhere.

The configuration method today is being supplemented by the teaching of phonic skills, by what many call decoding skills, and which are referred to here as recoding skills. Teaching of phonics can take two forms: whole-word phonics and synthetic phonics. Examine now a method that incorporates whole-word phonics teaching.

THE LINGUISTIC METHOD*

Since the whole-word sight-configuration method does not work with all children, and since of itself it does not develop a code for identifying words, it is necessary to look elsewhere to supplement it. One such avenue is the linguistic method. It is difficult to label this method. It is analogous to an analytic whole-word phonics method or a phonemic-word approach because the structure of the language is studied through symbol-sound relationships in whole words.

Bloomfield and Barnhart (1961) have presented a linguistic approach whose central thesis is that the major task facing the child is the mastery of the graphic system that reflects the spoken language system. They point out that there is an inseparable relationship between the words as they are printed and the sounds for which the letters are conventional signs, and that converting letters to meaning requires a concentration upon letter and sound to bring about an automatic association between them as rapidly as possible.

Bloomfield's view is that initial teaching of reading for meaning is incorrect and that meaning will come quite naturally as the alphabet code is discovered. Perhaps the easiest way to explain this is to use a diagram (Figure 8-7). Pupils generally come into the reading situation with meaning (unconditioned response) already attached to the spoken word (unconditioned stimulus); what they need to learn is to associate meaning with a written word (conditioned stimulus). The pupil thus needs to learn how the configuration *cat* graphically represents /kăt/. This is a problem of deciphering the alphabetic code, but once the pupil can "see" /kăt/ in *cat*, meaning tends to be rather automatically associated with the printed symbol. Lefevre (1964) was critical of Bloomfield's approach, on the grounds of its being largely confined to phonemic analysis and neglecting intonation, syntax, and ultimately meaning.

The presentation that follows is in the nature of a harmonization of variant linguistic approaches. It begins with a focus on meaningful language patterns and the reading of total language structures (which is the focus of Lefevre and the psycholinguists), but also emphasizes that for most children teaching has to come down to the level of the individual word identification and the association of letter and sound patterns.

Reading of Meaningful Language Patterns

Writing and print have as their chief function the recall of entire language patterns, especially sentence-level utterances. Comprehension of printed materials requires the perception of entire language stuctures, the perception, that is to say, of sentences. The sentence is the basic unit of meaning; it is the basic meaning-bearing pattern.

* The linguistic method is used in the *Merrill Linguistic Readers* (Charles E. Merrill); in the *Linguistic Readers* (Benziger); in the *Miami Linguistic Readers* (D. C. Heath); in the *Harper & Row Basic Reading Program;* and in *Let's Read* by Leonard Bloomfield (Clarence L. Barnhart).

Unconditioned Stimulus (US)	Unconditioned Response (UR)
/kăt/	meaning
Conditioned Stimulus (CS)	Conditioned Response (CR)
cat	meaning

Figure 8-7

Pupils are ready for reading when they realize that the languages they hear and speak can be represented graphically in writing and print, and that print says something.

After pupils have learned to identify and to name the configuration which represents their name, they should be introduced to reading complete sentence units, even though it is only a three-word sentence. The pupils should be exposed to words within the context of a total sentence.

Inability to deal with language patterns plays a decisive role in reading failure. The disabled reader's basic problem often is that of word-by-word reading without any sentence sense. The disabled reader often misses language structures completely (Lefevre 1964).

The teacher should be satisfied only when the child's oral reading of a sentence indicates, through the features of pitch, sequence, and stress, that the child in fact understands the total meaning. The very least the teacher should accept in the beginning is that children can "say" the sentence as they would "talk" it to a friend.

The words used and the meanings coveyed in initial reading experiences should generally include only those in the actual linguistic experience of the pupils. The pupils should be in full control of the language material, including the grammatical signals. The language-experience approach, as already indicated, appears to have the most to offer in this regard in beginning reading. It is built on the language structures that the child brings to school, and for this reason is a suitable means for introducing the child to reading meaningful sentence units.

Breaking the Alphabetic Code

Even though the psycholinguist believes that reading involves the reading of total language structures or sentences, and that the language-experience approach offers the most opportunity for doing this in beginning reading, one of the learner's first tasks in learning to read is to break the alphabetic code. It is at this point that the observations of Bloomfield and Fries have relevance.

The easiest form of word identification is to name a configuration, but because pupils need to acquire a method of identification that helps them to identify other words with ease, they need to learn a coding system. This system, as was noted earlier, is the sequence of letters and the phoneme-grapheme correspondences.

Despite its many imperfections, the English writing system is basically alphabetic, and reading usually requires the act of responding vocally to the printed letter as it functions with other letters. Words are constructed alphabetically, and the reader can learn to sound out the name of a new configuration from the letters of the word itself. The alphabet characters represent unit speech sounds, so the way of writing each word bears a close relationship to the speech sounds which make up that word. The letter is not sounded alone; it is sounded in the context of other letters or of the total word. The sounds represented by *b*, *c*, and *d* exist only in the context of a word or syllable. The correspondence between written and spoken English is weak if one attempts to relate individual letters and sounds, but if the graphemic unit is a letter pattern, words, or word groups, a high degree of correspondence is found.

Early linguistic materials, and indeed basal readers, presented a very restricted vocabulary. There probably is a happy medium between undue restriction and unwise variation. The sentences should be legitimate meaning-bearing patterns. They should provide contextual settings that permit words to be learned in a natural linguistic environment. However, the beginning reader is intrigued by the magic of the recoding process. Figuring out the word often is its own adequate motivation. There seems to be some legitimacy in controlling the introduction of phoneme-grapheme correspondences, and indeed teachers are finding that recent basal reading series have perhaps gone too far in removing syntactic controls. Words, particularly when they are used to teach the fundamental structures of language, should be graded for their phonetic difficulty (rather than semantic difficulty). Regular phoneme-grapheme correspondences should be emphasized initially. The rate of phoneme-grapheme correspondences should be controlled so that the pupil will more quickly and more easily master the principles that undergird morphology (word structure). It seems easier for children to learn to break the alphabetic code when they are introduced to words in which the letters behave consistently or in which they have only one phonetic value.

Auditory and Visual Discrimination

The readiness of pupils to learn the phoneme-grapheme correspondences or the alphabetic code is dependent upon their proficiency in auditory and visual discrimination. In the area of auditory discrimination, pupils must be able to isolate individual phonemes, must notice similarities or differences between phonemes or between a pair of spoken words, must be able to tell whether a given phoneme occurs at the beginning, middle, or end of the word, and must remember the sequence of phonemes.

In the area of visual discrimination, the first set of recognition responses children need to learn is for the letters of the alphabet. The letters must be identified as contrasting shapes. Pupils must visually discriminate each letter from every other letter, must note similarites and differences between pairs of words, must be able to name the letters, and must remember the sequence of the letters in a word. To be good readers, they must eventually be able to match a visual sequence of letters with an auditory sequence of sounds. Bloomfield has recommended that pupils be taught the capital letters before the lowercase letters and that reading begin only after pupils have learned the letters.

The Spelling Patterns

The linguistic method is organized around the basic spelling patterns of vowels and consonants in English: cvc—*bat;* vc—*at;* cv—*go;* cvc¢—*time;* and cvvc—*coat.* These spelling patterns are used to teach the phoneme-grapheme correspondences. Thus, the pupil learns that in the pattern cvc (*bat*), the *a* represents its short sound because it occurs in a monosyllable word and is followed by a single consonant. Fries (1963: p. 200) notes that "in the three letter word . . . *man,* it is not the single letter A that indicates the vowel sound [æ]. It is the spelling-pattern *m a n* in contrast with the spelling-pattern *mane* . . . . that signals the different words." In the spelling pattern cvc¢ (*mane*), the *a* represents its long sound.

This spelling-pattern approach teaches pupils to associate letter patterns with sound patterns—to respond to the contrastive features that identify and differentiate whole-word patterns. Pupils are taught to associate a sequence of letters with a sequence of sounds. Only complete words are pronounced; thus pupils attach the pronunciation to the total spelling pattern. From the beginning pupils learn to visually scrutinize all the letters in a word, the beginning consonant, the middle vowel, and the end consonant. Reading is not the matching of words, letter by letter, with words, sound by sound. Pupils are not taught that *b* says /bŭh/, but that it says the sound heard at the beginning of the word *boy.* Pupils will have attained a significant level of maturity when their responses to the spelling patterns have become so automatic that the graphic shapes sink below the threshold of attention, leaving only a consciousness of semantic and syntactic meaning.

Principle of Minimum Contrast

The principle of minimum variation or minimum contrast is the second major identifying characteristic of the linguistic method. The understanding of the difference that any particular letter makes in the spelling pattern is developed through the experience of pronouncing a variety of contrastive word pairs with minimum differences in their spelling patterns, for example, *bat-at; bat-fat; bat-pat,* and the like (Fries 1963).

Presenting /*bat*/ fifty times, in a variety of ways and in a variety of contexts, and telling the pupils it is /*bat*/ does not help to discriminate the word. Pupils learn what they need to learn only when *fat* and /*bat*/ are contrasted and when it becomes clear that the words are not functionally equivalent, in other words, only when the pupils are exposed to other contrastive words that are not *bat.* Thus, the linguistic method not only teaches pupils what the word *is;* it also teaches them what it *is not.*

In distinguishing the word *John,* good cues may be the length of the word, the two upright strokes, or the shape of the fishhook at the beginning, but these cues lack transferability. They do not help the reader to identify other words. They work as long as the pupil does not have to say what the word *John* is not. If the cue is the *J* or fishhook, the pupil cannot discriminate *John* from *Jack*. Smith (1971, 1978) notes that until pupils are shown what to distinguish *John* from, they will not acquire an appropriate set of distinctive features for identifying that word. They have to see a representative sample of words that are not *John* in order to find out in what respects *John* is different.

Rather than emphasizing only the word's configuration, the teacher might thus accomplish more by helping children to note the differences between words, by calling attention to the salient and distinctive characteristics of words and the sequence of letters within the word. The pupil must learn that each word has an individual, idiosyncratic graphic representation and that the sequence of letters gives it its identity.

The linguistic method teaches the pupil to associate specific letters in words with specific sounds, without conscious analysis of a word into its individual sounds, but by studying the whole word in lists and contexts.

Presenting the letter (for which a phoneme-grapheme association is to be learned) in color increases attention and emphasizes the unit to be studied.

The pupil learns the phoneme-grapheme interrelationships and the principle of minimum variation most easily by practicing with monosyllabic words. When all words are made up of three letters, the pupil cannot use the length of the word to identify it, and quite frequently cannot use the configuration either. With *bat—hat*, for example, both words obviously have the same configuration. In the beginning, the practice words used in developing the code contain only short vowels. The goal of this approach to reading instruction is to familiarize children with the phonetic consistencies of the language as a basis for generalizations to new words.

Some variation, however, is desirable. It has been found that training on only regular sound-to-spelling correspondences is less than optimal for transfer. Levin (1966) suggests that it seems reasonable for children early in their schooling to simultaneously learn more than one associated sound for letters and letter groups. The indication is that this will lead to greater flexibility in trying out sounds when the child meets new instances. Levin's *study* showed that dual associations were more difficult to acquire, but that once acquired they facilitated the pupil's learning to read new words.

In teaching initial-consonant discrimination, only the beginning consonant is varied in the pair of contrasting words (*c̲at-f̲at*); gradually, the median vowel (*ca̲t-cu̲t*) and ending consonant (*cat̲-can̲*) are varied.

Teaching Nonalphabetic Words

Alphabetically, irregular words with high utility (for example, *was, one*) must be taught as sight words. These words do not fit any spelling pattern; they are exceptions and from the beginning must be labeled as exceptions. Pupils should be taught from the beginning that nearly every generalization has exceptions and that if the word does not make sense in the sentence they should try another approach.

If the word is actually regular (for example, *came*) but the pupil has not yet been formally introduced to such words or to the principles governing the sounding of such words, the word might simply be pronounced, and teaching the appropriate word-analysis skills might be deferred until later. There is no reason to insist that children learn the word as a sight word or configuration, if by application of the principle of pacing they will soon know and understand it as an alphabetically consistent word.

Both the whole-word sight-configuration method and the kinesthetic method are useful in developing recognition of words that are not alphabetically regular.

Steps of the Linguistic Method

The steps of the linguistic method are

1. Present a word which exemplifies one of the basic spelling patterns (cvc—*man*), clearly written in manuscript, on a 4-by-6-inch card, on chart paper, or on the chalkboard.
2. Pronounce the word, making sure that the pupils look at the word as it is pronounced.
3. Have the pupils pronounce the word.
4. Spell the word, drawing attention to each letter, and pronounce the word again.
5. Have the pupils spell the word, pointing to each letter as the pupils say the name of the letters, and then have the pupils say the word.
6. Present the word in a sentence, written on the back of the card or on the chalkboard.
   a. Read the sentence to the pupils.
   b. Have the pupils read the sentence aloud.
   c. Have the pupils identify and underline the word being taught.
7. Have the pupils make a sentence using the word.
8. Have the pupils read the sentence aloud; let them identify the word, and let them underline it, frame it, or trace it in color.
9. Present another word exemplifying the same spelling pattern, and only minimally different from the first word (cvc—*ran*). Align this second word under the first word:

   man
   ran

10. Pronounce the second word (*ran*), making sure that the pupils look at the word as it is pronounced.
11. Have the pupils pronounce the word.
12. Show how the two words differ.
13. Have the pupils spell the word, pointing to each letter as the pupils say it, and have them say the word.
14. Have the pupils make a sentence using the word.

15. Introduce a third and fourth word, having the same spelling pattern and being only minimally different from the first two words (*fan* and *can*).
16. Have the pupils compose sentences using the new words:

    The man ran.
    The man has a fan.
    The man can fan.

    Write these sentences on the back of the card or on the chalkboard.
17. Have the pupils read the sentences aloud; let them identify the words learned, and let them underline the words, frame them, or trace them in color.
18. Present the words again in isolation.

The significant difference between the linguistic method and the sight-configuration method lies in the addition of spelling (Steps 3 and 6), in the spelling-pattern approach, and in the principle of minimum contrast (Step 9).

THE KINESTHETIC-TACTILE METHOD

Neither the configuration nor the linguistic or whole-word phonics approach meets the needs of every pupil. Some children have much difficulty in developing a visual image. With these, the kinesthetic or VAKT method, originally developed by Grace Fernald (1943), might be used.

The steps of the VAKT (visual, auditory, kinesthetic, tactile) method are:

1. A word is chosen from a sentence that the pupils are learning to read.
2. The teacher writes the word in large cursive writing on a 4-by-10-inch strip of paper or on the chalkboard. Manuscript writing may be used if the pupil has not yet mastered cursive writing.
3. The teacher pronounces the word and the pupils pronounce the word.
4. The pupils trace the word with a forefinger (or pencil), saying each part or syllable of the word as they do the tracing.* In the Fernald method tracing continues until the pupils can reproduce the word from memory.
5. The pupils write the word without the benefit of copy. They say the word to themselves, whenever they write it. The pupils may be aided by having a copy of the word before them initially. However, eventually the pupils must learn to write the word from memory.
6. The word is typewritten and included in the list of words that the pupils know.

As pupils become more proficient in word recognition, the need for tracing decreases, but pronouncing the word while writing it is always an essential feature. At this stage the VAKT method merges into a VAK method. The pupils then look at the word, say it to themselves, try to "see" or form a mental image of the word with their eyes shut and write it from memory. They compare it with

---

* Monroe (1932) in her synthetic phonetic approach, used pencil tracing.

the model and write it until they can do it correctly from memory. Instead of large script, the words are now written on index cards and filed alphabetically.

The kinesthetic-tactile method is time consuming, but it has many advantages. It emphasizes careful and systematic observation and visual scrutiny and study of the word; it enforces consistent left-to-right direction in reading; and the sensory impressions from tracing and writing reinforce the visual impression. Some suggest that the enforced attention to details in sequence rather than the tactile-kinesthetic sensation is the significant aid to learning. Use of the method in addition teaches phoneme-grapheme correspondences, helps children to overcome problems such as reversals, and teaches basic syllabication skills. Furthermore, it allows for immediate notation and correction of errors and for observation of progress at each stage.

However, tracing can become quite boring. There are numerous variations of the simple tracing technique. One of these is to print the words in broken lines (*want*) and have the pupil trace the word with a finger, crayon, pencil, or fiber-tipped pen.

When a pupil has an abnormal amount of difficulty in identifying the word visually, the Fernald method is recommended if the pupil does not know the letters; *the Gillingham method* (Gillingham and Stillman 1966) might be best used if the pupil has adequate control over the letters. The VAKT method is also useful in teaching words with irregular grapheme-phoneme correspondences, as is done in the Gillingham method. *

Niensted (1968) adapted the Fernald method to group use with high school juniors. The method involves teacher-prepared duplicated manuscripts to be traced by the students as the graphemes are pronounced, followed by an underlining of the syllables, and a reading of the passage using meaningful phrasing.

AN ECLECTIC READING METHOD**

Consider now a synthesis of the three basic whole-word methods: the configuration method, the linguistic method, and the VAKT (or VAK) method. It seems desirable at times to capitalize on all three methods, to incorporate the best of each into a unified method. It is not necessary to use every step with every pupil in every situation; instead, the eclectic method represents a multisensory multifaceted approach suitable to the needs of different readers.

* For an explanation of the Gillingham method, see Gillingham and Stillman (1966).
** For a more complete discussion of the eclectic position, see Dechant's "Why an Eclectic Approach in Reading Instruction?" *Vistas in Reading*, Proceedings of the Eleventh Annual Convention, International Reading Association (Newark, Del., 1967), pp. 28-32; also see Dechant's *Improving the Teaching of Reading*, 1970: pp. 234-238.

The following steps outline the sequence of steps of this method:

1.   Present the spelling pattern (cvc—*man*) in either manuscript or cursive form in a sentence on the chalkboard; underline, frame, or color the word. Later individual pupils transmit the word to a 4-by-6-inch card.
2.   Pronounce the word for the pupils.
3.   Have the pupils pronounce the word.
4.   Present another word exemplifying the same spelling pattern (*ran*) and pronounce it. Align this second word under the first word:

     man
     ran

     The second word should be a contrastive word which is only minimally different (beginning consonant) from the first word.
5.   Have the pupils pronounce the word.
6.   Spell the words and again pronounce them.
7.   Have the pupils spell the words orally, pointing to each letter as they say the name of the letter, and have them say the word.
8.   Have the pupils trace the words with a forefinger or pencil, making certain that the pupils pronounce the word while tracing it.
9.   Have the pupils write the words from memory, again making certain that they say the words while writing them.
10. Present the words in written sentence contexts:
     a.   Read the sentences to the pupils
     b.   Have the pupils read the sentences aloud.
     c.   Have the pupils identify the words and then underline (or frame or trace) them in color.
11. Have the pupils make sentences using the words learned.
     a.   Have the pupils read the sentences aloud.
     b.   Have the pupils identify the specific words learned.
     c.   Have the pupils underline, frame, or trace the words in color.
12. Present the words again in isolation.

The first two steps in developing word discrimination are similar in each method. Step 4 represents a modification of the sight-configuration method. It is designed to help the pupil to break the alphabetic code and to learn the phoneme-grapheme correspondences, using the spelling-pattern method and the principle of minimal variation. Initially the only variation is that of the beginning consonant (*fat-cat*). It necessarily follows that if only the first letter in a monosyllabic word is changed, the pupil will get practice in working with the same phonogram, or word family.

After the pupil has pronounced the word, the teacher spells the word for the pupil (Step 5) and the pupil then spells the word (Step 7). These steps take advantage of the alphabet method. Neither the sight-configuration method nor the VAKT method require the pupil to spell the word. Hinshelwood (1917) had the pupil develop an auditory memory for words by spelling aloud the word letter by letter.

A key reading skill is the ability to hear and see sequences in words. Disabled readers are almost universally unable to do this. Spelling requires this skill and teaches this skill. It teaches pupils to visually analyze *all* the letters in the word in sequence: the beginning consonant, the medial vowel, and the ending consonant. The pupils say the word after they have spelled it: *cat = /see-ay-tee/ = /kăt/*.

Step 8 requires the pupil to trace the word. This step, from the VAKT method, may not be needed in most cases. Tracing helps to stamp in the visual image. The normal sequence in kinesthetic identification of a word is tracing, matching, copying from a dotted outline form, copying from a sample, and writing from memory. Spelling and writing (Step 9) have the added advantage of developing a left-to-right direction in word attack.

Step 10 adds the dimension of color. Presenting the letter or the word to be learned in color intensifies the pupil's preception of it. Color is particularly useful with the pupil who has difficulty with figure-ground discriminations. If the discrimination task is one of identifying a whole word, the whole word may be presented in color. If it is a matter of teaching initial-consonant discrimination, only the initial consonant is in color.

A part of Steps 10 and 11 is having the pupil locate a particular word in a sentence. This is an example of successive discrimination and aids visual memory for the symbol (Hall 1976b.) Children commonly do not have particular difficulty in repeating short sentences, but many cannot identify the separate words in a printed sentence. They have no idea that spoken sentences consist of separate words: thus, *give me the* becomes *gimmethe.*

SYNTHETIC PHONIC METHODS*

Up to this point, the emphasis has been on four whole-word methods of teaching word identification. Unfortunately, not every pupil can learn to identify words in this way. Some pupils need to have the word broken down into its more simple units.

The synthetic phonic method does this. It starts with individual graphemes and phonemes. In synthetic phonic methods the pupil first learns to associate a distinct and separate phoneme with a letter or letter combination (*th, ng, sh,* and the like). The process is completed by blending the separate sounds into phonemic families or phonograms and words.

Synthetic phonic approaches may begin with consonants (*Monroe Method,* Monroe 1932: pp. 111-136), short vowels (*Color Phonics System,* Educators Publishing Service), or long vowels (*Phonetic Keys to Reading,* Economy Company).

---

* Three synthetic phonic basal-reading programs are: *Keys to Reading* (Economy); *Lippincott's Basic Reading Program* (J.B. Lippincott Company); and *Open Court Basic Readers* (Open Court).

In early phonic training it is desirable to concentrate on the teaching of the symbol-sound associations of perhaps three to five consonants (*b, d, m, p, t*) and one vowel. One by one the consonants are joined with each of the other vowels.

Each phoneme should be correlated with a key word. The key words for vowels may take two forms. The vowel sound may occur at the beginning of the key word (/ă/-*apple*, _at_; /ĕ/-*elephant*, _Eskimo_; /ĭ/-*Indian*, _igloo_, _it_; /ŏ/-*ostrich*, _octopus_, _on_; /ŭ/-*umbrella*, _up_), or the vowel may be taught using a key word in which the vowel occurs in the middle of the word as in c_a_t, b_e_d, f_i_sh, t_o_p, d_u_ck.

The method presented here is a synthetic phonic method clearly reflecting the present writer's biases. It starts with a target word (Step 1) whose meaning the pupil knows. In some synthetic phonic methods pupils are not introduced to words until they have mastered the basic phoneme-grapheme correspondences. The steps of a synthetic phonic method are:

1. Write the target word (*bat*) on the chalkboard or on a 4-by-6-inch card, using clearly written manuscript form.
2. Write the letter that represents the grapheme portion of a phoneme-grapheme correspondence, and which needs to be taught, on the chalkboard or on a 4-by-6-inch card and identify it by underlining it, framing it, or coloring it.
3. Name the letter (*b* = /bē/).
4. Say the phoneme that the letter represents: *b* = /bŭh/.
5. Have the pupils say the phoneme, making sure that they look at the letter (*b*) when saying the phoneme.
6. Have the pupils *name* the letter.
7. Have the pupils *trace* the letter, *copy* it, and *write* it from memory, saying the phoneme as they write it.
8. Teach the vowel phoneme-grapheme correspondence (*a* = /ă/) and the end-consonant phoneme-grapheme correspondence (*t* = /t/) in the same way.
9. Have the pupils blend /ă/ with /t/ to form /ăt/.
10. Have the pupils blend /b/ with /ăt/ to form /băt/.
11. After a number of target words have been learned, present the words in written sentence context.
    a. Read the sentence to the pupils.
    b. Have the pupils read the sentence aloud.
    c. Have the pupils identify the words and underline the words.
12. Have the pupils make a sentence using the words.
13. Have the pupils read the sentence aloud, let them identify the words, and let them underline, frame, or trace them in color.
14. Present the words again in isolation.

Step 2 simply calls the pupils' attention to the letter. It teaches the pupils that letters are parts of words and then lets the pupils know that the letter can be treated separately. At this stage pupils learn that the little squiggle is a letter, and they are taught that it has linear and curvilinear aspects. The pupil should be taught both capital and lowercase letters.

Step 3, naming of the letter, is frowned upon in many synthetic methods. Comment has been made elsewhere on the importance of letter naming.

Step 4, saying the phoneme, is the distinctive element in the synthetic phonic method and yet it allows for much variation. Some reading specialists teach /b/ as /bŭh/, noting that this is a necessary device in the beginning. Others note that it is impossible to blend *l-i-t*, if *l* is sounded /lŭh/. Still others concentrate on the movement of the lips when making the sound and teach children the speech mechanisms involved in making the sound.

Some methods (for example, the phonovisual method) teach the unvoiced consonants /p/, /t/, /k/, /th/, /f/,/s/, /sh/, /ch/, /wh/, /h/ or the breath consonants first. These may be sounded (for example, *p* = /phhh/) without a vowel. The voiced consonants, /b/, /d/, /g/, /th/, /v/, /z/, /j/, /zh/, /r/, /l/, /y/, /w/, on the other hand can only be pronounced with a vowel. The consonants /m/, /n/, and /ng/ are also voiced, but can be sounded individually (*m* = /mmm/). Perhaps the voiced consonants need to be taught as /bŭh/, /dŭh/, /gŭh/, with the /ŭh/ minimized as much as possible. Of course, the teacher may want to borrow from the linguists and teach the /b/ as the sound heard at the beginning of words like *boy*, *bet*, or *box*. Some suggest that all the pupil needs to learn is the mouth geography of the sound, how to sound it, without doing any actual vocalizing.

When Step 7 has been mastered, the pupils have now named, traced, written, and sounded the letter. The teacher may use exercises such as the following to reinforce the associations:

1. Say the phoneme and have the pupils write the letter that represents the sound.
2. Say the name of the letter and have the pupils say the phoneme that it represents.
3. Say the phoneme and have the pupils provide the name of the letter that represents it.

ADDITIONAL APPROACHES IN READING

The last twenty years have witnessed the proliferation of methods, theories, approaches, and programs. There is at least some indication that the complexities of English orthography may cause children to have major difficulties in identifying words. Many approaches have been made to this problem. One approach is to change the alphabet. The printed symbols themselves are modified so as to make the relationship more consistent. Briefly examine some of these approaches, beginning with the alphabet modifications.

The Initial Teaching Alphabet (ITA)

One alphabet model is the Initial Teaching Alphabet. It is designed to make reading easier by means of regularizing the coding of the basic sound units of English. There is one symbol for each single sound.

The ITA model presents a total of forty-four symbols. The basic thesis is that children should use a more reliable alphabet until they have acquired proficiency in it, at which point they should switch to the traditional alphabet and spelling.

Systems similar to the ITA system began as early as 1551. In that year John Hart suggested a new set of principles of spelling, and in 1569 in *Orthographie* he proposed to teach reading by using an alphabet that has as many letters as there are sounds or voices in speech. By 1845 there were twenty-six "phonetic alphabets" for teaching reading, including those of Benjamin Franklin and Brigham Young.

Figure 8–8 illustrates the ITA alphabet.

The Diacritical Marking System

Edward Fry (1964) suggested the use of diacritical markings to indicate how each of the traditional letters should be pronounced or to regularize the phoneme-grapheme relationship. Fry refers to this as the diacritical marking system or DMS. The diacritical markings are meant to be temporary, soon to be replaced by normal spelling and writing.

Figure 8–8   Initial Teaching Alphabet

The value of the system is said to lie in (1) the ease with which children can transfer their learning to regular orthography, because the basic word shape is preserved, and (2) the fact that difficulty with spelling is not increased, as is the case with ITA.

Fry recommends that (1) regular consonants and short vowels be unchanged; (2) that silent letters bear a slash mark (*wrīte*); (3) that long vowels have a macron over the vowel (*māde*); that *schwa* sounds be marked with a dot (*àgō*); that digraphs have a bar under both letters (*shut*); and that other exceptions have an asterisk above the letter (o*f*).

Words in Color

Caleb Gattegno, in *Words in Color*, 1977 (Educational Solutions), proposes a synthetic phonic approach using color as a cue to pronunciation and meaning. Each of the forty-seven sounds (twenty-seven consonants, twenty vowels) is represented by one color, even though it can be *written* in numerous ways. For example, the sound of short *i* may be written as *a (senate)*, *ai (mountain)*, *ay (always)*, *e (pretty)*, *ea (guinea)*, *ee (been)*, *ei (forfeit)*, *eo (pigeon)*, *ey (money)*, *i (sit)*, *ia (carriage)*, *is (sieve)*, *o (women)*, *u (busy)*, *ui (build)*, or *y (hymnal)*, but in Gattegno's system these letters would all be colored red. The letter *a*, colored white, represents the /ă/ in *bat*; when colored blue-green, it is the /ā/ in *lane*. The u as in *but* is yellow, the *i* as in *pin* is red, the *e* as in *pet* is blue, and the *o* as in *pot* is orange. The consonant *p* is brown, the *t* is purple, *s* is dark lilac, and so on. Unfortunately, discrimination of the individual hues is not easy for some children.

Programmed Learning Models

Today numerous materials designed to teach reading are being presented in programmed form. Programmed materials are an innovation emphasizing self-instruction, increased pupil participation, and almost immediate feedback of results. Programmed materials have the following obvious advantages:

1. They provide immediate knowledge of success or failure.
2. They permit each pupil to advance at his or her own success rate.
3. They require pupils to progress through a logical sequence of steps of increasing difficulty, each step being so small that it can be met successfully, and yet leading pupils closer to full mastery.
4. They prohibit the bypassing of any step without mastery.
5. They provide for readiness by presenting material of appropriate difficulty.
6. They provide the teacher with a rather accurate measure of where the pupils are and thus may lead to more meaningful homework and study.
7. They require pupils to listen or read carefully and to give their full attention. Unlike what is possible in the classroom, the teaching material cannot flow on without the pupil's attention. The program sits idle if the learner is not concentrating on the task at hand.

Examples of programmed materials are:

1. *The Macmillan Reading Spectrum* (Macmillan).
2. *Peabody Rebus Reading Program* (American Guidance Service).
3. *Programmed Reading*, 3rd Edition (Webster-McGraw-Hill).
4. *Distar* (Science Research Associates).
5. *Phonics for Pupils* (Croft Educational). Two programs covering the entire phonics program.
6. *Building Reading Power* (Charles E. Merrill). Seven booklets on contextual clues and structural analysis for upper grade students.
7. *Mott Reading Programs* (Allied Educational Council). Phonics Workbooks.

Individualized Models

Three computer-program models designed to individualize instruction are *Individually Prescribed Instruction*, developed at the University of Pittsburgh; *Computer-Assisted Instruction in Reading*, developed at Stanford University; and the *Wisconsin Design for Reading Skill Development*, developed at the University of Wisconsin.

Individually Prescribed Instruction assigns individual lessons to each child on the basis of pretest information and teacher observation. Objectives are arranged in sequential order by area of study.

Computer-assisted instruction has generally been restricted chiefly to the teaching of word-recognition skills. It replaces both teacher and book as the primary instructional aids and substitutes the computer. The Stanford project, *Computer-Assisted Instruction in Reading*, originated by Richard Atkinson, has received a good deal of attention. Atkinson feels that the computer should be used as a tool to free the teacher for more creative forms of instruction.

In Atkinson's program, visual material is presented on a screen, which is the face of a cathode-ray tube, and auditory stimuli are presented on a tape recorder. Responses are made with a light pen. When the light pen touches the face of the cathode-ray tube, the computer determines from the location touched whether the response was correct or wrong.

The computer flashes on the screen: "Name and number, please." The pupil types out her name and identification number: "Amy, 1026." The computer greets the pupil back: "Hello, Amy." After each drill exercise, the computer records the number and percentage of right and wrong answers and diagnoses Amy's weak areas. Each time Amy sits down to the terminal, the computer gives her a lesson where she needs more practice. The computer may say: "One of your words (*coat, caught*) is spelled wrongly. Type it correctly." If the pupil types *caught*, a star appears on the screen, giving immediate reinforcement. If she had given a wrong answer, the computer would have said: "Please try again."

The Wisconsin Design for Reading Skill Development stresses word attack, comprehension, study skills, self-directed reading, interpretative reading, and creative reading.* It is a management system designed to individualize instruction. Diagnostic tests are used by the teacher to assess pupil competency in each skill area. The teacher then directs each pupil to appropriate reading activities, using a resource file keyed to hundreds of commercially available texts. Progress tests keyed to specific objectives measure pupil mastery of each skill. The foundation of the entire Design is the outline of reading skills. It is a scope-and-sequence program of reading skills for kindergarten through grade six.

SUMMARY

Chapter 8 has described three ways of introducing reading, outlined the directed reading activity, discussed the difference between identification and recognition, identified word-identification strategies, developed a categorization of reading methods (analytical-synthetic), and outlined five general methods for teaching reading. Four of these were whole-word methods (the whole-word sight-configuration method, the linguistic method, the kinesthetic method, and the eclectic method); another group of methods begins with word parts (the synthetic phonic method).

There is no one best method for teaching word identification. There may be a best method for a given learner. There may be a best method for a special segment of the learner population. There may even be a best method for a given teacher because he or she is most comfortable with it. Teachers of reading thus have to look at many methods. Because they do not know which reading method may prove the best for them, they ought to consider a variety of possibilities, each of which might have some merit and validity in a specific teaching situation. There certainly is little justification for a situation which results in the same treatment for everyone year after year.

There is something to be learned from each of the methods, and best teaching may include all of the following:

1. Teach pupils a coding system that they can apply to other words. This comes to mean
    a. Pupils need to identify the sequences of letters and the sequences of sounds in words.
    b. Pupils need to learn the phoneme-grapheme correspondences.
    c. They can learn these best in the context of a whole word, using the principle of minimal difference to do so. Children are viewed as learners capable of discrimination and generalization who can, with guidance, learn a generalized coding system which they can use in identifying numerous words not previously seen.

* Available from National Computer Systems, Inc., 4401 West 76th Street, Minneapolis, Minn. 55435.

2. Use all senses. Have the pupils see, hear, say, and write the word. The effect of the engagement of all pathways to the brain is to strengthen the memory for automatic recall of all the associated patterns.

3. Have the pupils trace the letter or word.

4. Use a spelling-writing approach. Sooner or later the learner must be able to spell and write the letter or the word from memory.

5. Teach pupils the phonograms: have pupils hear, say, write, and read the phonogram.

6. Use color and diacritical markings to regularize the phoneme-grapheme correspondences.

7. Have children say the sentence, after they have read it mechanically, as they would "talk it" to a companion.

8. Use the oral neurological-impress method (Heckelman 1969) the imitative method, or the repeated reading method (Dahl and Samuels 1975; Samuels 1979) to develop fluency in reading and automaticity in sounding words. For a description of these, see p. 239.

9. If the pupil does not or cannot identify the word through the whole-word methods, use a synthetic phonic approach. In general, research and experience have shown that an analytical or whole-word approach has worked with most children. However, they have also shown that the analytic method has not worked with all children and that the synthetic method has worked with some children.

Perhaps a few generalizations are apropos in closing this chapter.

1. Most children learn to read regardless of the method chosen for teaching them. Many different methods can and do eventually lead to reading proficiency. One type of program does not seem to be clearly superior to all others or best for all children.

2. The choice of method *can* make a world of difference for the individual child, however. Reading disability seems to require both a predisposition in the pupil and an initial approach that ignores pupil differences.

3. The method that works best for a given child depends on the individual child. Not all children profit to the same extent from a given method. The task facing teachers is that of identifying the pupil who learns best with a given method. Until it is possible to standardize youth, it seems unwise to standardize reading method. If children were all alike, we might look for *the* method. Indeed, we would have found it long ago. If all children were identical, with identical experiences, we would not find individual differences among them. And without the individual differences, we would have no need for a variety of methods. If there were no differences, there would be no need to differentiate. But the fact is that children are different from one another intellectually, physically, emotionally, socially, and perceptually, and they seem to be differentiated on the basis of the reading method that is most beneficial to them.

4. No one program seems to provide for *all* the child's reading requirements. The effectiveness of any one method is increased when it includes other instructional components.

5. The "best" method for *most* children has both an analytical *and* a synthetic emphasis. Today most teachers use a combination or eclectic approach. Some begin with the total word and then *more or less* simultaneously break it down into its phonemic elements (analytic-synthetic method). Others begin with the phonemes and then combine these to form meaningful words (synthetic-analytic method).

Children need to perceive the whole word while at the same time taking in those characteristics that individualize the word.

6. Some teachers do not make use of the best material that is available, but if the teacher is a good teacher, other factors often pale into insignificance.* Differences in program effectiveness often can be attributed to teacher effectiveness. The teacher's effectiveness with a specific method depends to a great degree on understanding the pupil being taught. The really successful teacher is one who has developed an extraordinary sensitivity to the differences among children in the classroom and makes adjustments for them. A method of teaching is adequate only if the teacher knows enough about the child to be able to adapt the method to the child.

7. A given method may well produce excellent results under one set of conditions, but may result in failure under a different set of circumstances.

QUESTIONS FOR DISCUSSION

1. What are three major ways of introducing the pupil to reading and what are the relative strengths and weaknesses of each?

2. Discuss the merits of the directed reading activity in teaching both word identification and comprehension.

3. What are the differences between word identification and word recognition?

4. Discuss the application of the various word-identification strategies in acquiring a sight vocabulary.

5. Identify the specific merits of the five major methods discussed in the chapter.

6. How does the pupil develop a coding system for identifying words?

7. What are the major values of ITA, words in color, and the diacritical marking system?

8. Discuss the thesis that good readers must develop some sort of coding system which permits them to achieve independence in attacking words.

9. Discuss:
   a. The unit of meaning and of recognition may not be the unit of identification.
   b. The basic pattern or gestalt in language is the phoneme-phonogram interrelationship rather than the size or shape of the word.
   c. The good identifier of words learns a coding system based on the transitional probabilities that characterize letter sequences in English and that characterize the sound-print relationships of the language.
   d. The basic identification skill is the "seeing" of the sound in the printed symbol.

* See Dechant 1965a.

9

TEACHING THE CONSONANT PHONEME– GRAPHEME CORRESPONDENCES

Chapter 8 presented the basic word-identification strategies and stressed the significance of pupils' learning a code that will help them to identify words with ease. The within-word cues that pupils can use to identify words include configuration cues, phonic cues, and structural or morphemic analysis cues. Chapters 9 and 10 focus on the phonic cues. They emphasize the development of an understanding of the correspondences between the English spelling system and the English sound system, or in other words, the grapheme-phoneme correspondence.

The purpose of phonics instruction is to help the pupil to associate printed letters with the sounds that they represent. It is not implied, however, that reading is simply the recognition of the symbol-sound correspondences to the point where the reader responds to the marks with appropriate speech. The pupil must learn to crack the graphic code (the letter-sound relationships), but reading should not be equated with cracking the code. Reading is more than simply pronouncing.

Why phonics? Why is it necessary to teach phonics? Perhaps the answer to this question is best attained and illustrated by using an example. In the sentence, "The boy fell down the _____," the blank line might be completed by any number of words: *stairs, steps, hill, cellar*, among others. Only by using phonic skills can the pupil arrive at the correct word.

As indicated in Chapter 8, children need to learn a coding system which permits them to attack new words with ease and with accuracy. In 1964, in our book *Improving the Teaching of Reading*, we wrote: In reading, good teaching seems to mean that the teacher must devise techniques of instruction which help the pupil to construct a generic code or a coding system that has wider applicability in reading than would the rote identification of individual words and which permits the pupil to analyze new words without having to learn a new configuration each time.

Chapters 9 and 10 are designed to provide teachers with the principles and the knowledge necessary to help the pupil develop such a coding system. Teachers must know *what* phonic skills need to be taught, *when* to teach them, *why* they should be taught, and *how* they should be taught. If the pupil needs to learn to identify the word using the idiosyncratic features that individualize each word and if these are the grapheme-phoneme correspondences, then it follows that the teacher must know what correspondences to teach.

Phonics instruction and knowledge of the characteristics that individualize words present so many elements that the end result might be confusion rather than clarity of insight. If children had formally to be taught and to learn every contrast as an individual unit of knowledge, or indeed even if they had to formally learn every principle or generalization proposed in this and the subsequent chapter before learning to read, few might be termed readers and those of us who are readers would gladly exclaim, "Thank God, I have learned to read."

Yet the good reader has a functional knowledge of the phonic skills discussed in this section. And if the pupils are ever to become mature readers, they must be adept in the use of the graphic or written code of language.

It would also seem that the artful teacher needs a much vaster, more systematic, and more generalized knowledge than the good reader. Teachers need to know *why* a word is pronounced as it is. They need to be familiar with the complexities of the language. They need to know this information so that they can diagnose where the pupil's reading deficiency lies.

The teacher should remember that phonic skill is not developed overnight. It is impossible to suggest at what time children should have mastered the phonic skills or indeed whether they ever need to master all of them. Not every child can learn every skill. There will be and should be individual differences in this area as in most other areas of human accomplishment. A great amount of phonics emphasis may be contraindicated for slow learners and for those with language or auditory deficiencies.

TERMINOLOGY

Before getting into the specifics of phonics instruction, examine a few terms. The terms that are of interest here are phonology, phonetics, phonemics, phonemes, morphology, syntax, phonics, graphemes, letters, orthography, alphabet, and morphemes.

1. *Phonology* is the study of speech sounds; it includes the study of both phonetics and phonemics. In most communication, and hence in language, there is the **intention** to communicate something; the **intention** is then translated or encoded into symbols or words, and the necessary sounds are emitted. This latter process is termed phonation. The receiver of the communication in turn must hear the sounds (audition), must translate them (recoding), and must comprehend them (decoding).

2. *Phonetics* is the study of speech production; it is the study of the sound or phones used in speech, including their pronunciations, the symbolization of the sounds, and the action of the larynx, tongue, and lips in sound production. Phonetics does not concern itself with the ways words are spelled by the traditional alphabet. It seeks to develop phonetic alphabets which represent graphically the actual pronunciations of linguistic forms. Dictionaries contain phonetic transliterations. Phonetics furthermore deals with the variant pronunciations in different regions of a country and with the perception of speech sound by the hearing mechanism. *Applied* phonetics includes (1) correction of defective speech; (2) teaching of "standard" speech in a given region; and (3) devising symbols to represent speech sounds.

3. *Phonemics* is the study of how sounds function to convey differences of meaning; it is the study of the speech sounds that are used in a language. It is thus a study of phonemes. Phonemic analysis deals only with those sounds that are significant in the language (the phonemes) and ignores the nonsignificant differences (the allophones). The *p* sound in *pet, spot, suppose,* and *top* is slightly different in each instance, but the difference is considered to be nonsignificant.

   Basically two kinds of sound are produced by the human speech mechanism. Phones are speech sounds of any kind. Young children always produce a far greater number of sounds than they later use in the language. Phonemes are speech sounds that are a part of the language; phones are not. Thus, all phonemes are phones, but not all phones are phonemes.

4. The *phonemes,* of which there are forty-four in the English language, have one prime purpose in language. They are the smallest units of sound that can differentiate one utterance from another. For example, a single letter, representing a simple sound, completely changes the meaning in the following sentences: "A stitch in time saves none" "There's no business like shoe business."

   Phonemes are not single sounds; they are rather a collection of sounds; they are a class of closely related sounds; they are perhaps better described as a network of differences between sounds (Hockett 1958).

5. *Morphology* is the study of the meanings of language and of word form and word structure. Morphology and syntax compose the grammar of the language.

6. The smallest unit of printed word structure is the *grapheme.* The *morpheme* is the smallest unit of word structure that has meaning. A grapheme is a class of closely related graphs (*letters* or combinations of letters, for example *sh*) constituting the

smallest unit of writing that distinguishes one printed word from another. The grapheme as such has no meaning. The writing of graphemes in proper order to form morphemes is *orthography* or spelling. The set of graphic shapes that represent the phonemes of the language is the *alphabet*.

The grapheme is described as the counterpart of a phoneme. This distinguishes it from a letter. There are twenty-six letters in the alphabet, but there are many more graphemes. The word *cat* has three letters and three graphemes; the word *that* has four letters, but only three graphemes. The combination *th* is one grapheme. The word *brag*, has four letters and four graphemes; the *b* and *r* in *br* do not lose their individual identity. *Th* is a digraph, but *br* is a blend.

7. *Syntax* is the manner in which words are grouped into utterances or sentences. An utterance is a series of words that is spoken at one time.

Figure 9–1 illustrates the various facets of language.

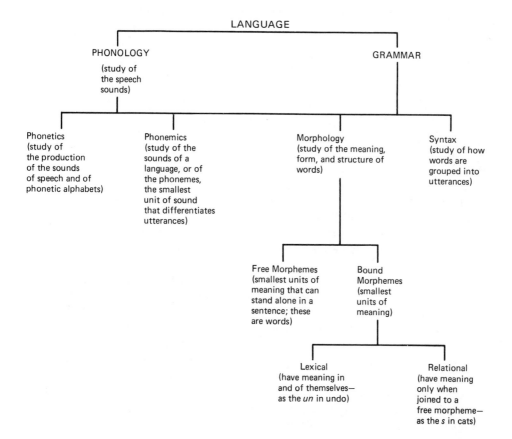

Figure 9–1 Various Facets of Language

THE NATURE OF PHONICS

Phonics relates the phonemes (the smallest units of sound) *to the graphemes* (the smallest units of printed word structure that differentiate printed words). Since phonics is the major concern of this chapter, let us single it out for more extensive treatment.

Phonics is the study of the phoneme-grapheme correspondences. It is the study of the speech equivalents of printed symbols and the use of this knowledge in identifying and pronouncing printed words. It is the study of the sound-letter relationships or of the relationships of phonemes to the printed or written symbols that represent them (the graphemes) and their use in discovering the pronunciation of printed and written words. Phonics is therefore the part of phonology and phonetics that is most involved in reading instruction (Harris and Sipay 1975).

Phonics instruction represents the various teaching practices that aim to develop the pupil's ability to sound out a word by matching the letters by which a word is spelled with the specific sounds which these letters represent. Phonic analysis is the actual process of sounding out letters or letter combinations to arrive at the pronunciation of the word.

Phonics is not intended to teach children how to pronounce the word. They already know that. What pupils need to learn is that printed symbols represent the sound or pronunciation of a word that they have already learned to say.

Word analysis is an inclusive term that subsumes all methods of identifying words. Phonics is one form of word analysis.

Phonics instruction (and consequently phonic analysis) is not reading; it is only one of the skills required for successful reading. It is not even the only method of word attack. Other ways of identifying and recognizing a word include the use of picture clues, the configuration of the word, context clues, and structural analysis. Children use all types of cues (phonic, grammatical, and meaning) to recognize words, but toward the end of first grade children become more reliant upon phonic cues. High-achieving children use phonic cues to a greater degree than do low achievers.

Word-attack skills are needed to attain one of the basic goals of teaching reading. It is hoped that readers eventually will commit the word so well to memory that they can respond to it spontaneously without having "to figure it out"; each word should then become a sight word that is instantly recognized.

The teaching of the phoneme-grapheme correspondence is built upon (1) the identification and discrimination of one sound from another, and (2) the visual discrimination of the letters that represent language sounds. Pupils should be able to see differences in printed letters and words, and they should learn to differentiate the separate sounds in spoken words. The teaching task that remains is one of developing an association or correspondence between the phoneme and grapheme.

Consider now the specifics of phonic instruction.

TEACHING THE BEGINNING
CONSONANT CORRESPONDENCES*

Pupils need to learn what is meant when the teacher says, "This word begins with an *m, t, h, p,* or *n* sound." Pupils must also learn to deal with beginning consonant substitution. They need to learn what changing the initial consonant does to the sound and the meaning of a word.

For years educators have debated the question whether consonants or vowels should be introduced first. The question is somewhat irrelevant. If pupils are to begin with complete words, consonants and vowels must necessarily be introduced concomitantly. Nevertheless, most word-identification methods introduce consonants before vowels, and the reasons usually include the following:

1. There is a greater correspondence between the consonant sounds and the letters used to represent them than between the vowel sounds and the letters used to represent them. Many consonants represent only one sound.
2. Consonant letters are more significant in the perceptual image of a word (thus, "J-hnn-- h-t th- b-s-b-ll" is more readily identified than "-o---ie -i- --e -a-e-a--").
3. Consonant letters to a great degree determine the sound of the vowel, whereas vowels rarely affect the sound of the consonant. For example, in one-syllable words the vowel is usually short when it is in the beginning or the middle position and followed by a consonant.
4. Most of the words met in beginning reading begin with consonants. Some 80 percent (175 words) of the 220 words on the Dolch Basic Sight Word List begin with consonants.
5. It makes sense to have the child work through the word from left to right, and this means beginning with the first letter, which commonly is a consonant.

The Consonant Sounds
of the Language

Table 9–1 summarizes the twenty-five consonant sounds of the English language. Each of the individual consonant letters (with the exception of *c, q,* and *x,* represents a distinct phoneme, resulting in a total of eighteen distinct phoneme-grapheme correspondences. There are seven additional consonant phonemes: /ch/, /sh/, /th/, /th/, /ng/, /hw/, and /zh/. The digraph *th* represents /th/ as in *either* and /th/ as in *ether; wh* represents /hw/; and the /zh/ sound occurs in the language, but not so the letter combination *zh.*

Consonant sounds are either *voiced* or *unvoiced.* They are voiced if they

---

* Numerous commercial materials are available for teaching the variant consonant phoneme-grapheme correspondences. Dechant (1981b), lists materials useful in teaching the consonant correspondences, pp. 77–97; and also lists materials designed specifically for teaching beginning consonants, pp. 97–100; for teaching end consonants and the phonograms, pp. 100–107; and for teaching beginning and ending consonant clusters, pp. 107–110.

Table 9-1 The Consonant Sounds of the Language

PLOSIVES		FRICATIVES		NASALS	SEMIVOWELS	
Voiced	*Unvoiced*	*Voiced*	*Unvoiced*	*Voiced*	*Voiced*	*Unvoiced*
/b/	/p/	/th/	/th/	/m/	/r/	/h/
/d/	/t/	/v/	/f/	/n/	/l/	/hw/
/g/	/k/	/z/	/s/	/ng/	/y/	
		/zh/	/sh/		/w/	
		/j/	/ch/			

are accompanied by vibration of the vocal cords; they are unvoiced if there is no vibration of the vocal cords.

The voiced consonants (/b/, /d/, /g/, /j/, /l/, /m/, /n/, /ng/, /r/, /**th**/, /v/, /w/, /y/, /z/, /zh/) can only be vocalized in connection with a vowel sound (for example, /bē/). The sound represented by *f*, on the other hand, can be made with the upper teeth and the lower lip without using the vocal cords; it is therefore termed an unvoiced sound, and the consonant *f* is an unvoiced consonant. The unvoiced consonants are /ch/, /f/, /h/, /hw/, /k/, /p/, /s/, /sh/, /t/, and /th/.

Table 9–2 lists the consonant letters and also the twenty-five distinct consonant sounds of the language. The consonants *b*, *f* (except in *of*), *h*, *j*, *k*, *l*, *m*, *p*, *r*, *v*, *w*, and *y* represent only one sound. The table also includes the variant spellings of each of the consonant sounds.

Introduction of the Initial Consonants

The pupil encounters difficulty with consonants on three levels: (1) Not all sounds are equally easy to articulate; (2) not all letters are equally easy to identify; and (3) some consonant letters may represent an unusual number of sounds. Look at each of these.

First, there is an order of primitivity of sounds. Sounds generally are produced by children in the following sequence: /m/, /p/, /b/, /t/, /d/, /n/, /h/, /w/, /f/, /v/, /k/, /g/, /h/, /th/, /sh/, /zh/, /ch/, /j/, /s/, /z/, /r/, and /l/. Most articulatory errors made by primary children involve /f/, /l/, /r/, /s/, /sh/, /k/, /th/, and /ch/.

Second, the letters themselves present problems for the pupil. The most frequently confused pairs of letters, in rank order, by nonreading kindergarteners are: *p-g*, *d-b*, *d-q*, *d-p*, *b-p*, *h-u*, *i-l*, *k-y*, *t-u*, *c-e*, *d-h*, *h-n*, *h-y*, *j-k*, and *n-u*.

Third, some letters may represent more than one sound: for example *c* may represent /k/ *cat*, /s/ *city*, or /sh/ *vicious*. The letter *x* represents five distinct sounds: the sound of /ks/ in *box*, of /gz/ in *exist*, of /ksh/ in *anxious*, of /gzh/ in *luxurious*, and of /z/ in *xylophone*.

Many errors in reading arise from the fact that children cannot or do not

Table 9–2 Consonant Phoneme-Grapheme Correspondences

GRAPHEME	PHONEME	SPELLING OF THE PHONEME
b	/b/ bat	bad, rabbit
c	/k/ cat; /s/ city /sh/ vicious	
d	/d/ dog; /j/ soldier /t/ helped	did, add, filled
f	/f/; /v/ of	fat, effort, laugh, phrase
g	/g/ go; /j/ giant; /zh/ garage	go, egg, ghost, guest, catalogue
h	/h/ hat	he, who
j	/j/ judge	jam, bridge, verdure, tragic, exaggerate, soldier
k	/k/ key	coat, account, chemistry, back, acquire, sacque, kind, folk, liquor
l	/l/ lamp	land, tell
m	/m/ mask	drachm, paradigm, calm, me, climb, common, solemn
n	/n/ not; /ng/ finger, bank	gnaw, knife, mnemonic, no, manner, pneumonia
p	/p/ pet	cup, happy
q(u)	/kw/ quit; /k/ liquor; /k-w/ liquid	
r	/r/ run	run, rhythm, carry, wrong
s	/s/ see; /z/ his; /sh/ sure; /zh/ treasure	cent, nice, psychology, say, scent, schism, miss
t	/t/ top; /ch/ picture; /sh/ nation	stopped, bought, ptomaine, tell, Thomas, button
v	/v/ van	of, Stephen, very, flivver
w	/w/ west	choir, quick, will
x	/ks/ box; /gz/ exact; /z/ xylophone; /ksh/ anxious; /gzh/ luxurious	
y	/y/ yes	opinion, hallelujah, yes
z	/z/ zoo; /s/ waltz; /zh/ azure	has, discern, scissors, Xerxes, zero, buzz
ch	/ch/ church; /j/spinach; /sh/ chef /k/ Christmas	child, watch, righteous, question, future
ng	/ng/ ring	ink, long, tongue
sh	/sh/ ship	ocean, machine, special, pshaw, sure, schist, conscience, nauseous, she, tension, issue, mission, nation
th	Unvoiced /th/ thin Voiced /t͟h/ then, /t/ Thomas	thin then, breathe
wh	/hw/ wheat; /h/ who /zh/	where garage, measure, division, azure, brazier

discriminate certain sounds orally and consequently neither make the sound properly nor form the proper association between the spoken element and the written element. The teacher thus must determine what phonetic elements should be taught, in what order they should be taught, and how they might be taught best.

The presentation that follows deals with each of the consonant letters and the sounds that they represent in the following order:

1. *B, C (hard sound), D, G (hard sound), H, J, M, N, P, T, W*
2. *F, L, R, S*
3. *C* (soft sound), *G* (soft sound)
4. *K* and *Q*
5. *V, X, Y, Z*

The purpose in this material is twofold: (1) to identify the sounds that the individual consonants represent in the initial position—hence, the initial-consonant grapheme-phoneme correspondences; and (2) to identify all of the pronunciations that each of the consonant letters represents, even though some of these occur only in the middle or at the end of words.

The Letters B, C (Hard Sound), D, G (Hard Sound), H, J, M, N, P, T, W

The letters *b, h, j, m, p,* and *w,* represent only one sound. In the initial stages of phonic teaching, or at the preprimer level, the pupils should be taught each of these letters and the sounds that they represent. The common sounds of *c*/*k*/, *d*, *g*/*g*/, *n*, and *t* are also taught at this level. The variants of *c*/*s*/ as in *city*, of *g*/*j*/ as in *giant*, and of *d*, *n*, and *t* need to be taught somewhat later.

Examine now the less common representations of *d, n,* and *t.*

THE SOUNDS REPRESENTED BY D: /d/, /j/, /t/

The letter *d* usually represents /d/ as in *danger.* It may also represent /j/ as in *soldier* or *individual.* It is silent before *g* (*badger, dodger, edge*) and in such words as *adjunct, adjust, handkerchief, handsome,* and *Wednesday.*

D in combination with *u* often is pronounced /j/ as in *gradual, deciduous, schedule, fraudulent, nodule, pendulum, graduate, individual, residual,* and *incredulous*; it may also represent /d/ as in *dual, duel,* and the like. *D* in combination with *i* has the /j/ sound in only two words: *soldier* and *cordial.* In the combination *ed,* the *d* represents /t/ when *ed* follows an unvoiced consonant (/ch/, /f/, /h/, /hw/, /k/, /p/, /s/, /sh/, /t/, /th/) as in *puffed, packed, dipped,* and *wished.*

THE SOUNDS REPRESENTED BY N:
/n/, /ng/

The letter *n* generally represents the voiced /n/ heard in *not* or *fan*. It represents the voiced /ng/ when it occurs before *k* (*bank, drink, dunk,* or *monk*); when it comes before a *c* that represents /k/ as in *uncle;* and when it occurs before a *g* pronounced /g/ as in *finger* /*fing-ger*/, *linger, single,* (but not in *singer*). It is silent after *m* as in *autumn, column, condemn, damn,* and *hymn.*

THE SOUNDS REPRESENTED BY T:
/t/, /ch/, /sh/

The consonant letter *t* represents unvoiced /t/ as in *tent* or *time* or unvoiced /ch/ when it is immediately followed by *ure* as in *picture* or *pasture*. In the combination *ti* (*nation, mention*) or *te* (*righteous*), the *t* may represent /ch/ or /sh/.

The *t* is silent in such words as *bustle, castle, chasten, chestnut, Christmas, fasten, hasten, hustle, listen, mortgage, mustn't, often, soften, thistle, whistle,* and *hautboy.*

For a listing of monosyllabic words containing short vowel sounds and the consonants *b, c* (sounded as /k/), *d, g/g/, h, j, m, n, p, t,* and *w,* see Appendix II.

The Letters F, L, R, S

Children generally have more difficulty articulating *l, r, s,* and at times *f* than the sounds previously considered. In some instances it is absolutely necessary to teach the physical formation of each sound (see Appendix I).

The *f* (with the exception of the word *of*), the *l,* and the *r* always represent one sound. The letter *s* presents more difficulties. It can represent: /s/ as in *see*—unvoiced; /z/ as in *his*—voiced; /sh/ as in *sure*—unvoiced; and /zh/ as in *treasure*—voiced.

The *s* represents /s/:

1. At the beginning of a word or a syllable: *sell, sunset.*
2. As the initial letter of a consonant blend: *best, task, spring.* This usage is regular with *sc, sk, sl, sm, sn, sp, st,* and *sw.* The consonant diagraph *sh* is an exception.
3. In conjunction with another *s* at the end of a word: *dress, miss, fuss, recess.*
4. After unvoiced consonants: *puffs, ducks, maps, cats, myths.*

The *s* represents /z/:

1. After voiced consonants: for example, *b* (*cobs*), *d* (*lids*), *g* (*gags*), *ge* (*judges*), *h* (*highs*), *l* (*pills*), *m* (*hams*), *n* (*vans*), *ng* (*sings*), *r* (*cars*), *v* (*lives*), *w* (*bellows*), voiced *th* (*lathes*).
2. After long vowels (*flies*).

3. At the end of some one-syllable words (*as, has, was, is, his*).
4. When the *s* occurs between two vowels (*closet, miser*). Words ending in *se* may have the sound of /s/ as in *house* or of /z/ as in *arose*.

The *s* represents /sh/ in such words as *mansion, sure, insure, assure, censure, nauseous, sugar;* and when double *s* is followed by a vowel, as *issue, tissue, pressure, fissure.*

The *s* represents /zh/ in words such as *vision, measure, treasure, usury, composure, exposure, fusion.*

The *s* is silent in such words as *aisle, fuchsia, bas-relief, Carlisle, debris, Illinois, island, isle, Louisville, viscount, chamois, corps, rendezvous.*

The Letters C (Soft Sound) and G (Soft Sound)

Before pupils are introduced to the /s/ sound of *c* and the /j/ sound of *g*, they should have learned the hard sound of both letters. The sound represented by *c* and *g* are as follows. The c represents: /k/ as in *cat*—unvoiced; /s/ as in *cent*—unvoiced; or /sh/ as in *vicious*—unvoiced. The g represents: /g/ as in *go*—voiced; /j/ as in *giant*—voiced; or /zh/ as in *garage*—voiced.

C and *g* generally represent a soft sound before *e, i,* or *y; c* becomes an /s/ as in *cede* and *g* becomes a /j/ as in *age*. Sometimes, *c* represents /s/ before *a* as in *façade* and is written *ç*. *C* becomes /sh/ when *c* is followed by *i* as in *vicious, electrician, social, ancient,* or by *e* (*ocean*).

G is /j/ after *e, i,* or *y* except in words like *get, give, girl, tiger, gift, geese, gear, geyser, giddy, gild, gill, gird, girdle,* and *finger.* In words borrowed from the French (*prestige, fuselage, beige, menage, montage, corsage, cortege, barrage, sabotage, espionage, entourage, camouflage, rouge, garage, mirage*) *g* is a /zh/ sound.

Words of one syllable ending with the sound of /j/ are usually spelled with the *dge* ending if the sound is immediately preceded by a short-vowel sound (*edge, fudge*), and with the *ge* ending if the sound is immediately preceded by a long-vowel sound or a consonant (*cage, change*).

G is silent before *n* (gnash, gnat, gnaw, align, arraign, benign) or *m* (*diaphragm*). *C* is silent after *s* (*ascend, ascent, descent, scene, muscle*) when the *sc* is followed by *e, i,* or *y,* in the combination *ck* (*back*), and in such words as *czar, indict, victuals.*

The *gu* combination represents /g/: *guard, guess, guide, guinea, guilt, guitar.* The *gu* in *penguin* represents /gw/; *gue* represents /g/ as in *plague, vague, fatigue, intrigue.*

The Letters K and Q

In the letters *k* and *q*, the consonant blends *nk* and *sk*, and the speech consonant *ck*, the pupil meets new phonic problems. The pupil needs to learn that certain sounds can be written in two ways. The much more common hard *c* and the *k* represent the same sound.

The letter *k*, pronounced /*k*/, occurs infrequently at the beginning of the word. The word *king* is an example of a word in which it does. More commonly the initial *k* sound is represented by *c*. However, the *k* is much more frequent than the *c* at the end of the word.

The speech consonant, *ck*, at the end of the word, preceded by a short vowel, is simply /*k*/ as, for example, in *back, click, cluck*. *Kn* is simply an /*n*/ as in *knack, knell, knit, knock, knob, knoll*.

The combination *nk* is commonly pronounced /*ngk*/. *Ank* is /ăngk/ as in *bank, drank, plant, prank*; *ink* is /ĭngk/ as in blink, drink, ink, pink; *unk* is /ŭngk/ as in *bunk, dunk, flunk, junk*; *onk* is /ŏngk/ as in *honk* or /ŭngk/ as in *monk*.

The letter *q* occurs only in the combination *qu* and usually has the sound of /*kw*/. It also may be simply a /*k*/ as in *liquor, quay, queue*, and *conquer*. Occasionally, the /*kw*/ sound is separated as in *liquid* /lik' wid/. *Que* at the end of a word is simply a /*k*/ sound: *unique, critique, picturesque, plaque*.

The Letters V, X, Y, Z

The *v*, *x*, *y*, and *z* represent many difficulties for children. The *x* can represent five distinct sounds; the *y* functions as a consonant and a vowel; and the *z* can represent /*z*/, /*s*/, or /*zh*/. The *v* represents only one sound.

Look at the *x*, *y*, and *z* in more detail. The sounds represented by *x* are /*ks*/ as in *box*—unvoiced; /*ksh*/ as in *anxious, luxury*; /*gz*/ as in *exact*—voiced; /*gzh*/ as in *luxurious*; and /*z*/ as in *xylophone*—voiced.

The consonant letter *x* usually represents /*ks*/ as in *ax, box, fix, fox*. When it occurs at the beginning of a word (*xylophone*) or in an unstressed syllable that precedes a vowel sound (*exact*), it represents /*z*/ or /*gz*/.

The letter *y* usually represents voiced /*y*/ as in *yacht, yard, year, yes, yet, your, you, yearn, yule*. It may also function as a vowel and then generally represents either /ī/ or /ĭ/. It may also represent other vowel sounds.

The consonant letter *z* usually represents voiced /*z*/ as in *blaze, zip*, or *frieze*. It may also represent unvoiced /*s*/ as in *waltz* or voiced /*zh*/ as in *azure, glazier, seizure*.

It is important to realize that many of the variant sounds of the consonants occur only in the middle or at the end of the word: *d* as /*j*/ (*soldier*); *n* as /*ng*/ (*bank*); *t* as /*ch*/ (*picture*); *s* as /*z*/ (*his*); *s* as /*sh*/ (*mansion*); *s* as /*zh*/ (vision); *x* as /*ks*/ (*box*); *x* as /*gz*/ (exact); *x* as /*ksh*/ (anxious); *x* as /*gzh*/ (luxurious).

Activities for Teaching
the Beginning-Consonant
Correspondences

Many factors may account for difficulties in learning phoneme-grapheme correspondences, among which is any factor that interferes with visual and auditory discrimination. Specific difficulty with phoneme-grapheme correspondences is sometimes referred to as an intersensory transcoding difficulty and may be caused by carelessness, defective hearing, inadequate instruction, or neurological factors.

The following steps outline instructional strategies that are useful in teaching initial-consonant phoneme-grapheme correspondences:

1. *Present the phonic element in context.*

    Present the word that contains the phonic element to be taught in a contextual or sentence setting. The sentence may be one that a pupil has used in a language-experience story, or it may be taken from a selection that the pupils are to read. Thus, if the intent is to teach the beginning *b-/b/* relationship, it may be represented as follows. Write the sentence on the chalkboard, underlining the letter *b* wherever it occurs: "The bug bit the boy on the finger." Tell the pupils that you will help them to identify words like *bug, bit, boy* that begin with the letter *b*.

2. *Associate the sound heard at the beginning of a word with a letter that represents it.*
    A. Have the pupils group under two sound cards or pictures representing *m* and *b* a number of cards with pictures whose names begin with either an *m* or a *b*. The picture cards may represent the following: moon, monkey, mittens, mop, man, mouse, money, map, mail, book, bell, boy, bike, box, bed, bus, bat, boat. The teacher points to the letter *m* on the sound card and says, "This letter says /m/ as in *milk*." The teacher then does the same for *b*. The pupils must say the name of each picture aloud and compare it with the sound card.* This is a picture-sound matching task.

m

b

    B. Have the pupils put a line through each picture that begins like the stimulus word *bell.*

        bell

        It is important that the pupils know the names of the pictures!
    C. Have the pupils look carefully at the letter beginning each of the words under the pictures, and give the letter a name or ask the pupils what the name of the letter is. Sound the words, making sure that the pupils listen carefully to the sound at the beginning of each word.

    * *Teach*, Int. M-1, Walker Educational Book Corporation.
    The art on this page is from Dechant 1981 (p. 278). Reproduced by permission.

D.   Color or underline the *b* at the beginning of each of the words.

E.   Print the letter *b* in color on the chalkboard, again repeat its name, and write out other words beginning with the *b* sound that the youngsters have mentioned. Have pupils name things in the room that begin with /b/.

F.   Associate the letter *b* with the key picture; in this instance with the picture of the bell. Refer to the *b* sound as the "bell" sound.

G.   Have the pupils draw a line from the letter *t* to the pictures whose names begin with the same sound.

H.   Teach pupils to associate the *b* sound with both the capital and lowercase letter *b*. Pupils may be shown that a word like *Ben*, which begins with a capital letter, is sounded in the beginning just like the word *bug*. It is helpful to show the pupils that if a personal name begins with *b*, the capital *B* must be used.

I.   Have the pupils read the sentence containing the target words.

3.   *Use the kinesthetic sense and other senses to reinforce learning.*

4.   *Teach the pupils to differentiate one phoneme-grapheme association from another.*
     In line with what was discussed earlier, the pupils must learn what a given letter does *not* represent. Thus, *b* does not represent /d/. Exercises such as the following teach the distinction between the variant consonants:

A.   Have the pupils draw a line through the two pictures in each row that begin with the same sound.

B.   Have pupils circle each word that begins like the name of the picture.

bat   cat   hog   bug

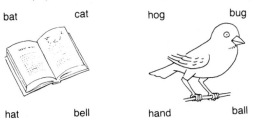

hat   bell   hand   ball

The art on this page is from Dechant 1981 (pp. 278–279). Reproduced by permission.

C. Have the pupils write or circle the proper consonant in various types of exercises.

(1) Have the pupils write the consonant that begins the name of a picture:

a. _____ is the sound that starts   b. _____ is the sound that starts

(2) Have the pupils circle the correct beginning letter sound.

b   b   b
h   d   h
m   h   m

D. Make a circular card with an opening cut in it, similar to the one below. Write a word-ending on the card and put initial consonants on a strip of paper. Have pupils pull the strip of paper through the opening, revealing new words.

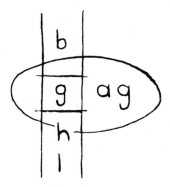

E. Have the pupils draw a line from words which have the same ending, but which begin with different consonants, to the picture which the word represents. This teaches that changing the beginning consonant alters the meaning of the word.

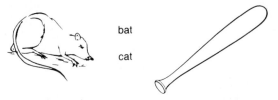

bat

cat

The art on this page is from Dechant 1981 (pp. 279–280). Reproduced by permission.

F. Have the pupils fill in the blank with one of the letters following the end of the sentence, thus giving meaning to the sentence.
   (1) *The pup __it the man.* (*h, b*)
   (2) *Ben has a pet __en.* (*h, b*)
G. Teach pupils the variant sounds of *c* and *g* with exercises such as the following:
   (1) Have students write /*k*/ or /*s*/ below each *c* in a list of words to indicate what the *c* represents. The same exercise also can be used to teach the sounds represented by *g*. The pupils write /*g*/ or /*j*/.

a.	circle	a. got
	/s/ /k/	/g/
b.	cut	b. gem
c.	city	c. give

   (2) Have the pupils make a rule for the sounds represented by *c* or *g* by filling in the blank spaces in a statement like the following: *C* usually represents a soft sound when it is followed by the vowel letters __, __, and __, and it represents a hard sound when followed by the vowal letters, __, __, and __.

Words to Teach Consonant Correspondences

Tables 1 and 2 in Appendix II provide lists of words helpful in teaching the initial consonant correspondences.

TEACHING THE END-CONSONANT CORRESPONDENCES

In whole-word phonics the pupil has to deal visually with the beginning consonant, the median vowel, and the *ending consonant* from the beginning. Consonants generally represent the same sound at the end of the word as at the beginning of the word. However some of the sounds associated with consonants (e.g. *n* = /*ng*/ *bank*; *s* = /*z*/ *has*; *z* = /*s*/ *waltz*) occur only in the middle or at the end of a word. The sounding of final *s* and the doubling of some final consonants call for additional comments.

S at the End of a Word

The letter *s*, at the end of a word, represents /*s*/ after another *s* (*dress, miss*) and after the unvoiced consonants (*puffs, ducks, maps, cats, myths*). It represents /*z*/ at the end of some one-syllable words (*as, has, is, was, his*), after the voiced consonants (gags, bibs, lids) and after long vowels (*flies*).

The *es* ending represents /*s*/ after unvoiced sounds (*takes*) except for sibilants (*s, ss, ch, sh, x*); it represents /*z*/ after the voiced sounds (*goes*) except for sibilants; it represents /*ĕz*/ or /*ĭz*/ after sibilants (*loses, Graces's*).

Doubling of Final Consonants

Some of the consonant letters are doubled at the end of a word. The letters most frequently doubled are *f, l,* and *s.* Other consonants that may be doubled are *b*, *d*, *g*, *m*, *n*, *p*, *r*, *t*, and *z*; for example, *ebb*, *add*, *egg*, Finn, Lapp, *err*, *purr*, *mitt*, and *fuzz*.

The consonants *c*, *h*, *j*, *k*, *g*, *v*, *w*, *x*, and *y* are never doubled at the end of a word. When *cc* and *gg* are followed by *e*, *i*, or *y*, they represent two distinct sounds: *success, suggest*.

The learner's problem with double consonants is more of a spelling problem than a reading problem. The following list of words is useful in teaching the doubling of consonants.

Ending in *FF*	Ending in *SS*	Ending in *LL*		
cuff	*bass*	*all*	*sell*	*till*
huff	*mass*	*ball*	*tell*	*will*
muff	*pass*	*call*	*well*	*dull*
off	*less*	*fall*	*yell*	*bull*
puff	*mess*	*hall*	*fill*	*full*
	hiss	*tall*	*hill*	*pull*
	miss	*wall*	*ill*	
	boss	*bell*	*mill*	
	moss	*fell*	*pill*	
	toss			

The most common exceptions are *as, bus, gas, has, his, if, is, of, pal, plus, this, thus, us, was, yes, dwarf, golf, half, loaf, meal, mail, roof, self, soil, thief, wheel,* and *wolf*.

The techniques which were useful in teaching the beginning consonant may be used in teaching end-consonant substitution. Among these are:

1. Pronounce some words which end with the *t* sound such as *hat, but, net*. The end sound may be slightly elongated or stressed, but it should not be distorted.

2. Have the pupils give other words ending with a *t* sound.

3. Pronounce words, some of which end with the *t* sound and some of which do not. Have pupils raise their hands when the word ends with a *t* sound. The teacher may put pictures (such as those illustrated below) on the board, first asking the pupils to name the picture, and then asking them to identify the pictures or words that have the same ending sound.

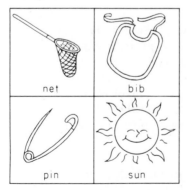

The art on this page is from Dechant 1981 (p. 284). Reproduced by permission.

4. Print the letter *t* on the blackboard and write out the words, *hat, but, net,* or any other word ending with a *t* that the youngsters mentioned.

5. Have the pupils read the words in unison.

6. Show the pupils how substituting one final consonant for another completely changes the word. The word *pet,* for example, may become *pen* or *pep; tan* may become *tap* or *tab.* The pupil must learn that changing the final consonant both alters the word and falsifies the meaning. At this stage the pupil is learning consonant substitution.

Workbooks and other teacher-prepared materials may then be used to teach the end sounds. The following exercises are illustrative:

1. Have the pupils check whether the names of a series of pictures end like a given key word.

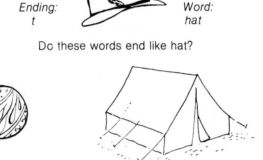

Ending: *Word:*
   t   *hat*

Do these words end like hat?

yes   no   yes   no

2. Have pupils pick from a series of letters the one that completes a word.

b   m   n   p   t

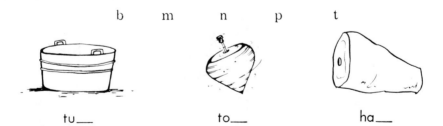

tu___   to___   ha___

3. Have pupils write the proper consonant letter in the blank space. In this exercise the letters are not listed as in exercise two.

The art on this page is from Dechant 1981 (p. 285). Reproduced by permission.

to-   fa-   su-

4. Have the pupils circle the word that the teacher reads. The teacher says "cat" and the pupil must select the correct word from *can, car, cat, cap.*

5. Have the pupils note whether a given letter occurs first or last in a word.
   Is the letter sound above the picture first or last in the word? Circle the correct answer:

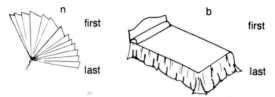

n   first   b   first

last   last

6. Have the students write the beginning and ending letter of the name of a picture.

What letters come before and after the vowel letters?

e   u   i   i

7. Using the principle of minimal contrast, have pupils discriminate between words whose only difference is at the end of the word: *cap, cat*

8. Teach pupils to differentiate between the *s* and *z* sounds with exercises such as the following:
   A.

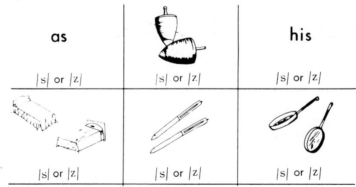

as		his
$\|s\|$ or $\|z\|$	$\|s\|$ or $\|z\|$	$\|s\|$ or $\|z\|$
$\|s\|$ or $\|z\|$	$\|s\|$ or $\|z\|$	$\|s\|$ or $\|z\|$

The art on this page is from Dechant 1981 (pp. 285–286). Reproduced by permission.

as		*his*
/s/ or /z/	/s/ or /z/	/s/ or /z/
/s/ or /z/	/s/ or /z/	/s/ or /z/

B. Have pupils write /s/ or /z/ below each *s* in a list of words to indicate the sound that the *s* represents

ha<u>s</u>	i<u>s</u>
z	z
puff<u>s</u>	pan<u>s</u>
cat<u>s</u>	thi<u>s</u>

TEACHING RHYMING AND THE PHONOGRAMS

After pupils have learned to discriminate auditorially the final consonants, they are generally introduced to rhyming. Thus, pupils first learn to listen to the ending *t* sound as in *bat, bit, lot, hut,* but soon learn that *bat, cat, fat, hat,* and *mat* rhyme. In being introduced to rhyming, pupils are simultaneously being introduced to phonograms or word families. When they learn that *fat* and *cat* rhyme, they are also learning the *at* phonogram.

One of the basic patterns in the language is the phonogram. Some even suggest that the phonogram is the natural unit of the English language. The phonogram is a closed syllable which begins with a vowel (as, for example, *eg, eb, ac, in, ill, ate, ing, oat*) and which produces a single speech sound. The phonogram is generally phonetically stable and regular in sounding, its form is consistent, and it has a basic utility in reading. Thus *an* is a stable unit whether it occurs in initial, medial, or lateral positions: initial—<u>an</u>*imal;* medial—*adv*<u>an</u>*cing;* and lateral—*r*<u>an</u>.

Joos (1966) notes that the sounding of vowels is regulated in most cases by the letter pattern that follows the vowel, and that since the phonogram (*if, ite, ate, ike*) has the vowel plus its following letter pattern, the reader can quickly learn to see the entire pattern as a unit. Joos adds that experience justifies this observation. Pupils taught to analyze words into phonograms quickly read sound-symbol patterns and are safely past letter-by-letter perception.

By the time pupils have mastered the beginning and end consonants and short vowels, they should be able to deal with the following phonograms:

ab	*as*	*ell*	*ib*	*im*	*izz*	*ot*	*um*
ac	*at*	*em*	*ic*	*in*	*ob*	*ox*	*un*
ad	*ax*	*en*	*id*	*ip*	*od*	*ub*	*up*
aff	*az*	*ep*	*if*	*is*	*og*	*ud*	*us*
ag	*eb*	*ess*	*iff*	*iss*	*om*	*uff*	*uss*
am	*ed*	*et*	*ig*	*it*	*on*	*ug*	*ut*
an	*eg*	*ex*	*ill*	*ix*	*op*	*ull(dull)*	*uzz*
ap							

Some other phonograms that pupils might profitably learn in the elementary years are as follows:

ace	ape	ear	ibe	irt	oft	ord	ude
ack	ar	ease	ice	ise	oid	ore	udge
act	ard	eat	ich	ish	oil	ork	uge
ade	are	eck	ick	isk	oke	orn	ule
aft	ark	edge	ide	ist	old	orse	ult
age	arm	eed	ife	itch	ole	ort	umb
aid	arn	eek	ift	ite	oll	ose	ume
ail	arp	eel	igh	ith	olt	oss	ump
aim	art	eem	ight	ive	omb	ost	und
ain	ase	een	ike	ize	ome	otch	une
air	ash	eep	ild	oach	one	ote	ung
ait	ask	eer	ile	oad	ong	oth	unk
ake	ast	eet	ilk	oak	onk	ouch	ur
alk	atch	elm	ilt	oal	ood	ough	ure
all	ate	elt	ime	oam	oof	ought	urn
alt	ave	emp	ince	oan	ook	ound	urt
ame	ay	end	ind	oap	ool	our	use
amp	aw	ent	ine	oar	oom	ouse	ush
and	aze	erd	ing	oast	oon	out	usk
ane	ead	ern	inge	oat	oop	ow	ust
ance	eak	esk	ink	obe	oor	owe	utch
ang	eal	est	int	ock	oot	own	ute
ange	eam	etch	ipe	ode	ope	oy	uy
ank	ean	ew	ird	odge	or	ube	
ant	eap	ey	ire	off	orb	uck	

The following exercises are useful in developing the rhyming skill:

1. Explain the meaning of rhyme and illustrate it by providing words that actually rhyme: *ham, jam, pam,* or *hat, cat, rat, fat.*

2. Have pupils circle the word that rhymes with the name of the picture.

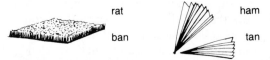

3. Have pupils provide rhymes for simple words such as *cat* or *bed.* The game "Quiz Panel" is quite adaptable to this task. The teacher first selects a panel of four pupils who sit in the front of the room, and then pronounces a word for which individual members of the panel must provide a rhyming word. When panel members miss, they are replaced by other members of the class. A variant form of this exercise involves picture reading. The pupil is shown three pictures, the first of which is of a bat. Of the other two pictures, only one rhymes with *bat.* The teacher asks the pupil to pick out the one that rhymes with *bat.*

The art on this page is from Dechant 1981 (p. 288). Reproduced by permission.

4. Suggest three words, two of which rhyme. Have pupils pick out the word that does not rhyme with the other two words.

5. Have the pupil match pictures (band-hand) whose names rhyme.*

6. Present pairs of words written on cards ⟨ *sing sink* ⟩ , and have the pupils indicate whether or not the words rhyme.

7. Have pupils draw a line from each word in Column 1 to a word that rhymes in Column 2:

1.	2.
bake	*meet*
nose	*rose*
feet	*cake*
tree	*see*

8. Have pupils circle the words that rhyme with the first word: *lone—done, bone, rock, took, some.*

9. Organize words into linguistic spelling patterns and have the pupils suggest other words that fit the pattern:

	a	*e*	*i*	*o*	*u*
b	*bat*	*bet*	*bit*		*but*
c	*cat*			*cot*	*cut*
h	*hat*		*hit*	*hot*	*hut*
p	*pat*	*pet*	*pit*	*pot*	
s	*sat*	*set*	*sit*		

Knafle (1973) found that color or underlining may be effectively used as cues to enhance children's learning of pattern similarities such as *cat, mat, fat.* Color cues and underlining appear to aid the subjects in detecting structure.

TEACHING THE BEGINNING- AND ENDING-CONSONANT CLUSTERS

After pupils have learned to deal with single consonants they should be introduced to consonant clusters. The term, *consonant clusters* includes consonant blends, consonant digraphs, and consonant trigraphs.

Beginning Consonant Blends

Consonant blends consist of two or more letters each having its own distinct sound. The following two-letter beginning consonant blends occur: *bl, br, cl, cr, dr, dw, fl, fr, gl, gr, pl, pr, sc, sk, sl, sm, sn, sp, sq, st, sw, tr,* and *tw*.

The sounds represented by the consonant blends are those exemplified by key words in the following lists:

* *Teach*, A-D-5, Walker Educational Book Corporation.

bl /bl/ as in *blue*	sc /sk/ as in *scold*
br /br/ as in *bring*	sk /sk/ as in *skate*
cl /kl/ as in *clean*	sl /sl/ as in *sleep*
cr /kr/ as in *cream*	sm /sm/ as in *smoke*
dr /dr/ as in *dress*	sn /sn/ as in *snow*
dw /dw/ as in *dwarf*	sp /sp/ as in *spoon*
fl /fl/ as in *flag*	sq (u) as in *squat*
fr /fr/ as in *free*	st /st/ as in *stand*
gl /gl/ as in *glass*	sw /sw/ as in *swing*
gr /gr/ as in *grass*	tr/tr/ as in *tree*
pl /pl/ as in *play*	tw /tw/ as in *twig*
pr /pr/ as in *pride*	

For additional words illustrative of beginning and ending consonant blends see Appendix II.

Ending Consonant Blends

After pupils have learned to handle some of the beginning consonant blends, they are ready to learn the end consonant blends. A list of final consonant blends includes the following combinations.

ct (act)	lk (elk)	nk (bank)	rd (lard)	rt (art)
ft (raft)	lm (elm)	ns (lens)	rf (dwarf)	sc (disc)
lb (bulb)	lp (alp)	nt (ant)	rl (snarl)	sk (desk)
lc (talc)	lt (fault)	pt (apt)	rm (arm)	sm (spasm)
ld (bald)	mp (pump)	rb (garb)	rn (barn)	sp (clasp)
lf (elf)	nd (band)	rc (arc)	rp (harp)	st (nest)

Consonant Digraphs: ch, sh, th, wh, ng, gh, ph

The letter clusters *ch*, *sh*, *th*, *wh*, and *ng* represent sounds different from every other consonant sound. The consonant clusters *gh* and *ph* are also digraphs, but they represent previously learned consonant sounds; *gh* can represent either /g/ or /f/; *ph* can represent /f/, /v/, or /p/. Digraphs are not a blend of two letters.

THE DIGRAPH *ch*

Ch can represent /ch/ as in *church*; /j/ as in *spinach* or *Greenwich*; /sh/ as in *chef*; and /k/ as in *Christmas*. The /sh/ sound occurs in words of French derivation: *cache*, *chagrin*, *Chicago*, *gauche*, *machine*, *chauffeur*, *chassis*, *chic*, *parachute*, *chaperon*, *brochure*, *charlatan*, *echelon*, *chiffon*, *machinery*, *mustache*. *Ch* has a /k/ sound in some words derived from the Greek and Hebrew such as *chasm*, *chorus*, *Christ*, *Christmas*, *chrome*, *scheme*, *ache*, *chemist*, *chloride*, *choral*, *orchid*, *school*, *echo*, *chaos*, *chord*, *orchestra*, *character*, *architect*, *archives*, *catechism*, *cholesterol*, *chronic*, *hierarchy*, and *oligarchy*. In *drachm*, *schism*, *yacht*, and *fuchsia* the *ch* is silent.

The Digraph *sh*

The diagraph *sh* presents no special problems. It always represents the same sound.

The Digraph *th*

Th can represent the following sounds:

1. Unvoiced /th/ as in *ether:*
   A. When *th* occurs at the end of a word (*bath*) except in *with* and *smooth*; the *th* in *with* may also be unvoiced.
   B. In the combination *ths* when it is preceded by a short vowel sound (*deaths*) or by a consonant (*months*).
2. Voiced /t͟h/ as in *either:*
   A. In the plural of some words (*mouths*).
   B. When *th* is at the beginning of some words (*the, them, there, this, thither*).
   C. In *the* endings (*bathe*).
   D. In *with* and *smooth*.
3. /t/: *Thomas, Esther, Thompson.*
4. /th/ or /t͟h/: in *cloths, truths, youths, wreathes.*
5. *Th* is silent in *asthma.*

The Digraphs *wh, gh, ph, ng*

The combination *wh* may be pronounced as /hw/ (*wheel*), or simply as /h/ before *o* (*who, whom, whole*). The combination, *gh,* may be pronounced as a simple /g/ (*ghost*), it may be an /f/ (*enough*), or it may be silent (*eight, freight, neigh, neighbor, sleigh, straight, weigh, weight*). *Ph* commonly represents /f/ (*phase*). It also may be sounded as /v/ (*Stephen*), as a /p/ (*diphthong, diphtheria, naphtha*), or it may be silent (*phtalin*).

The digraph *ng* represents /ng/ (*sing, rang, long*). The combination *ng* is not always a digraph. In plurisyllables such as *linger, finger,* and *stronger* the *ng* represents /ng-g/. In words like *strange,* the *ng* represents /nj/.

The Phoneme /zh/

The /zh/ sound is never written *zh*. It may be represented by *g* (*garage*), by *s* (*division*), or by *z* (*azure*).

Three-Letter Blends

The pupil also needs to learn to deal with three-letter clusters: *chr, phr, sch, scr, shr, spl, spr, str,* and *thr.* A few illustrative monosyllabic words beginning with these combinations are:

chr /kr/:   *Christ, chrome*
phr /fr/:   *phrase*

sch /*sk*/:	*scheme, school*
scr /*skr*/:	*screech, screen, scroll, script, scrunch*
shr /*shr*/:	*shred, shrewd, shriek, shrill, shrimp, shrub, shrug*
spl /*spl*/:	*splash, spleen, splice, splint, split, splotch, splurge*
spr /*spr*/:	*sprain, sprang, sprawl, spray, spread, spree, spring, sprint, sprite, sprout, spruce, sprung*
str /*str*/:	*strain, strait, strand, strap, straw, stray, streak, stream, street, strength, stress, stretch, stride, strife, strike, string, stripe, strive, strode, stroll, strong, struck*
thr /*thr*/:	*thrash, thread, threat, three, threw, thrice, thrift, thrill, throat, throb, throng, through, throw, thrust*

Consonant Trigraphs

The consonant trigraphs, representing a single speech sound, are *chm* /*m*/ as in drachm; *tch* /*ch*/ as in match; *ght* /*t*/ as in *thought; sch* /*s*/ as in *schism; cht* /*t*/ as in *yacht; chs* /*s*/ as in *fuchsia;* and so forth.

Additional Digraphs

Digraphs are often formed by combinations of letters in which one letter is pronounced and the other is silent. Common combinations are *kn* (*know*), *wr* (*write*), *bb* (*rabbit*), *ff* (*cuff*), *ck* (*lack*), *ll* (*call*), *nn* (*inn*), *rr* (*purr*), *ss* (*hiss*), *tt* (*mitt*).

Other examples include

Silent b after *m:*	*bomb, climb, crumb, dumb, lamb, limb, numb, plumber, succumb, thumb*
Silent b before all consonants except *l* and *r:*	*debt, debtor, doubt, doubtful, subtle (blue, brig)*
Silent c before *k:*	*back, tack*
Silent c after *s:*	*ascend, ascent, descend, descent, scene, scent, scepter, muscle, science, scissors*
Silent d before *g:*	*badger, dodger, edge, fudge*
Silent g before *m:*	*diaphragm*
Silent g before *n:*	*align, arraign, benign, campaign, design, ensign, feign, foreign, gnash, gnat, gnaw, reign, resign, sign, sovereign, mignon, impugn, malign*
Silent k before *n:*	*knack, knap, knee, kneel, knelt, knew, knife, knight, knit, knob, knock, knot, know, knuckle*
Silent m before *n:*	*mnemonic*
Silent n after *m:*	*autumn, column, condemn, hymn, solemn*

Other illustrations of words in which one consonant is not pronounced for one reason or another are

Silent h:	*aghast, ah, exhaust, exhibit, ghost, heir, hemorrhage, honest, honestly, honor, hour, hourly, oh, rhesus, rhetoric, rhinestone,*

rhinoceros, rheumatism, rhubarb, rhumb, rhyme, rhythm, rhythmic, shepherd, Thomas, Thomism, Thompson, Theresa, Thames, Thailand, vehement, vehicle

Silent *l*: *almond, alms, balk, balmy, behalf, calf, calk, calm, chalk, folk, folklore, half, jaywalk, kinsfolk, palm, polka, psalm, salmon, solder, talk, walk, yolk, could, should, would*

Silent *p*: *corps, cupboard, pneumatic, pneumonia, psalm, psalmist, psalter, pseudo, psychiatry, psychic, raspberry*

Silent *s*: *aisle, Arkansas, bas-relief, Carlisle, chamois, corps, debris, Illinois, island, isle, Louisville, rendezvous, St. Louis, viscount*

Silent *t*: *castle, chestnut, Christmas, fasten, hasten, hustle, listen, mortgage, mustn't, often, soften, thistle, whistle, jostle, nestle, rustle, trestle, wrestle*

Silent *w*: *awry, answer, bowler, enwrap, own, owner, rewrite, sword, swordfish, swordsman, toward, two, wrack, wraith, wrangle, wrangler, wrapper, wrath, wreak, wreath, wreck, wreckage, wren, wrench, wrestle, wrestling, wring, wrinkle, wrist, wristband, writ, write, writer, writing, wrong, wrongly, wrote, wrought, wrung, wry;* and in the ending *ow* as in *snow*.

Teaching the *initial consonant blends* begins with the same procedure as the teaching of the beginning consonants. Here are additional exercises:

1. Have the pupils put a line through the two pictures that begin with the same sound.

2. Have the pupils sound the blend at the beginning of the row and put a cross (x) through the picture in the row that begins with the same sound.

gl

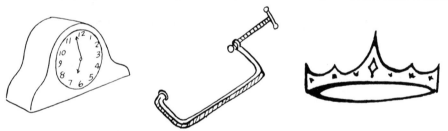

3. Have pupils circle each word that begins like the name of the picture.

The art on this page is from Dechant 1981 (p. 288). Reproduced by permission.

drink   clip   crab   drip

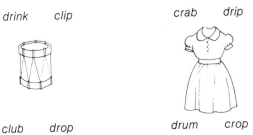

club   drop   drum   crop

4. Have the pupils write or circle the proper consonant blend in various types of exercises.

A. Have the pupils circle the correct beginning letter sound:

dr   br   dr
dw   cl   cr
cr   cr   dr

B. Have the pupils write under each picture the initial consonant blend of the name of each picture:

____og   ____y   ____obe

5. Have the pupils circle the word that gives meaning to the sentence and that agrees with the picture at the end of the line:

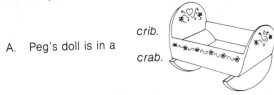

A. Peg's doll is in a   crib.

crab.

6. Have the pupils fill in the blank in the sentence with one of the letters at the end of the sentence, thus giving meaning to the sentence.

A. He is ____apping. (cl, cr)

7. Have the pupils circle the letters that stand for the sound heard at the beginning of a nonsense word: glock = pl, gl, gr, bl.

8. Have the pupils circle the correct one of two printed words, one of which the teacher reads. The teacher reads chair and the pupil selects between chair and share.

The art on this page is from Dechant 1981 (p. 290). Reproduced by permission.

9. Have the pupils write the letters representing the initial sound in a nonsense word such as: *chot, shet, thub.*

Exercises such as the following will be useful in teaching the *end-consonant blends:*

1. Have the pupils check whether the name of a series of pictures ends like a given key word:

ck   duck

Does the word end like du*ck*?

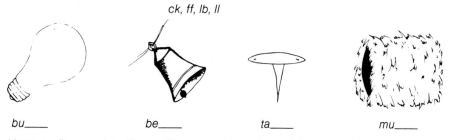

yes   no   yes   no   yes   no

2. Have pupils pick from a series of consonant blends the one that completes the name of a picture:

ck, ff, lb, ll

bu____   be____   ta____   mu____

3. Have pupils complete the spelling of each word by adding *k* or *ck:*

mil____   du____   in____

Another variant of this exercise requires the pupil simply to circle the correct ending:

The art on this page is from Dechant 1981 (pp. 290–291). Reproduced by permission.

4. Have the pupils complete exercises like the following by filling in the correct consonant ending:

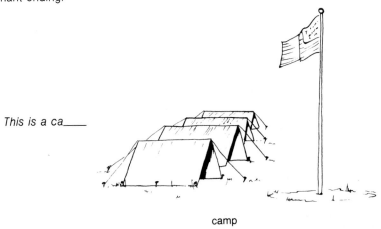

This is a ca____

camp

The following exercises are useful in teaching *consonant digraphs.*

1. Have the pupils look at a picture, say the name of the picture, and select the consonant digraph that represents the beginning or end sound of the name. The first picture illustrated teaches the beginning consonant digraph and the second one teaches the ending consonant digraph.

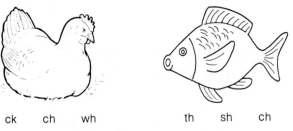

ck   ch   wh   th   sh   ch

2. Have the pupils note whether *ch* occurs at the beginning or end of a word:

Beginning   Beginning   Beginning
CHAIR   **WATCH**   **CHICKEN**
End   End   End

The art on this page is from Dechant 1981 (p. 291). Reproduced by permission.

3. Have the pupils discriminate between the various sounds for the same digraph:

ch: ch, j, sh, k
sh: sh
th: the voiced *th* and unvoiced *th*
wh: hw and h
gh: g, f, or silent
ph: f, v, p, or silent

4. In teaching the discrimination of the various sounds of consonants and digraphs, the teacher may have pupils write the correct sound below each underlined letter combination in a series of words:

butcher	chivalry	this
/ch/	/sh/	/th/
chemist	spinach	physical
/k/	/j/	/f/
Stephen	laugh	whom
/v/	/f/	/h/

METHOD OF TEACHING

The method of word identification that has most to offer in teaching the phoneme-grapheme correspondences would clearly seem to be the linguistic method. It is the only whole-word method that is explicitly designed to develop a code that will permit the pupils to identify words other than through shape or length. It does this by its emphasis on spelling patterns, spelling, and the principle of minimum contrast. Other approaches recommended for automatizing word identification skills and for developing fluency in reading are the neurological impress method, the imitative method, and the repeated reading method. The neurological impress method (Heckelman 1969) is a system of unison reading whereby the student and the teacher read aloud simultaneously at a rapid rate. This approach is especially effective with those who are phonics-bound or who have had intensive phonics training but still are not reading fluently. Langford (1974) found the method to be effective with severely retarded readers.

Hollingsworth (1978) found that the neurological-impress method was effective with fourth-to-sixth-grade remedial-reading pupils when used with as many as ten pupils at a time. Group use was made possible by using the EFI Multi-Channel Wireless Language System.

Other similar approaches are the imitative method (tape a story on the pupil's instructional level and have the pupil listen to the tape and follow along in the book until the pupil can read the story perfectly, fluently, and with expression) or the repeated reading method (Dahl and Samuels 1975; Samuels 1979) which requires pupils to read a passage of one hundred words or less on their instructional level again and again until they can read it fluently without error.

SUMMARY

Chapter 9 has dealt with the consonant phoneme-grapheme correspondences. The following chart summarizes these and may be used as a quick reference.

Consonant Phoneme-Grapheme Correspondences

SINGLE CONSONANTS	CONSONANT COMBINATIONS

Single Consonants Representing One Phoneme

Initial-Consonant Blends

b, f (except in *of*), *h, j, k, l, m, p, r, v, w, y*

bl, br, cl, cr, dr, dw, fl, fr, gl, gr, pl, pr, sc, sk, sl, sm, sn, sp, sq(u), st, sw, tr, tw, chr (kr), phr (fr), sch(sk), scr (shr), shr, spl, spr, str, thr

Single Consonants Representing Two or More Sounds

End-Consonant Blends

c	= /k/ *cat;* /s/ *city;* /sh/ *vicious*
d	= /d/ *dog;* /j/ *soldier;* /t/ *helped*
g	= /g/ *go;* /j/ *giant;* /zh/ *garage*
g(u)	= /g/ *guest, catalogue*
n	= /n/ *not;* /ng/ *finger, bank*
q(u)	= /kw/ *quit;* /k/ *liquor;* /k-w/ *liquid*
s	= /s/ *see;* /z/ *his;* /sh/ *sure, nauseous;* /zh/ *treasure, division*
t	= /t/ *top;* /ch/ *picture;* /sh/ *nation*
x	= /ks/ *box;* /gz/ *exact;* /z/ *xylophone;* /ksh/ *anxious;* /gzh/ *luxurious*
z	= /z/ *zoo;* /s/ *waltz;* /zh/ *azure*

ct, ft, lb, lc, ld, lf, lk, lm, lp, lt, mp, nd, nk, ns, nt, pt, rb, rc, rd, rf, rl, rm, rn, rp, rt, sc, sk, sm, sp, st

Consonant Digraphs Representing a Distinct Phoneme

ch	= /ch/ *church;* /j/ *spinach;* /sh/ *chef;* /k/ *Christmas*
sh	= /sh/ *ship, fish*
th	= /th/ *either;* /th/ *ether;* /t/ *Thomas*
wh	= /hw/ *whee;* /h/ *who*
ng	= /ng/ *sing;* /ng-g/ *finger;* /nj/ *strange*

Additional Consonant Digraphs

bb	= /b/ *rabbit*	*kn*	= /n/ *know*	*sc*	= /z/ *discern*
bd	= /d/ *bdellium*	*lf*	= /f/ *calf*	*sch*	= /s/ *schism*
bt	= /t/ *debt*	*lk*	= /k/ *folk*	*sch*	= /sh/ *schist*
cc	= /k/ *account*	*ll*	= /l/ *call*	*sci*	= /sh/ *conscience*
chm	= /m/ *drachm*	*lm*	= /m/ *alms, calm*	*ss*	= /sh/ *issue*
chs	= /s/ *fuchsia*	*mb*	= /m/ *climb*	*ss*	= /s/ *dress*
ck	= /k/ *back*	*mm*	= /m/ *common*	*ss*	= /z/ *scissors*
ct	= /t/ *indict*	*mn*	= /n/ *mnemonic*	*st*	= /s/ *castle*
cz	= /z/ *czar*	*ngue*	= /ng/ *tongue*	*sw*	= /s/ *answer, sword*
dd	= /d/ *add*	*nn*	= /n/ *manner, inn*	*tch*	= /ch/ *catch*
dge	= /j/ *judge*	*pb*	= /b/ *cupboard*	*tg*	= /g/ *mortgage*
dk	= /k/ *handkerchief*	*ph*	= /f/ *graph;* /p/ *diphthong;* /v/ *Steven*	*tt*	= /t/ *button, mitt*
dn	= /n/ *Wednesday*	*pn*	= /n/ *pneumonia*	*tw*	= /t/ *two*
ds	= /s/ *handsome*	*pp*	= /p/ *happy*	*vv*	= /v/ *flivver*
ff	= /f/ *effort, bluff*	*ps*	= /s/ *psalm*	*wn*	= /n/ *owner*
ft	= /f/ *often*	*psh*	= /sh/ *pshaw*	*wr*	= /r/ *write*
gg	= /j/ *exaggerate;* /g/ *egg*	*pt*	= /t/ *ptomaine*	*xh*	= /x/ *exhaust*
gh	= /g/ *ghost;* /f/ *rough*	*rh*	= /r/ *Durham, myrrh*	*zz*	= /z/ *buzz*
ght	= /t/ *thought*	*rps*	= /r/ *corps*		
gm	= /m/ *paradigm*	*rr*	= /r/ *carry, err*		
gn	= /n/ *align, gnaw*	*sc*	= /s/ *scent*		

QUESTIONS FOR DISCUSSION

1. Define phonics, describe its purpose, and discuss the reasons for studying it.
2. Diagram language and show how phonics relates to language.
3. Outline the basic consonant phoneme-grapheme correspondences, including in your answer:
   A. The total number of phoneme-grapheme correspondences.
   B. How one moves from twenty-one consonant letters to twenty-five distinct consonant phonemes.
   C. The difference between voiced and unvoiced sounds and what consonants these include.
   D. The letters and the variant sounds that they represent.
4. Give three reasons why phonics presents special problems for the pupil.
5. Under what conditions does the *s* represent /s/ and /z/?
6. Which letters tend to double at the end of a word? Give some exceptions to the rule.
7. Describe the three steps in teaching phonographs, defined phonograms, and describe how phonogram teaching might be simplified.
8. List and give examples of the variant beginning- and ending-consonant clusters.

10
TEACHING THE VOWEL PHONEME– GRAPHEME CORRESPONDENCES

Pupils must from the beginning learn to break the alphabetic code, as noted in Chapter 9. This means they must be able to deal with both consonants and vowels. They must become fluent with the short vowel sounds that they hear in words like *bat*, *net*, *pin*, *cot*, and *hut*, but they also need to learn the long *a* sound as in *age*, the long *e* as in *be*, the long *i* sound as in *bite*, the long *o* sound as in *go*, the special *o* sounds as in *off* and in *orb*, and the long *u* sound as in *use* and *rule*.

Since the short vowel occurs much more frequently than the long vowel, the pupil should be taught to sound the vowel as a short sound. If the word thus formed does not sound like a word that the pupil already knows or if it does not make sense in the context, then another attempt must be made.

There are four principles that may help more advanced pupils in arriving at the correct word: the principle of variability, the principle of position, the principle of silentness, and the principle of context.

Before considering these, a few observations seem in order:

1. The pupil learns vowel generalizations or rules best by frequent experiences with words that exemplify the rule.

2. These experiences should be consistent. Thus, exceptions should be learned as sight words.
3. Only those rules which have wide applicability are worth teaching.

The *principle of variability* simply means that the pronunciation of the written vowel may change from one word to another or that the same vowel letter can represent more than one sound. The letter *e* may represent /ĕ/ as in *bed* or /ē/ as in *he*. The pupil gradually must learn and apply such basic variations as the following:

a	*e*	*i*	*o*	*u*	*misc.*
/ă/ hat*	/ĕ/ bed	/ĭ/ bit, crypt**	/ŏ/ lot	/ŭ/ hut	/oi/ toil, boy
/ā/ fade	/ē/ be	/ī/ bite, cry	/ō/ so	/ū/ /yü/ /yōō/ use	/ou/ /aú/ house, now
/ä/ car	/ė/ /ûr/ term		/ȯ/ off, orb	/ü/ /ōō/ rule	
/â/ care				/u̇/ /o͞o/ pull	/ə/ ever

Table 10–1 summarizes the nineteen vowel variations and the variant spellings of each sound.

Examine now the teaching of the short vowel correspondences in more detail.

TEACHING THE SHORT-VOWEL CORRESPONDENCES

Children early learn to articulate both the short and the long vowel sounds. The short vowels or unglided sounds are usually introduced before the long vowels because they occur most frequently in monosyllabic words, are alphabetically more consistent, and occur more frequently in words that pupils meet in initial reading.

As pupils meet the short vowel in words, they gradually become familiar with the second vowel principle, namely, the *principle of position*. The principle of position simply means that the sound represented by the vowel letter changes depending upon its position in the word. The first vowel rule that flows from the principle of position is: *A single vowel letter at the beginning or in the middle of a one-syllable word usually represents its short sound (am, an, as, at, if, in, is, it,*

---

* The semi-circle over a vowel (ă) is a breve; the line over a vowel (ā) is called a macron; the two dots over a vowel (ä) are called a dieresis; the peaked sign over a vowel (â) is termed a circumflex.

** The *y* also functions as a vowel when it immediately follows another vowel letter in a word, as in key.

Table 10-1 Vowel Phoneme-Grapheme Correspondences

GRAPHEME	PHONEME	SPELLING OF PHONEME
a	/ă/ hat	hat, plaid, half, laugh
	/ā/ age	age, aid, gaol, gauge, say, they, basin, break, melee, vein, weigh
	/â/ care	care, air, prayer, where, pear, their
	/ä/ car	father, sergeant, heart
e	/ĕ/ net	many, aesthetic, said, says, let, bread, heifer, leopard, friend, bury
	/ē/ be	Caesar, quay, equal, team, bee, key, these, receive, people, machine, believe, Phoenix
	/ẽr/ or /ûr/ term (accented syllable)	pearl, stern, first, word, turn, journey, myrtle
i	/ĭ/ pin	England, been, bit, carriage, sieve, women, busy, build, hymn
	/ĭ/ or /ē/	here, fear, weird, deer, bier, fakir
	/ī/ ice	aisle, aye, height, eye, ice, lie, high, choir, buy, coyote, sky, rye, type
o	/ŏ/ cot	watch, odd, honest, knowledge
	/ō/ go	hautboy, beau, yeoman, sew, open, boat, toe, home, oh, brooch, soul, though, low
	/ô/ orb, off, all, law	all, Utah, walk, Arkansas, taught, law, order, broad, memoir, bought
oi	/oi/ toil	coil, boy
ou	/ou/ or /aů/ house	house, bough, now
u	/ŭ/ hut	come, does, flood, trouble, cup, twopence
	/ū/ or /yü/ or /yo͞o/ use	beauty, feud, queue, few, ewe, view, use, cue, you, yule
	/ů/ or /o͝o/ put	wolf, good, should, full
	/ü/ or /o͞o/ food	maneuver, threw, adieu, move, shoe, food, croup, through, rule, blue, suit, fruit, two
schwa	/ə/	*Except for the short i /ĭ/ (as in senate, forfeit), the vowel sound in the unstressed syllable almost always becomes /ə/:* about, taken, April, lemon, circus, villain, pigeon, porpoise, vicious.
	/ər/	liar, mother, elixir, honor, honour, augur, zephyr

of, on, up, us, top, hat, pig). Most vowels in monosyllabic words follow this rule. You will recall that the linguistic method is based on the principle that the spelling pattern in which the vowel is placed determines the sound of the vowel: thus, in a cvc or vc word, the vowel letter tends to represent its short sound.

Vowel rule one also commonly applies to monosyllabic words in which the median vowel is followed by a double consonant. In general, the vowel is short: for example, *back, fact, raft, lamp, band, sang, tank, chant, dash, task, last, deck, elm, hemp, bend, lent, desk, west, milk, tilt, sing, sink, hint, fish, risk, fist, sock, duck, cult, jump, fund, sung, sunk, rush.* However, in *igh, ind, ild, old, oll, olt,* and the like, the vowel is long. These combinations are best taught as phonograms or as word families. For example:

<table>
<tr><td>1. Long i with igh:</td><td>bright, fight, flight, fright, high, knight, light, might, night, right, sigh, sight, slight, thigh, tight</td></tr>
<tr><td>with ind:</td><td>bind, blind, find, grind, hind, kind, mind, rind, wind (also wĭnd)</td></tr>
<tr><td>with ild:</td><td>child, mild, wild; also pint, climb</td></tr>
<tr><td>2. Long o with old:</td><td>bold, cold, fold, gold, hold, mold, old, scold, sold, told</td></tr>
<tr><td>with oll:</td><td>boll, droll, knoll, poll, roll, toll, scroll, stroll</td></tr>
<tr><td>with olt:</td><td>bolt, colt, jolt;</td></tr>
<tr><td>Also:</td><td>gross, ghost, host, most, post, both, comb, don't, won't</td></tr>
</table>

Frequently, the *o* represents the /ȯ/ sound: *broth, cloth, moth; boss, cross, floss, gloss, loss, moss, toss; cost, frost, lost; off, scoff; loft, oft, soft.* In *gong, long, prong, throng, strong, song, tongs,* and in *honk,* the *o* may represent either *ŏ* or *ȯ.*

In words like *range, change,* and *strange,* the *a* represents its long sound. In words like *edge, dodge, fringe, singe, tinge, hedge, ledge, wedge, lodge, binge,* and *cringe,* the vowel represents its short sound. Note that the middle vowel is followed by a double consonant and a silent *e.*

The pupil, besides having to learn the regular short-vowel correspondences in monosyllabic words, also needs to gradually become familiar with certain variants: the *ä* sound of *a,* the *ȯ* sound of *a* followed by *ll,* the short *u* sound of *o,* the short *o* sound of *a,* the *ȯ* sound of *a* following *w, the ȯ* sound of *o,* and the *schwa* sound.

THE *ä* SOUND OF *a*

Early in their phonic training pupils need to learn the /ä/ sound of *a.* This is the sound which the pupil meets in such words as *bar* or *car.* The following words are helpful in teaching the sound:

bar	*jar*	*star*	*dark*	*mark*
car	*scar*	*tar*	*hark*	*park*
far	*spar*	*bark*	*lark*	*spark*

THE *ȯ* SOUND OF *a* FOLLOWED BY *ll*

The /ȯ/ sound of *a* occurs when the *a* is followed by *ll.* The following words illustrate this use:

all	*call*	*mall*	*wall*	*fall*	*squall*
ball	*hall*	*tall*	*small*	*stall*	*walleye*

The /ȯ/ sound of *a* also occurs when *a* is followed by single *l* (*talk, walk, salt, halt, walnut, walrus, waltz*).

THE SHORT *u* SOUND OF *o*

The *o* frequently represents /ŭ/. The following words are illustrative:

son	dove	above	dozen	monkey	stomach
ton	glove	among	govern	month	someone
won	love	become	honey	mother	sometime
one	none	coming	lovely	oneself	sometimes
come	shove	cover	money	oven	
done	some	donkey	Monday	shovel	

It is interesting to note that in most instances the *o* is followed by *m*, *n*, *p*, *t*, or *v*. In words of more than one syllable, the *u* sound of *o* occurs in the accented syllable.

THE SHORT *o* SOUND OF *a*

The *a* often represents a short *o* sound when it follows *w*. The following words illustrate this use:

swamp	wasp (also wȯsp)	wallow
swan	watch (also wȯtch)	washrag
swap	watt	washer
swat	what (also hwŭt)	washroom
wad	swallow	watchful
wand	tightwad	watchman
want (also wȯnt)	waffle	water (also wȯter)
was (also wŭz)	wallet	
wash (also wȯsh)	wallop	

The short *a* sound of *a*, following *w*, also occurs: *wacky*, *wag*, *wagon*, *wax*.

THE *o* SOUND OF *a* FOLLOWING *w*

The *o* sound of *a* occurs when *a* is followed by *r* and when the *ar* follows *w*:

dwarf	warm	warden	wart
swarm	warn	wardrobe	warlike
war	warp	warmly	

THE ȯ SOUND OF *o*

In words like *fog*, *hog*, and *log* the *o* may represent the short *o* sound or the ȯ sound.

The Schwa

In a two-syllable word the vowel sound in the unstressed syllable often is a softened sound and is represented by the symbol "ə". It is termed the *schwa* sound. Illustrative words are:

mantel	*blossom*	*apron*	*ballot*
medal	*bottom*	*bacon*	*bigot*
metal	*seldom*	*button*	*carrot*
model	*symptom*	*cotton*	*parrot*
pistol	*wisdom*	*crayon*	*riot*

**Activities for Teaching
the Short-Vowel
Correspondences**

Teaching of the short-vowel correspondences may proceed through the following steps.

1. Pronounce some words that contain the short-*a* sound, such as *bat, fat, cat, rat, cap, sat, Ann, at, am,* and *apple,* and tell students that the vowel sound they hear is the short-*a* sound. The *ă* sound may be slightly elongated. The teacher may identify each sound with a jingle such as the following:

   Aa*
   Apple, apple
   Come to me
   From the big,
   Tall apple tree.

   Ee*
   Egg, egg
   I like it best.
   The hen will lay one
   In her nest.

2. Pronounce words, some of which contain the short-vowel sound and some of which do not, and have the pupils raise their hands when the word contains the short-*a* sound.

3. Have pupils give other words containing the short-*a* sound.

4. Print the letter *a* on the blackboard and write out words such as *at, am, bat, mat, hat.* Underline the letter *a* and note that in each instance one consonant follows the vowel. This is a good time to teach that the vowel letters may represent both a long- and a short-vowel sound, and that the name of the letter gives its long sound. Then tell pupils that today they are learning the short-*a* sound. The teacher may give a key picture for each of the vowel sounds. For *a,* it might be an apple; for *e,* an egg or an elephant; for *i,* an insect or ink; for *o,* an ox or an ostrich; and for *u,* an umbrella. The teacher may associate the short *a* with an apple and may call it the "apple sound."

5. Post different pictures on the blackboard and ask pupils to draw a line under any pictures whose names contain a short-*a* sound.

6. Write a name under each picture whose name contains a short-*a* sound. Underline the letter *a* and note that it represents the short-*a* sound. The teacher sounds the words, moving a finger across the word from left to right, and makes sure that the

* Reprinted by permission from *Time for Phonics, Book A* by Louise Binder Scott. Copyright 1962 by McGraw-Hill, Inc.

pupils listen carefully to the sound in the middle of the word. The teacher should give the short-*a* sound a slight emphasis.

7.   Have the pupils say the words in unison or individually.

8.   Teach pupils to associate the short-*a* sound with both the capital and the lowercase letter.

9.   Have pupils print the letter *a*, both as a capital and in lowercase.

Workbooks and other teacher-prepared materials may now be used to teach the correspondences. The following exercises are illustrative:

1.   Have the pupils put a line through each picture that has a short *a* sound in the middle.

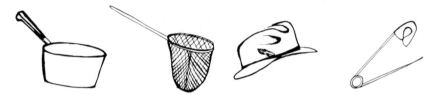

2.   Have the pupils write the missing vowel letter.
      h__t
      c__t

3.   Have the pupils draw a line from the letter *e* to the pictures whose names have the same sound as that represented by the letter *e* in *egg*.

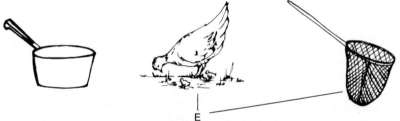

As soon as the pupils have mastered more than one vowel letter-sound correspondence, exercises such as the following are helpful.

1.   Have the pupils circle the word that rhymes with the name of the picture and let them write the word.

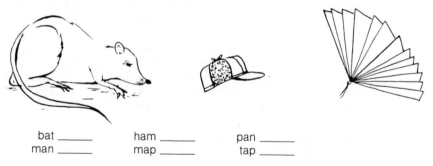

bat _____   ham _____   pan _____
man _____   map _____   tap _____

The art on this page is from Dechant 1981 (pp. 282–283). Reproduced by permission.

2. Have the pupils write the missing vowel letter.

$$\underline{s} \quad \underline{n} \quad \quad \underline{h} \quad \underline{g}$$
     x   x

3. Have the pupils identify the word *duck* in a list of four words: *dock, Dick, deck, duck*. Such an exercise presumes that the pupils have learned the respective short sounds of the five vowels.

4. Have the pupils circle the vowel sound that they hear.

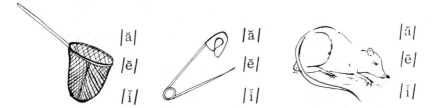

|ă| |ă| |ă|
|ĕ| |ĕ| |ĕ|
|ĭ| |ĭ| |ĭ|

5. Make a circular card similar to the one below. Write the beginning and ending consonant letter on the card and put the vowel letters on a strip of paper. Have the pupils pull the strip of paper through the opening, revealing new words.

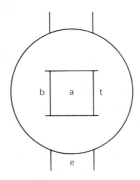

6. Have the pupils fill in the missing vowel letter in exercises such as the following:

    This is a p____n.
    This is a t____p.

The art on this page is from Dechant 1981 (p. 283). Reproduced by permission.

7.   Have the pupils circle the correct pronunciation in an exercises such as the following:

	tun			sun	
a. A ton		of gold.	c. A son		of Jim.
	ton			son	

	lot			dun	
b. A lot		of fish.	d. He has done		his job.
	lut			don	

This last exercise teaches the pupils to discriminate between the short-*o* and the short-*u* sound of *o*. Through exercises like those above, the pupils should learn the following:

1.   The letters *a, e, i, o,* and *u* are vowel letters.

2.   When these letters are pronounced like their names, they have a long sound.

3.   These vowel letters also represent a short sound.

4.   Changing the vowel letters alters both the appearance of the word and its meaning. Students must be taught medial-vowel substitution inductively. They must see what changing the vowel letter does to the form of the word, to its pronunciation, and to its meaning.

5.   When there is only one vowel *sound* in a word, that word is a one-syllable or monosyllabic word.

6.   When there is only one vowel *letter* in a word (as in words like *at* and *bat*), and when that vowel letter is followed by a single consonant letter (*at* or *bat*), then the vowel usually represents its short-vowel sound. Gradually the pupil should learn to verbalize the first vowel rule: *A single vowel letter at the beginning or in the middle of a one syllable word usually represents that letter's short sound.*

TEACHING THE LONG-VOWEL CORRESPONDENCES

In learning long vowel correspondences, pupils first learn that long vowels generally represent the same sound as that indicated by their names. They then learn a further extension of the principle of position: namely, that the vowel letter receives its long sound when a single vowel letter comes at the end of a one-syllable word or when it is placed in a cv spelling pattern: for example, *a, be, he, she, me, we, I, go, no, so, by, cry, fly, fry, my, sky, sly, spy, try, why.* Exceptions are: *ha, do, to, too, two,* and *who.* These really are not exceptions to the rule since the vowels are long, but the words are not alphabetically regular. A second vowel rule may be stated thus: *A single vowel letter at the end of a one-syllable word usually represents a long sound.*

Long Vowel and Silent E

The *principle of silentness* frequently operates in monosyllabic words in which there are two vowel letters, one of which is an *e* that is not pronounced. The principle of silentness simply notes that certain vowel letters are not pronounced.

When the *e* comes at the end of a monosyllabic word (*late, fire, store, cure*), it frequently is silent, and the normally short sound in the middle of the word becomes a long vowel. A third vowel rule may be stated thus: *In one-syllable words in which there are two vowel letters, the second one being a silent e preceded by a single consonant, the initial vowel letter represents a long-vowel sound.* Common exceptions to the rule are:

are	*gone*	*move*	*sure*
come	*have*	*none*	*there*
done	*live*	*one*	*were*
dove	*lose*	*prove*	*where*
give	*love*	*some*	*whose*

Many two- or three-syllable words also do not follow the general principle, with the first vowel either taking on a short sound or a different long-vowel sound.

ace: solace, furnace, Horace, menace, palace, preface, surface.

age: adage, advantage, average, baggage, bandage, bondage, breakage, cabbage, carnage, carriage, cleavage, coinage, cottage, courage, damage, dosage, drainage, forage, garbage, homage, hostage, image, language, leakage, luggage, manage, marriage, message, mileage, mortgage, orphanage, package, passage, pillage, postage, pottage, roughage, rummage, salvage, sausage, savage, scrimmage, sewage, seepage, soilage, soakage, spoilage, village, vintage, voltage, voyage, wastage, wattage, wreckage, yardage

ege: college, privilege

ige: prestige

ase: purchase

ate: chocolate, climate, deliberate, delicate, delegate, desolate, duplicate, frigate, palate, prelate, private, senate, separate, temperate

ice: chalice, complice, crevice, justice, malice, notice, novice, office, practice, service; caprice, police

ile: docile, fertile, fragile, futile, hostile, missile, mobile, sterile, tactile

ile: automobile

ine: doctrine, engine, ermine, famine, genuine, determine, examine

ine: carbine, machine, marine, morphine, ravine, routine, sardine, vaccine, vaseline, magazine

ise: premise, promise, treatise; valise

ite: respite, favorite

ive: active, captive, festive, massive, motive, passive, tractive; naive

ome: become

ose: purpose

ove: above, improve

uce: lettuce

A new sound occurs in words such as *blare, care, dare, fare, flare, glare, hare, mare, rare, scare, snare, stare,* and *ware.* This /â/ sound is a more open sound than the long-*a* sound and occurs commonly in accented syllables and in conjunction with the *r* sound. There is no great need to distinguish it for pupils from the long *a* sound.

The pupil also needs to learn the distinctive sounds of *u* in such words as *use* and *rule*. The sound in *use* occurs also in such words as *beauty, feud, few, cue, you*. The sound in *rule* (also in *threw, move, shoe, food, croup, through, blue*) occurs commonly after *j, r,* and *l,* especially when these consonants are preceded by another consonant (*brute*). The sound in *use* is symbolized by /$\bar{u}$/, /y$\ddot{u}$/, or y$\overline{oo}$; the sound in *rule*, by /$\ddot{u}$/ or /$\overline{oo}$/.

Vowel Combinations:
Second Vowel Silent

The pupil also must learn further extensions of the principle of silentness. Thus, the fourth vowel rule reads: *In certain vowel combinations, for example, ai, ay, ea, ee, oa, oe, ow, ue, ui, the second letter may be silent and the first letter represents the long-vowel sound.*

ai: The *ai* combination has the long /$\bar{a}$/ sound about 75 percent of the time, (*aid, bait*); in 15 percent of the cases, it is followed by *r* and is pronounced /$\hat{a}$/ as in *air, chair, fair, flair, hair, lair, pair,* and *stair.* The other pronunciations should be learned as sight words: *aisle, plaid, said, again.* In *mountain, villain, fountain, curtain, chieftain, certain, captain, bargain,* and the like, the *ai* becomes a *schwa* (ə).

ay: The *ay* combination as in *play, ray,* and *hay* represents the /$\bar{a}$/ sound about 95 percent of the time. Common exceptions are *aye, says, yesterday.*

ee: The *ee* combinations as in *bee* or *beet* represents /$\bar{e}$/ about 85 percent of the time. In words like *beer, cheer, deer, jeer, peer, sheer, sneer, steer,* and *veer,* the double *e* represents /$\breve{i}$/ or /$\underset{\smile}{e}$/. This is a lowered long *e* sound and occurs only in conjunction with *r.* A common exception is *been.*

oa: The *oa* combination as in *coat* or *boat* is sounded like a long *o* about 95 percent of the time. The *oa,* pronounced as in *broad,* /$\dot{o}$/ occurs the remaining 5 percent of the time. Common examples are *roar, oar, soar,* and *hoard.* Some of the latter (*board*) can also be /$\bar{o}$/.

oe: The *oe* combination is pronounced as long *o* (*foe, hoe*) 60 percent of the time; as long *e* (*Phoebe*) about 20 percent of the time; and as /$\overline{oo}$/ or /$\ddot{u}$/ in such words as *shoe, snowshoe, canoe,* and *horseshoe,* about 20 percent of the time. A common exception is *does.*

ow: The *ow* combination is listed here because in about 50 percent of the cases it follows the general principle of silentness. Thus, in *snow, blow,* and *glow,* the *w* is not pronounced, and the *o* is given its long sound. In the remaining cases it is pronounced as /a$\dot{u}$/ (*town, gown*). The *w* in words like *down, blew, shown* functions like a vowel. In *shown* the *ow* functions as a diphthong.

ea: The principle of silentness also applies to certain words having an *ea* combination. This group of words is by far the least consistent. The pupil will have to learn many of the words as sight words. In attacking words with the *ea* combination the pupil's best guess is the long *e* sound (*beach, bean, clean*). It occurs about 65 percent of the time. The next most common usage is that of the short *e* /$\breve{e}$/ as in *bread, dead, deaf,* and *head.* The pupil must learn that *great*, *break*, and *steak* are pronounced as /grāt/, /brāk/, /stāk/. The ending *ear* may be pronounced four ways: as /ē/ or /ĭr/ in *beard*, *dear*, *ear*; as /â/ in *pear*, *bear*, *wear*; as /ėr/ or /ûr/ in *earth*, *earn*, *pearl*; and as /ä/ in *heart*. The pronunciations of *ea* are summarized below:

The Pronunciations of *ea*

Ea

ē		/ĕ/				/ā/
beach	cream	bread	deaf	dreamt	spread	great
beak	deal	breath	death	head	sweat	break
beam	dream	dead	dread	health	thread	steak
eat	east					

Ear

/ēr/	/ĭr/		/â/	/ėr/	/ûr/	/ä/
clear	gear	shear	bear	earn		heart
dear	hear	smear	pear	earth		hearth
beard	near	spear	swear	hearse		
ear	rear	tear	wear	pearl		
fear	sear			search		

ue: The *ue* combination generally represents one of the long *u* sounds:
      ue as /ū/: *cue*, *due*, *hue*, *imbue*, *statue*, *tissue*.
      ue as /ü/: *blue*, *clue*, *flue*, *glue*, *rue*, *slue*, *true*, *accrue*, *bluegill*, *bluegrass*, *blueprint*, *construe*, *gruesome*, *rueful*, *untrue*, *sue*.

ui: The *ui* combination also represents for the most part one of the long *u* sounds:
      ui as /ū/: *nuisance*.
      ui as /ü/: *bruise*, *cruise*, *juice*, *sluice*, *grapefruit*, *fruitcake*, *juicy*, *recruit*.
      ui can also represent /ĭ/: *build*, *built*, *guilt*. (*Suite* is an exception.)

Table 10–2 shows the interrelationships between the principles of position and silentness, the spelling patterns, and the vowel rules:

Table 10-2   Interrelationships between Vowel Principles, Spelling Patterns, and Vowel Rules

VOWEL PRINCIPLE	SPELLING PATTERN	VOWEL RULE
Principle of Position	vc—ăt cvc—hăt vcc—ănt	Vowel Rule I: Vowel represents its short sound
	cv—gō	Vowel Rule II: Vowel represents its long sound.
Principle of Silentness	cvcȼ—firȼ	Vowel Rule III: First vowel represents its long sound; second vowel letter is not sounded.
	cvvc—boȧt	Vowel Rule IV: First vowel represents its long sound; second vowel letter is not sounded.

THE PRINCIPLE OF CONTEXT

The fourth principle to the learned is the principle of context. Since a single vowel letter or a group of vowel letters in a word can represent one of two or three sounds, if in a given word the number and position of the vowel letter or group of vowel letters do not indicate which vowel sound is to be applied, word meaning or context must be used as a clue to pronunciation.

The context provides a significant means for confirming the sounds of the vowel combinations and is especially useful in dealing with some of the following variants. If the relationship between a vowel letter and a vowel sound is one that occurs in only a few words, the words should be taught as sight words. The following lists give examples where context plays a major role; under this general heading, too, are grouped additional vowel combinations (*ei, ie, oo, ou*) which sometimes follow the principle of silentness, but where the variants are so numerous that context often is the only clue as to what the word is.

1. *Sounds of a*
    /ĕ/ as in *any*
    /ĭ/ as in *senate*
    /ä/ as in *mama*

2. *Sounds of e*
    /ĭ/ as in *pretty*
    /ō/ as in *sew*
    /ä/ as in *sergeant*

3. *Sounds of i*
    /ē/ as in *ski, broccoli, police, spaghetti, machine, unique, fatigue*
    /y/ as in *familiar, peculiar, genius, behavior, junior, senior, Indian, brilliant, Italian, valiant, onion, Spaniard, spaniel, congenial, convenience, convenient, obedient, period, ratio, curious*

4. *Sounds of o*
    /ĭ/ as in *women*
    /u̇/ or /o͝o/ as in *wolf*
    /ü/ or /o͞o/ as in *do, to, who*
    /ŭ/ as in *come*

5. *Sounds of u*
    /ĕ/ as in *bury*
    /ĭ/ as in *busy*
    /u̇/ or /o͝o/ as in *bull, full, pull, put*

6. *Sounds of ei (ey)*
    A common pronunciation for *ei* is that of a long *a*. The following words are illustrative: *beige, deign, feign, feint, reign, rein, reindeer, seine, skein, veil, vein, eight, freight, neigh, sleigh, weigh,* and *weight.* In words like *heir* and *their,* the *ei* is *â.*

    In some instances *ei* is simply pronounced as a long *e,* the second vowel letter being silent; thus the following: *ceiling, deceive, conceive, receive, leisure, seize, either, neither.*

    The *ei* may be pronounced as long *i* as in *height,* short *e* as in *heifer,* and short *i* in *forfeit, sovereign,* and *foreign.*

    The *ey* is pronounced as /ē/ as in *barley, honey, kidney, key.* It is pronounced as long *a* in *hey, obey, prey, they, whey.* This latter sound is common in monosyllables and when *ey* occurs in a stressed syllable ending a word: *obey, convey.* It also occurs as long *i: eye, eyeball, eyebrow, eyelash.*

7. *Sounds of ie:*
   Ie may be a long *e*, a short *i*, a long *i*, or a short *e*. The long *i* sound is common when *ie* is at the end of a word (*die*) and in the ending *ied*. In words of more than one syllable when *ie* ends the word, *ie* often represents /ē/: *cookie, collie, prairie, brownie, lassie.*

   Long *e: brief, chief, field, fierce, frieze, grief, grieve, niece, piece, priest, shield, shriek, siege, thief, wield, yield*

   Long *i: die, fried, lie, pie, tried, applied, belie, implied, untie, untried*

   Short *e: friend, befriend, friendless, friendly, friendship*

   Short *i: sieve*

8. *Sounds of oo:*
   Oo is pronounced as /ü/ or /ōō/ (*bloom*), as /ú/ or /ŏŏ/ (*cook*), as /ō/ (*door*), and as short /ŭ/ (*blood*). The latter two occur infrequently and should be taught as exceptions. The combination *ook* occurs frequently enough in words so that one may speak of the /ŏŏk/ words. Some examples are *book, brook, cook, hook, nook, rook, shook,* and *took.* Only *spook* is an exception.
   The following words are illustrative of the *oo* combinations:

   Oo as /ü/: *bloom, boom, boot, booth, broom, choose, cool, doom, drool, droop, food, fool, gloom, goose, groove, hoof, hoop, mooch, mood, moon, moose, noose, pooch, pool, proof, roof, room, roost, root, school, scoop, scoot, shoot, smooth, snoop, snoot, snooze, soon, spook, spool, spoon, stooge, stoop, swoop, too, tool, tooth, troop, zoo, zoom*

   Oo as /ú/: *book, brook, cook, crook, foot, good, hood, hook, look, nook, shook, soot, stood, took, wood, wool*

   Oo as /ō/: *brooch, door, floor*
   Oo as /ŭ/: *blood, flood*

9. *Sounds of ou:*
   Ou has numerous pronunciations: as /ou/ or /aú/ in *blouse,* in which case it represents a diphthong; as long *o* in *course; as /ü/* in *group;* as /ú/ in *could; as /ó/* in *bought* or *cough;* as short *ŭ* in *touch,* as /ŏ/ in *hough,* as /ə/ in *vigorous,* and as /ėr/ or /ûr/ in *flourish* or *journey.*

   Ou as /ou/ or /aú/: *blouse, bough, bounce, bound, bout*
   For additional examples refer to the diphthongs.

   Ou as /ō/: *dough, furlough, mould, soul, though, although, doughnut, thorough, poultry*

   Ou as /ü/ or /ōō/ or as /ū/ (yü or yōō): *coup, group, route, soup, through, wound, you, youth, cougar, coupon*

   Ou as /ŭ/: *cousin, country, couple, double, enough, tough, rough, touch, trouble, young*

   Ou as /ó/: *bought, brought, cough, nought, fought, ought, sought, thought, wrought*

   Ou as /ú/: *could, should, tour, would, your*

   Ou as /ə/: *vigorous*

   Our as /ėr/ or /ûr/: *adjourn, journal, journey, flourish*

ADDITIONAL VOWEL COMBINATIONS

Some vowel combinations characteristically represent a sound distinct from that represented by either of the vowel letters: for example, *au, aw, eu, ew,* or they may follow the principle of silentness, but it is the first vowel that is silent:

Sounds of au and aw

The combination *au* is pronounced /ȯ/ (*ought*) about 95 percent of the time; the principal exceptions are *draught, gauge, aunt, chauffeur,* and *laugh. Aw* is always pronounced as /ȯ/ (*law*) when it occurs at the end of the word or syllable or is followed by *k, l,* or *n.* The /ȯ/ sound is represented by *au* or *aw* in the beginning and the middle of the word (*August, awe, cause, crawl*), but at the end of a word it is always *aw* (*law*).

Au as /ȯ/: aught, caught, caulk, cause, fault, faun, flaunt, fraud, Gaul, gaunt, gauze, haul, haunch, haunt, jaunt, laud, launch, naught, naughty, Paul, paunch, pause, sauce, Saul, staunch, taught, taunt, vault, vaunt, applaud, applause, auburn, audit, auger, augment, augur, August, auster, auto, because, naughty

Aw as /ȯ/: awe, bawl, brawl, claw, craw, crawl, dawn, draw, drawl, drawn, fawn, flaw, gawk, hawk, jaw, law, lawn, paw, pawn, thaw, awful, gnaw, hacksaw, jigsaw

Sounds of eu and ew:

Eu as /ǖ/ (*yü*): deuce, feud, feudal, teuton, neutral, neural, neuter, neutron, Europe

Eu as /ü/ or /o͞o/: maneuver

Ew as /ǖ/ (*yü*): few, mew, new, pew, spew, stew, view, sinew, nephew

Ew as /ü/ or /o͞o/: blew, brew, crew, drew, flew, grew, Jew, shrewd, slew, threw, Hebrew, jewel

Ew as /ō/: sew (this in an exception)

THE DIPHTHONGS

Diphthongs are digraphs that represent a gliding monosyllabic speech sound. They are two succeeding vowel sounds that are joined in a single syllable under a single stress. The sound is distinct from that represented by either of the single letters. The most common such combinations are *oi, oy, ou* (*house*), and *ow* (*brow*).

Diphthong sounds of oi, oy, ou and ow

Oi: The sound of *oi* as in *boil* (*broil, choice, coil, coin*) occurs about 98 percent of the time. A common exception is *choir.*

Oy: The sound of *oy* as in *boy* (*joy, toy*) also occurs about 98 percent of the time. An exception is *coyote.*

Ou: The diphthongal sound of *ou* occurs in such words as:

cloud, couch, count, crouch, flour, foul, found, fount, gouge, grouch, ground, hound, hour, house, loud, mound, mount,

> *mouth, noun, ouch, ounce, our, oust, out, plough, pouch, pounce, pound, pout, proud, round, rout, scour, scout, shout, south, about, aloud, around*

Ow: The dipthongal sound of *ow* occurs about 50 percent of the time, particularly at the end of words, and is illustrated in the following words:

> *bow, brow, brown, browse, chow, clown, cow, crowd, crown, down, dowse, drown, frown, gown, growl, how, howl, jowl, owl, plow, prow, prowl, scowl, town, wow*

THE EFFECT OF R
ON A PRECEDING VOWEL

Pupils must also be able to cope with *ar, er, ir, or,* and *ur.* The consonant sometimes influences the sound represented by the vowel letter. The letter *r,* when following a single vowel letter, changes the sound of the vowel, which is then neither long nor short.

> *The sounds of ar*
>
> /är/ as in *car, park*
>
> /âr/ as in *care* and as in *parent* or *Mary*
>
> /ăr/ as in *paradise, paradox, barrel*
>
> /ȯr/ as in *warm, ward, war, wart*
>
> /ər/ as in *liar, granular, westward,* or in *maroon* when the *a* is the final letter in an unaccented syllable.
>
> /ĕr/ in the suffix *ary: stationary, legendary, sanitary*

When the *r* is followed by a silent *e* as in *care* or *fare,* or when it is the final letter in an accented syllable and is followed by a vowel as in *parent* or *Mary,* the *a* is frequently pronounced /âr/. When the *a* is the final letter in an unaccented syllable and is followed by an *r* in the next syllable, it is /ə/: *maroon* and *cataract.*

In the suffix *ward* and in some final syllables, *ar* is also pronounced /ər/: *liar, granular, westward, pillar, dollar, orchard, Tartar, circular, lizard, wizard, mustard.* The sound /ȯr/ is common when *ar* is immediately preceded by *w*: *war, warm, ward, dwarf, swarm, wart, warble.* In the suffix *ary, ar* is pronounced as /ĕr/: *stationary, legendary, sanitary.*

> *The sounds of er*
>
> /ėr/ or /ûr/ as in *her, revert, adverb*
>
> /ər/ as in *hotter, baker*
>
> /ĕr/ as in *meridian, merry*
>
> /ē/ or /ĭr/ as in *here*
>
> /âr/ as in *there, where, very*

Er in monosyllabic words (*her*), generally in accented syllables (*revert*), and in unaccented syllables in which the *er* is followed by a consonant (*adverb*) is sounded as /ėr/ or /ûr/. When it names a person (*baker*) or has a comparative meaning (*hotter*), it is usually pronounced as /ər/. It may also be /ĕr/ as in *meridian,* /ē/ or /ĭr/ as in *here,* or /â/ as in *there, where, ferry, herring, very,* or *perish.*

> *The sounds of ir*
>
> /ėr/ or /ûr/ as in *firm*

/ər/ as in *tapir, elixir*
/ī̇r/ as in *dire*
/ĭr/ as in *virile*

Ir is sounded as /ėr/ or /ûr/ in monolyllables (*firm*) and in accented syllables (*firkin*). It may be sounded as /ər/ (*tapir*) in an unaccented syllable, /ī̇r/ (*dire*) in a vcv¢ spelling pattern, or /ĭr/ (*virile, irrelevant, irritate*).

The sounds of or

/ȯr/ as in *for* or *fork*
/ėr/ or /ûr/ as in *word*
/ōr/ as in *more*
/ər/ as in *doctor*

Or is sounded as /ėr/ or /ûr/ when *or* follows *w* as in *word, work, world, worship, worm, worse, worth.* In other monosyllabic words it is sounded as /ō/ or as /ȯ/. The most common pronunciation is /ȯ/: *born, cord, cork, corn, for, fork, gorge, horn, horse, Lord, morn, norm, north, or, orb, scorch, scorn, short, snort, sort, sport, stork, storm, torch, worn, fort, porch.*

When *or* is immediately followed by a silent *e* at the end of a monosyllable, or syllable in a polysyllabic word, it usually represents /ōr/ as in *store, more, before, soreness*. The *or* may also be pronounced as /ər/ as in *inventor*.

The sounds of ur

/ėr/ or /ûr/ as in *hurt*
/ər/ as in *liturgy, murmur, augur*
/ū̇r/ as in *cure*
/u̇r/ as in *sure, jury, rural, hurrah*

Ur is sounded as /ėr/ or /ûr/ in monosyllabic words and in the accented syllable of polysyllabic words. *Ur* also may be /ər/ (*liturgy*), /ū̇r/ (*cure*), and /u̇r/ (*sure, jury, hurrah, rural*).

When *ar, er, ir, or,* or *ur* are followed by a second *r*, the vowel is usually short: *barrel, barren, sparrow, barrack, derrick, error, terrier, errand, irrelevant, irritate, mirror, borrow, horror, sorry, corrupt, torrent.*

The vowel also is frequently short when the *r* is followed by a vowel: *charity, tariff, lariat, parachute, paratroop, parasol, paradise, paradox, parapet, parallel, parasite, parable, ceremony, America, very, inherit, peril, verity, merit, cleric, spirit, miracle, direct, quorum.*

Sometimes the *r* is separated from the vowel preceding it and has no effect on its pronunciation: *arise, around, arena, spiral, Irish, erect, erupt, hero, irate, siren, uranium, pirate, virus, furious, spirant, wiry, glory, tyrant, mores, oral, story, Tory.*

ACTIVITIES TO TEACH LONG-VOWEL CORRESPONDENCES

Exercises such as the following are especially helpful in teaching the various vowel letter and sound correspondences:

1. Have the children memorize a little ditty such as the following:

A is called ă,
When it tells of the cat,
Which stumbled and fell
When chasing the rat.

A is called ā,
When it tells of the cake
That Mama will bake
And that I'll help her make.

2. Have the pupils put a line through each picture that has a long *a* sound.

3. Have the pupils circle the correct *a* sound.

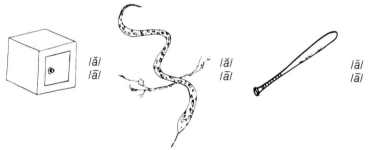

/ă/
/ā/

/ă/
/ā/

/ă/
/ā/

4. Have the pupils write the missing vowels. This exercise is useful in teaching long vowels followed by silent *e*.

p___p___   f___l___   f___r___

5. Have pupils turn words such as *at, can, cap, cut, dam, din, fat, grim, grip, hat, hid, hop, Jan, kit, mad, not, pal, pan, pin, pip* into other words by adding *e*.

6. Provide a list of words with the long vowel missing and let the pupils add it.

b____, cr____, pl___te, b___ke, c___ke, d___me.

7. Have pupils indicate by number the picture that has the same vowel sound as the word.

The art on this page is from Dechant 1981 (p. 293). Reproduced by permission.

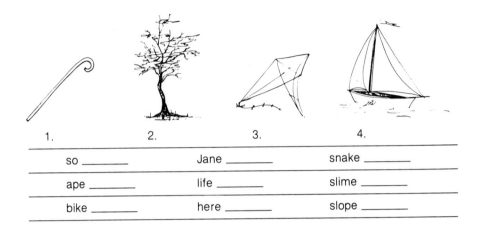

	1.	2.	3.	4.
so _____		Jane _____	snake _____	
ape _____		life _____	slime _____	
bike _____		here _____	slope _____	

8. Besides learning to discriminate between long and short vowels, pupils need to learn how to designate long and short vowels and how to indicate silent letters. An exercise like the following teaches this by requiring pupils to put proper diacritical marks on a series of words.

āt	blow	hay	fan
hŏt	got	duke	jail
dīnȩ	soap	bed	see
gō	sleep	fun	rake
gĕt	joke	fame	brute
fēȧst	tube	Brad	name
cŭt	bike	sat	like

9. Have pupils match the vowel sound in a picture with a sound that they already know.

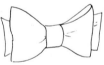

bow (ō)

a. snow _____
b. down_____
c. owl _____
d. gown_____
e. brown _____

clown (ou)

f. plow _____
g. blow _____
h. clown _____
i. how _____
j. slow _____

The art on this page is from Dechant 1981 (p. 260). Reproduced by permission.

260

10. Have the pupils select the correct pronunciation for a given vowel combination.

ā   ō   ē

ă   ŏ   ĕ

11. Have pupils learn phonograms containing a long vowel sound; for example, *ite, eat, ike, ail.*

12. Remind students of the six basic vowel-pattern groups:
    a. The single vowel-letter pattern as in *bat* or *at* (this is a clue to the short-vowel sound).
    b. The open-vowel pattern as in *be* or *me*
    c. The vowel letter with a final *e* as in *rope* or *use*
    d. The double vowel-letter pattern as in *rain*
    e. The modified vowel pattern as in *bird, word, all, far*
    f. Exceptions or words that do not fit any of the above patterns

    Then present a list of words and let students indicate which pattern the underlined letters fit.

thru̲sh _____	la̲rge _____	lea̲ve _____
scre̲ech _____	la̲ys _____	bo̲red _____
bela̲bor _____	ama̲zed _____	enca̲mp _____
rea̲lized _____	justi̲fiable _____	urchi̲n _____
rhuba̲rb _____	repro̲ach _____	bu̲rlap _____

SUMMARY

Chapter 10 has dealt with the vowel phoneme-grapheme correspondences. The following chart summarizes these and may be used as a quick reference.*

Vowel Phoneme-Grapheme Correspondences

SINGLE VOWELS	VOWEL COMBINATIONS	
Short Vowels	*Vowel Digraphs: First Vowel Long, Second Silent*	
ă hat (note a /ŏ/ wasp)	ai /ā/ aid	ee/ē/ bee
ĕ den	ay /ā/ play	ei /ē/ seize
ĭ kin, hymn	ea /ē/ cream	ey /ē/ key, barley

* For further materials to teach and develop the vowel correspondences, see Dechant 1981b: pp. 77–97, 116–120.

The art on this page is from Dechant 1981 (p. 294). Reproduced by permission.

Vowel Phoneme-Grapheme Correspondences (*continued*)

SINGLE VOWELS	VOWEL COMBINATIONS

SINGLE VOWELS

ŏ *lot* (note o /ŭ/ *son*)
ŭ *but*

Long Vowels

ā *fate*
ē *be*
ī *fine, rye*
ō *go, store*
ū yü *few, use*
ü o͞o *rule;* also o as /ü/ *to, who*

Long Vowels in Special Combinations

a /ā/ *strange*
i /ī/ *bind, child, pint, climb, high, fight*
o /ō/ *roll, cold, don't, gross*

Mixed Vowels

a /ä/ *car*
a /ȯ/ *call*
a /ȯ/ *war*
a /â/ *care*
o /ȯ/ *log, off, toss, cloth, strong, orb*
u / u̇/ *full, put, sure*

Schwa: (ə): *about, taken, April, circus, pigeon,
lemon, villain, porpoise, vicious.*

VOWEL COMBINATIONS

ie /ī/ *pie*
oa /ō/ *boat*
oe /ō/ *foe*
oo /ō/ *door*
ou /ō/ *soul*

ow /ō/ *show*
ue /ū/ *cue*
ue /ü/ *blue*
ui /ū/ *nuisance*
ui /ü/ *cruise*

Additional Vowel Digraphs

ai /â/ *chair*
au /ȯ/ *aught*
aw /ȯ/ *law*
ea /ā/ *great*
ea /ä/ *heart*
ea /ĕ/ *bread*
ear /âr/ *pear*
ear /ĭr/ *fear*
ee /ĭ/ or /ȩ̄/ *cheer*
ei /ā/ *veil, eight*
ei /ī/ *height*
eir /ĭr/ *weird*
eu /ü/ or /o͞o/ *maneuver*
ew /ū/ or /yü/ *few*
ew /ō/ *sew*
ey /ā/ *obey*
ey /ī/ *eye*
ie /ē/ *chief*

ie /ĕ/ *friend*
ie /ĭ/ *sieve*
oa /ȯ/ *board*
oe /ü/ or /o͞o/ *shoe*
oe /ē/ *Phoebe*
oo /ü/ *moon*
oo /u̇/ *book*
oo /ŭ/ *flood*
ou /ū/ or /ü/ *you, soup*
ou /ȯ/ *ought*
ou /u̇/ *could*
ou /ŭ/ *cousin*
our /ər/ *journal*
uy /ī/ *buy*
ui /ĭ/ *build*

Vowel Blends (Diphthongs)

oi /oi/ *toil*
oy /oi/ *boy*
ou /ou/ or /au̇/ *house*
ow /ou/ or /au̇/ *bow*

Vowel + R

ar /är/ *arm*	ar /ər/ *liar*	ar /ȯr/ *war*	ere /â/ *there*
er /ėr, ûr/ *term*	er /ər/ *mother*	are /â/ *care*	ire /ī/ *fire*
ir /ėr, ûr/ *dirt*	ir /ər/ *elixir*	ear /ĭr/ or /ȩ̄/ *fear*	ore /ō/ *store*
or /ėr, ûr/ *word*	or /ər/ *honor*	ear /âr/ *pear*	our /ər/ *journal*
/ȯr/ *for*	ur /ər/ *augur*	ear /ėr/ *pearl*	our /au̇/ *hour*
ur /ėr, ûr/ *hurt*	yr /ər/ *zephyr*	eer /ĭr/ *cheer*	ure /ū/ *cure*
yr /ėr/ *myrtle*	. . . .	eir /ĭr/ *weird*	ure /u̇/ *sure*
. . . .	air /â/ *chair*	ere /ĭ/ or /ē/ *here*	

QUESTIONS FOR DISCUSSION

1. Identify the nineteen vowel phonemes and give the appropriate diacritical markings for each.
2. Relate the four principles that govern vowel sounding to the five basic spelling patterns and to the four vowel rules.
3. Although Vowel Rule I ordinarily applies when a double consonant follows a single vowel in a syllable (*ent*), list exceptions to this situation.
4. List exceptions to the rule that a single vowel letter in a syllable followed by a single consonant receives its short sound.
5. Identify by symbolism and example the two sounds of long *u*.
6. To what vowel rule are the following words exceptions?

bind	*stroll*	*boss*	*cold*
bar	*son*	*ball*	*swat*
war	*who*	*are*	*to*
live	*dare*	*some*	*scarce*
here	*been*	*said*	*does*
guilt	*earth*	*heart*	*put*

7. Identify the usual sounds of the following vowel combinations:

an	*eu*	*oi*	*ou*
aw	*ew*	*ey*	*ow*

11

TEACHING THE STRUCTURAL OR MORPHEMIC ANALYSIS SKILLS

The intraword cues available to the reader in identifying words are configuration cues (discussed in Chapter 8), phonic cues (discussed in Chapters 9 and 10), and morphemic cues. Phonic cues help the reader to sound out the word, and if the word thus sounded is in the pupil's aural-oral vocabulary, the pupil can associate meaning with it.

Morphemic or structural analysis helps the reader get the pronunciation of a word by breaking the word into its parts, and it helps the reader get directly to the meaning by breaking the word into its meaning parts (*cat—s, class—room, trans—scribe*). Morphemic analysis deals with the examination of the elements within the unidentified word itself. It is an analysis of the meaningful elements within a derived word: the root itself, the prefixes and suffixes, the inflectional endings, and so forth. By examining the structure of a long, unknown word and identifying its meaningful parts (the morphemes), the pupil is more likely to be able to understand the meaning of the word and indirectly to work out its pronunciation.

Morphology, the study of word structure and word meaning, permits the introduction of minute changes into the word to produce a special meaning. Morphemic analysis is an analysis of the word into its morphemes, the smallest units of language that convey meaning. The morpheme may be either free or bound. A free morpheme is the smallest unit of meaning that can stand alone; it is a word. The word *book* is one morpheme when it denotes a bound set of printed pages; it is a different morpheme when the word designates the function of an arresting police officer (Smith and Barrett 1974). The bound morpheme tends to be a smaller unit of meaning than the free morpheme, and it cannot stand alone in a sentence. The free morpheme has lexical meaning if it has a meaning of its own (for example, prefixes and suffixes), and it has relational meaning if it has a grammatical meaning. For example, in the sentence, "She insists on it", the *in* in *insists* has lexical meaning; it has meaning wherever it occurs. The *s* at the end of the word has no meaning of itself; it has meaning only to the extent that it makes the verb a third person singular: it is said to have relational meaning. The *s* may also take on a relational meaning when it changes a noun from the singular to the plural or when it denotes the possessive case.

The bound morpheme is always attached or affixed to a free morpheme (for example *un—do; hit—s*). Prefixes and suffixes are bound morphemes. Thousands of words, especially long words, consist of a root and affixes (a combination of free and bound morphemes) or possibly two roots (a combination of two free morphemes).

Structural or morphemic analysis deals with eight different situations:*

1. Inflectional endings of words such as *s, es, ed, ing.*
2. Inflectional changes such as changing *y* to *i*; dropping the final *e*; doubling the final consonant; or changing *d* to *t.*
3. Compound words which are combinations of two free morphemes.
4. Contractions with *t.*
5. Hyphenated words.
6. Derived words, constructed of a root and affixes (both prefixes and suffixes).
7. Syllabication.
8. Accent.

Consider individually now the development of the various subskills in morphemic analysis, beginning with the teaching of the inflectional endings.

TEACHING
THE INFLECTIONAL ENDINGS

Inflectional endings are a class of suffixes. They include the possessive of nouns (cat's), plural of nouns (cats), the third person singular (talks), the present participle (talking), the past tense (talked), and the comparative (colder), superlative (coldest), and the adverbial *ly* (boldly). The plural of nouns and the third-person singular are formed by *es* when the root word ends in a hissing or sibilant sound (*ss, sh, ch, x*).

* For commercial materials designed to aid in the development of the structural analysis skills, see Dechant 1981b: pp. 121–140.

Teaching S

The earliest structural analysis skill to be learned by the pupil is the ability to deal with the inflectional ending *s*. The *s* can change the word in three ways: (1) It changes the verb into third person singular; (2) it makes a noun plural in form; and (3) it changes the word into its possessive form. The teaching of the *s* plural is easier when it is accompanied by another word in the sentence that suggests the plural. The sentence, "Tom has ten pets," is an example of this.

Plural *s* is normally taught at the preprimer level; third-person singular *s*, possessive *s*, *ed*, *ing*, and *er*, at the primer level; *es* and *est*, at the first-reader level.

The use of the apostrophe *s* is also introduced in the first grade. Beginning with the vocabulary that the pupil already knows, the pupil is shown what the addition of *s* does to the word.

Exercises like the following teach the use of the third-person singular *s* and the plural *s*.

1. *Teaching the third person-singular s*
   Have the pupils circle the correct verb in an exercise such as the following:

	bat.		hop.
Ben		Bob	
	bats.		hops.

2. *Teaching the plural s*
   Have the pupils circle the correct word in an exercise such as the following:

nut   nuts   hen   hens   mat   mats

The art on this page is from Dechant 1981 (p. 296). Reproduced by permission.

3. *Teaching the possessive s*

An exercise such as the following differentiates the possessive use of *s* from the other uses of *s:*

This is _____ book.
(Pams, Pam's)

Teaching ing

The endings *ed,* *'s,* and *ing* are introduced to pupils shortly after teaching the plural and third-person singular *s.* The teacher demonstrates how *ing* can be added to verbs to form two-syllable words such as *hitting, hopping,* or *running.* The pupil has to learn that when a monosyllabic word ends in a single consonant letter preceded by a single vowel letter, the consonant is doubled before adding the *ing* and that the second consonant is silent (*bat—batting*).

In words of more than one syllable, if the last syllable is stressed and ends with a single consonant letter preceded by a single vowel letter, the consonant letter is doubled before adding *ing* (*omitting, regretting*). The final consonant is usually not doubled if the accent is on any syllable other than the last (*labeling, remembering*).

After pupils can deal successfully with long vowels in various combinations and after they have mastered the regular uses of *ing* as discussed above, they need to expand their uses for *ing:* Whenever *ing* is added (1) to monosyllabic words ending in a vowel, diphthong, or double vowel (*being, doing, crying, playing, fleeing, hoeing, blowing*), (2) to monosyllabic words ending in a single consonant preceded by a double vowel (*failing, creeping, boasting, dreaming*), (3) to monosyllabic words ending in a double consonant (*asking, barking, drinking*), or (4) to words ending in *ow* (*blowing*), no doubling of the letter preceding *ing* occurs.

Monosyllabic words ending in a silent *e* drop the final *e* before adding *ing* (*praise—praising; smile—smiling; give—giving; come—coming*). *Hoe-hoeing* is an exception.

The principles suggested apply not only to *ing* but to any suffix beginning with a vowel. The most common such suffixes are: *able, ably, ability, age, ance, ant, ard, ary, ation, ed, en, ence, ent, er, ern, ery, es, est, ion, ish, ity, ive, or, ous,* and *y.* Words ending in *ce* or *ge* retain the *e* before a suffix beginning with *a* or *o.*

Exercises such as the following teach the use of *ing:*

Tom digs.
Tom is
digging.

She pets
her dog. She
is _____
her dog.

The art on this page is from Dechant 1981 (p. 296). Reproduced by permission.

Teaching the Past Tense
with ed

The pupil also must be introduced to the past tense formed by *ed*. In reading *ed* pupils meet certain problems. The *e* is silent (*begged, canned, hoped*) except after *d* and *t* (*batted, nodded, cheated, drifted*), and the vowel in the root word, if it represents a long-vowel sound, retains its long sound (*hoped*). The *d* is pronounced as /*t*/ after the unvoiced consonants such as *f* (*puffed*), *k* (*peeked*), *p* (*dipped*), *sh* (*wished*), but not after *t*; it is pronounced as a /*d*/ after the voiced consonants (*begged, canned*). The past participle of *dream, learn,* and *spell* may be pronounced with a /*t*/ or a /*d*/ sound.

Exercises such as the following develop skill in the use of *ed*.

1. Have pupils indicate whether the *ed* ending is pronounced, *t, d,* or *ed.*
   a. The dog begged (*begd*) for a catfish.
   b. The cop nabbed (*nabd*) the gunman.
   c. She nodded (*nod-ed*) to the man.
   d. He petted (*pet-ed*) his wet cub.
   e. She napped (*napt*) on her bed.

2. Have pupils check the correct pronunciation of *ed.*

d	*d*	*d*
nabbed *ed*	mopped *ed*	batted *ed*
t	*t*	*t*
t	*d*	*d*
gagged *ed*	nipped *ed*	tipped *ed*
t	*t*	*t*

3. An exercise requiring the pupil to select one of three words that fits syntactically can be used to teach the variant uses of *s, ing,* and *ed:* "The boy was _____ in the building." (looks, looked, looking)

4. The inflectional endings (*s, ed, ing, er, 's*) may all be taught by using a simple word wheel.

TEACHING INFLECTIONAL CHANGES

Inflectional changes take many forms. The pupil must be taught to:

1. Drop final *e* before adding a suffix or an inflectional ending beginning with a vowel:
   > *bake—baking, baked, baker.*
2. Change *y* to *i* when adding a suffix or an inflectional ending beginning with a vowel:
   > *busy—busier, busiest*
   > *happy—happier, happiest*

3. Retain the *y* when the suffix is *ing:*
   copy—copying

4. Form the plural of a word ending in *y* by changing the *y* to *i* and adding *es:*
   city—cities
   baby—babies

5. Change the *f* to *v* in plurals and add *es:*
   loaf—loaves
   wife—wives

The first four of these inflectional changes are introduced at the first reader level; changing *f* to *v* is taught at the second reader level.

TEACHING COMPOUND WORDS

As the pupils' skill in structural analysis develops, they may identify two simple words in one larger word. They may see *tea* and *pot* in *teapot; some* and *thing* in *something;* or *bat* and *boy* in *batboy.* The ability to see two words in a longer word is helpful in pronouncing the word, but also in associating meaning with it.

Pupils also need to learn that one-syllable words have only one vowel sound, and that compounds have two or more vowels, each of which is sounded, and that they are therefore called two- or multi-syllable words. Pupils need to learn this inductively.

There are numerous compounds that are teachable at the primary or even the primer level. On more advanced levels the pupil should learn more difficult words, beginning with those compounds that keep the basic meaning of each word making up the compound. For example, a classroom is a room where class is held. Other words useful in teaching this skill are *campfire, cornstalk, cowboy, earthquake, eyelash, hillside, hilltop, railroad, rosebush, watchman, weekend, steamboat, workbook, snowshoes, sawdust, sandhill, newsboy, seasick, housework, windshield.*

Frequently, the meaning of the compound is completely new—for example, *broadcast, township,* or *wholesale.* Some compounds are written as two words—for example, *ice cream, living room, dining room, sea power, post office, oil painting, air brake, parcel post, money order,* or *school spirit.*

Compounds frequently used in children's books include the following words:

airplane	bedroom	blacktop	boxcar	cannot
another	bedside	blackboard	broadcast	cardboard
anyone	bedtime	blueberries	broomstick	carhop
anything	beehive	bobcat	breakdown	childhood
backbone	beeline	bobsled	bulldog	classmate
bagpipe	bellhop	bobwhite	buttermilk	classroom
barnyard	bigtop	boldface	byways	cobweb
baseball	birthday	bloodshed	campfire	corkscrew

cornstalk	gumdrop	northwest	shipshape	touchdown
cowboy	halfway	offset	sideline	township
daylight	hamlet	onset	sidetrack	trailways
daytime	haystack	outgrow	signpost	treetop
dishpan	hedgerow	outline	smokestack	upkeep
downtown	herself	outskirts	snowbank	uplift
dragnet	himself	package	snowshoes	upon
drumstick	hillside	pancake	soapsuds	upset
earthquake	hilltop	peanut	somebody	vineyard
elsewhere	horseback	pigpen	something	warehouse
everywhere	housekeeper	plaything	sometimes	watchdog
everything	hubbub	playtime	somewhere	watchman
eyebrow	indeed	policeman	stagecoach	waterfall
eyelash	inland	popcorn	starfish	waylay
farmhouse	inside	popgun	statehood	weekend
farmland	instep	postman	steamboat	whoever
fireman	into	pullman	subway	whatever
fireplace	itself	quicksand	sunburn	wholesale
fishhook	jackknife	railroad	sunburst	wigwam
forbid	kidnap	rainbow	Sunday	wishbone
forget	lemonade	ransack	sundown	withdraw
foreman	limestone	roommate	sunlit	within
footprint	lonesome	rosebush	sunset	without
footstep	lookout	runway	sunshade	withstand
footstool	makeshift	sandhill	sunshine	windshield
gatepost	mankind	sandwiches	sunstroke	woodpile
godchild	maybe	sawdust	sunup	woodland
grandchildren	milkman	scarecrow	tadpole	workbag
grandfather	milkshake	seacoast	Thanksgiving	workbook
grandmother	milkweed	schoolbook	tiptop	yardstick
grandstand	newsboy	schoolhouse	tomtom	yearbook
grapevine	newsgirl	schoolroom	tonight	yuletide
graveyard	nighttime	seesaw	toothbrush	

Teaching pupils to read compounds includes exercises such as the following:

1. Have pupils write or copy words that have been formed from two simpler words:

The art on this page is from Dechant 1981 (p. 298). Reproduced by permission.

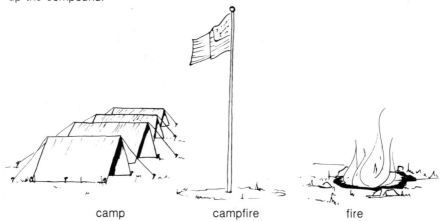

pig ⟍
     pigpen
pen ⟋

mail ⟍
     mailman
man ⟋

This is a _____   This is a _____

2. Have pupils see that compounds often keep the basic meaning of each word making up the compound:

     camp   campfire   fire

3. Have pupils join a word in column I to a word in column II to form a compound word:

I	II	Compound Word
1. bell	1. top	1. bellhop
2. big	2. set	
3. sun	3. dog	
4. for	4. hop	
5. bull	5. get	

4. Have pupils look at two pictures and ask them to produce the compound. Initially pupils may be required only to pronounce the compound word. Later, they may have to write the word.

     fishhook

5. Have the pupil draw a line between the two words making up the compound word: cow/boy.

6. Have pupils, using a dictionary, find the meaning of compounds that do not keep the basic meaning of each word making up the compound: *township, wholesale, broadcast, indeed, outline, ransack, seesaw, tadpole, pullman,* and so forth.

The art on this page is from Dechant 1981 (p. 298). Reproduced by permission.

TEACHING THE CONTRACTIONS

The use of the apostrophe to denote the possessive case is introduced to the pupil in the first grade. The pupil also needs to become familiar with the use of the apostrophe in contractions which is introduced later in the first grade. The contractions the pupil must learn are as follows:

FIRST READER	SECOND READER	THIRD READER	(OR LATER)
can't	aren't	ain't	they're
didn't	couldn't	hasn't	we'd
doesn't	hadn't	he'd	weren't
don't	haven't	he'll	we've
I'd	he's	here's	where's
I'll	I've	she'd	who'd
I'm	let's	she'll	who'll
isn't	she's	there'll	who's
it's	they'll	there's	wouldn't
that's	wasn't	they'd	you've
what's	we'll		
you'd	we're		
	won't		
	you'll		
	you're		

The levels for teaching the contractions are merely suggestive.
Exercises useful in teaching contraction skills include the following:

1. Have the pupils write out the two words that the contraction represents:

    didn't did not   who'll ____ ____
    she's ____ ____   we've ____ ____

2. Have pupils write the contraction after they have been given the regular, noncontracted form:

    Pam _____ in school today.
        (was not)

3. Have pupils match contractions with the noncontracted form:

    she'll   is not
    isn't   it is
    it's   she will

4. Have the pupils circle the correct contraction that finishes a sentence:

    a. I _____ go to the movies today.
        (can't, let's, it's)

    b. Please _____ pick the carnations.
        (can't, don't, won't)

TEACHING ROOTS, PREFIXES, AND SUFFIXES

Being able to break a word into its root, prefix, and suffix is another valuable aid in identifying a word and in developing meaning for a word.

In teaching students the structural skill here indicated, certain definite steps must be followed. The teacher must show the students that most two- and three-syllable words are composed of a root, and either a prefix, or a suffix, or both. Next, the teacher develops meaning for the words *root*, *prefix*, and *suffix*.

The root is the main part of a word. It is the reservoir of meaning. The prefix is another word part that is put before the main part of the word or at the beginning of the word.

The teacher should demonstrate to the pupils that prefixes change the meaning of a word, much as an adjective changes the meaning of a noun. For example, *circumnavigate* is composed of the prefix *circum* and the root *navigare*. *Navigare* is a Latin word meaning "to sail." The prefix *circum* means "around," and the entire word, *circumnavigate*, means "to sail around." The prefix *circum* thus changes the meaning of the root by indicating that in this instance *navigate* is not just sailing but is actually a particular type of sailing.

The suffix is another part of many two- or three-syllable words. It comes at the end of the word. The suffix frequently indicates what part of speech the word is. Thus, *ly* (*badly*) is a suffix and usually indicates that the word is an adverb. The *ion* (*condition*) is a suffix and usually indicates that the word is a noun. This might be termed the grammatical function of the suffix. The suffix also has a meaning function. The suffix *able* means "capable of," as in the word *durable*. Suffixes also serve as an important structural clue and are therefore helpful in the word-recognition program.

Five combinations of root, prefix, and suffix are immediately indicated:

1. Root by itself as in *stand*.
2. Prefix + root as in *prefix*.
3. Root + suffix as in *badly*.
4. Prefix + root + suffix as in *interchangeable*.
5. Root + root as in *cowboy*.

Studies have shown that a few Latin and Greek roots are very helpful in deciphering the meanings of thousands of words. The list that follows contains the nineteen most common Latin roots:

LATIN WORD (PRINCIPLE VERBAL PARTS)	MEANING	RELATED ENGLISH WORDS
agere, ago, egi, actum	to act, do, arouse, to set in motion, drive, transact, sue	agent, act, action, actuality, actual, active, actor

LATIN WORD	MEANING	RELATED ENGLISH WORDS
cedere, cedo, cessi, cessum	to give ground, to yield, to seize	seceded, cede, secession
ducere, duco, duxi, ductum	lead	duct, conduct, ductile, abduct
facere, facio, feci, factum	to do, make	fact, factory, benefit, factor, fashion, factual
ferre, fero, tuli, (tolerabilis, tollere, tolerare), latum	bear, carry	ferry, oblation, tolerate, ferret, tolerant, toleration, transfer
legere, lego, legi, lectum	choose, collect, gather, read	elect, reelect, select, lector, lecturer
mittere, mitto, misi, missum	send	emit, mission, remit, submit, admit, missive
movere, moveo, movi, motum	move, arouse, excite	move, mobility, movable, movement, mover
plicare (complicare), (com)plico, (com)plicavi, (com)plicatum	to fold, confuse	complicate, duplicate, plicate, complication
ponere, pono, posui, positum	put, place	pose, opposite, post, position
portare, porto, portavi, portatum	carry	comport, port, export, import, report
regere, rego, rexi, rectum	to rule, guide, direct	direct, regular, rector, rectory, rex
scribere, scribo, scripsi, scriptum	to write	script, transcript, manuscript, inscription
specere, specio, spexi, spectum	to see	specious, specter, spectre, inspect, spy
stare, sto, steti, statum	to stand, remain, endure	statue, insist, stationary, station
tenere, teneo, tenui, tentum	hold, have	tenuto, tenet, tenor, tenaculum, tenacious
tendere, tendo, tentendi, (tensum)	stretch out, extend, march toward	tend, tendency, tension, tender
venire, venio, veni, ventum	to come	event, convene, convention
videre, video, vidi, visum	to see	view, vision, visible, visit

Greek roots are also helpful in arriving at the meanings of words. Here are twenty Greek roots, of which the first two are by far the most common.

GREEK WORD	MEANING	RELATED ENGLISH WORDS
graphein, grapho, gegrapha	to write, inscribe	graph, phonograph, monograph, graphic
legein, lego	to tell, to say	(see logos)
aer	air, atmosphere	aerodonetics, aerate
autos	self	automatic, automobile
bios	life	autobiography, biography, biology
geos	earth, land	geologist, geometry
heteros	other	heterodox, heterogeneity
homoios	like, same	homogeneity, homogeneous
logos	word, thought, study	geology, biology
micros	small	microscope, microcosm
monos	alone, only, once, one	monochord, monochrome
philos	friend	philanthropy
phone	sound, tone, voice	telephone, phonic
physis	nature	physics, physical
polys	many	polygamy, polygamist
pseudos	lie, false	pseudonym
psyche	breath, life, spirit	psychic, psychology
sophos	wise, clever	philosopher, philosophy
tele	far	television, telepathy
telos	end	telephone, telegraph

The following prefixes are used most frequently:

PREFIX	MEANING	EXAMPLES
ab, a	away from, from	abstract, absent, avert
ad, a, ap, at, as, acc, app, add, al	to, toward	ascend, advent, allocate
be	by, thoroughly, make	beguile, belittle
com, co, cor, con, col, cum	with, joint, equally	cooperate, communication, coauthor, coextensive
de	from	deduce, depress
dis, di, dif	apart, opposite of	discontent, disentangle
epi	upon	epigram, epidermis, epitaph
ex, e, ef, es	out of	exit, exhale, eject, extract
in, en, im, em	in, into	immigrant, impel

PREFIX	MEANING	EXAMPLES
in, ir, il	not	inactive, indomitable
inter, enter, intro	between	interchangeable, interpose, interscholastic
mis	wrong	misconstrue, misspell, mislead
mono	alone, one	monograph, monologue
non	not	nonreligious, nonconform
ob, op, of, opp, off	against	obstacle, offend, occasion
pre	before	precede, prefect, prefer
pro	in front of	proceed, pronoun
re	back, again	recede, reanimate
sub, succ, suff, susp, supp	under	subterranean, suffix
trans	across	transgress, transcend
un	not, reverse an act	unjust, unfair, unequal

Many suffixes are also helpful in working out the meanings of words. The following are common:

SUFFIX	MEANING	EXAMPLES
able, ible, ble	capable of, worthy	durable, credible, detachable
age	act or state of	dotage, bondage
al, eal, ial	relating to that which	naval, terminal, regional
an, ian	relating to, belonging to	urban, Christian
ance, ancy, ence, ency	quality or state of	temperance, violence
ant	quality of (adj.)	reliant
	one who (n.)	truant
ar, er, or	related to (adj.)	popular
	one who (n.)	scholar, author
arium	a place for	aquarium
ary	related to (adj.)	planetary
	signifying office	notary
	a place for (n.)	granary
at(e)	cause to be (v.)	liberate
	quality of (adj.)	moderate
	office (n.)	pastorate
ation	cause to be, or of the act of	creation
ative	tending to, or of the nature of	palliative

SUFFIX	MEANING	EXAMPLES
cle	diminutive ending	particle
cy	state of (n.)	bankruptcy
	quality of	constancy
	office of	superintendency
	rank of	captaincy
dom	fact of being, state, condition	kingdom, wisdom
eer	one who deals with, is connected with	auctioneer
en	made of	woolen
en	to make	lengthen, strengthen
en	to make plural	oxen
ent	being	adjacent
er	one who, that which	pointer
est	superlative degree	slowest
ful	full of	graceful, blissful
fy	to make	glorify, falsify, classify
ial	pertaining to	official
ic	pertaining to	classic, metallic
	belonging to	Germanic
	connected with	domestic
	of the nature of	philosophic
ical	belonging to	comical
	related to	medical
ier	one who	carrier
ion	act of, process of, state of	vision, suspension
ish	like	foolish
ist	one who	communist, violinist
ite	native of	Gothamite
ity, ty	state of	unity, ability
ive	having the nature or quality of that which	suggestive, abusive, destructive
ize	to subject to the action or treatment denoted by the verb *to make*	modernize memorize
	to treat or combine	oxydize
	to practice	temporize
less	without	motionless
ly	like in appearance characteristic	brotherly, ably, gently slowly, lastly
ment	result of, act of doing state or quality of	astonishment, increment, enjoyment
ness	state, quality of, degree of	preparedness, blindness

SUFFIX	MEANING	EXAMPLES
or	agent or doer	editor
	state or quality of	candor
orium	place for	auditorium
ory	of or belonging to, place of	auditory, laboratory
ose, ous	full of	comatose, piteous
ous, ious, eous	full of or abounding in	joyous, courteous
ry	quality, character conduct of, place of art or trade	foolery bakery archery
sis	state or condition of	peristalsis
tion, sion, xion	act, state, result of	contention, condition
tude	quality or degree of	servitude
ty	quality or state of	liberty
ure	act of being result of an act state body	censure picture judicature legislature
ward	toward	southward

It is probably best to begin the teaching of affixes by teaching suffixes before prefixes. This permits the child, moving left to right, to encounter the root word first. *

Approximate levels at which to introduce the suffixes and prefixes are as follows:

SUFFIXES

FIRST READER	SECOND READER	THIRD READER		THIRD READER AND ABOVE			
ar	er	able	sion	age	cle	ial	ive
ed	ful	an	tion	al	com	ic	like
est	less	ation	ward	ance	eer	ical	ory
ing	ment	hood		ancy	en	ier	ose
ly	ness	ian		ant	ence	ious	ous
	y	ible		arium	ency	ism	some
		ish		ary	ent	ist	tude
		or		ate	ery	ity	ty
		ship		ative	fy	ize	ure

* For a more complete listing of roots, prefixes, and suffixes see Dechant 1973: pp. 215–238.

PREFIXES

SECOND READER	THIRD READER		THIRD READER AND ABOVE			
a (ab)	ad	in	ante	extra	mid	super
be	anti	ob	bi	fore	mis	supra
en	com	over	col	il	non	sur
ex (e)	de	per	con	ir	post	tele
re	dis	pre	em	inter	semi	trans
un	im	pro	epi	intro	sub	ultra

Teaching pupils how to use roots, prefixes, and suffixes as cues to meaning may be done by exercises such as the following:

1. *Teaching Roots*
   A. Ask the pupils to write out the root word.

   cried *cry*   happiest _____
   carried _____   flies _____
   easier _____   dried _____

   B. Have the pupils write the root and the suffix on separate lines.

	Root	*Suffix*
selling	sell	ing
cooked	_____	_____
rains	_____	_____

   C. Have the pupils add *er, ed, ing,* or *s,* where appropriate, to the root word.

	Add er	*Add ed*	*Add ing*	*Add s*
stay	_____	stayed	staying	stays
cook	_____	_____	_____	_____
bat	_____	_____	_____	_____
walk	_____	_____	_____	_____

2. *Teaching Prefixes*
   A. Ask the pupils to work out the meaning of a word when the prefix and its meaning are given.
      (1) transport _____
          trans—across
      (2) deduct _____
          de—from, away from

   B. Have the pupils identify the word when the meaning and prefix are given.
      (1) to send out of the country
          (ex) export
      (2) to turn a pupil away from school
          (ex) _____

C. Have the pupils give a definition or synonym for an underlined prefixed word.
   (1) We have a *semimonthly* meeting. (twice a month)
   (2) It is questionable that we can *disentangle* ourselves from the internal strife of other people.
   (3) Is there really so much virtue in being a *nonconformist?*

D. Have the pupils select the word that means the same as the underlined word.
   (1) The virtuosa announced her encore, but because of the applause her words were only *half-heard.*
       _____ audible
       _____ semiaudible
       _____ inaudible

   (2) Randy thought of trading in his Fury I on a GTO, but the dealer obviously *put too low a value* on his car.
       _____ valueless
       _____ undervalued
       _____ invaluable

   (3) The teacher was *extremely critical* of my performance.
       _____ uncritical
       _____ ultracritical
       _____ overcritical

3. *Teaching Suffixes*
   A. Some suffixes, when added to a word, form a personal noun and mean "one who." For example, *farmer* refers to one who farms. Have the pupils indicate what noun may be formed from each of the following definitions:

   One who manages . . . . manager
   One who speaks . . . .
   One who exports . . . .
   One who theorizes . . . .
   One who paints . . . .
   One who organizes . . . .

   B. Some suffixes when added to a word form an adjective. For example, *teachable* pertains to someone who can be taught. Have the pupils give the meanings of words such as the following:

   childish . . . . acting like a child
   poetic . . . .
   illusory . . . .
   peerless . . . .
   honorary . . . .
   compulsory . . . .
   dreamy . . . .
   spacious . . . .

   C. Have the pupils give the suffix, suffix and word meanings, and part of speech for each of the following words:

	Suffix	Meaning of Suffix	Meaning of Word	Part of Speech
falsify	fy	to make	to make false	verb
occurrence				
motherhood				
feverish				
usually				
generous				
braggart				

   D. Have the pupils select the word that says the same thing as the italicized words in sentences such as the following:

      (1) The dog was *watching* the child carefully lest she wander onto the street.
           watchful
           watcher

      (2) The sky was *without a cloud.*
           cloudless
           cloudy

      (3) The man *did not move a muscle.* He waited for the judge's verdict.
           movable
           motionless

      (4) Are you *the person who will help me* with this job?
           helpful
           helper

   C. Have the pupils identify the number of prefixes, suffixes, or both, in the words such as

        compulsory   Prefixes: 0 1 2   Suffixes: 0 1 2

   D. Have the pupils read prefixed and suffixed nonsense words:

unpan	prohit	cupable	wellful
exlike	prestand	floorent	gating

TEACHING HYPHENATED WORDS

Learning hyphenation skills occurs generally at the fourth-grade level. Whenever a compound word is used as a modifier and occurs before the word that it modifies, it is hyphenated: thus, *living-room furniture,* or *fourth-grade level.* The hyphen also is used with *self* (*self-denial, self-confidence, self-control*) and with compound numbers from 21 to 99 when they are spelled out (*twenty-six men*).

DEVELOPING SYLLABICATION SKILLS

Syllabication must receive attention at all levels of reading instruction. For most pupils, learning in this area is greatest during the intermediate grades. However, even in the first grade the pupil must be trained to hear the distinct vowel sounds that occur in a word. Gradually, some children will learn that the number of vowel sounds heard indicates the number of syllables in a word.

Glass (1967) questions the value of syllabication. He notes that usually the syllabication is done only after the sounds in words become known. No one in his study seemed to use syllabication rules to discover the sounds in words; rather, the sounds were used to determine syllable division. To determine correct syllable boundaries the pupil must first pronounce the word; the division of a word rests on its pronunciation. Glass thus notes that word analysis is not needed once the sound of the word is known and asks: "Why syllabicate?" Glass concludes that he can discover no reason why syllabication activities should be included in a word-analysis program. Not all reading specialists agree with these observations.

There is an additional confusion involved in the issue of syllabication in that lexicographers divide words by structure and linguists divide them by pronunciation. Linguists have argued that the syllable is a phonological unit, not a graphemic unit.

At any rate, good readers know how to divide words accurately and rapidly. This does not mean that they divide every word that they come to in their reading or that they know the rule for dividing it. The former would slow down reading and might even interfere with good comprehension. The latter is not necessary for good reading.

The first principle to be learned is that every syllable contains a sounded vowel. At times, a vowel itself constitutes a syllable: *a-corn, I, vi-o-let, lin-e-ar, lin-e-al, cer-e-al, o-pen, i-de-a.* The student must also learn that a syllable may contain more than one vowel letter. The number of syllables a word has is dependent upon the number of vowels *heard*, not on the number of vowel letters *seen*. A spoken syllable is thus defined as a unit of pronunciation or as an uninterrupted unit of speech containing one vowel phoneme or sound that is pronounced with one impulse. It may consist of the vowel sound alone (*I*); a vowel sound either preceded or followed by a single or multiple consonant sound (*go, at, ant, brat*); or a vowel sound both preceded and followed by a consonant sound (*cat*). Syllables are in this sense units of sound, in contrast to morphemes which are units of meaning. The syllable may also be defined as the part of a word that contains a vowel and receives some stress. Phonetically, it is a speech segment having a single vocal impulse.

The spoken syllable does not always correspond exactly to the written or printed syllable. Printing conventions for the division of words at the end of a line have not always followed the pattern of speech syllables. However, speech syllables and printed syllables do correspond with enough regularity that the printed syllable can be used in dividing words into parts which in turn can be readily analyzed and blended to pronounce words. Thus, a printed syllable will be considered as the sequence of letters more or less approximating the syllable of speech.

A word of one syllable is called a monosyllable, and a word of two or more syllables is called a plurisyllable. A word having more than three syllables may be referred to as a polysyllable.

Syllables are of two kinds: *closed* syllables and *open* syllables. A closed syllable is one that ends with a consonant: *cat*, *basis*, and *magnetic*. The vowel in a closed syllable usually represents a short vowel sound.

An open syllable is one that ends in a vowel: *cry, by*. The vowel in an open syllable is usually a long vowel. At one time, the *y* at the end of a word was often pronounced as a short *i*; today, it is a long *e* (*baby, shabby*).

A number of syllabication generalizations have been developed for helping children pronounce unfamiliar words. The following generalizations seem to have the highest validity:

RULE I: DOUBLE CONSONANTS (vc/cv)

When two consonant letters follow a vowel letter (as in *after, kitten, pencil, summer*, and *butter*) *the word is divided between the two consonants, and the first syllable ends with the first consonant.* In instances of this kind the second consonant is silent when the consonants are the same except in compounds (*bookkeeper*). Since the first vowel is followed by a consonant, it usually is given its short sound.

Not all double consonant letters can be divided, however. Consonant blends and speech consonants fall into this category (*gam-bler, re-shape*).

RULE II: SINGLE CONSONANTS (v/cv)

When only one consonant letter or a digraph follows a vowel letter (as in *paper, bacon, prefer, begun*, and *reshape*) *the word is usually divided after the first vowel letter, and the consonant or consonant digraph begins the second syllable.* The first vowel letter, in that it ends a syllable, is usually given its long sound (*si-lent, no-mad, ba-sin, da-tum, mi-nus, to-tal, ha-zel, si-nus, fa-tal, ca-det, ce-ment*).

EXCEPTIONS AND OBSERVATIONS

A. Not all words follow the above rules. For example, *planet, solid, robin, travel, study, record*, river, primer*, cabin, tropic, present*, timid, habit, pity, body, quiver, copy, lily, bigot, honor, venom, olive, legend, lemon, valid, limit, dragon, wagon, digit, solid, cherish, volume, lizard, snivel, cherub*, and *profit* join the consonant to the first vowel. This makes the first vowel short, and the accent is on the first syllable.

B. Suffix *ed:* The suffix *ed* is a syllable only when it follows the sound *d* or *t: bunted, handed*.

C. Whenever *le* ends a word and is preceded by a consonant, the last syllable consists of the consonant and the *le:* thus, *ta-ble, mid-dle, peo-ple*. When *le* is preceded by *ck*, *le* is a separate syllable: *freck-le, buck-le*. When *gle* is preceded by *n*, as in *bungle, jingle, mangle, mingle, single, spangle, tangle, tingle*, it is pronounced as /gg'l/. The *e* in *ble, tle, ple*, and *dle* is silent. Some authors, however, suggest that *le* is pronounced /əl/ with the *e* being shorter than usual and called *schwa*.

---

* These may be divided according to both rules, dependent upon their meaning in the sentence.

Observe that in *tle* the *t* sometimes is silent and at times may be pronounced. Thus, in *battle, bottle, brittle, mantle, cattle, little, rattle,* and *tattle* the *t* is pronounced; in *castle, hustle, jostle,* and *rustle* (words in which the *tle* follows the letter *s*) it is silent.

D. Sometimes it is necessary to divide between two vowels: *cre-ate.* Examples of this include the following:

    oi: *archaic, laity, mosaic*
    ea: *cereal, create, delineate, fealty, laureate, lineate, linear, permeate*
    ei: *being, deity, reinforce, reinstate, spontaneity*
    eu: *museum, nucleus*
    ie: *client, diet, dietary, expedient, orient, piety, propriety, quiet, science*
    oa: *coadjutor, coagulate, oasis*
    oe: *coefficient, coerce, coexist, poem*
    oi: *egoist, going*
    oo: *cooperate, coordinate, zoology*
    ue: *cruel, duel, duet, fluent, fuel, gruel, influence, minuet*
    ui: *altruism, ambiguity, annuity, fluid, fruition*

E. *Compound Words:* In a compound word the division comes between the two words making up the compound: *post-man.*

F. *Root Words and Affixes:* Prefixes and suffixes are usually set apart from the rest of the word: *go-ing, trans-port.*

Teaching of syllabication may begin when pupils are introduced to words ending in *ing* and to simple compounds, hence in first grade. In second grade pupils should learn to hear the number of vowel sounds in a word, learn the basic syllable generalizations (vc/cv as in *after* and v/cv as in *bacon*), and learn to apply the short-vowel rule to the stressed syllable in two-syllable words. In third grade the pupils should learn to hear and mark syllable division, to syllabicate two and three-syllable words, and to know the syllabication exceptions.

Betts (1961) outlined the steps in applying syllabication, accent, and phonics skills to the syllables of words:

1. Pupils must first learn to hear the number of syllables in spoken words.
2. Pupils must learn to identify syllables in printed words. Early in the grades pupils need to learn that some words ending in *ed* have only one syllable (*cooked*), whereas others have two syllables (*landed*).
3. Pupils must learn to accent the proper syllable. Accentuation should be taught only after pupils have mastered steps one and two and after they have learned something about prefixes and suffixes. These latter rarely are accented (*intend, fishing*).
4. Pupils must learn to apply phonic skills to the separate vowels in words; they need to be able to apply the short-vowel rule to the stressed syllable (*rabbit*).
5. Pupils must check to see if the word makes sense in the sentence.

Remediation of syllabication difficulties may take many forms. Teachers may pursue some of the following courses:

1. Provide training in dictionary usage.
2. Provide ear training, teaching the pupil to hear the syllables within words. Have pupils say their names in unison: *Ted-dy*, *Sar-a*, *Jim*, *Bobb-y*.
3. Pronounce words having one or two syllables and let pupils clap or raise their hands when they hear a word of two syllables.
4. Have pupils listen to words and indicate the number of vowels actually heard.

mercury	3	inaccurately	_____
wherewithal	_____	bridge	_____
tuberculosis	_____	humiliate	_____
calculate	_____	thoroughbred	_____
accumulate	_____	arguments	_____

5. Present the same exercise as in #4, but have the written form of the word in front of the pupil.
6. Have pupils divide words of more than one syllable.

witness	wit-ness	allegiance	_____
idea	_____	lonely	_____
pebble	_____	stomach	_____
minstrel	_____	squirrel	_____
completion	_____	camera	_____

7. Have pupils identify the number of vowels, the number of vowel sounds, and the number of syllables in words.

	VOWELS	VOWEL SOUNDS	SYLLABLES
summer	2	2	2
lonely	3	2	2

8. Help the pupil to use diacritical markings.
9. Teach the basic syllabication rules using numerous examples to illustrate the generalization. For example:
   Have the pupil divide words such as *basket*, *witness* and such words as *pilot*, *motel*, *bacon* and let them verbalize the principle involved.

DEVELOPING ACCENTUATION SKILLS

A word of two or more syllables generally is pronounced with more stress on one syllable. This is termed *accent*. In most dictionaries the accent mark (') is placed just after the syllable that receives major stress. In words of three or more syllables there may be a secondary accent, as in *lo' co mo' tive*.

    Accentuation is taught only after the pupil has learned to hear the number of syllables in spoken and written words. This usually occurs in second grade. In third grade the use of stress marks should be taught and some basic generalizations should be introduced. Exercises in accentuation should always use words that the pupil knows. After pupils have learned the meaning of accent and the way the dictionary identifies the accent or stress point, they may gradually be introduced to the following generalizations:

1. Words of two syllables, in which two consonants follow the first vowel, generally accent the first syllable: thus, *after, kitten, puppet,* and *butter.* This also occurs in many words in which only one consonant follows the vowel: *bacon, pilot,* but there are many exceptions: *begin, prefer.*

2. When a two-syllable word contains two vowels in the second syllable but only one is pronounced, the second syllable generally is accented: *abide, abode, above, about, aboard, delay, and proceed.* Usually the last syllable contains a long vowel sound.

3. Compound words usually carry the primary accent on (or within) the first word: *bellhop, bulldog, carhop, dishpan, godson, pigpen.* There are many exceptions to this rule: *another, forget, upon.*

4. Syllables beginning with a consonant followed by *le* (*circle, rabble*) are not accented.

5. In three-syllable words, in which the root word's second syllable ends in a silent *e* and is accented (*advise, excite, translate*), the accent is often on the second syllable: *adviser, excited, translated.* Other three-syllable words have their accent on the first syllable: *piloted, traveled, shivered.*

6. Root-word syllables, when preceded by prefixes or followed by suffixes, usually are accented: *amuse, amusement.*

7. Words ending in *ion, ity, ic, ical, ian,* or *ious* have the accent immediately before these suffixes: *consternation, athletic, immersion, harmonious, humidity, psychological, historian.*

8. Words of three or more syllables ending in a silent *e* usually accent the third-to-last syllable: *graduate, accommodate, anticipate.*

9. Homographs or words with identical spellings receive their accent from the context in which they are used: *con'tract—con tract'.*

In introducing pupils to accent and syllabication, the teacher needs to use words that the pupils know. Repeated exercise with actual words will help pupils obtain a functional knowledge of the generalizations stated above.

Initially, the teacher may pronounce a word orally and let the pupils indicate by one or two fingers whether the word has one or two syllables, and whether the accent falls on the first or second syllable. Gradually, the pupils should learn to write a word, divide it, and indicate its accent. At the upper grade levels, pupils should be able to give the rules which govern a word's syllabication and accentuation.

Exercises* useful in developing proper accentuation skills are

1. Pronounce a word such as *basket,* putting the accent on the first syllable and then on the second syllable, and have pupils select the correct pronunciation. The word should be used in a sentence and it should be in the pupils' aural-oral vocabulary.

* For materials designed to teach each of the structural analysis skills, see Dechant 1981b: pp. 121–140.

2.   Using known words, have pupils circle the word that is accented properly:

    a. fáther   fathér   c. bácon   bacon′
    b. colór   color′   d. bégin   begin′

3.   Teach pupils that the use and meaning of a word have a bearing upon the accent of the word:

    a. He made a *récord* of the proceedings.
    b. Will you *record′ the proceedings of today's meeting?*

    Words useful in developing these discriminations are: *august, buffet, compact, present, annex, contract, conduct, content, convict, excuse, produce, record, object, combine, rebel, protest, permit, minute, perfect, subject, abstract.* The pupil should learn that this shift of accent occurs especially when a noun is used as a verb or as an adjective: *presént—present′*; *mínute—minuté.*

4.   Introduce pupils to some of the compound words given earlier and let them see that in compound words the accent is usually placed on the first word: *doorway, rainbow,* and the like.

SUMMARY

Chapter 11 has examined the teaching of structural or morphemic analysis skills. Morphemic analysis skills are meaning skills that the reader may use not only to develop meaning for words but also to aid in the identification of words. When readers use them in the latter fashion, they generally syllabicate the word, pronounce the syllables, blend the resultant sounds, and check whether the word so formed makes sense in the sentence.

QUESTIONS FOR DISCUSSION

1.   What are the eight facets with which morphemic or structural analysis usually deals?
2.   Differentiate between inflectional endings and suffixes.
3.   Identify the difficulties of teaching compounds.
4.   What are the definitions and functions of roots, prefixes, and suffixes?
5.   What types of words are usually hyphenated?
6.   What are the basic syllabication rules?
7.   Discuss the importance of structural analysis in word identification and comprehension.
8.   What principles guide the accentuation of words?

12
DEVELOPING WORD–MEANING SKILLS

It is at this point that you should recall that reading is a twofold process. First, it requires *word identification* (visual discrimination of the word, and recoding or the ability to pronounce the word), which is generally effected by configuration cues, phonic cues, morphemic analysis cues, and sometimes by picture and context cues. Second, reading requires *comprehension* (decoding or associating meaning with the symbols that comprise the word). Reading is an interpretative process; it is a conceptual and thinking process; it is thinking through print.

In the next few chapters the emphasis is on reading as a comprehension process. The goal of all reading is the comprehension of meaning. Comprehension in reading depends upon the ability to deal with individual word meanings, but also upon the ability to reason with words. Chapter 12 focuses on the first of these, that is, with the association of an experience with a given symbol. This is absolutely necessary, but it nevertheless is the most elemental form of comprehension. Complete meaning is not conveyed by a single word. Good readers must learn to interpret words in their contextual setting. They must comprehend words as parts of phrases, clauses, and sentences. Chapters 13 and 14 will deal with this phase of reading.

Word knowledge is the most important factor for reading comprehension or for reading with meaning in the elementary and secondary school years. Studies generally indicate that vocabulary is highly related to comprehension. Even when allowance is made for intellectual differences, there still is a sufficiently high relationship between reading comprehension and vocabulary proficiency to justify attempts to improve comprehension through vocabulary training.

DIFFICULTIES IN DEVELOPING MEANINGS FOR WORDS

Developing word meaning is one of the teacher's most important tasks. Even though pupils possess the meanings needed for the comprehension of the reading materials available to them, the teacher constantly must expand the pupils' semantic meanings and check upon the adequacies of the pupils' present meanings.

Fortunately, it appears that children have a far greater knowledge of the literal meaning of words than is usually credited to them. First graders generally have a speaking vocabulary of over 2500 words and possibly a recognition vocabulary of over 20,000 words. Certainly no teacher ever taught a child even most of the words the child knows.

However, few students have had sufficient experience to appreciate all the connotations or multiple meanings of a word. They have not developed precision in meaning. This knowledge comes only through experience. Some students, even if they have a broader understanding of a word, are often content to settle for the first meaning that comes to mind. Poor readers, especially if they are inclined to be impulsive, tend to do this.

The word *run*, for example, according to the American College Dictionary, has 109 distinct meanings; the word *take* has 76 meanings, and the word *round* has 83 different meanings. *Run* can mean to move swiftly, to go back and forth between two locations, to participate in an election, to win a race, to get into debt, to trace a story back to its source, to smuggle contraband, and to operate a store. These are only a few examples. In addition, we speak of a run of fish, a run of bad trouble, a run on the bank, a running brook, the ordinary run of people, and a cattle run.

The teaching of meanings for words involves a threefold process, each part of which is significant. The pupils must be taught the basic, literal meaning of the word; they must be taught the more common alternate meanings (in other words, they must learn all the significant meanings); and they must be taught to select from the list of multiple meanings the correct meaning which fits the context.

Multiple meanings are not the only ambiguities of language that make the apprehension of meaning difficult. Two different words may have the same or similar meanings, and two words which are pronounced alike may have different spellings and meanings (*blue-blew*). These latter words are termed homonyms. The same words may have different pronunciations and meanings (*wĭnd-wīnd*). Such words are called homographs or heteronyms. Numerous idiomatic and figurative expressions add to the reader's predicament.

Some words are used in their generic sense or are much more abstract than are others. The word *dot* may allow for only slight variations of meaning. The word *democracy* has an invariant meaning, but it also allows for a multitude of differing interpretations. Often familiar terms are used in an unfamiliar sense. This is especially so in the content areas. And words may have different syntactical functions and a variety of inflectional endings. The word *best*, which usually has an adjectival function, becomes a noun in a sentence such as, "Your best is not good enough." The word *cat's* is indeed different from the word *cat* and has an added meaning dimension.

There are some general principles that should guide the teacher in the dealing with the difficulties in developing meaning:

1. Words by themselves are not inherent, valid units of meaning. The meanings connoted by a word have been arbitrarily assigned to the symbol.
2. Most words have more than one meaning. Generally, the more frequently a word is used, the more meanings it tends to have.
3. The number of meanings actually elicited by a word depends on the number and quality of experiences that the reader has associated with the word. Each new level of meaning requires a corresponding broadening of experience with objective reality.
4. The specific meaning elicited by a word is a function of the context in which the word occurs, both the verbal or semantic context and the syntactic context. Syntax helps to determine which of the semantic meanings is the appropriate one.

READING AS AN ASSOCIATIVE PROCESS

Before looking at the techniques for teaching word meaning, examine how meaning is associated with the printed symbol in the first place. Meaning can be associated with the printed word only by associating the word with an experience, whether real or vicarious, or by associating it with another symbol (the spoken word) that has meaning for the child. For most children the latter is a natural process. The child is asked to look at the word *cat*, and is told that it is pronounced /kăt/. It is assumed that the child will bring the meaning to the printed word that was previously associated only with the spoken word.

It may be well at this point to reacquaint yourself with classical conditioning, for as one examines how a child learns to read, one sees a striking similarity between these processes and the classical conditioning experiments.

In Pavlov's experiment (Pavlov 1927), the problem was one of getting the dog to salivate to the sound of a metronome or a bell. Pavlov found that the dog would salivate (unconditioned response—UR) immediately when a plate of powdered food (unconditioned stimulus—US) was placed before it. In the experimental situation, a tone was sounded (conditioned stimulus—CS) and the dog then was presented with a plate of powdered food (US). Naturally the dog would salivate. After about thirty such trials the dog salivated (conditioned response—CR) when only the tone was sounded. The dog had become conditioned to the tone.

Conditioning, then, denotes that a stimulus which is inadequate for some response (CS) can become adequate by being combined one or more times with a stimulus which is adequate for the response (US) (Razran 1955).

Generally, children have already developed most of the meanings that they encounter in their early reading experiences, and they have also associated these meanings or experiences with a spoken symbol. Teaching these children to read then means that the teacher must get them to identify the visual symbol and to associate with it the meaning that has already been associated with a spoken symbol. Children must associate the spoken and written word a sufficient number of times so that they come to react to the written word with the same meaning that was previously taken to the spoken word. Printed words are symbols of sounds and are formed from letters which are symbols of sounds. A printed word has meaning because it is a symbol of sound, a spoken word, that already has meaning for the child (Terman and Walcutt 1958).

Thus, for children learning to read, the spoken word is the unconditioned or familiar stimulus and the written word is the conditioned stimulus. Gradually, with repeated associations between the written and the spoken word, children bring to the written word the same meanings that they previously attached to the spoken word. Through association, meaning becomes attached to the written word. Figure 12–1 illustrates this process.

Some children have great difficulty in associating meaning with the written word. Sometimes the child simply has not had the experiences necessary to develop meaning. Few pupils have had sufficient experience to appreciate all the connotations or implied or inferred meanings of a word. Some may not identify the word correctly and thus never associate the meaning with a given symbol. It is not uncommon to find that the pupil will know a word on the flash card, but will not know it when it appears in contextual reading. The word may have been

Figure 12-1   Conditioning and Reading

PAVLOV			READING	
US Powdered Food	UR Salivation		US Spoken Word	UR Meaning
CR Bell	CR Salivation to Bell		CS Written Word	CR Meaning Associated with Written Word

identified as "the one that appears on the card with the broken corner." Children need to be taught to pay attention to the distinctive features of words.

Finally, the association process itself may break down. Children generally need more than one association between stimulus and meaning. They need to see the word in many and varied situations. Varied practice extends and refines the meaning; repetitive practice makes the association habitual.

TECHNIQUES FOR DEVELOPING MEANING*

The word-identification strategies, discussed in Chapter 8, are each useful in developing meaning. Briefly, these are illustration or picture cues, structural or morphemic analysis, phonic cues, context cues, and dictionary cues. Phonic analysis, for example, helps a pupil to obtain meaning through the correct pronunciation of the word. However, this technique works only if the pupil recognizes the word when it is spoken.

The guided or directed reading activity (DRA) provides the format for the teaching of meaning. The basic steps of the DRA are

1. Building readiness for reading a selection by building concept and vocabulary background, by creating interest and motivation, and by creating a purpose for reading.
2. Guided silent reading.
3. Checking comprehension.
4. Oral rereading of the material.
5. Extending word-recognition and comprehension skills: learning and practicing new skills.
6. Enrichment and follow-up activities: supplementary reading, dramatization, and other creative activities.

Of interest here is the development of the word-meaning skills. The teacher selects from the material to be read those words with which the pupils are likely to have difficulty and develops recognition and meaning for these words. The DRA is so important in the development of meaning that the reader should again review the DRA in Chapter 8.

In the group situation where the DRA format is used, pupils of a particular basal level meet with the teacher who motivates them toward the selection by posing questions about the theme or setting or other aspects of the story. The pupils read the selection silently (and/or orally) and orally answer specific teacher-developed questions. Unfortunately, it is extremely difficult to use the DRA with as many as three different subgroups in a classroom and still do quality

* For materials designed to develop each of the word-meaning skills, see Dechant 1981b: pp. 145–171.

teaching. Even within the same subgroup it is difficult to evaluate *each* pupil's progress. Charnock (1977) suggests that above the second-grade level, pupils should be required to write out their answers to specific questions about the story. Occasionally students can meet as a subgroup, read and discuss the story, and then develop group-written responses to the questions. Sometimes pupils may pair with one another to complete the assignment. Charnock suggests that this approach allows for better class management, better monitoring of pupil abilities and progress, and more original thinking. He notes that some children dislike being put on the spot to answer a tough question, resent those who know it all, and are slowed by the less skilled and perceptive.

In developing meaning for words teachers have essentially two options: they may use either a direct- or a vicarious-experience approach:

1. *The direct-experience, observation, or participation approach* includes such activities as field trips or visits to a farm or factory, thus broadening the pupil's experiential background.
2. *The vicarious-experience approach* may take three forms:
   a. Direct instruction in vocabulary: This includes teaching the use of morphemic, phonic, and context cues, together with the dictionary, and the study of word lists, word parts, word origins, and the like. It involves pronunciation of words, association of words with pictures, and the use of words in discussion. Studies (Vaughan, Crawley, and Mountain 1979) generally show that direct instruction in vocabulary is superior to incidental instruction.
   b. Incidental experience approach: This involves the use of pictures and illustrations, oral discussion, storytelling, films, filmstrips, slides, models, rhyme and puzzle games, dramatization, pageants, picture dictionaries, picture word-games that require the matching of words with pictures, and the like. Association of the printed word with a picture is perhaps the most used technique in the primary grades.
   c. Wide or extensive reading: Reading, in and of itself, is a valuable aid in acquiring word meanings and in developing one's vocabulary.

The twenty techniques that follow are illustrative of the above approaches to the development of meaning. Most of them involve direct instruction. The first seven techniques were for the most part discussed at length in Chapter 6, and thus do not require additional comment here. The techniques are

1. Provide experience with the concrete object or event. Direct experience is still the best way to develop meaning for a word.
2. Label objects and make extensive use of signs in the classroom; have pupils cut out and label pictures.
3. Teach the pupils to read pictures, illustrations, charts, graphs, and maps. It is difficult to learn what an architect's scale is without an accompanying illustration. Pictures promote mental imagery and memory for a word's meaning.
4. Use riddle, rhyme, and puzzle games to illustrate meaning.
5. Have pupils construct and use picture dictionaries.

6. Use picture word cards, flash cards and lotto games; read easy stories; build sentences with word cards; make scrapbooks; and pursue other similar activities.

7. Have pupils place words in the category to which they belong. For example, the pupils might be required to classify things one might find on a street; things found on a farm; things to eat; things to ride in; things that are animals, plants, fruit, birds, countries, clothing, colors, insects; or things that fly, run, or float.

    Categorizing or grouping for memory aids in recall. It permits greater amounts of material to be transferred into the long-term memory (Vaughan, Crawley, and Mountain 1979). For additional aids in teaching categorization skills, see p. 298.

8. Teach the pupil the use of the context as a cue to word meaning. A later section (page 299) treats context more completely. A simple context exercise requires the pupil to deal with sentences such as the following:

    a. Father bought the apples at the _____. (story, store)

    b. Pass the salt and _____.

    c. Each dog wants a new _____. (book, bone, apron)

9. Have pupils develop the concept of multiple meanings with an exercise such as the following:

    Read the following sentences. The word run *is used in each of the sentences, but it has a different meaning in each. Write the meaning of the word* run *in the blanks provided.*

    a. The boat runs between Georgia and New York. *sails (between two places)*

    b. The two-year-old filly ran first in the Belmont Stakes. *ran (and won) a race*

    c. I ran the story back to its source. *traced*

    d. We saw a run of fish. *school (of fish)*

    e. The man had a run of bad fortune. *series (of unlucky events)*

    f. The brook runs by the cottage. *goes, is located*

    g. He belongs to the ordinary run of people. *(common) kind*

    h. He runs contraband between the Middle East and Europe. *smuggles*

10. Teach pupils the meanings of heteronyms, words whose pronunciation and meaning change depending upon their use in the sentence. Thus:

    a. The *wind* is blowing through the trees.

    b. Some people *wind* their clock before going to bed every evening.

    Examples of heteronyms are: *abstract, annex, august, bass, bow, buffet, close, combine, compact, conduct, console, consort, content, contract, convict, desert, digest, dove, entrance, excuse, incense, intern, invalid, lead, live, minute, object, permit, present, primer, produce, project, protest, read, rebel, record, refuse, sow, subject, tear, wind, wound, convert, perfect, relay.*

11. Teach pupils to use the cloze procedure to develop meaning. This procedure enables readers to use the context to identify the word that completes a passage. The technique is discussed later in this chapter.

12. Teach pupils to use structural words as cues to meaning. In the sentence, ''Ed was talkative while Bill remained taciturn,'' the word *while* signals that *taciturn* is the opposite of *talkative*. Structural words, and in particular their function in the reading of a sentence, are discussed more fully in Chapter 13.

13. Teach pupils the meaning of homonyms (homophones). Homonyms are words that sound alike but have different spellings and meanings. They frequently lead to

recognition and meaning difficulties. To illustrate their difference, the teacher must use them in various contexts. Thus, the difference between *blue* and *blew* is brought out in the following sentences:

a.   The wind *blew* down the house.

b.   Mary wore a *blue* dress.

Labov (1966) notes that dialect can increase the number of homonyms in the spoken language, leading to confusion in interpretation of the written language and the need to put extraordinary reliance on context. The omission of the /r/ in *guard* makes homonyms of *guard* and *god;* omission of the /l/ in *toll* makes homonyms of *toll* and *toe.* Some common homonyms are:

ail-ale	forth-fourth	peace-piece	stile-style
ate-eight	foul-fowl	peek-peak	straight-strait
arc-ark	four-for	peel-peal	sun-son
awl-all	gail-gale	peer-pier	sweet-suite
bail-bale	groan-grown	plane-plain	tail-tale
base-bass	hair-hare	pore-pour	teem-team
be-bee	hale-hail	praise-prays	their-there
bear-bare	haul-hall	principal-principle	through-threw
beat-beet	heel-heal	rain-rein-reign	thrown-throne
bell-belle	here-hear	raise-raze	tide-tied
berth-birth	hew-hue	rap-wrap	to-too-two
blue-blew	horse-hoarse	read-red	toe-tow
bored-board	hour-our	read-reed	tolled-told
bow-bough	led-lead	reel-real	vale-veil
break-brake	leek-leak	road-rode	vane-vein-vain
bread-bred	loan-lone	sail-sale	wade-weighed
buy-by	lye-lie	sea-see	waist-waste
cell-sell	made-maid	seem-seam	wait-weight
cellar-seller	mail-male	seen-scene	wave-waive
cent-sent-scent	mane-main	seer-sear	way-weigh
course-coarse	mantle-mantel	sew-so-sow	week-weak
dear-deer	meet-meat-mete	sight-site-cite	whole-hole
do-dew-due	new-knew	slay-sleigh	wood-would
doe-dough	night-knight	sole-soul	wring-ring
fair-fare	no-know	some-sum	write-right
feet-feat	one-won	sore-soar	wrote-rote
fir-fur	or-ore	staid-stayed	you-yew-ewe
flee-flea	owe-oh	stare-stair	
flew-flue	pain-pane	steak-stake	
flower-flour	pair-pare	steal-steel	

14.   Teach pupils to use high imagery words and to analyze the sense appeal of words. Exercises such as the following develop this ability:

a.   The bumpy highway caused the car to *creak* and *rattle,* but we went merrily on our way.
Creak appeals to the sense(s) of _____ (touch, sight, sound, taste, smell).
Rattle appeals to the sense(s) of _____ (touch, sight, sound, taste, smell).

b.   Icicles, hanging from the roof of our battered cabin, *dripped* and *peppered* the snow beneath *with holes* where *melted* water fell.
The pupils are required to indicate which senses the words *dripped, peppered with holes,* and *melted* appeal to.

Some words useful in teaching the differences in sense appeal of words are:

TOUCH	SIGHT	SOUND	TASTE	SMELL
cold	green	mellow	sweet	fresh
warm	rippled	bang	sour	pungent
hot	spotted	crash	bitter	stuffy
rough	glistening	thud	salty	fragrant
bumpy	ruffle	bellow	smoky	choking
sandy	pale	thumping	ripe	clean
soft	grassy	thrashing	tender	stifling
sticky	whirling	around	tasty	aroma
wet	weather-	stampeding	well-	burning
limp	beaten	splash	seasoned	rancid
sturdy	shadowy	shuffle	tart	moldy
smooth	billowing	honk	spicy	sickening
sleek	lightning	snort	sage	stenchy
frozen	darkness	rumble	biting	
sharp	dense	lapping	sugary	
waxy	bright	growl	bland	
damp	swirling	murmuring		
gentle	hair-	rustle		
crisp	raising	buzzing		
frosty	crouching	purring		
thick	trembling	moan		
tender	fluffy	howl		
stinging	foamy	chirp		
snapping	blossoming	hissing		
icy	brilliant	creaking		
icy cold	windblown	thunderous		
thin	snowy	whine		

Wolpert (1972) found that high imagery words are learned significantly more easily than low imagery words and that imagery value has a substantially greater effect on learning than has word length or shape. Hargis and Gickling (1978) found that high imagery words are more readily learned as sight words and remain in memory storage longer.

15. Teach pupils to use the root of a word as well as prefixes and suffixes as cues to meaning. This technique was covered in Chapter 11.

16. Teach pupils how to work out the meaning of compound words. The problems and techniques of teaching compounds were discussed in Chapter 11.

17. Teach pupils how to read words used in a figurative sense. This skill is dealt with later in this chapter.

18. Help pupils to use the dictionary. This skill is examined later in this chapter.

19. Have pupils study technical vocabularies. Knowing technical vocabularies is particularly important in the content areas. The primary types of technical vocabularies are (1) words that are peculiar to a given subject area; (2) words that are common to all content areas but that have a special meaning in a given content area; and (3) symbols used in a given content area (Dillner and Olson 1977).

    Examples of these categories are as follows:

	Words Peculiar to the Area	Common Words with Special Meaning	Signs and Symbols
History	homestead fascism	cold war grandfather clause	NATO UNESCO
Mathematics	monomial polygon	empty set acute	$\sqrt{}$ $\emptyset$
Biology	ecosystem oogenesis	elements collision	DNA RNA
English	adverb adjective	case dash	& ?

20. Have pupils study the origin of words and how they change, or in other words, the etymology of words. The following exercises are useful:

    a. Study the surnames of children in the class. For example, names like *Baker, Butler, Binder, Bishop, Cook, Brewer, Dechant, Dreher, Engel, Geist, Guard, Hunter, King, Miner, Miller, Pfeifer, Rider, Sander, Schuchman, Schumacher, Shearer, Skinner, Smith, Spicer, Taylor, Teller, Walker,* and *Weaver* identify occupations.

        Other surnames represent objects: for example, *Ball, Bell;* some surnames identify certain characteristics of an object or person: thus *Belle, Breit, Fair, Good;* some identify colors: *Black, Braun, Brown, Gray, Green, Roth, Schwartz (Schwartzkopf),* and *White;* and finally, some are animal names: thus, *Beaver, Bee, Bird, Crow,* or *Ochs.*

    b. Study the foreign origin of words. The Dutch, the French, the Germans, and the Italians have given us many words; here are just a few: Italian (*soprano, piccolo, piano, contralto*); French (*carburetor, chauffeur, coupe, beau, chateau, trousseau, chamois, machine, boudoir, bouquet, barrage, croquet, sachet, ballet*); and German (*kindergarten, waltz, sauerkraut, wiener*). Words of Latin and Greek origin are so numerous that a list is not necessary.

    c. Study new words in the language. Examples of words which are themselves new or are used today in a new sense are as follows:

ack-ack	biodegradable	ecocide	imploit
amtrac	cherrypick	ecofreak	intercom
audiophile	chicken dog	ecophobia	interrobang
ambudsman	chopper-copper	ecosystem	jawboning
big wheel	cloverleaf	emcee	junkie
Black Panther	commune	freeway	klutz
blitz	calypso	frozen rope	liquidate
blue meanie	cloverleaf	genocide	LSD
boogie-woogie	crewcut	ghetto	maxi
brainwashing	cowabunga	goldbrick	meat packer
bellyland	cybernetics	grasshopper	medevac
bamboo curtain	dartchery	grass roots	megaton
bazooka	deicer	glasphalt	me-tooism
beachhead	deltiology	hardtop	mini
bebop	discophile	hi-fi	Molotov cocktail

moto-cross	poodle cut	rhubarb	supermarket
needle (v)	poptop	satellite	slapshot
nitty-gritty	prefab	schmo	spinoff
Oscar	paramedic	sexism	transsex
oreo	rabbit ears	snow (television)	tripsit
pedal pusher	ragarock	spelunker	urbicidal
ponytail	rev	split-level house	

Consider now some of the techniques for developing word meaning in greater detail, including the teaching of specific meanings, the use of context cues, the use of the cloze procedure, the interpretation of figurative and idiomatic expressions, the study and use of the dictionary, and the teaching of space, numerical, and time concepts. Begin with techniques designed to develop specific meanings for words.

DEVELOPING SPECIFICITY OF MEANING

All words have slightly different meanings. The term *synonym* stands for "something like," not for "the same as" (Johnson and Pearson 1978). The exercise that follows, from Johnson and Pearson (1978: pp. 38–42) is helpful in teaching pupils the meaning differences of words:

1. Have the pupils select a category (such as conveyances) and have them identify various types of conveyances (car, truck, bicycle, motorcycle, bus, train, airplane). List these in a column. Then have pupils suggest features or attributes possessed by at least one of the conveyances, and list these across the top of the blackboard or paper. Now have pupils indicate by pluses or minuses if a given conveyance possesses the attribute.

CONVEYANCES	WHEELS	TIRES	ENGINE	HANDLEBAR	MOVES IN AIR
Car	+	+	+	−	−
Truck	+	+	+	−	−
Bus	+	+	+	−	−
Train	+	−	+	−	−
Bicycle	+	+	−	+	−
Airplane	+	+	+	−	+

2. Have pupils suggest additional attributes and have them expand their list of conveyances.
3. Help pupils to realize that if enough attributes are considered, no two words have the identical pattern of pluses and minuses, and hence, that no two words have identical meanings.

Additional exercises may require the pupil to

1.   Rank on the basis of one feature (such as intensity) a series of words of similar meaning (such as *loathe, hate, despise, abhor, dislike*).

2.   Select from a list of words the one word that does not belong with the others: *loathe, hate, love, dislike.*

3.   Group under each of three categories (such as birds, insects, animals) such words as *tern, ferret, gnu, cicada, emu, plover.* This exercise often requires the use of the dictionary.

INFERRING MEANING
FROM CONTEXT CUES

Another major technique for developing meaning for words consists of teaching pupils to use context cues. Pupils' first reading experiences encourage them to use the verbal context in which a word occurs in order to decipher the meaning of the sentence and indeed to identify the word. In Chapter 7 it was suggested that pupils be taught to use the beginning consonant letter and the context to identify the word. In Chapter 8 the use of context cues in identifying words was given further consideration. Reading teachers have always suggested that pupils should look at the word, that they should not guess, and that they should try to anticipate or predict meaning. The reader needs to think along with the author.

The testimonials to the importance of context cues are many. Context is considered one of the most important aids to word identification and to interpretation. Emans (1968) notes that context cues help students to (1) identify words they previously identified but forgot; (2) check the accuracy of words tentatively identified by the use of other cues; (3) develop rapid recognition of words by permitting them to anticipate what a word might be; and (4) identify words that are not identifiable in any other way.

Steiner, Wiener, and Cromer (1971) found that poor readers fail to extract contextual cues essential for identification; they seem to be identifying words as if the words were unrelated items unaffected by syntactical or contextual relationships. They are so preoccupied with details that they read a word into the sentence that makes little or no sense. They struggle unsuccessfully to sound out words whose meaning is completely obvious from the surrounding context.

Skill in using the context needs constant refinement, and indeed it becomes increasingly more valuable as a pupil advances through school. Some pupils, however, rely too much on the context. Context cues are seldom adequate alone because they provide only one aid to word recognition. In some instances context may even lead to confusion or error. The reading makes sense, but sometimes it is not the meaning intended by the writer. The reading of pupils who misuse context is often quite inaccurate. Such pupils may skip over words or add new words, but their most frequent error is that of substituting what they think the story should say.

Pany and Jenkins (1977) found that relying on context to teach word meanings or simply telling meanings to children is not as effective as giving pupils practice in stating meanings. In general, pupils should be taught to combine the sense of the sentence with phonic or other cues.

Contextual signals work as clues to an unknown word's meaning because of the readers' reasoning ability, their past experience, their knowledge of the topic, and the store of meanings that they possesses.

There are various types of contextual aids or cues which can be useful in interpreting what one is reading:

1. Typographical aids, such as quotation marks, parentheses, italics, boldface type, and footnotes or glossary references.
2. Structural aids, such as indications of comparison and contrast.
3. Verbal context or substitute words, such as linked synonyms or antonyms, summarizing words, definitions, examples, restatements, and words of description, direct explanation, or contrast.
4. Word elements, such as roots, prefixes, and suffixes; in other words, morphemic cues.
5. Figures of speech, such as similes or metaphors.
6. Pictorial representations or illustrations; that is, accompanying pictures, diagrams, charts, graphs, and maps (picture cues).
7. Inferential cues, as when cause-effect relationships lead the reader to a new meaning.
8. Subjective cues, such as tone, mood, setting, and intent.
9. Presentation cues, such as the position of words, the sequence of a sentence or paragraph, the general organization of a selection, or cues derived from a pattern of paragraph organization involving a main idea and supporting details.

To assure that pupils will be successful in utilizing context cues in developing meaning for words, the teacher should constantly broaden pupils' experiences, thus increasing their store of meanings; make certain that the material being read is not too difficult; help pupils to develop adequate word-recognition skills and adequate sight vocabulary (especially of the core words); encourage wide reading; and provide systematized instruction in the use of context cues.

Teaching pupils to use context cues may include exercises in areas such as the following:

1. Have pupils use picture cues to help determine meaning. For example, have them circle a picture that completes a sentence: The small boy hit the _____ a long way.

The art on this page is from Dechant 1981 (p. 318). Reprinted by permission.

2. Teach pupils to use synonyms as cues to word meaning. Synonyms are a part of the context. They are defined as one or more words or expressions of the same language that have the same or nearly the same meaning. Thus, a synonym for *azure* may simply be *blue;* more correctly it is the *blue color of a clear sky.*

Pupils reap much benefit from exercises with the synonyms of words. Initially these exercises are oral. The teacher asks, "What word has the same meaning as *azure?*" An exercise is more effective when pupils use the word in a sentence and then substitute their own synonym. A synonym may be a simple word, or perhaps a phrase or definition. The following exercises teach the use of synonyms as cues to meaning:

a. There are many *utensils* or instruments that one uses daily in a kitchen, a bakery, or on a farm:

  (1) _____ (a vessel used in a kitchen)
  (2) _____ (a tool or instrument)

b. Below is a list of words. Each of the words is a synonym for one of the words in the boxes. Be sure to use each word:

conceal	impede	prohibit
throttle	eulogy	trivial
fret	miniature	prevent
detain	deaden	stifle
diminutive	whine	bewail
laud	disguise	commend

praise	hide
muffle	hinder
complain	small

3. Teach the pupil to use antonyms as cues to word meaning. Antonyms are words opposite in meaning to other words. Useful exercises are:

a. Fill in the word opposite in meaning to the italicized word in these sentences:

  (1) Today the sky is *bright*, but yesterday it was _____.
  (2) Do you like *sweet* or _____ pickles?
  (3) Do you want to be _____ or *last* in the parade?

b. Below is a list of words. Each of the words is an antonym for one of the words in the boxes. Be sure to use each word:

totter	exacting	succeed
palatable	guilty	topple
extravagant	wasteful	tasty
stern	stagger	prevail
delinquent	lavish	culpable
triumph	delectable	demanding

lenient	saving
fail	disagreeable
stand upright	innocent

c.   Match each word with its antonym:

(1)   eminent   (a)   indolence
(2)   alacrity   (b)   light
(3)   awkward   (c)   adroit
(4)   benevolent   (d)   malignant
(5)   frugal   (e)   include
(6)   dusky   (f)   unknown
(7)   exclude   (g)   extravagant

d.   Indicate whether the paired words are synonyms or antonyms:

blunt-sharp _____
crooked-straight _____
regret-sorry _____
horrible-dreadful _____

4.   Have pupils identify the meaning of the italicized word from the definition, explanation, description, or reason accompanying it in the sentence or paragraph. For example:

a.   The pupils are studying the structure of the *bat*. It is the only placental mammal that is capable of flying. (*placental mammal*)

b.   A *stalactite,* an iciclelike formation hanging from the roof of the cave, is created when lime-water drips from the cave ceiling.

c.   He *brandished* his sword fiercely, but the enemy soldier also waved his own sword in a threatening manner.

d.   Mary and Bill are sister and brother; they are *siblings.*

e.   The first *cartologist* was making maps long before the discovery of America.

f.   A *speleologist* is a scientist who studies and explores caves.

g.   The seats upon which we were to sit were *littered* with paper and other trash; in fact, they were absolutely filthy.

h.   It was so *frigid* outside that I quickly buttoned up my coat.

USE OF THE CLOZE PROCEDURE

Developed by Wilson Taylor in 1953, the cloze procedure, which calls for the reading of a passage from which certain words have been deleted, may be used to estimate both the readability or difficulty level of materials, and the pupil's instructional reading level. It also functions as an effective instructional tool in developing comprehension by focusing on the use of contextual cues (both semantic and syntactic) as aids in word recognition and comprehension. Pupils need to be good readers of the context if they are to supply the missing word for the blank space in the cloze passage; if the pupils cannot do this task, the cloze technique may be used to teach it. The pupil's score on a cloze test is an index of the pupil's ability to comprehend reading matter.

Zintz (1977) notes that the term *cloze,* from the gestalt term *closure,* describes the tendency of the individual to anticipate what will complete an unfinished pattern. In reading, successful anticipation depends on the ability of the readers to use the context to identify the word that will complete a passage. It is assumed that the better the readers are in understanding the passage, the more likely it is that they will be correct in guessing the missing word.

Cloze passages have every *nth* word (usually every fifth word) deleted; the pupil is expected to fill in the missing word. The technique is useful in teaching such skills as mastery of structural and functional words (prepositions, conjunctions). Deleting every *nth* word forces the reader to generate words for the blank spaces that meet the syntactic and semantic constraints of the sentence (Ammon 1975). It forces the reader to deal with such situations as "Bill went _____ the hill." The pupil will have to use the context to come up with the word (*up, down,* or another).

One variation of the cloze procedure is to delete preselected words, such as every *nth* noun or verb. Another variation is to delete a portion of a word. The latter technique is particularly helpful in teaching joint use of phonic skills and context cues. In "The boy threw the _____," the sentence structure makes it clear that only a noun can be used to complete the sentence. Semantic and syntactic context suggests that relatively few nouns (for example, *baseball, football*) are possible. Adding a *b* (a phonic cue) to the left side of the blank space restricts the choices even more. Additional cues, other than the beginning letter, might be given to help the pupils figure out the missing word. For instance, the number of letters in the word might be given, or the pupils might be given four words from which to choose the correct one.

It appears that adverbs, adjectives, and prepositions are hardest for children to produce. Also, cloze tests with deleted *content* words (nouns, verbs, and adjectives) are significantly more difficult than the cloze tests with every *nth* word deleted.

Pupils are considered to be reading on an independent level when they can replace 61 percent or more of the deleted words, on the instructional level when they can replace 41 percent or more of the deleted words, and on the frustrational level, when they can replace no more than 40 percent of the deleted words (Rankin and Culhane 1969). These criteria apply only when the exact word is counted as correct.

A caution is in order. Cloze measurements have limited usefulness. They are applicable only to the specific material from which the exercise was taken, although a low score indicates that the pupil cannot utilize context cues and the redundancy of the language to gain help in reading with meaning.

INTERPRETING FIGURATIVE AND IDIOMATIC EXPRESSIONS

It has already been indicated that numerous idiomatic expressions cause meaning problems. Among these expressions are *Jack-of-all-trades, devil-may-care attitude, penny-wise and pound-foolish, to be down-and-out, going to the root of the matter, to be in hot water, don't cry over spilt milk, to cost a pretty penny, to burn the candle at both ends, to blow off steam, to play with fire, to get down to brass tacks, to have an ax to grind, to cook someone's goose, to talk through one's hat, to sit on the fence, to put through the mill, to read between the lines, raining cats and dogs, to take with a grain of salt, snake in the grass, to smell a rat, to weasel out of a situation,* or *a rough row to hoe.*

The above are only a few samples of figures of speech. The major figures of speech may be categorized as follows:

Figures of Resemblance

An *allegory* is a prolonged metaphor (as in *The Pilgrim's Progress*).

Onomatopoeia is the use of words whose sounds suggest the meaning (*buzz, bowwow, splash, crackle,* "the murmurous haunt of flies").

A *metaphor* is an analogy or expression of comparison which, unlike the simile, does not use *as* or *like* ("You're a clumsy ox").

Personification is the endowment of an inanimate object or abstract idea with personal attributes ("The leaves danced in the wind"; "The flames ate hungrily at the wooden foundation").

A *simile* compares two objects or actions and usually joins them with *as* or *like* ("My car goes like the wind").

Metonymy is the use of one word for another, the first word being suggestive of the other ("The woman keeps a good table"; "The pen (power of literature) is mightier than the sword (force)").

Figures of Contrast or Satire

Antithesis is a strong contrasting of ideas ("Man proposes, God disposes"; "Give me liberty or give me death").

An *epigram* is a short, terse, satirical, or witty statement.

In *irony* the implied evaluation is the opposite of that stated.

Apostrophe is the addressing of the dead as living, or the absent as present ("Arise dead sons of the land and sweep the enemy from our shore").

Figures of Exaggeration

Hyperbole is an exaggeration ("His eyes opened wide as saucers"; "The story is as old as time").

Euphemism is the substitution of an inoffensive expression for one that may be considered unpleasant (*mortician* for *undertaker; underachiever* for *disabled reader; plump* for *fat*).

Synecdoche is the use of the part for the whole ("Five hundred hands (persons)"; "My *set of wheels* takes me where I want to go").

Exercises like the following help pupils to read words used in a figurative sense:

1. Teach pupils the meanings of such terms as metaphor, simile, allegory, irony, antithesis, hyperbole, euphemism, synecdoche, epigram, apostrophe, metonymy, personification, onomatopoeia.

2.   Have pupils define the italicized words in sentences such as:
   a.   I was *tickled to death.*
   b.   Garden flowers *laughed merrily.*
   c.   The squirrel *froze* in its tracks.

3.   Have pupils choose meanings for the italicized words in examples such as:
   a.   You cannot trust him. He's a *wolf in sheep's clothing.*
      (1)   He howls like a wolf.
      (2)   He looks like a wolf, but dresses well.
      (3)   He is mean and cunning but pretends to be meek and innocent like a sheep.
   b.   *I'll stand by* you whenever you need me.
      (1)   I'll wait alongside.
      (2)   I'll be ready to help.
      (3)   I'll be near.

4.   Illustrate figurative language with pictures. Have pupils look at the illustrations and select the one that best describes the meaning of the sentence.

A ___
B ___

1. Boats were dancing up and down on the waves.

A ___
B ___

2. The ship plows the sea.*

5.   Have pupils write out the meaning of sentences containing various figures of speech:
   a.   I laughed until I thought I would die. (hyperbole)
   b.   Her face turned as red as a beet. (simile)
   c.   The summer months sure fly by. (personification)

* The sentences and illustrations are from Groesbeck (1961) and are used with her permission.

  d. "Zzzingg! Yowww!" howled the saw. (onomatopoeia and personification)
  e. Neighbors from near and far gathered there. (antithesis)
  f. Arise dead sons of the land and sweep the enemy from our shores. (apostrophe)
  g. She gave her hand in marriage. (synecdoche)
  h. We zipped up our summer cottage and headed for home. (metaphor—cottage described as a garment)
  i. I bought two seats for the play. (metonymy)

STUDY AND USE OF THE DICTIONARY

Although pupils may have learned to use the context and other cues to decipher the meaning of words, they must still sometimes go to the dictionary. The meaning of some words may best be learned by looking the words up in the dictionary. Picture dictionaries can be used as early as the primer level of first grade, and simple glossaries can be introduced at the third-grade level. Standard dictionaries can be introduced at about the fourth-grade level.

To learn to use the dictionary, the pupil needs to

1. Develop alphabetization skills, beginning at about the second-grade level.
2. Understand the use of guide words and be able to locate dictionary entry words quickly. This skill should be learned at the third-grade level even though many nine-year-olds have not mastered the skill of using guide words (Reading in America 1976). Pupils frequently cannot locate the entry word if they are not familiar with roots and affixes.
3. Understand dictionary symbols (the breve, macron, circumflex, tilde, and the like), and understand each item included in an entry. To do this the pupil needs to be able to deal with such abbreviations as *cap* (capitalized), *cf* (compare, see), *esp* (especially), *exc* (except), *fr* (from), *i.e.* (that is), *illus* (illustration), *mod* (modern), *opp* (opposite), and *orig* (originally).
4. Understand how to work out the pronunciation of words and to identify accents, derivations, and parts of speech. The dictionary's pronunciation key and pronunciation guide are both needed to do this.
5. Examine the dictionary to learn the various meanings of a word as given by the dictionary in order to select the definition that applies to the word as it is used in a particular sentence.

The following exercises are designed to teach the basic dictionary skills:

1. Have pupils alphabetize a list of letters and words.
  a. Have the pupil arrange alphabetically four to six noncontiguous letters: *x, c, n, b, k, o.*
  b. Have the pupil supply the preceding and following letter:

   ____ k ____ ____ x ____ ____ o ____ ____ d ____
   ____ b ____ ____ s ____ ____ p ____ ____ f ____

  c. Let the pupil arrange a series of last names in alphabetical order.
  d. Have the pupil alphabetize a series of words beginning with the same letter or

blend, and indicate the alphabetization by numbering the words in proper sequence:

shear _____	Shilluk _____	shoal _____
shingle _____	shindig _____	shifty _____
Shingon _____	shibboleth _____	ship _____

   e. Have pupils place extra words in a list of already alphabetized words so that the entire list is alphabetized:

equal	_____	matter
farther	guilt	_____
_____	_____	_____
gadget	_____	rate

Extra words:

gloss	horrible	nuance
freeze	manage	rat

2. Starting with known sight words, have students identify the correct pronunciation of words by checking them in the dictionary:

	kōm		măk-ə-nou
come		mackinaw	
	kŭm		măk-ə-nȯ
	pŭt		mə-skēt-ō
put		mosquito	
	pu̇t		mos-skēt-ō

3. Have pupils underline the listed words that would appear between given guidewords, such as *gust* and *haet:*

gutteral	haggle
gunpowder	hackney
gyroscope	hockey

4. Teach the basic dictionary symbols: the diacritical markings, such as the breve, macron, circumflex, and tilde; and the basic abbreviations, such as *cap* (capitalized), *cf* (compare), *esp* (especially), and *i.e.* (that is).

5. Have pupils put a check (✔) opposite words that are incorrectly accented:

_____a.	se′•ri′•ous	_____ f. throt′•tle′
_____b.	ge•og′•ra•phy′	_____g. in′•te•ri•or′
_____c.	neg′•a•tive′	_____h. tem′•po•rar′i•ly
_____d.	cor′•rec′•tion	_____ i. dec′•la•ra′•tion
_____e.	sanc′•tu•ar•y	_____ j. his•to′•ri•an

6. have pupils select from the dictionary the definition or meaning that fits the specific use of the word in the sentence:

   man da rin (man′ də rin), n. 1. under the Chinese empire, an official of high rank. 2. *Mandarin,* the main dialect of the Chinese language, spoken by officials and educated people. 3. kind of small, sweet, spicy orange with a very loose peel; tangerine. [<Chinese Pidgin English<Pg. *mandar* to order (<L *mandare*), blended with Malay *mantri*<Hindu.<Skt. *mantrin* advisor]

   Example: "He ate the mandarin, but he would have preferred a California orange." What does *mandarin* mean in the preceding sentence? Which definition applies?

7. Have students identify the dictionary entry word that would be used to look up the marked word in these sentences:

   a. He was *terribly* confused about the whole situation. *terrible*

   b. As the candle burned lower, the light in the room became *dimmer.* _____

   c. Jack was *unearthing* some fossils. _____

8. Have pupils develop skill in using the reference materials in the dictionary by asking then to locate such information as:

   a. Abbreviations:

CBD	Ci	fm
CSF	KKK	pizz
Ark	id	MP

   b. Arbitrary signs:

$$\triangle \qquad \Sigma$$
$$\neq \qquad \widehat{}$$
$$3 \qquad \beta$$

   c. Biographical names:

Baring	Dreyfus
Charlemagne	Kipling
Cezanne	Lombard

   d. Geographical locations:

Ardennes	Djakarta
Baton Rouge	Oshkosh
Dvinsk	Shantung

   e. Colleges and universities:

Dekalb College	Fairleigh Dickinson University
Erskine College	Puget Sound University

9. Have students indicate how the dictionary identifies the following:

   a. Main entry   e. Definition
   b. Pronounciation   f. Special usage
   c. Part of speech   g. Synonyms
   d. Derivation   h. Pronunciation key

10. A good definition groups the object described into a class of things and then differentiates it from all other members of that class.

Have pupils look up a word in the dictionary and note both its class aspects and its differentiae:

WORD	CLASS	DIFFERENTIA
plow		
potash		
echidna		
eel		

DEVELOPING SPACE, NUMERICAL, AND TIME CONCEPTS

There are many words or concepts that do not have clear and definite referent points. Among these are space concepts and some quantitative and time concepts.

Space words or concepts that need to be taught include: *bottom, under, beside, in front, toward-away, beyond, up-down, round, flat, straight, join, moving-still, deep-shallow, top, through, away from, next to, inside, middle, far-thest, around, over, between, nearest, corner, behind, under, side, below, right, forward, above, separated, left, in order.* Quantitative words or concepts to be taught include *big-small, tall-short, long-short, wide, fat-narrow, thin, some, not many, few, widest, most, whole, second, several, almost, half, as many, not first or last, medium sized, zero, every, pair, equal, third, least.* Time words or concepts that need to be taught include *follow, fast-slow, now, early-late, past, start, begin-stop-finish, after, beginning, never, always.* The pupil must also learn such concept words as *different, other, alike, matches, skip, open-closed, soft-hard, easy-hard, dark-light, loud, light-heavy, with-without.*

A suggested sequence for teaching these basic concepts (Boehm manual: p. 16) is as follows:

1. Present the concept through the use of concrete materials.
2. Specifically label the concept.
3. Use the concept in several concrete situations, thus broadening its referent base.
4. Illustrate the concept in a photo, picture, or drawing. Using the word in a phrase with an accompanying picture is especially helpful.
5. Use the concept in a sentence.
6. Demonstrate that the word (for example, *through*) can have different meanings.
7. Show that an object can be both long and short, depending upon the referent object.
8. Use concepts in combination: "Point to the *last* box in the *first* row."
9. Focus attention on opposites: *left-right; top-bottom.*
10. Focus on degree: *far, farther, farthest.*

SUMMARY

To be readers, children must be able to identify words and to associate some meaning with them. But children cannot do this unless they have had the opportunity to develop meaning. Generally, meaning is acquired through some form of direct or vicarious experience. Perhaps the emphasis on learning from experience is too great. More emphasis should perhaps be given to learning from instruction, and this has been the intent of this chapter. The chapter has reviewed a good many techniques for developing meaning. The following summary can be put on a large chart and may serve to call the pupil's attention to word study.

A SUMMARY OF TECHNIQUES FOR IMPROVING VOCABULARY

1. Broaden your experiences. Be alert for new ideas and always learn to describe them in clear terminology. Read and discuss. Listen and write!
2. Develop a regular and systematic method of studying words.
3. Keep a vocabulary notebook (or 3-by-5-inch cards) in which you write the words you want to master. Include the pronunciation and meanings of each word.

4. Learn the common meaning of the word first. Gradually expand your knowledge to include special meanings.
5. Study the word in its context.
6. Associate the word with a mental picture.
7. Break the word into its basic elements—the root, prefix, and suffix.
8. Associate the root word with its synonyms (words with similar meanings) and antonyms (words with opposite meanings).
9. Study carefully those words that are pronounced alike, but that have different spellings. Such words are called homonyms. Examples of these words are: f-a-r-e/f-a-i-r.
10. Use new words in writing and in speaking.
11. Develop an interest in the origin of words.
12. Introduce yourself to the new words in the language.
13. Learn the fine shades of meanings of words. Instead of the word *little,* you may at times wish to use *small, minute, microscopic, tiny, petty, dwarfed, stunted, diminutive, Lilliputian, short, puny,* or *miniature.*
14. Finally, study the technical vocabulary of your subject matter.

QUESTIONS FOR DISCUSSION

1. What are some of the hindrances to the easy development of meanings for words?
2. What are some appropriate techniques for teaching meaning at the kindergarten level?
3. What are additional appropriate techniques for teaching meaning at the primary and intermediate levels?
4. Discuss and illustrate the various ways of using the context to infer the meaning of a word?
5. Discuss ways of developing meaning for figurative expressions?
6. What dictionary skills should the pupil develop in the intermediate years?
7. Discuss the following statements:
    a. The specific meaning elicited by a word is a function of the content in which it occurs.
    b. Reaction to a word is more directly a function of experience than of context.

13

DEVELOPING HIGHER–LEVEL COMPREHENSION SKILLS

This chapter goes beyond simple word meaning. It is designed to teach phrase, clause, sentence, and paragraph comprehension. It is intended to teach literal, organizational, interpretative, critical, and appreciative comprehension.

THE NATURE OF COMPREHENSION

Reading comprehension is difficult to define. In fact, no one has as yet been able to identify the components of reading comprehension. Comprehension includes the correct association of meanings with word symbols, the selection of the correct meaning suggested by the context, the organization and retention of meanings, the ability to reason one's way through smaller idea segments, and the ability to grasp the meaning of a larger unitary idea. Thorndike (1917) described reading comprehension simply as thinking.

To comprehend, a pupil needs to understand language patterns, to recognize the structural elements composing a sentence, and to perceive the syntactic interrelationships of these elements. In other words, the pupil must understand syntax.

Davis (1944, 1972) early noted that underlying comprehension are two general mental abilities: the ability to remember word meanings (word knowledge) and the ability to reason with verbal concepts, and hence with words. It may not be possible to teach and develop the two basic comprehension skills which depend on these abilities. They may well be a part of one's native endowment. The very fact that poor readers fail to correct their errors in oral reading suggests that the problem is one of associating the material after it gets to the brain.

Comprehension is a thinking process; it is thinking through reading. As such, it is dependent upon the learners' basic cognitive and intellectual skills; upon their background of experience (vocabulary, knowledge, concepts, and ideas); and upon their language skills (knowledge of morphology, syntax, and grammar).

Readers use their thinking and verbal-reasoning skills to read for main ideas, for details, for organization, for evaluation, and for appreciation. Whether pupils can read for comprehension and at what level they do so also depends upon the difficulty of the material and upon such physical factors such as the lighting and format, and the size, style, and legibility of the type.

Figure 13-1 outlines the various facets of reading comprehension as they are examined in Chapters 12, 13, and 14.

The previous chapter's concern was the development of word meaning or the association of meaning with a single word, which is the most elemental form of comprehension. This chapter is more concerned with the ability to reason with words or with verbal concepts. To achieve the higher forms of comprehension, the pupil must be helped to comprehend units of increasing size, and to move from literal comprehension to interpretative, critical, and creative reading. This latter ability is here described as higher-level comprehension. Examine now these various levels of comprehending.

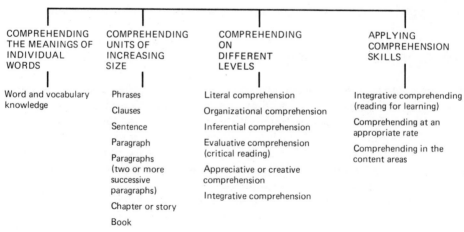

COMPREHENDING THE MEANINGS OF INDIVIDUAL WORDS	COMPREHENDING UNITS OF INCREASING SIZE	COMPREHENDING ON DIFFERENT LEVELS	APPLYING COMPREHENSION SKILLS
Word and vocabulary knowledge	Phrases	Literal comprehension	Integrative comprehending (reading for learning)
	Clauses	Organizational comprehension	Comprehending at an appropriate rate
	Sentence	Inferential comprehension	Comprehending in the content areas
	Paragraph	Evaluative comprehension (critical reading)	
	Paragraphs (two or more successive paragraphs)	Appreciative or creative comprehension	
	Chapter or story	Integrative comprehension	
	Book		

Figure 13-1 The Facets of Comprehension

LEVELS OF COMPREHENSION

Learning to comprehend involves a complex of skills. Various writers have at-tempted to categorize these into three or four levels. Lanier and Davis (1972), in summarizing comprehension skills, categorize them as literal skills (recognizing and recalling facts, details, sequence, main idea, directions, organization, and the like); interpretative skills (inferring, drawing conclusions, generalizing, deriving meaning from figurative language, predicting, anticipating, and sum-marizing); critical skills (judging, detecting propaganda, analyzing, checking validity, checking the author's biases and purposes); and creative skills (applying information, responding emotionally).

Barrett's (Barrett 1972; Barrett and Smith 1974, 1979) taxonomy includes literal comprehension, reorganization (this aspect is not included in the 1974 or 1979 version of Barrett's taxonomy as a separative category), inferential com-prehension, evaluation, and appreciation.

Literal comprehension requires the identification, recognition, and recall of ideas, information, or happenings that are explicitly stated in the selection.

Reorganization requires the analysis and synthesis or organization of ideas or information explicitly stated in the materials read. It includes classifying, outlining, summarizing, and synthesizing.

Inference requires an integration of the content of a selection which alone can lead to inferences about the material. It involves a combination of conjecture and explanation based on a synthesis of the literal content, personal knowledge, intuition, and imagination. It goes beyond the printed page.

Inference can take the form of either convergent or divergent thoughts. Convergent thinking is involved in such skills as identifying topic sentences, determining sequence, and recalling details; it calls for some commonness of meaning or convergence between writer and reader. Convergent inferences cause the reader to come to a specific correct answer or an agreed-upon hypothesis that may be verifiable through the data supplied by the writer. A divergent inference, on the other hand, calls for imagination or creative thinking. It is an inference that does not have to be judged as right or wrong. In divergent thinking the in-dividual develops alternative answers, none of which is necessarily correct but none of which is incorrect either. Divergent thinking is a synonym for creative thinking (Harris and Sipay 1975). When pupils are asked to give *their* interpreta-tion of a poem, *their* opinion of a character, or *their* evaluation of a situation, *their* answer will, by definition, always be acceptable.

Evaluation or critical reading requires the reader to make evaluative judgments about the content, using external or internal criteria as points of reference. The external criteria might be those of the teacher or the authorities on the subject; internal criteria might be the reader's personal experiences and knowledge or the internal logic or consistency of the passage or article. Evaluative thinking includes judgments about seeming reality or fantasy, fact or opinion, as well as judgments of adequacy or validity, of appropriateness, worth, desirability, completeness, suitability, truthfulness, and probability of occurrence.

Appreciation requires the reader to become aware of the literary techniques, forms, and styles employed by the writer to stimulate emotional response. It includes the emotional response to the plot or theme, identification with the characters and incidents, and reactions to the author's use of language and imagery.

Integrative comprehension is reading for learning. It involves the ability to retain information, to apply and integrate information with one's past experiences, to locate information, to read graphs, maps, and charts, and to use the dictionary. Integrative comprehension is discussed in Chapter 14.

Reading comprehension, on all levels, but especially when it involves units larger than a single word, is obviously a complex of abilities. The good comprehender possesses the ability to:

1. Associate experiences and meaning with the graphic symbol (have an adequate meaning vocabulary).
2. Understand words in context and select the meaning that fits the context.
3. Give meaning to units of increasing size: the phrase, clause, sentence, paragraph, and whole selection.
4. Develop literal and denotative meaning (be able to answer literal questions about a passage):
   a. Detect and understand the main idea.
   b. Recognize and recall significant facts or details.
   c. Follow directions given in the material.
   d. Recognize the sequence of a passage.
   e. Identify explicitly stated expressions of relationships, such as cause-effect, contrast, comparison.
5. Develop an understanding of the organization (be able to answer questions calling for an analysis, synthesis, or organization of ideas and information explicitly stated):
   a. Identify the basis of paragraph organization; for example, comparison-contrast, cause-effect, classification or categorization, enumerative sequence, time sequence, size, distance, position or degree, general to specific, thesis-proof pattern, opinion-reason pattern, problem-solution pattern, narrative-description pattern, definition pattern.
   b. Summarize, outline, underline, and take notes on the material read.
6. Develop inferential, interpretative, or connotative meaning of the material read (be able to get implied meaning of what is read):
   a. Make inferences, draw conclusions, generalize, speculate, or predict.
   b. Interpret figurative expressions.
   c. Supply implied details.
   d. Anticipate outcomes.
7. Make judgments or critical evaluations about the material:
   a. Evaluate the quality, accuracy, truthfulness, and appropriateness of what is read.
   b. Determine whether the text affirms, denies, or fails to express an opinion about a supposed fact or condition.

    c.   Detect propaganda, one-sided presentations, prejudices, biases, and faulty inferences.

    d.   Evaluate the writer's reputation, biases, purposes, and motives.

    e.   Detect errors of reasoning, analogy, overgeneralization, oversimplification, and distortion.

8.   Read for learning:

    a.   Retain ideas.

    b.   Apply ideas and integrate them with past experiences.

    c.   Locate information in encyclopedias, card catalog, almanacs, and the like, and use table of contents, index, or appendix of a book.

    d.   Read maps, graphs, charts.

    e.   Use the dictionary.

9.   Read for appreciation:

    a.   Recognize literacy and semantic devices.

    b.   Identify the tone, theme, mood, and intent or purpose of the writer.

The above skills and their development comprise the content of Chapters 13 and 14. Before examining each of them in detail, consider another element that will help you come to a better understanding of comprehension—namely, the differences between good and poor comprehenders.

CHARACTERISTICS OF THE GOOD AND POOR COMPREHENDER

Good and poor comprehenders differ (1) in decoding skills, (2) in lexical access, and (3) in text organization (Golinkoff 1975–76). If reading is the extraction of information or meaning from the text and not simply the recoding of written symbols to sound, readers must have cracked the written code and so be able to recognize printed words (decoding); they must have stored in semantic memory the meanings for printed words (lexical access); and they must be able to extract meaning from units larger than a single word, hence from phrases, sentences, and paragraphs (text organization).

Reading comprehension is not possible without the ability to pronounce the printed word (recoding). Poor readers tend to have poor recoding skills. They make more than twice the number of oral reading errors per hundred words than do good readers. Good comprehenders, on the other hand, are capable of rapid and accurate word recognition. They have automatized the basic recoding skills. They have committed thousands of words to their sight vocabulary and can recognize them instantly and with minimum language cues.

Lexical access does not appear to be a major problem of poor comprehenders, nor do they appear to have difficulty with the notion that a symbol can stand for meaning. But although the poor comprehender is generally able to obtain the meaning of single printed words without experiencing difficulty, the need to focus too much on the word's phonological features may even destroy this ability.

Ability to read the text organization may be the chief distinguishing characteristic between the good and the poor comprehender. Good comprehenders treat the sentence as a unit of meaning. They read in phrase-like units and are flexible in their pattern of reading, varying their eye movements, and changing the size of the processing unit. They regress only after they are unsuccessful in grasping the meaning of a larger segment of text. The good comprehenders pay most attention to the information relevant to their purpose, ignore useless information, read in the largest unit appropriate to the task, and process the least amount of graphic information possible. The end result of this is that the good comprehenders seem to use a scan-for-meaning pattern. They treat reading as a process of information getting.

The poor comprehenders, on the other hand, are more concerned with word identification. They are unable to use interword and intraword redundancy to help them identify and read single words. They are so concerned with recoding each word that they fail to utilize the interword relationships within the text that could increase their recoding rate and permit more efficient sampling of the text. They are unable to organize the text. They read the text in a word-by-word manner with a minimum of text organization.

The following observations, in addition to those just made, summarize the deficiencies of disabled readers:

1. The reading comprehension of poor comprehenders is often substantially lower than their listening comprehension. They can understand materials at a higher level when the materials are read to them than when they read the materials themselves. They obtain a higher instructional-level score on a reading inventory when the material is read to them than when they read it.
2. They cannot read textbooks or materials at their grade level on an instructional level, that is, with 95 percent accuracy in word recognition and 75 percent accuracy in comprehension.
3. They have greater difficulty recoding unfamiliar words.
4. They recode even familiar words more slowly than does the average pupil at their age or grade level.
5. They produce a greater number of reading errors that do not conform to the semantic meaning of the selection.
6. They make more uncorrected errors (especially in oral reading) that disturb the meaning of the text. They frequently fail to correct their errors or do not notice when they make a mistake.
7. Their mistaken readings do not conform to the syntactic structure of the sentences in which they are substituted.

DEVELOPING COMPREHENSION IN THE CLASSROOM

Two widely accepted requirements for the development of comprehension in the classroom are (1) establishing a purpose prior to reading and (2) asking questions before, during, and after the reading. This methodology has come to be known as the guided or directed reading activity. The teacher manuals of basal programs thus contain questions to be asked before the reading and questions to be asked after the reading. This phase was discussed in Chapter 12, and you may want to refer to that section as well as to the discussion of the directed reading activity given in Chapter 8.

Other techniques for developing comprehension include

1.   Having pupils show by an illustration of the events (a drawing, map, chart, diagram, or graph), by retelling the story, or by demonstration, that they have understood the content of what they have read.

2.   Having pupils identify and state the topic sentence, write a title for the paragraph or story, or identify the details, directions, or sequence of material read.

3.   Having pupils develop a formal outline of what they have read.

4.   Having pupils summarize what they have read.

5.   Having pupils provide the ending for a story which has not been read to completion or having them suggest alternate endings to a story that has been read completely.

6.   Having pupils match pictures with sentences.

For best results in comprehension teaching, the teacher should always have the pupils read at their instructional or independent reading level, should make sure that the materials are interesting to the pupils, should establish a background of experience and knowledge for the reading assignment, and should teach pupils to use punctuation and to read in phrase and thought units.

Peters (1977) notes that much confusion in teaching comprehension arises from the failure to clearly distinguish between instructional outcomes and instructional techniques. Later in the chapter, reading for the main idea will be discussed. The teacher needs to see this as an instructional outcome, and must clearly differentiate it from the related instructional technique or enabling skill which is the ability to select the topic sentence. For example:

Instructional Outcome	*Enabling Skill or Instructional Technique*
1. Reading for the main idea (recognizing the central thought of a passage).	1. Ability to select the topic sentence.
	2. Ability to state the topic sentence in one's own words.

A major emphasis in this chapter is to identify the instructional outcomes, but there is an even greater concern with the enabling skills or the instructional technique, hence with the practical aspects of teaching and with remediating specific difficulties in comprehension.* Direct your attention now to the develop-

---

* For a listing of materials designed to develop each of the comprehension skills, see Dechant 1981b: pp. 175–207.

ment of literal, organizational, inferential, and evaluative comprehension skills, beginning with literal comprehension.

DEVELOPING LITERAL
AND DENOTATIVE MEANING

The primary skill that pupils need to acquire in order to read a sentence or a paragraph is the ability to get the direct, literal meaning of a word and sentence. They must be able to recognize, locate, and recall the ideas that are explicitly stated: the main idea, the significant details, sequence, directions, and so forth; and they must be able to answer questions regarding the literal, denotative meaning.

Two basic types of exercise that teach literal comprehension skills are

1. Ask questions about the material read which require pupils to identify, recall, or supply the names of the characters, to describe a very specific incident, to state the main idea, to state the order of events, and so forth.
2. Have pupils demonstrate that they have gotten the literal meaning by
    a. Illustrating the story.
    b. Showing or demonstrating the sequence of events.
    c. Retelling the story.

Even though comprehension tasks such as those just described often involve pupils in the retrieval of trivial factual data (Guszak 1967), or in parroting back what they have read, literal comprehension is important. Literal comprehension is the basis of all higher-level comprehension skills.

Kottmeyer (1974) notes that simple literal meanings are derived from a combination of the lexical meanings of words (words are the distillation of our experiences) and the structural meanings of the word sequences that are termed sentences. Pupils, if they are to be good literal comprehenders, must then be able to decipher the literal meanings of units of increasing size: words, phrases, sentences, and paragraphs. Examine each of these individually.

Word Reading

As was indicated in Chapter 12, without a knowledge of key words and concepts the pupil's comprehension will always be limited. Only if readers know the words can they chunk information into meaningful units—Pearson (1975) calls these semantic chunks—or into memory storage units that facilitate the synthesizing process of cementing ideas together (Peters 1977). And yet the meaning of a sentence is not obtained by piling up, as it were, the meaning of individual words. Comprehension is not simply a process of recognizing individual words, and then stringing them together like beads, to come up with the full meaning of a sentence. The directed reading activity and other techniques for teaching word meaning discussed in Chapter 12 are pertinent here, as are the concept-development models presented in Chapter 6, and by Frayer, Frederick, and Klausmeier (1969). From such models, exercises like the following may be derived:

1. Have the pupils identify a concept's relevant attributes: its unchanging core of experience, its invariant characteristics: for example, a globe is spherical and it represents the earth.

2. Have pupils identify the concept's irrelevant attributes: the size of the globe is an irrelevant attribute.

3. Have pupils identify a non-example of the concept or have them contrast the concept with a non-example: a wall map is a non-example of a globe; it is nonspherical.

4. Have pupils identify the relationship that the concept has to other concepts: globe and map both represent the earth.

Vocabulary development should be concerned with the teaching of various conceptual relationships: members of the concept, non-members of the concept, and idiosyncratic and invariant characteristics of the concept.

Phrase Reading

Along with competency in word reading, the pupil needs to learn to comprehend phrase units. Good readers are able to organize what they have read into meaningful phrase and even sentence units. Poor readers, on the other hand, are often characterized by word-by-word reading. Their memory images for words are so short-lived that they have difficulty reading phrases.

Many researchers look upon the phrase as the unit of reading (Golinkoff 1975–76). Separating sentences into phrases is a way for the reader to organize the sentence into grammatical and semantic units. However, a recent study indicates that students (nine-, thirteen-, and seventeen-year-olds) have more difficulty in identifying the meaning of specific word groups than in identifying the overall meaning of a passage, suggesting that it may be easier to read a sentence than a phrase (Reading in America 1976).

Phrase reading attempts to get the pupil away from word-by-word reading. The latter usually results from slowness and inaccuracy in word recognition. Thus, the materials used to develop phrase-reading ability should present few or no difficulties in word recognition or word meaning for the learner.

Exercises helpful in developing phrase-reading ability include

1. Have pupils practice reading sentences with idiomatic expressions and proverbs:
   a. A rolling stone *gathers no moss.*
   b. Smooth seas *make poor sailors.*

2. Read to pupils, emphasizing or stressing the phrase units, and making sure that pupils identify them as phrase units.

3. Have pupils read in unison with the teacher.

4. Have pupils read sentences which have been divided into phrase units:
    a. The mailman / left us / a most welcome package / this morning.

5. Have pupils mark off sentences into phrase units.

6. Have pupils rearrange the phrases in a sentence into a correct order:
    a. the next block / my friend, Jack / lives on /

Reading the Sentence

Huey (1912) wrote that language begins with the sentence. Comprehension of printed materials requires the perception of complete language structures such as the sentence. The sentence is the basic meaning-bearing pattern. The word may be the basic unit of identification, but the basic unit of reading is surely the sentence.

Good comprehenders have developed skill in associating meaning with individual words, but they can also read sentences. They can grasp the meaning of larger segments of the text and have learned that the full meaning of a sentence depends on the punctuation, the word order, and the grammatical inflections signaling tense, number, and possession, and on such function words as *because* or *nevertheless*.

Poor readers, on the other hand, cannot grasp the meaning of larger segments of the text (phrase, clause, sentence, paragraph). They cannot integrate individual word meanings within sentences; they cannot relate the meanings of several sentences contained in a passage; they cannot use redundancy cues to work out the meaning of a sentence; and they have poor sentence sense. This is often demonstrated by word calling or simply sounding the words without knowing what they mean.

Sentences present numerous difficulties for the reader. The difficulty of the vocabulary is first, but sentence length and complexity are also factors. The longer the sentence, the more difficult it usually is to comprehend. Long sentences tend to contain dependent clauses, variations in word order, and greater use of connectives and function words, all of which make it more difficult to understand what one is reading.

The ability to read sentences improves as the pupil grows in the ability to deal with word meanings and in the ability to read phrases, to use punctuation, and to deal with basic sentence patterns and sentence structure. The first two have already been discussed. Examine the remaining three, beginning with reading punctuation.

Reading the Punctuation

Punctuation is frequently looked upon merely as a discipline in writing rather than as a help in reading. Yet writers punctuate not for themselves, but for the reader. Punctuation is not only a set of rules to be learned, but also a means of facilitating the grasp of meaning. Punctuation represents the intonation pattern in speech—the pauses, pitch, and stress.

Exercises such as the following teach pupils how to read the punctuation:

1. Teach the functional difference between the period and the question mark with simple sentences:
    a. Mary has a kitten.
        Does Mary have a kitten?

2. Show how a misplaced comma falsifies the intended meaning of a sentence:
    a. The school, kitchen, cafeteria, and auditorium are off bounds during regular school hours.
        The school kitchen, cafeteria, and auditorium are off bounds during regular school hours.
    b. "The man," said the boy, "broke the window."
        The man said the boy broke the window.

Reading the Sentence Patterns

To be proficient in sentence comprehension, the pupil also needs to learn the basic sentence patterns: noun-verb or subject-verb (people talk); noun-verb-noun or subject-predicate-direct object (Ann plays baseball); noun-verb-noun-noun or subject-verb-indirect object-direct object (Jim gave Tom a watch); noun-linking verb-adjective or subject-linking verb-adjective (Flowers are pretty); and noun-linking verb-noun or subject-linking verb-predicate noun (He is (my) brother).

Exercises such as the following teach this skill:

1. Have pupils identify the sentence pattern of a series of sentences. The pupils should indicate whether the pattern is (1) subject-verb; (2) subject-predicate-object; (3) subject-linking verb-adjective; (4) subject-linking verb-noun.
    a. The art show exhibited the most famous western art.
    b. Lori became president of the Young Democrats.

2. Have pupils identify the who or what in a sentence; the happening indicated; and the why, where, or when, if the sentence contains answers to these questions.
    a. Late last night a burglar entered the home of Jack Perkins on Market Street, apparently to steal several valuable paintings.
        Who did what? Where? When? Why? How?

Pupils need to learn that signals for *where* are words like *under, over, in, on, at, to, between, among, behind, in front of;* for *when,* words like *before, after, later, while, now, then;* and for *how,* words like *as* or *like,* or adverbs ending in *ly.*

Pupils also need to become familiar with the common transformations of basic sentences: passive voice (The boy was given a watch); questions, negative sentences, imperative sentences, and sentences beginning with *It* or *There* (There are six girls in the classroom).

Reading the Syntactic Structure

The structure of the phrase, sentence, or paragraph serves as a further cue to the fuller meaning of what is written. Written English presents special difficulties in this regard. It is less redundant than oral English, often containing logical and subordinate connectives, thus increasing sentence complexity.

Next to intonation and sentence order (including basic sentence patterns), the most significant cues to language patterns are the structure words, markers, or the so-called empty words. These are discussed in this chapter under the heading, "Reading the Organization." Nouns, verbs, adjectives, and adverbs present the fewest meaning problems.

Reading the Paragraph

Up to this point, word reading, phrase reading, and sentence reading (including reading of the punctuation, of sentence patterns, and of syntactic structure) have been examined. Now consider the paragraph.

An organization, which lists reading of paragraphs under literal comprehension, as is done here, may be questionable since reading of units of increasing size (phrases, sentences, and especially paragraphs) requires comprehension skills other than literal comprehension, such as inferential, organizational, and evaluative comprehension. Phrase, sentence and paragraph reading are thus listed here simply because the reader must first learn to obtain a literal comprehension of the sentence and paragraph before learning to read between the lines or before making critical evaluations of what is read.

Paragraph reading depends upon the ability to identify the main idea and to group details (including directions and sequence) about this main idea. Examine first the matter of reading for the main idea.

READING FOR THE MAIN IDEA

The most important skill required for comprehending a paragraph is the ability to identify the main idea or the central thought in what one reads. All the other interpretative reading skills are secondary. Pupils who do not get the main idea cannot identify the theme of a paragraph, cannot understand the implied meanings, and usually cannot organize or summarize what they have read.

Reading for the main idea requires the pupil to distinguish between essentials and nonessentials and between the most important idea and subordinate details (Harris and Sipay 1975). Since it is a form of intellectual reasoning requiring categorization and synthesis, children with below-average intelligence have more difficulty in identifying the main idea than in identifying details.

The ability to read for the main idea may be developed through exercises such as the following:

1. Have pupils identify the main idea of a sentence by underlining key words.

2. Have pupils select the topic sentence or the sentence which best identifies the main idea of a paragraph. For example,

> The thermostat, an invention of the twentieth century, has been designed to substitute machinery for man's brain and nervous system. This device is an example of the simple analog computer and controls the temperature of a room automatically. When the temperature of a room changes, a signal is sent to the starting switch of the furnace. What makes the switch work? The signal sent by the thermostat turns on the switch when heat is needed or turns it off when enough heat has been manufactured.*

> Mark the topic sentence of the above paragraph:
> _____ a. "The signal sent by the thermostat turns on the switch . . . manufactured."
> _____ b. "The thermostat . . . has been designed to substitute machinery for man's brain and nervous system."
> _____ c. "What makes the switch work?"
> _____ d. "When the temperature of a room changes, a signal is sent to the starting switch of the furnace."

3. Have pupils choose from a prepared group of sentences (based on a paragraph that they have read) those that agree or disagree with the general idea of the paragraph.

4. Have pupils restate the topic sentence in their own words.

5. Have pupils select from a series of sentences the one that does not stay on the topic. For example,

> It was the last of the seventh. The Mexican juniors were about to bring home the Little League baseball championship. It was ten degrees below zero in Canada. The crowd was on its feet eagerly waiting for the final pitch of the game.

6. Have pupils write a title for a paragraph.

7. Have pupils select the best title from several prepared by the teacher. For example,

> It was a summer's day late in the 1870's. High in the southern sky the hot noonday sun blazed down upon ripening grainfields and far-reaching stretches of unbroken prairie. Not a breeze rippled the prairie grasses! Not a birdcall broke the hot, dead stillness in which ears attuned to listening might have heard the corn grow.**

> Which of the following titles best fits this paragraph?
> a. "The Stillness of a Hot Summer Afternoon"
> b. "A Hot Afternoon"

8. Have pupils identify the main idea of a poem. For example,

> The night shall be filled with music,
> And the cares that infest the day
> Shall fold their tents like the Arabs,
> And as silently steal away—Henry Wadsworth Longfellow

---

* *Listen and Read*, GHI (1), 12, Educational Developmental Laboratories, Huntington, N.Y., 1969.

** Mabel O'Donnell, Engine Whistles, *The Alice and Jerry Basic Readers*, "Puffing Billy," p. 5. Copyright 1957, 1954, 1947, 1942 by Harper & Row, Publishers.

9. Have pupils turn the subheads or subtitles into a question. The answer to the question generally gives the main idea of the paragraph.

10. Have pupils locate the function words in the paragraph that tie the sentences together: *then, therefore, and, but,* and the like.

Pupils do not only read simple sentences and paragraphs. More frequently they have to interrelate a number of paragraphs. The main idea may very well be spread over two or three paragraphs.

The following exercises are helpful in teaching this skill:

1. Have pupils locate the topic sentences of all the paragraphs in an essay or story and relate these to obtain the larger idea conveyed in the selection.

2. Have pupils read the title, the subheads, and the summary of a chapter and tell in a simple sentence what the chapter or selection is about.

3. Have pupils skim the chapter or selection in order to get a general idea of the selection.

4. Present first one paragraph and then two other related paragraphs and let the pupils determine which of the last two supports and logically follows the first paragraph.

Reading for Details
(Directions and Sequence)

Along with reading for and stating the main idea, the pupil must learn to read for details. Reading for details becomes especially important in functional reading and in study-related reading—in other words, in science, geography, arithmetic, home economics, and history.

Developing the pupil's ability to read for literal details, including reading for *directions* and *sequence*, may be accomplished through exercises such as following:

1. Have pupils look at a picture and then let them describe what they saw.

2. Ask pupils to note the details in a paragraph after you have stated its main idea.

3. Have pupils read a paragraph into which have been inserted some irrelevant sentences and let them identify these sentences.

4. Have pupils analyze a written paragraph into its main and supporting ideas by making a formal outline of it.

5. Let pupils read and then carry out simple directions on how to do something or how to play a game. Children may develop direction charts. Common activities include how to care for a plant, pet, or garden; how to cook a simple dish; how to make a dictionary; how to use the reading table.

6. Have pupils respond to directions such as
    a. Draw a circle around the longest word in this sentence.
    b. Write the abbreviation for the third month of the year.
    c. Write the following words in alphabetic order: *bird, box, brush, bench, bag, bush.*

7. After giving pupils a paragraph to read, ask questions about it that call for detail. Multiple choice, completion, and true-false questions are especially appropriate in eliciting answers concerning the details of a paragraph.

8. Have pupils develop a chart, diagram, or map of the sequence of events, described in a story they have read.

Learning to follow directions through reading is essentially reading for details. In following directions every little step is significant. The pupil must give full attention to all the data and must also look for a definite sequence of data. Following directions is particularly important in doing arithmetic and in carrying out experiments.

READING THE ORGANIZATION

Good readers also comprehend the organization of what is being read; they think with the reading material, organizing, summarizing and outlining it as they go along. Good comprehenders see the relationship between the main and the subordinate ideas and arrange these in some logical order.

Bruner (1966) notes the importance of structure for learning. Structure makes understanding easier, by simplifying information and by increasing the manipulability of a body of knowledge. Without structure, knowledge is more readily forgotten. Bruner notes that the key to retrieval (or recall of the information) is organization. Organization of information reduces the aggregate complexity of material by embedding it into the learner's cognitive structure.

Reading in the content areas, especially, depends upon proficiency in organization skill. Textbooks have a characteristic paragraph organization. The topic sentence sets the theme of the paragraph. A sequence of details follows. The paragraph is concluded by a summarizing sentence.

The SQ3R method, which will be discussed in Chapter 14, and the directed reading activity (DRA), which was discussed in Chapter 8, serve to organize the material for the learner.

Paragraphs tend to be organized according to characteristic patterns. Niles (1965) suggests the following patterns of paragraph organization: enumerative sequence of events, time sequence (indicated by such words as *next, while, when, later*), cause-effect, and comparison-contrast. Other authors speak of organization by size and distance, by position or degree, by classification or categorization, by a description pattern, by a definition pattern, from general to specific ideas, or from specific to general ideas. Birkley (1970) speaks of the thesis-proof pattern (a thesis followed by a series of proofs), the opinion-reason pattern (most common in editorials), the problem-solution pattern, the information pattern, and the narrative pattern. Niles adds that efficient study is a matter of perceiving these organizational patterns as one reads and responds to what one has read. The good reader knows how paragraphs are organized.

Numerous activities help pupils learn to organize what they are reading. Among these are the following:

1. Teach the use of the SQ3R method of study (as described in Chapter 14) or the DRA model.

2. Have pupils group a series of pictures in a logical or chronological sequence.

3. Have pupils organize information about a given subject, such as animals, using a chart similar to the following:

ANIMAL	WHERE DOES IT LIVE?	WHAT DOES IT EAT?	HOW DOES IT MOVE?	HOW DOES IT DEFEND ITSELF?	OTHER CHARACTERISTICS
lion					
chimp					

4. Have pupils group a series of details about a main idea.

5. Let pupils develop an outline for a story, with major headings and subheadings.

6. Have pupils arrange records, directions, or ideas in a sequential order.

7. Have pupils assemble various bits of information about a selected topic and group them into an informative story.

8. Have pupils write a number, letter, or word that best completes the grouping (this exercise also teaches classification):
   a. 2, 4, 6, 8, _____
   b. A, E, I, 0, _____
   b. dog, cat, horse, cow, _____
   d. Sunday, Monday, Tuesday, _____

9. Teach pupils how to identify a paragraph's organization with exercises such as the following which require them to identify the type of organization. Prepare questions about the paragraphs which help pupils to identify the organization:
   a. *Organization by Contrast*

   The speed of animals varies greatly. Land animals generally are more speedy than water animals, but less so than air animals. Nevertheless, individual differences within each group are considerable. A goldfish swims about four miles an hour; a trout, five miles an hour; a sailfish and a barracuda, thirty miles an hour.

   Among land animals, the slowest is the turtle, which travels about one-tenth of a mile an hour, and the fastest is the cheetah, which travels up to sixty-five miles an hour. Man can swim about five miles an hour but can run twenty miles an hour. Among air animals, the housefly is the slowest, traveling about five miles an hour; the duck hawk flies 175 miles an hour.

   b. *Organization on a Cause-Effect Basis*

   What causes a cyclone, a tornado, and a hurricane? A cyclone is caused by a low-pressure area in which the winds move counter-clockwise in a spiraling-upward fashion. A tornado also is a low-pressure area but smaller and more violent than a cyclone. A hurricane is a huge mass of air whirling about a calm center.

c. *Organization by Chronological Sequence*

   On June 7, 1896, Samuelson and Harbo, in an eighteen-foot boat, rowed out of New York in the evening tide. They wanted to cross the Atlantic by rowboat. They rowed for nine hours and then rested for an hour; at night each man rowed for three hours while the other rested. A month out of New York the boat was overturned, but they managed to right it. Fifty-two days after leaving New York harbor they landed on the Scilly Islands, near France.

The reason poor readers or poor comprehenders have so much difficulty in using sentence and paragraph structure to identify meaning is that they are unable to summarize and outline the material, and they are unable to use the markers, or the structure words, (the so-called empty words) as cues to paragraph organization. First consider summarizing and outlining.

Summarizing and Outlining

Summaries help to preserve the essential facts and the main ideas in capsule form. They are particularly useful when reading stories, essays, or social science materials; they are not so useful in chemistry, physics, or biology. A summary or synopsis is all that may be necessary for retaining important information about the former. As for the latter, a summary may be longer than the original.

Outlining is just another way of organizing information. It is closely related to summarizing. When readers own their books, they sometimes outline them by underlining and by using letters and numbers to designate main and subordinate points.

Exercises useful in teaching the summarizing and outlining skills are

1. Have pupils write a one-sentence summary of a paragraph.

2. Have pupils select the main idea of a paragraph from four possible choices. For example,

   Transportation developed step by step. In the beginning people used logs to move down the stream. The lake or stream was the first roadway. Then people taught animals to pull heavy loads on sledges. The land became the natural roadway. Finally, people discovered the wheel. This led to the invention of the stagecoach.

A good summary for this paragraph might be:

a. People used logs to move down the streams.

b. The problems of transportation were overcome by the invention of the wheel.

c. Transportation passed through the stages of log travel, sledge travel, and stagecoach travel.

d. The land became the natural roadway.

3. Have the pupils read poetry and select the best summary from a series of four choices. Poetry usually presents one main idea or moral (all the words are so interrelated that they dovetail into one main idea),

   Not enjoyment, and not sorrow,
   Is our destined end or way:
   But to act, that each to-morrow
   Find us farther than to-day.
   —Henry Wadsworth Longfellow

A good summary of this poem might be:

a.   People must take what comes.

b.   People can do something about their destiny.

c.   All of us are doomed to sorrow.

4.   Have pupils summarize a message so that it would be suitable for sending by telegram (reduce a fifty-word message to a twenty-word message).

5.   Have pupils write summaries of stories that they have read.

6.   Have pupils select from three summaries that which best summarizes a series of paragraphs.

7.   Have pupils write headlines for the school paper.

8.   Have pupils do exercises requiring them to summarize material using the outline form.

9.   Have the pupils, especially in the middle grades and junior high, paraphrase passages that they have read (Sullivan 1978).

Reading Structure Words

Being able to identify the relationships that conjunctions signal also has a positive effect on reading comprehension (Stoodt 1972). Key structural words assist the reader in following the author's transition from idea to idea and from paragraph to paragraph.

Shepherd (1973) grouped structure words as follows. Some additional words have been included.

I.   *Structure words indicating additional ideas*

   A.   *Words pointing to supporting or coordinating ideas, adding to the total thought, or marking a pairing of ideas*

and	furthermore	besides	likewise	the main point is
also	plus	too	similarly	since then
another	otherwise	after that	again	not only,
in addition	moreover	as well as	since	but also
				both-and

   B.   *Words pointing to final or concluding ideas or that indicate that the point being made flows from previous statements*

consequently	in conclusion	then	thereupon
thus	in summation	to sum up	accordingly
hence	at last	in brief	
therefore	finally	in the end	

II. *Structure words indicating contrast, a change in ideas, or that a contradictory statement is about to be introduced*

opposed to	on the other hand	nevertheless	whereas
in contrast	but	yet	while
to the contrary	in spite of	still	rather
conversely	although	even if	not withstanding
however	either-or	if	except
even though	unless		

III. *Structure words indicating concrete application of a thought: cause and effect relationships, introduction of an example, classification, etc.*

therefore	as a result	specifically
accordingly	hence	for instance
it follows	consequently	provided
thus	in conclusion	like
in order that	since	because
for example	so that	

IV. *Structure words pointing to relationships among and between ideas*

A. *Time relationships*

in the first place	last	previously	when
at the same time	now	hereafter	afterward
thereafter	later	at last	during
in retrospect	after	at length	in the meantime
meanwhile	before	following	subsequently
finally	immediately		

B. *Space relationships*

here	close	by	farther on	to the east	around
there	far	away	above	westward	over
yonder	near	under	across	beneath	everywhere

C. *Relationships of degree*

many	little	some	best	fewer	greater
more	less	all	worst	fewest	greatest
most	least				above all

D. *Relationships of emphasis*

this	that	one	some	few
these	those	several		

The most difficult conjunctions are *when, so, but, or, where, while, how, that, if;* the easiest are *and, how, for,* and *as.* Such words as *however, thus, which, although,* and *yet* are difficult even in the intermediate years (Katz 1968; Robertson 1968).

Specific exercises in teaching pupils to read structure words might be:

1. Present two or more structure words in the same sentence and have students indicate whether the substitution has altered the meaning (Peters 1977).

   a. Football is my favorite sport, *but* my parents will not let me play it.

   b. Football is my favorite sport, *although* my parents will not let me play it.

   c. Football is my favorite sport; *consequently,* my parents will not let me play it.

   d. Football is my favorite sport; *moreover,* my parents will not let me play it.

   e. Football is my favorite sport, *and* my parents will not let me play it.

   f. Football is my favorite sport; *however,* my parents will not let me play it.

2. Before reading key passages, have students underline important structural words and then have them indicate whether the structure word suggests that an additional idea is being presented, whether a contradictory statement is being made, whether a cause-effect relation is indicated, and so forth.

DEVELOPING INFERENTIAL
READING SKILLS

Inferential comprehension, the third level of comprehending, goes beyond the printed page or beyond the explicitly stated content. Good comprehenders can and do read for implied details and for implicit or latent meanings. They can read between the lines, use verbal reasoning to infer additional supporting details, make inferences as to the main idea and the sequence or what might happen next, predict outcomes, and answer questions about material calling for inferential, interpretative, or connotative meaning.

A study of the reading abilities of nine-, thirteen-, and seventeen-year-olds (Reading in America 1976) shows that all age groups improved over the last four years in literal comprehension, but when the comprehension items became more difficult, either as a result of lengthy, complex passages or because of questions that required some manipulation of the information, the thirteen- and seventeen-year-olds performed less well than four years ago. The older pupils generally did not do as well on the inferential comprehension and reference (study) skill items.

Inferring meanings is based upon a firm foundation in using context clues, in understanding word and sentence meanings, in finding main ideas and related details, and in organizing and classifying facts (Burg et al. 1978). Inferential comprehension depends upon the ability of the readers to synthesize information from their experience with information from the reading content.

Activities designed to develop inferential reading include the following:

1. Have the pupils respond to questions calling for divergent inferences:
   a. How do you interpret this poem?
   b. What is your opinion of the main character?
   c. What might have been the motives of the main character?
   d. Could you provide a new ending?
   e. Do these people live in the way we do?
   f. Where do you think the incident took place?

2. Have pupils respond to questions asking for implied meaning: "It was so *frigid* outside that I quickly buttoned up my coat." What is the meaning of the word *frigid*? (It is logical that the reason the person buttoned his or her coat was that it was cold.)

3. Have pupils read to draw conclusions: "Pam went merrily down the street, whistling to herself." (Pam was happy, sad, worried.)

4. Give several endings to a story and let pupils pick the one that would be the best conclusion.

5. Have pupils read to predict the outcome. Ask questions such as: What will happen next?

6. Have the pupils read and try to guess the answer to riddles.

7. Have the pupils interpret cartoons in the editorial section of the daily newspaper.

8.   Have pupils respond appropriately to teacher-developed exercises modeled after test items; for example, the pupil is required to read a paragraph and then to select from five possible answers the one that answers an inferential question about the paragraph. Sample question and answers are "During the period described in the selection, poets were apparently considered: A. Quite important, B. Somewhat important, C. Not particularly important, D. Somewhat unimportant, E. Quite unimportant". (Comprehension subtest of the *Nelson-Denny Reading Test*)

READING FOR EVALUATION
(CRITICAL READING)

Critical reading involves literal comprehension, but it is also demands that the reader evaluate or pass judgment on the quality, logic, reliability, value, accuracy, and truthfulness of what is read. It involves the evaluation of the validity and intellectual worthwhileness of printed materials. It means that the reader must be able to recognize the author's intent and point of view, and to make judgments and inferences. The good reader looks for contradictory material, relates the material to personal experience, distinguishes fact from fiction or opinion, is concerned with the timeliness of the material, and tries to understand the author's motives. The good comprehender reads beyond the materials.

Critical readers are as much interested in why something is said as in what is said, are sensitive to how words are used and slightly suspicious of the author's biases, and pay particular attention to words with several meanings. They check the copyright data, the author's credentials, and the publisher's past performance. Critical readers look for errors of reasoning, of analogy, of overgeneralization, of oversimplification, and of distortion; they look for one-sided presentations, prejudices, faulty inferences, and propaganda; they avoid jumping to quick conclusions.

Critical reading is slow, sentence-by-sentence, and thought-by-thought reading. The reader needs to be able to follow inductive and deductive argument, to spot generalizations, to be sensitive to analogies and such simple devices as guilt through association. Critical reading requires the reader to carefully analyze the writer's words, purpose, and implications.

The teacher can lessen the difficulties of critical reading with exercises such as the following:

1.   Have students read newspapers, magazines, editorials, and cartoons critically.

2.   Ask questions that require an evaluative response.

3.   Stop students before they come to the writer's conclusion and let them state all the possible solutions.

4.   Have pupils react critically to such words as *fascist, communist, socialist, conservative, capitalist, liberal,* and the like.

5. Have pupils select from three or four stated purposes the one that best represents the writer's purpose.

6. Have pupils engage in group discussions as a way of getting at assumptions or preconceptions.

7. Teach pupils to recognize the difference between connotative and denotative meanings of words.

8. Help pupils to identify an unstated premise or conclusion.

9. Help pupils to distinguish between subjective and objective evidence.

10. Teach pupils to detect common techniques used by writers to sway public opinion:
   a. False or glittering generalization
   b. Bias or prejudice
   c. Unwarranted inference or cliché
   d. Confusion of fact and opinion
   e. Distortion of truth
   f. Misleading headline
   g. Bandwagon appeal
   h. Card stacking (relating only to one side)
   i. Appeal to emotions
   j. Assuming all relationships are causal
   • k. Name calling
   l. Begging the question
   m. False analogy
   n. Error in inductive or deductive reasoning
   o. Ignoring alternatives
   p. Oversimplification
   q. Changing the meaning of terms
   r. Questionable sampling
   s. Testimonial (using prominent names to bolster one's view)
   t. Transfer techniques ("I drink A and B")
   u. Failure to cite sources of one's information
   v. Use of straw issues

11. Teach pupils to discriminate between factual news reporting and editorial writing.

12. Teach pupils to distinguish literary genres such as fantasy, realistic and historical writing, and biography.

13. Have pupils match propaganda techniques with statements, as in the following examples:

Propaganda Techniques

a. Citation of authority or testimonial
b. Bandwagon or "everybody is doing it" technique
c. Glittering generality
d. Transfer technique (similar to testimonial, but supporting statement is not directly associated with what is being advocated)
e. Name calling

Statements

_____1. Mr. Bott says there is no need to fear snakes.
_____2. Everybody is going to Lakewood Park on Sunday afternoon.
_____3. Grand Park is the finest park in central Missouri.
_____4. Don't be a wallflower.
_____5. A and B tastes best. Everybody drinks A and B.
_____6. When you wear a hat you are more of a man and people hire men.
_____7. There's nothing like wood to add to the decor of your home.
_____8. The best music comes from a Cunningham radio.
_____9. People who know drink their beer out of a glass.

14.   Have pupils evaluate the reliability of information by collecting several viewpoints from different sources on the same topic.

SUMMARY

Essentially, this chapter has concerned itself with advancing the pupil's comprehension skills. From the literal interpretation the pupil must advance to cause-and-effect reasoning and to the drawing of inferences; to making generalizations and arriving at conclusions; to the interpretation of the deeper meanings; and to appreciation. Appreciation, which is discussed in Chapter 14, involves all the other cognitive dimensions of reading.

Although each of the specific skills discussed here reaches its culmination only in the upper grades and frequently not even then, the teacher of reading, as indeed all teachers, must encourage the development of each skill early in the primary grades. Even critical reading should begin in the primary grades. It is not what to teach but how to teach the skills that causes difficulty.

The ability to comprehend printed material is not, of course, entirely subject to development. Teaching cannot accomplish everything. The ability to remember word meanings and the ability to reason with verbal concepts are probably a part of the child's native endowment. Skill development is subject to the potentialities that already exist.

QUESTIONS FOR DISCUSSION

1.   What comprehension skills seem not amenable to training? Which seem most amenable to training?
2.   What principles in addition to those mentioned in this chapter should guide the teacher in the development of word meanings?
3.   What types of organization do paragraphs normally fall into? Either write or locate materials that illustrate various organizations and that might be used at junior high school level.
4.   Discuss:
    a.   The specific meaning elicited by a word is a function of the context in which it occurs.
    b.   Drill and training in comprehension increase comprehension achievement rather than comprehension potential.
    c.   Comprehension depends upon such variables as vocabulary, intelligence, perception, interpretation of language (getting meaning from context), and speech.
    d.   Organizing what is read, as for example by summarizing or outlining, is positively related to comprehension.
5.   Apart from variations in the ability to read, what are the most important differences between good and poor readers?

6. What is critical reading? How might newspapers be used to develop critical-reading skills?
7. How else may critical reading be taught?
8. What special skills and attitudes are needed for critical reading?
9. Diagram and identify the various facets of comprehension.
10. Differentiate between good and poor comprehenders.
11. Offer eight suggestions for developing comprehension skills.

14

DEVELOPING FUNCTIONAL READING SKILLS

Chapter 14 continues the examination of the comprehension skills. It deals with three special facets of reading: reading for learning, developing the rate of comprehension, and reading in the content areas.

The three facets of reading discussed in this chapter are somewhat diverse and not readily classifiable. In the discussion of the facets of comprehension in the introduction to Chapter 13, the three topics that are the concern of this chapter were described as involving the application of the basic comprehension skills. Clearly all three require competency in the comprehension skills already discussed, but they also require skills beyond those discussed. The purpose of this chapter is to identify the additional comprehension skills needed for competency in each of these facets of reading. First consider reading for learning.

READING FOR LEARNING

Complete reading is said to involve four steps: recognition, understanding, reaction, and integration. Ultimately, it is hoped that the reading a child does will influence and direct some future activity. In a very real sense, then, whenever children integrate what they are reading, they are studying. This may be the ultimate in comprehension. Gray (1957) points out that integration is "the heart of the learning act in reading." The reading act is complete only when that which is read becomes assimilated.

Integrative reading is commonly identified with study-related reading. Herber (1969) defines study skills in reading as work skills that produce useful knowledge for a learner; they are reading skills especially adapted to execute particular tasks. They help the student to develop ideas, to remember ideas, and to use ideas.

Poor readers, however, often cannot read for learning or for study purposes. They almost universally have difficulty reading textbooks. They may be able to recognize the words and comprehend their meaning, but often cannot integrate or assimilate the material read. Specifically, the disabled reader

1. Cannot use the dictionary: cannot locate words in a dictionary; cannot use diacritical markings to determine the correct pronunciation of the word; cannot find the meaning appropriate to the context; cannot use guide words, accent, and syllabication cues; cannot interpret phonetic respellings; cannot use cross references; and cannot determine the plural, the part of speech, or the sense of a word, from the information as it is given.

2. Has not developed an effective method of study-related reading, such as the SQ3R method.

3. Cannot locate information in encyclopedias, card catalogs, or almanacs; and cannot use the table of contents, index, or appendix of a book.

4. Cannot read maps, graphs, charts, and the like.

5. Cannot adjust the method or rate of reading to the purposes and nature of the material.

6. Cannot retain what has been read.

Dictionary skills were discussed in Chapter 12. Examine now the second area in the list above; in particular, consider the SQ3R method of study.

SQ3R METHOD OF STUDY

The SQ3R method of integrative reading, proposed by Robinson (1961), involves five steps: survey, question, read, recite, and review (thus SQ3R). The SQ3R method is especially designed for history, social science, science, and prose materials.

Surveying is the first step in the SQ3R method and is the process of becoming familiar with the broad outlines, the chapter title, the main headings, the topic sentences, and the summary. Good students get an overall picture of what they are reading or studying. The reason is obvious. Students must know what kind of article they are reading before they can choose their techniques well.

In surveying a book, one first of all looks at the title. The title tells in general what the book is about; the preface gives a more detailed statement. In the preface the writer tells why the book was written and what he or she seeks to accomplish. The table of contents gives a more detailed outline of the book. It gives clues to the writer's organization. The chapter titles, headings, and summaries should come next. The chapter headings are especially important; they are the clues to the chapter organization. In general, the chapter title identifies the chapter's main idea. The major headings give the broad outlines of the chapter and show how the writer supports the main idea. Under each major heading may be one or more side headings.

In surveying paragraphs, the topic sentence is especially important. It summarizes the paragraph. It contains the main idea of the paragraph and usually is the first sentence in a paragraph.

Surveying thus allows the reader to warm up to the reading task ahead. It gives an overall view of the material. It is a preview. Elementary teachers have always prepared children for the reading task. They have made certain that children had the necessary experience for understanding and that they had a purpose for reading. This is what surveying accomplishes for the student. Surveying serves the same function as does the first step of the directed reading activity.

Smith and Hesse (1969), in a study of 340 eleventh-grade students, found that listening to a cognitive organizer or preview had a positive effect on the attitudes of poor readers and on their ability to identify the main idea. It did not have the same effect on good readers. It seemed that the good readers had sufficiently well developed styles of organizing themselves cognitively to be able to comprehend what they read.

Skimming is frequently used in previewing or surveying. Skimming gives a quick glimpse of the organization. It is a sort of threshing process in which the wheat is separated from the chaff. The reader is seeking certain information or perhaps wishes to decide whether or not to read the selection more intensively.

The second step in integrative reading is the *question*. Sometimes the writer poses questions at the beginning or at the end of the chapter. The teacher may suggest questions as a part of the assignment. Pupils need to learn to make their own questions by turning the main headings or italicized words into questions.

Melnick (1965) notes that questions establish a basis for identifying and clarifying the purpose for reading. The first step in the directed reading activity involves the asking of a question that focuses attention on the purpose for reading. Rothkopf (1970) suggests that questions asked after reading are more important for understanding and retention than are those asked before reading.

Melnik lists two main functions of the question. As a diagnostic tool, the unstructured question permits the teacher to observe a variety of individual responses: how the pupil approaches the reading passage; the pupil's tendency to relate ideas or perhaps to focus on isolated details; the pupil's ability to organize what is being read. As an instructional tool, the question helps the pupil to identify the author's purpose and to clarify meaning. The question technique tends to surpass both careful reading without questions and rereading of the same material.

Students should write down their questions, whether developed before, during, or after the reading, as a basis for review. Formulating questions before reading certainly encourages readers to seek answers as they read.

The third step of an effective study procedure is the *reading* itself. The elements necessary for purposeful reading include the following:

1. Have a definite reason for reading.
2. Define clearly the problem that is to be solved.
3. Focus attention on the main points.
4. Try to group the supporting details with the main idea.
5. Keep in mind the nature of the assignment.
6. Pay special attention to illustrations of all kinds: graphs, maps, charts, and the like.
7. Be a flexible reader, adjusting the rate of the reading to the purpose of the reading and the nature of the material.
8. Seek to answer questions.

Study-related reading frequently is intensive reading. It is careful, rather slow reading, with emphasis upon remembering details. Intensive reading requires that upon reaching the end of the chapter the reader recognize the main idea. The reader should know where the author is heading, should form an outline of what is read, and should identify the major and supporting points.

The fourth step of Robinson's SQ3R study method, to *recite*, is literally a self-examination. Here pupils attempt to answer for themselves the questions that were posed, without referring to their notes or other aids. Only when the pupils cannot answer the questions should they consult notes or refer to the book. Self-recitation directs attention to specific questions, thereby aiding concentration. Generally it is recommended that the recitation should occur as soon as possible after the reading.

Self-recitation makes a number of contributions to effective learning. Pupils are immediately aware of how well they have read, how accurately they have accomplished their purposes, and whether they can express their new found knowledge in their own words. If they can verbalize their knowledge to their own satisfaction, they can generally explain or recite to another. This kind of recitation is the heart of effective study; it is the seeking of answers to self-imposed questions, and rather than settling for rote memorization, it puts one's new learnings into one's own words.

The fifth and final step of Robinson's method is *review*. Study is not complete until it includes a plan for retention. If learning is to be of any use in later situations, the student must remember what has been learned. Review, whether through studying one's notes, through recall, self-recitation, class discussion, tests, summaries, or rereading, should be an exercise in critical reading and thinking and should involve assimilation, integration, and organization. Review is critical reexamination with the goal of integrating the content and acquiring useful generalizations. Unless something is done to slow it, forgetting proceeds at a rapid pace immediately after learning. Thus review should come as soon as possible. And generally more than one review is needed.*

Developing Location and Reference Skills

A second major study skill is the ability to locate information. The good student is one who has learned to locate information. This means a familiarity with library aids and with such library resources as the Dewey and Library of Congress classification systems, the card catalog, and various indexes, encyclopedias, and almanacs. It also means the ability to find the desired material within a book, a chapter, a paragraph, or a sentence. It means that students should know how to use a book's table of contents, footnotes, or appendix.

Location and reference skills may be taught with exercises such as these:

1. Have pupils locate the pages in which an encyclopedia treats given content matter: "On what page would you find something about George Washington?" "Find a description of an elephant." "In what volume(s) and on what page or pages is atomic energy discussed?"

2. Teach pupils how to use the volume designation on the back of encyclopedias to locate quickly the subject matter for which they are looking.

3. Teach the meaning and use of guide words and cross references in encyclopedias.

Examine now another specific study skill, namely, the ability to read maps and graphs.

Reading Maps, Graphs, and Tables

When writers cannot accurately put into words alone what they want to say, they frequently use pictures, maps, graphs, and diagrams. However, the pupil gets what the writer has intended from such materials only if the new symbols incorporated into these illustrations are understood.

Children can be taught to read maps, charts, and graphs, perhaps as early as first grade. The more capable first-grade children can learn to handle simple graphs. Children can interpret pictorial graphs most easily; next in order of difficulty come circle or pie graphs, two-dimensional graphs, and line graphs.

---

* For a listing of materials useful in teaching location and reference skills, use of library resources, alphabetizing and dictionary skill, proper use of an encyclopedia, reading of maps, charts, and graphs, general study skills, such as the SQ3R method, note-taking, using a table of contents, and the index, outlining, and the like, see Dechant 1981b: pp. 208-218.

Vertical bar graphs seem to be easier to read than horizontal bar graphs, but ultimately, the ease or difficulty children experience in reading graphs depends on the materials and the context in which they are used.

READING MAPS

Teaching pupils to read maps includes the following procedures:

1. Studying the title of the map.
2. Studying each symbol (the legend).
3. Noting direction on the map.
4. Analyzing and applying the map scale.
5. Relating the area under study to a more general or larger area: Kansas in relation to the United States
6. Knowing different types of maps: physical and relief maps, political maps, maps depicting crops, rainfall, population, vegetation, windbelts, ocean routes, rivers and lakes, continents and islands, railroads and highways.
7. Studying map colorations.

Exercises designed to improve map reading skills are as follows:

1. Relate map study to pictures and aerial photographs.
2. Demonstrate how a small map or globe represents a large territory.
3. Have the pupils make a map of their hometown or of the immediate environment (school building, school grounds).
4. Let pupils answer true or false statements such as the following:
    a. My home is north of the post office.
    b. East of our school is the public library.
5. Have the children locate their town on a map.
6. Teach that shading from green through yellow, brown, and red indicates an increase in altitude.
7. Ask the pupils to locate on the map an example of each of the following:

archipelago	coastline	highland	ocean
basin	continent	inlet	peninsula
bay	delta	island	plateau
boundary	desert	isthmus	port
branch	dike	jungle	reef
canyon	divide	lake	river
cape	estuary	marsh	sea
channel	fiord	mesa	strait
city	gulf	mountain	swamp
cliff	harbor	oasis	tributary
			valley

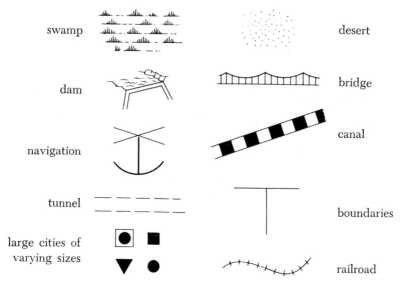

swamp	desert
dam	bridge
navigation	canal
tunnel	boundaries
large cities of varying sizes	railroad

Figure 14-1 Geographical Symbols

8. Teach the representation of elevation and slope through contour lines.

9. Study the meanings of terms such as these:

apogee	isobar	altitude
contour line	isotherm	longitude
divide	meridian	parallel
equinox	perigee	meridian
international date line	satellite	Mercator's projections

10. Have pupils match picture symbols with word symbols, as in Figure 14–1.

11. Have pupils make up and answer questions based on maps.

READING GRAPHS

Children also need help in learning to read graphs, of which there are four kinds. The *pictorial* graph (see Figure 14–2) uses pictures to show relationships between realities. This kind of graph, in which the units are expressed in picture form, is the easiest to read. The *bar* graphs (see Figures 14–3 and 14–4) express amounts or compare the size of quantities. For example, one may want to compare the heights of various buildings or dams in the United States or the number of ticket sales made by the children in two different classes. In each instance, the bar graph shows how much more or less one category contains when measured against another. A bar graph may be either vertical or horizontal.

The *line* graph (see Figure 14–5) shows changes between quantities. It indicates what has happened over a period of time: whether there has been an in-

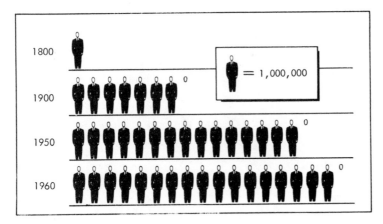

1800

1900

= 1,000,000

1950

1960

Figure 14-2   Population Growth in the United States: A Pictorial Graph (Pictograph)

crease or a decrease, for example, in the amount of rain, in the price of food, or in the daily temperature. The *circle* or *pie* graph (see Figure 14–6), shows the relation of parts to a whole. It may be used, for example, to indicate the percentage of As, Bs, Cs, and Ds in a certain class; how much of the family budget goes to

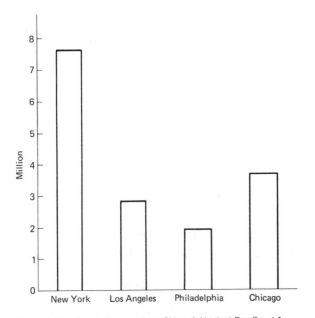

Figure 14-3   Populations of Major Cities: A Vertical Bar Graph*

* Figures 14–3 through 14–6 are reprinted by permission from the *Listen and Read Workbook*, copyright 1961, and *Listen and Read*, MN, copyright 1969, by Educational Developmental Laboratories.

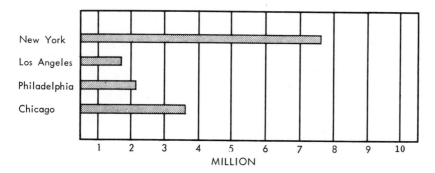

Figure 14-4 Populations of Major Cities: A Horizontal Bar Graph*

food, clothing, shelter, savings, car, miscellaneous; or what percentage of the school budget is allotted to such categories as salaries, maintenance, and the general operation of the school plant.

To read graphs of one kind or another, pupils should learn to observe the following steps:

1. Read the title of the graph—this tells what the graph is about.
2. Discover what is being compared—persons, places, or things.
3. Be able to interpret the legend and the meaning of the vertical and horizontal axes.
4. Identify the scale of measure that has been used. What does each figure represent?
5. Discover what conclusions can be drawn from the graph.

The exercises that follow are illustrative of how pupils might be helped to read graphs of various types.

1. Have pupils identify the percentage increase in the population of the United States from 1800 to 1900 or the total population growth from 1950 to 1960, using Figure 14–2 to do so.

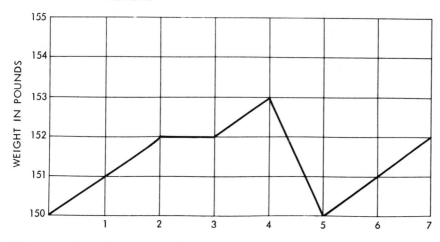

Figure 14-5 Weight Gain for Patient X Over a Seven-Week Period: A Line Graph*

Where it comes from...

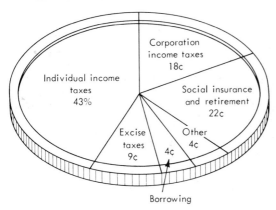

Figure 14-6 Income for Governmental Expenses: A Circle or Pie Graph*

2. Have pupils identify the approximate population of New York City, using Figures 14–3 or 14–4. Have pupils rank the cities by population.

3. Have pupils determine from the graph in Figure 14–5 the week during which patient X weighed the least and the week during which patient X weighed the most.

4. Have pupils use Figure 14–6 to identify the greatest single source of governmental income.

READING TABLES

A table is a simple listing of facts and information. In reading a table, students should first look at the title, and then look at the headings of the various columns, with their major headings and subheadings if there are any. Finally, students must read the details which are usually written in the left-hand column. Figure 14–7 teaches all of these skills.

Figure 14-7 Going to Europe: Who Spends What

FAMILY INCOME	NUMBER OF TRAVELERS	NUMBER OF DAYS	AMOUNT SPENT PER DAY	TOTAL SPENT
$5,000 or less	181,500*	51	$ 9.60	$495
$5,000–$10,000	557,700	36	$13.20	$474
$10,000–$15,000	435,160	32	$15.10	$487
$15,000–$20,000	305,140	29	$16.54	$473
$20,000 and up	720,500	26	$25.39	$671
All Travelers	2,200,000	33	$16.73	$552

* All figures are for 1967

Source: U.S. Treasury

344

DEVELOPING RATE
OF COMPREHENSION*

In addition to learning to read for study purposes, pupils must learn to adjust their rate of reading to fit the purposes of the reading and to fit the nature of the materials.

Rate of reading may be described as rate of comprehension or as speed in grasping the meanings intended by the writer. Rate has no meaning apart from comprehension. No one actually reads faster than he or she comprehends, but many read much more slowly than their comprehension permits. Generally the limiting factor to rate improvement is the mind rather than the eye. The central cognitive processes involving the storage of information in memory play a critical role in the performance of skilled readers.

Relationship Between Rate
and Comprehension

The relationship between rate and comprehension is important to the teacher because the teacher must decide when to stress rate improvement and when to emphasize comprehension skills. A reader who is low in both comprehension and rate will generally not benefit from an emphasis on speed. Such a pupil needs training in basic comprehension skills as indeed does the pupil who reads rapidly but with low comprehension. However, one who reads all materials slowly but with good comprehension may well profit from training in speed. Perhaps this is because rapid reading requires the pupil's full attention, whereas when the pupil plods along, attention wanders.

In mathematics and science the correlations between comprehension and rate of reading tend to be low and negative. In general, the faster students read in these areas, the less they tend to understand.

The Value of Speed Reading

Despite the ambivalence of some of the research, rapidity in reading seems to have an economy value in its own right and should be investigated as a separate skill. Rate training should be included in developmental reading programs and should begin at or above the sixth grade. Most readers cease improving in rate, if no attempts are made to increase it, by about the sixth grade.

However, rate of reading is not the primary goal in reading. The ultimate aim is comprehension according to the reader's abilities and needs. This means that the good reader is a flexible reader. Just as cars have in them the power to go slowly or rapidly as the occasion demands, so too good readers can slow down or

* See Dechant's "Rate of Comprehension—Needed Research" (1961); for materials designed to develop rate of comprehension, see Dechant 1981b: pp. 218–225.

speed up as the nature and difficulty of the material and their own needs and purposes change. The good reader can shift gears in reading.

Flexibility appears to be the critical difference between good and poor readers. Good readers set comprehension as their goal and adjust rate rather automatically. Poor readers mechanically plod from word to word. Efficiency in reading means simply this: with some purposes and some materials one should read slowly; with others, one should read more rapidly.

Skimming and Scanning

Skimming is selective reading. In skimming, readers choose what they want to read. They select those sentences, clauses, and phrases that best serve their purposes, get a general impression of the selection, and decide on the basis of this examination whether to read the selection more intensively. A quick glance is given to the table of contents, the index, the chapter titles, the paragraph headings, the topic sentences, and the summary. These provide valuable clues to the main idea.

In scanning, readers run their eyes down the page with the purpose of finding an answer to a specific question, of locating a specific date or number, a reference, a name, a city, or a quotation.

Skimming and scanning are not accelerated reading. When engaging in them, readers switch from looking to reading to looking and back again to reading. They look back and forth and down the page in a floating manner, taking in words, ideas, and organization at a subliminal level. In fact, there is usually less reading than looking, and when the skimmer or the scanner read, they read in the usual way.

Research tends to indicate that reading rates above 800 words per minute are in the nature of skimming and scanning. When skimming, the reader characteristically omits part of the content and reads with considerably less comprehension.

Improving Rate of Reading

Rate of reading can undoubtedly be improved. Students who have undertaken some form of rate-improvement training do increase their speed and will generally read faster than those who have not had such training.

Rate of reading should always be dependent on the purposes, intelligence, experience, and knowledge of the reader and upon the difficulty level of the material. The rate is always affected by the psychological and physical state of the reader, by the reader's motivation and mastery of the basic reading skills, and by the format of the materials. More specifically, factors that affect speed and comprehension are the following: the size and style of the type; the blackness and sharpness of the print; the quality and tone of the paper; the size of the page; the physical organization of the material; the amount of white space; the kind and placement of the illustrations, headings and subheadings; the style and clarity of the writing; the field of knowledge from which the writing is drawn; the complexity of the ideas; and the kind of writing (poetry, narrative, or descriptive) being read; together with the reader's mental ability, reading skill, likes and dislikes, background of experience, purpose, interest in the field being presented, and familiarity with the peculiarities of the author's style and phraseology.

Readers get into trouble in reading and must proceed more slowly in the following situations: when the writer's style is too difficult; when the ideas are too abstract; when trying to learn and to remember what they are reading; when following directions such as the carrying out of an experiment; when reading poetry; when reading critically—trying to evaluate what they read; and when reading in such specialized fields as science.

Advocates of rate-improvement programs claim that such programs may lead to more accurate and more precise perception; more accurate and more rapid visual discrimination; wider span of apprehension and of perception; increased span of recognition; better attention and concentration; shorter reaction time; fewer regressions; decrease in the number and duration of fixations; reduction of vocalization; better comprehension; general improvement in perceptual skills; and increased ability in organizing perceived material.

Spache (1976) notes that rate training may develop a set for faster reading, greater use of contextual cues, better visual discrimination, more rapid and more accurate recognition of word gestalts, reduction of cues needed for word recognition, better perception of what one sees peripherally, and reduction of the caution exhibited in slow or word-by-word reading.

Rate training is counterindicated, however, for pupils who show any coordination or fusional difficulties or tendencies to suppression (Spache 1976). And rate improvement cannot be built on inadequate word-perception and word-recognition skills.*

Mechanical Devices
for Rate Improvement

Mechanical devices designed to improve rate are tachistoscopes and accelerating devices.

TACHISTOSCOPES

Tachistoscopes expose numbers, letters, words, phrases, or other images for short periods of time, usually ranging from 0.01 to 1.5 seconds. Most training on these machines is at the higher speeds.

Tachistoscope training, whether individual or group, primarily develops the pupil's perceptual intake skills. By forcing the pupil to cope with intake

---

* The reader may want to consult Chapter 11 in *Psychology in Teaching Reading* (Dechant and Smith 1977) for a summary of rate-improvement studies and an evaluation of rate-improvement programs.

speeds of 0.1 seconds or less, the tachistoscope requires the pupil to see more rapidly, more accurately, and in a more orderly fashion, to pay more attention, and to organize what is seen. The pupil also develops better directional attack.

Tachistoscopic training has greatest value in the elementary years when the pupil is "learning to see." Since much of the material is designed to develop accuracy of seeing and retention of the particular placement or sequence of certain elements (for example, the pupil needs to see and remember 24571 in definite order), it may have value in a word-attack program.

ACCELERATING DEVICES

The accelerating devices provide rate training for the competent reader. Such devices (for example, the *Controlled Reader*, Educational Developmental Laboratories) are said to lead to a reduction in fixations and regressions, better attention and concentration, more rapid thinking, and improved organization of what is read. Much group training with accelerators is at far point. This is undesirable for students with myopic vision and for those who have difficulties with fusion, because they are required to improve rate while handicapped visually. At far point the person can also "read" more words than in normal reading. It is possible that this explains the relatively little transfer that occurs from machine programs to normal book reading.

Evaluation of Mechanical Rate-Improvement Training

No one suggests that reading instruments make a total program. On the other hand, few deny that they have a legitimate role in a balanced reading program. In evaluating their effectiveness, one must always be cautious about generalizing from one instrument to all others. Each has its own strengths and weaknesses and must be separately evaluated.

Certain principles, however, guide evaluation of all rate-improvement programs. It is not enough to simply look for rate gains. The reader's relative efficiency is more than a matter of the reading rate; it is also a function of the fixations and regressions.

$$\text{Relative Efficiency} = \frac{\text{Rate}}{\text{Fixations} + \text{Regressions}}$$

An increase in rate is significant only when it is accompanied by a reduction in fixations and regressions.

How good are rate-improvement devices, or for that matter, other rate improvement activities? The answers are mixed:

1. Reading speed can be improved, and gains in rate tend to have an adequate degree of permanency.

2. Improved rate is not automatically transferred to all types of material, however, and the amount of transfer of rate gains from machine-oriented programs to more typical reading is quite variable and unpredictable.

3. The improvement through mechanical devices seems to be no greater than that resulting from motivated reading alone.

4. The visual or perception span can be increased both vertically and horizontally through tachistoscopic training.

5. Mechanical devices may result in an inflexible approach to the reading task.

6. Rate gains that do occur through tachistoscopic training may be due to the elimination of regressive eye movements and better use of peripheral vision.

7. The tachistoscopic span (visual span) is already much larger than the recognition span of the average reader.

8. The mind, not vision, is generally the limiting element in reading. Fast and slow readers are differentiated on the basis of the central processes. Reading is primarily a perceptual function. Those who excel in rate of thinking tend to be high in rate of comprehension. Rate of association may be the critical factor. The increase in mental activity may also account for the better comprehension and retention that accompanies rate improvement.

9. The more significant the material is to the reader, the wider the reader's recognition span will be.

10. The machine and the purr of the motor have a psychological and motivational effect on machine-conscious students, especially boys. They do not stretch the visual span but rather spur the mind.

11. Rather than speed training, with some students it might be better to improve poor vocabulary and word-recognition and word-analysis skills. Weaknesses in basic reading skills should be diagnosed and corrected before any consideration is given to rate of reading.

12. If, in fact, good readers react to ever decreasing or minimal cues, then mechanical training may at times be successful simply because it teaches students to read with fewer cues, to guess better what they see peripherally, and to be more confident in dealing with indistinct portions of words (Spache 1976).

13. Motivational factors, verbal set, or mind set, may be the most significant in improving both rate and permanency of rate.

14. The best use of mechanical devices may be with average and better-than-average readers having specific problems in rate of reading.

15. Fast readers tend to use contextual clues more efficiently. In effect, they see fewer words when reading. If this is so, then instruction in key-phrase reading should be encouraged (Rose 1969). Phrase-reading training increases perceptual span, reading comprehension, and rate.

16. Research shows that it is desirable to say the word subvocally while reading. The fade-out of the visually acquired stimulus seems rapid if it is not recoded in acoustic form (Rose 1969). An acoustic factor seems to be involved in immediate memory and recall. And if this is so, it seems that instruction in fast reading should not do away with inner speech.

17. Mechanical training may develop a set for faster reading, may increase the use of contextual cues, lead to better visual discrimination, and perhaps even increase acute attention. Machines are thus best used in developmental reading. Perhaps their major contributions are more rapid and more accurate recognition of word gestalts and a reduction in the cues needed for word recognition (Spache 1976).

Educational Implications

There seems to be little justification for emphasis on speed of reading in the primary school years. The intermediate pupil and the high school students, on the other hand, must be taught to adjust their reading speed to the materials and purposes of reading. They must be taught, either through book or machine programs, facility and speed in perceiving words and relating them to their meaning. They must be taught to read in thought units. They must be helped to overcome such faulty habits as moving the lips, pointing to words, or moving the head while reading.

Pupils should be encouraged to move their eyes as rapidly across the line of print as is possible. Too frequently, pupils *can* read faster, but they have developed the habit of reading slowly. To overcome this habit, pupils should time themselves on passages of a particular length. In the beginning the passages should be simple and interesting. If the print is in narrow columns, as in newspapers, pupils should be encouraged to make only one fixation per line, forcing themselves to move their eyes down the page.

Readers are constantly tempted to regress so that they can read more accurately. Normally this may be good procedure, but it does not lead to increased speed. Too cautious readers must fight against this. They can be helped to overcome excessive caution by using a moving-slot device. Moving a piece of paper (from which a line-sized slot has been cut) down the page forces readers to move ahead and keeps them from looking either back or too far ahead. Another device consists simply of a sheet of paper which may be moved down the page, covering a line at a time.

Rate Skills and the Poor Reader

The rate of comprehension of poor readers is often significantly below the norm for their age and grade level. They cannot read as many words per minute as would be normal for a pupil their age. Causes commonly adduced to explain a slow reading rate are

1. The pupil moves the lips and vocalizes excessively during silent reading. An overemphasis on auditory methods of oral reading may lead to excessive lip movements, inner vocalization, and word-by-word reading. Movement of the lips is an indication of inner vocalization. Even though vocalization may have its own merits (see point 16, page 349), it does affect rate of reading.
2. The pupil is a word-by-word reader.
3. The pupil sounds out every word.
4. The material is too difficult; the pupil has not had the experiential background or lacks the intellectual maturity to bring meaning to the printed materials.
5. The pupil's eye-movements are inflexible; the pupil does not vary eye movements with the difficulty of the reading matter or a change of purpose.
6. The pupil's eye movements lack rhythm and the return sweep may be faulty.
7. The pupil sequences too slowly with resultant overfixation. He or she is a perseverative reader and cannot change fixation easily.

8. The pupil has slow word recognition; he or she decodes even familiar words slowly.
9. The pupil has binocular or fusion difficulties.
10. The pupil has inadequate comprehension ability.
11. The pupil's perception span, eye memory, and eye-voice spans are too narrow.
12. The pupil makes too many regressions.
13. The pupil cannot read in thought units.
14. The pupil has developed the habit of finger pointing while reading.

The following techniques may be used to increase rate:

1. Use phrases on flash cards to speed up word recognition.
2. Call pupils' attention to their lip movement. If, when pupils read easy material, lip movement (and voicing) do not cease, it may indicate that pupils are moving their lips out of habit. Vocalization generally indicates that pupils are encountering difficulty. Vocalization thus is a symptom rather than a cause of the difficulty. Sometimes, however, and in young children particularly, vocalizing may aid comprehension.
3. Have pupils read simple materials as rapidly as they can. This practice should be repeated frequently and should include the charting of their progress by the pupils.
4. Have pupils time their reading.
5. Have pupils skim a page in a textbook to find the answer to a question, to locate a new word, or to identify a quotation. Use materials at or below the instructional reading level of the pupils.
6. Have pupils skim an encyclopedia article for a specific fact.
7. Have pupils determine purposes for reading and then discuss the appropriateness of various rates for various reading purposes. Teach pupils how to read a telephone book, a newspaper, a history assignment, a science experiment, a mathematics problem, and so forth. This helps pupils to be flexible readers.
8. Have pupils read to music and rhythm.
9. Use tachistoscopes and accelerating or controlled reading devices which require reading at a rate too rapid for voicing of the words.* Commercially available tachistoscopes are:
   AVR Eye-Span Trainer (AVR E-S-T 10) (Audio-Visual Research).
   TAC-III and TAC-II (A/V Concepts)
   TAC-Mate (A/V Concepts)
   Rapid Reading Kit (Better Reading Program, Inc.)
   T-Scope Tachistoscopic Projector (Califone)
   EDL Flash-X (Educational Developmental Laboratories)
   EDL Tach-X (Educational Development Laboratories)
   Tach-Mate (Instructional/Communications Technology, Inc.)
   Vu-Mate (Instructional/Communications Technology, Inc.)
   Tac-Ette (Keystone View)
   Electro-Tach (Lafayette Instrument Company)
   Attachable Lens Barrel Tachistoscope (Lafayette Instrument Company)
   Automatic Projection Tachistoscope (Lafayette Instrument Company)

* For a listing of book-centered and machine rate-improvement programs, see Dechant 1981b: pp. 218–225.

Selectro Tach 40020V (Lafayette Instrument Company)
Tachomatic X 500 (Psychotechnics, Inc.)
T-Matic X 150 (Psychotechnics, Inc.)
Speed -I-O-Scope (Society for Visual Education)

Accelerating devices provide rate training for competent readers and are most useful in the upper elementary years and in junior high school. Commercially available accelerators include:

Readamatic Pacer (Americana Interstate Corporation)
FS50, FS-150N, or FS500N (A/V Concepts)
AVR Reading Ratemeter (Audio-Visual Research Company)
Craig Reader (Craig Education)
Controlled Reader Senior (EDL-McGraw-Hill)
EDL Controlled Reader Jr. (EDL/McGraw-Hill)
EDL Combo-8 Controlled Reader (EDL/McGraw-Hill)
EDL Skill Mate (EDL/Mc-Graw-Hill)
EDL Skill Builder (EDL/McGraw-Hill)
EDL Skimmer (Educational Developmental Laboratories/McGraw-Hill)
Guided Reader (Instructional/Communications Technology, Inc.)
P.D.L. Perceptoscope Mark III, Model 100 (Perceptual Development Laboratories)
Shadowscope Reading Pacer (Psychotechnics, Inc.)
Prep Pacer (Reading Lab Inc.)
SRA Reading Accelerator (Science Research Associations)

READING IN THE CONTENT AREAS*

A major functional reading skill, and the third to be discussed in this chapter, is the ability to read in the content areas. The acid test of a reading program is the transferability of the learning it provides to content areas. The pupils are not just reading; they are reading in a given area. As one child said, "You can't read readin', you gotta read sumpin'." A goal of the developmental reading program has to be the infusion of reading-skills instruction into every subject area where reading is a prime medium for learning (Early 1969). Research shows that general reading ability alone is often not enough to assure reading improvement in content courses; pupils must be equipped with special skills to meet their needs. As pupils advance through school, it becomes increasingly difficult for them to be weak in reading and strong in the content subjects.

At one time, the ability to read was considered to be a general skill applicable to any reading material, and reading ability was measured by a general reading test. Today it is accepted that reading consists of many skills, that reading comprehension in a given subject area can be broken down into many

---

* For a listing of materials designed to teach reading in the content fields, see Dechant 1981b: pp. 226–231.

subskills and abilities, and that a pupil might read exceptionally well in a given content area but extremely poorly in another.

Each reader's background of vocabulary and experience will vary from one content area to another. Consequently, in a given content area, equally intelligent readers may greatly differ in readiness for reading. And each area possesses its own problems. Specialized vocabulary, maps, tables, graphs, abbreviations, indexes, diagrams, and footnotes are but a few of the new problems that readers must deal with as they learn to read effectively in different content areas. In addition, as children progress through school, new terms are introduced faster and with fewer repetitions, more facts are presented, and greater retention and application are expected.

Vocabulary is a distinct problem in each of the content areas. That vocabulary development is particularly significant in content-area reading should not be surprising. Words are "advance organizers" and provide cues to the structure of the materials. Ausübel (1960) noted that the learning and retention of unfamiliar but nevertheless meaningful verbal material can be facilitated by the advance introduction of relevant subsuming concepts. These concepts and the words that represent them help learners to mobilize the most relevant existing concepts they already possess (past learning) and provide anchorage for (help organize) the new material that must be learned.

Review now the specific reading demands of the content areas, beginning with those demanded in the reading of literature.

Literature

The goals in the reading of literature are somewhat different from those of the other content areas. The reading of literature calls for an emotional involvement not generally demanded by other types of content-area reading. It requires special appreciation of the mood and style of the author; it requires the reader to respond to form, sometimes to rhyme, to connotative meanings, and to emotional overtones; and it requires the reader to deal with such literary forms and devices as the sonnet, the essay, and the metaphor. Readers must find in literature reflections of the ever-flowing stream of human behavior and emotions. They must analyze the characters, appreciate the style, and digest the sequence of development (Tremonti and Algero 1967). Reading literature requires literal understanding, analysis, appreciation, critical insight, symbolic interpretation, aesthetic appreciation, and recognition of the relevance of literature to life. Students need to go beyond mere passive acceptance of literal comprehension; they must do something with what they read (Simmons 1965). They need to get involved.

Chapter 13 identified various levels of comprehension, the last of which was appreciation. Reading for appreciation is what the reading of literature is all about. Appreciation skills include appreciation of the various types of literature (poetry, prose, drama, and so forth), of style or manner of expression, and of such aspects as tone (serious or humorous). Unfortunately, poor readers often cannot identify the mood, tone, theme, intent, and purpose of the writer; they cannot differentiate between the denotative and connotative use of words; they cannot answer questions requiring an awareness of the literary techniques, forms, and styles used by the writer; and they cannot perceive the literary and semantic devices by means of which writers accomplish their purposes.

Examine some of these factors, beginning with the types of literature. Each literary form has its own mode of expression.

Fiction is the biography of conflict in human motives. It traces the conflict from its inception to its conclusion. Since motives are within the individual, the writer must "psychoanalyze" the fictional character, report what the character is saying to him- or herself, use soliloquies or asides in which the character tells the audience what his or her motives are, or portray the character's motives through appearance, speech, or action. The successful reader of literature must understand these literary contrivances of the author and read between the lines for a comprehension of the basic meaning.

In *poetry*, the writer communicates through words and concepts, but also through tone, mood, repetition, rhythm, and rhyme. Poetry is literary work in metrical form. It is the art of rhythmical composition.

Poetry presents all kinds of grammatical and structural difficulties. The syntax may be irregular; it is sometimes difficult to identify the verb; the juxtaposition of words for auditory and aesthetic effects is often peculiar; and the writing may be marked by irregular constructions. To read poetry successfully, it is necessary to understand metaphors.

In reading *drama*, it is necessary to understand the action and the setting. The latter is largely supplied by stage directions which may break up the dialogue, making it more difficult to follow the sequence of events. The students must also learn to visualize various actions going on at the same time.

In *essays*, the mood may take a formal, pedantic, humorous, satiric, philosophical, inspirational, persuasive, or political form. The *short story* presents its own literary contrivances. It is characterized by uniformity of tone and plot and by dramatic intensity.

To appreciate the various literary forms (fiction, poetry, drama, essays, short stories) the pupils must to learn to analyze the elements of plot, characterization, style, and theme.

PLOT

The pupils must learn to ask a series of questions. Did I like the ending? How would I have changed it? Did the writer use surprise, suspense, or mystery to keep me interested? What was the conflict or the major motive of the story? What time and place or settings are depicted? Is it fanciful or realistic literature?

An exercise like the following teaches pupils to appreciate plot:

1. Read the following sentences and select the word that best characterizes the plot:

    > We stood on the bridge not knowing whether to go forward, backward, or just remain where we were. In front of us and behind, the flood waters were rushing across the highway. Broken tree limbs, barrels, and household goods were floating by.

    This series of sentences indicates that the plot is based upon

    a. surprise.
    b. suspense.
    c. adventure.
    d. intrigue.

CHARACTERIZATION

The pupils should ask: What character did I like best? Which one would I like to be? Were the characters true to life?

Pupils learn characterization skills by analyzing statements and answering certain questions about them. For example

1. Read the following description:

    > The man just sat. His eyes stared into empty space. No smile or grin ever adorned his face. When he spoke, it was about the wickedness of man and the burning fires of hell.

    This series of sentences describes a person who is probably

    a. discontented with life.
    b. satisfied with life.
    c. successful in life.
    d. proud of living.

Or the teacher may require the pupils to underline the one word out of three that best characterizes the person described in key sentences. For example

1. Jim grabbed Johnny by the shoulder and threw him against the wall. "That's for ratting on me."

    Jim is: generous, *unethical*, brave.
2. Mary's eyes shot darts of fire at anyone who in the slightest way disagreed with her.

    Mary is: rude, generous, *opinionated*.

STYLE

The pupils should ask: What was the writer's style? What figures of speech did the author use? What was the general mood or tone of the writing?

At the junior high and high school levels, students' comprehension of what they read is aided significantly by the ability to identify the writer's style. Shaw (1958) points out that a writer's rhetorical and grammatical contrivances characterize his or her writings. Shaw notes that much like the ice-cream cone which is both container and confection, the contrivances of the writer both support ideas and are themselves digestible. The writer often has so many peculiar characteristics that readers obtain a better conception of what the writer is trying to say if they reread the material. The mood of the writer colors the meaning of what is written and frequently can be identified only by reading between the lines.

The reader operates within the context of a particular writer, but to get the most of what is read, the reader also needs to become familiar with the rhetorical devices used in poems, plays, short stories, essays, novels, and bibliographies. Unless readers have at least some experience with the topic, are familiar with the specific rhetorical devices used, and can process the language and stylistic features of the writer, it is unlikely that they will be able to make accurate predictions of the writer's meaning.

THEME

The pupils should ask: What was the moral of the story? Which character best exemplifies the morals and the ideals of the writer? How do the ideas portrayed fit my own ideas?

Social Studies

Effective reading in the social studies presents three principal difficulties that require the development of specialized background and skills:

1. The vocabulary may be highly specialized and the reading material is likely to make use of fairly complex concepts.
2. The diagrammatic materials may require considerable interpretive skill for their effective use.
3. The content is frequently emotionally weighted and controversial. A critical evaluation rather than blind acceptance is required.

In teaching students to read social studies content one must begin with social studies materials. The teacher must know what specific skills to teach and how they should be taught. The following statements might guide instruction in reading in the social studies area:

1. Call attention to the words, duplicate them for the pupils, have pupils consult the dictionary definition, use the words in the appropriate context, give attention to root words and shades of meaning, use Latin derivatives and prefixes to increase vocabulary, pay special attention to words of foreign origin, require pupils to use the words in meaningful sentences, and have pupils develop their own dictionary.

2. Use films, charts, pictures, recordings, dramatizations, cartoons, models, exhibits, and the like to illustrate new concepts.

3. Teach the technical meanings of such words as *gold rush, cold war, diet, raw materials,* and the like.

4. Require pupils to read for special purposes—to answer a question, to identify the cause, to locate a certain fact, to verify an opinion, to compare different points of view—and to adjust speed of reading to purpose and type of content.
   a. Teach the value of skimming in preparation of assignments.
   b. Encourage pupils to experiment with different reading rates for different materials and purposes.
   c. Require intensive SQ3R reading of the textbook.
   d. Have those who experience difficulty understanding or retaining the material take notes or make an outline.

5. Teach pupils how to locate materials. Teach library usage, use of the Reader's Guide, card catalog, and sources of social studies materials.

6. Provide numerous activities that stimulate critical thinking and analysis and that teach pupils to infer, to evaluate, and to integrate what they read.
   a. Discuss steps to follow in problem solving.
   b. Teach pupils how to develop their own point of view.
   c. Use the discussion method and require pupils to state their own opinions and how they arrive at them.
   d. Use a debating model of presentation of beliefs and supporting factual evidence to teach pupils how to collect and evaluate facts and how to relate facts to points in an outline.

7. Make assignments specific enough so the pupils will know *how* to read. For example, the teacher may require the pupils to identify the author's point of view.

8. Test and constantly evaluate the pupils' proficiency in reading social studies materials:
   a. Prepare a self-evaluation checklist, use class evaluation of oral and written reports, and evaluate the adequacy of outlines and summaries.
   b. Organize interrogation periods in which pupil leaders ask questions about material read and evaluate responses.

9. Teach pupils to perceive the organization of materials.
   a. Have them identify the main idea, details, and structure of the writing.
   b. Have them find and understand the purpose of cue words, such as *furthermore, nevertheless, moreover, since, because.*

Mathematics

Reading in mathematics requires pupils to comprehend a new set of symbols. They must react to numerical symbols that synthesize verbal symbols, must be able to read *and* compute, and must know both the individual and combined meanings of verbal symbols and mathematical signs; they must read deductively, must translate formulas into significant relationships, and must in general read slowly.

In learning to read in mathematics, pupils should do the following:

1. Read the problem quickly to get an overview.

2. Read for main ideas or the specific question asked.

3. Learn technical mathematical terms.

o read

ʒad the organization, listing in one column the points given and in the second the /oints needed.

Translate the verbal symbols into mathematical symbols and formulas.

Read for relationships and translate these into an equation.

. Analyze carefully mathematical symbols and formulas.

8. Analyze carefully all graphs, figures, illustrations, and the like.

9. Follow a definite procedure:
   a. Learn the meaning of all words.
   b. Find what the problem asks for.
   c. Decide what facts are needed to find a solution to the problem.
   d. Decide what mathematical process is required (addition, subtraction, and so forth).
   e. Identify the order for solving the problem.

10. Make a drawing of the problem. A problem such as the following can be easily represented by a drawing:

    Harry has fifteen pictures. If he can paste three pictures on each page of his scrapbook, how many pages will be filled?

11. Proceed slowly and be willing to reread.

12. Learn to follow directions.

Science

Reading in science requires the ability to follow a sequence of events. It requires an orderly, systematic approach, including the ability to classify, categorize, and memorize. Technical vocabulary must be mastered, formulas must be learned, and theory must be understood.

Directions become very important. The success of an experiment depends on the pupil's ability to follow directions. Reading in science, as in mathematics, is usually careful, analytical, and slow. It puts a premium on inductive reasoning and on detail. Every formula, chart, and graph is important. It demands a problem-solving approach similar to the steps of the scientific method. The pupil must learn to follow the scientist as he or she states the problem, enumerates the facts, formulates a hunch or hypothesis, investigates the facts to test the hypothesis, works toward the conclusion, and makes the verification. The pupil must observe the facts, keep them in mind, relate them to each other, and determine whether or not they support a theory.

Difficulties encountered in problem solving may be due to (1) inability to read analytically in order to select details, locate and remember information, organize what is read, separate essential data from nonessential data, distinguish between what is known and what is unknown; (2) failure to understand what is read because of lack of experience; (3) lack of knowledge of the quantitative relationships implied; (4) lack of a basic understanding of the differences between the fundamental operations; (5) inability to determine the reasonableness of the answer; (6) inability to translate verbal statements into mathematical sentences; or (7) failure to see the relationship between reality and the situation being presented in the verbal problem (Davis 1973).

Science reading is especially difficult because

1. There is a continuing and tremendous growth of new vocabulary and an accelerated obsolescence of other vocabulary.
2. Science teaching often suffers from lack of sequence, with great overlap between grade levels, and thus is not conducive to developing a sequence in reading skills from grade level to grade level.
3. Scientific ideas are becoming increasingly complex, and it is difficult to utilize a one-syllable word for a ten-syllable science concept.
4. Writers of science materials do not agree on what the readability level of books should be.
5. Many of the terms used are mathematical.
6. Many common words are used in a special sense (*force, body*).
7. Statements are concise (laws, definitions, formulas).
8. Special reading facility is required in dealing with equations, formulas, scales, cross-section and longitudinal models, and flow charts.

Helping the poor reader in science may include

1. Simplifying the vocabulary for pupils (a meteorologist is simply a weatherman). The pupil needs to be taught how to comprehend technical symbols, graphs, maps, charts, diagrams, formulas, scales, and equations. It may be useful to
   a. Have pupils compile a science dictionary or develop a word-card file of science words and symbols.
   b. Have pupils read the section in the textbook that describes the way the technical vocabulary is handled and that alerts the pupil to bold-face or italicized terms, definitions, key words, and the like:
2. Having pupils read for the main idea: "The purpose of this experiment is. . . .".
3. Having pupils organize the material by jotting down the steps in an experiment.
4. Using films to illustrate and develop concepts.
5. Helping pupils adjust their reading speed to the difficulty of the material, the purpose for reading, and their own familiarity with the material.
6. Teaching pupils to use a problem-solving technique: formulating the hypotheses, collating the evidence, evaluating and organizing the evidence, forming a conclusion, and testing the conclusion.
7. Teaching pupils to recognize the sequence of steps.
8. Conducting hunts for information requiring the use of bibliographies, encyclopedias, card catalog, glossaries, indexes, dictionaries.
9. Directing the pupils in developing summaries and outlines.
10. Having pupils express formulas in their own words.
11. Developing competency in reading scales and diagrams and in understanding formulas and equations.

SUMMARY

This chapter has summarized the comprehension skills that go beyond mere comprehension of word meaning, and indeed beyond the general comprehension skills. The focus has been on reading for learning, development of rate of comprehension skills, and reading in the content areas. In each section techniques and materials have been suggested for development of the specific skills.

QUESTIONS FOR DISCUSSION

1. What are the steps of the SQ3R method of study or integrative reading, and what is the function of this method in improving the reading skills of children?
2. What are the special problems of map reading?
3. Discuss four kinds of graphs and the problems they present in interpretation.
4. What are the special reading problems in literature, mathematics, science, and social studies, and how might they be dealt with in the daily class session?
5. How are rate and comprehension related to one another?
6. Outline a program for rate improvement at the junior high level.
7. What is the value of machine-centered rate improvement programs?

15

DEVELOPING ORAL READING SKILLS

Even though the major emphasis in reading today is on silent reading, children need to become good oral readers. The advantages of oral reading are

1. *Pupils benefit educationally by reading prose, poetry, and dramatic works aloud.* There are many benefits in choral reading or oral reading by a group. It leads to better appreciation of literature and to improved pronunciation, phrasing, interpretation, rhythm, and flexibility.

2. *Oral reading teaches pupils that writing is a record of the oral language.* Right from the beginning pupils should read the whole sentence aloud. This develops an awareness of the intonation pattern and is probably the best preventer of word-by-word reading. Unfortunately, the intonation pattern cannot be fully represented by writing. The tone of voice (the paralanguage) and the gestured bodily movements are only crudely represented by underlined words, exclamation points, or word choice *(sauntered, gesticulated).* Oral reading also provides practice in pronouncing words and in grammatical usage. Through it the child's speaking vocabulary may be developed, and poise and voice control may be fostered.

3. *Oral reading also has diagnostic values.* It is especially helpful in testing for fluency and accuracy in reading and gives clues to a child's eye movements and speech defects. Children below third-grade level in reading ability need to be carefully evaluated by the teacher to see how accurately they are reading. By listening to a

pupil's oral reading, the teacher can note errors of mispronunciation, repetition, omission, addition, and the like. These errors reflect many of the mistakes that the pupil is making in silent reading. Since reading usually requires the association of a printed form with an oral equivalent, especially at the learning-to-read level, it would seem only logical that oral reading be used to examine this relationship.

Examine now how oral reading differs from silent reading.

DIFFERENCES BETWEEN ORAL AND SILENT READING

Oral reading calls for all the sensory and perceptual skills required in silent reading, such as visual discrimination, rhythmic progression along a line of print, and the ability to take to the word those experiences that the writer, by his or her peculiar choice and arrangement of words, hoped to call to the reader's attention.

Oral reading also requires skills beyond those needed in silent reading. Many aspects of oral reading differ from those associated with silent reading. In oral reading there are generally more fixations, more regressions, and longer pauses. Oral reading is generally slower than silent reading. In oral reading, reading rate is limited by pronunciation; in silent reading, it is limited only by the ability to grasp meaning. Oral reading calls for interpreting to others; in silent reading, one interprets only to oneself. Oral reading demands skills in voice, tempo, and gesture and in sensing the mood and feeling intended by the author.

If silent and oral reading are not the same process, then it is important to know what the basic oral reading skills are. The discussion that follows addresses this point.

ORAL READING: A COMPLEX OF SKILLS

Oral reading, like silent reading, consists of a complex skills. The good oral reader

1. Interprets the author's meaning accurately.
2. Transmits correctly the author's meaning to the listener.
3. Makes a proper interpretation of the author's feelings and moods: the reading is expressive.
4. Reads in meaningful thought units.
5. Demonstrates clarity and accuracy in articulation, enunciation, and pronunciation; the pupil's reading is essentially free from errors of omission, addition, substitution, reversals, and the like.
6. Gives an accurate translation of the writer's punctuation marks into pauses, stops, and so forth; phrasing is correct and inflection of the voice is appropriate.
7. Is fluent and smooth in reading, keeping the eye well ahead of the voice; the pupil has an appropriate eye-voice span.

8. Has suitable quality and volume of voice: the voice is audible.
9. Has suitable pitch: the voice is not too high pitched.
10. Avoids labored precision in reading aloud; the pupil is not a word-by-word reader.
11. Has appropriate rate: the reading is neither too slow nor too rapid.
12. Has proper posture.
13. Looks at the audience at frequent intervals.

Oral reading is certainly not a basic reading skill in the same way that word recognition, comprehension, and rate are. Instead, oral and silent reading are two ways of reading, and children must become proficient in both. Both require skill in word recognition, comprehension, and rate. Thus oral reading requires all the skills of silent reading and some special ones of its own. Seen in this light, oral reading may itself be termed a special reading skill.

Good oral readers must understand the author's meaning, sense the author's moods, and be able to convey both meaning and mood to others. They must be able to recognize words instantly and use good phrasing and pronunciation and proper voice inflection. Good oral readers need to adapt their voices to the room and must have auditory and visual contact with the audience. They should be poised and confident, and be able to assume the proper posture; they must keep their eyes well ahead of their voices, must enunciate clearly, pronounce correctly, and hold the attention of the audience. There are certain things, as well, that good oral readers *cannot* be: they cannot, for example, be word callers, jerkily attacking one word at a time in a high-pitched monotone, and reading as though they were reading a grocery list, giving little consideration to meaning.

Oral reading should not ordinarily be done without previous silent reading. In the primary grades, particularly, where pupils have not yet developed an adequate sight vocabulary and adequate recognition skills, pupils should not be allowed to read their stories aloud to the class without a preliminary silent reading. From the beginning, too, stress should be on naturalness of tone. The teacher should encourage this by asking pupils to read sentences in the manner in which they would be spoken, since the best model for oral reading is speech. Passages frequently should be read to the pupils to give them a feeling for conversational tone.

The teacher also needs to pay particular attention to each child's articulation, enunciation, and pronunciation. The emphasis should be on simple rhymes and stories, using the sounds needed at the child's specific stage of development. Pronunciation should be corrected tactfully, without embarrassing the child. Mispronounced words should be practiced in their correct form as parts of a sentence.

Pupils also must learn appropriate pitch, quality, and volume of voice. Voice factors are important for the listener; listening is more or less difficult depending on the voice qualities of the reader. Each pupil needs to be given the opportunity to read to a single child and to a group, and to engage in choral reading.

Two vital vocal skills are phrasing and smoothness. Readers must be able to keep their eyes well ahead of their voices so they can organize and group the words, giving them the proper inflections. This means that children should read simple materials without too many new words. Generally, materials written by the children, which are based on the vocabulary known to them, are most effective. Many errors of communication are the result of faulty phrasing or faulty grouping of words. Generally, phrasing will be appropriate if the reader understands what is being read; sentences can then be broken into meaningful phrases and clauses. Oral readers also must learn to emphasize particular words properly, by giving a word more stress, by elongating the pronunciation, or by using a higher pitch.

In oral reading, the eye-voice span takes on special significance. This is the space (measured in words) between the word being vocalized and the word being fixed by the eye (in the eye fixation). Good readers tend to have a much wider span and more moment-to-moment variations in span than do poor readers. This allows the good reader's voice to proceed smoothly even though the reader's eyes may have to stop for a time on difficult words.

The teacher can check on eye-voice span by first asking pupils to read two or three lines aloud and then stopping them. The pupils then have to say aloud additional words that they have read silently, but that they have not yet read aloud. A narrow eye-voice span indicates that the pupil needs help in looking ahead.

IDENTIFICATION AND ANALYSIS OF THE PUPIL'S ORAL READING MISCUES

It has generally been assumed that an identification and analysis of the pupil's errors in oral reading would furnish valuable clues about the pupil's silent reading ability. Unfortunately, the correlation between oral reading and silent reading, especially after the primary years, is not of sufficient magnitude to permit accurate prediction of silent reading comprehension from oral reading scores. Furthermore, word-identification errors elicited on tests in isolation do not constitute a solid basis for predicting errors in connected text. All the fourth graders in a study by Allington and McGill-Franzen (1980) did better in identifying words in connected text than in isolation from a text.

Such an analysis is not useless, however. The analysis of the pupil's oral reading habits and of the errors he or she makes in oral reading does make it possible to glean some understanding of the pupil's typical behaviors in both oral and silent reading. Oral reading errors do tend to carry over to silent reading. Conversely, it is reasonable to expect that silent reading errors generally should decrease as oral reading improves. If pupils can read well orally, it is likely that they will be able to read well silently.

Oral reading analysis should focus on positive aspects. It should help the teacher to understand the pupil's gradual development of word-recognition and word-analysis skills, point the teacher to the instructional needs of the pupil, emphasize *what the pupil can do*, indicate the kinds and types of reading experiences that should be provided, and lead to the identification of the areas where most of the mistakes occur and toward which remedial teaching ought to be directed.

Goodman's (1969) analysis of oral reading errors, or miscues as he refers to them, focuses on the reader's dependence upon phonic strategies, on grammatical accuracy, on semantic or meaningful reading, on the degree of self-correction that the reader exercises, and on the influence of dialect and intonation upon miscues. Graphic and phonemic similarity between the printed word and the reader's oral response is analyzed. Miscues are coded according to the degree that the oral response diverges from the syntax and the meaning of the printed word. Miscues are interpreted as indicators of strength when the language and meaning are kept intact; when this does not occur, they are indicators of weakness. Syntactic acceptability is judged in terms of the dialect of the reader.

Miscue analysis thus concerns itself with such questions as these: How much do the two words (the printed word and the reader's response) look alike (graphic similarity) or sound alike (phonemic similarity)? Is the grammatical function of the reader's oral response the same as that of the printed word? Does the reader substitute a verb for a verb or a noun for a noun? Is the sentence that contains the miscue syntactically (grammatically) and semantically acceptable? Does the reader's correction of his or her own miscues make the sentence semantically acceptable? Goodman's analysis indicates that many errors are made as a result of trying to make better sense out of the context, and he suggests that these should not be considered errors.

According to miscue analysis,

1. Substitutions of similar-appearing words (instances of graphic similarity) which adhere to the meaning of the sentence indicate greater reading maturity.

2. The greater the proportion of miscues *spontaneously* corrected, the greater is the pupil's reading maturity. Too much dependence upon word-analysis techniques actually results in a decrease in self-corrections.

3. Substitutions of similar function words (such as noun for noun, adverb for adverb) represent a more mature reading response. Poor readers give grammatically incorrect responses or even ones that in grammatical terms are totally implausible solutions.

4. *Dialect* errors should not be counted as errors. Black children, Chicanos, and minorities generally make errors which merely reflect their culture:
   Black children will exhibit the following:
   a. Omission of /r/ or /l/: *guard/god/*; *help/hep/*; omission of final consonants: *past/pass/*.
   b. Substitution of /i / for /e/: *pen/pin/*; of /v/ for final /th/: *breathe/breav/*; of /f/ for unvoiced final /th/: *breath/bref/*.

   c. *Additions:* plurals in *sts* become *stes: pests/pestes/.*

   d. *Syntax:* omission of final *s* in third person singular: *wonders-wonder;* omission of *s* in possessives; omission of prepositions: *He goes to school-He goes school;* and double negatives.

   e. *Word order: Why won't she come?* turns into *Why she won't come?*

Spanish children confuse:

   a. Certain sounds:

      /s/ for /th/: *thin /sin/.*
      /ch/ for /j/: *judge /chudge/.*
      /s/ for /z/: *zinc /sinc/.*
      /p/ for /b/: *bar /par/.*
      /b/ for /v/: *vote /bote/.*
      /t/ for /d/: *den /ten/.*
      /c/ for /g/: *goat /coat/.*
      /d/ for /th/: *this /dis/.*
      /s/ for /sh/: *shoe /soe/.*
      /sh/ for /ch/: *chew /shew/.*
      /j/ for /y/: *yellow /jellow/.*
      /n/ for /m/: *dime /dine/.*
      /gw/ for /w/: *way /gway/.*

   b. Negatives: *Mary no here.*
   c. Verb forms: *The boy eat.*
   d. Word order: *The dress red.*

5. When the printed word and the oral error or miscue resemble each other phonemically or semantically (the substituted word maintains the meaning of the sentence), it is a sign of reading maturity.

6. Good readers' miscues tend to maintain the syntax (tense, word function, word order) of the sentence. Syntax is disturbed when the reader is not comprehending.

It would appear that pupils are better served when the observations made by Goodman are given consideration in oral reading analysis. In addition, analysis of oral reading should be based on selections whose readability level parallels the pupil's instructional level. And analysis of errors should be based on an adequate sample of errors; fewer than 25 errors is probably too little to produce a reliable evaluation.

It is probably best to use a tape recorder to record oral reading errors. Another approach is to simply check the pupil's error, and then after testing, to have the pupil reread that part of the passage in which the error occurred and analyze the error more thoroughly.

CAUSES AND REMEDIATION OF POOR ORAL READING

Consider now the causes of poor oral reading and some general techniques for improving oral reading

The causes of inadequate oral reading generally include

1. Carelessness, inattention, or habit.
2. Immaturity.
3. Lack of instruction in oral reading.
4. Reading orally before reading silently.
5. Inadequate sight vocabulary.
6. Inadequate word-recognition skills.
7. Tenseness while reading.
8. Inappropriate eye-voice span.
9. Improper phrasing, resulting in word-by-word reading or in a clustering of words that do not fit into thought units.
10. Ignoring of punctuation.
11. Improper rate of reading.
12. Eye or visual defects.

Techniques for improving oral reading usually involve one or a combination of the following activities:

1. Tape the pupil's reading after teaching the pupil to read the materials as they were spoken in the first place. Have the pupil listen to and analyze the reading. Have the pupil reread the story orally, again on tape, and then let the pupil compare the results.
2. Provide choral reading opportunities.
3. Encourage dramatizations.
4. Make sure that silent reading precedes oral reading and that oral reading is fluent.
5. Let pupils see how a shift of stress in a sentence alters the meaning of the sentence.
6. Develop the pupil's eye-voice span.
7. Stress naturalness of tone.
8. Let the pupils read to a single pupil as well as to a group.
9. Let the pupils read materials that they have written.

DEALING WITH SPECIFIC MISCUES
IN ORAL AND SILENT READING

Chapter 16 suggests numerous ways of identifying pupil achievement in reading. Most of these involve oral reading: for example, the informal reading inventory, the oral reading tests, and the various word lists. By listening to pupils' reading the teacher can get a better understanding of the errors that the pupils are making and that keep them from making an accurate identification of words. This is the diagnostic function of oral reading. It is also important to note that poor readers make twice as many oral reading errors as do good readers.

This section gives consideration to the specific miscues in oral reading and provides an understanding of why the miscues occur and what to do when they do occur.

Attempting to assign an exact reason or cause for each oral reading error is literally impossible. The teacher should note both the quantity and quality of errors. The proportions of various errors, the types that are excessive, the part of the word in which errors are concentrated all call for examination.

Not all errors have the same implications. Reading the sentence, "He saw a house on a hill," leads to entirely different qualitative errors if the reader identifies the word *house* as *home* or *horse*. In general, when errors are concentrated at the beginnings of words, they indicate failure in sight vocabulary or difficulty with consonants and consonant blends. With errors occurring in the middle of words, vowel letter-sound correspondences may be the problem.

The oral reading errors examined here are

1. Omissions of a word or part of a word.
2. Additions or insertions of a word or part of a word.
3. Substitutions or mispronunciations, including contractions or misplaced accents.
4. Repetitions of a word or part of a word, and regressions.
5. Words pronounced for the pupil by the examiner.
6. Word-by-word reading.
7. Phrasing errors and ignoring of punctuation.
8. Losing the place while reading.
9. Vocalizing and moving the lips.
10. Hesitations.
11. Pointing at the word.
12. Eye movement difficulties.

Reversal errors and transpositions were examined in Chapter 7. Self-corrections, if they are made within about a five-second span, are not considered as errors.

The research data show that substitutions and repetitions increase during the first three grades, but omissions and words requiring aid tend to decrease. Schlieper (1977), studying grades one to three in Montreal, found that third-grade pupils who were good readers produced more repetitions and attempted more words than the first graders; but their errors were grammatically acceptable; omissions decreased. Third-grade poor readers, on the other hand, made more omissions *and* repetitions than did the first-grade good readers.

Consider the oral reading errors now in some detail.

Omissions

Some pupils have a tendency to skip letters or even whole words; their omissions increase with age or as speed in oral reading increases. When pupils omit too much, vision should be checked. A marker may help such readers to keep on line.

Causes generally adduced to explain omissions are

1. Carelessness, inadequate attention, or habit. The pupil may not attempt to recode unknown words.

2. Dialect: omission of *r* or *l* in *guard/god; help/hep;* dialect errors are not normally considered as errors.
3. Poor word-attack skills.
4. Inadequate preparation in structural analysis, especially inflectional endings and suffixes.
5. Inadequate sight or recognition vocabulary causing pupils to skip over the unknown word.
6. Impulsiveness.
7. Too rapid reading.
8. Inability to use context.
9. Poor comprehension.
10. Heterophoria, expecially exophoria, causing pupils to lose their place while reading.

Remediation of omissions may take multiple forms. Sometimes, if the cause is readily identifiable, for example, e.g., heterophoria, it is easy to know what to do. Usually the problem is more complicated.

1. If the cause of the omission error is chiefly one of carelessness or faulty habit, call the pupil's attention to any error that is made; often this alone is adequate. Sometimes the problem is solved by having the pupil slow down.
2. Since omissions are generally centered on the middles and endings of words, show the pupil the target word (*cat*) for two seconds and then require the pupil to select it from three words in which only the middle vowel or the ending consonant is different (*car, cat, cab*).
3. Teach the pupil to scan the word thoroughly.
4. Use choral reading.
5. If the cause is an inadequate sight vocabulary or inability to use context cues, teach the core words.
6. In many instances omissions reflect inadequate phonic and structural analysis skills; these need to be developed.

Additions and Insertions

Some pupils add letters or even total words. The causes generally suggested to explain additions and insertions are

1. Dialect: plurals in *sts* become *stes* (*pests /pestes/*).
2. Lack of comprehension: the pupil tries to smooth out or elaborate upon the text.
3. Attempt to correct a previous error.
4. Overdependence upon context or failure to follow the context.
5. Lack of sentence sense.
6. Inability to recognize words quickly and easily.

Remediation of additions or insertions includes (1) calling attention to the insertion or addition; (2) having the pupil engage in choral reading; and (3) having the pupil read along with a taped reading. The latter two recommendations help the pupil to develop sentence sense. Some additions to words, such as an *s* to a verb, reflect an inability to see the interrelatedness of the words in a sentence.

Substitutions (Mispronunciations, Contractions, Misplaced Accent)

The most frequent oral reading errors are those of substitution, including mispronunciations, contractions, and misplaced accent. Substitutions generally take the form of (1) substitution of words of similiar appearance and of similar meaning (*house* for *home*); (2) substitution of words of similar appearance but different meaning (*horse* for *house*); (3) meaningless or wild guessing at words that leads to nonsensible sentences; and (4) substitution of words that fit grammatically and syntactically (substitution of one verb for another verb).

Causes adduced to explain substitutions are

1. Carelessness or inattention to word parts.
2. Inability to sustain fixation or rapid shifts of attention while reading.
3. Overreliance on the initial elements in words: the pupil looks only at the first part of the word. The impulsive reader is particularly likely to do this.
4. Overreliance on context or not using the context.
5. Failure to scan the word thoroughly enough to identify the order of the letters and to be certain that the word is just this word and not another.
6. Inadequate word-recognition and decoding skills.
7. Astigmatism causing confusion of similar-appearing words.
8. Binocular difficulties (strabismus, lack of fusion, or aniseikonia) causing the reader to see two of everything, for example, or causing the image to be badly blurred.
9. Overreliance on configuration cues.
10. Inadequate sight vocabulary.

When pupils substitute words of similar appearance and meaning, they may be attending to only one part of the word or may not be using phonic skills. When pupils substitute words of similar appearance but different meaning, they are probably relying too much on configuration cues. When pupils substitute words that lead to nonsensible sentences, or which are frankly impossible substitutions, it indicates little attention to either word form or context. Such pupils probably have a meager sight vocabulary and poorly developed word-attack skills, are not paying attention to meaning, and do not understand the purposes of reading. When the substitution fits the grammatical and syntactical context, it indicates that the reader is demanding meaning from the text and at least on that basis it is a sign of reading maturity.

Mispronunciation (poor articulation and inaccurate enunciation) is a form of substitution. It is caused by

1. Carelessness, inattention, or habit.
2. Poor auditory discrimination skills.

3. Hearing defects.
4. Reading too rapidly.
5. Inadequate phonics ability.
6. Faulty vision.
7. Foreign or bilingual background or dialect.
8. Speech organs not correctly formed.
9. Poor syllabication and accentuation skills.
10. Focusing too much or exclusively on the beginnings of words.
11. Inadequate sight vocabulary.

If mispronunciations or other substitutions are caused chiefly by carelessness, the teacher should call the pupils' attention to it and help them to correct the error. The teacher may have pupils engage in choral reading, have them follow in a book a passage that has been tape recorded, or may encourage pupils to slow down their reading. Pupils frequently feel that they have to produce a constant stream of response (that their reading cannot have any interruption), and when confronted with a strange word, they thus substitute any word that comes into their mind rather than try to analyze the word.

Remediation of mispronunciations includes in addition:

1. Teaching pupils the use of diacritical markings in the dictionary to work out the pronunciation of the word.
2. Teaching pupils the difference between sounds by using the concept of minimal difference as used in linguistic methods.
3. Training in word analysis and syllabication.
4. Drill on common sight words.
5. Use of proper pronunciation by the teacher.
6. Practice with rhyming words.
7. Helping pupils to place their lips and tongues properly in making the sound.
8. Teaching the pupils to listen *through* (from start to finish) the word.
9. Evaluating pupils' hearing and auditory discrimination skills and remediating these if needed.

Remediation of meaningless guessing may include (1) teaching the importance of precise and accurate word recognition; (2) teaching the varied methods of word identification (configuration cues, meaning cues, phonetic and structural analysis cues, dictionary use, and the like); and (3) emphasizing the importance of using context cues.

Errors resulting from misuse of contractions and accent and their remediation were discussed in Chapter 11.

Repetitions and Regressions

Repetitions are often attempts to aid comprehension or to regain the train of thought. Repetitions or regressions within the same word are particularly significant for diagnosis. Repetitions frequently affect comprehension adversely, reduce reading rate, and cause unrhythmical oral reading.

The causes generally adduced to explain *repetitions* are:

1. Poor word-analysis skills or slowness in word recognition.
2. Faulty directional attack, moving the eyes from right to left during reading.
3. Attempts to stall while analyzing the word repeated or one near it; often the pupil cannot identify the word immediately following the one being repeated.
4. Efforts to correct a miscue; the pupil realizes that the first reading did not make sense.
5. Tension or embarrassment.
6. Low intelligence.
7. Eye defects that affect focus or fusion such as exophoria or heterophoria.
8. Poor sight vocabulary.
9. Too difficult materials.
10. Speech impediment.

The causes generally adduced to explain *regressions* are:

1. Interruption of the flow or pattern of thought.
2. Habit.
3. Lack of confidence; the pupil feels a constant need to reread.
4. Eye defects that prevent accurate perception.
5. Missing some of the material.
6. Failure to recognize the basic meaning.
7. Need to verify what was read or to analyze the phrase or sentence.

Remediation of repetitions and regressions includes the following procedures:

1. Use choral reading and mechanical devices (such as the Controlled Reader, Educational Developmental Laboratories) which prohibit the pupil from regressing or repeating.
2. Have the pupil read silently before reading orally.
3. Have the pupil move the eyes rhythmically and rapidly from left to right.
4. Use easier and more interesting material.
5. Use phrase cards.
6. Help the pupil develop an appropriate stock of sight words.
7. Provide training in word analysis.
8. Help the pupil increase the eye-voice and the eye-memory span.
9. Help the pupil develop fluency of oral expression.
10. Provide practice in reading along with a tape recording of the printed material.

Words Aided

The poor reader has to be aided far more frequently than the good reader. The number of words with which the pupil needs help is a good indication of reading skill. Sometimes the teacher is too quick in saying the word for the pupil. The pupil could be helped more by being encouraged to take a risk. The pupil often prefers not to attempt a reading. Werner (1948) indentifies this with the analytic stage of development and suggests that in the beginning reader it may indicate a deficiency in letter-sound knowledge; in the disabled reader it may indicate an unwillingness to take a risk or be wrong again. A pupil who is the beneficiary of much teacher assistance will naturally make fewer other errors. Conversely, the pupil who makes many other errors may have received little teacher help.

Causes commonly adduced to explain a pupil's need for constant help in reading are:

1. Poor sight vocabulary.
2. Poor word-analysis skills.
3. Too much dependence on others.
4. Unwillingness to attempt to identify the word.

Remediation should involve building up the pupil's confidence, developing adequate word-attack skills and an adequate sight vocabulary, and encouraging the pupil to take a risk. Such pupils are particularly benefited from learning to combine phonic skills with context skills.

Word-by-Word Reading

Word-by-word readers or word callers plod along slowly, tend to disregard punctuation, make frequent phrasing errors, read in a monotone, point at words, and frequently lose the place. Beginning readers are often word-by-word readers, but soon pass this stage. Word-by-word readers, struggling to pronounce the word, also have difficulty getting the meaning. Because the pauses between the words are too long, the pupils simply cannot retain ideas long enough to relate one word to another and thus comprehend what is being read.

Causes commonly adduced to explain word-by-word reading are:

1. Poor word-identification skills; the pupil may have a meaning for a word in his or her semantic reservoir but cannot decipher the word's printed form.
2. Lack of sight vocabulary.
3. Inability to use the context; the pupil may be especially deficient in using the context together with the beginning consonant to identify the word.
4. Habit; this is generally the cause when, if given materials substantially below his or her reading level, the pupil is still doing word-by-word reading.
5. Short fixation span.
6. Perfectionism; pupil was taught to do only word-perfect reading.
7. Too much emphasis on phonics and sounding out of words; pupil was taught to sound out all unknown words.
8. Too difficult material.
9. Low intelligence.
10. Short eye-memory or eye-voice span.

11. Immaturity.
12. Finger pointing.
13. Lip movement and inner vocalization.
14. Inability to associate the word with concepts; the pupil has not learned that the word stands for an idea or concept and thus is simply a word caller.

If on materials which the pupil is reading word by word, the pupil can answer about 75 percent of the questions testing comprehension, the difficulty is probably a matter of word recognition; if, on the other hand, comprehension falls below 75 percent, the problem is probably in the area of comprehension.

Remediation of word-by-word reading can take many forms:

1. If the pupil's word-by-word reading is out of *habit*,
   a. Tape the pupil's reading and let the pupil listen to it.
   b. Give the pupil experience and practice in choral reading.
   c. Use mechanical pacing devices (such as the Controlled Reader, Educational Developmental Laboratories) that require the pupil to move at a certain pace.
   d. Use tachistoscopic exercises that teach phrase reading.
   e. Have the pupil move a piece of cardboard from the top to the bottom of the page in reading, forcing the reading process to move more quickly than usual.
   f. Teach the pupil how to read in phrases and in thought units.
   g. Have the pupil read independent-level materials (interesting but relatively easy) at a rate faster than the pupil is accustomed to.
   h. Use the neurological impress method (see Heckelman 1969), with teacher and pupil reading together at a rapid rate.
   i. Use flash cards, exposing phrases for only a short time.
2. If the pupil's word-by-word reading stems from difficulties in *word recognition*,
   a. Have the pupil read materials on a lower level of difficulty.
   b. Use the language-experience approach, letting the pupil write and read his or her own stories.
   c. Use flash cards to develop a better sight vocabulary.
   d. Have the pupil read along with materials recorded on tape.
3. If the pupil's word-by-word reading stems from difficulties in *comprehension*, teach reading for meaning and use of context clues.

Poor Phrasing

Poor phrasing is indicated when pupils fail to pause at the proper places, often totally ignoring the punctuation, especially the commas.

Common causes of poor phrasing are

1. Ignoring the punctuation.
2. Inadequate word identification skills.
3. Inadequate comprehension.
4. Habit; when the pupil reads everything in a word-by-word manner.
5. Not reading the structure and organization of the material.
6. Simple nervousness.
7. Short eye-memory or eye-voice span.
8. Short-lived memory images for words.

If the pupil fails to recognize about 95 percent of the words on material that he or she is reading, word recognition difficulties may be a major cause of the poor phrasing; if he or she cannot answer comprehension questions about the material (with at least 75 percent accuracy) but knows 95 percent of the words, comprehension difficulties may be causing the poor phrasing.

If word recognition is a major cause of poor phrasing, the difficulty may be remedied by increasing the pupil's sight vocabulary. The teacher may also use phrase cards; have pupils practice on common prepositional phrases; have pupils listen to tape recordings of a reading properly phrased; and have pupils read materials on their independent level.

If the problem is chiefly one of poor habits in reading, pupils should be taught the meaning of punctuation and the use of the punctuation marks to aid proper phrasing. The teacher may stress punctuation marks by coloring them. Pupils should be taught the relationship between the inflection of the voice and the use of various punctuation marks. Pupils may also be required to practice reading sentences that have been broken into phrases: *Pam and Lori------went fishing------this morning.* Another exercise may have the pupils do choral reading.

Loss of Place

Loss of place, including inability to follow words sequentially on a line, misplacement of a word to a line above or below, jumping of lines, or difficulty in moving from the end of one line to the beginning of another, is another frequent problem of poor readers.

Causes of loss of place in reading are

1. Binocular or fusion difficulties (heterophoria, hyperphoria, exophoria).
2. Poor lighting.
3. Improper position of the book.
4. Lack of attention.
5. Problems with direction.
6. Tendency of pupil to look at the teacher when having difficulty in pronouncing a word.
7. Injury in the right posterior cerebral hemisphere.

Remediation may include allowing the pupil to use a liner to mark each line.

Hesitations

Hesitations are caused by inadequate sight vocabulary, poor word-identification skills, and a short eye-voice span. Generally, if the pupil can identify the word in five seconds or less, a hesitation is not counted as an error. Remediation should include practice with easy materials, and practice in phrase reading.

Vocalizing and Moving the Lips

Vocalizing and moving the lips while reading are appropriately discussed together. Movement of the lips is symptomatic of inner vocalization. Vocalization, as already noted, is itself a symptom; it is rarely a cause; it indicates that the pupil is encountering difficulty in reading.

Buswell (1947) believed that silent reading should be a process of association between perceptual stimulation and meaning "without a mediating subvocalization." And the psycholinguists maintain that the fluent reader decodes directly from the graphic symbol to meaning.

However, moving the lips and vocalizing may not be the ogre that some people believe. It seems likely that speech traces are a part of all or nearly all thinking and even of "silent" reading. Jacobsen (1932) found that the muscles controlling the eyes contract during imagination as though the individual were looking at the object. Furthermore, when people think, the muscles of the tongue and upper lip vibrate as if they were saying the words. Edfeldt (1960), studying the electromyographic records of college students, found that all engaged in silent speech while reading. Good readers engaged in less silent speech than poor readers, and the more difficult the material, the more silent speech occurred.

Recent analyses of brain-wave research indicate that when speech is imminent, the Broca-Wernicke area of the brain sends out word waves a fraction of a second before the word is vocalized, signaling the vocal cords, mouth, and throat to form the words. The interesting point is that the brain sends out the word waves even if the person does not speak the word but only thinks it.

That speech aids thinking has been fully recognized by philosophers and psychologists. The Greeks used the same word, *logos*, for both thinking and speech. Watson (1920) referred to thought as the "subvocal use of language."

Certainly little children are constantly using speech to make sense out of their world. Young children constantly talk to themselves, dripping speech as it were, because for them inner thinking and mental imagery are closely associated with vocal expression. Speech aids their thinking. It appears that vocalizing similarly aids young children in comprehending what they are reading. Motor dysfunctions, resulting from lesions in the motor association areas in the brain and in the speech sensory areas, disrupt internal speech (self-commands and subvocalization) and thus affect reading. It is a common observation that children who are not allowed to articulate words, to rehearse them as it were, make more spelling errors.

Research also provides other data that indicate that it may be desirable to say the word subvocally while reading. The fade-out of the visually acquired stimulus seems to be rapid if it is not recoded in acoustic form (Rose 1969). An acoustic factor seems to be involved in immediate memory and recall.

Although the evidence suggests a close relationship between implicit speech, thinking, and reading, it certainly does not mean that to proceed from graphic symbol to meaning always means going through the auditory-vocal counterparts of the printed symbol. Furthermore, vocalizing is not without its drawbacks. A common cause of vocalizing worth countering is the pupil's feeling that he or she must "read" every word in order to comprehend. And whatever its cause, once silent reading attains the maximum speed of oral reading, vocalizing may block further increases in rate.

Remediation of excessive vocalization should:

1. Call the pupil's attention to his or her lip movement (and vocalization).
2. Use appropriate rate-improvement activities. Excessive vocalization is a frequent cause of slow reading.
3. Have the pupil read easy material, material on his or her independent reading level. If, when the pupil reads easy material, the lip movement (and voicing) continues, it may indicate that the pupil is moving his or her lips out of habit.

Pointing at the Word

Some students use a finger to follow words in a line of print. This necessarily slows reading and destroys rhythmical reading. The reasons for finger pointing generally are (1) the habit of doing so was developed in the early grades; (2) defective vision prevents clear and sustained reading; (3) the print may be too small for the pupil's age.

Remediation of finger pointing may include:

1. Have the pupil's eyes checked. If the cause is visual, the optometrist may be able to help the pupil more than can the teacher.
2. Teach the pupil how to scan. The pupil soon learns that the finger is not needed as a crutch.
3. Have the pupil read materials on a screen, which makes it impossible to do finger pointing.

Eye-Movement Difficulties

Disabled readers, and indeed beginning readers, often have numerous eye-movement difficulties. They:

1. Make too many fixations and regressions for their age and grade level.
2. Produce fixations in reading that are too long; conversely, their fixation or recognition span is too narrow—it does not include as many letters or words as it might.
3. Sequence eye movements too rapidly, thus skipping material, or perseverate, sequencing too slowly with resultant overfixation. In the latter situation pupils read slowly and hesitantly.
4. Show inflexibility in eye movements; the pupils do not change their eye movements to fit the difficulty of the material or a change of purpose for reading.
5. Lack rhythm in reading.
6. Have difficulty in moving from the end of one line to the beginning of another; the return sweep is faulty.
7. Have relatively low reading efficiency, generally below their age or grade level. The relative efficiency is computed thus:

$$\frac{\text{rate (wpm)}}{\text{fixations and regressions per 100 words}}$$

An R. E. (Relative efficiency) of 0.29 is equivalent to a 1.0 grade level; one of 1.71, to 9.0 grade level; and one of 2.95, to a 14.0 grade level.

8. Have a short eye-memory and eye-voice span.

Causes commonly adduced to explain eye-movement difficulties are:

1. Too difficult material; material is not on the pupil's instructional level.
2. Inappropriate format with regard to the pupil; the print is too small or the lines of print too long.
3. Too much pain to read well being taken by the pupil.
4. Lack of adequate word-recognition skills.
5. Lack of familiarity with the material being read.
6. Difficulty in assimilating ideas.
7. Difficulties in binocular coordination.
8. Word pointing, which prohibits smooth movement of the eyes across the line of print.

Remediation may take the following lines:

1. Let the pupil read easier material.
2. Teach the pupil to counteract the natural impulse to look back and thus to regress or to be too cautious.
3. Teach the pupil to read in thought units.
4. Teach pupils to read in phrase units, thus getting him or her away from word-by-word reading.
5. Help the pupil to automatize the word-identification skills.
6. Check the pupil's vision, particularly whether he or she has difficulties in binocular coordination.

SUMMARY

Chapter 15 has summarized basic data about oral reading. It has distinguished between oral and silent reading, discussed the identification and analysis of oral reading errors, attempted to identify the causes for these errors, and suggested appropriate remediation. The chapter closed with suggestions for dealing with fourteen distinct oral reading errors.

This chapter completes Part IV of this book. Part IV has dealt with the skills that need to be taught and learned if the pupil is to be a good reader. Part IV examined methods of word identification, stressed the teaching of the consonant and vowel phoneme-grapheme correspondences and of structural or morphemic analysis skills, and studied the word-meaning, comprehension, and functional reading skills. All of these skills have an implied context, namely, silent reading. Chapter 15 has pointed out that the silent reading skills are also important in oral reading, and that for good oral reading additional skills must be mastered.

Finally, one should not ignore the important diagnostic value of oral reading. This value will become more obvious as you study Chapter 16.

QUESTIONS FOR DISCUSSION

1. What are some of the major differences between oral and silent reading?
2. What are the major purposes and values of oral reading?
3. Describe the implications of miscue analysis, particularly in evaluating the pupil's reading maturity?
4. What oral reading miscues appear to have greatest diagnostic value?
5. Is it possible to read without vocalizing? Give reasons for your answer.

PART V

diagnostic teaching
of reading

The concern Part V addresses is this: a substantial number of pupils are not reading up to their ability level, an even larger number are not performing up to grade level, and many cannot read their textbooks or the reference materials used on their grade level.

A basic assumption in dealing with children who are not achieving as well as they might achieve has been that pupils can come closer to realizing their potential if they are given the type, quality, or sequence of learning experiences needed to free them from deficit behavior. The average reading teacher begins with the conditions that are present and which prevent the pupil from achieving. The teacher begins with the problem as the pupil presents it and helps the pupil rather immediately in solving it.

This remedial position strikes directly at the problem behavior itself, attempts to break the nonproductive pattern, and seeks to substitute more effective behavior. It assumes that one can identify a definable criterion behavior which the effectively learning child displays and by means of which, with proper educational intervention or remediation, the child who has lacked this ability can learn to achieve the expected level of performance. This position is often described as the deficit behavior or task approach (Johnson and Morasky 1977).

Chapter 16, the only chapter in Part V, attempts to lead the teacher at least somewhat beyond the approach just described. Looking beyond purely symptomatic treatment, it suggests that causes are significant and that remediation should be programmed to the symptoms *and* the causes. Chapter 16 seeks to help the teacher get a better overall view of the diagnostic process; it should help the teacher be a better teacher.

16

DIAGNOSIS AND REMEDIATION IN THE CLASSROOM

Previous chapters have focused on how a pupil becomes a reader. In Chapter 16 the concern is with reading disability; the chapter outlines the procedure for diagnosing reading disability and for remediating difficulties that do exist.

Disabled readers may well be with us always; at any rate, there is at present no reading method or approach that guarantees total freedom from disability. The teacher thus needs to become versed in dealing with the child who is drifting or has drifted into trouble. That is the significance of this chapter. There is no intent here to present a complete diagnostic program.* The chapter does outline the diagnostic process, especially the assessment of pupil achievement in reading.

Although the nature and severity of a reading problem sometimes calls for the intervention of the reading specialist, the main responsibility always remains with the classroom teacher (Otto and Chester 1976). The classroom teacher is the first intervening agent. The competent classroom teacher is the surest means of prevention of reading disability. And reading failures can be prevented only if every reading lesson is a diagnostic lesson. Diagnosis identifies minor difficulties

---

* This has been done in Dechant's *Diagnosis and Remediation of Reading Disabilities* (1981a).

before they become disabilities and thus occasions adjustments in instruction that might remove these difficulties. Problems that are diagnosed early are less firmly entrenched and more easily treated (Johnson and Morasky 1977). Thus, it does not make sense to delay remedial instruction until, say, the third grade. We cannot permit children to become imprisoned in faulty learning habits. At the first instance the teacher notices that the child is not progressing satisfactorily, diagnostic study and appropriate remedial education are indicated.

Schiffman (1964), in a survey of 10,000 children, found that pupils with reading problems who were identified and received remedial education in the second grade had ten times as great a chance for successful outcome of the remedial treatment as those identified only at the ninth-grade level. Kraus (1973), in a longitudinal study of elementary and secondary students in New York City, found that children who received remedial help from a trained remedial teacher at an early age were able to attain their potential level by ninth grade. Those who did not receive remedial help were unable to catch up.

That the problem of reading disability is serious is well documented. Recent studies lead to the conclusion that approximately 10 to 15 percent of school children are not reading up to their ability level. A substantially larger number are not reading up to grade level.

A DEFINITION
OF READING DISABILITY

Before venturing into the techniques for identifying reading disability, perhaps we should come to terms with the definition of reading disability. Disabled readers are those whose reading capacity is considerably greater than their reading achievement. These pupils' reading performance is substantially below their potential. Disabled readers should be differentiated from slow learners whose performance in reading is substantially below age or grade level but often is up to ability level. However, slow learners may also be disabled readers when their reading performance is substantially below ability level.

Satisfactory proficiency at times means reading at grade level; in other instances it may mean reading below grade level or substantially above grade level. Some children (such as slow learners) simply cannot, in terms of the requisites for success, achieve at their chronological grade level; others (gifted children) perhaps should be reading three or four years above grade level. Otto and Chester point out that "we are so determined to get 'grade level' performance out of everybody that we forget that many children should be doing substantially better" (1976: p. 216).

Disabled readers, then, are readers who "should be" doing better than they are. They exhibit an achievement level that is not explainable by lack of potential.

There are, of course, other definitions of reading disability. Wilson (1967) suggests that on the high school level the disabled or problem reader is one who cannot read textbooks effectively. Harris and Sipay (1975) identify reading disability with reading performance that is significantly below expectancy for the reader's age and intelligence and that also is disparate with the reader's cultural, linguistic, and educational experience.

From the foregoing statements, it should be clear that reading disability cannot be defined without some reference to the degree of disability. A disabled reader may be more disabled or less disabled in reading. A retardation of six months at the first-grade level is more serious, for example, than is a retardation of six months at the sixth-grade level.

It is probable that a reader should be considered a disabled reader if the discrepancy between performance and potential exceeds nine months in the primary years, twelve months in grades four and five, and eighteen months in grades six and above.

MEASURING PUPIL POTENTIAL

Since reading disability can be most usefully defined as achievement in reading that is significantly below potential, it becomes imperative that a fair estimate of pupil potential be obtained. This comprises Step I of the diagnostic reading procedure.

Various ways of assessing reading potential or expectancy have been tried. The tests most frequently used and the best available to assess reading potential are scholastic-aptitude tests. The following group tests are useful for identifying and for initial screening of scholastic aptitude:

1. *California Short Form Test of Mental Maturity*, 1963 (California Test Bureau/McGraw-Hill). Grades K–13.
2. *Cognitive Abilities Test*, 1974 (Houghton Mifflin). Grades K–12. This test, Primary Batteries I & II, grades K–3, and Multi-Level Edition, grades 3–12, evolved from the *Lorge-Thorndike Intelligence Test*.
3. *Henmon-Nelson Tests of Mental Ability*, 1973 (Houghton Mifflin). Grades K–12.
4. *Kuhlmann-Anderson Tests: A Measure of Academic Potential* (Scholastic Testing Service). Grades K–12.
5. *Kuhlmann-Finch Scholastic Aptitude Test*, 1960 (American Guidance Service). Grades 1–12.
6. *Otis-Lennon Mental Ability Test*, 1979 (Psychological Corporation). Grades K–12.

The scholastic-aptitude tests usually yield an I.Q. or a mental-age score. Every pupil whose I.Q. score falls below 90 or below the 25th percentile on a group test requiring reading should be given an individual intelligence or scholastic-aptitude test. An individual I.Q. test should also be given when the pupil's reading-level score, as determined by a reading-achievement test, is significantly below the pupil's grade level, or falls below the 25th percentile. Poor readers tend to do poorly on I.Q. tests which require reading to get the correct answer, and for this reason need to be retested. Here are a few tests that are specifically designed to deal with this problem. Most of these tests are individual tests and some of them require special training for their administration.

1. *IPAT Culture Fair Intelligence Tests,* 1973 (Institute for Personality and Ability Testing). Ages 4 to adult; part group, part individual; 40–60 minutes.
2. *Peabody Picture Vocabulary Test,* 1981 (American Guidance Service). Ages 2.5–40.
3. *Slosson Intelligence Test for Children and Adults* (SIT), 1981 (Slosson Educational Publications). Infancy and up.
4. *Stanford-Binet Intelligence Scales,* 1972 norms (Houghton Mifflin). Ages 2 to adult.
5. *Wechsler Intelligence Scale for Children* (WISC), ages 5–15; and *Wechsler Intelligence Scale for Children-Revised* (WISC–R), 1974, ages 6–16.9, (Psychological Corporation).

The measurement of scholastic aptitude is perhaps the most confused and strongly attacked area of educational assessment, but if used correctly scholastic-aptitude tests do provide the best information about the pupil's problem-solving ability. They indicate whether the pupil is processing information at a level appropriate for his or her age.

The I.Q. score is a mathematical or numerical score which provides an estimate of the pupil's ability to learn, solve, and understand problems. It expresses the pupil's rate of mental development, and indicates what might be expected of the pupil.

The I.Q. score should not and cannot be used as an absolute measure. Nevertheless, though perhaps too simple an estimate of the pupil's present academic potential, the I.Q. is the best that we have. It is indicative of the minimum that we might expect from the pupil; it is certainly not indicative of the maximum of which the pupil is capable. It does not estimate the pupil's ability to profit from future instruction or the future achievement that might result if a particular instructional program is instituted or if the source of the disability is alleviated or removed (Burg et al. 1978).

If the goal of reading instructions is reading achievement that approaches the limit of each pupil's capacity (Otto 1977) and if education is intended to take pupils where and as they are, and lead them to the maximum level of which they are capable, then there is need for a measure of reading expectancy. The scholastic-aptitude test, especially the individual test, and the listening-comprehension test provide the best estimate of this characteristic available today. The assumption is that the pupil's reading-achievement score ought to be comparable with his or her listening-comprehension score.

ASSESSING PUPIL ACHIEVEMENT

The average classroom teacher is more interested in obtaining a measure of the pupil's achievement in reading than in measuring the pupil's potential. Usually schools examine reading achievement in school-wide reading-assessment programs, using the norm-referenced reading-survey test to do so.

Norm-Referenced Survey Tests

A norm-referenced survey test assesses general achievement in reading and is typically the first reading-achievement test that the teacher will use. Usually it emphasizes vocabulary knowledge, comprehension of sentences or paragraphs, and perhaps speed of comprehension. It gives a general picture by identifying broad areas in which the pupil excels or is weak.

Standardized, norm-referenced survey tests may be used to measure the effectiveness of instruction, to classify pupils according to their abilities, to determine the average as well as the range of reading ability in the classroom, to subgroup for instructional purposes, to identify the specific phase of silent reading in which individual pupils or the whole class is deficient, to aid in the selection of reading materials of appropriate difficulty that the pupil may be expected to use with understanding, and to measure the general level of pupil progress (Harris and Sipay 1975). The tests thus may tell that a certain pupil is reading at a level typical of children one or more grades above or below his or her present grade level.

Some common survey tests are the following:

1. *California Achievement Tests*, Forms C & D: *Reading*, 1977 (CTB/McGraw-Hill). Level 10 (Kindergarten) measures letter forms, letter names, listening for information, letter sounds, visual discrimination, and sound matching. Level 11 (K.5–1.9 grade level) measures phonic analysis, vocabulary and comprehension. Levels 12 and 13 (grades 1.5–3.9) in addition measure structural analysis. Levels 14–19 (grades 3.5–12.9) simply measure vocabulary and comprehension.
2.. *Gates-MacGinitie Reading Tests*, 1978 (Houghton Mifflin). Grades 1.5–12. This test provides reading measures for Primary (grades 1, 2, and 3) in vocabulary and comprehension, for Primary CS (grades 2 and 3) in speed and accuracy. Survey D (grades 4–6), Survey E (grades 7–9), and Survey F (grades 10–12) each measure vocabulary, comprehension, speed, and accuracy.
3. *Iowa Silent Reading Test*, 1973 (Psychological Corporation). Grades 6–12. This test on three levels (Level I for grades 6–9 and for high school students reading below grade level; Level II for grades 9–14; and Level III for academically accelerated high school and college students) includes subtests for vocabulary, reading comprehension, directed reading (study skills), and reading efficiency (speed and accuracy).
4. *Metropolitan Reading Tests*, 1978 (Psychological Corporation). Grades K–12.9. The Preprimer level is designed for grades K.0 to K.5; the Primer level (grades K.5–1.4) measures visual discrimination, letter recognition, auditory discrimina-

tion, sight vocabulary, phoneme-grapheme consonants, and comprehension; the Primary 1 level (grades 1.5–2.4) measures auditory discrimination, sight vocabulary, phoneme-grapheme consonants, word-part clues, vocabulary in context, and comprehension; the Primary 2 level (grades 2.5–3.4) measures sight vocabulary, phoneme-grapheme consonants and vowels, word-part clues, vocabulary in context, and comprehension; the Elementary level (grades 3.5–4.9) adds rate of comprehension to the Primary 2 level; the Intermediate level (grades 5.0–6.9) measures phoneme-grapheme consonants and vowels, word-part clues, vocabulary in context, rate of comprehension, skimming and scanning, and comprehension; and the Advanced 1 level (grades 7.0–9.9) measures vocabulary in context, rate of comprehension, skimming and scanning, and reading comprehension. The 1978 version of the test has added the Advanced 2 (grades 10–12) level. The Metropolitan reading tests are a part of the *Metropolitan Achievement Tests.* Available to the user is a Dual Stanine Report which compares reading scores with the 1979 edition of *Otis-Lennon Mental Ability Test.* It aids in the identification of pupils with an atypical relationship between scholastic-aptitude and reading-achievement scores. The 1978 edition of these tests yields instructional reading-level scores that help the teacher to decide which book to use with each pupil and offers both norm-referenced and criterion-referenced measurements. The test also offers an estimate of achievement expectancy based on socioeconomic data.

5. *Nelson-Denny Reading Test,* Forms C and D, 1973 (Houghton Mifflin). Grades 9–12 and college. This 30-minute test measures vocabulary, comprehension, and rate.

6. *Nelson Reading Skills Test,* 1977 (Houghton Mifflin). Grades 3–9. This test, available in 3 levels (3–4, 5–6, 7–9) consists of an 8-minute word meaning test and a minute comprehension test. For grades 3–4 an optional test, Word Parts, is provided. It measures sound-symbol correspondence, root words, and syllabication. A reading rate test is optional for grades 5–6 and 7–9.

7. *Peabody Individual Achievement Test* (PIAT), 1970 (American Guidance Service). This individual test is designed for kindergarten through adult level and consists of 5 subtests: Mathematics, Reading Recognition, Reading Comprehension, Spelling, and General Information. The test plates are contained in 2 Easel Kits. Areas measured in reading are letter names, letter sounds, visual discrimination of letters and words, and comprehension of sentences. Testing time is 30–40 minutes.

8. *Stanford Reading Tests* (Psychological Corporation). Grades 1.5–9.5. These tests are designed for Primary 1 (grades 1.5–2.4); Primary 2 (grades 2.5–3.4); Primary 3 (grades 3.5–4.4); Intermediate 1 (grades 4.5–5.4); Intermediate 2 (grades 5.5–6.9); and Advanced (grades 7–9.5). The tests measure vocabulary, reading comprehension, word-study skills, and listening comprehension.

Criterion-Referenced Tests

The reading-achievement tests that have just been examined are each silent, norm-referenced reading tests. They compare the pupil's score with that of others, indicating the pupil's placement in relation to a group. The criterion-referenced tests estimate the pupil's mastery of a specific skill or content and establish an expected level of achievement on an individual basis. For example, criterion-referenced assessment might describe the pupil "as having mastered the sounds of all the vowels and consonants, including blends, except for 'str', and 'thr', and 'scr', instead of designating him as one who reads orally at a grade equivalent of 2.2" (Hammill and Bartel 1978: p. 11). Criterion-referenced instruments are used to determine whether pupils have met specific instructional objectives or whether they have attained specific reading competencies. They measure mastery level rather than grade level. They are particularly useful in evaluating intraindividual growth (Kirk, Kliebhan, and Lerner 1978).

Teachers tend to be especially enthusiastic about criterion-referenced assessments. Knowing that a pupil has not yet mastered three specific blends is more helpful to the teacher in making day-to-day instructional decisions than is knowing that the pupil reads at a grade equivalent of 2.2 (Hammill and Bartel 1978).

Among the more notable programs using criterion-referenced measures are the following:

1. *Croft Teacher Training System* (Croft).
2. *Fountain Valley Teacher Support Systems* (Richard I. Zweig Associates).
3. *Individual Pupil Monitoring System-Reading* (Houghton Mifflin).
4. *Prescriptive Reading Inventory and PRI Instructional Management System* (CTB/McGraw-Hill).
5. *Skills Monitoring System-Reading* (Harcourt Brace Jovanovich).
6. *Wisconsin Design for Reading Skill Development* (National Computer Systems).
7. *Instructional Management System* (Harper & Row).
8. *Read-On* (Random House).
9. *Phonics Dart* (Modern Curriculum Press).

Read-On provides 60 criterion-referenced tests on audio-tape cassettes for grades 1–4. Areas covered are auditory-visual discrimination, phoneme-grapheme correspondence, structural analysis, word recognition, and comprehension.

The Fountain Valley Teacher Support System in Reading provides self-administered and self-scoring tests on audio tape, grades 1–6, measuring skill in phonetic analysis, structural analysis, vocabulary development, comprehension, and study skills.

NCP Phonics Dart is a criterion-referenced testing program for the primary level. It consists of 10 tests measuring visual discrimination, rhyming words, auditory discrimination, alphabet recognition, letters in beginning and ending position, consonant blend recognition, consonant digraphs, sentence meaning, *y* as a vowel, hard and soft *c* and *g*, murmur diphthongs, plural endings, prefixes, dropping final *e*, doubling final consonant, irregular double vowels, diphthongs, suffixes: *ing, ed, er, est, ly, ness, less, ful,* contractions, synonyms, antonyms, homonyms, recognition of syllables, compound words, syllabication: root + prefix or suffix, two or more consonants between two vowels, one consonant between two vowels, and vowels sounded separately.

Instructional Objectives Exchange (Box 24095, Dept. G, Los Angeles, California, 90024) offers measurable objectives collections for the decoding skills, reading comprehension, structural analysis, and study and reference skills for grades K–12 and criterion-referenced tests for word-attack skills and comprehension skills for grades K–6.

Criterion-referenced testing using the informal reading inventory and other instruments, will be examined in detail later, but first examine a technique for analyzing the test data derived from assessment of the pupil's potential and achievement.

ANALYSIS OF THE TEST DATA

There is not much value in administering scholastic-aptitude and reading-survey tests unless the data are analyzed and used. Only by analyzing the data is it possible to say whether a genuine discrepancy exists between expectancy level and achievement and whether the discrepancy, if one exists, is of sufficient magnitude to necessitate further analysis.

The following data, on three eighth-grade pupils, were obtained from scholastic-aptitude testing and survey testing. Only enough data are included here to illustrate the technique involved.

PUPIL	READING SCORE AT GRADE LEVEL	I.Q. SCORE	CHRONOLOGICAL AGE
1	8.3	122	13.9
2	6.0	101	13.3
3	6.3	83	14.0

One way of expressing the relationship of attainment to expectancy is to compare pupils' reading age (RA) with their mental age (MA). (It would also be possible, of course, to compare reading age with listening age, as determined from a listening-comprehension test.) The purpose of the comparative procedure is to determine whether the reading score (reading-age score) is substantially below the mental-age score (or the listening score, as the case may be).

The difference between the mental age and the reading age tells whether pupils are doing as well as they should, or whether pupils are disabled in reading, and if so, what the degree of disability might be.

Normally, the teacher will have three kinds of data for each pupil: (1) the pupil's score on a reading-achievement test which has been converted into a reading grade-level score; (2) the pupil's I.Q. score; and (3) the pupil's chronological age. What must the teacher do with these data?

First: It is necessary to convert the reading-grade score into a reading-age score. This is done by adding 5.2 to the grade score (see Figure 16–1). The average pupil enters first grade at the age of 6.2. There thus tends to be a difference of 5.2 (6.2 minus 1) between chronological age and grade placement. The

Figure 16-1 Reading Disability of Three Students

PUPIL	READING GRADE SCORE	READING AGE (RA) SCORE	CHRONOLOGICAL AGE	I.Q. SCORE	MENTAL AGE	DIFFERENCES BETWEEN MA & RA
1	8.3	13.5	13.9	122 (13.9 x 1.22)	17.0	−3.5
2	6.0	11.2	13.3	101 (13.3 x 1.01)	13.4	−2.2
3	6.3	11.5	14.0	83 (14.0 x .83)	11.6	−0.1

reason for subtracting 1 from the pupil's age is that the pupil starts school in grade 1.

Second: It is necessary to compute the mental age. This may be done (as shown in Figure 16–1) by multiplying the age by the I.Q., being careful to put a decimal point at the proper place in the I.Q.

Third: It is necessary to subtract the reading-age score from the mental-age score (see Figure 16–1). The difference between these scores represents the degree of disability, if indeed there is any.

It is desirable that the scholastic-aptitude test and the reading-achievement test be given at approximately the same time. If they have been administered at different times, it is necessary to use the pupil's obtained mental age at the time that the reading-achievement test was administered, in order to compute the discrepancy between mental age and reading achievement. This means that the chronological-age factor in the mental-age formula needs to be adjusted to fit the age of the pupil when the reading test was given.

Using the criteria given earlier, namely, a difference between expectancy and achievement of more than eighteen months at the eighth-grade level, pupils 1 and 2 would certainly be considered disabled in reading. Using two different formulas—the Bond-Tinker (1967) and the Harris-Sipay (1975) formulas—on the same data gives the following:

Pupil #1

1. *Personal Data:*   IQ = 122; CA = 13.9; MA = 17;
                      Reading Grade Score = 8.3.
2. *Bond-Tinker Formula:* Grade Expectancy is equal to $(\frac{IQ}{100}$ X Years in School) + 1.0. Substituting appropriate data in the formula indicates that this student's Grade Expectancy is equivalent to $\frac{(122 \times 7.6)}{100}$ + 1.0 = 10.27. Subtracting 8.3 (the student's actual reading grade score) from the Grade Expectancy (10.27 − 8.3) gives 1.97. The Bond-Tinker formula thus estimates that the pupil's reading performance is 1.97 grade levels below expectancy (Degree of Retardation).
3. *Harris-Sipay Formula* (1975: This formula begins with the computation of the pupil's Reading Expectancy Age (R Exp. A). This is equal to $\frac{2 \text{ MA} + \text{CA}}{3}$. Substituting appropriate data into the formula indicates that this student's R Exp. A is equivalent to $\frac{2(17) + 13.9}{3}$ = 16. Converting the Reading Expectancy Age to a Grade Expectancy (R Exp. A minus 5.2 or 16 − 5.2 = 10.8) gives 10.8. The degree of retardation or disability is equal to the Grade Expectancy (10.8) minus the pupil's actual reading performance (8.3) or 2.5. The Harris-Sipay formula thus suggests that the pupil's reading performance is 2.5 grade levels below expectancy (Degree of Retardation).

In general, the Bond-Tinker formula sets unduly high expectancies for the dull and too low expectancies for the bright. Unfortunately, this is what prevails in many schools: slow learners are probably reading as well as they can and gifted learners often read at a level substantially below their ability level.

Harris and Sipay (1975: p. 146) also suggest an objective numerical measure of severity of disability (the Reading Expectancy Quotient or R Exp. Q); set a specific cutoff point (R Exp. Q of 90); and differentiate among disabled, underachieving, and slow learners (using the Reading Quotient or RQ). They obtain the Reading Expectancy Quotient by dividing the attained reading age (RA) by the expectancy age (R Exp. A): $R \text{ Exp. } Q = \dfrac{RA \times 100}{R \text{ Exp. } A}$. Reading achievement is considered satisfactory when the Reading Expectancy Quotient is above 90 or when reading achievement is 90 percent of expectancy. If it falls below 90, a genuine disability is considered to exist, and the lower the expectancy quotient is, the more severe the disability tends to be. A quotient below 85 indicates that the disability is severe.

Harris and Sipay's formula also allows for differentiation between genuine cases of disability in reading and the poor reading of the slow learner and the underachiever in reading. The Reading Quotient (RQ) is used to do this where $RQ = \dfrac{RA}{CA} = 100.$

When both R Exp. Q and RQ are below 90, the learner's reading performance is significantly below both the pupil's own expectancy and below the normal performance for the pupil's age.

When the R Exp. Q is below 90, but the RQ is 90 or above, the pupil is probably achieving above age or grade level, but significantly below ability level.

When the R Exp. Q is 90 or above, but the RQ is below 90, the pupil is probably doing as well as he or she can, but performance is substantially below age or grade level.

These observations may be summarized as follows:

	R. EXP. Q	RQ
Normal Reader	90 or above	90 or above
Disabled Reader	Below 90	Below 90
Underachiever in Reading	Below 90	90 or above
Slow Learner	90 or above	Below 90

Computing the Reading Expectancy Quotient and the Reading Quotient on pupil #1 reveals the following:

a. $R \text{ Exp. } Q = \dfrac{RA \times 100}{R \text{ Exp. } A}$

$\dfrac{13.5 \times 100}{16} = 84$

Since pupil #1's R Exp. Q is below 85, he or she probably has a severe reading disability.

b.   RQ = $\dfrac{RA \times 100}{CA}$

$\dfrac{13.5 \times 100}{13.9} = 97$

Since the RQ is 97, the Harris-Sipay formula would classify the reader as an underachiever in reading. The pupil is achieving at grade level, but substantially below ability level. The pupil needs substantial help to attain his or her potential.

Pupil #2

1.   *Personal Data:*   I.Q. = 101; CA = 13.3; MA = 13.4; Reading Grade Score is 6.0.

2.   *Bond-Tinker Formula:* $\dfrac{(\text{I.Q.} \times \text{Years in School})}{100} + 1$

$\dfrac{(101 \times 7.6)}{100} + 1 = 8.68$

8.68 − 6 (Reading Grade Score) = 2.68 (Degree of Retardation)

3.   *Harris-Sipay Formula:*

a.   R Exp. A = $\dfrac{2MA + CA}{3}$

$\dfrac{2(13.4) + 13.3}{3} = 13.4$

R Exp. A − 5.2 = Grade Expectancy

13.4 − 5.2 = 8.2

8.2 − 6 = 2.2 (Degree of Retardation)

b.   R Exp. Q = $\dfrac{RA \times 100}{R \text{ Exp. A}}$

$\dfrac{11.1 \times 100}{13.4} = 84$

c.   RQ = $\dfrac{RA \times 100}{CA}$

$\dfrac{11.1 \times 100}{13.3} = 84$

Since both the Reading Expectancy Quotient and the Reading Quotient are below 85, the pupil is probably severely disabled in reading and is also achieving significantly below grade level. The pupil's reading-grade score is 6 even though he or she is in the eighth grade.

Pupil #3

1.   *Personal Data:*   I.Q. = 83; CA = 14.0; MA = 11.6; Reading Grade Score is 6.3.

2.   *Bond-Tinker Formula:* $\dfrac{(\text{I.Q.} \times \text{Years in School})}{100} + 1$

$\dfrac{(83 \times 7.6)}{100} + 1 = 7.31$

7.31 − 6.3 (Reading Grade Score) = 1.01 (Degree of Retardation)

3. *Harris-Sipay Formula:*

   a. $R \text{ Exp. A} = \dfrac{2MA + CA}{3}$

   $$\dfrac{2(11.6) + 14}{3} = 12.4$$

   $R \text{ Exp. A} - 5.2 = \text{Grade Expectancy}$

   $12.4 - 5.2 = 7.2$

   $7.2 - 6.3 = 0.9 \text{ (Degree of Retardation)}$

   b. $R \text{ Exp. Q} = \dfrac{RA \times 100}{R \text{ Exp. A}}$

   $$\dfrac{11.5 \times 100}{12.4} = 93$$

   c. $RQ = \dfrac{RA \times 100}{CA}$

   $$\dfrac{11.5 \times 100}{14} = 82$$

Pupil #3 is doing about as well as expected. The pupil is reading substantially below grade level, but the reading-age score is approximately the same as the mental-age score. The pupil is a slow learner. This is indicated by the Reading Expectancy Quotient of 93 and a Reading Quotient of 82.

Summarizing the data on the three students, using the various formulas, yields the following variations in degree of reading retardation.

	#1	#2	#3
Mental Age	−3.5	−2.2	−0.1
Bond-Tinker	−1.97	−2.68	−1.01
Harris-Sipay	−2.5	−2.2	−0.9
R Exp. Q	84	84	93
RQ	97	84	82

Each of the formulas identifies the disability of pupils 1 and 2, even though pupil 1 is reading approximately up to grade level. Furthermore, all the formulas identify pupil 3 as a slow learner. Using these formulas (observing the cautions earlier noted) can help to identify those readers whose reading performance is substantially at variance with potential. It should identify those students who need further analysis and study.

The limitations inherent in the discrepancy model and hence in each of these formulas preclude putting total faith in the ability of such formulas to predict reading disability. There are inherent difficulties in dealing quantitatively with the concept that disabled readers are readers who are not performing up to their ability level or up to their potential. It is of course for this reason that some prefer to use simpler criteria of reading disability, such as that the pupil cannot read the textbook; that the pupil's reading achievement is substantially below age or grade level; or that the pupil makes more than five word-recognition errors per 100 words or fails to achieve a 75 percent comprehension score on questions about materials generally read by children at the same age or grade level. The last mode employs a criterion-referenced instrument which will be examined here shortly, the informal reading inventory. In many reading programs the analysis of the pupil's performance on the reading inventory is the only analysis that occurs and is the one which determines what kind and what level of intervention is needed.

DIAGNOSTIC TESTING

The initial part of this chapter has dealt with Step I of the diagnostic procedure. Step I is primarily concerned with the identification of the reading difficulty. It is a process of screening. By completing Step I, one should have greatly reduced the number of pupils who need special attention. Step I should have differentiated pupils who are genuinely disabled in reading and who need corrective and remedial instruction from those who simply need adapted instruction. At a minimum, it ought to provide differential early programming for some children who may not be progressing adequately. It ought to identify the pupils for whom Steps II, III, and IV of the diagnostic process have significance.

Step II, diagnostic testing, involves a substantial amount of assessment. It is the beginning of detailed and individual diagnosis. Only those pupils who were identified in the screening process (Step I) as not achieving in reading at an appropriate level need the intensive and detailed analysis that takes place in Step II of the diagnostic process.

Step II deals with the simple question: Does the pupil possess the enabling skills that make achievement in reading possible? Step II answers the additional question: What reading errors or miscues does the reader make that cause him or her to be described as a disabled reader? It identifies the specific behaviors or symptoms that describe the reader's disability and that need to be remediated. The principal goal or purpose of Step II is the determination of the syndrome of symptoms or the symptomatology of the case. Its concern is with *how* the pupil reads. And Step II is directed toward identifying the severity or *type* of disability (as contrasted to *level* of disability which is the focus of Step I) from a study of the pupil's miscues and symptomatology. The teacher studies symptoms to make educated guesses about the severity of the pupil's reading problems. Collectively, the symptoms or significant behaviors exhibited by disabled readers amount to a definition of the reading problem (Otto et al. 1974).

On this level the teacher is not satisfied to know that the pupil is reading on a second-grade level when in fact he or she might be able to read on a fourth-grade level. The teacher wants to know the specific reasons for the overall low performance: Is it a lack of adequate vision or hearing? Is it a deficiency in auditory or visual discrimination? Is it the inability to attack words? Is it limited vocabulary? Is it a failure to use context? Is it the lack of ability in auditory blending? Is it an orientational difficulty? Or is it a combination of factors?

Step II of the diagnostic process ideally includes the following assessments:

1. *Assessment of the pupil's vision, hearing, and eye-movement.* (See Chapter 5 for a description of vision and eye-movement screening tests and for audiometric measurements.)

2. *Assessment of the pupil's visual perception skills,* especially visual discrimination, visual-motor integration, and visual memory.

3. *Assessment of the pupil's auditory perception skills,* especially auditory discrimination, blending, and memory.

4. *Assessment of the pupil's preferred mode of learning.* This aspect is generally not included in assessment programs simply because there is some question whether this can be done. Nevertheless, there seems to be value in assessing whether the pupil is primarily a visual, auditory, or kinesthetic learner, especially since the major methods of teaching word identification are the sight-configuration method, the linguistic or whole-word phonic method, the synthetic phonic method, and the kinesthetic method.

5. *Assessment of laterality and directionality.* The instruments of concern here measure laterality or left-right motor dominance, knowledge of left and right, directional confusion, reversal tendency, and spatial orientation.

6. *Assessment of knowledge of the core words* without which it is impossible to make use of the context in reading. (See Chapter 8 for a description of such lists, including the *Dolch Basic Sight Word List.*) Words from these lists can be used to estimate the pupil's reading level. The use of such lists for this purpose has been especially popular in the primary grades.

7. *Assessment of the pupil's word-recognition skills.* This assessment overlaps point 6, but adds to the overall understanding of the pupil's word-recognition skills (in other words, of the pupil's sight vocabulary.) The instruments used in this assessment provide measurements of sight or recognition vocabulary that go beyond the core vocabulary.

8. *Assessment of independent, instructional, and frustration level in word recognition and comprehension in both oral and silent reading.* The informal reading inventories, the oral reading tests, and other so-called individual diagnostic tests may all be used to do this.

9. *Assessment of the pupil's proficiency in both phonetic and structural analysis skills.*

The forms of measurement described in points 7, 8, and 9 will concern us now, beginning with the measurement of the pupil's sight or recognition vocabulary.

MEASUREMENT OF SIGHT OR RECOGNITION VOCABULARY

A number of instruments or tests that measure the ability to "read" or pronounce a set of printed words have been developed. Among these are:

1. *Slosson Oral Reading Test (SORT),* 1963 (Slosson Educational Publications). Grades 1–12. This is an individual test and is based on the ability to pronounce

words at different levels of difficulty. It consists of 10 lists of 20 words from the primer level through the eighth grade. An additional list is provided for high school. The examiner starts on a list where the pupil can pronounce all 20 words. The pupil's score is obtained by adding up all the correct responses as well as those words below the pupil's perfect starting list. This sum is then converted into a grade-level score. Testing takes about 3 minutes.

2. *Wide Range Achievement Test* (WRAT), 1978 (Western Psychological Services; Copyright, 1976, by Guidance Associates of Delaware, Inc.). Ages 5–adult. This test is an individual test of word recognition, spelling, and arithmetic computation. The Reading section contains words, ranging in difficulty from age 5 to college level. The Pre-Reading section has pupils write their names, name 2 of the letters in their names, name 13 capitals, or if they can't do this, match 10 capitals. The pupils read aloud the words in Level I if they are under 12. Level II is used with pupils over 12. Level I has 75 words; Level II contains 74 words. Testing is discontinued after 12 consecutive failures. Whenever failures occur in the first line of the reading test, the 3 pre-reading parts are administered. Grade norms for Level I range from pre-kindergarten to grade 16.2; for Level II they range from pre-kindergarten to grade 19.5.

Instruments such as these assume of course that the pupil's ability to pronounce words is an adequate measure of ability to read materials in which words are strung together, or in other words, of ability in sentence or paragraph reading. Such tests do appear to be able to provide a quick assessment of the pupil's reading level, especially in the early grades, but for best diagnosis of why pupils are not reading up to their ability level, there is need for assessment and evaluation using the instruments that will be described next.

MEASUREMENT OF INDEPENDENT, INSTRUCTIONAL AND FRUSTRATION LEVEL IN WORD RECOGNITION AND COMPREHENSION IN BOTH ORAL AND SILENT READING

Different types of instruments may be used to assess reading level in word recognition and comprehension in both oral and silent reading. Among these are the informal reading inventories and the oral reading tests, as well as some other diagnostic tests. Begin with the informal reading inventories.

The Informal Reading Inventory

As indicated earlier, survey testing or testing on standardized reading-achievement tests generally provides the teacher with an estimate of the pupil's grade-level performance (for example, that the pupil is reading on a 2.2 grade level) but it provides little information about

1. The conditions that cause the problem in reading.
2. The symptoms that identify the disabled reader: the actual reading behavior,

observable characteristics, or the errors or miscues that cause the reader to be described as disabled.

3. The reasons for the reader's overall low performance in reading.

4. The type or severity of the disability.

The informal reading inventory is programmed to provide the information suggested in these four points. It is probably the most frequently used mode of (1) identifying actual reading level and (2) identifying actual reading behaviors, even though oral reading tests, diagnostic reading tests, and some other tests designed specifically for these purposes all do about the same thing; the latter tests will be examined later in this chapter.

The teacher must decide how many and what types of the available instruments are needed to get a good understanding of the pupil's reading behavior. First consider the use of the teacher-made informal reading inventory in determining pupil reading level and specific strengths and weaknesses in reading.

The informal reading inventories are individual tests which require pupils to read increasingly difficult material, both silently and orally, until they reach the frustration level either by making too many word recognition errors or by obtaining a too low comprehension score. The inventories thus consist of a series of graded reading selections. They are designed to help teachers in determining the reading levels of children in the classroom or to estimate the level of material that is most suitable for a reader. Their main purpose often is to determine how difficult a book the pupil can read at an instructional level.

Three Reading Levels

In the preceding paragraph two terms were introduced: instructional level and frustration level. To these may be added a third: the independent level.

The *independent* reading level is the highest level at which the pupil can read fluently, with few word-recognition errors and with good comprehension. It is about one year below the instructional level. Materials that the pupil can read at the independent level normally comprise the pupil's free-time or recreational reading fare. The *instructional* level is the level at which both word recognition and comprehension are satisfactory, but where the pupil needs the teacher's help. It is the level where systematic instruction can be initiated and where indeed instruction is best applied to upgrade the pupil's reading competency. It is the teachable level. On this level, instructional guidance is needed for best performance. The material is difficult enough to require instruction, but easy enough so as not to be frustrating. At the *frustration* level, the pupil's reading is full of word-recognition and comprehension errors, fluency disappears, and the pupil shows signs of frustration, tension, and discomfort. The material is too difficult to even allow for growth. The pupil is simply not ready for the material.

Betts (1957) considers pupils to be reading on a frustration level if they read with less than 75 percent comprehension and less than 90 percent accuracy in word recognition. Pupils read on an instructional level if they read with 75 percent comprehension and 95 percent accuracy in word recognition. And pupils read on an independent level if they read with 90 percent comprehension and 99 percent accuracy in word recognition.

Why use informal reading inventories to identify the pupil's reading level when this has probably been done already through a standardized reading achievement test? Standardized tests tend to overestimate the instructional level by as much as two years, and thus pupils matched to materials on the basis of the survey reading test score may be forced to read on a frustration level. Standardized tests thus are not particularly helpful in identifying a book that the pupil can read on an instructional level.

Construction of Informal Reading Inventories

The teacher can construct informal reading inventories in two ways. After selecting reading passages at or near the pupil's grade level, the teacher performs a readability check for each passage, determines difficulty level, and prepares comprehension questions to measure pupil competency. The readability check will help to identify the reading level of the material. Thus, if the readability level of a passage is 3.5 grade level and if the pupil can read this material with no more than five recognition errors per 100 words and no less than a 75 percent score on the comprehension questions, the pupil is presumed to be reading on at least a 3.5 grade level.

In a second approach, principally concerned with whether the pupil can read a given book, the teacher selects three passages from a graded book, usually a basal reader, prepares comprehension questions about the material, and determines whether the pupil reads this material on an independent, instructional, or frustration level. Dependent upon the pupil's ability to answer the comprehension questions satisfactorily, the teacher learns either that the material has a suitable difficulty level, that it is too difficult, or that it is too easy.

One might presume that passages taken from a graded third-grade reader would all have a third-grade difficulty level, but this is not always so; thus, it is best to do a readability check on this material also. However, since the purpose is not so much to identify the pupil's reading level as to identify a book that he or she can read on an instructional level, the readability check may not be needed.

It is generally recommended that on the preprimer level the passages used in testing be about 50 words in length. On the primer and first-reader level, they should be 100 words in length. Above second grade they might be between 200 and 250 words long.

If the first approach is used, various reading selections should be developed for each grade level. The range of difficulty levels should be as large as is the reading ability of the students in a given grade. Thus, on the sixth-grade level it is desirable to have materials with readability levels going from about the third to the ninth grade.

At least *two* selections are needed at each difficulty level: one to evaluate silent reading ability and another to evaluate oral reading ability. Whether the teacher has the pupil read paragraphs of varying lengths and various difficulty levels or whether the pupil reads paragraphs from graded readers, the pupil should always be required to read two selections, one silently and another orally.

Comprehension is generally measured over material that the pupil has read silently. Five to ten comprehension test questions should have been prepared prior to the reading, using both literal and inferential questions. Sometimes a free-response kind of comprehension check is used. If this is done, the teacher should have prepared an outline of the selection so the concepts can be checked off as the pupil tells what he or she has read.

Although the oral reading of the selection is generally used to diagnose word-recognition strengths and weaknesses, oral reading comprehension should also be measured. If silent reading comprehension is substantially better than oral reading comprehension, it may indicate special skill in context reading; it may also suggest that the pupil's word-recognition ability is not advancing at the rate of the pupil's contextual reading ability.

The pupil's ability in word recognition may be measured either through the use of a separate, graded word list, or by having the pupil read orally the passages which he or she previously read silently, or by a combination of the two approaches. If a graded word list is used, the pupil's oral reading generally begins at the level where the pupil performed adequately on the word list.

After the pupil has read the passage silently, the teacher may read the passage aloud, beginning at the level at which the pupil failed the silent reading criterion. Comprehension is then checked in the usual manner. Differences between the comprehension score after silent reading and after having the passage read aloud by the teacher may indicate genuine differences in silent reading comprehension and listening comprehension. The highest level at which pupils can understand material read aloud to them is considered to be their *reading capacity level* or potential reading level at that age. This mode of determining discrepancy between achievement in reading and potential in reading may be as valid as one which bases determination of potential on scholastic-aptitude test scores.

Determining Readability Level

Readability refers to the success that a group of readers has with a book. Thus, a book or a passage labeled as grade-three readability level supposedly can be read comfortably by pupils with an instructional reading level of grade three. The teacher is interested in the measurement of the comprehensibility (readability) of materials. However, if teachers are to select materials of appropriate difficulty, they must also be able to quantify the difficulty or comprehensibility of the material.

One way of quantifying the difficulty of materials is through the use of readability formulas. The formulas that have been used most widely are the Spache (1953, 1966) formula, designed for grades one to three; the Dale-Chall (1948) formula for grades four to six; and the Flesch (1943, 1948) formula for grades above five.

A simpler mode of determining readability than any of the above was developed by Fry in 1961 and revised in 1977 (Fry 1977). The revised version of Fry's Readability Graph, like the earlier versions, provides readability estimates for materials designed for grade one through college, extending readability estimates throughout each of the college years.

Figure 16–2 pictures the Fry Readability Graph and provides guidelines for its use. The Fry graph is based on the number of syllables and the number of sentences per 100 words. The longer the sentences (and hence the fewer the number of sentences per 100 words) and the greater the number of syllables (long words have more syllables), the more difficult the material is assumed to be.*

Expanded Directions for Using the Fry Readability Graph

1. Randomly select three sample passages and count out exactly 100 words each, beginning with the beginning of a sentence. Do count proper nouns, initializations, and numerals.

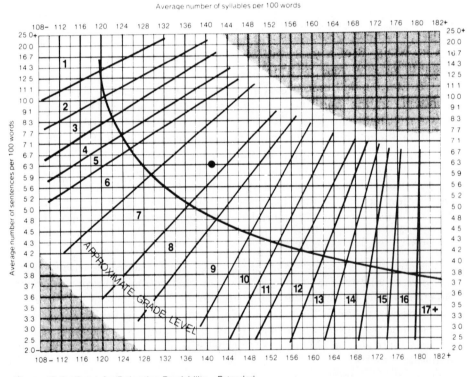

Figure 16-2 Graph for Estimating Readability—Extended

* Fry, E., "Fry's Readability Graph: Clarifications, Validity, and Extension to Level 17," *Journal of Reading* 21 (December 1977), pp. 242–252. The *Fry Readability Scale*, a simplified form of the graph, is available from Jamestown Publishers, P.O. Box 6743, Providence, Rhode Island 02940.

2. Count the number of sentences in the 100 words, estimating the length of the fraction of the last sentence to the nearest one-tenth.

3. Count the total number of syllables in the 100-word passage. If you do not have a hand counter available, an easy way is to simply put a mark above every syllable over one in each word; then when you get to the end of the passage, count the number of marks and add 100. Small calculators can also be used as counters by pushing numeral 1, and then pushing the + sign for each word or syllable when counting.

4. Enter on the graph the average sentence length and average number of syllables; plot dot where the two lines intersect. Area where dot is plotted will give you the approximate grade level.

5. If a great deal of variability is found in the syllable count or the sentence count, putting more samples into the average is desirable.

6. A word is defined as a symbol or a group of symbols bounded by a blank space on either side; thus, *Joe, IRA, 1945,* and *&* are each one word.

7. A syllable is defined as a phonetic syllable. Generally, there are as many syllables as vowel sounds. For example, *stopped* is one syllable and *wanted* is two syllables. When counting syllables for numerals and initializations, count one syllable for each symbol. For example, *1945* is four syllables, *IRA* is three syllables, and *&* is one syllable.

8. Few passages or books will fall in the graph's gray area; but when they do, grade-level scores are invalid.

9. Example:

	syllables	sentences
first 100 words	124	6.6
second 100 words	141	5.5
third 100 words	158	6.8
average	141	6.3

Readability: 7th grade (see dot plotted on graph)

Computerized readability summaries are available from Britton & Associates, Inc. (Instructional Materials Analysis Service, 1054 N. W. Fillmore, Corvallis, Oregon 97330) for the basal reading series, *Reading 720* (Ginn), *Reading Unlimited* (Scott, Foresman), *Houghton Mifflin Reading Series, Keys to Reading* (Economy), *Reading Perspectives* (Heath), *Merrill Linguistic Reading Program, Holt Basic Reading System,* and *Reading Basics Plus* (Harper & Row).

Fox Reading Research Company (P.O. Box 1059, Coeur d'Alene, Idaho 83814), offers the *Foxies Reference,* 1979, which lists the readability level for over 7,890 stories in 32 basal series.

Evaluation of Reading Inventories

Informal inventories are especially helpful in making continuous evaluations of pupils' progress. Pupils' reading tells something of their background of experience, of their vocabulary knowledge, of their reading habits (slowness in reading, excessive lip movements or vocalization, finger pointing, lateral head movement which may reduce speed in reading, or eratic eye movements), of their comprehension, and of their specific difficulties.

As a given pupil reads, the teacher looks for pupil interest in materials, concentration, attention span, impulsiveness, refusal to try to decode words, speed with which the reading is completed, willingness to read orally, and ability to follow directions. The first sign indicative of poor reading is often the pupil's attitude toward reading. A pupil who does not read well generally is not willing to read aloud, and would rather hear others read.

The teacher is particularly interested in the pupil's oral reading errors or miscues, including reversals, number of words aided or pronounced by the teacher, omissions, insertions, additions, repetitious, word-order confusions, substitutions, mispronunciations, and hesitations.

Usually if it takes the pupil more than five seconds to pronounce the word, it is counted as an error or miscue. Some do not count it as a miscue if pupils correct themselves within a five-second span. Miscues that conform to dialect, hesitations, and ignoring of punctuation marks are often not counted as miscues in scoring. Repeated errors on the same word are generally considered to be one miscue.

Dunkeld (1970) reports that a word-recognition score based on a miscue count of mispronunciations, substitutions, words pronounced for the learner, insertions, and reversals showed a higher correlation with comprehension than did any other combination of miscues. Oral reading errors, their causes and remediation, were discussed in detail in Chapter 15.

The teacher needs to have a copy of the passages that the pupil is reading in order to follow the pupil's reading and to mark the reading errors. Various systems of marking errors have been developed; each of the published informal inventories presents its own system. It is strongly recommended that the pupil's oral reading be taped so the teacher can analyze it in detail at his or her own leisure.

The chief weakness of the informal inventories is that they provide no validity and reliability data. Their strength comes from the understanding and insight with which they are interpreted.

However, the values of the inventories outweigh their deficiencies. They furnish information about the thinking and reading strategies that the pupil employs to reconstruct the writer's message. Furthermore, they can be developed for subject-matter content that is comparable to the content the pupil has to deal with in the classroom. Thus, evaluation of the pupil's reading deficiency is conducted with the same or similar material as that which the pupil is using for instructional purposes. And inventories deal very directly with intraindividual differences. For example, a pupil's word recognition skills normally develop in close relationship to his comprehension skills. It is when they do not do so that difficulties occur and that a differential diagnosis becomes necessary. Not only do pupils grow, develop, and mature at an *individual* rate, but so does competency in various skills. The chief concern in reading has unfortunately been how one child differs from another. The informal reading inventory helps to focus on the way an individual reader differs within himself or herself. Many important instructional decisions can and must be based on an analysis of these differentials in performance.

Published Informal Reading Inventories

Classroom teachers often use published reading inventories to estimate the pupil's reading level. These generally consist of graded word lists and graded reading selections, with questions prepared in advance to test the reader's oral and silent reading comprehension.

The major published reading inventories are:

1. *Botel Reading Inventory*, 1978 (Follett Educational Corporation). Grades 1–12.
2. *Classroom Reading Inventory*; Nicholas Silvaroli, 3rd edition, 1976 (Wm. C. Brown Company). Preprimer to tenth-grade level.
3. *Standard Reading Inventory*; Robert A. McCracken, (Klamath Printing Company). Preprimer to tenth-grade level.
4. *Reading Miscue Inventory*; Yetta Goodman and Carolyn Burke, 1972 (Macmillan). Grades 1–7.
5. *Individual Reading Placement Inventory*; Edwin H. Smith and Weldon G. Bradtmueller, 1970 (Follett Educational Corporation). Youth and adults reading below seventh grade.
6. *Ekwall Reading Inventory*, 1979 (Allyn and Bacon). Preprimer to ninth-grade level.
7. *Reading Placement Inventory*; Floyd Sucher and Ruel A. Allred, 1973 (Economy Company). Grades 1–9.

Only the *Classroom Reading Inventory*, useful in grades 2–10, will be described.

The *Classroom Reading Inventory* is composed of two main parts: Part I, Graded Word Lists and Part II, Graded Oral Paragraphs. Part III, A Graded Spelling Survey, may also be administered. Parts I and II must be administered individually; Part III may be administered to groups. The inventory may be administered quite easily in about 15 minutes.

The Graded Word Lists, containing 20 words each, are designed for preprimer to sixth grade. The pupil, beginning on preprimer level, pronounces each word. Testing is discontinued at the level at which the child mispronounces 5 of the 20 words. Corrected errors are counted as acceptable responses.

The Graded Oral Paragraphs are begun at the highest level at which the pupil recognized all the words on the Graded Word Lists section. They range from 24 words at the preprimer level to 174 words at the eighth-grade level. They are used to estimate the pupil's independent and instructional reading levels, to identify word-recognition errors made in oral reading, and to measure reading comprehension.

The Graded Spelling Survey gives 10 words for each level from first to sixth grade. Testing is discontinued when the pupil makes 5 spelling errors in any one level.

The errors noted in the inventory are those of repetition (⌒), insertion (⌄), substitution (——), omission (◯), and where the pupil needed assistance (P). An example would look like this:

   is   old   P

It was the day to go to the farm. "Get in the bus," said Mrs. Brown.

Comprehension is tested by five questions at each level. Each level of the Oral Paragraphs includes a system for determining the pupil's rate (words per minute) of reading.

The instructional level is identified with 95 percent accuracy in word recognition and 75 percent comprehension on the oral reading paragraphs. A scoring guide identifying independent, instructional, and frustration levels accompanies each oral selection. A hearing capacity level is identifiable and is the level at which the pupil can comprehend 75 percent of the material when it is read to him. It is the pupil's listening comprehension level.

Oral Reading Tests

The oral reading tests measure essentially the same skills as the reading inventories. They rely on graded word lists and paragraphs read orally to measure oral reading comprehension and to evaluate accuracy in oral reading.

Two oral reading tests that are commonly used are

1. *Gilmore Oral Reading Test*, 1968 (Psychological Corporation) Grades 1–8, 15–20 minutes. This individual test consists of 10 paragraphs, measuring comprehension, speed, and accuracy of oral reading. Pupil errors can be recorded: substitutions, mispronunciations, insertions, omissions, words pronounced by examiner, disregard of punctuation, hesitations, and repetitions.
2. *Gray Oral Reading Tests*, 1967 (Bobbs-Merrill Educational Publishing). Grades 1–12. This test consists of 13 graded passages in each of four forms. It is designed to measure growth in oral reading, to help in diagnosing reading difficulties, and to provide beginning placement in grade or reading groups.

The *Gilmore Oral Reading Test* provides teachers with a means of analyzing the pupil's oral reading performance. Pupils begin reading in a selection two grade levels below their grade placement or at the level where they make no more than 2 errors on a paragraph. The pupils are tested on successively more difficult paragraphs until they make 10 or more errors. Rate of reading is determined by dividing the sum of all the words read, by the total number of seconds elapsed, in all the test paragraphs.

The Gray Oral Reading Tests are useful for grade one to college. Three reading selections are usable on the first grade level, five are for grades two to six, and the last five measure up to college level.

The Gray Oral Reading Test may be used to assess general level of reading for a new pupil entering a school and thus helps in placing the pupil in a reading group. It provides a measure of oral reading achievement and of fluency and accuracy of oral reading, rather than of comprehension even though literal comprehension is tested.

Beyond the primary grades, testing begins two passages below the pupil's grade level or in a passage where the pupil can read without any errors. Testing continues until the pupil makes 7 or more errors on each of the two successive passages.

Errors recorded are words aided, gross mispronunciations, partial mispronunciations, omissions, insertions, substitutions, repetitions, and inversions. The comprehension questions ask only for literal meaning and the details of what is read. The time required to read a passage is recorded, and time and the total number of errors are used to determine the grade equivalent in oral reading.

Individual Diagnostic Reading Tests

The diagnostic reading test, like some of the instruments already described, seeks to discover specific strengths and weaknesses. It is especially useful in planning remedial procedures. In a diagnostic test, as already indicated, it is the mistakes that the pupil makes that indicate the pupil's areas of need. The exact identification of the types of errors thus directs the examiner to specific remedial needs. The total score may be indicative of the degree of personal need.

The diagnostic test is the basis of the diagnostic-prescriptive approach: diagnose-teach-diagnose-teach. The survey test groups pupils by reading level; the diagnostic test groups according to needs (phonics, comprehension, and the like). The most effective use of the diagnostic test is for individual tutoring.

Of the various diagnostic tests available, the *Diagnostic Reading Scales* (Spache, 1981, CTB/McGraw-Hill, grades 1–8 and retarded 9–12, no time limit) are most useful for classroom diagnosis. These scales are individually administered tests designed to identify reading deficiencies that hinder pupils from reading adequately. The scale is recommended for normal and retarded readers at the elementary, junior high, and senior high levels. The test battery comprises 3 word-recognition lists, 22 reading passages, and 12 supplementary tests measuring consonant sounds, vowel blends, consonant blends, common syllables, blending, letter sounds, initial-consonant substitution, and auditory discrimination, etc. Three reading levels are yielded for each pupil: instructional level in oral reading, independent level in silent reading, and potential level in auditory comprehension.

ASSESSMENT OF THE PUPIL'S PROFICIENCY IN BOTH PHONETIC AND STRUCTURAL ANALYSIS SKILLS

A very significant part of any reading assessment is an analysis of the pupil's word analysis skills. Earlier chapters (Chapters 9 to 11) were devoted to the development of these skills. The assessment of these skills is also of great importance.

Tests which have been designed specifically to measure skill in word analysis, both phonic and structural, are:

1. *Doren Diagnostic Test of Word Recognition Skills*, 1973 (American Guidance, Inc., Publishers Building, Circle Pines, Minnesota 55014). Grades 2–3. This group test measures for letter recognition, beginning sounds, whole-word recognition, words within words, speech consonants, ending sounds, blending (use of consonant blends), rhyming, vowels, discriminate guessing (use of context clues), spelling, and sight words. The test is most effective when given individually. Each of the subtests has from 15 to 45 items. The test is untimed. Test scores are recorded on an individual skill profile, and a score of 7 or more errors indicates that that specific skill area needs remedial teaching.

2. *Lane Diagnostic Test of Word Perception Skills*, 1975 (Economy Company, P.O. Box 25308, 1901 North Walnut, Oklahoma City, Oklahoma 73125). This test, designed for grades 4–12, has two parts: Phonetic Analysis and Structural Analysis. Phonetic Analysis consists of subtests on vowel symbols, initial vowel sounds, medial vowel sounds, vowel sounds determined by letter positions and spelling, initial consonant sounds, final consonant sounds, sounds of consonant blends, sounds of consonant digraphs, consonant sounds determined by letter positions and spellings, and sounds of final syllables and suffixes. Structural Analysis consists of syllable discrimination, word division, compound words, and affixes. A cassette tape is available as an aid in administering the test.

   The self-scoring answer sheet serves also as a profile, indicating specifically where the pupil's deficiency lies. Part II, Structural Analysis, profiles scores into three levels indicating competency, reinforcement needed, or reteaching needed.

3. *Murphy-Durrell Prereading Phonics Inventory*, 1976 (Borg-Warner Educational Systems, 600 West University Drive, Arlington Heights, Illinois 60004). This test consists of four parts: Lower-Case Letter Names (26 items), Letter Name-Sounds (22 items), Writing Letters from Dictation (26 items), and Syntax Matching— matching words in speech with words in print (10 items). Test 1 measures the child's ability to hear the name of a letter and to circle the letter named. The names of the letters (except for *h*, *p*, *w*, and *y*) contain their phonemes, with each spoken letter name requiring the same phonetic vocal gymnastics as the phoneme. Test 2 tests the child's awareness of letter names as initial sounds in spoken words (long vowels—*acorn, eagle, iron, old, uniform;* 8 consonants whose names consist of their phoneme plus long *e*—*beach, ceiling, deep, genius, peach, teeth, veal, zebra;* the consonants whose names consist of short *e* plus their phonemes—*effort, elephant, emerald, engine, Esther, extra;* and *j, k,* and *r* by *jail, Kate, arm*). This is a test not used in any other instrument. Test 3 requires the pupil to write letters from dictation of the letter names. Test 4 is new in readiness testing. It is based on the fact that children have no difficulty repeating short sentences attached to pictures, but many cannot identify the separate words in a printed sentence. Many children have no idea that spoken sentences consist of separate words. The directions for an item on this test are: "Put your finger on the brush. Brush your *hair.* Find *hair* on your paper and circle it." The profile on the *Murphy-Durrell Prereading Phonics Inventory* groups pupils, on the basis of test scores, into four groups: A (the top third), B (the middle third), C (the low third), and D (the bottom 5 percent). Pupils identified as C (or D) tend to have serious difficulty in reading.

   Murphy and Durrell have developed an 8-week intervention program called

Sound Start that has been quite effective in dealing with the deficiencies discovered by testing with this Inventory.

For a discussion of this test, see Donald D. Durrell and Helen A. Murphy, "A Prereading Phonics Inventory," *The Reading Teacher* 31 (January 1978), 385–390.

4. *Roswell-Chall Diagnostic Reading Test of Word Analysis Skills*, 1979 (Essay Press). Revised version; this individual test of phonic and word recognition skills, for grades K–4, takes 10 to 15 minutes to administer. It covers sight recognition of high frequency words, naming capitals and lowercase letters, consonant blends and digraphs, short vowels, long vowels with *e*, long vowel combinations, writing and spelling cvc words, and the like.

GROUP DIAGNOSTIC INSTRUMENTS

The best available instrument that may be used to make diagnostic evaluations of *groups* of students in such significant areas as auditory discrimination, phonetic and structural analysis, vocabulary, comprehension, and even rate of comprehension is the *Stanford Diagnostic Reading Test*, 1976 (Psychological Corporation), which tests for four levels: Red Level (grades 1.6–3.5), Green Level (grades 2.6–5.5), Brown Level (grades 4.6–9.5), and Blue Level (grades 9–13). The Red Level measures auditory vocabulary, auditory discrimination, phonetic analysis, word reading, and reading comprehension. The Green Level adds structural analysis. The Brown Level includes a test of reading rate. The Blue Level measures reading comprehension, word meaning, word parts, phonetic analysis, structural analysis, scanning and skimming, and speed reading. The test has been specifically designed for low-achieving pupils. The test generally measures decoding skills, vocabulary skills, comprehension skills, and rate skills. In the early years the emphasis is on the decoding skills; in the middle grades and beyond greater emphasis is placed on vocabulary and comprehension, and eventually rate. Testing time ranges from 1 hour and 43 minutes to 2 hours and 25 minutes.

The areas measured by each of the Levels are*

Auditory Discrimination and Phonetic Analysis test consonant and vowel sounds; Structural analysis measures word division and blending; Reading Comprehension on the Red Level is directed toward sentence reading and paragraph comprehension; on the upper grade levels, 2.6 to 12, it measures literal and inferential comprehension.

The *Stanford Diagnostic Reading Test* provides a computer-analyzed profile for each pupil that makes instructional suggestions. This service, termed the Instructional Placement Report, is very helpful to the teacher.

---

* See the Manual for *The Stanford Diagnostic Reading Test*, p. 72.

Subtest or Total

RED LEVEL	GREEN LEVEL	BROWN LEVEL	BLUE LEVEL
Auditory Discrimination →	Auditory Discrimination		
Phonetic Analysis →	Phonetic Analysis →	Phonetic Analysis →	Phonetic Analysis
	Structural Analysis →	Structural Analysis →	Structural Analysis
			Decoding Total
			Word Meaning
			Word Parts
Auditory Vocabulary →	Auditory Vocabulary →	Auditory Vocabulary →	Vocabulary Total
Word Reading			
Reading Comprehension			
	Literal Comprehension →	Literal Comprehension →	Literal Comprehension
	Inferential Comprehension →	Inferential Comprehension →	Inferential Comprehension
Comprehension Total →	Reading Comprehension Total →	Reading Comprehension Total →	Reading Comprehension Total
			Fast Reading
			Scanning and Skimming
		Reading Rate →	Rate Total

READING ASSESSMENT CHECKSHEET

The teacher doing the assessment is aided in the compilation of information about a pupil by using a simple checklist. A sample follows. The checksheet should be adapted to the specific skills (or errors) measured in the pupil assessment program.

Let us now summarize what Step I and II of the diagnostic procedure have accomplished. Up to this point in the diagnostic process the teacher should have:

1. Made a comparison of the pupil's capacity or reading expectancy and his or her actual achievement in reading. Questions such as the following should have been answered: Is the pupil a disabled reader, a slow learner, a slow learner who is also a disabled reader, or is the pupil an underachiever, a gifted learner who is reading up to grade level but substantially below ability level? What are the pupil's learning strengths and weaknesses? What is the degree of severity of the disability?

2. Identified whether the pupil has the enabling skills (adequate vision and visual discrimination, adequate hearing and auditory perception skills, adequate direction and sequence sense) that make it possible to become a reader.

3. Identified the pupil's preferred mode of processing information, using the pupil's previous achievement (for example, achievement in phonics) as the best and most reliable gauge of what is the pupil's best mode of learning.

4. Evaluated the pupil's recognition of the core sight words of the language, using such lists as the *Dolch Basic Sight Word List*.

5. Identified the pupil's word-recognition level beyond the recognition of simple core words: (1) by using the graded word lists of the inventories and oral and diagnostic reading tests; (2) by evaluating the pupil's oral reading of a passage and noting accuracy and errors while reading; or (3) by testing the pupil with a word-recognition test.

6. Identified the student's independent, instructional, and frustration levels, using informal inventories or the oral or diagnostic tests to do so.

7. Identified the pupil's silent and oral reading comprehension level using either teacher-constructed questions or questions developed by the test author.

8. Identified the pupil's strengths and weaknesses in phonetic and structural analysis. Ability to decode (to deal with the grapheme-phoneme correspondences) is absolutely necessary to become a good reader.

DETAILED INVESTIGATION OF CAUSALITY

Step III of the diagnostic process is the detailed investigation of causality. It calls for a thorough analysis of the reading disability, leading to an identification of the causal factors involved.

Numerous hypotheses have been advanced to explain reading disability, or why pupils are not achieving as well as they should. The *deficit hypothesis* assumes that some personal trauma has interfered with the ability to read. The

READING DIAGNOSIS CHECKSHEET*

NAME _____ GRADE _____

SCHOOL _____ TEACHER _____

			YES	NO
READING BEHAVIORS	1.	Moves lips during reading		
	2.	Vocalizes excessively		
	3.	Uses fingers to hold his place		
	4.	Is tense or nervous while reading		
	5.	Holds book too close or too far away		
	6.	Frequently loses his place		
ORAL READING ERRORS	7.	Omissions		
	8.	Additions and insertions		
	9.	Substitutions, mispronunciations		
	10.	Repetitions or regressions		
	11.	Words aided		
	12.	Reversals		
	13.	Word-by-word reading		
	14.	Poor phrasing		
	15.	Hesitations		
EYE-MOVEMENT DIFFICULTIES	16.	Too many fixations and regressions		
	17.	Fixations are too long		
	18.	Eye-movements are inflexible		
	19.	Reading lacks rhythm		
	20.	Return sweep is faulty		
	21.	Sequences eye-movements too rapidly		

		YES	NO
PHONEME/GRAPHEME CORRESPONDENCES (PHONICS)	22. Knows consonant phoneme/grapheme correspondences		
	23. Knows vowel correspondences		
	24. Knows blend and digraph correspondences		
	25. Uses beginning consonant and the context to identify the word		
STRUCTURAL ANALYSIS SKILLS	26. Has adequate structural analysis skills		
	27. Can identify the number of syllables in spoken and printed words		
	28. Can identify the accented syllable in words		
SIGHT WORDS	29. Sight vocabulary is adequate for his age and grade level		
	20. Knows the basic core (Dolch) words		
SILENT AND ORAL READING COMPREHENSION	31. Comprehends when reading grade level materials silently		
	32. Comprehends when reading grade level material orally		
	33. Comprehends better when materials are read to him		
	34. Makes many errors (especially in oral reading) that disturb the meaning of the text		
	35. Uses syntactic cues to identify the word and to read with comprehension		
	36. Has an inadequate meaning vocabulary		
	37. Can use context cues to work out the pronunciation and meaning of a word		
	38. His rate of comprehension is significantly below the norm for his age and grade level		
	39. Can read his textbooks on an instructional level		

* Adapted from Eldon E. Ekwall, *Locating and Correcting Reading Difficulties*, third ed. (Columbus, Ohio: Charles E. Merrill Publishing Company, 1981, p. 5).

solution to the problem is presumed to lie in a compensatory program to deal with the pupil's "disadvantagedness." (Hittleman 1978: p. 410). Attempts to identify pupil deficiencies in visual and auditory discrimination fit here.

The *developmental hypothesis* suggests that pupils' reading achievement depends on how they have developed. The problem involves timing rather than potential. The diagnostic role becomes one of identifying the pupil's state of development. Pupils lacking appropriate readiness appear to be learning disabled, but the apparent disability may be merely a maturational lag, "the slow or delayed development of those brain areas which mediate the acquisition of age-linked development skills" (Hittleman 1978: p. 410). In fact, the deficits observed in poor readers, rather than representing a unique deficit or syndrome, often do parallel the behavior patterns of younger children.

Disability may also be the result of different modes of *processing information* and of solving problems. Hittleman notes that all pupils are disabled when expected to perform tasks in a manner not consistent with their mode of processing information.

Which hypothesis explains reading disability? Deficit hypothesis? Developmental lag? Preferred mode of processing information? They are probably all partially right, but also partially wrong.

If you recall, Chapters 4 and 5 (Part III of this book) dealt with the causes of reading ability and disability. Those chapters made a detailed study of the correlates of disability and related patterns of deviance (as measured in Step II) to specific causal events. Such areas as inadequate experiential background, inadequate language background, inadequate maturation, inadequacies in intellectual-social-emotional development, lack of motivation, instructional inadequacies, visual and auditory inadequacy, and deficiencies in other physical-physiological areas were discussed. You may want to review that section.

Step III of diagnosis relates reading behaviors to causes and projects a relationship between what the pupil does or does not do and what might be the underlying reason. The teacher or diagnostician needs to ask: Is the pupil a corrective or remedial reader? Is the pupil's poor reading performance basically in the area of comprehension skills, word-identification skills, rate skills, oral reading, or a combination of these. Is there a basic deficiency in the enabling skills that must be remedied before moving into the improvement of reading? Are there other factors that interfere with the pupil's reading? Is the pupil from a low socioeconomic background, with a simultaneous scarcity of reading materials in the home and a paucity of experience, or are dialect, articulation difficulties, and poor auditory discrimination substantive inhibitory factors? Is the pupil's disability explainable by less than 20/60 visual acuity at near point, by fusion problems, by high-frequency hearing losses, by attention difficulties (short attention span, undue amount of distractibility, impulsivity, hyperactivity), by inadequate cognitive development, by poor memory for sequences, by poor sentence sense, by low self-image, or by poor motivation and concentration? Is the disability explainable by difficulties in visual form perception or in eye-hand coordination? Are the pupil's difficulties in reading attributable to retarded speech development, inadequate listening comprehension, or a limited vocabulary? Is the disability explainable by a maturational lag or a delay in the development of certain neurological functions? Does the pupil have unusual difficulty with the orientation of figures in space, with the ordering of sounds in time, or with relating two or more perceptual modalities? Is the pupil's difficulty caused by an inability to code (label) or synthesize (chunk) information for effective storage and retrieval? Is the problem basically a memory problem? Many similar questions might and should be asked. The object of these questions is to identify both the type of disability and its causes, so that proper intervention may be applied.

As the diagnostician or teacher evaluates the symptomatology in a given case, the following questions should always be asked (Wilson 1967):

1. Did the pupil make the same error on both easy and difficult material, or were the errors chiefly the result of having to read material which was on a frustration level for the pupil? Diagnostic conclusions and remediation should not be based on errors made on material that is clearly too difficult for the pupil.
2. Were the pupil's slowness in reading and constant need to regress while reading the result of poor reading skill or simply of the desire to read carefully? Diagnostic conclusions should not be based on comprehension errors made over material that the pupil did not have time to read. Sometimes pupils' reading grade levels are inaccurate because they answered questions incorrectly on a test that they did not have time to finish.
3. Was the pupil's performance reliable or was it poorer than usual because he or she was nervous, upset, or distracted during the testing situation?

Most remedial programs move from the symptom or symptoms directly to remediation. At times this is all that can be done. Symptomatic treatment, not unlike the prescription of aspirin for a headache, is surely simpler than trying to identify causes, but it is also less fruitful and at times may be quite dangerous. Problem readers come in many varieties; their symptoms may be different, but so may be the causes. Differences, for example, between the reading problems of the disabled reader and those of the slow learner are identifiable both on a symptomatological and a causal level.

Consider now a few observations about Step IV of diagnosis.

REMEDIATION OF THE DISABILITY

Step IV of diagnostic procedure is the development of a plan for remediation. Identification of symptoms and causes is simply not enough. Diagnosis is meant to lead to remediation; it must serve as a blueprint from which remediation is structured. It must be directed toward formulating methods of remediation. Educational diagnosis is productive only if it is translated into specific educational strategies.

Differential diagnosis and precise assessment are the basis for effective educational programming. From a study of the diagnostic data, the teacher evolves a plan through which it is hoped the learner will improve in reading. Unfortunately, too often there is little or no correspondence between diagnosis and the precise specification of remediation procedures. Too often diagnosis serves only to emphasize the point that there is a problem which requires contact with the remedial service.

The remedial phase of diagnosis is by far the most significant. It translates the diagnostic data into statements about "what to do." The resultant remedial plan should help the remedial or classroom teacher develop and carry through the best possible corrective procedures. Step IV, the remedial planning phase, needs to address itself to each of the following areas:

1. It must specify what skills (of word recognition, comprehension, and so forth) need to be taught. Specificity is extremely important. The goals or objectives need to have the specificity of the following:
   a. The pupil will perceive rhyming words.
   b. The pupil will be able to carry out simple directions.
   c. The pupil will recognize and name all upper- and lowercase letters.
   d. The pupil will write upper- and lowercase letters when named.
   e. The pupil will recognize and use initial and final single consonants.

   In general, specific objectives need to be identified in the areas of auditory and visual perception, phonetic analysis, structural analysis, vocabulary development, and comprehension skills, including literal, interpretative, organizational, evaluative, and appreciative comprehension.

2. It must indicate what type of teaching is needed. Teacher objectives must be translated into pupil tasks. The diagnosis should include recommendations as to how the pupil should be taught. And it should provide insight into why a given method is recommended.

3. It should develop a plan for remediation, should establish an instructional sequence, and should establish priorities in teaching the deficient skills. It should plan for the development of those skills and abilities which are most necessary for immediate, successful reading.

4. It should identify the most efficient materials (both as to ability and interest level). Bond and Tinker emphasize that "there should be no compromise with difficulty even to get material of high interest" (1967: p. 454). The remedial plan should suggest materials that the pupil can handle and will be interested in. To do this, the teacher needs to know the pupil's instructional level. It is very important to remember that reading skills do not operate in a vacuum. The teacher needs proper materials. The recommendations thus should be quite specific as to the materials and should include suggestions for appropriate readability level of materials. Basal readers may be used if the pupil has not been exposed to them previously. Usually, modified basal readers (high interest, low readability level) or use of the language experience approach are preferable. Linguistically oriented readers may be indicated if the pupil needs to learn a large number of sight words in a relatively short time. Programmed materials may be suggested when the pupil needs step-by-step sequential presentation of materials or has a constant need for confirmation of progress.

5. It should indicate where the remedial work might best be done. The pupil may need to be taken out of the classroom or provided with a carrel.

6. It should recommend what the proper length of the remedial instructional period might be. The length will depend upon the skill being taught and on the physical and social-emotional maturity of the child. Half-hour sessions are probably suitable for first and second graders; eighth graders might be able to handle hour-long sessions.

7. It should indicate what adjustments need to be made for the pupil's special interests, for any emotional or physical defects, or for conditions in the child's home and community that may block reading growth.

8. It should offer suggestions on how to interpret to the pupil and to others the progress to be made. The remedial plan should develop in the pupil a feeling of responsibility for his or her own progress. It is important that the student realize that remediation is a result of personal effort; it cannot be donated by the teacher. Not only must the teacher give, but the student must be able and willing to take and to utilize the help given. Progress charts should be developed. The units of improvement need to be small enough so that progress can be recorded at frequent intervals.

9. It should suggest independent work activities for the pupil.

Certain additional principles should guide the teacher in corrective and remedial instruction:

1. Discover the child's area and level of confidence. Start where the pupil knows something. Nothing succeeds quite like success. One of the most therapeutic experiences for disabled readers is success. Thus, remedial instruction should begin at the level at which the pupil can succeed, probably about one grade level below the pupil's ability. This may be the pupil's instructional, or even independent, level. It must begin where the pupil is, not where the curriculum guide suggests that average sixth-grade learners, for example, are. It should begin with short assignments, inspire confidence, and restore status to the child in the eyes of his or her peers, parents, and teachers. It should remediate areas of weakness and capitalize on areas of strength. The teacher should work with deficit areas only after a pattern of success has been established.

    In dealing with corrective or remedial cases it is necessary to remember that

    a. The pupil is generally anxious and fearful of discussing his or her problem with an adult.

    b. The pupil's anxiety and guilt are especially high when he or she has experienced parental disapproval.

    c. One cannot *reteach* a pupil who never learned. One cannot remedy what was always lacking. Children receiving remedial education are distinct from normal readers in that they did not learn as a result of the educational procedures that were effective with most children. The methods and principles of remedial teaching and developmental teaching are distinguishable, if at all, by the emphasis on individualization. The remedial teacher may delve more precisely into the causes of the reading problem, may use a greater variety of materials and motivational devices, and may individualize the program to a greater degree. Diagnosis may be more intensive, instruction is perhaps more focused and more carefully paced, reinforcement may be more systematic, and assessment of mastery may be more vigorous, but remedial teaching is no more than this. It is not a magic hocus-pocus of special methods, but rather a more intense and personal application of the techniques used with others.

2. It is not uncommon to find children getting the correct answer using an incorrect method. An incorrect method is one (such as guessing) that will hinder future progress.

3. If a pupil is cured, it does not necessarily mean that the correct method of cure has been found. The intangibles of teacher-pupil motivations and teacher effectiveness generally play an important role. The good teacher may have good results regardless of the method used. The poor teacher may experience only failure.

4. No one remedial method has universal application. The remedial teacher should select the methods of instruction that are in harmony with the best mode of learning for a given child.

5. In dealing with remedial cases, psychotherapeutic principles should be incorporated into the process. The teacher should
    a. Develop a constructive relationship with the pupil (rapport). Drop the role of an authoritative teacher. Become an interested teacher.
    b. Be a genuine person.
    c. Totally and unequivocally accept the pupil despite the pupil's frequent failure in school.
    d. Have complete faith in the pupil's improvability and ability to read. It is a fact that if the significant adults in a pupil's life believe that he or she can succeed, his or her chances for success are appreciably improved.
    e. Develop a feeling of empathy, not sympathy. Objectivity must be maintained. If sympathy develops, the pupil feels that he or she has to please the teacher and that he or she cannot make mistakes. This often leads to tension.

6. Base teaching on sound learning principles: Speak slowly and give only a few directions at a time; allow the pupil to use his or her finger or marker if it is needed to focus attention; do not overload the pupil; provide frequent reinforcement; provide constant and varied drill (the pupil's short attention span and distractibility require it); break up assignments into small parts; call attention to the details in words; and have the pupil overlearn perceptual and associational responses until they become automatic. Remember that with severely disabled readers, violation of learning principles produces negative learning; for the disabled reader, remediation that does not help is likely to harm.

The classroom teacher, who finds that some students are not making the progress that they should, may benefit from a much broader exposure to remedial education than it is possible to give here, but he or she should be guided by two principles:

1. Develop those *skills* which are most necessary for immediate successful reading.
2. Identify and apply those *methods* which deal with both symptom and cause and which bring about proper remediation.

This book's primary emphasis has been on these important points. It shows the teacher how to develop the enabling or readiness skills (Chapters 6–7), the basic phonic and structural analysis skills (Chapters 9–11), the word-meaning skills (Chapter 12), and the comprehension and functional reading skills (Chapters 13–15). And Chapter 8 introduces the reader to reading methods.

We began this chapter with the premise that reading disability occurs when achievement in reading falls substantially below potential. It behooves the teacher then to help the pupil to achieve up to ability. This is surely the major purpose of remedial instruction.

There will be occasion to comment further on remediation in Chapter 17, the final chapter, which outlines the mechanics of corrective and remedial instruction.

SUMMARY

Chapter 16 has dealt with the basic aspects of the diagnostic process—screening, diagnostic testing, identification of causes, and remediation. These aspects reflect a central concept of diagnostic teaching. Diagnostic teaching of reading implies that the classroom teacher can work with students of varying levels of potential and achievement. A diagnostic teacher knows where the pupil is, where he or she could be, and at what level he or she should be aiming. The teacher has the ability to identify the pupil's level of achievement, to estimate potential for achievement, and to diagnose and prescribe for skill needs. Unless the teacher knows the pupil's potentials, teaching may be geared to previous levels of achievement and not to potentials *for* achievement.

Chapter 16 has outlined how to measure potential, how to assess achievement, and how to estimate the discrepancy between the two, if indeed there is such a discrepancy. It has suggested a program of assessment, to include assessment of the pupil's knowledge of the core words, assessment of instructional level in word recognition and comprehension in both oral and silent reading, and assessment of phonic and structural analysis skills. It has stressed in particular the use of criterion measures to identify skill needs.

QUESTIONS FOR DISCUSSION

1. Discuss prevention of reading disability as an important principle in the teaching of reading.
2. What does a comprehensive individual diagnosis consist of?
3. What are the criteria for estimating a child's independent and instructional reading levels?
4. Discuss the advantages and disadvantages of the informal reading inventory.
5. Which diagnostic test would you recommend for grade levels four through six?
6. Identify basic symptoms of reading disability and suggest possible causes for each. How would you go about identifying the specific cause?

PART
VI

organizing the elementary reading program

Part VI consists of only one chapter, Chapter 17, which bears the same title as Part VI. Chapter 17 distinguishes between developmental, corrective, and remedial instruction and discusses them each as a phase of the developmental reading program. This final section of the book discusses the characteristics of a good reading program and examines the needs (and how to meet them) of the slow learner, the corrective reader, and the remedial reader. The peculiar needs of the reluctant reader were discussed in the course of the text.

Of perhaps special significance in this chapter is the section that deals with planning and organizing for learning, and especially with the importance of skill or task training, functional analysis, process training, and the use of the process-task approach. Chapter 17 also describes the planning of a lesson and provides some guidelines for evaluating instruction.

17

ORGANIZING
THE ELEMENTARY
READING PROGRAM

The major concern in this final chapter is the organization of an effective reading program. It would be desirable if one could say "This is the way to organize for effective instruction," or "Here is a blueprint for an ideal program," but no one is that fortunate nor that omniscient.

Various innovative practices exist today, such as performance contracts by private industries, use of tutors, teacher aides, or other para-professionals, individualized instruction, programmed materials, and use of multimedia approaches and computers; but a good reading program cannot be lifted from a book and it cannot be purchased from a commercial source. It must be developed locally by a fully committed staff. Flashy hardware, shelves of material, and even specialized personnel do not make a good reading program. That is the product of the coordinated efforts of many people working over a long period of time (Otto and Smith 1970).

The position taken here is that there is only one reading program, and that is the developmental program. There are variant forms of instruction: developmental, corrective, and remedial; but diagnosis and corrective and remedial instruction must be an integral part of the developmental program. They must accompany all effective teaching.

DEVELOPMENTAL PROGRAM

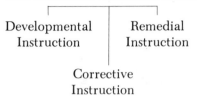

Developmental
Instruction

Remedial
Instruction

Corrective
Instruction

PRINCIPLES OF A GOOD
READING PROGRAM

Perhaps before venturing into the specifics of the developmental program, it will be helpful to identify the basic concepts and principles characteristic of a good reading program. These principles seem especially pertinent:

1. The most significant prerequisite seems to be administrative conviction, direction, and provision. The administrator alone possesses the prestige and persuasion to carry through a sound reading program. He or she must encourage the development of the program and insure that the reading philosophy is implemented in logical and innovative ways. The administrator needs to provide the impetus for defining the reading program's philosophy and must be the facilitator of that philosophy by extending it to the entire school.

   In Step I of the diagnostic process (see Chapter 16), the concern was to identify and classify pupils according to a taxonomic strategy: Is the pupil disabled in reading or not? It is a tragedy indeed to do this successfully only to find that either the program, the personnel, or the time are unavailable to provide specific intervention. The administrator is the only one who can make the reading program happen.

2. It must be clear why the program exists. Its purpose, goals, and objectives must be closely identified and stated behaviorally, and the objectives must be explicitly defined in terms of student needs.

3. Facilities, materials, and equipment must be adequate. Materials should vary in type, in interest, and in range of ability. The procedures for reinforcing the objectives and skills must be clearly identified.

4. The effectiveness of the program needs to be continuously appraised.

5. Reading instruction needs to have the support of the parents and must be developed conjointly with them. The educational remediation plan for a disabled learner, in particular, should be jointly determined by teacher, parents, and if possible, the pupil, and agreed to in writing by the parents and the school personnel. The agreement should state the objectives to be achieved, the teaching resources to be used (such as personnel, material, and space), the schedule for attaining these objectives, and last but not least, a plan for evaluating progress toward these objectives. When appropriate, this agreement should also list the specific obligations of the parent, the child, and the school.

6. Even when the reading program grows out of sound developmental principles, careful decisions must be made about *what to teach* (content), *how to teach* whatever needs to be taught (pedagogy), *in what sequences* to introduce skill teaching, and *where to teach* (the learning environment).

424

Because of the nature of the reading process and the individuality of learners, it seems illogical to suggest that certain learnings are peculiar to third grade, to seventh grade, or to senior high school. *Skill development does not come in capsule form.* One cannot dish out to seventh graders the seventh-grade capsule and to twelfth graders the twelfth-grade capsule.

It is for these reasons that all teachers including those engaged in remedial instruction, should be familiar with the *total* reading program. Each teacher needs to appreciate the program's continuity, each needs to know at what level the pupil is working, what the pupil has learned, and what he or she probably needs to learn. Introduction of reading skills is useless unless the pupil's subsequent reading experiences serve to maintain those skills.

If children are to receive adequate education, the teacher must also know *how* to teach the basic skills. The teacher must know what method to use in teaching skills and must be able to construct and use special projects that illustrate, organize, and develop the skills.

Where pupils are taught is almost as significant as *what* and *how* they are taught. The teacher (and indeed the parent) should ask: Does the pupil need a special class or should he or she be kept in the regular classroom? Where is it most likely that people will build on the pupil's strengths and remediate the pupil's deficiencies? Will what the pupil learns compensate for what he or she loses by being taken out of the regular classroom? In the future, grouping practices may become more flexible, with more subgrouping in the classroom and with specialists assisting regular teachers in the individualization of instruction.

7. There are other readers, besides disabled readers, who need special help. Among these are slow learners and disadvantaged or experientially deprived children. However, the slow learner usually does not need remedial instruction; he or she usually benefits most from paced instruction.

8. In the learning of basic skills there clearly are differences among children in *rate* of learning. The differences in learning *capacity* are just as significant. Some children may never master all the skills. This again reinforces the need for individualization of each pupil's reading program. The teacher must start the child at the point of success that he or she has attained and must permit the pupil to advance as far and as rapidly as he or she can.

THE MECHANICS
OF DEVELOPMENTAL, CORRECTIVE,
AND REMEDIAL INSTRUCTION

With the principles just stated to serve as a guide, examine now the mechanics of developmental, corrective, and remedial reading instruction.

Grouping for Developmental Instruction

Developmental instruction emphasizes reading instruction that is designed to systematically develop the skills and abilities considered essential at each level of reading advancement. Developmental instruction is the type of instruction that is given to the majority of children in the regular classroom. The entire book's focus has been on that type of instruction, and it bears no repetition here.

However, there are some observations to be made about grouping for instruction. Originally, the major adjustment made for individual differences in achievement was to fail the weak students and accelerate the gifted students. Historically, the next approach was some form of homogeneous grouping. Homogeneous grouping attempts to bring together those children who are most similar in age, ability, industry, previous experience, or other factors that affect learning. Age groups were used initially, but children of the same age did not necessarily achieve similarly. In the 1880s educators were already complaining about the lockstep in reading education. The complaint was that all students of similar age were forced to advance along a common front at the same rate of speed. Each student had the same book, was asked to learn the same material, and was judged by the same academic standards.

With the increased emphasis on individual differences in the 1920s, and with the publication of the twenty-fourth yearbook of the National Society for the Study of Education, *Adapting the School to Individual Differences*, came a new classroom organization. It was termed ability grouping and resulted in pupils being grouped into average, below-average, or above-average subgroups.

Frequently, reading ability has been used as the basis for forming instructional groups, with classes or subgroups within a class being organized on the basis of how well children read. The major problem pervading all attempts to group homogeneously, even on the basis of reading ability, is that children in the same grade have many differences, both inter- and intrapersonal, in addition to their differences in reading ability.

The advantages of ability groupings are said to be:

1. It makes it easier for the teacher to provide the experiences and materials of instruction which each level needs.
2. It does not waste the time of the superior readers nor bore them.
3. It does not undermine the self-esteem of the poor readers by throwing them into constant comparison with the superior readers.
4. It is more economical; there is obviously no economy in trying to teach students what they are not ready to learn or for that matter in making students who have already learned a skill mark time until all others in the class have learned the same skill.

Ability grouping, unfortunately, has not done what its proponents claimed. It has not appreciably reduced the variances in pupil performance and has often been accompanied by feelings of inferiority, frustration, and failure.

Today, although realizing that they must make curricular changes and class organizational changes that give consideration to pupil differences, teachers generally feel that this is best accomplished through heterogeneous groups with flexible subgrouping within the class.

The classroom teacher commonly spends some time with the entire class at the beginning of the class hour to introduce a new unit or topic or to give special assignments and directions. The class is taught as a whole if the teacher finds that all or most of the pupils are deficient in a particular skill, such as the rules of punctuation. Some time is spent with the entire group at the end of the period to summarize and to make homework assignments. Between the beginning few minutes and the end of the class, the teacher frequently finds it necessary to subgroup the youngsters according to their similarity of needs. Table 17–1 shows an organization of the reading period that makes group instruction possible and that permits greater individualization through the process of subgrouping.

The organization suggested in Table 17–1 permits the teacher to deal simultaneously with three groups, each at a different *level* of reading performance, each using its own set of materials, and each advancing at its own success level. Dividing the class into three groups according to reading levels permits the teacher to use basal readers more closely approximating the individual pupil's achievement level.

In another situation, where grouping is on a needs basis, one subgroup may be working on word recognition, another on comprehension, and a third on rate improvement, even though the youngsters composing a given subgroup might be reading on different levels. Thus a child reading on a third-grade level might be working with one reading on a fourth-grade level. Both of them may need help with diphthongs, consonants, or speech consonants.

If the situation prevails where all children on the same reading level are grouped together for reading instruction as in cross-grade or cross-age grouping, there still may be need of flexible subgrouping, as for example into the following

Table 17-1   The Reading Hour

9:00–9:10	Common Activities
9:10–9:55	Subgrouping within the Classroom
9:55–10:00	Common Activities

Group I 9:10–9:25 Directed reading	Group II 9:10–9:25 Free reading	Group III 9:10–9:25 Reading group with teacher
(Practice on what has been taught)	(Application of what has been taught)	(Actual teaching)
1. Workbooks 2. Mimeographed seat work 3. Questions on the board to answer 4. Use of programmed materials 5. Use of listening stations	1. Games 2. Free reading of library books—recreational reading 3. Seat work exercises	1. Basal reading instruction 2. Specific skill instruction
9:25–9:40 Free reading	9:25–9:40 Reading with teacher	9:25–9:40 Directed reading
9:40–9:55 Reading with teacher	9:40–9:55 Directed reading	9:40–9:55 Free reading

three groups: those receiving actual instruction, those practicing what has been taught, and those applying what has been taught.

Subgroups may be formed on the basis of a specific learning task, on an achievement basis, on an interest basis, or on a need (the need for the same skill development) basis. Students may be grouped to help each other in a learning activity (tutorial grouping). Such groups may be labeled *team groups.* The teacher may form intraclass groups for the purpose of reinforcement, reteaching, or independent work. Groups may also be formed on the basis of friendship patterns (sociometric techniques may be used to group on this basis).

When flexible subgrouping is used, the number of groups formed depends on such factors as the size of the class, the range of abilities and needs of the groups, the length of the reading period, the social maturity of the class, and the teacher's skill.

Grouping patterns, besides flexible subgrouping within the classroom, may take any one of the following forms:

1. Team teaching, permitting the grouping of children into very small groups when needed.
2. Half of the children reporting an hour early and leaving an hour early, with the other half coming an hour later, providing the teacher with a smaller group at both ends of the day. Reading and related language arts may be taught in these periods of reduced class size. Lunch periods might also be staggered with similar effect.
3. Reserve teachers or supplemental teachers working with groups of eight to twelve for one hour each day to help the lowest reading groups.
4. Master teachers (on the basis of one master teacher to six to ten less experienced teachers) working with small groups.
5. Remedial reading teachers giving demonstrations for classroom teachers.
6. Parents or other paraprofessionals being present in the classroom to listen to pupils read, help pupils select books, help pupils carry out assignments or directions, correct workbooks, supervise seat work, help pupils complete makeup activities, direct remedial drill, operate audiovisual equipment, distribute and collect materials, help pupils use the library, and help the teacher with record keeping.

Teaching method always functions in the context of a specific type of classroom organization. The good educational program has always had some aspect of the individualized program, and the individualized program does not eliminate all group aspects. If indeed teachers believe in the individuality of the learner, then it is difficult to ignore either approach, for one student may learn better in group situations, another in independent study. And even the same student may learn better when shifting from one approach to another as the occasion and his or her own needs demand. Some types of learning may best be obtained through individualized instruction; others, through group instruction. Groups of five may be best for discussion purposes; groups of two or three may be best for practice exercises.

With this in mind, consider a few observations:

1. At times it is desirable to teach a class as a whole.
2. Homogeneous grouping may reduce or narrow but will not completely eliminate the range of differences or achievement in a group.
3. Teachers often seem to prefer homogeneous grouping.
4. Grouping on the basis of *one* criterion does not necessarily make individuals more alike or other measures, nor is the particular trait chosen for the grouping necessarily the dominant determinant of behavior in the group.
5. Flexible subgrouping may prevent the stigma of failure. The pupil sees that the grouping is temporary and is designed to help him or her overcome a specific weakness. Pupils are not set apart permanently from their peers. Even the slow pupil may be helped to realize that slowness in one area does not mean slowness in all areas.
6. Combinations of group and individual instruction seem to be indicated at present.
7. No organizational plan of itself insures reading success. Even the most careful grouping does not eliminate the need for teaching reading to several different levels at the same time.
8. The search for a happy balance between grouping and individualization is still in progress. It would seem that heterogeneous grouping with mobile, flexible subgrouping, rather than homogeneous grouping, has the most to offer in the regular classroom. Flexible subgrouping permits the organization of clusters or subgroups of students with common reading needs. This appears to allow for the greatest amount of the individual growth.

Grouping for Corrective Instruction

Corrective instruction is a form of educational planning within the regular classroom. It stresses sequential development in word attack and comprehension skills but uses special techniques and materials and concentrates on a particular reading deficiency. Corrective instruction is given in addition to regular reading instruction. It refers to situations in which remedial activities are carried on in the regular classroom. Flexible subgrouping seems especially helpful in dealing with the problems of students who need corrective reading instruction.

Grouping for Remedial Instruction

Remedial instruction consists of remedial activities for the seriously disabled reader. It generally takes place outside of the framework of regular class instruction and is usually conducted by a remedial reading teacher or a special teacher of reading. Remedial instruction should thus be restricted to a small clinical group with severe symptoms of reading disability—those having difficulty mastering even the simplest mechanics of reading. In some schools there is no classroom space available, and the school may have to use mobile equipment to house the remedial program. In other schools, the remedial teacher may function out of the reading materials center.

Regardless of where the remedial room is, it should probably have two glass-partitioned offices: one for the remedial teacher and one for testing purposes. The glass partition permits the teacher to observe the testing from his or her own office. The room should also contain an audiovisual center, small-group practice areas, individual practice cubicles, desks, chairs, bookshelves, and office furniture.

Organizing for remedial instruction requires that pupils be dismissed from the regular classroom at scheduled times during the regular school day so that they can go to the remedial class or room for special instruction. The pupil reports to the remedial class for perhaps one lesson a day and then returns to his or her own classroom. It is important that the pupil get back to the regular classroom reading program as soon as possible. It is recommended, therefore, that every nine weeks the following question should be asked and answered about every pupil: Is the pupil ready to return to the regular classroom for work in reading?

Harris (1978) suggests that a forty-to-forty-five minute remedial session might be divided as follows: five minutes for assignments, getting materials together, and so forth; ten minutes for a teacher-directed group session, often centered on introducing a new skill; fifteen minutes of follow-up exercise on the group lesson; and ten minutes for individual activities.

The remedial room should be equipped with audiovisual materials of various types: filmstrip projector, tachistoscopes, accelerating devices, record players, children's records, tape recorder, listening stations, flash cards, and art supplies. It should contain books of all types, supplementary readers, programmed reading materials, multilevel reading laboratories, testing and diagnostic materials, magazines, games, and all kinds of word-recognition and comprehension-development materials.

In the remedial setting there needs to be a reduction in the pupil-teacher ratio. In the first place, pupils needing special attention exhibit a wider range of individual differences, have more frequent and greater psychological and physical limitations, and show a greater variation of reading difficulties. Secondly, the remedial teacher needs more time for individual diagnosis and remediation, for record keeping, and for consultation with parents, classroom teachers, and such specialists as physicians, psychologists, audiologists, psychiatrists, social workers, neurologists, neuropsychologists, and pediatricians.

Remedial teaching, because of its expense, is necessarily limited. It is a slow process and has to be conducted on a one-to-one basis or at most on the basis of one teacher to three to five students. Harris (1978) notes that groups of five or six are probably the maximum that allow for individual attention, and he adds that the total load at any one time of a remedial reading teacher should probably range between thirty-five and fifty children. Because of the expense involved, even when a special remedial teacher is available it is probable that instruction will be individualized rather than strictly individual.

The focus of remedial instruction is upon each individual learner, not upon groups of learners or upon grade-level performance. It is not what the group does that is important, nor even whether an individual measures up to grade level. The chief concern is that the individual learner do as well as he or she can.

Remedial teaching is empathic, well-focused, realistically paced, assessment-based instruction that facilitates learning (Otto 1977). It transcends methods, materials, and techniques, and even organizational schemes; it involves observable acts and demands a rigorous assessment of mastery. Otto contends that if remedial teaching is to be properly focused, paced, and individualized, it must be based on thorough and specific information about the learner, and that it must also give consideration to available resources, viable teaching alternatives, and realistic outcomes.

PROVIDING FOR THE PROBLEM READER

The problem readers are not simply disabled readers. They include the slow learner, the reluctant reader, the disadvantaged reader, the gifted under-achiever, and the disabled reader—both the corrective reader and the remedial reader.

The disabled reader's performance is by definition below his or her potential. The slow learner's performance, on the other hand, is substantially below age or grade level, but often is up to ability level. The pupil may not be a disabled reader even though he or she is a poor or problem reader.

The slow learner is often wrongly considered to be a disabled reader because grades in school are based on absolute performance rather than on how well pupils use their ability. The pupil is a poor reader in that he or she scores below grade level, but reading achievement might be quite appropriate and thus the slow learner should not be viewed as a disabled reader.

The gifted learner, even though reading at or above grade level, is often reading substantially below his or her ability level. Such a pupil is, in fact, a disabled reader but is sometimes euphemistically referred to as an underachiever in reading. Unfortunately, too many gifted learners have been allowed to underachieve.

The reluctant reader and the disadvantaged reader almost always read below their ability level and quite frequently below their age or grade level. Table 17–2 identifies characteristics of the various poor readers.

Chapter 4 outlined what provisions might be made for the reluctant reader. Consider now provisions for slow learners, corrective readers, and remedial readers.

THE SLOW LEARNERS

Slow learners may or may not be disabled in terms of their ability level, but they are retarded as to grade level. They generally have an I.Q. of between 70 and 90, and thus the major deficiency is in the area of intellectual development. These pupils often begin to read at age seven or later, read slowly and haltingly, and achieve below grade level in areas other than reading, such as spelling or

Table 17-2 Characteristics of Various Poor Readers

SLOW LEARNER	RELUCTANT READER	DISADVANTAGED READER	DISABLED READER	UNDERACHIEVER
Ability level is below 90 I.Q.	Can read but will not.	Potential often far exceeds performance.	Is usually of average or above average intelligence, although a disabled reader could also be a slow learner.	Ability level is substantially above average.
Generally reads on ability level.	The root of the reading difficulties is the mental attitude of the pupil.	Generally can learn and wants to learn.	Does not read on ability level.	Generally reads at or above grade level.
Generally reads below grade level; in terms of the requisites for success the pupil cannot achieve at his or her chronological grade level.	Solution to the reading problem must begin with a change of attitude.	The major deficiencies are language- and experience-related.	May or may not be reading below grade level.	Reads substantially below ability level.
Instruction needs to be adapted to the pupil's limited ability; the pace of instruction and teacher expectations must be realistic.		Often is deficient in auditory attention.	May show blocks to learning, especially emotional or neurological, which keep the pupil from learning to read.	
		Needs to learn how to learn.		

arithmetic. They do not need a remedial program. In fact, pushing them may only hurt them. They may interpret it as dissatisfaction with their wholehearted efforts.

Certainly major adjustments must be made for slow learners. They require a longer readiness program than does the average child. To begin formal reading instruction for these pupils before they have a mental age of six or more wastes the time of both teacher and pupil and results in pupil discouragement. The extended readiness program for the slow learner requires a variety of concrete experiences. It must progress slowly, with an emphasis on pupil activity.

Reading charts built from the direct experiences of the children are especially useful with slow learners. These charts will be read and reread with pride and satisfaction by slow-learning pupils at chronological ages considerably beyond those at which they can be used with the average child. In the early stages of their learning, listening will need to be stressed more than reading.

In the slow learner's reading program, considerable time should be spent on phonetic and structural analysis and on the mastery of simple comprehension skills. Slow learners appear to have little need for rapid reading skills. They will not read many different materials. The reading of the slow learners, especially when they are about ready to leave school, should be functional in nature.

Since the instruction of the slow learner occurs principally in the regular classroom, teachers may help the slow learner most by making adjustments in their own *expectations* of the pupil, in the *content* of the reading program, and in the *pace* and *rate* set for progressing through it. Some of the following techniques can be usefully applied to the slow learner in particular:

1. Provide a friendly, accepting, and encouraging relationship. Teacher attitudes substantially affect the performance of the slow learner: the teacher must believe in the improvableness of the learner.
2. Create a learning environment where simple reading is important: each learning experience should grow out of a need. Teach the pupil to read road signs, city directories, a letter from a friend, want ads, newspapers, an application blank, a menu; the slow learner needs to learn the working vocabulary required to function effectively as a citizen.
3. Pace the learning according to the student's ability:
    a. Introduce only a few materials at any given time.
    b. Review daily.
    c. Introduce materials in varied contexts.
    d. Simplify materials, explanations, and techniques.
    e. Use short periods of instruction.

    The basic vocabulary needs to be carefully controlled. Build many reading situations which require pupils to use their limited vocabulary over and over again. These students need aural-oral experience with words. The use of workbooks is especially recommended.
4. Coordinate all the language arts. Let the pupils do oral reading; sometimes they need to hear themselves say the word to understand what they are reading. A multisensory approach makes learning a concrete process for these pupils.

5. Do not underestimate the slow learner's ability to learn. Do not simply let these pupils do busy work.

6. Have the student see his or her progress in each lesson through individual and objective evidence. Nothing succeeds like observed and tangible success.

   a. Have the pupil keep a card file of words that he or she has learned to spell or read.

   b. Have the pupil construct a picture dictionary, perhaps of shop tools. The teacher needs to provide opportunities for the student to shine in some area.

   c. Have the pupil graph his or her progress each day.

7. Provide drill on new words.

   a. Let the student write, pronounce, and read the words.

   b. Use all the sense avenues.

8. Provide ample opportunity for review, repetition, and overlearning. Slow learners have difficulty with both immediate and delayed memory. They profit greatly from repetition which they need in order to retain information and to reinforce learning. They may get the gist of a story only in spurts, so that each rereading adds more to their understanding. The teacher needs to spend a great deal of time in developing new concepts. Slow learners also need step-by-step instruction. And they must be permitted to use their knowledge in various contexts.

9. Individualize instruction. The teacher needs to give as much individual help as possible.

10. Do not put the pupil into a remedial program simply because he or she is reading below grade level. Far too many slow learners fill Title I classes.

11. Use concrete illustrations to develop concepts and generalizations. Slow learners have difficulty with abstract reasoning. They are slow to perceive relationships, to make inferences, to draw conclusions, or to generalize. They need to be helped to reason through discussion periods, dramatization, and other such activities.

12. Provide short-range goals. Projects should not be too long, and rewards should be frequent.

13. Emphasize the visual and auditory characteristics of words. Word analysis is very helpful. The teacher may encourage lip movements, vocalization, and pointing to a word. The teacher needs to emphasize phoneme-grapheme relationships.

14. Break complex learning tasks into small steps. Programmed materials and teaching machines are especially recommended because they divide the task into small steps and use frequent repetition and other supportive cues to make the correct response dominant.

15. See to it that all directions are definite, specific, and detailed.

THE CORRECTIVE READERS

Corrective readers are either partially disabled readers or readers with a specific skill deficiency. The following statements characterize these readers.

TYPE 1: PARTIAL DISABILITY

1. The pupil's reading level is considerably lower than the pupil's mental age, but no other specific problem exists.

2. The pupil learns only after undue and laborious effort. He or she is like the

underweight child whose eating habits are not conducive to gaining weight but who, if a proper diet is followed, will gain.

3. The pupil learns after inhibiting factors have been removed.

4. The pupil's reading profile is relatively uniform.

5. The pupil may not have been ready for initial reading experiences and may have gradually fallen behind as schooling continued.

6. Instruction and reading materials generally have been above the pupil's level of ability and above his or her level of achievement in word-recognition and comprehension skills.

7. The pupil may have been absent from school at critical periods.

8. The pupil needs more experience in reading, including systematic instruction at his or her level of ability. Usually a visual-auditory technique or method is adequate. There is a need for major adjustment in materials and instruction and for a reading program that motivates the pupil to learn.

TYPE 2: SPECIFIC DISABILITY

1. Learning capacity is adequate, but skill deficiencies in regard to certain specifics in word analysis or comprehension indicate that the pupil has not profited from regular classwork as well as he or she might. The pupil has missed or has not profited from basic instruction in a given area.

2. The pupil's reading performance may be adequate overall in relation to ability, but diagnostic testing will reveal a low subscore on a test.

3. There is usually a need for training in the area of weakness rather than a need for total remediation in the basic skills.

4. The pupil should be kept in the regular classroom, but the specific skill deficiency should be dealt with in subgroups of three to five.

THE REMEDIAL READERS

Remedial readers or severely disabled readers tend to exhibit a common set of characteristics. In summary, these are as follows:

1. The remedial reader is more often a boy than a girl.

2. Severely disabled readers are clearly more likely to have been premature or to have survived some complication of pregnancy. Prematurity is commonest among mothers at the lowest socioeconomic level. However, some studies indicate that premature children who later became disabled readers often have brothers and sisters who were not premature and did not suffer from pregnancy complications but who still were disabled readers. This would indicate that prematurity may not be the significant factor.

3. There is also some evidence (Yahraes and Prestwich 1976) that frequently among disabled readers there is a disproprotionate number of adopted children.

4. The disabled reader's I.Q. is usually in the normal range, but the verbal I.Q. tends to be significantly below the performance I.Q.

5. There is more persistent and frequent left-right confusion and inappropriate spatial orientation of graphemes.

a. There is a greater incidence of reversal of concepts ("floor" for "ceiling," "go" for "stop," "east" for "west"). The remedial reader frequently makes kinetic reversals (*b-d*). The pupil reads entire words backward (*saw-was*), transposes letters (*flim* for *film*), and inverts letters. The pupil may perform as well if the book is held upside down.

b. The pupil often comes from a family in which there is a history of left-handedness.

c. The pupil shows evidence of delayed or incomplete establishment of one-sided motor preferences. He or she tends to be ambidextrous, or shows mixed dominance.

d. The pupil has difficulty in telling right from left.

6. Disabled readers generally exhibit disturbances in motor and visual-motor patterning and inadequate figure-ground discriminations. Clumsiness in manipulation of small muscle groups (such as in writing) is rather common. The execution in writing is jerky and arrhythmic. Penmanship is characterized by poorly formed and irregular characters, malalignment, omissions, linkages that are too short or too long, and fusion of letters.

7. Remedial readers often have poor auditory discrimination skills. They are unable to deal with the temporal order of phonemes. Doehring (1968) found in his study of thirty-nine disabled readers, aged ten to fourteen, that deficiencies in sequential processing abilities, both visual and verbal, were intrinsically associated with reading disability.

8. The disabled reader often has speech difficulties. The jerkiness in writing described in point 4 is often accompanied by jerky, stumbling, and explosive speech (cluttering). Stuttering, lisping, and stammering are also quite common. Failure to understand what is said and slowness in learning to talk are often indicative of later problems in reading.

9. The disabled reader tends to be hyperactive, distractive, distractible, and impulsive. The pupil has a short attention span, perseverates excessively, and has a low frustration tolerance (Orlow 1974; Hartman 1974). There is some evidence that disabled readers are unable to shift attention, an ability required for successful reading.

Sawyer (1974), noting that problem solving requires the ability to direct one's attention to relevant information, points out that some learners may be disabled because they have constricted attention abilities. Disabled readers are likely to attend equally to all stimuli, thus finding it difficult to withhold attention from some stimuli (Santostefano, Rutledge, and Randall 1965). Good learners exhibit flexible attention abilities, being able to attend to some stimuli while ignoring others.

Consider now in greater detail the behaviors that characterize the reading of the remedial reader. These behaviors generally relate to the identification of the symbols, the identification of the phonemes and the association of the phonemes with the symbols, and the association of meaning with the symbols. At each of these points difficulties can arise.

DEFICIENCY IN VISUAL IDENTIFICATION

This deficiency reveals itself in many ways and can be described in many ways. The learner may have a letter- or a word-naming difficulty (anomia). The pupil may have poor visual discrimination skill, be weak in visual imagery, and have poor memory for visual sequences. The learner may have great difficulty with visual recognition and recall of familiar words.

The following observations relating to deficiencies in visual identification are common when one deals with a severe disability:

1. The pupil does not experience the flash global identification of a word as a whole. He or she cannot develop a gestalt for the word or indeed for the letter. Because of inadequate figure-ground discrimination the pupil sees words on the printed page as an undifferentiated design rather than as an entity.
2. The letter standing alone has no language identity. *S* may be described as a traffic sign.
3. Spelling of words may be peculiar. This is because the pupil ignores many details in words.
4. The reading is arrhythemical and replete with word-recognition errors. The pupil demonstrates more vowel, consonant, reversal, omission, addition, substitution, perseveration, and repetition errors than is usual.
5. The pupil will ask again and again for help with the same word.
6. The pupil cannot pronounce unfamiliar words. The pupil has a tendency to guess wildly at words. He or she pays attention to specific letters and guesses wildly at the rest (*horse* becomes *house*). The rendition of a word is often phonetically unrelated to the desired response (*dog* becomes *chay*).
7. The pupil has an unusual amount of difficulty with similar-appearing words (*bed-fed*).
8. The pupil vocalizes excessively while reading silently.

Readers who have difficulty in identifying the word visually might be helped by kinesthetic-tactile techniques (the Fernald method) if they have not yet acquired visual recognition for letters. Remedial phonics (such as the Orton-Gillingham approach) may be used if letter recognition has occurred. For a description of these methods, see Chapter 8.

DEFICIENCY IN ASSOCIATING PHONEME AND GRAPHEME

The basic deficiency here is one of inability to relate symbols, to associate the proper phoneme with the proper shape, or to match a visual sequence with an auditory sequence. There is an intersensory transcoding difficulty or a recoding difficulty. The pupil has great difficulty acquiring phonic skills. Sometimes this happens because the auditory symbols fail to achieve identity. The pupil cannot differentiate between the sounds that are heard, or as a result of inadequate figure-ground discrimination, the pupil hears speech as an undifferentiated noise.

There are numerous examples of the phoneme-to-grapheme mixup in the English language; the phoneme /f/, for example, can be written as *f* (*scarf*), *ff* (*chaff*), *gh* (*laugh*), and *ph* (*graph*). Another term for the mixup is *irregular orthography*. The mismatching of phoneme and grapheme is the heart of the problem for many reading-disabled children (Bannatyne 1971a).

DEFICIENCY IN ASSOCIATING
MEANING WITH SYMBOLS

The disabled reader also has meaning and comprehension problems. Such pupils frequently exhibit an associative learning disability, making it impossible for them to associate experiences and meanings with symbols. On more advanced levels (ten to fourteen years) they will have difficulty organizing what they read or study.

Rutherford (1971) notes that the inability to generalize from word to concept seems to be one of the three most limiting features of dyslexia. The others, according to Rutherford, are the inability to translate from sound to symbol and faulty memory for sequences. The symbolic abilities are impaired, with the result that even though the learner has conceptual strengths he or she cannot come up with proper symbolic designations (*height* for "tallness" or *summer* for "hot weather"). The pupil cannot translate perceptions into symbols (Zintz 1972). Comprehension is poor, and rate of comprehension is significantly below the norm.

The Severely Disabled Readers

In *Diagnosis and Remediation of Reading Disabilities* (Dechant 1981a), we described various models of reading disability. Let us briefly summarize here our own model. This is, a functional-structural model which groups all reading disabilities into six types, with four of these types being considered severe reading disabilities (see Figure 17–1) or disabilities associated with remedial readers. In other words, when one studies remedial readers, four strands of severely disabled readers emerge, namely, secondary dyslexia, maturational dyslexia, primary dyslexia, and alexia. Begin with cases of secondary dyslexia or disability.

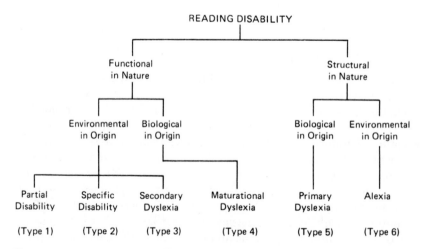

Figure 17-1   Dechant's Grouping of Types of Reading Disability.

438

Type 1: secondary dyslexia. Secondary dyslexia or reading disability is by far the most common form of disability seen in remedial readers. This syndrome is characterized by the following:

1. The learner's problems are more severe than those of the corrective reader and include inability to use contextual clues, poor comprehension, wild guessing at words, inability to deal with individual letter sounds or to move from sound to symbol, reversal tendencies, and difficulty in structural analysis.
2. There is usually no single identifiable cause of the disability. Multiple causality is indicated, with the reading disability closely related to intellectual, emotional, environmental, psychological, or educational factors. It is probable that some one factor is the precipitating cause; other factors are contributing causes.
3. The capacity to read is intact. This learner reads poorly, but he or she has a normal reading potential. The disability is not innate or the result of a deficit in structure or functioning of the brain. The causation is not primarily within the nervous system. There is usually no familiar history of reading disability.

Diagnosis of secondary dyslexia concerns itself with the conditions that are now present in the learner in order to give direction to a program of reeducation. The diagnostician is concerned with the reading strengths and limitations of the learner and with those conditions within the educational environment that need to be corrected before remedial instruction can be successful and the pupil can be expected to make maximum progress.

Learners whose reading disability is found to be secondary dyslexia should be taught in small groups in a remedial setting.

Type 2: maturational dyslexia. Maturational dyslexia is a severe reading disability in which a maturational lag, or a delay in the development of certain neurological functions that children must possess in order to learn to read, is the primary causative agent.

The developmental-lag hypothesis was first proposed by Samuel T. Orton. Orton (see Chapter 5) noted that children with severe reading disabilities had difficulty in orientation (*b* was perceived as *d*), in sequencing (letters within words were transposed: *split* became *spilt*), and in recognizing and copying shapes. Orton gave these behaviors a maturational-lag interpretation. According to Orton, the lag is caused by inadequate development of cerebral dominance, and Orton suggested that the learner in these instances lacks the neurological development needed to succeed in reading.

Maturational dyslexia thus indicates the presence of some brain pathology (which may have an inherent biological basis), but the disability is not aphasic in nature. There is no structural defect or deficiency. The condition flows from cerebral immaturity or a maturational lag or slowness in certain specialized aspects of neurological development. There is a basic disturbance in the pattern of neurological organization without evidence of any definite brain damage; the disorder is a problem of neurophysiological variation, not a defect or disease. Brain dysfunction is not always the result of brain damage; it may be hereditary or developmental in etiology, and maturational dyslexia represents such a dysfunction. There is delayed or irregular neurological development. The potential is there, but it has not yet been realized. Such pupils are late bloomers. They are not yet matured, but they are capable of maturing.

There is frequently a familial history of reading disability and generalized language disturbances associated with maturational dyslexia, with the problem more commonly being inherited through the father's side of the family. Orton (1928) repeatedly noted family histories showing the existence of language disabilities and confused dominance among the family members. Hallgren (1950), Norrie (1960), Herrmann (1959), Bakwin (1973), and Geschwind (1971) all supply strong evidence for the familial nature of some forms of reading disability.

Type 3: primary dyslexia. Primary dyslexia is more difficult to describe than maturational dyslexia because there is no single clinical feature that can be accepted as pathognomonic. There is no invariable core of symptoms. It is a defect in the visual interpretation of verbal symbols and in the association of sounds with symbols. Children with primary dyslexia fail to learn to read even though they have had appropriate instruction, come from a culturally adequate home, are properly motivated, have adequate sensory equipment, have normal intelligence, and show no gross neurological defect or brain pathology (Eisenberg 1966). The disability nevertheless is based on some organic incapacity (Quadfassel and Goodglass 1968). The neurological signs are minimal but they are inborn or genetically rather than environmentally determined.

With primary dyslexia there is a *structural* variation that makes it difficult to learn to read. There is a loss of function rather than simply an absence of function as is the case in maturational dyslexia. It could be considered a massive unreadiness for reading (Money 1962). The student is deficient in even the most fundamental basic reading skills; it is almost as though he or she had never been in school. Remedial instruction often seems to have little effect, and where it is effective, it may well be that the learner is a maturational dyslexic rather than presenting a genuine case of primary dyslexia.

Primary dyslexia may be differentiated from other forms of dyslexia chiefly in these ways: there is a neurological, organic, or structural cause for the disability; and there tends to be a family history of disability.

Type 4: alexia. Alexia is the loss of the ability to read as a result of damage, injury, or lesion to the association and connection areas in and around the angular gyrus of the language-dominant cerebral hemisphere. For most of us this is the left hemisphere. With alexia there is clear brain pathology which prevents the learner from becoming a reader, or which takes away the reading ability that once existed. The person may see black marks on paper but does not recognize that they represent words. The past history of such an individual often reveals normal speech development initially, and there usually is no family history of reading difficulty.

Instructional techniques alone cannot come directly to grips with the reading problem. This is a reader who is neurologically unable to read. The reading disability is actually a symptom of an earlier lesion to the nervous system.

Neurological signs may be soft (poor ocular convergence, hyper- or hypoactivity, and difficulty sustaining attention) or hard (problems with muscle tone, muscle strength, and synergy or the ability of muscles to carry out a joint operation). Other indications of brain injury are abnormal responses of deep reflexes (those of the knee or the sole of the foot) and the cogwheel-type rigidities such as bringing the arm down in a series of ratchetlike movements. The brain-injured child tends to be hyperactive, to have a short attention span, to be impulsive, and to exhibit a low frustration level. The pupil may flit from one activity to another without apparent purpose or meaning.

If the symptoms described predominate in a given case, the teacher may suspect neurological impairment, especially when there is a history of neurological dysfunction in the family, when there have been certain complications of pregnancy (German measles, Rh incompatibility, threatened abortion) or birth (prematurity, Caesarean, forceps delivery, asphyxia), when the child was poisoned, or when he or she suffered a head injury resulting in unconsciousness. Alexia differs from primary dyslexia principally in that in alexia the neurological dysfunction is environmentally induced and the condition is not family-related.

PLANNING AND ORGANIZING FOR EFFECTIVE LEARNING

To this point the discussion has identified the principles of a good reading program, discussed the mechanics of developmental, corrective, and remedial instruction, especially the pros and cons of grouping, and given some suggestions for providing for the problem readers: the slow learner, the corrective reader, and the remedial reader. The present section deals with planning and organizing for effective learning.

The teacher of reading needs to have specific plans for organizing effective instruction. This is particularly so when performance problems appear. Then the teacher must have a set of problem-solving tools for restoring appropriate performance. Four such tools are (1) skill or task training, (2) functional analysis, (3) process or ability training, and (4) process-task training (Kirk 1976).

Skill or Task Training

Task training involves the identification of daily objectives to be attained and the division of lessons into subskills. It involves an analysis of the behaviors needed to succeed in the task, a definition of behavioral objectives, and the organization of a program of instruction.

The development of a unit of instruction usually involves five steps: task analysis; preparation of criterion measures; preparation of objectives, if needed;

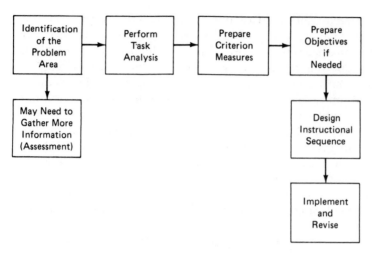

Figure 17-2 Skill of Task Training: Developing a Unit of Construction.

preparation of the instructional sequence; and finally, implementation, testing, and revision (Johnson and Morasky 1977). These steps are outlined in Figure 17–2.

The various steps or phases of the instructional cycle coincide to a great degree with what has become known as the Individual Educational Plan (IEP). The IEP is a requirement of the Education of All Handicapped Children Act (P.L. 94–142). This law mandates that every handicapped child must have an individually planned and implemented educational program. While the IEP is required only of handicapped children, we believe that it is equally appropriate for all children who have been singled out to receive special instruction or services. An IEP includes the assessment of the child, the formulation of long-range goals and short-term objectives, a description of the proposed educational intervention with specification of type and duration of each aspect of instruction, and an evaluation of the effort.

Step I, *task analysis*, is the identification of the behaviors, subtasks, discriminations, and the like which the pupil must possess in order to perform the task successfully. It is the isolation, description, and sequencing of the necessary subtasks which, when mastered, enable the pupil to perform the objective (Bateman 1971). Task analysis is the breaking down of a body of content into its component parts; it is the differentiation of tasks into micro units or subskills which the learner can master a step at a time. The teacher must decide *what* he or she expects the pupil to learn. "Until this is done, there is no basis for *focusing* instruction" (Otto 1977: p. 202). A central purpose for diagnosis (Otto et al. 1974) is to decide *what* to teach. Diagnosis helps the teacher to determine what the pupil needs.

Teaching children to swim (the task) may require teaching children how to kick their legs, how to tread water, how to keep from breathing under water,

442

and so forth. These are the subtasks. Task training assumes that the pupil's problem is lack of experience and practice with the task.

The *criterion measures*, Step II, are tests used by the teacher to identify whether the pupil can do the subtasks required to perform the task. If the pupil can complete each criterion measure adequately, then he or she has the skills needed for the overall task. The criterion measures are the enabling objectives; they are referred to as criterion measures because the teacher determines the level of performance that is adequate.

A criterion measure for the blending task may require the pupil to recognize and say the phonemes in sequence in four out of five teacher-presented words. Such an investigation might reveal, for example, that the pupil can successfully perform some of the subtasks or enabling objectives but not enough of them to be successful in blending. The pupil would then be considered as unable to blend.

The *objectives*, Step III, are descriptive statements indicating the goal to be attained. Thus, the objective might be expressed as follows: Given some words pronounced by the teacher, the pupil is able to identify the letter that represents the initial sound of each word eight times out of ten. The objective is thus a description of the pupil's behavior after instruction. It is a restatement of the goal in behavioral terms or in terms of pupil behavior, and for this reason is termed a behavioral objective. It focuses on the observable outcome of instruction, hence the observable performance.

Stating of behavioral objectives should specify (1) the type of behavior that will be accepted as evidence of mastery, (2) the conditions under which the behavior is expected to occur, and (3) the criteria of acceptable performance or mastery. In this version of the example given earlier—*Given some words pronounced by the teacher*, the pupil is able to identify the letter that represents the initial sound of each word EIGHT TIMES OUT OF TEN—the italicized portion represents the conditions, and the capitalized portion represents the criterion of acceptable performance.

It is not always necessary to state the objective. The final task description may be an adequate statement of the objectives.

Since the writing of objectives is often a difficult process, the following are offered as models:

1. Given a list of words, the pupil will identify all those that contain consonant blends and consonant digraphs and will put one line under the blends and two lines under the digraphs.
2. Given words containing the vowel-consonant-silent *e* combination, the pupil will identify the vowel as representing a long sound.
3. Given a list of singular nouns, the pupil will add either *s* or *es* to form the plural of each word.
4. Given sets of words with *not* and *will*, the pupil will combine these words to form contractions.

5. Given a paragraph in which the main idea is clearly stated, the pupil will identify the main idea by drawing a line under it.
6. Given examples of open and closed syllables, the pupil will identify the vowel sound as representing either a long or a short sound.
7. Given a paragraph with a main idea and a number of details, the pupil will put two lines under the main idea and one under the supporting details.
8. Given words containing the letter c, the pupil will put a check mark beside each word that contains a soft c sound.

The *instructional sequence*, Step IV, includes the design and construction of procedures and materials that will be used in teaching the skills identified in the task analysis. A second purpose of diagnosis is to help the teacher to decide *how* to teach what needs to be taught (Otto et al. 1974). Diagnosis attempts to match learner and means of instruction. Diagnosis should identify what skills need to be taught, give information about the pupil, and lead to the identification of the most promising instructional strategies.

The teacher may put the entire instructional program on tape so pupils can use the materials independently. This technique would be quite helpful in developing auditory discrimination of sounds. Pupils might begin by listening for differences and similarities in a group of parallel words (*car-bar*) and recording their answers in a workbook.

Implementation, testing, evaluation, and revision, Step V, allow the teacher to establish empirically that the instruction package is valid—that it actually teaches the behaviors described in the objectives. It is also important that what has been learned leads to functional changes in reading which result in increased ability on the task. The whole purpose of task or skill training, together with objective-based instruction, is improved ability to read connected text.

Functional Analysis

Functional analysis is another tool available to the teacher, one which identifies the relationships between behavior and environmental events. It requires the teacher to ask the following questions (Towle and Ginsberg 1975):

1. What is the exact behavior being examined? (Is it possible to describe the action?)
2. How frequently does the behavior occur?
3. What conditions precede the occurrence of the behavior?
4. What events immediately follow the behavior?

The teacher can isolate the events that influence the pupil's performance (1) by analyzing the pupil's performance in different settings and (2) by comparing the setting conditions. From such analysis should emerge a knowledge of the conditions which produce errors and the contexts within which they occur.

Process or Ability Training

Process training focuses on the process rather than the product. For example, children need to develop adequate visual discrimination if they are to be able to read. The assumption is that increasing the pupil's visual discrimination will increase reading ability.

Process training assumes that there exists within the pupil a particular disability that inhibits the learning process, irrespective of the teacher's restructuring of the task. The explanation for an individual's inability to swim, for example, might be identified as weak upper arm and shoulder muscles, and remediation might consist of arm and shoulder exercises, weight lifting, and the like. A case of severe reading disability may be explained as the result of visual memory deficit (Hinshelwood's (1917) concept of "word blindness," for example), and amelioration might be sought in improving the ability to remember (Kirk and Gallagher 1979). Development of the enabling skills discussed in Chapter 8 is a process approach.

The Process-Task Approach

The process-task approach is also termed the aptitude-instructional interaction (Kirk, Kliebhan, and Lerner 1978) or aptitude-task interaction (Kirk and Gallagher 1979). It requires both task analysis and pupil analysis and both task training and process training. Instruction is matched to pupil aptitude (or lack of aptitude) to produce the best interaction between the two. Thus, remediation may involve the teaching of visual discrimination (process) of letters and words (task) rather than of geometric figures. This approach is synonymous with the diagnostic-prescriptive method. The emphasis is on training in the process of visual discrimination of the task needed to do well in reading.

Corrective reading generally involves task or skill training; the pupil may need help in word recognition, vocabulary, phonics, or some other skill. Remedial reading generally calls for process-task training as well. The Fernald method is an example of a process-task remedial procedure. It attempts to remediate a developmental disability (inadequate visual memory) in the task of reading, teaching the pupil visual sequential memory and attention to detail through the process of writing words from memory (Kirk and Gallagher 1979).

Reading disabilities should not be isolated from the instructional factor. What has been learned about children with reading disabilities should be related to both developmental and remedial instruction. Symptomatological treatment is not enough; somehow the teacher must tie together symptom, cause, and remediation. It may not be the visual discrimination deficit alone, for example, that causes a disability, but the use of inappropriate methods for a given pupil. We have indeed come full circle. The attempts to identify children's preferred modes of processing information now make sense. The choice of methods for a pupil depends on this information. And because of the aptitude-instructional interaction, causes and indeed correlates (such as the relationship between visual discrimination and reading) take on new significance. The aptitude-instructional interaction explains why the pupil with high frequency hearing losses who is taught by a phonics method becomes a reading disability.

The implications of this method are

1. The teacher should remediate the pupil's deficit by using a reading task. (This would explain, for example, why matching of geometric forms, as indicated earlier, would not be too effective.)
2. Instructional adaptations can ameliorate or compensate for the correlates that might otherwise interfere with the pupil's ability to learn to read.

PLANNING A READING LESSON

It is now possible to present a lesson plan based on one of the tools for effective instruction just described. The lesson plan presented in Figure 17–3 is a simplified version of the task approach. The task analysis, criterion measures, and objectives are all stated in Column 1. Columns 2 (Materials) and 3 (Instructional Strategies and Procedures) are two separate parts of the process of designing the instructional sequence.

A good lesson plan should thus state (1) the specific purposes, goals, or objectives of the lesson, (2) the materials needed to achieve the objectives of the lesson, (3) the procedures required to achieve the objectives, and (4) the amount of time that will be allotted to each activity. Figure 17–3 summarizes a portion of a good lesson plan.

The objectives should be challenging but well within the learner's potential to master. Since young children and disabled readers tend to have short attention spans and low tolerance for sustained work, each activity should be timed so the pupil can complete the activity without undue fatigue, boredom, and frustration.

It is important that the objectives of successive lesson plans are hierarchically organized. There needs to be some continuity from lesson to lesson. The lesson plan should identify exactly what materials will be used, including for printed materials the name of the publisher, the title, the page on which the activity is located, and the level for which is it intended.

It is extremely important to chart pupil progress. Pupils should be actively involved in selecting and developing the type of progress chart that will record their progress. Skills to be learned should be taught in hierarchical sequence as much as possible, even though Chall (1976) questions whether we have the knowledge, based either on research or clinical experience, to arrange skills hierarchically. Nevertheless, the teacher is aided by checking his or her sequence against one of the many hierarchical lists of the word recognition and comprehension skills.

The use of context cues should be taught during each remedial session.

DAILY LESSON PLAN

Pupil _____ Lesson _____

Age _____ Instructional Level _____

SPECIFIC OBJECTIVE	MATERIALS	INSTRUCTIONAL STRATEGIES AND PROCEDURES	TIME IN MINUTES
Pam will be able to pronounce five new words from the Dolch Basic Sight Word List. 1. laugh 2. warm 3. together 4. again 5. please	Words from the Dolch *Word List* ——————— 4" x 6" cards with words printed on front and teacher-produced sentence using the word on the back ——————— Felt tip pen or crayon	1. Present words, one at a time, pronouncing them for the pupil. 2. Have the pupil pronounce the word. 3. Present the sentence on back of the card and have the pupil underline the word. 4. Have the pupil make up a sentence using the word. The teacher records the sentence and has the pupil underline the word and read the sentence. 5. The pupil again pronounces the word. 6. After all 5 words are presented in this manner, shuffle the cards and present them for a mastery check.	10
Pam will be able to answer correctly at least 3 of 4 questions after reading "silently."	The four questions Pam will answer are: 1. _____ 2. _____ 3. _____ 4. _____ (Teacher will indicate whether the question calls for literal, inferential, evaluative, or appreciative comprehension)	The teacher will set purposes for reading and after the reading will ask the questions. The 4th question will be an inference question, calling for an understanding of: 1. Implied meaning 2. Anticipating outcomes	10

Figure 17-3 Daily Lesson Plan

The DRA, or a portion of it, should be used in every lesson. Finally, it is absolutely imperative that the teacher log each activity. Specificity is the chief criterion. What was the miscue made by the pupil? What kind of comprehension question was missed? Clear and accurate data of this sort are crucial to the testing and revision phase where the teacher modifies instruction as pupil needs demand.

Teachers may think it too much of a challenge to develop a lesson plan for each pupil. Nevertheless, there should be a lesson plan for the class as a whole, for each of the subgroups, and if individualization means anything there must ultimately be one for each individual pupil.

GUIDELINES FOR EVALUATING INSTRUCTION

Consider now some guidelines for evaluating instruction. The teacher needs to determine the effectiveness of various procedures in terms of the gains in reading achievement. Over the course of years many quite different procedures have been suggested for evaluating instruction, especially remedial teaching, but too few data are available concerning their relative effectiveness. Young (1938) suggested that the personality of the teacher and his or her ability to enlist each child's active cooperation are more important than the specific method used. On the other hand, numerous studies of remedial and diagnostic methods indicate that reading difficulties can be either entirely or at least largely eliminated by the use of the appropriate instructional method.

Guthrie, Seifert, and Kline (1978), in an analysis of fifteen studies, found substantial evidence that remedial reading instruction can help pupils to learn to read. Successful programs shared the following characteristics: the pupils were of elementary age, of average intelligence, and of middle socioeconomic backgrounds; the teacher-pupil ratio was no higher than one to four; and the program lasted at least fifty hours.

Balow (1965) found that remedial instruction was effective in dealing with the problems of the disabled reader, but he also noted that severe reading disability is not corrected by short term intensive treatment and should instead be considered a relatively chronic illness needing long term treatment rather than the short course typically organized in current programs.

Rankin and Tracy (1965) and Tracy and Rankin (1967) list three methods of measuring and evaluating individual differences in reading improvement.

1. *Crude gain.* In this situation comparable tests are given before (pretest) and after (posttest) a remedial program. The score at the start of the program is subtracted from the score at the end of the program, and the difference is considered as improvement.

2. *Percentage gain.* In this approach the gain between the pretest and posttest is expressed as a percentage of the initial score. The formula then is percent of
   $$\text{gain} = \frac{\text{pretest-posttest}}{\text{posttest}}$$

3. *Residual gain.* This is the difference between the actual posttest score and the score that was predictable from the pretest score.*

* For a discussion of this third procedure the reader may want to consult the articles by Rankin and Tracy cited above in the *Journal of Reading,* March 1965, and March 1967.

Ekwall (1972) suggests three methods for measuring pupil progress: (1) comparing pretest and posttest results; (2) using a control group; and (3) using the ratio-of-learning criterion, which is a measurement of children's learning rates (amount learned per year) prior to entering a special program versus their learning rate during the program.

Many faulty conclusions apparently have been drawn from reading research because residual gain was not considered. As Sommerfield (1957) points out, there is a natural tendency for those people who score at the extremes of a distribution on the first test to score closer to the mean of the distribution on the second test. The scores tend to regress toward the mean. However, Harris (1978) observes that children who are not given remedial help simply do not regress toward the mean; instead they fall farther behind.

Dolch (1956) has cautioned that research can come up with the wrong answers unless it is carefully planned and watched. He recommends vigilance in these areas:

1. Compare equally able teachers working equally hard.
2. Compare pupils of equal ability and equal home influences.
3. Compare equal school times and emphases.
4. Watch size of class carefully.
5. Beware of misleading averages.
6. Watch for unmeasured results.

In discussing these points, Dolch emphasizes that the teacher who is using the method is frequently far more important than the method used. Teacher competency, rather than the system of instruction, is often the critical determinant of achievement. Numerous variables enter into any experiment. The reported results of experimental reading programs may be influenced by the subjects involved, the techniques and materials used, the conditions under which the study was done, the tests employed, the statistical devices used, and undoubtedly the bias or misinterpretations of the investigator.

Studies often do not make allowance for the differences in both skill and motivation among teachers. Control groups tend to be taught by the "regular" teachers, experimental groups by teachers who have a special interest in the project and can give more time to their students. Studies do not control for the Hawthorne effect, namely, the learning that results simply because the program is new and presents for students and teachers alike an opportunity for recognition. Results are frequently evaluated by means of test scores, but this is not necessarily the significant, and the significant is not necessarily measurable. There are no published tests available, for example, that measure how well students read to gain information in specific courses. In many instances achievement at the moment is evaluated; the transfer value of what has been learned is rarely evaluated.

There also is a difference between educational significance and statistical significance. Sometimes a difference of one-tenth of a year is significant at the .05 level of confidence, but it may have no practical significance.

Weiner (1961) notes that to evaluate changes in reading behavior one must consider all relevant functions: perceptual, integrative, and motivational. It is necessary to evaluate processes rather than simply end products, to evaluate measurable and nonmeasurable changes, and to evaluate changes in self-concept and attitudes as a result of remedial programs. It is necessary to find ways of analyzing the process that produced the outcome and of determining cause-and-effect relationships. Weiner points out that evidence of improvement involves greater accuracy in responses to printed material, greater dependability, greater retention of and confidence in one's responses, and greater speed.

In advancing a clinical concept of assessment, Weiner stresses the qualitative aspects of assessment and suggests that gains must be measured from the point of actual departure and not from an arbitrary zero point on a grade-level scale. Pupils in need of remedial services start not from scratch, but from behind scratch.

Harris (1978) suggests two criteria for judging whether a pupil is ready to succeed without further remedial help: (1) the ability to read required classroom assignments with passable comprehension and (2) the establishment of the habit of reading for pleasure, and thus being able to continue to practice the new skills.

SUMMARY

This final chapter of the book has offered some practical suggestions for organizing for effective instruction, for meeting the needs of slow learners and of corrective and remedial readers, for organizing the learning or teaching process, for planning a lesson with the disabled reader, and for evaluating instruction.

As we close this book we hope that we may have suggested some new practices, helped the reader to select some of the most promising practices from the vast array of prevailing procedures, and offered some reasons why certain practices are preferred over others.

Chall (1978), summarizing research on reading and learning disabilities, reports that most studies which have compared reading instruction with perceptual training have found that reading instruction is more effective; that task analysis and direct teaching of skills is to be recommended; and that the most efficient way to remediate reading problems is to teach reading (language structure, phonetic skills, phoneme sequencing, and so forth). Interwoven in the data is the repeated observation that a teacher possessing sound principles of education is the key to the child's success. There is no substitute for adequate teaching. The teacher, which you either are or are about to become, is of tremendous importance in preventing and in treating children's reading and learning disabilities.

Appendix

PRODUCTION
OF THE
CONSONANT SOUNDS

B is produced by closing the lips tightly and holding the teeth slightly apart. The lips are blown apart with a voiced breath. The *p* is made like the *b*, but there is no voicing. The breath comes out between the lips in a soft voiceless puff.

D is produced by pressing the tip of the tongue against the upper teeth ridge, just behind the upper front teeth, and by blowing down the tongue while starting the voice at the same time. The sides of the tongue lie against the side teeth. The teeth are slightly separated. The tongue is suddenly lowered, allowing the breath to escape in a slight voiced explosion. The sound of *t* begins like *d*, but the blowing is so rapid that the breath escapes with an explosive result.

The *t* sound is an unvoiced dental plosive. It is made by obstructing the air stream and is followed by a sudden release of air. The soft palate is raised so the air does not pass through the nose. There is no vibration of the vocal cords in making the *t* sound, and it therefore is called an unvoiced sound. It is called a dental because in making the sound the tongue touches the upper gum ridge and then is quickly released, freeing a puff of air.

G is produced with the lips and teeth slightly separated. The back of the tongue is raised against the back roof of the mouth. The tip of the tongue is kept behind the lower front teeth and the tongue is blown down suddenly with a voiced breath. *K* is made like *g* except that the slight explosion is voiceless. With the teeth and lips slightly apart, the back of the tongue is lifted against the soft palate. The breath bursts out in a voiceless puff.

The fricative or spirant consonants, *f, v, th,** *s, z, sh, zh, j,* and *ch* are formed by partially closing the air passage. These sounds can be prolonged indefinitely and usually are accompanied by friction. To produce the labiodental fricatives, the unvoiced *f* and the voiced *v*, the upper teeth are in contact with the lower lip. Breath is forced out as the teeth and lip touch. When the sound is voiced, it is a *v*; when it is unvoiced, it is an *f*.

The production of both the voiced and unvoiced dental fricative *th* requires contact between the tip of the tongue and the back of the upper front teeth. The teeth and lips are slightly apart.

To produce the unvoiced *s* the air stream is allowed to pass through a narrow opening between the tip of the tongue and the gums. The front teeth are closed and the entire tongue is raised and grooved along the midline. The tip of the tongue is placed about a quarter of an inch behind the upper teeth. The soft palate is raised. The *s* sounds like air going out of a tire. The voiced *z* requires a slightly larger opening and the teeth are separated.

The unvoiced *sh*, as in *ship*, is produced much like the *s*, but the air stream is forced over a broader surface than for the *s*. The tongue is raised and drawn back, the lips are rounded, and the soft palate is raised. The *zh* is the same sound as the *sh* except that it is voiced.

The unvoiced *ch* is produced by making the *t* sound and quickly exploding it into a *sh* sound. The tip of the tongue touches the upper gum ridge and then is quickly released, freeing a puff of air and producing a *t* sound. This then is quickly changed to the *sh* sound. The *j* sound is voiced and made by raising the front part of the tongue toward the teeth ridge and hard palate. The sounds *ch* and *j* (which is produced like *ch*) sometimes are called plosives. More correctly, they are affricates in that they begin as plosives and end as fricatives.

The nasals or linguals, *m, n,* and *ng,* are formed by completely closing the mouth and allowing the air to escape through the nasal cavities. The soft palate is lowered and each sound is voiced. Closed lips prevent the air from passing through the mouth in the production of *m*. The teeth are slightly apart and a humming sound is sent through the nose. For *n* the tip of the tongue is pressed against the gums. The tongue is not dropped and the mouth is not closed until the sound has been made. For *ng* the tongue is raised against the soft palate. The tongue is kept in this position until a voiced sound is sent through the nose.

The semivowels or glides, *y, hw, w, l, r,* and *h,* are produced by a gliding movement of the tongue or lips from one place to another. They are produced

---

* *Th* as in *then* (voiced) and in *thin* (unvoiced). The unvoiced *th* occurs, for example, in *birth, booth, breath, broth, cloth, both, death, depth, doth, earth, faith, fourth, length, mouth, north,* and *path*. The voiced *th* occurs in *than, that, their, these, they, therefore, those, thus, bathe, breathe, clothe, scathe, smooth, sooth, with, although, brother, either, father, other,* and *gather*.

when the vocal organs are getting ready to produce another sound. The passage from the vocal cords to the outside is partially blocked. The voiced *r* before a vowel, as in *rabbit* or *train*, is produced by raising the tip of the tongue toward the gum ridge without actual contact. The teeth are slightly separated and a curl is formed down the middle of the tongue.

The voiced *l* is produced by elevating the tip of the tongue toward the upper gum ridge. Contact is made, and the air passes over the sides of the tongue. The soft palate is raised for making both sounds. Some describe the *l* sound as the "peanut butter sound." As the sound is made, it feels as if one were licking peanut butter from the roof of one's mouth.

The *hw* is produced like a *w* without vocal cord vibration. It is an unvoiced fricative. To produce the voiced *w* the lips are rounded and an opening is left for the air to emerge from the mouth. The tip of the tongue is raised in back of the lower teeth. In teaching the sound, the teacher might ask the child to blow out a lighted candle while saying *while* or *what*. The *w* is like a vowel in that it is pronounced in a vowel position and like a consonant in that it is pronounced with audible friction. *H* generally is an unvoiced sound; *y* is a voiced sound.

Like the *w*, the *y* has the position of a vowel but the friction of a consonant. The front tip of the tongue is raised nearly to the hard palate behind the upper teeth. The side of the tongue touches the side of the teeth, and the teeth and lips are slightly apart. *H* should be sounded with a vowel. When *h* occurs between vowels it may be a voiced sound. The vowel determines the position of the tongue and lips. The air is blown outwards, and the tongue is behind the lower teeth.

Appendix II
WORD LISTS

Word lists given in this appendix provide the teacher with a ready source of words to teach the skills.

The following list gives monosyllabic words containing short vowels that are helpful in teaching the consonants *b*, *c*, (sounded /*k*/), *d* (sounded /*d*/), *g* (sounded /*g*/), *h*, *j*, *m*, *n* (sounded /*n*/), *p*, *t*, (sounded /*t*/), and *w* in the beginning position.

1. MONOSYLLABIC WORDS FORMED BY B,C,D,G,H,J,M,N,P,T, AND W

bad	bit	cob	dam	dot	gun	hub
bag	Bob	cod	Dan	dub	had	hug
ban	bog	cog	den	dug	ham	hum
bat	bud	con	did	gab	hem	hut
bed	bug	cop	dig	gad	hen	jab
beg	bun	cot	dim	gag	hid	jam
bet	but	cub	din	gap	him	Jan
bib	cab	cud	dip	get	hit	Jed
bid	can	cup	Doc	God	hog	jet
big	cap	cut	dog	got	hop	jib
bin	cat	dad	Don	gum	hot	jig

Jim	mob	not	pig	tat	tug
job	mop	nub	pin	Ted	tut
jog	mud	nun	Pip	ten	was (wŭz)
jot	mug	nut	pit	tic	web
jug	mum	pad	pop	Tim	wed
jut	nab	Pam	pot	tin	wet
Mac	nag	pan	pun	tip	wig
mad	Nan	pat	pup	Tip	win
man	nap	Pat	put (pùt)	tit-tat	wit
map	Ned	peg	tab	Tom	won (wŭn)
mat	net	Peg	tag	ton (tŭn)	
men	nib	pen	tam	top	
met	nip	pep	tan	tot	
Mig	nod	pet	tap	tub	

Adding the sounds /f/, /l/, /r/, and /s/ to the above consonant phonemes as in the next list, permits the teacher to introduce many additional alphabetically consistent words. The asterisked words should be taught as sight words.

2. MONOSYLLABIC WORDS FORMED BY B,C,D,F,G,H,J,L,M,N,P,R,S,T,W AND THE SHORT VOWELS

as (ăz)*	fop	lag	or (òr)*	rod	sip
	for (fòr)*	lap		rot	sir (sèr)*
bus	fun	led	pal	rub	sit
	fir (fèr)*	leg	pus	rug	sob
	fur (fèr)*	let		rum	sod
		lid	rag	run	son (sŭn)*
fad	gas	lip	ram	rut	sop
fan	Gus	lit	ran		sub
fat		log (lòg)*	rap	sad	sun
fed	has (hăz)*	lot	rat	sag	sum
fib	her (hèr)*	lug	red	Sal	
fig	his (hĭz)*		rib	Sam	
fin			rid	sap	us
fit	if	nor (nòr)*	rig	sat	
fog	is (ĭz)*		rim	set	was (wŭz)*
		of (ŭv)*	rip	Sid	
	lad	off (òf)*	rob	sin	

The following list (on page 456) of words is useful in teaching the doubling of the *f*, *l*, and *s* at the end of the word.

3. THE DOUBLING OF *F,L,S,* AT THE END OF WORDS

Ending in ff	*Ending in ss*		
cuff	bass	hiss	cuss
duff	mass	miss	fuss
huff	pass		muss
muff		joss	
puff	Bess	boss (bòs)	
riff-raff	less	moss (mòs)	
ruff	mess	toss (tòs)	

Ending in ll			
all (òl)	bell	Bill	cull
ball	dell	dill	dull
call	fell	fill	gull
fall	hell	hill	hull
gall	jell	ill	lull
hall	mell	Jill	mull
pall	Nell	mill	null
tall	sell	pill	bull (bùl)
wall	tell	rill	full (fùl)
	well	sill	pull (pùl)
		till	
		will	

4. SOFT *C* AND *G*

The following lists are useful in teaching the soft *c* and *g* sound.

bounce	dunce	lace	place	splice
brace	face	lance	pounce	spruce
cede	farce	mice	prance	stance
cell	fence	mince	price	thence
cent	fierce	nice	prince	thrice
chance	fleece	niece	quince	trace
choice	flounce	once	race	trance
cinch	force	ounce	scarce	trice
cite	glance	pace	since	twice
cyst	grace	peace	slice	vice
dance	hence	pence	sluice	whence
deuce	ice	piece	source	wince
dice	juice	pierce	space	

age	budge	dirge	forge	gene
badge	bulge	dodge	fringe	gent
barge	cage	dredge	fudge	germ
beige	change	edge	gage	gibe
bilge	charge	flange	gauge	gin
bridge	cringe	fledge	gem	gist

gorge	huge	pledge	siege	strange
gouge	judge	plunge	sledge	surge
grange	large	purge	sludge	tinge
grudge	liege	rage	smudge	trudge
gym	lodge	range	splurge	urge
hedge	merge	ridge	sponge	verge
hinge	nudge	rouge	stage	wage
hodge-podge	page	sage	stooge	

K and *Q* may be taught using the following lists.

5. MONOSYLLABIC WORDS FORMED WITH *K* AND *Q* AND THE PREVIOUSLY LEARNED CONSONANTS AND VOWELS

ark	crock	hock	knell	park	rock	speck
ask		honk	knit	peck		spunk
	dark	hulk	knob	pick	sack	stack
back	deck	husk	knock	plank	sank	stalk (ȯ)
balk (bōk)	Dick		knoll (nōl)	pluck	sick	stark
bank	disk	ilk	knot	plunk	silk	stick
bark	drank	ink		prank	skid	stink
bask	drink		lack	prick	skiff	stock
black	duck	junk	lark	punk	skill	stuck
blank	dunk		lock		skim	stunk
blink	dusk	keg	luck	quack	skin	sulk
brink		kept		quaff	skip	swank
brisk	elk	kick		quart (ȯ)	skit	
buck		kid	mark	quell	skulk	tack
bulk	flank	kill	mask	quest	skull	talk (tȯk)
	flask	kiln	milk	quick	skunk	tank
calk (kȯk)	flunk	kilt	mink	quill	slack	task
cask	folk (fōk)	kin	monk	quilt	slick	tick
click	frank	king	muck	quit	slink	trek
clink	Frank	kink	musk		smock	trick
cluck	frisk	kiss		rack	snack	
crick		kit	nick	rink	sock	walk (wȯk)
	hack	knack	Nick	risk	spank	wick
						wink

Words representative of the *v* and *z* sounds are found in the following lists.

6. *V* AND *Z*

V

brave	curve	eve	heave	love	rove	starve
breve	dive	five	hive	move	save	stove
cave	dove	gave	hives	pave	salve	vail
clove	drive	give	jive	peeve	selves	vain
cove	drove	grave	knave	prove	sleeve	vale
crave	Eve	have	live	rave	solve	van

vane	veil	vet	vine	vote
vase	vein	vex	vise	vouch
vast	vend	vie	vogue	waive
vat	vent	view	voice	wave
veal	verb	vile	void	wives
veer	vest	vim	volt	wave

Z

blaze	doze	froze	jazz	size	zest	zoom
breeze	faze	fuzz	phiz	sneeze	zinc	
bronze	fez	gauze	prize	snooze	zing	
buzz	fizz	gaze	quiz	squeeze	zip	
craze	freeze	glaze	raze	wheeze	zone	
daze	frieze	haze	razz	zeal	zoo	

WORDS TO TEACH THE BEGINNING AND ENDING CONSONANT CLUSTERS

Word lists such as the following provide the teacher with a ready source of words to teach the beginning- and end-consonant clusters.

7. BEGINNING BLENDS

bl

blot	blotter	blue	blacktop	bliss	bled
blanket	black	blob	blame	bluff	blaze
blade	block	blank	bless	blink	

br

brad	bred	branch	bread	bracket
brag	brim	bridle	bridge	brute
bran	bring	briefcase	brick	broke
brass	broom	bridegroom	brown	brave
brat	bracelet	bride	broomstick	brace

cl

clad	cliff	club	clamp
clam	cling	clown	clove
clan	clip	cloud	click
clap	clod	clock	cluck
class	clog	claw	clink
clef	clot	classroom	close

cr

crayon	crown	crime
cracker	crate	cry
croquet	crack	crave
crowbar	crock	craze
cross	crane	

dr

dress	dresser	drank
drumstick	dryer	drunk
drink	drape	dry
drawer	drugstore	drive
dragon	druggist	

dw

dwarf
dwell
dwelling

fl

flapjack	flower	fling	flank
flagpole	fly	flame	flask
flashlight	flake	fluke	flunk

fr

freighter	Frank
friar	frisk
frame	fry
fruit	froze

gl

globe
glove
glasses
glare

gr

grapefruit	grape	grime	grace
grandstand	green	gripe	grass
griddle	gray	grade	
grave	grasshopper	graze	

pl

plate	plow	pluck
plume	plane	ply
planter	plank	place
pliers	plant	

pr

pretzel	protractor	prove	prize
prune	priest	prose	price
present	prime	prank	
propeller	probe	pry	

sc

scooter	scarecrow
scale	scare
scarf	scope

sk

skate	ski	skid	skit
skull	skillet	skiff	
skeleton	skirt	skim	
skunk	sky	skin	

sl

slide	slime	sly
slack	slope	slice
slate	slick	

sm

smack
smoke
smock
smile
smite

sn

snake	snowshoes	snore
snowman	snail	
snack	snare	

sp

spade	sparrow	sparkle	spine
spy	spider	spare	speck
spank	spoon	spire	spunk
sparkplug	spool	spike	space

sq

squat
squall
squid
squint

st

stagecoach	stove	stapler	stink	stole
starfish	stick	statute	sty	stone
stoplight	stool	store	stack	
steamboat	stairs	stunk	stale	
stop sign	stake	stuck	stare	
steeple	stable	stock	stoke	

sw

swing	sweat
sweater	switch
swallow	sweeper
swan	

tr

train	triangle	tramp	trike
truck	trunk	trailer	try
tree	tray	tripod	trace
tractor	trinket	trash	
trick	tricycle	trade	
track	trophy	tribe	

tw

twenty	twinkle	twice
twelve	twins	
tweezers	twine	

8. ENDING-CONSONANT COMBINATIONS

ck *

back	crack	kick	prick	rock	luck
hack	slack	lick	slick	sock	suck
jack	smack	Mick	stick	tock	tuck
lack	snack	nick	trick	block	cluck
Mack	stack	Nick	tick	clock	pluck
pack	track	pick	wick	crock	stuck
quack	deck	quick	cock	flock	truck
rack	heck	sick	dock	frock	
sack	neck	brick	hock	smock	
tack	peck	click	lock	buck	
black	Dick	flick	mock	duck	

ct

act	fact	tract
pact	duct	pict
tact	sect	strict

ff *

staff	miff	whiff	buff	muff
chaff	skiff	doff	cuff	puff
gaff	sniff	scoff	fluff	scuff
quaff	stiff	off	gruff	stuff
cliff	tiff	bluff	huff	tuff

ft

raft	deft	drift	loft
draft	left	swift	oft
craft	cleft	gift	soft
graft	theft	shift	tuft
shaft	lift	thrift	daft
aft	rift	sift	

*The asterisked endings are digraphs, although *lf* and *lm* may also be blends.

lb

bulb
alb

lc

talc

ld

bald	meld	cold	hold	sold
scald	weld	fold	mold	told
held	bold	gold	old	

*lf**

calf	self
half	golf
elf	wolf
self	

*ll**

all	tall	spell	fill	rill	full
ball	wall	swell	frill	shrill	pull
call	bell	tell	gill	sill	cull
fall	cell	well	grill	skill	dull
gall	dell	yell	hill	spill	gull
hall	dwell	bill	ill	still	hull
pall	fell	brill	kill	thrill	skull
small	sell	chill	mill	will	
squall	shell	dill	pill	doll	
stall	smell	drill	quill	bull	

*lm**

balm	palm	helm
calm	elm	realm
psalm	whelm	film

lp

alp	yelp
scalp	gulp
help	pulp

lt

fault	dealt	smelt	jilt	stilt
halt	dwelt	welt	kilt	bolt
malt	felt	built	lilt	colt
salt	knelt	gilt	tilt	jolt
vault	melt	guilt	wilt	cult
belt	pelt	hilt	silt	

*mb**

climb	bomb	comb	numb	limb
lamb	tomb	dumb	crumb	womb

mp

pump	crimp	cramp	pomp	slump
stamp	camp	damp	stomp	trump
tramp	hump	lamp	bump	hemp
clamp	stump	tamp	lump	imp
ramp	clump	limp	plump	jump
blimp	dump	romp	rump	primp

nd

band	hand	bend	mend	trend	blond
bland	land	end	rend	wend	pond
brand	sand	blend	send	wind	fund
gland	stand	fend	spend	bond	
grand	wand	lend	tend	fond	

*ng**

bang	sang	king	sting	long	rung
fang	slang	wing	swing	song	slung
gang	tang	ping	ting	pong	stung
hang	bing	ring	bong	tong	sung
pang	bring	sing	dong	clung	swung
rang	ding	sling	gong	flung	

nk

bank	flank	kink	brink	junk	stunk
sank	frank	link	drink	punk	trunk
tank	plank	mink	slink	sunk	
blank	prank	pink	stink	drunk	
clank	spank	sink	honk	flunk	
crank	tank	wink	bunk	skunk	
drank	fink	blink	dunk	spunk	

*nn**

Finn
inn

ns

lens

nt

ant	scant	sent	flint	tint	grunt
can't	slant	spent	glint	font	hunt
grant	want	tent	hint	front	punt
pant	bent	went	mint	blunt	runt
plant	dent	dint	print	brunt	stunt
rant	lent	lint	stint	bunt	

pt

apt	kept	swept
rapt	slept	wept

rb

garb
barb

rc

arc
marc

rd

lard	yard
bard	curd
card	lord
hard	chord
ward	cord

rf

dwarf	surf
wharf	turf
serf	scarf

rl

snarl	churl	pearl
gnarl	curl	swirl
Carl	furl	whirl
earl	girl	uncurl
twirl	hurl	unfurl
Burl	knurl	

rm

arm	alarm	worm
farm	charm	squirm
harm	storm	term
warm	form	

rn

barn	yearn
darn	fern
warn	urn
earn	turn
learn	concern

rp

harp	sharp	slurp	chirp
carp	warp	burp	

rr*

parr

rt

art	part	hurt	pert
Art	smart	curt	sort
cart	tart	dirt	court
dart	wart	shirt	

sc

disc

sk

desk	mask	tusk	husk
disk	ask	dusk	musk
flask	bask	frisk	risk
cask	task	brisk	

sm

spasm
prism
ism

sp

clasp	grasp	rasp
asp	lisp	hasp
gasp	crisp	wisp

*ss**

pass	hiss	bass
miss	toss	

st

nest	crust	best	twist	west	must
mast	blast	blest	bust	trust	past
fist	last	rest	crest	crust	
cast	dust	rust	gust	fast	
mist	lost	pest	hast	grist	
frost	test	just	jest	host	

tt

mitt
putt

9. DIGRAPH *Ch*

arch	botch	chain	charm	cheer	chill	chose
batch	branch	chair	chart	cheese	chin	chow
beach	breach	chalk	chase	chess	chip	chuck
beech	breech	champ	chaste	chest	chirp	chug
belch	broach	chance	chat	chew	choice	chum
bench	brooch	change	cheap	chick	choke	chunk
birch	bunch	chant	cheat	chide	choose	church
bleach	catch	chap	check	chief	chop	churl
blotch	chaff	charge	cheek	child	chore	churn

chute	fetch	launch	patch	reach	smutch	thatch
cinch	filch	leach	paunch	retch	snatch	torch
clench	flinch	leech	peach	rich	snitch	touch
clinch	flitch	lunch	perch	roach	speech	trench
clutch	French	lurch	pinch	scorch	splotch	twitch
coach	grouch	march	pitch	scotch	squelch	vetch
couch	gulch	match	poach	scratch	stanch	vouch
crotch	hatch	mooch	pooch	screech	starch	watch
crutch	haunch	much	porch	scrunch	staunch	welch
ditch	hitch	mulch	pouch	search	stench	winch
drench	hunch	munch	preach	sketch	stitch	witch
Dutch	inch	notch	punch	slouch	stretch	wrench
each	itch	ouch	quench	smirch	switch	wretch
etch	latch	parch	ranch	smooch	teach	

10. DIGRAPH *Sh*

ash	mesh	share	shell	shop
bash	mush	shark	sherd	shorn
brash	plush	sharp	shield	short
brush	rash	shave	shift	should
bush	rush	shawl	shin	shout
cash	sash	shay	shine	shove
clash	shade	she	ship	show
dash	shaft	sheaf	shirk	shun
dish	shag	shear	shirt	slash
fish	shake	sheath	shoal	slush
flush	shale	sheathe	shoat	smash
fresh	shall	sheave	shock	splash
frosh	shalt	shed	shod	squash
gnash	sham	sheen	shoe	trash
harsh	shame	sheep	shone	wish
hush	shank	sheer	shoo	
josh	shan't	sheet	shook	
lash	shape	shelf	shoot	

11. DIGRAPH *Th*
Voiceless /th/

bath	faith	ninth	theme	threat	thud
berth	fifth	north	thick	three	thump
birth	filth	oath	thief	thresh	thwart
booth	forth	sixth	thigh	threw	tooth
breadth	fourth	sloth	thin	thrice	truth
breath	froth	Smith	thing	thrift	twelfth
broth	growth	sooth	think	thrill	warmth
cloth	hath	south	third	throat	wealth
couth	health	strength	thirst	throb	width
dearth	hearth	teeth	thong	throng	worth
death	heath	thank	thorn	through	wraith
depth	mirth	thatch	thought	throw	wrath
doth	mouth	thaw	thrash	thrush	wreath
earth	myth	theft	thread	thrust	youth

Voiced /~~th~~/

baths	soothe	thence	though
bathe	that	there	thus
breathe	the	these	thy
clothe	thee	they	with
scathe	their	this	wreathe
scythe	them	those	writhe
smooth	then	thou	

12. DIGRAPHS *wh*, *gh*, and *ph*

Wh sound

whack	whelm	which	whip	*Wh* represents /*h*/
whale	whelp	whiff	whirl	before the letter *o:*
wharf	when	whig	whish	who
what	whence	while		whole
wheat	where	whilst		whom
wheel	whet	whim		whoop
wheeze	whew	whine		whose

Silent Gh

aught	dough	light	ought	though
bough	drought	naught	plough	thought
bought	eight	neigh	sleigh	through
brought	freight	night	sought	weight
caught	height	nought	straight	wrought

Gh as /f/

cough	laugh	slough	trough
draught	rough	tough	

Gh as /g/

ghost
ghoul
ghetto
ghastly

Ph as /f/

phase	alphabet	autograph	asphalt	saxophone
phew	hyphen	nephew	prophet	sophomore
phlegm	phonograph	philosophy	phobia	geography
telephone	phone	typhoon	symphony	phonics
photograph	graph	orphan	physical	pamphlet
phrase	photo	physics	sphere	biography

Ph as /v/

Stephen

Ph as /p/

diphthong
diphtheria
naphtha

Words using a long vowel-silent *e* combination may be taught from the following list.

13. MONOSYLLABIC WORDS WITH A SILENT *E* AT THE END AND A LONG VOWEL SOUND IN THE MIDDLE OF THE WORD

ape	crude	flake	June	muse	quite	slime	tile
are /ä/	cruise	flame		mute	quote	slope	time
ate	cube	flare	Kate			smile	tire
	cute	fluke	kite	name	rake	smite	tome
babe		fuse		nape	rape	smoke	tone
bade	dame		lake	nine	rare /â/	smote	tote
bake	Dane	gale	lame	node	rate	snake	trade
bale	dare /â/	game	lane	none*	ride	snare /â/	tribe
bane	date	gape	late	nose	rife	snipe	tripe
base	dime	gate	life	note	rile	snore	tube
bate	dine	give /ĭ/	line	nude	rime	sole	tune
bide	dire	glade	lobe		ripe	some*	twine
bike	dome	glare /â/	lode		rise	spade	
bile	done*	gone /ò/	lone	ode	rite	spare /â/	vale
bite	dope	grate	lube	one*	robe	spate	vane
blade	dose	grime	lure		rode	spike	vile
blame	dote	gripe	lute	pale	role	spine	vine
bone	dove*	grope		pane	rope	spire	vise
bore	drape		made	Pete	rude	spite	vote
bride	drive	hare /â/	make	pike	rule	spume	
brine	drove	hate	mane	pile		stake	wade
brute	dude	have /ă/	mare /â/	pine	safe	stale	wake
	duke	here /ĭ/	mate	pipe	sake	stare /â/	wane
cake	dupe	hide	mere /ĭ/	plane	sale	stile	ware
came		hike	mete	plate	sate	stipe	waste
cane		hire	Mike	plebe	scale	stoke	were /è/
cape	eke	hole	mike	plume	scape	stole	wide
care /â/		home	mile	poke	scare /â/	sure	wife
chore	fade	hone	mine	pole	scope	swine	wile
clove	fake	hope	mire	pope	sere /ĕ/	swipe	wine
code	fame	hose	mite	pose	shake		wipe
coke	fare /â/		mode	prime	side	take	wire
come*	fate	jade	mole	probe	sire	tale	wise
cone	fife	Jane	mope	prone	site	tame	
cope	file	jibe	mote	prose	skate	tape	
crate	fine	joke	move /ü/	prune	slate	tide	yoke
crime	fire	Jude	mule	pure	slide	tike	Yule

---

* O frequently is a short *u* as in *some, come, dove, love, done, none, one. Dove* can also be /dōv/.

Words that use a combination of two vowels will be found in the list that follows.

14. TWO-VOWEL COMBINATIONS

Ai as /ā/	maize	clay	eel	reel	coat	Joe
aid	paid	day	feed	see	croak	shoe*
aide	pail	flay	feel	seed	float	toe
ail	paint	gay	feet	seem	foal	
aim	pair	hay	flee	seen	foam	*Ow as /ō/*
ain't	plaid*	may	fleet	seep	gloam	blow
air	plaint	nay	free	sleek	gloat	bow
aisle*	praise	play	geese	sleep	goad	bowl
bail	quail	pray	Greek	sleet	goal	crow
bait	quaint	ray	green	sneer	goat	flow
braid	raid	say	greet	speed	groan	flown
brail	rain	says*	heed	steed	load	glow
brain	raise	slay	heel	steel	loaf	grow
claim	said*	stay	jeep	steep	loam	grown
drain	sail	tray	jeer	steer	loan	know
fail	saint	way	keel	sweep	moan	low
faille	slain		keen	sweet	moat	mow
fain	snail	*Ee as /ē/*	keep	teem	oak	owe
faint	staid	bee	knee	teens	oat	own
fair	stain	beech	kneel	tree	road	row
flail	stair	beef	leek	tweed	roam	show
flair	tail	been*	lees	tweet	roan	slow
gain	taint	beer	meet	wee	roast	snow
gait	trail	beet	need	weed	soak	stow
hail	train	bleed	peek	week	soap	throw
hair	trait	breed	peel	weep	toad	tow
jail	waif	creed	peep		toast	
laid	wail	creek	peer	*Oa as /ō/*		
lain	waist	creel	preen	boast	*Oe as /ō/*	
lair	wait	creep	queen	boat	doe	
maid		creese	queer	broad*	does*	
mail	*Ay as /ā/*	deed	reed	cloak	foe	
maim	aye*	deem	reef	coal	goes	
main	bay	deep	reek	coast	hoe	

* Aisle (il); plaid (plăd); said (sĕd); aye (ī); says (sĕz); been (bĭn); broad (brȯd); does (dŭz); shoe (shü). Words in air are pronounced /âr/; those in eer, /ir/ or /ẹr/.

REFERENCES

ALEXANDER, DUANE, and JOHN MONEY, "Reading Disability and the Problem of Direction Sense," *The Reading Teacher* 20 (1967), 404–409.

ALLINGTON, RICHARD L., and ANNE McGILL-FRANZEN, "Word Identification Errors in Isolation and in Context: Apples vs. Oranges," *The Reading Teacher* 33 (1980), 795–800.

AMMON, RICHARD, "Generating Expectancies to Enhance Comprehension," *The Reading Teacher* 29 (1975), 245–249.

ANSHEN, RUTH N., "Language as Idea," in *Language: An Inquiry Into Its Meaning and Function*, ed. Ruth N. Anshen. New York: Harper & Brothers, 1957.

ARNOLD, RICHARD, and JOHN MILLER, "Reading: Word Recognition Skills," in *Reading*, ed. Pose Lamb and Richard Arnold. Belmont, Calif.: Wadsworth Publishing Co., 1976.

ARNOLD, R. D., and A. H. WIST, "Auditory Discrimination Abilities of Disadvantaged Anglo and Mexican-American Children," *The Elementary School Journal* 70 (1970), 295–299.

ATKINSON, RICHARD C., *Contemporary Psychology*. San Francisco: W. H. Freeman & Company, 1971.

AUSUBEL, D., "The Use of Advance Organizers in the Learning and Retention of Meaningful Verbal Material," *Journal of Educational Psychology* 51 (1960), 267–272.

BAKWIN, H., "Reading Disability in Twins," *Developmental Medicine and Child Neurology* 15 (1973), 184–187.

BALLER, WARREN R., and DON C. CHARLES, *The Psychology of Human Growth and Development.* New York: Holt, Rinehart & Winston, 1961.

BALOW, BRUCE, "The Long-Term Effect of Remedial Reading Instruction," *The Reading Teacher* 18 (April 1965), 581–586.

BALOW, BRUCE, et al., *Perinatal Events or Precursors of Reading Difficulty* (Interim Report No. 17). Washington, D.C.: National Institute of Education, 1974.

BANKS, ENID, "The Identification of Children with Potential Learning Disabilities," *Slow Learning Child: The Australian Journal on the Education of Backward Children* 17 (1970), 27–38.

BANNATYNE, ALEXANDER D., *Language, Reading, and Learning Disabilities: Psychology, Neuropsychology, Diagnosis and Remediation.* Springfield, Ill.: Charles C Thomas, 1971. (a)

BANNATYNE, ALEX, "Spelling and Sound Blending," *Academic Therapy* 7 (1971), 73–77. (b)

BANNATYNE, ALEX, "Reading: An Auditory-Vocal Process," *Academic Therapy* 9 (1973), 429–431.

BARRETT, THOMAS C., "Visual Discrimination Tasks as Predictors of First-Grade Teaching Achievement," *The Reading Teacher* 18 (1965), 276–282.

BARRETT, THOMAS C., "Performance on Selected Prereading Tasks and First-Grade Reading Achievement," in *Vistas in Reading.* Newark, Del.: International Reading Association, 1967.

BARRETT, THOMAS, C., "Taxonomy of Reading Comprehension," *Reading 360 Monograph.* Lexington, Mass.: Ginn, 1972.

BARRETT, THOMAS C., "Educational Implications of Minimal Brain Damage," *The Reading Teacher* 27 (1974), 662–668.

BARRETT, THOMAS C., and RICHARD J. SMITH, *Teaching Reading in the Middle Grades.* Reading, Mass.: Addison-Wesley, 1974, 1979.

BARTON, ALLEN, "Social Class and Instructional Procedures in the Process of Learning to Read," in *Twelfth Yearbook of the National Reading Conference,* ed. Y. Melton Culbreth and Ralph C. Staiger. Milwaukee, 1962.

BATEMAN, BARBARA, "Learning Disabilities—Yesterday, Today, and Tomorrow," *Exceptional Children* 31 (December 1965), 167–176.

BATEMAN, BARBARA, *Essentials of Teaching.* Dimensions in Early Learning Series. San Rafael, Calif.: Dimensions Publishing Co., 1971.

BEERY, KEITH E., *Visual Motor Integration.* Chicago: Follett Publishing Co., 1967.

BENSON, J., "Teaching Reading to the Culturally Different Child," in *Readings on Reading,* ed. Alfred R. Binter, John Diabal, and Leonard Kise. Scranton, Pa.: International Textbook Co., 1969.

BENTZEN, FRANCIS, "Sex Ratios in Learning and Behavior Disorders," *American Journal of Orthopsychiatry* 33 (January 1963), 92–98.

BETA UPSILON CHAPTER, PI LAMBDA THETA, "Children's Reading Interests Classified by Age Level," *The Reading Teacher* 27 (1974), 694–700.

BETTS, EMMETT A., *Foundations of Reading Instruction.* New York: American Book Company, 1957.

BETTS, EMMETT, "Issues in Teaching Reading." *Controversial Issues in Reading,* Tenth Annual Reading Conference, Lehigh University (April 1961).

BIRKLEY, MARILYN, "Effecting Reading Improvement in the Classroom Through Teacher Self-Improvement Programs," *Journal of Reading* 14 (1970), 94–100.

BLOOMFIELD, L., "Linguistics and Reading," *Elementary English* 19 (1942), 125–130, 183–186.

BLOOMFIELD, L., and CLARENCE L. BARNHART, *Let's Read: A Linguistic Approach.* Detroit, Mich.: Wayne State University Press, 1961.

BOND, GUY L., and MILES A. TINKER, *Reading Difficulties: Their Diagnosis and Correction.* New York: Appleton-Century-Crofts, 1967.

BONEAU, C. ALAN, "Paradigm Regained? Cognitive Behaviorism Restated," *American Psychologist* 29 (May 1974), 297–309.

BRUNER, J. S., "Going Beyond the Information Given," in *Contemporary Approaches to Cognition.* Cambridge: Harvard University Press, 1957. (a)

BRUNER, J. S., "On Perceptual Readiness," *Psychological Review* 64 (March 1957), 123–152. (b)

BRUNER, J. S., *On Knowing.* Cambridge: Harvard University Press, 1962.

BRUNER, J. S., *Toward a Theory of Instruction.* Cambridge: Harvard University Press, 1966.

BRUNSWICK, EGON, "Scope and Aspects of the Cognitive Problem," in *Contemporary Approaches to Cognition.* Cambridge: Harvard University Press, 1957.

BRZEINSKI, JOSEPH E., "Beginning Reading in Denver," *The Reading Teacher* 18 (October 1964), 16–21.

BRZEINSKI, JOSEPH, M. LUCILE HARRISON, and PAUL McKEE, "Should Johnny Read in Kindergarten? A Report on the Denver Experiment," *NEA Journal* 56 (March 1967), 23–25.

BUGELSKI, B. R., *The Psychology of Learning Applied to Teaching.* Indianapolis, Ind.: Bobbs-Merrill, 1964.

BURG, LESLIE A., et al., *The Complete Reading Supervisor.* Columbus, Ohio: Charles E. Merrill, 1978.

BUSWELL, G. T., "An Experimental Study of the Eye-Voice Span in Reading," *Supplementary Educational Monographs*, No. 17. Chicago: University of Chicago, 1920.

BUSWELL, G. T., "Perceptual Research and Methods of Learning," *The Scientific Monthly* 64 (1947), 521–526.

CALLAWAY, BYRON, "Pupil and Family Characteristics Related to Reading Achievement," *Education* 92 (1972), 71–75.

CARHART, RAYMOND, "Auditory Training" and "Conservation of Speech," in *Hearing and Deafness: A Guide for Laymen*, ed. Hollowell Davis. New York: Murray Hill Books, 1947.

CHALL, JEANNE S., "The Influence of Previous Knowledge on Reading Ability," Ohio State University, *Educational Research Bulletin* 26 (December 1947), 225–230.

CHALL, JEANNE S., *Reading and Development.* Newark, Del.: International Reading Association, 1976.

CHALL, JEANNE S., "A Decade of Research on Reading and Learning Disabilities," in *What Research Has to Say About Reading Instruction*, ed. S. Jay Samuels. Newark, Del.: International Reading Association, 1978.

CHARNOCK, JAMES, "An Alternative to the DRA," *The Reading Teacher* 31 (December 1977), 269–271.

CHOMSKY, CAROL, "Stages in Language Development and Reading Exposure," *Harvard Educational Review* 42 (February 1972), 1–33.

CHOMSKY, NOAM, *Syntactic Structures.* The Hague: Mouton, 1957.

CHOMSKY, NOAM, "Phonology and Reading, in *Basic Studies in Reading*, ed. Harry Levin and Joanne P. Williams. New York: Basic Books, 1970.

COHEN, ALICE, and GERALD G. GLASS, "Lateral Dominance and Reading Ability," *The Reading Teacher* 21 (January 1968), 343–348.

CRIBBIN, JAMES J., "The Teacher: Hercules, Tantulus or Sisyphus?" *Education* 80 (October 1959), 100–105.

DAHL, PATRICIA R., and S. JAY SAMUELS, Teaching High-Speed Word Recognition and Comprehension Skills." Unpublished paper, University of Minnesota. 1975.

DALE, EDGAR, and JEANNE CHALL, "A Formula for Predicting Readability," *Educational Research Bulletin* 27 (January 1948), 11–20.

DALLMANN, MARTHA, ROGER L. ROUCH, LYNETTE Y. C. CHAR, and JOHN J. DeBOER, *The Teaching of Reading*. New York: Holt, Rinehart & Winston, 1978.

DAVIS, DAVID. "An Indispensable Sight Vocabulary." Unpublished monograph, University of Wisconsin, 1973.

DAVIS, FREDERICK B., "Fundamental Factors of Comprehension in Reading," *Psychometrika* 9 (September 1944), 185–197.

DAVIS, FREDERICK B., "Psychometric Research on Comprehension in Reading," *Reading Research Quarterly* 7 (Summer 1972), 628–678.

DeBOER, J. J., and MARTHA DALLMANN, *The Teaching of Reading*. New York: Henry Holt, 1960.

DECHANT, EMERALD, "Rate of Comprehension-Needed Research," in *Changing Concepts of Reading Instruction*, ed. J. Allen Figurel. International Reading Association Conference Proceedings, Vol. 6. New York: Scholastic Magazines, 1961.

DECHANT, EMERALD, "Teacher Differences and Reading Method," *Education* 86 (September 1965), 40-43. (a)

DECHANT, EMERALD, "The Philosophy and Sociology of Reading," in *The Philosophical and Sociological Basis of Reading*. Milwaukee: National Reading Conference Yearbook, 1965. (b)

DECHANT, EMERALD, *Diagnosis and Remediation of Reading Disability*. West Nyack, N.Y.: Parker Publishing Company, 1968.

DECHANT, EMERALD, *Improving the Teaching of Reading*. Englewood Cliffs, N.J.: Prentice-Hall, 1964, 1970.

DECHANT, EMERALD, *Detection and Correction of Reading Disability*. New York: Appleton-Century-Crofts, 1971.

DECHANT, EMERALD, *Reading Improvement in the Secondary School*. Englewood Cliffs, N.J.: Prentice-Hall, 1973.

DECHANT, EMERALD, *The Diagnostic Process*. Hays, Kans.: Author, 1975.

DECHANT, EMERALD, "Motivation Revisited," *Improving Instruction* 11 (January 1977).

DECHANT, EMERALD, *Diagnosis and Remediation of Reading Disabilities*. Englewood Cliffs, N.J.: Prentice-Hall, 1981.(a)

DECHANT, EMERALD, *Teacher's Directory of Reading Skill Aids, Techniques and Materials*. West Nyack, N.Y.: Parker Publishing Company, 1981.(b)

DECHANT, EMERALD, and HENRY P. SMITH, *Psychology in Teaching Reading*. Englewood Cliffs, N.J.: Prentice-Hall, 1961, 1977.

DeHIRSCH, KATRINA, and JEANNETTE JANSKY, "Kindergarten Protocols of Failing Readers," in *Reading Diagnosis and Evaluation*, vol. 13, ed. Dorothy L. DeBoer. Newark, Del.: International Reading Association, 1970.

DeHIRSCH, KATRINA, JEANNETTE J. JANSKY, and WILLIAM S. LANGFORD, *Predicting Reading Failure*. New York: Harper & Row, 1966.

DENBURG, SUSAN D., "The Interaction of Picture and Print in Reading Instruction," *Reading Research Quarterly* 12, no. 2 (1976–1977), 176–189.

DEUTSCH, C. P., et al., *The Disadvantaged Child: Studies of the Social Environment and the Learning Process*. New York: Basic Books, 1967.

DILLNER, MARTHA H., and JOANNE P. OLSON, *Personalizing Reading Instruction in Middle, Junior and Senior High Schools*. New York: Macmillan, 1977.

DOEHRING, DONALD G., *Patterns of Impairment in Specific Reading Disability: A Neurological Investigation*. Bloomington, Ind.: Indiana University Press, 1968.

DOLCH, E. W., "A Basic Sight Vocabulary," *The Elementary School Journal* 36 (1936), 456–460.

DOLCH, E. W., "School Research in Reading," *Elementary English* 33, (February 1956), 76–80.

DUNKELD, COHN G. M., "The Validity of the Informal Reading Inventory for the Designation of Instructional Reading Levels." Unpublished doctoral dissertation, University of Illinois, 1970.

DURRELL, DONALD D., *The Improvement of Basic Reading Abilities*. Yonkers, N.Y.: World Book Co., 1940.

DURKIN, DOLORES, "The Achievement of Pre-School Readers: Two Longitudinal Studies," *Reading Research Quarterly* 1 (1966), 5–36.(a)

DURKIN, DOLORES, *Children Who Read Early*. New York: Teachers College Press, 1966.(b)

EAMES, THOMAS H., "The Effect of Endocrine Disorders on Reading," *The Reading Teacher* 12 (April 1959), 263–265.

EARLY, MARGARET J., "What Does Research in Reading Reveal About Successful Reading Programs?" in *What We Know About High School Reading*. Champaign, Ill.: National Council of Teachers of English, 1969, 40–53.

EDFELDT, AKE W., *Silent Speech and Silent Reading*. Stockholm: Almquist and Wiksell, 1959; Chicago: University of Chicago Press, 1960.

EISENBERG, LEON, "Epidemiology of Reading Retardation," in *The Disabled Reader*, ed. John Money. Baltimore: John Hopkins Press, 1966.

EKWALL, ELDON E., "Measuring Gains in Remedial Reading," *The Reading Teacher* 26 (1972), 138–141.

EMANS, ROBERT, "Context Clues," in *Reading in the Total Curriculum*, International Reading Association Conference Proceedings. Newark, Del.: International Reading Association, 1968.

EMANS, ROBERT, "Oral Language and Learning to Read," *Elementary English* 50 (1973), 929–934.

ENTUS, A., *Hemispheric Asymmetry in Processing of Dichotically Presented Speech and Non-speech Sounds of Infants*. Denver: Society of Research in Child Development, 1975.

ENTWISLE, DORIS R., "A Sociologist Looks at Reading," in *Reading Problems: A Multidisciplinary Perspective*, ed. Wayne Otto, et al., Reading Mass.: Addison-Wesley, 1977.

FEINGOLD, BEN, "Hyperkinesis and Learning Disabilities Linked to Artificial Food Flavors and Colors," *American Journal of Nursing* 75 (May 1975), 797–803.

FERNALD, G. M., *Remedial Techniques in Basic School Subjects*. New York: McGraw-Hill, 1943, 1966.

FILDES, LUCY G., "Experiments on the Problem of Mirror-Writing," *British Journal of Psychology* 14 (1923), 57–67.

FIRESTER, LEE, and JOAN FIRESTER, "Wanted: A New Deal for Boys," *Elementary School Journal* 75 (1974), 28–36.

FLESCH, RUDOLF, *Marks of Readable Style: A Study in Adult Education*. New York: Bureau of Publications, Teachers College, Columbia University, 1943.

FLESCH, RUDOLF, "A New Readability Yardstick," *Journal of Applied Psychology* 32 (June 1948), 221–233.

FRASURE, NANCY E., and DORIS R. ENTWISLE, "Semantic and Syntactic Development in Children," *Developmental Psychology* 9 (1973), 236–245.

FRAYER, DOROTHY A., WAYNE C. FREDERICK, and HERBERT J. KLAUSMEIER, *A Schema for Testing the Level of Concept Mastery*. Madison: University of Wisconsin, April 1969.

FRIES, CHARLES C., *Linguistics and Reading*. New York: Holt, Rinehart & Winston, 1963.

FRY, EDWARD, "A Diacritical Marking System to Aid Beginning Reading Instruction," *Elementary English* 41 (May 1964), 526–529, 537.

FRY, EDWARD, "A Readability-Formula that Saves Time," *Journal of Reading* 11 (April 1968), 513–516, 575–577.

FRY, EDWARD, "Fry's Readability Graph: Clarifications, Validity, and Extension to Level 17," *Journal of Reading* 21 (December 1977), 242–252.

GARDNER, HOWARD, "Developmental Dyslexia," *Psychology Today* 7 (1973), 62–67.

GAARDNER, K. R., "Eye Movements and Perception," in *Early Experience and Visual Information Processing in Perceptual and Reading Disorders*, ed. F. Young and D. Lindsley. Washington, D.C.: National Academy of Sciences, 1970.

GATES, ARTHUR I., *The Improvement of Reading*. New York: Macmillan, 1927.

GENTILE, LANCE M., "Effect of Tutor Sex on Learning to Read," *The Reading Teacher* 28 (1975), 726–730.

GESCHWIND, N., "The Organization of Language and the Brain," *Science* 170 (1971), 940–944.

GIBSON, ELEANOR J., "Experimental Psychology of Learning to Read," in *The Disabled Reader*, ed. John Money. Baltimore: John Hopkins University Press, 1966.

GIBSON, ELEANOR J., and HARRY LEVIN, *The Psychology of Reading*. Cambridge: M.I.T. Press, 1975.

GILLINGHAM, ANNA, and BESSIE W. STILLMAN, *Remedial Training for Children With Specific Disability in Reading, Spelling, and Penmanship*. Cambridge: Educators Publishing Service, 1966.

GINSBURG, G. P., and ANN HARTWICK, "Directional Confusion as a Sign of Dyslexia," *Perceptual and Motor Skills* 32 (1971), 535–543.

GLASS, GERALD G., "The Strange World of Syllabication," *Elementary School Journal* (May 1967), 403–405.

GLASS, GERALD G., and ELIZABETH H. BURTON, "How Do They Decode? Verbalizations and Observed Behaviors of Successful Decoders," *The Reading Teacher* 26 (March 1973), 645.

GOLDSTEIN, KURT, *The Organism*. New York: American Book Company, 1934.

GOLDSTEIN, KURT, "The Problem of the Meaning of Words Based Upon Observation of Aphasic Patients," *Journal of Psychology* 2 (July 1936), 301–316.

GOLDSTEIN, KURT, and MARTIN SCHEERER, "Abstract and Concrete Behavior: An Experiment with Special Tests," *Psychological Monographs* 2 (1941).

GOLINKOFF, ROBERTA MICHNICK, "A Comparison of Reading Comprehension Processes in Good and Poor Comprehenders," *Reading Research Quarterly* 11 (1975–1976), 623–659.

GOODMAN, KENNETH S., "A Psycholinguistic View of Reading Comprehension," in *New Frontiers in College-Adult Reading*, ed. George B. Schick and Merrill M. May. Milwaukee: National Reading Conference, 1966.

GOODMAN, KENNETH S., "Reading: A Psycholinguistic Guessing Game," *Journal of the Reading Specialist* 4 (May 1967), 126–135.

GOODMAN, KENNETH S., "Analysis of Oral Reading Miscues: Applied Psycholinguistics," *Reading Research Quarterly* 5 (Fall 1969), 9–30.

GOODMAN, KENNETH S., "Comprehension-Centered Reading," *Claremont Reading Conference Yearbook* 34 (1970), 125–135.

GRAY, W. S., "Is Your Reading Program a Good One?" University of Kansas Conference of Reading, International Reading Association, October 12, 1957.

GRIFFIN, DONALD C., HOWARD N. WALTON, and VERA IVES, "Saccades as Related to Reading Disorders," *Journal of Learning Disabilities* 7 (1974), 52–58.

GROESBECK, HULDA GWENDOLYN, "The Comprehension of Figurative Language by Elementary Children: A Study in Transfer." Unpublished doctoral dissertation, University of Oklahoma, 1961.

GROFF, PATRICK, *The Syllable*. Portland, Ore.: Northwest Regional Educational Laboratory, 1971.

GROFF, PATRICK, "Reading Ability and Auditory Discrimination: Are They Related?," *The Reading Teacher* 28 (1975), 742–747.

GUNDERSON, DORIS V., "New Developments in the Teaching of Reading," *Elementary English* 50 (1973), 17–21, 148.

GUSZAK, FRANK J., "Teaching Questioning and Reading," *The Reading Teacher* 21 (December 1967), 227–234, 252.

GUSZAK, FRANK J., "Reading: Comprehension Skills," in *Reading*, ed. Pose Lamb and Richard Arnold. Belmont, Calif.: Wadsworth Publishing Co., 1976.

GUTHRIE, JOHN T., "Reading Comprehension Processes and Instructions," in *Cognition, Curriculum, and Comprehension*, ed. J. T. Guthrie. Newark, Del.: International Reading Association, 1977.

GUTHRIE, JOHN T, et al., "Clues from Research on Programs for Poor Readers" in *What Research Has to Say About Reading Instruction*, ed. S. Jay Samuels. Newark, Del.: International Reading Association, 1978.

HADDOCK, MARYANN, "Teaching Blending in Beginning Reading Instruction Is Important," *The Reading Teacher* 31 (March 1978), 654–658.

HALL, MARYANNE, *Teaching Reading As a Language Experience*. Columbus, Ohio: Charles E. Merrill, 1976. (a)

HALL, MARYANNE, "Prereading Instruction: Teach the Task," *The Reading Teacher* 30 (October 1976), 7–9. (b)

HALL, MARYANNE, SARA MORETZ, and JODELLANO STATOM, "An Investigation of Early Writing: Research Report." College Park: University of Maryland, 1973.

HALLGREN, BERTIL, "Specific Dyslexia (Congenital Word Blindness)," *Acta Psychiatrica Et Neurologica*, Supplement No. 65. Copenhagen: 1950, 1–287.

HAMMILL, DONALD D., and NELLIE R. BARTEL, *Teaching Children With Learning and Behavior Problems*. Boston: Allyn & Bacon, 1978.

HAMMILL, DONALD D., and STEPHEN C. LARSEN, "The Effectiveness of Psycholinguistic Training," *Exceptional Children* 41 (September 1974), 5–14.

HARGIS, CHARLES H., and EDWARD E. GICKLING, "The Function of Imagery in Word Recognition Development," *The Reading Teacher* 31 (May 1978), 870–874.

HARRINGTON, SISTER MARY JAMES, and DONALD D. DURRELL, "Mental Maturity versus Perception Abilities in Primary Reading," *Journal of Educational Psychology* 46 (1955), 375–380.

HARRIS, ALBERT J., "Lateral Dominance, Directional Confusion, and Reading Disability," *Journal of Psychology* 44 (October 1957), 283–294.

HARRIS, ALBERT J., *Effective Teaching of Reading*. New York: David McKay Co., 1962.

HARRIS, ALBERT J., *How to Increase Reading Ability*. New York: David McKay Co., 1956, 1961.

HARRIS, ALBERT J., "Practical Suggestions for Remedial Teachers," *The Reading Teacher* 31 (May 1978), 916–922.

HARRIS, ALBERT J., and EDWARD R. SIPAY, *How to Increase Reading Ability*. New York: David McKay Co., 1975.

HARTLAGE, LAWRENCE C., "Vision Deficits and Reading Impairment," in *Basic Visual Processes and Learning Disability*, ed. Gerald Leisman. Springfield, Ill.: Charles C Thomas, 1976.

HARTMAN, NANCY C., "Response: Low Tolerance for Frustration: Target Group for Reading Disabilities," *The Reading Teacher* 27 (1974), 675.

HEBB, D. O., *A Textbook of Psychology*. Philadelphia: W. B. Saunders Co., 1958.

HECKELMAN, R. G., "A Neurological-Impress Method of Remedial Reading Instruction," *Academic Therapy* 4 (Summer 1969), 272–282.

HEILMAN, ARTHUR W., *Principles and Practices of Teaching Reading*. Columbus, Ohio: Charles E. Merrill, 1961, 1972.

HEILMAN, ARTHUR W., *Phonics in Proper Perspective*. Columbus, Ohio: Charles E. Merrill, 1976.

HENRY, JULES, *Culture Against Man*. New York: Random House, 1963.

HERBER, HAROLD L., "Study Skills: Reading to Develop, Remember and Use Ideas," in *Reading in the Content Areas*. Syracuse, N.Y.: Syracuse University Press, 1969.

HERRMANN, KNUD, *Reading Disability: A Medical Study of Word-Blindness and Related Handicaps*. Springfield, Ill.: Charles C Thomas, 1959.

HERRICK, JUDSON, *The Evolution of Human Nature*. Austin: University of Texas Press, 1956.

HILDRETH, GERTRUDE, *Teaching Reading*. New York: Holt, Rinehart & Winston, 1958.

HILLERICH, ROBERT L., *PDQ: Prediction with Diagnostic Qualities*. Wilmette, Ill.: Eduscope, 1974.

HILLERICH, ROBERT L., "A Diagnostic Approach to Early Identification of Language Skills," *The Reading Teacher* 31 (January 1978), 357–364.

HINSHELWOOD, JAMES, *Congenital Word Blindness*. London: H. K. Lewis, 1917.

HITTLEMAN, DANIEL R., *Developmental Reading: A Psycholinguistic Perspective*. Chicago, Ill.: Rand McNally College Publishing Co., 1978.

HOCHBERG, J., "Attention and Perception in Reading," in *Early Experience and Visual Information Processing in Perceptual and Reading Disorders*, ed. F. A. Young and D. B. Lindsley. Washington, D.C.: National Academy of Sciences, 1970.

HOCKETT, CHARLES F., *A Course in Modern Linguistics*. New York: Macmillan Publishing Co., 1958.

HOFFMAN, M. S., "Early Indications of Learning Problems," *Academic Therapy* (Fall 1971), 23–35.

HOLLANDER, SHEILA K., "Reading: Process or Product," *The Reading Teacher* 28 (March 1975), 550–554.

HOLLINGSWORTH, PAUL M., "Can Training in Listening Improve Reading?" *The Reading Teacher* 18 (1964), 121–123, 127.

HOLLINGSWORTH, PAUL M., "An Experimental Approach to the Impress Method of Teaching Reading," *The Reading Teacher* 31 (March 1978), 624–626.

HORN, ERNEST, *Methods of Instruction in the Social Studies*. New York: Charles Scribner's Sons, 1937.

HOSKISSON, KENNETH, and BERNADETTE KROHM, "Reading by Immersion: Assisted Reading," *Elementary English* 51 (September 1974), 832–836.

HUEY, EDMUND B., *The Psychology and Pedagogy of Reading*. New York: Macmillan, 1912.

HULL, F., et al., *National Speech and Hearing Survey*. Project No. 50978, Bureau of Education for the Handicapped, U.S. Office of Education, Department of Health, Education and Welfare, Washington, D.C., 1976.

HURVICH, LEO M., and DOROTHEA JAMESON, "Opponent Processes as a Model of Neural Organization," *American Psychologist* 29 (February 1974), 88–102.

JACOBS, J., "Experiments in Prehension," *Mind* 12 (1887), 75–79.

JACOBSEN, EDMUND, "Electrophysiology of Mental Activities," *American Journal of Psychology* 44 (October 1932), 677–694.

JAMES, WILLIAM, *Principles of Psychology*. New York: Holt, Rinehart & Winston, 1890.

JAMES, WILLIAM, *Talks to Teachers on Psychology*. New York: Holt, Rinehart & Winston, 1920.

JANSKY, JEANNETTE, and KATRINA DeHIRSCH, *Preventing Reading Failure: Prediction, Diagnosis, Intervention*. New York: Harper & Row, 1972.

JENKINS, JOSEPH R., R. B. BAUSELL, and L. M. JENKINS, "Comparisons of Letter Name and Letter Sound Training as Transfer Variables," *American Educational Research Journal* 9 (1972), 75–85.

JOHNS, JERRY L., "A Supplement to the Dolch Word Lists," *Reading Improvement* 7 (Winter 1971–1972), 91.

JOHNSON, DALE D., and P. DAVID PEARSON, *Teaching Reading Vocabulary*. New York: Holt, Rinehart & Winston, 1978.

JOHNSON, DORIS J., "Treatment Approaches to Dyslexia," in *Reading Disability and Perception*, ed. George D. Spache. Newark, Del.: International Reading Association, 1969.

JOHNSON, STANLEY W., and ROBERT L. MORASKY, *Learning Disabilities*. Boston: Allyn & Bacon, 1977.

JOLLY, ALLISON, *The Evolution of Primate Behavior*. New York: Macmillan, 1972.

JOOS, LOYAL W., "Linguistics for the Dyslexic," in *The Disabled Reader*, ed. John Money. Baltimore: Johns Hopkins University Press, 1966.

JUDD, C. H., and G. T. BUSWELL, "Silent Reading: A Study of the Various Types," *Supplementary Educational Monographs*, No. 23. Chicago: University of Chicago Press, 1922.

KASS, C. E., "Psycholinguistic Disabilities of Children with Reading Problems," *Exceptional Children* 32 (April 1966), 533–539.

KATZ, E. W., "Understanding Connectives," *Journal of Verbal Learning and Verbal Behavior* 7 (1968), 501–509.

KELLER, HELEN, *The Story of My Life*. New York: Doubleday, 1920.

KENDLER, HOWARD H., "Stimulus-Response Psychology and Audiovisual Education," *AV Communication Review*, 9, no. 5 (1961), 33–41.

KIRK, S. A., "Learning Disabilities: Reopening Pandora's Box." Speech Delivered at the 27th Annual Conference of the Orton Society, New York City, December 14, 1976.

KIRK, S. A., and J. ELKINS, "Characteristics of Children Enrolled in the Child Service Demonstration Centers," *Journal of Learning Disabilities* 8 (1975), 630–637.

KIRK, S. A., and JAMES T. GALLAGHER, *Educating Exceptional Children*. Boston: Houghton Mifflin, 1979.

KIRK, S. A., SISTER JOANNE MARIE KLIEBHAN, and JANET W. LERNER, *Teaching Reading to Slow and Disabled Learners*. Boston: Houghton Mifflin, 1978.

KLASEN, EDITH, *The Syndrome of Specific Dyslexia*. Baltimore: University Park Press, 1972.

KLEIN, HOWARD A., "Cross-Cultural Studies: What Do They Tell About Sex Differences in Reading?" *The Reading Teacher* 30 (May 1977), 880–886.

KNAFLE, JUNE D., "Word Perception: Cues Aiding Structure Detection," *Reading Research Quarterly* 8 (1973), 502–524.

KOTTMEYER, WILLIAM, *Decoding and Meaning*. New York: McGraw-Hill, 1974.

KRAUS, PHILLIP E., *Yesterday's Children: A Longitudinal Study of Children from Kindergarten into the Adult Years*. New York: John Wiley, 1973.

KRISE, MORLEY, "Reversals in Reading: A Problem in Space Perception?" *Elementary School Journal* 49 (1949), 278–284.

KRISE, MORLEY, "An Experimental Investigation of Theories of Reversals in Reading," *Journal of Educational Psychology* 43 (1952), 408–422.

LABOV, W., "Linguistic Research on Non-Standard English of Negro Children." Paper read at New York Society for the Experimental Study of Education, New York City, 1965.

LABOV, W., *Some Sources of Reading Problems for Negro Speakers of Non-Standard English*. Bethesda, Md.: National Cash Register Co., 1966.

LADD, ELEANOR M., "Individualizing Instruction in Classroom Corrective Situations," in *Vistas in Reading*, vol. 2, part I. Newark, Del.: International Reading Association, 1967.

LANGE, K., *Apperception: A Monograph on Psychology and Pedagogy*, ed. Charles De Garma. Boston: D. C. Heath, 1902.

LANGER, SUSANNE K., *Philosophy in a New Key*. New York: Mentor Books, New American Library, 1948.

LANGFORD, KENNETH, et al., "An Examination of Impress Techniques in Remedial Reading," *Academic Therapy* 9 (Spring 1974), 309–319.

LANGMAN, MURIEL POTTER, "The Reading Process: A Descriptive, Interdisciplinary Approach," *Genetic Psychology Monographs* 62 (August 1960), 1–40.

LANIER, RUBY JEANNE, and ANITA PRICE DAVIS, "Developing Comprehension Through Teacher-Made Questions," *The Reading Teacher* 26 (1972), 153–157.

LASHLEY, K. S., "Persistent Problems in the Evolution of Mind," *Quarterly Review of Biology* 24 (1949), 28–42.

LAURITA, RAYMOND E., "Bringing Order to the Teaching of Reading and Writing," *Education* 93 (February, March 1973), 254–261.

LAWRENCE, DENIS, "An Experimental Investigation into the Effects of Counseling Retarded Readers," in *New Horizons in Reading.* Newark, Del.: International Reading Association, 1976.

LEARY, BERNICE E., "Developing Word Perception Skills in Middle and Upper Grades," *Current Problems in Reading Instruction.* Pittsburgh: University of Pittsburgh Press, 1951.

LEFEVRE, CARL A., "Language Patterns and Their Graphic Counterparts: A Linguistic View of Reading," in *Changing Concepts of Reading Instruction*, ed. J. Allen Figurel. International Reading Association Conference Proceedings, vol. 6. New York: Scholastic Magazines, 1961.

LEFEVRE, CARL A., "Reading Our Language Patterns: A Linguistic View—Contributions to a Theory of Reading," in *Challenge and Experiment in Reading*, International Reading Association Conference Proceedings, vol. 7 (1962).

LEFEVRE, CARL A., *Linguistics and the Teaching of Reading.* New York: McGraw-Hill, 1964.

LERNER, JANET W., *Children with Learning Disabilities: Theories, Diagnosis, and Teaching Strategies.* Boston: Houghton Mifflin, 1976.

LEVIN, HARRY, and E. A. TURNER, *Sentence Structure and the Eye-Voice Span.* Project No. B.R. 5–1213–9–OEC–6–10, September 1966.

LINDER, RONALD, and HENRY T. FILLMER, "Auditory and Visual Performance of Slow Readers," *The Reading Teacher* 24 (1970), 17–22.

LIVINGSTON, ROBERT B., et al., *Report for the International Brain Research Foundation*, quoted in the *New York Times*, November 2, 1975, p. 38.

LONDON, PERRY, *Beginning Psychology.* Homewood, Ill.: Dorsey Press, 1975.

LUNDSTEEN, SARA W., "Levels of Meaning in Reading," *The Reading Teacher* 28 (December 1974), 268–272.

LYLE, J. G., "Certain Antenatal, Perinatal, and Developmental Variables and Reading Retardation in Middle-Class Boys," *Child Development* 41 (1970), 481–491.

MARCHBANKS, G., and LEVIN H., "Cues by Which Children Recognize Words," *Journal of Educational Psychology* 56 (April 1965), 57–61.

McBROOM, M., J. SPARROW, and C. ECKSTEIN, *Scale for Determining a Child's Reader Level.* Iowa City: Bureau of Publications, State University of Iowa, 1944.

McLEOD, JOHN, *Dyslexia Schedule.* Cambridge, Mass.: Educators Publishing Service, 1969.

McLEOD, JOHN, "Reading Expectancy from Disabled Learners," *Journal of Learning Disabilities* 1 (February 1968), 7–15.

McNEIL, MALCOLM R., and C. E. HAMRE, "A Review of Measures of Lateralized Cerebral Hemispheric Functions," *Journal of Learning Disabilities* 7 (1974), 51–59.

MELNICK, AMELIA, "The Formulation of Questions as an Instructional—Diagnostic Tool," in *Reading and Inquiry.* Conference Proceedings, International Reading Association, vol. 10, (1965).

MOLFESE, D., "Cerebral Asymmetry in Infants, Children and Adults: Auditory Evoked Responses to Speech and Musical Stimuli," *Journal of the Acoustical Society of America* 53 (1973), 363.

MONEY, JOHN, *Reading Disability Progress and Research Needs in Dyslexia*. Baltimore: John Hopkins University Press, 1962.

MONEY, JOHN, *A Standardized Road-Map Test of Direction Sense*. San Rafael, Calif.: Academic Therapy Publications, 1976.

MONEY, JOHN, D. ALEXANDER, and H. T. WALKER, JR., *A Standardized Road-Map Test to Direction Sense*. Baltimore: Johns Hopkins University Press, 1965.

MONROE, MARION, *Children Who Cannot Read*. Chicago: University of Chicago Press, 1932.

MONTGOMERY, DIANE, "Teaching Prereading Skills Through Training in Pattern Recognition," *The Reading Teacher* 30 (March 1977), 616–623.

MOORE, RAYMOND S., and DOROTHY N. MOORE, *Better Late Than Early: A New Approach to Your Child's Education*. New York: Reader's Digest Press, 1975.

MORENCY, ANNE, "Auditory Modality and Reading: Research and Practice," in *Perception and Reading*, ed. Helen K. Smith, vol. 12, part 4. Newark, Del.: International Reading Association, 1968.

MOYER, SANDRA B., and PHYLLIS L. NEWCOMER, "Reversals in Reading: Diagnosis and Remediation," *Exceptional Children* 43 (April 1977), 424–429.

MUEHL, SIEGMAR, and ETHEL M. KING, "Recent Research in Visual Discrimination: Significance for Beginning Reading," in *Vistas in Reading*. Newark, Del.: International Reading Association, 1967.

NAIDEN, NORMA, "Ratio of Boys to Girls Among Disabled Readers," *The Reading Teacher* 29 (1976), 439–442.

NEISSER, ULRIC, "The Processes of Vision," in *Contemporary Psychology* (1968), San Francisco: W. H. Freeman & Company, 1971.

NICHOLSON, ALICE, "Background Abilities Related to Reading Success in First Grade," *Journal of Education* 140 (1958), 7–24.

NIENSTED, SERENA, "A Group Use of the Fernald Technique," *Journal of Reading* 11 (1968), 435–437, 440.

NILA, SISTER MARY, O.S.F., "Foundations of a Successful Reading Program," *Education* 73 (1953), 543–555.

NILES, O. S., "Organization Perceived," in *Developing Study Skills in the Schools*, Perspectives in Reading, no. 4. Newark, Del.: International Reading Association, 1965.

NORBERG, KENNETH, "Perception Research and Audio-Visual Education," *Audio-Visual Communication Review* 1 (Winter 1953), 18–29.

NORBERG, KENNETH, "Perception Research and Audio-Visual Education," in *Readings for Educational Psychology*, ed. W. A. Fullagar, H. G. Lewis, and C. F. Cumbee. New York: Thomas Y. Crowell, 1956.

NORRIE, E., "Word Blindness in Denmark: Its Neurological and Educational Aspects, *Independent School Bulletin* 3 (1960), 8–12.

NORVELL, GEORGE W., *The Reading Interests of Young People*. Boston: D. C. Heath, 1950.

NORVELL, GEORGE, W., *What Boys and Girls Like to Read*. Morristown, N.J.: Silver Burdett Company, 1958.

OHNMACHT, D. D., "The Effects of Letter Knowlege on Achievement in Reading in the First Grade." Paper presented at American Educational Research Association Conference, Los Angeles, Calif., 1969.

OLSEN, WILLARD C., "Seeking Self-Selection, and Pacing in the Use of Books by Children," *The Packet*, 7, no. 1. Boston: D. C. Heath, 1952.

OLSON, ARTHUR V., "Growth in Word Perception Abilities as It Relates to Success in Beginning Reading," *Journal of Education* 140 (1958), 25–36.

ORLOW, MARIA, "Low Tolerance for Frustration: Target Group for Reading Disabilities," *The Reading Teacher* 27 (1974), 669–674.

ORTON, SAMUEL T., "An Impediment to Learning to Read: A Neurological Explanation of Reading Disability," *School and Society* 28 (1928), 286–290.

ORTON, SAMUEL T., *Reading, Writing and Speech Problems in Children*. New York: W. W. Norton, 1937.

OTTO, WAYNE, "Orientation to Remedial Teaching," in *Reading Problems: A Multidisciplinary Perspective*, ed. Wayne Otto et al. Reading, Mass.: Addison-Wesley, 1977.

OTTO, WAYNE, and ROBERT D. CHESTER, *Objective-Based Reading*. Reading, Mass.: Addison-Wesley, 1976.

OTTO, WAYNE, and RICHARD SMITH, *Administering the School Reading Program*. Boston: Houghton Mifflin, 1970.

OTTO, WAYNE, et al., *Focused Reading Instruction*. Reading, Mass.: Addison-Wesley, 1974.

PANY, DARLENE, and JOSEPH R. JENKINS, "Learning Word Meaning." Champaign: Center for the Study of Reading, University of Illinois, March 1977.

PARK, GEORGE F., and KENNETH A. SCHNEIDER, "Thyroid Function in Relation to Dyslexia (Reading Failures)," *Journal of Reading Behavior* 7 (1975), 197–199.

PAVLOV, I. P., *Conditioned Reflexes*. London: Oxford University Press, 1927.

PEARSON, DAVID P., "The Effects of Grammatical Complexity of Children's Comprehension, Recall, and Conception of Certain Semantic Relations," *Reading Research Quarterly* 10 (1975), 155–192.

PEARSON, DAVID P., "Some Practical Applications of a Psycholinguistic Model of Reading," in *What Research Has to Say About Reading Instruction*, ed. S. Jay Samuels. Newark, Del.: International Reading Association, 1978.

PETERS, CHARLES W., "The Comprehension Process," in *Reading Problems: A Multidisciplinary Perspective*, ed. Wayne Otto et al. Reading, Mass.: Addison-Wesley, 1977.

PIERONEK, FLORENCE T., "Using Basal Guidebooks—The Ideal Integrated Reading Lesson Plan," *The Reading Teacher* 33 (November 1979), 167–172.

PLESSAS, GUS P., and CLIFTON R. OAKES, "Prereading Experiences of Selected Early Readers," *The Reading Teacher* 17 (January 1964), 241–245.

POOLE, I., "Genetic Development of Articulation of Consonant Sounds in Speech," *Elementary English Review* 11 (1934), 159–161.

POPE, LILLIE, *Learning Disabilities Glossary*. Brooklyn, N.Y.: Book-Lab, 1976.

PORTER, WILLIAM E., "Mass Communication and Education," *The National Elementary Principal* 37 (February 1958), 12–16.

QUADFASSEL, F. A., and H. GOODGLASS, "Specific Reading Disabilities and Other Specific Disabilities." *Journal of Learning Disabilities*, vol. 1 (1968) 590–600.

RAMSEY, W., "Evaluation of Assumptions Related to the Testing of Phonics Skills," Washington, D.C.: *National Center for Educational Research and Development*, 1972.

RANKIN, E., and ROBERT J. TRACY, "Residual Gain as a Measure of Individual Differences in Reading Improvement," *Journal of Reading* 8 (March 1965), 224–233.

RANKIN, EARL, and J. CULHANE, "Comparable Close and Multiple Choice Comprehension Test Scores," *Journal of Reading*, 13 (1969), 193–198.

RAZRAN, GREGORY, "A Note on the Use of the Terms *Conditioning* and *Reinforcement*," *American Psychologist* 10 (1955), 173–174.

READ, MERRILL S., "The Biological Bases: Malnutrition and Behavioral Development," *Early Childhood Education*, Chicago, Ill.: 71st Yearbook of the National Society for the Study of Education, 1972.

Reading in America, Reading Report, No. 06–R–01. Denver: National Assessment of Educational Progress, 1976.

REED, DAVID W., "A Theory of Language, Speech and Writing," *Elementary English* 42 (December 1965), 845–851.

RITTY, J. MICHAEL, "Assessing and Alleviating Visual Problems in the Schools," *The Reading Teacher* 32 (April 1979), 796–802.

ROBECK, MILDRED C., "An Ounce of Prevention," in *Remedial Reading: Classroom and Clinic*, ed. Leo M. Schell and Paul C. Burns. Boston: Allyn & Bacon, 1972.

ROBECK, MILDRED C., and JOHN A. R. WILSON, *Psychology of Reading*. New York: John Wiley, 1974.

ROBERTSON, JEAN E., "Pupil Understanding of Connectives," *Reading Research Quarterly* 3 (1968), 387–417.

ROBINSON, FRANCIS P., *Effective Study* (rev. ed.). New York: Harper & Brothers, 1961.

ROEDER, HAROLD H., and NANCY LEE, "Twenty-five Teacher-Tested Ways to Encourage Voluntary Reading," *The Reading Teacher* 27 (1973), 48–50.

ROGERS, CARL, *On Becoming a Person*. Boston: Houghton Mifflin, 1961.

ROSE, LYNDON, "The Reading Process and Some Research Implications," *Journal of Reading* 13 (1969), 25–28.

ROSNER, JEROME, "Language Arts and Arithmetic Achievement and Specifically Related Perceptual Skills," *American Educational Research Journal* 19, no. 1 (1973), 59–68.

ROSNER, JEROME, "Auditory Analysis Training with Prereaders," *The Reading Teacher* 27 (1974), 379–384.

ROSS, ALAN O., *Psychological Aspects of Learning Disabilities and Reading Disorders*. New York: McGraw-Hill, 1976.

ROSS, RAMON, "Teaching the Listener: Old Mistakes and a Fresh Beginning," *Elementary School Journal* 66 (February 1966), 239–244.

ROSSI, GIAN F., and GUIDO ROSADINI, "Experimental Analysis of Cerebral Dominance in Man," in *Brain Mechanisms Underlying Speech and Language*, ed. C. H. Millikan and F. L. Darley. New York: Grune & Stratton, 1967.

ROTHKOPF, ERNEST Z., "The Concept of Mathemagenic Activities," *Review of Educational Research* 40 (1970), 325.

ROUSSEAU, JACQUES, *Emile*. New York: Appleton-Century-Crofts, 1899.

RUDDELL, R. B., "Language Acquisition and the Reading Process," in *Theoretical Models and Processes of Reading*, ed. H. Singer and R. B. Ruddell. Newark, Del.: International Reading Association, 1970.

RUDDELL, R. B., *Reading-Language Instruction: Innovative Practices*. Englewood Cliffs, N.J.: Prentice-Hall, 1974.

RUTHERFORD, WILLIAM L., "Letter-Name Versus Letter-Sound Knowledge in Learning to Read," *The Reading Teacher* 24 (1971), 604–608.(a)

RUTHERFORD, WILLIAM L., "What Is Your DQ (Dyslexia Quotient)?" *The Reading Teacher* 25 (1971), 262–266.(b)

RYSTROM, RICHARD, "Psycholinguistics and the Reading Process," in *Improving Reading in Middle and Secondary Schools*, ed. Lawrence E. Hafner. New York: Macmillan, 1974.

SAMUELS, S. JAY, "The Effect of Letter-Name Knowledge on Learning to Read," *American Educational Research Journal* 9 (1972), 65–74.

SAMUELS, S. JAY, "Success and Failure in Learning to Read," *Reading Research Quarterly* 8 (Winter 1973), 200–239.

SAMUELS, S. JAY, "The Method of Repeated Readings," *The Reading Teacher* 32 (January 1979), 403–408.

SANTOSTEFANO, S. L., RUTLEDGE, and D. RANDALL, "Cognitive Styles and Reading Disabilities," *Psychology in Schools* 2 (1965), 57–63.

SAPIR, EDWARD, *Language: An Introduction to the Study of Speech*. New York: Harcourt, Brace and World, 1921.

SAWYER, DIANE J., "The Diagnostic Mystique—A Point of View," *The Reading Teacher* 27 (1974), 555–561.

SCHEERER, MARTIN, "Cognitive Theory," in *Handbook of Social Psychology*, vol. 1, ed. Gardner Lindzey. Reading, Mass.: Addison-Wesley, 1954.

SCHEERER, MARTIN, "Spheres of Meaning: An Analysis of Stages from Perception to Abstract Thinking," *Journal of Individual Psychology* 15 (May 1959), 50–61.

SCHIFFMAN, GILBERT, "Early Identification of Reading Disabilities: The Responsibility of the Public School," *Bulletin of the Orton Society* 14 (1964), 42–44.

SCHIFFMAN, GILBERT B., "An Interdisciplinary Approach to the Identification and Remediation of Severe Reading Disabilities," in *Junior College and Adult Reading Programs*. Milwaukee, Wis.: National Reading Conference, 1967.

SCHLIEPER, ANNE, "Oral Reading Errors in Relation to Grade and Level of Skill," *The Reading Teacher* 31 (December 1977), 283–287.

SCHUBERT, D. G., and T. L. TORGERSON, *Improving the Reading Program*. Dubuque, Iowa: Wm. C. Brown, 1972.

SEIDERMAN, A. S., "An Optometric Approach to the Diagnosis of Visually Based Problems in Learning," in *Basic Visual Processes and Learning Disability*, ed. Gerald Leisman. Springfield, Ill.: Charles C Thomas, 1976.

SEMELMEYER, MADELINE, "Can Johnny Read?," *Education* 77 (April 1957), 505–512.

SEXTON, PATRICIA L., *The Feminized Males: White Collars and The Decline of Manliness*. New York: Random House, 1969.

SHAW, PHILIP, "Rhetorical Guides to Reading Comprehension," *The Reading Teacher* 11 (1958), 239–243.

SHEPHERD, DAVID, *Comprehensive High School Reading Methods*. Columbus, Ohio: Charles E. Merrill, 1973.

SILVER, ARCHIE A., and ROSA A. HAGIN, "Maturation of Perceptual Functions in Children with Specific Reading Disability," *The Reading Teacher* 19 (1966), 253–259.

SILVER, ARCHIE A., and ROSA A. HAGIN, *Search and Teach*. New York: Walker Educational Book Corporation, 1976.

SIMMONS, JOHN S., "Reasoning Through Reading," *Journal of Reading* 8 (April 1965), 311–314.

SINGER, HARRY, "Active Comprehension from Answering to Asking Questions," *The Reading Teacher* 31 (May 1978), 901–908.

SINGER, HARRY, S. JAY SAMUELS, and JEAN SPIROFF, "The Effect of Pictures and Contexual Conditions on Learning Responses to Printed Words," *Reading Research Quarterly* 9, no. 4 (1973–1974), 555–567.

SMITH, D. E. P., and PATRICIA M. CARRIGAN, *The Nature of Reading Disability*. New York: Harcourt, Brace and Co., 1959.

SMITH, FRANK, "Making Sense of Reading—And of Reading Instruction," *Harvard Educational Review* 47 (August 1977), 386–395.

SMITH, FRANK, *Understanding Reading: A Psycholinguistic Analysis of Reading and Learning to Read*. New York: Holt, Rinehart & Winston, 1971, 1978.

SMITH, HENRY P., "The Sociology of Reading," in *Exploring the Goals of College Reading Programs*, Fifth Yearbook of the Southwest Reading Conference for Colleges and Universities. Fort Worth: Texas Christian University Press, 1956.

SMITH, HENRY P., and EMERALD V. DECHANT, *Psychology in Teaching Reading*. Englewood Cliffs, N.J.: Prentice-Hall, 1961.

SMITH, MONTE D., et al., "Intellectual Characteristics of School Labeled Learning Disabled Children," *Exceptional Children* 43 (March 1977), 352–357.

SMITH, RICHARD J., and THOMAS C. BARRETT, *Teaching Reading in the Middle Grades*. Reading, Mass.: Addison-Wesley, 1974, 1979.

SMITH, RICHARD J., and KARL D. HESSE, "The Effects of Prereading Assistance on the

Comprehension of Good and Poor Readers," *Research in the Teaching of English* 3 (1969), 166–177.

SMITH, RICHARD J., and DALE D. JOHNSON,   *Teaching Children to Read.* Reading, Mass.: Addison-Wesley, 1976.

SOFFIETTI, J. P.,   "Why Children Fail to Read: A Linguistic Analysis," *The Harvard Educational Review* 25 (Spring 1955), 63–84.

SOMMERFIELD, ROY E.,   "Some Recent Research in College Reading," in *Techniques and Procedures in College and Adult Reading Programs*, Sixth Yearbook of the Southwest Reading Conference. Fort Worth: Texas Christian University Press, 1957.

SONENBERG, CHARLOTTE, and GERALD G. GLASS,   "Reading and Speech: An Incidence and Treatment Study," *The Reading Teacher* 19 (December 1965), 197–201.

SOUTHGATE, VERA,   "The Language Arts in Informal British Primary Schools," *The Reading Teacher* 26 (1973), 367–373.

SPACHE, GEORGE,   "A New Readability Formula for Primary Grades Reading Materials," *Elementary English* 53 (March 1953), 410–413.

SPACHE, GEORGE,   *Good Books for Poor Readers.* Champaign, Ill.: Garrard, 1966.

SPACHE, GEORGE,   *Diagnosing and Correcting Reading Disabilities.* Boston: Allyn & Bacon, 1976.

SPENCER, L. PETER,   "The Reading Process and Types of Reading," in *Claremont College Reading Conference*, Eleventh Yearbook. Claremont, Calif., 1946.

STEINER, ROLLIN, MORTON WIENER, and WARD CROMER,   "Comprehension Training and Identification for Poor and Good Readers," *Journal of Education Psychology* 62 (December 1971), 506–513.

STEPHENS, W. E., E. S. CUNNINGHAM, and B. J. STIGLER,   "Reading Readiness and Eye-Hand Preference Patterns in First Grade Children," *Exceptional Children* 33 (1967), 481–488.

STOODT, BARBARA D.,   "The Relationship Between Understanding Grammatical Conjunctions and Reading Comprehension," *Elementary English* 49 (1972), 502–504.

STOTT, D. H.,   "Some Less Obvious Cognitive Aspects of Learning to Read," *The Reading Teacher* 26 (1973), 374–383.

STRAG, GERALD A., and BERT O. RICHMOND,   "Auditory Discrimination Techniques for Young Children," *Elementary School Journal* 73 (1973), 447–453.

STRICKLAND, RUTH G.,   "Children, Reading and Creativity," *Elementary English* 34 (1957), 234–241.

SULLIVAN, HOWARD J., MASAHITO OKADA, and FRED C. NIEDERMEYER,   "Learning and Transfer Under Two Methods of Word-Attack Instruction," *American Educational Research Journal* 8 (1971), 227–239.

SULLIVAN, JOANNA,   "Comparing Strategies of Good and Poor Comprehenders," *Journal of Reading* 21 (May 1978), 710–715.

SUTTON, MARJORIE H.,   "Readiness for Reading at the Kindergarten Level," *The Reading Teacher* 17 (January 1964), 234–239.

SWENSON, I.,   "Word-Recognition Cues Used in Matching Verbal Stimuli Within and Between Auditory and Visual Modalities," *Journal of Educational Psychology* 67 (1975), 409–415.

TAYLOR, E. A.,   *Eyes, Visual Anomalies and the Fundamental Reading Skill.* New York: Reading and Study Skills Center, 1959.

TAYLOR, STANFORD E.,   *Speed Reading vs. Improved Reading Efficiency.* Huntington, N.Y.: Educational Developmental Laboratories, 1962.

TAYLOR, STANFORD, E., and HELEN FRACKENPOHL,   *Teacher's Guide: Tach-X Flash-X.* Huntington, N.Y.: Educational Developmental Laboratories, 1960.

TAYLOR, STANFORD E., H. FRACKENPOHL, and I. L. PETTEE,   *Grade Level Norms for the Components of the Fundamental Reading Skill.* Huntington, N.Y.: Educational Developmental Laboratories, Bulletin 3, 1960.

TERMAN, SIBYL, and C. C. WALCUTT, *Reading: Chaos and Cure*. New York: McGraw-Hill, 1958.

TERRY, PAMELA, "The Effect of Orthographic Transformations Upon Speed and Accuracy of Semantic Transformations." *Reading Research Quarterly* 12, no. 2 (1976–1977), 166–175.

TERRY, PAMELA, S. JAY SAMUELS, and DAVID LaBERGE, "Word Recognition as a Function of Letter Degradation, Spacing and Transformation." Minneapolis: Center for Research in Human Learning, University of Minnesota, 1976.

THORNDIKE, E. L., "Reading as Reasoning; A Study of Mistakes in Paragraph Reading," *Journal of Educational Psychology* 8 (June 1917), 323–332.

THORNDIKE, ROBERT L., *Children's Reading Interests*. New York: Bureau of Publications, Teachers College, Columbia University, 1941.

THORNDIKE, ROBERT L., *Reading Comprehension Education in Fifteen Countries*. International Association for the Evaluation of Educational Achievement. New York: Halsted Press, 1973.

TIMKO, HENRY G., "Configuration as a Cue in the Word Recognition of Beginning Readers," *Journal of Experimental Education* 39 (1970), 68–69.

TINKER, MILES A., "The Use and Limitations of Eye-Movement Measures in Reading," *Psychological Review* 40 (1933), 381–87.

TINKER, MILES A., and CONSTANCE M. McCULLOUGH, *Teaching Elementary Reading* (4th ed.). Englewood Cliffs, N.J.: Prentice-Hall, 1975.

TOWLE, MAXINE, and ALLEN GINSBERG, "An Educator's Mystery: Where Do Performance Problems Come From?" *Journal of Learning Disabilities* 8 (October 1975), 18–21.

TRACY, ROBERT J., and EARL F. RANKIN, JR., "Methods of Computing and Evaluating Residual Gain Scores in the Reading Program," *Journal of Reading* 10 (March 1967), 363–371.

TREMONTI, JOSEPH B., and CELESTINE ALGERO, "Reading and Study Habits in Content Areas," *Reading Improvement* 4 (1967), 54–57.

TURAIDS, DAINIS, JOSEPH WEPMAN, and ANNE MORENCY, "A Perceptual Test Battery: Development and Standardization," *Elementary School Journal* 72 (1972), 351–361.

TYLER, LEONA E., "Individual Differences," in *Encyclopedia of Educational Research* (4th ed.), ed. Robert L. Ebel and Victor H. Noll. New York: Macmillan, 1969.

VAN RIPER, CHARLES, and KATHARINE G. BUTLER, *Speech in the Elementary Classroom*. New York: Harper & Row, 1955.

VAUGHAN, SALLEY, SHARON CRAWLEY, and LEE MOUNTAIN, "A Multiple-Modality Approach to Word Study: Vocabulary Scavenger Hunts," *The Reading Teacher* 32 (January 1979), 434–437.

VERNON, M. D., *Backwardness in Reading*. London: Cambridge University Press, 1957.

VEATCH, JEANNETTE, and PHILIP J. ACINAPURO, *Reading in the Elementary School*. New York: John Wiley, 1978.

WALCUTT, CHARLES C., JOAN LAMPORT, and GLEN McCRACKEN, *Teaching Reading*. New York: Macmillan, 1974.

WARDHAUGH, RONALD, "Reading: A New Perspective," in his *Reading: A Linguistic Perspective*. New York: Harcourt Brace Jovanovich, 1969.

WATSON, JOHN B., "Psychology as the Behaviorist Views It," *Psychological Review* 20 (1913), 158–177.

WATSON, J. B., "Is Thinking Merely the Action of the Language Mechanism?" *British Journal of Psychology* 11 (October 1920), 87–104.

WECHSLER, DAVID, *The Measurement of Adult Intelligence*. Baltimore: Williams and Wilkins, 1944.

WEINER, BLUMA B., "Dimensions of Assessment," *Exceptional Children* 28 (September 1961), 483–486.

WERNER, H., *Comparative Psychology of Mental Development*. New York: International Universities Press, 1948.

WHEAT, H. G., *Foundations of School Learning*. New York: Knopf, 1955.

WHEELOCK, WARREN H., and NICHOLAS J. SILVAROLI. "Visual Discrimination Training for Beginning Readers," *The Reading Teacher* 21 (November 1967), 115–120.

WHISLER, NANCY G., "Visual-Memory Training in First Grade: Effects on Visual Discrimination and Reading Ability," *Elementary School Journal* 75 (1974), 51–54.

WHORF, BENJAMEN L., "Science and Linguistics," *Technology Review* 42 (1939–1940), 229–231, 247–248.

WILLIAMS, JOANNA P., ELLEN L. BLUMBERG, and DAVID W. WILLIAMS, "Cues Used in Visual Word Recognition," *Journal of Educational Psychology* 61 (1970), 310–315.

WILLOWS, DALE M., "Reading Between the Lines: Selective Attention in Good and Poor Readers," *Child Development* 45 (June 1974), 408–415.

WILSON, ROBERT W., "Diagnosing High-School Students' Reading Problems," in *Junior College and Adult Reading*. Milwaukee: National Reading Conference, 1967.

WILSON, ROBERT W., *Diagnostic and Remedial Reading*. Columbus, Ohio: Charles E. Merrill, 1967, 1972.

WOLPERT, EDWARD M., "Length, Imagery Values and Word Recognition," *The Reading Teacher* 26 (November 1972), 180–186.

WOODWORTH, R. S., *Psychology*. New York, Holt, Rinehart and Winston, 1921.

YAHRES, HERBERT, and SHERRY PRESTWICH, *Detection and Prevention of Learning Disorders*. U.S. Department of Health, Education and Welfare, No. (ADM) 76–337, 1976.

YOUNG, ROBERT A., "Case Studies in Reading Disability," *American Journal of Orthopsychiatry* 8 (April 1938), 230–254.

YOUNG, ROSS N., *Reading in the Junior and Senior High School*. Minneapolis: Educational Test Bureau, 1927.

ZINTZ, MILES V., *Corrective Reading*. Dubuque, Iowa: Wm. C. Brown Co., 1972, 1977.

ZINTZ, MILES V., *The Reading Process: The Teacher and the Learner*. Dubuque, Iowa: Wm. C. Brown Co., 1980.

index